Contents

PART IV   CONTEXTS

List of Figures and Tables

Figures

Tables

List of Contributors

Frank R. Ankersmit is Professor for Intellectual History and Philosophy of History at Groningen University, The Netherlands.

Laure Bereni is a Postdoctoral Fellow at the Centre Maurice Halbwachs, Paris, France.

Jens Borchert is Professor of Political Science and Political Sociology at the University of Frankfurt, Germany.

Hubertus Buchstein is Professor for Political Theory and the History of Political Ideas at the University of Greifswald, Germany.

Gonzalo Capellán de Miguel is Lecturer in Contemporary History at the University of Cantabria, Spain.

Christine Fauré is Director of Research at the Centre National de la Recherche Scientifique (CNRS), Triangle-Université de Lyon, France.

Simona Forti is Professor of Political Philosophy at the University of Piemonte Orientale, Italy.

Olivia Guaraldo is Lecturer in Political Philosophy at the University of Verona, Italy.

Mogens Herman Hansen is Lecturer in Classical Philology, SAXO Institute, University of Copenhagen, Denmark.

Irène Herrmann is Associate Professor of Modern European History at the University of Fribourg, Switzerland.

Uffe Jakobsen is Associate Professor and Director, Centre for Baltic Sea Region Studies, Department of Political Science, University of Copenhagen, Denmark.

Jussi Kurunmäki is a Research Fellow (Swedish Research Council) at the Department of Political Science, Stockholm University, Sweden.

Marcus Llanque is Professor for Political Theory and the History of Political Ideas at the University of Augsburg, Germany.

Chantal Mouffe is Professor of Political Theory, Centre for the Study of Democracy, University of Westminster, London, UK.

Kari Palonen is Academy of Finland Professor at the University of Jyvaskyla, Finland.

Tuija Pulkkinen is Professor of Women's Studies at the University of Jyvaskyla, Finland.

José María Rosales is Lecturer in Moral and Political Philosophy at the University of Malaga, Spain.

Meike Schmidt-Gleim is Marie Curie Fellow at the University of Piemonte Orientale, Italy.

Anna Schober is a Research Fellow at the Institute of Contemporary History, University of Vienna, Austria.

Pierre-Antoine Schorderet is Acting Professor of Political Science, Institut d'Etudes Politiques et Internationales, University of Lausanne, Switzerland.

Gabriella Silvestrini is a Research Fellow at the Facoltà di Scienze Politiche, University of Piemonte Orientale, Italy.

Quentin Skinner is Regius Professor of Modern History in the University of Cambridge, UK.

Claudia Wiesner is a Research Fellow at the Zentrum für Konfliktforschung/Centre for Conflict Studies, University of Marburg, Germany.

Acknowledgments

This book is one of the outcomes of The Politics and History of European Democratization research network. We are grateful to the European Science Foundation for its funding, and to the Universities of Copenhagen, Greifswald, Jyvaskyla, Malaga and Piemonte Orientale for additional financial help.

The network was chaired by Kari Palonen and coordinated by a team of ten members, including Tuija Pulkkinen, the Vice-chair, Frank Ankersmit, Hubertus Buchstein, Christine Fauré, Simona Forti, Uffe Jakobsen, Oleg Kharkhordin, Chantal Mouffe, Pierre Rosanvallon and José María Rosales.

After a public call in 2003, we selected some thirty young scholars to participate in the network. We had received more than seventy applications from all over Europe. The response was so enthusiastic that we changed our original programme, and managed to invite quite a few of them to the series of five workshops held between 2003 and 2005.

None of this would have been possible without the enduring support from the ESF staff. We would like to thank Henk Stronkhorst, Head of the Social Sciences Unit, who assisted us during the initial phase of the network, and Monique van Donzel, Head of the Humanities Unit, who has skilfully and encouragingly supervised the network proceedings and helped us in innumerable instances. Special thanks go to Madelise Blumenroeder for her expert and dedicated assistance in administrative matters.

In preparing the Malaga workshop, the first one in the series, we would like to acknowledge the support of the Research Vice-Rectors Professors Adelaida de la Calle and José Angel Narváez. Marta Postigo helped with the practical arrangements. For the efficient Jyvaskyla workshop, we thank Dr Oili Pulkkinen, who took care of its practical preparations, the Faculty of the Social Sciences for the additional funding of the event, and the Rector of the University, Professor Aino Sallinen, for her inaugural lecture on Finnish political rhetoric. The Turin workshop was co-funded by the Fondazione Einaudi. We gratefully recognize its support and the invaluable contribution by Simona Forti and Gabriella Silvestrini.

The following workshop was held in Greifswald. We thank the Dean of the Faculty of Philosophy, Professor Manfred Bornewasser, for his support, and Hubertus Buchstein and Stefan Fietz for their competent help. The last one was held in Copenhagen. For the practical arrangements, we thank the following members of the local organizing committee: Mimi Larsson, Tina-Marie Samson Markussen, Helle Pedersen and Uffe Jakobsen. We also thank Professor Jens Bartelson for the opening speech, and Head of Department Lars Bille for the welcome speech at the opening reception. Last but not least, we thank the Department of Political Science for hosting and providing additional funding for the successful event.

We would like to mention the names of specially commissioned discussants, session chairs and of a number of workshop participants who have greatly contributed to our debates but whose papers have been published elsewhere: Gonzalo Arruego, Nere Basabe, Adriana Cavarero, Tristan Coignard, Ulku Doganay, Max Edling, Henrik Enroth, Javier Fernández Sebastián, Stefan Fietz, Elisabetta Galeotti, Rebekka Göhring, Kathrin Groh, Roberta Guerrina, Tim Knudsen, Ayça Kurtoglu, Alice Ludvig, Artemy Magun, Oliver Marchart, Iivi Masso, Sinikka Mustakallio, Thomas Poell, Tuija Parvikko, Ove K. Pedersen, Johannes Pollak, Cécile Rol, Harmut Rosa, Sia Spiliopoulou-Åkermark, Suvi Soininen, Asil Telli-Aydemir, Tapani Turkka, Nadia Urbinati, Wim Weymans and Linda Zerilli.

The production of this research companion has taken over a year. All the papers selected have been thoroughly rewritten and carefully revised according to an editorial plan devised to turn the original collection of papers, inter-connected as they were, into a research companion. We thank Ashgate's anonymous reviewers for their insight and suggestions.

The copy-editing has been a very interesting and engaging process, English being a second language for most of the authors. We have coordinated the work by Daniel Blackie, Satu Marjaana Halle, Bruce Henry Leitman, Tuija Modinos, Elizabeth Moulton, Samantha Novello, Violette Oudkerk and David Westacott. At Ashgate, we have been grateful for the continuing support of Kirstin Howgate and Margaret Younger, and the expertise of the editorial team. Finally, for us as editors, the preparation of the book has been a rewarding experience. We have been fortunate to have cooperated with such an outstanding team.

On the Politics, Concepts and Histories of European Democratization

Tuija Pulkkinen and José María Rosales

'Democratization' is a frequently encountered concept in academic book titles, often used under the assumption that Western democracies should be the normative reference regarding democratization elsewhere. Yet only a handful of studies deal with the initial breakthrough of democratization in Europe more than two hundred years ago, or with the fairly recent changes in democratic ideals and practices due to social movements and gender issues. This research companion presents a complementary view that questions the validity of the ready-made model of Western democracy. It studies the details of political struggles that have led to the present-day situation within the processes of democratization in Europe. Reading history this way highlights neglected features of democratization, such as rhetorical manoeuvres by political agents, conceptual changes, gender struggles and time conditions for political action – all of which are aspects that reveal the history of democratization to be much more contingent than it is usually taken to be.

The project is a result of a research network funded by the European Science Foundation, The Politics and History of European Democratization, which convened scholars from different parts of Europe into five workshops over three years. The main objective of the network was to discuss the politics, concepts and histories involved in democratization as a complex of changes that has altered the conditions of political action and debate on the Continent for the past two centuries. Instead of pursuing a comprehensive overview of every move in democratization, and to provide a feasible comparative approach, we have applied what Kenneth Burke calls 'representative anecdotes' through a contingent selection of case studies and research methods. From this vantage point, the chapters in this volume convey a vivid image of the crossroads of democratization with continuing debates and varying episodes and circumstances.

Democracy is a contingent phenomenon, yet at the moment, so it seems, it is a political system increasing in popularity. According to surveys by the United

Nations and other organizations such as Freedom House, by 2007 barely less than half of the two hundred states in the world were democracies and nearly half the world population lived under democratic regimes as the numbers were increasing. However, democracy is not necessarily a success story, let alone a one-way road. There are dangers reflected in some of the chapters of this collection, mostly in terms of violence, but also in terms of totalitarian gestures. Moreover, the very popularity of the concept of democracy renders the concept inherently controversial in both its content and its range of reference.

This volume aims to render the politics and history of European democratization into a complex, plural, contingent and open-ended experience that presents a colourful picture of the manifold and unexpected movements between ideas, concepts, languages, countries and political agents by conveying the process. The democratization of European politics is but a surprising result that has required both skillful rhetorical conceptualization and new forms of legitimization of changes for overcoming the resistance of traditions and institutions. In the end, democratization becomes a story which may take new turns, the future of which remains to be seen.

Democratization is thus a polyvalent concept that describes the changes either between various types of rulership or within them. Under this general usage, it is imbued with a diffuse assumption that in many cases, if not all, those changes arise from comparable antecedents and produce similar results. However, there is no single model, but a differentiation of political regimes in varying combinations of institutional factors, such as constitutions, elections, parties, parliaments and civic activity. If a historical survey of political regimes sheds light on the diverse models of democracy, the genealogical study of democracies provides a nuanced picture of democratization as a set of interacting strategies and procedures.

For all the vagueness surrounding it, though, the concept of democratization captures the idea of movement towards democracy in a very intuitive and comprehensible way, opening up the perspective of contingency and action for the future. In each particular case, a closer analysis of the use of the concept would clarify whether the hopes or expectations concerning democratization were irrational or reasonable, self-defeating or feasible, but the most intriguing aspect of the concept is its capacity to express the expectations for democratic change.

Democratization describes a procedure and outlines the conditions behind it. In many comparative case studies, the sequence of events and the claimed causes provide a view of the past, but the lessons for the future are the most instructive political aspect of any such reconstruction. Yet comparative studies are based on empirical and processed data that usually exclude, or underestimate, the non-linear aspects of political events, most notably the conflicting and the rhetorical features of politics. For the present volume, the contingency of democratization and the dissensus as the main characteristic of a democratic regime have been the guiding heuristic principles. Not surprisingly, despite the increasing tendency to give 'democracy' a positive connotation, the content of the concept 'democracy' itself, as well as the vocabulary around it, have remained as a topic of lively conversation during the two centuries of democratization. Acknowledging its conceptual openness, the chapters of this volume take up the concept from different perspectives while also recounting its historical change.

We have considered three general types of studies on democratization, in most cases combined with each other. In the first type, political imagination has been used to discern the singularity of events within a process of democratization either as a conceptual change or as a change of the political regime. Thought experiments, application of conceptual models and construction of historically significant ideal types in the analysis and appreciation of some possible or viable ways of democratic change are characteristic of several chapters presented here. In addition, the volume contains several historical studies, which interpret and evaluate changes, events, processes or movements that are well known in themselves, but deserve a novel appreciation from the perspective of democratization in Europe in general. Furthermore, we present a number of critical reviews of documents, political actions and actors to examine the discursive aspects of politics, and to analyze the rhetorical conditions, moves and strategies used in the struggles around democratization.

Modern democracy is most commonly defined in opposition to ancient and direct democracy through its representational character. Representation, however, poses a number of difficult questions for democratic theory. What is representation, and how should political representation be organized? How should the criteria for representation be set in order to satisfy the conditions of a democratic system? How do democratic participation and representation relate to each other? Answers to these questions are and have been debated – and by no means along any straightforward lines – in the rich history of democratic theory and practice as reflected in the accompanying chapters.

Gender is also one of the most persisting themes of discussion and arguments for political reform in the process of democratization. Since the time of the French Revolution, women's representation has been one of the sore points in the definitional paradoxes of liberal democracies. Paying tribute to gender as one of the significant stories in the history of representative democracy, our collection includes a number of chapters on the history and present state of struggles over gendered issues. The topics range from the conquest of universal suffrage and persistent controversies about modes of participation and representation to specific methods and concepts used by women and feminists in political action. How it was possible to think of democratic representation as universal and representative for so long while half of the population was not considered a legitimate part of it still remains an enigma.

Unlike political institutions, the specific nature of acting and thinking that democratic deliberation enhances is rarely paid attention to in the vast literature on democracy. This volume aims to correct this deficit by devoting several chapters to the specific types of conduct that democratic political systems have brought with them. These types of conduct involve not only particular modes of rhetoric cultivated within democratic regimes, but also ways of interpreting the past or ways of thinking of political times, for example. Also included are reflections on the role of passion in politics, as well as the histories of entire professions and ways of life that have come to existence, and in some cases also died out, within the process of European democratization.

In the course of the history of democratization, the methods of democratic political combat itself have been plentiful and have changed over time. The means of politics proper in democracy is undoubtedly speech, following the famous Arendtian dictum, and consequently, the main focus of this collection is on the rhetoric of politics. In politics, the rhetorical field of action extends from parliamentary discussions and political debates to media coverage and academic treatises, political pamphlets and other publications and forms of acting. The companion also pays due attention to other means of political tactics of persuasion all the way to violence and terrorism, not bypassing street action as part of democratic politics.

Likewise, a fair amount of European history, covering contexts from local to transnational, is present in the pages that follow. The authors analyze discussions by studying primary sources in a number of countries and languages with the aim of situating the results in a broader European context. Most of the chapters also engage in debates of political theory on how to understand democracy and how to judge its value in comparison to other ways of ruling.

***

The volume consists of 23 chapters divided into four parts focusing on European democratization from different historical and analytical perspectives. Regarding methods and contents, though, most of the papers intersect with several parts, which makes for an integrated project organized by four guiding threads: concepts, practices, changes, and contexts of democratization.

Part One, 'Concepts', focuses on conceptual shifts and controversies surrounding democratization moves. While tracing the theoretical discussions concerning the elective processes that begin with the choice of representative over direct democracy, the chapters deal with politically contested concepts such as representation, sovereignty, state, gender, violence, passions, subjects and citizenship. In Part Two, 'Practices', the attention turns to the operative, time-bound practices in the politics of democratization. The chapters in this part discuss different rhetorical strategies developed during the history of democratization. By examining the intellectual and political backgrounds of the rhetoric of democratization, they shed light on the evolving methods of political struggles, and prove the decisive role played by political and civic practices in the transformation of institutional politics.

By contrast, Part Three, 'Changes', surveys some long-term historical and political democratizing changes. They affect both practices and, above all, institutions. In all the cases discussed, democratization reveals a profound metamorphosis of the political culture. Lastly, the chapters of Part Four, 'Contexts', explore national and thematic contexts of democratization. Changes and contexts prove the historical and contingent nature of democratic systems, although they also reveal the comparable features present in many democratization processes. Besides, they point out how contingent and diverse the conceptualizations of democratic systems have been.

Concepts

Through the second half of the eighteenth century, 'democracy' referred to direct democracies of the ancient and medieval cities only. During the American and French Revolutions, a crucial semantic and institutional transformation took place, producing the synthesis (Paine) of democratic ruling and representation. Yet even then, allusion to the ancient model was present in the debates, and most of the time adduced to claim the impossibility of keeping the ideal of direct ruling in modern societies. In the end, it was the idea of representation that updated and adapted the ancient ideal for modern times.

In the first two chapters, both Frank R. Ankersmit and Mogens Herman Hansen discuss the merits of representative democracy with respect to direct democracy. Representation remains the key concept of modern democracy, since modern democratic political systems crucially rely on this principle. Many of the chapters included here deal, in one way or another, with the notion of representation. Against theorists who understand the main problem of democracy as the correct mirroring of the represented, both Frank Ankersmit in Chapter 1 and Tuija Pulkkinen in Chapter 7 emphasize the creative and performative power of representation.

In Chapter 1, 'Representative Democracy: Rosanvallon on the French Experience', Ankersmit examines theories of representation, particularly resemblance theory, reflecting simultaneously on the writings of Pierre Rosanvallon, one of the leading contemporary historians of democracy. Following Rosanvallon's presentation of the history of representative democracy in France, Ankersmit argues that after the Revolution, in nineteenth- and twentieth-century France, discussion about political representation was inspired by a search for the nature of the 'right' projection rules for representation under the meaning of resemblance theory. Ankersmit explores Rosanvallon's history of democratization in France in detail, as a series of inter-related debates concerning the correct projection rules. He argues that the weakest point in the resemblance theory of representation is its dependence upon prior projection rules. Accordingly, he points out that because there is no true representation independent of projection rules, representation is always anti-foundationalist. Yet Ankersmit also defends the notion of representation as foundational, in the sense that it founds a political order. Direct democracy, he points out, could never create a nation. He defends the primacy of representative democracy over direct ruling because, he argues, only representative democracy obliges citizens to look at themselves from the perspective of the others.

In spite of its apparent weaknesses, direct ruling is still considered an ideal of democracy in contemporary discussions. In Chapter 2, 'Direct Democracy, Ancient and Modern', Mogens Herman Hansen points out that the only real-life example of direct democracy was that of the Greek city-states from *c.* 500 BC to the end of the Hellenistic period. About half of the city-states were democracies, most of them direct democracies. Hansen describes how the institutions of Athenian direct democracy worked: from regular voting by ordinary citizens to the separation of initiative from decision, the appointment of magistrates, jurors and legislators by the drawing of lots and their short-term office, maximum one year, with a ban on iteration creating constant rotation, and political pay, which made decision-making and deliberation possible for less wealthy citizens too. Hansen contemplates whether this model of decision-making by amateurs could be transferred to our world of telecommunications and electronic voting, as the proponents of direct democracy would have it. The contemporary models of direct democracy which Hansen studies in detail include both the referendum procedure and experiments on random choice for creating a 'minipopulus'. Whether the direct form of democracy is inferior or superior to the prevailing form of representative democracy remains an open question, the answer to which depends on what democratic features are considered most valuable. The last related argument seems, though, out of the question. Hansen concludes that based on the historical evidence of ancient Greece, direct democracies cannot be expected to be more prone to peace than representative ones.

Long before the democratization process progressed seriously, Europeans discussed the procedures and practices deployed in parliaments and other representative assemblies. Related to these discussions, the composition and constitutional functions of representative assemblies were much debated, but rarely did those disputes concern the democratic nature of such institutions before the French Revolution. In the next two chapters, Gabriella Silvestrini and Christine Fauré present episodes of argumentation on key political notions, such as democracy and sovereignty, and government models, such as representative and republican, pointing out surprising contingencies and discrepancies in the arguments of authors like Rousseau and Sieyès.

'Democracy' was most often taken as an ancient model contrasted with monarchies and oligarchies and essentially understood as the rule by majority. In Chapter 3, 'Neither Ancient nor Modern: Rousseau's Theory of Democracy', Gabriella Silvestrini argues that contrary to what is generally suggested, Jean-Jacques Rousseau's idea of democracy had very little to do with majority rule. His model entails a high degree of constitutional constraints on the rule of majority, whereas democracy was identified with majority rule primarily by absolutist authors, such as Hobbes and Pufendorf. In the perspective of the modern theories of sovereignty, Silvestrini holds that even as it seems that Rousseau radically dismisses representative democracy, his position can actually be interpreted as being very close to the modern distinction between ordinary laws and constitutional norms. According to Rousseau's model of democracy, Silvestrini claims, the sovereignty of the people, which cannot be handed over to representatives, comprises the power to enact fundamental laws, as well as the power to choose and regularly control the rulers, while ordinary laws can be passed by representatives.

However, one of the major discussants and proponents of the ideal of good government before and during the French Revolution, Abbé Sieyès, took Rousseau as an advocate of direct democracy, which he himself strongly opposed. Traditionally, most scholars have considered Sieyès an advocate of representative government and a critic of the republican model, establishing a causal relation between both positions. Yet, as Christine Fauré documents in Chapter 4, 'Representative Government or Republic? Sieyès on Good Government', a closer reading of Sieyès's papers allows for a novel interpretation. Fauré points out the remarkable dissociation he made between representative government and the republican concept of power, associated with Rousseau and direct democracy. Sieyès proposed to maintain a king, but interestingly enough, an elected one. In this way, claims Fauré, Sieyès's elective monarchy resembles the contemporary institution of the President of the Republic.

Democracy involves not only structures such as parliaments and procedural rules such as elections, but also heated and passionate debates. Chantal Mouffe argues that democratic political theory should take the agonistic dimension of politics as the key to understanding democracy. In Chapter 5, 'Democratic Politics and the Dynamics of Passions', she defends her renowned conception of democracy as a model which aims to transform antagonisms into agonism. When democracy is theorized as a form of action, some consider the representation of interests as the key motivation of political actors, and others stress the role of reason in democratic deliberation. The sheer pleasure and thrill of passion for *pro* and *contra*, and the conflict therein that politics gives an opportunity to, is often forgotten. Mouffe argues against both the deliberative and the aggregative models of democracy, and also suggests that an agonistic understanding is better for coming to terms with the challenges democratic politics confronts today.

Mouffe and the authors of the two final chapters of Part One argue in the context of contemporary contexts of democratic theory, taking up some key concepts and understandings of democracy and politics. The next conceptual explorations deal with the role of violence in politics and with the concept of 'subject' as a gendered subject in democratic representation.

Violence, unlike passion, is by definition ruled out of the democratic realm of argumentation. Yet, the discursive dimension of politics, essential for democracy, is but a permanent counterweight to violent modes of collective action. The tension proves inexorable, though. As argued by Olivia Guaraldo in Chapter 6, democratic systems build on state structures, which rely on their monopoly of violence to keep violence away from the democratic debates. Inspired by the writings of Adriana Cavarero and Judith Butler, in 'Disobedient State and Faithful Citizen? Re-locating Politics in the Age of Globalization', she studies the connections between violence and politics from a perspective of re-thinking the human condition in its exposure to violence. Guaraldo traces the challenges that representative democracy faces at present to the early modern anthropological premises of politics based on the immune individual as a fictitious entity.

Approaching democracy through the existentialist notion of human condition is, in contrast, criticized by Tuija Pulkkinen in Chapter 7, on the basis of the problematic implications for understanding gender. In 'The Gendered "Subjects" of Political Representation', Pulkkinen scrutinizes the concept 'subject' in the context of contemporary feminist political theory. Examining Linda Zerilli's view, according to which subject issue dominates the feminist democratic theory, Pulkkinen detects a politics of philosophy involved in Zerilli's presentation by revealing some existentialist presuppositions. In Part One's final chapter, Pulkkinen brings the discussion back to the notion of representation, drawing attention to the performative effects of the history of democratization, one of which is the creation of a political subject, 'women'. She argues that there are three different gendered subject issues created within the history of democratization, and although the political subject 'women' is a troublesome heritage within feminism, the question of subjection to gendered norms remains an issue relevant for democratic political theory.

Practices

As different as the agendas and itineraries of democratization have proved within European history, no democratization process has ever been possible without people overcoming the resistance of the old order and without the legitimization of the changes involved. In terms of justification practices, democratization is always a result of rhetorical struggles among contemporary agents, as well as among later historians who attempt to understand the changes produced. Part Two presents a number of case studies on the rhetorical struggles, strategies and devices which first rendered democratization possible, then kept the new regimes going, and finally provided the means for their life. The history of democratization has created specific types of acting and speaking, including styles of parliamentary debating, as well as imaginative forms of political demonstrations.

Political debates are conducted by rhetorical means. Among them, maybe the most effective and extreme is the recourse to ridicule – making the enemy appear laughable – as argued by Quentin Skinner in Chapter 8, 'Political Rhetoric and the Role of Ridicule'. Skinner notes that in the beginning of the European democratic practices during the early-modern period, political speeches and writings surprisingly closely followed the rules of rhetoric, in the deliberative mode, of the textbooks of Roman and Greek authors. Aristotle, as well Quintilian and Cicero, all tell us that laughter is a sign of scorn and contempt, and that ridicule is considered the most powerful of all rhetorical weapons. Succeeding in exciting pity and scorn supports the argument, and at the same time discredits the adversaries. In early seventeenth-century England at the time of the Civil War, which is one of the first stages of modern European parliamentary rule, the weapon of ridicule was keenly made use of by King Charles I and his advisers to discredit the Parliamentary cause. Skinner shows how, by deploying every technique recommended by the theorists of rhetoric on ridicule, the king demonstrated by mockery that he regarded the Parliament beyond argument, and was prepared to fight the Parliamentary cause with all methods.

Political games within parliamentary regimes testify to the importance of rhetorical practices. The interplay between government and opposition is constantly mediated by the rhetorical moves of political actors. But even if politicians train their oratorical competences to perform properly in the public sphere, they have to undertake a crucial task of learning – that of playing with political times – argues Kari Palonen in Chapter 9, 'Political Times and the Rhetoric of Democratization'. Time is present in democratic politics in multiple forms. To begin with, democratic regimes distinguish themselves from monarchies and bureaucracies exactly on the basis of their temporary nature – the routine of the administration, for example, can always be interrupted by the next elections. But perhaps the most interesting aspect of the time condition of politics has to do with the ways it affects political performance. Politicians are extremely sensitive to time, notes Kari Palonen, and this fact is not a mere technical remark. On the contrary, it carries a more existential meaning with it. Palonen portrays politicians in democratic regimes as individuals exposed to situating their activities in time and to using time as a political tool. He suggests that the process of democratization has accentuated the timeliness of political activity. Simultaneously, it has valued the short term over the long, and required a reinterpretation of long-term concerns accordingly.

Time in the form of history is yet another tool in the hands of political agents, and it often provides a means of argument for and against democracy. A couple of such instances of arguing with history are analyzed in Chapter 10, 'Democratization and the instrumentalization of the Past'. Dirk Hermann takes up the political (ab)uses of history in countries as dissimilar as Switzerland and Russia. In the decisive moments in the history of democratization in both these countries, historians have in fact taken part in politics by evoking history. In Switzerland, the time of the French Revolution was recounted in competing narratives by the patriots and the reactionaries, who both evoked the past by referring to the founding myths of the country. In the democratization of Russia, the period immediately after the collapse of the Soviet system was rich in rhetorical uses of history. Herrmann illustrates the typical features of the process of democratizing a country, and indicates internal contradictions that undermine partisan history and democracy.

Historians influence public opinion by providing documented and reasoned accounts of the past. Needless to say, any reconstruction is an exercise in interpretation, inescapably linked to political connotations. Another indirect way of expressing an opinion in order to influence political decision-making is examined by Marcus Llanque in Chapter 11, 'The Rhetoric of Intellectual Manifestos from the First World War to the War against Terrorism'. Intellectual manifestos are oratorical attempts to persuade an audience, which may be local, but also national or even global. Furthermore, manifestos are a special kind of collective work, judged from the point of view of the intellectual authorship, and also a distinctive form of public intervention in politics. Very often intellectuals make an effort to be seen to represent a public position although they, of course, are no representatives and have not been elected. Llanque points out that sometimes in exceptional circumstances, like in times of warfare, defenders of the democratic idea become very ideological when praising democracy against ideological or totalitarian systems. Reflecting on the 2002 'What we are fighting for' manifesto by US intellectuals defending the 'war on terror', Llanque reminds us of the enduring temptation of intellectuals who identify with democracy to force democratization with non-democratic methods.

Unlike historical interpretations and statements by intellectuals, public performances, from demonstrations to the occupation of public spaces, are a means of both influencing opinions and political participation. Anna Schober analyzes from multiple perspectives the political significance of public actions that seem like mere aesthetic manifestations. Chapter 12, 'City Squats and Women's

Struggle: Feminist Political Action as Public Performance', shows how feminist non-professionals of politics have often made use of the practice of occupying public spaces for performances, making the absence of persons and topics in parliamentary politics visible by aesthetic means. Schober reconstructs the long and variable history of such theatrical politics of representation from the scene of the market women created in 1789 Paris, when they streamed from les Halles to the city hall, to the extraordinary emphasis on aesthetic style and bodily presence of the contemporary 'Women in Black' groups.

Part Two concludes with Chapter 13 by Simona Forti on 'Spectres of Totality'. 'Totalitarianism' is the term which in the course of the twentieth century has increasingly replaced the earlier counter-concepts of democracy – autocracy, tyranny and dictatorship. Forti studies closely the dangers that perpetually haunt democracy in the form of totalitarian practices. She names the three ever-haunting possibilities of conduct as spectres of 'hyper-humanity' (or the bio-political spectre), absolute lie (the spectre of the crisis of reality) and the normality of evil (or the spectre of organized irresponsibility). Arguing against those who would locate the totalitarian experience solely in the past of Europe, she maintains that within the history of European democratization, the dimension of totalitarianism is constantly present, much closer and less exceptional today than we tend to think, and never definitively over, as it is so commonly thought to be.

Changes

The most significant processes of change within the course of democratization in Europe – distinguishing recent forms from ancient democracies and going on throughout the modern democratization – have been related to the ideal that democracy as a political system should treat people equally irrespective of their household (*oikos*) status. Ancient democracy was played exclusively between fully independent heads of household. The citizens had considerable means of subsistence, which included having dependent people under their rule. By contrast, in modern times, dependency in domestic life by birth, or lack of independent economic means in life have successively less and less been accepted as reasons for not holding positions of representative trust.

Most notably, this change has affected women. The idea and enactment of the *polis* as a sole male practice has changed into an ideal of democracy as a non-gendered system along with the change in the legitimization of personal household dependency. The change in the gendered rules of democracy has successively, and often in paradoxical forms, gained ground since the time of the French Revolution. Starting from, by definition, dependent members of a household, women have first fought for suffrage and later for representative positions in democracies. Till this day, in all democratic systems the majority of members of representative and governing bodies are male, although the numbers are constantly challenged. The first two chapters in Part Three explore the gender aspect of the transformation of parliamentary systems covering parts of the incomplete story of struggles over gender within the democratization of Europe.

In Chapter 14, 'Women's Partial Citizenship: Cleavages and Conflicts Concerning Women's Citizenship in Theory and Practice', Claudia Wiesner discusses women's citizenship, concentrating on the tension between the universalist claim by the theory of citizenship and its unequal practice. Wiesner provides a historical overview, particularly with respect to German and French struggles before and after the conquest of the female suffrage. She also analyzes the factors of women's contemporary partial citizenship in Europe. With clear numbers, Wiesner demonstrates that in practical terms, equality is not the state of affairs with respect to gender in the European democracies today.

To bridge the gap between the unequal numbers of gender in parliamentary representation, some European countries have discussed and introduced gender quotas. In France, action towards this direction was taken through an election reform titled 'Parité' in 2000. Chapter 15 by Laure Bereni, 'Gendering Political Representation? The Debate on Gender Parity in France', examines the argumentation of parity advocates in France. Bereni first pays attention to rhetorical traditions, such as academic feminism and debates within international organizations, which provided the background for taking up the case of parity in France during the 1990s. Looking more closely at the discursive strategies of the French parity campaigners, she then argues that in their case, they paid excessive tribute to the dominant discourse of republican universalism. In her view, this strategy led to the depoliticization of the parity claim: instead of asking people to fight gender discrimination, the campaigners presented their demand as a means of improving representative democracy. The two genders were, within this strategically successful but ultimately inherently apolitical argumentation, presented as eternal complementary partners, not as categories constructed through power relations.

The next two chapters look at another aspect in the same change, which ultimately has to do with acceptance of household dependency. An ideal produced within the process of modern European democratization, which distinguishes it from the ancient models, is that nobody should be so dependent economically as not to be able to serve as a representative. The idea of paying the delegates, to make it possible for persons of any class to devote the time required to deliberating on public matters without being economically dependent, means that the professionalization of political agents has gained ground enormously in the development of the modern forms of democracy. The following two chapters in Part Three look at the change process of professionalization.

Chapter 16, 'Political Professionalism and Representative Democracy: Common History, Irresolvable Linkage and Inherent Tensions', is an analysis of the field of problems caused by the process of professionalization of politics. Jens Borchert argues in this chapter that there is an inevitable vicious circle imbedded in the democratization. In his view, professionalizing political offices has been a necessary development within the history of democracy in Europe, but that adjustment, in its turn, creates practices which tend to violate democratic principles. Professional representatives almost inevitably seek to maintain their power, and look for means to ensure it. His view is not an entirely pessimistic one, however, as he argues that although attempts to reform this state of affairs are futile, they are nevertheless crucial for keeping democracy active. 'The trick is to keep the democratic patient alive, not to heal him,' Borchert states.

Hubertus Buchstein examines the process of professionalization from another angle – electoral procedures – in Chapter 17, 'Democratization and Professionalization: The Disappearance of the Polling Officer in Germany and the Introduction of Computer Democracy'. Those who take care of the rooms where voting takes place and those who count the votes are important in running a democratic system, and many countries use public funding for carrying out these tasks. Buchstein recounts the story of the polling officers in Germany, and then considers the contemporary discussions on the ways of cutting the costs of the system by electronic devices. He argues that the new level of professionalization required for casting and counting the vote by the electronic means violates the idea of democracy. In this case, not only are the politicians turned into professionals, but also the voters need a high degree of expertise to take part in elections in an electronic, computer-assisted democracy. More seriously, the voters' trust in the counting procedures would be at great risk, as the results would be transparent only to highly educated professional experts. This, Buchstein claims, would pave way to a new aristocracy.

In the last chapter of Part Three, 'The History of Parliamentary Democracy in Denmark in Comparative Perspective', Uffe Jakobsen takes up a comparative perspective to the history of European democratization. Adopting the recent processes of change, i.a. of transitions from the authoritarian rule to that of democracy, in Eastern Europe after 1989 as his point of reference, Jakobsen attempts to build a systematic view for looking at democratization of Denmark in the nineteenth century. Curiously enough, as Jakobsen shows, similar challenges emerged in the nineteenth and twentieth centuries on both sides of the Continent. The outcome invites, in his view, a reconsideration of the supposed specificity of the types and timing of changes within the historical processes of democratization in Western Europe.

Contexts

Part Four continues with closer examinations of particular cases of the European democratization, while simultaneously taking up crucial aspects of the democratic systems. In Chapter 19, 'A Long and Hard Process of Democratization: Political Representation, Elections and Democracy in Contemporary Spain', Gonzalo Capellán de Miguel provides an analysis of the lengthy and complex history of Spanish democratization ever since the beginning of the nineteenth century, with the formation of the first liberal governments, till 1977, when free elections were held after almost forty years of dictatorship. The whole period, Capellán notes, is characterized by an irregular succession of liberal and anti-liberal intervals, which made for intermittent conceptualizations of a corpus of liberal ideas, and likewise, for an accidental creation of representative institutions. Over the years, either in authoritarian or in democratic contexts, in times of lack of liberties and in times of full freedom, democratization has generated a political culture of its own. The 1977 general elections carried the double symbolism of inaugurating a new democratic period and of retrieving a stolen democratic legacy.

While the Spanish history of democracy is uneven and full of challenges, Switzerland is usually given as an example of long and steady rule of democracy with a much closer connection to the ancient direct democracy than that of the other European countries. In Chapter 20, 'Do Political Parties Matter? Direct Democracy and Electoral Struggles in Switzerland in the Nineteenth Century', Pierre-Antoine Schorderet argues that despite the common identification of the Swiss political regime with direct democracy, based on a millennial history of democratic self-government in the cantons, Swiss democracy has also traditionally functioned through representative institutions. What singles out the Swiss model, Schorderet claims, is a combination of procedures and practices of direct and representative democracy. Concerning the party system, for example, the institution of the referendum has proven to be in itself a result of electoral struggles, and a new resource, as well as a constraint, for the emergence of political parties.

Another national case study is presented by Jussi Kurunmäki, who in Chapter 21, 'The Breakthrough of Universal Suffrage in Finland, 1905–1906', studies the early stages of the democratic reforms in Finland, the first European country to exercise universal suffrage. Kurunmäki asks what made it possible for Finland, maintaining the last estate-based representation system on the Continent, to unexpectedly jump ahead of any other European country into introducing universal and equal male and female suffrage in the parliamentary elections of 1906. Paying attention to the different contexts, where demands for universal suffrage were made, from parliamentary discussions and initiatives to women's suffrage mobilizations and publicist debates in the press, Kurunmäki documents the singularity of Finland's path to democratization, in contrast to countries such as England or Sweden, with a long history of gradual reforms.

The next two chapters in Part Four provide a view of more contested environments and rarer and more recent examples within the European democratization processes. They both also involve challenges to democracy in the form of violence, but of a very different kind.

In Chapter 22, 'Nationalism, Constitutionalism and Democratization: The Basque Question in Perspective', José María Rosales focuses on the Basque Country, providing a perspective on the challenges a nationalist conflict poses to a democratic regime. Most, if not all, types of nationalism in European democracies endorse the principles of democratic theory and of liberal constitutionalism. Considered constitutionally, though, the normative consistency of democratic nationalism is but partial, argues Rosales. The chapter examines the intriguing relations between nationalism and democracy through the exceptional view of terrorist violence in the name of a nationalist cause.

Chapter 23, 'The Dis-/Appearance of the *Demos*', by Meike Schmidt-Gleim, takes up another case of outbreak of violence, now from the point of view of a self-diagnosis of a democratic system. Her case is the *banlieue* revolts in French cities during fall 2005. Schmidt-Gleim sees the danger, posed to the long history of democracy in France, in the way the government responded to the upheavals by ultimately demanding that the subjects obey the existing norms. Schmidt-Gleim argues that this means annihilating the *demos* and turning sovereignty into a governmental principle.

The volume closes with a postscript chapter on the future of democracy by Kari Palonen, who initiated as well as acted as the Chair of the Politics and History of European Democratization network. In 'The Past, Present and Future of Democratization', Palonen ends this research companion with a characteristically positive note on the future of democracy. In his 2006 book *La contre-démocratie*, Pierre Rosanvallon, also a member of the European Science Foundation network, names as 'counter-democratic' moments the new types of measures which can be used to complement the representative regime. Palonen notes that in his analysis, Rosanvallon ultimately remains critical of the depoliticizing and paralyzing effects of counter-democratic measures. The postscript briefly examines the current situation of democracy against the backdrop of its history, and takes another look at the old discussion surrounding representative democracy – the relationship between government and parliament, considering majority rule. A crucial issue for the success of democratic systems, Palonen concludes, is finding ways to prevent a majority from 'realizing' its programme too completely.

At the beginning of this Introduction, we mentioned some figures on the global spread of democracy, a process continually challenged by various threats. The comparative view can be updated continuously: democracy captivates the political imagination of people all over the world, and yet it is a fragile conquest, always in need of civic legitimization through the exercise of political agency and judgment by the citizens. Taking into account these conditions, this research companion aims to provide a more precise view of democratization. By presenting a multifaceted picture of democratization in Europe as an open-ended process, it suggests that there are no clear-cut solutions or trouble-free routes to one direction or another. Yet, notwithstanding all the elusiveness of the term, a positive conclusion on the basis of this state of affairs is that there is always room – and indeed, a need – for further democratization within political systems.

PART I

CONCEPTS

Representative Democracy: Rosanvallon on the French Experience

Frank R. Ankersmit

Introduction

In 1992, Francis Fukuyama published his *The End of History and the Last Man*. In this book, Fukuyama celebrated, among other things, the world-wide triumph of democracy. Since then, the facts have confirmed his view. Democracy has gloriously defeated all its rivals, and alternatives to democracy are nowhere taken seriously. But strangely enough, at the same time in most Western countries, citizens nowadays tend to be dissatisfied with their governments, they distrust their politicians more than was ever the case in the last few decades, they easily shift from one political party to another without expecting any real benefit from this, and they are almost unanimously far more focused upon what their democratic governments do wrong than on what they do right.

Of course, this is nothing new. We need only think of the Interbellum in order to recognize that dissatisfaction with democracy is far from being a new phenomenon. Or think of the late 1960s, when radicalist versions of direct democracy or of self-government were opposed to the representative democracies actually existing in the West. What is new, therefore, is that our present dissatisfaction with representative democracy does not go together with the hope of something better. We now seem to acquiesce in what dissatisfies us so much in our democracies, and seem not to be challenged by this into thinking how to improve our present political predicament. For example, when commenting on his own country, Pierre Rosanvallon writes: 'la France est devenue molle, la vie politique globalement terne, la mobilisation sociale réduite à quelques tensions passagères et les débats à l'étiage. Les passions se sont énervées, l'imagination s'est mise en sommeil' (Rosanvallon 1998, 329).

I quite deliberately chose for a quote from Rosanvallon's writings in order to illustrate our present state of mind with regard to (representative) democracy. For in the 1400 pages of his erudite and magisterial trilogy – *Le sacre du citoyen. Histoire du suffrage universel en France* (1992), *Le peuple introuvable. Histoire de la représentation démocratique en France* (1998), *La démocratie inachevée. Histoire de la souveraineté du peuple en France* (2000) – Rosanvallon gave us an account of the two hundred-year history and present state of representative democracy that does not have its counterpart anywhere else. It would be no exaggeration to say that what Braudel did for economic history in the 1960s and 1970s has its parallel for political history in the writings by Rosanvallon: Braudel gave us the *longue durée* of our economic past, and Rosanvallon that of democracy. It is true that Rosanvallon mainly writes about France, and one should certainly be careful when making inferences from his analysis of the French case to what the situation is like in other countries or to what might even be generally true of contemporary representative democracy. But one may hope that precisely this fact will challenge historians from other countries to emulate Rosanvallon's effort and show what their own country's contribution to democracy has been.

Moreover, whatever the results from such future books may be, we will have to agree with Rosanvallon's claim that the French experience with representative democracy since the French Revolution must be especially informative. The explanation is that the transition from older forms of government to representative democracy was far more gradual in countries like the UK or the USA than it had been in France, and that, since 1789, France has experimented with a whole series of more or less democratic forms of government. And avalanches of theoretical speculation accompanied each change in government. Taking the above into account, one might well agree with Rosanvallon when he says that representative democracy in all its imaginable (or unimaginable) variants has been more eagerly and more 'existentially' discussed in France than in any other country in the world – and that for this reason, the history of democracy in France ought to be of specific interest to the political philosopher (Rosanvallon 1992, 37–8).

So, if one wishes – and this will be my aim in this chapter – to discuss representative democracy not only from an exclusively theoretical perspective and include also what one might call the actual 'experience' of representative democracy, it is advisable to focus on France. And then we can choose no better guide than Pierre Rosanvallon.

Representation and Truth

Nevertheless, before getting down to the historical realities of representative democracy, a few theoretical comments have to be made on the notion, and on that of representation in particular. To begin with, from a historical perspective we can say that the classical notion of democracy has nothing to do with representation, and next, that the representation of the estates had nothing to do with democracy. It need therefore not surprise us that many authors in the eighteenth and nineteenth centuries found it difficult to fit 'representative democracy' into already existing political categories, and sometimes even believed it to be a wholly new kind of government that could not be accounted for in terms of accepted political wisdom (Rosanvallon 1998, 12).

In spite of the conceptual puzzles occasioned by the notion, it came into use in the second half of the eighteenth century. According to Rosanvallon, what we presently understand by the notion can already be found in the writings by the Marquis d'Argenson of the 1760s (Rosanvallon 2000, 24), whereas the phrase 'representative democracy' itself seems to have been used for the first time by Alexander Hamilton in a letter dated 19 May 1777 (Rosanvallon 1998, 11). So the notion was already current at the end of the eighteenth century; moreover, one quickly succeeded in identifying what are the crucial questions to be asked and discussed with regard to representative democracy, as has quite recently and most cogently been argued by Bernard Manin in his *Principles of Representative Government* (1997; for the nineteenth-century French authors see also Rosanvallon 1998, 235ff.); whereas, on the other hand, the adjective 'representative' leaves less, or even no room at all, for disagreement, and will thus be acceptable to anybody.

However, what meaning should we give to the adjective 'representative', if used in the context of democratic politics? When focusing on the philosophical discussion of the notion of representation, we will find that there are two theories of representation: the resemblance theory and the substitution theory of representation. According to the resemblance theory, a representation should *resemble* what it represents. A picture or painting of a tree is a good representation of that tree if and only if it resembles the tree in question. Though many philosophers will still agree that there is much of value in the resemblance theory, it never quite recovered from the criticism leveled at it by Nelson Goodman in his very influential *Languages of Art* of 1968. Goodman argued that the resemblance theory will inevitably get entangled in absurdities. For example, suppose you have the following three things: (1) Blenheim Castle, (2) a painting of Blenheim castle and (3) a painting of, let's say, the Duke of Marlborough. Assuming, then, the resemblance theory to be true, you would have to assert that (2) is a representation of (3) rather than of (1), since paintings resemble each other more (all consisting of paint on a canvas, with a frame around it, and so on) than a painting and a huge building resemble each other.

Goodman did not infer from this that representation should be an inconsistent notion. Rather, it was his argument that representation is always tied to a symbolic or notational system such as, for example, language – hence the title of his so very influential book. These symbolic or notational systems are always active between the represented and its representation (though sometimes these notational systems may be so natural and so widely shared by all of us that we tend to forget about their existence). But they are there, after all, and this makes the direct confrontation between the representation and its represented, which is presupposed by the resemblance theory, an illusion. Think, again, of language: words do not resemble what they stand for or represent. Or think of a historical text on some part of the past: such a text may be a most convincing representation of that part of the past, but it does not 'resemble' that part of the past in any accepted meaning of that word.

This brings me to the substitution theory that was, as far as I know, first proposed by Edmund Burke in his book *A Philosophical Enquiry into the Origins of our Ideas of the Sublime and the Beautiful* (1757). This theory takes the etymological meaning of the term 'representation' as its point of departure: a 're-presentation' makes something 'present' (again) that is absent, or, put differently, it is a *substitute* (hence the theory's name) or a *replacement* for something that is absent. Now, it should be emphasized that the substitution theory does not mention any criteria (resemblance or anything else) something has to satisfy in order to function as a representation of a represented. For example, Ernst Gombrich was quite explicit about his rejection of the resemblance criterion. Speaking about images of the Gods that were created at the dawn of mankind, Gombrich writes:

> in many cases these 'images' represent in the sense of 'substitution'. The clay horse or servant buried in the tomb of the mighty takes the place of the living. The idol takes the place of the God. ... Can our substitute take us further? Perhaps, if we consider how it could become a substitute. The 'first' hobby horse (to use eighteenth century language) was probably no image at all. Just a stick which qualified as a horse because one could ride on it. ... The tertium comparationis, the common factor, was function rather than form. (Gombrich 1961, 172)

Hence, for the child a hobby horse could be a representation of a real horse, not because it *resembled* a real horse, but simply because it could in the child's eyes *function* as a real horse. However – and this cannot be emphasized enough – this does not exclude that *under certain circumstances* it is resemblance that may make something into a believable substitute for something else, for a represented. In such cases, we have a kind of overlap of the two theories of representation. These cases are all the more interesting since they present us with what appeal the resemblance theory has for its adherents, and in continuation with this, how we should weigh the merits and shortcomings of the resemblance and the substitution theories.

We can sum up as follows. When comparing the substitution and the resemblance theory of representation, the first is undoubtedly the stronger of the two. For sometimes representations do not resemble what they represent or offer a reliable basis for true statements about a represented. Think of Gombrich's example of the hobby horse. But in other cases this may be different, and then true statements about the world can be derived from what is given to us in a representation. But this should not tempt us into seeing in truth our sole criterion for the reliability of representation, as the resemblance theory requires us to do. For even if a representation resembles its represented, there is a dimension in representation that cannot be reduced to issues of truth and falsity. And our conclusion must be that truth cannot be our compass in our search for reliable representation – aesthetic, historical, political or otherwise.

Implication for Political Representation

The main conclusion to be derived from the foregoing is that we should realize ourselves how helpless and insufficient the criteria of resemblance and truth are, in fact, in (political) representation. Take, again, the example of historical representation: these criteria may be fully satisfied in the sense that all the historian's statements on the past are true, and yet the resulting representation may be wholly unilluminating.

This may show us what is wrong with a whole set of theories of political representation. Think, for example, of the views of political representation that were put forward by the anti-Federalists during the debate about the American Constitution:

> the very term representative, implies that the person or body chosen for this purpose, should resemble those who appoint them – a representation of the people of America, if it be a true one, must be like the people ... They are the sign   the people are the thing signified .... It must then have been intended that those who are placed instead of the people, should possess their sentiments and feelings, and be governed by their interests, or in other words, should bear the strongest resemblance of those in whose room they are substituted. (quoted in Manin 1997, 110)

Obviously, we have to deal here with a translation of the resemblance theory of representation to the domain of political representation. When trying to identify the kind of (tacit) assumption of the resemblance theory of political representation, we had best consider the way the theory was formulated by Mirabeau: 'parlant de la bonne composition d'une assemblée, Mirabeau note en janvier 1789 qu'elle doit être "pour la nation ce qu'est une carte réduite pour son étendue physique; soit en partie, soit en grand, la copie doit toujours avoir les mêmes proportions que l'original"' (Rosanvallon 1998, 17).

Mirabeau's conception of political representation, described by Rosanvallon as 'l'approche "microcosmique" de la représentation', can be said to be an elaboration of the anti-Federalist argument. The anti-Federalist required the representative (or, rather, the representation of the people) to resemble what he represents, whereas Mirabeau offers a proposal for how to actually achieve this aim. And the intuition then is that there should be certain 'projection rules' – as there are rules for the projection of the surface of the earth on a map – that have to be applied in order to guarantee 'resemblance'. And, next, that if we are in possession of the right projection rules, a 'true' representation of the electorate or of the nation will be no less possible than a fully reliable map of a country.

It might well be said that a good deal of the reflection on political representation in nineteenth- and twentieth-century France – as recorded by Rosanvallon – was inspired by a relentless search for the nature of these 'right' projection rules. I'd like to illustrate this with two suggestive examples taken from Rosanvallon. I shall begin with a few comments on the so-called doctrinaire liberals. The doctrinaire liberals were a group of politicians and statesmen (such as Pierre Paul Royer-Collard, 1763–1845, or François Guizot, 1787–1874) or high-placed public servants, such as Prosper de Barante (1782–1866). The group always remained quite small. Nevertheless, the group was highly visible and most prominently present in public debate. For example, the electoral law of February 1817, with which the Ultras lost their grip on the electorate by the abolition of indirect vote, was mainly the work of Royer-Collard and of François Guizot (Rosanvallon 1992, 210). After the revolution of 1830, the doctrinaires came to power – and Louis Philippe's reign can well be seen as the regime of the doctrinaires.

The main and lasting contribution of the doctrinaire liberals has been the transformation of the still very abstract and strongly contractualist liberalism of the late eighteenth century to a thoroughly historicized liberalism, reminding the politician of the fact that he should always take into account the historical context within which he has to take his decisions. As they also argued, after 1815 France needed above all a politics aiming at 'impartiality' and at a transcendence of existing political divisions. From this perspective, the name of the doctrinaire liberals could not possibly have been more misleading (for a conjecture on the origin of the name of the doctrinaire liberals, see Kossmann 1987, 269). Moreover, they were the first liberals to be very much aware of the complexities of the post-revolutionary social order and of the implications that this observation should have for the politician. And certainly Guizot was, at times, capable of insights into the nature of the early nineteenth-century socio-political order that are sometimes even more penetrating and clairvoyant than Tocqueville's (see for this Rosanvallon's equally brilliant *Le moment Guizot*, 1985: for example, 55–72).

The sovereignty of Reason is the point of departure of all political wisdom for the doctrinaires, and it therefore need not surprise us that *Le Globe* could hail the idea as 'la théorie du siècle' (Rosanvallon 1992, 231). Much of the charm of this notion of sovereign reason for Guizot was that nobody, at any time, could really claim to be in possession of the sublime dictates of Reason. In this way, Guizot succeeded in killing two birds with one stone. For, in the first place, Reason would effect a laicization of political thought in so far as Reason belongs to a world in which God's Word is no longer decisive. But, next, since Reason was just as much out of the reach of anybody as God had been, the doctrinaires could call a halt to anybody claiming to possess supreme political wisdom and in terms of which liberal freedom might be threatened. In this way, civil freedom now found a most secure anchor in their political thought.

But there is a second dimension to this notion of the sovereignty of Reason: the notion will function much like a Kantian 'regulative idea' that should always guide and inform our efforts, while at the same time being forever beyond our reach. In this way, the notion of sovereign Reason mobilizes all of the social and political body in a common effort to improve the social and political world we are living in; in this way, it presupposes and stimulates a close interaction of state and society and the rejection of any attempt to create insurmountable barriers between the two (see Guizot 1851, 68).

Sovereignty is now *dynamized*; it has become a social and political force moving us to the future. The doctrinaires opted for a Reason that is, essentially, forward-looking, urging us to gather all the intimations of the rationalization to be found in the social and political world, while avoiding, as Burke had recommended, the eighteenth-century rationalist presumption that anything 'final' could ever be found in this way.

It will not be hard to spell out what this should mean for political representation. In agreement with the foregoing, Guizot argues that the main purpose of representation can only be to gather as well as possible these *disseminations* (a word that he much likes to use) of Reasons all over society. When claiming that representation is the discovery of political reason, Guizot insists: 'que le gouvernement représentatif n'attribue la souveraineté à personne, que tous les pouvoirs s'agitent dans son sein pour la découverte et la pratique fidèle de la règle qui doit présider à leur action, et que la souveraineté de droit ne leur est reconnue qu'à condition qu'ils la justifieront incessamment' (Guizot 1851, 93).

At first sight, Guizot's argument might seem to amount to a powerful justification of universal suffrage – for what a priori certainty would there be that no 'disseminations' of Reason could possibly be found in the lower strata of society as well? Contrary to the logic of his own argument, Guizot used it to excluding the majority of the French from the ballot. With this he stood, admittedly, in a long tradition going back to the physiocrats. And we should not forget that the Revolution itself, even in its more radical phases, still distinguished between 'active' and 'passive' citizens, of which only the former possessed the right to vote. (For a detailed account of the (pre-)history of universal suffrage during the French Revolution, see Rosanvallon 1992, 41–185. See especially p. 80 for the, to us, rather surprising lack of interest of even people like Robespierre and Pétion in the political exclusion of these passive citizens.)

In Guizot's case, the practical significance of his argument about sovereignty should be that only a tiny upper layer of wealthy bourgeois had the right to vote, since he believed that only these rich bourgeois had the 'capacity' of political Reason. So it all resulted in what Rosanvallon refers to as 'le régime capacitaire', whose alleged ineluctability was already derided by Tocqueville with his ironic caricature of the monarchy of July: 'la force des choses veut que les capacités gouvernent' (Tocqueville 1840 [1945], 73).

Discerning a liberating and a regressive dimension in it can best characterize the doctrinaire's argument in the history of political representation. The liberating dimension reveals itself in the dissemination of Reason in society, and in its appeal to society no less than to the political centre itself to collect and organize these manifestations of Reason into a coherent whole for the benefit of the entire nation. The theory and practice of the doctrinaire's policies can best be compared here with the breaking up of a hitherto uncultivated political wilderness and making it fit for political tillage. It is as if the doctrinaire has dug political canals over parts of a still pre-political landscape so that the political Reason scattered over the landscape can be led back via those canals to the center, where it can now be made useful for the nation.

In this way, political freedom is spread over part of the territory. But the regressive dimension of the doctrinaire's argument nullifies much of the promise of its liberating dimension by restricting the locations of Reason to the immediate neighborhood of these canals. All in all, it is as if somebody had made a hydrographic map of some part of a country carefully 'representing' all the canals in that part of the country, and who then says: 'Well, this is what the country really *is* like.' This person apparently believes that there is nothing in the world beyond what can be processed by the rules for cartographical projection. And such a person would, in this way, confuse description with representation. Indeed, this is, in fact, how Royer-Collard would look at political representation: he insists that it could never be more than a *metaphor*. For, so his (Rousseauist) argument goes, if taken *literally*, representation means that the representative has 'une véritable ressemblance' (!) with whom he represents (Rosanvallon 1998, 104; see also Rosanvallon 1992, 234). In this way, a misconception of representation on the one hand and bourgeois social prejudice on the other most unhappily mutually reinforced each other.

This brings us to another theoretically interesting proposal for political representation that is, in fact, both a kind of mirror image of the doctrinaire proposal for representation and its logical complement, taking us up to the early years of the Third Republic. At that time, one started to have one's misgivings about the individualism of traditional political representation: individual citizens vote for their assemblies, they do so in the isolation of the compartments of a polling station, which seems to symbolize the momentary suspension of all of their social affiliations. And yet these social affiliations are no less part of the social and political fabric than the voter in his 'naked' individuality. Put differently, was the traditional voting not an untoward homage to the methodological individualism of eighteenth-century contract theories? And was such a system, for this very same reason, not completely out of step with the demands of the time, now that the nineteenth century had been so successful in measuring the immense powers of history and of society? But when theorists attempted to derive a new representational system doing justice to the powers of history and society, the resemblance theory of representation was no less triumphant in their minds than it had been a century earlier in those of the anti-Federalists or of Mirabeau (see Rosanvallon 1998, 103).

Nevertheless, the task resemblance theory is now required to perform is quite different from the one expected from it by eighteenth- and early nineteenth-century theorists. To put it into one formula, previous applications of the resemblance theory were 'perspectivist'; that is to say, one required the political representation to resemble the nation itself *if seen from the perspective of the political center*. Ideally, it would have to make no difference whether the politician, located at the political centre and looking at the nation from that vantage point, would have to deal with the people's representatives or with the people *itself*.

Well, this perspectivism is completely reversed in the kind of theories Rosanvallon has in mind here. A quasi-metaphysical pretension has now crept in: one is no longer interested in the question of what the electorate may look like if seen from one perspective or another – one now rather asks the baffling question: 'What does the nation look like, if seen from the perspective of *itself*?' For only the answer to *this* question could show us what the nation *really* or *essentially* is like. And is it not the nation's essence, or its nature, that ought to be represented by the nation's representation? One opted for this proud alternative all the more easily and naturally since a perfectly satisfactory and self-evident answer could be given to the apparently so perplexing question of how to get to this essence or nature of the nation. For is this not simply what we have the social sciences for? We should not lose from sight that these nineteenth-century positivist conceptions anticipate the role granted to economic considerations in our contemporary democracies, where the economic argument often is a stronger determinant in public decision-making than the will of the electorate.

It was often argued by these theorists – such as philosopher Alfred Fouillée, the sociologist Thomas Ferneuil and Emile Durkheim himself – that French society is not 'une poussière d'hommes individuels', but an *organic* whole, whose parts cooperate closely with each other and which could even not exist without the interaction with these other parts of society. In practice, this resulted in proposals to discern in French society a number of (professional) groups held together by shared interests – and then the argument was that political representation should do justice, in one way or another, to these ineluctable facts about the social organization of France.

If we compare the doctrinaire's conception of political representation to the one defended by the social theorists, the main difference is undoubtedly that the former opened up the political domain from above, whereas the social science theorists propose to do so from below. But there is agreement between these two conceptions of representation on a more fundamental level. *For both embrace the resemblance theory of representation* – and both rely either implicitly or explicitly on what I'd like to call here certain rules for 'the projection' of the electorate on the much reduced scale of the 'map' of the representative assembly. In the case of the doctrinaires, a (fairly) naive theory about the dissemination of the *capacités* over the country's political surface could serve as such a rule of projection. *Mutatis mutandis*, the same is true of the social scientific model: the stratifications and categories that were deemed by the social scientists to be constitutive of the nation as a social whole, or as a social organism, would have to be respected for an optimal political representation. And in both cases, the decisive argument for these intuitions has been that only thanks to the application of such rules for 'representational projection' could 'resemblance' of the representation to the represented both be achieved and ascertained. In the case of the doctrinaires, the projection rule of the *capacités* would ensure that the Reason embodied by the nation's representatives would closely 'resemble', or even be identical with, the Reason that is disseminated all over the nation. And in the case of the social scientific model, social scientific theory would even offer a scientific guarantee for the 'resemblance' between the nation's political representation and the electorate it represents.

It should be observed, in this context, that the wrestling with these questions of resemblance and of how to achieve it had an urgency in France that one will rarely encounter in other major Western democracies. Rosanvallon mentions several explanations for this. Above all, we should never forget the suddenness and the staggering proportions of the political challenges the French revolutionaries saw themselves confronted with in the years after 1789. After one had wiped away the monarchy and all that went with it, the clergy, the aristocracy, the Parlements, the *corps intermédiaires* and so on, no political institution of Ancien Régime France had been allowed to stand. Everything had been razed to the ground, and therefore everything now had to be built from scratch again.

The only two things left were, in fact, the revolutionary government in Paris and the indiscriminate mass of the French people. So the real problem was how to (re-)establish contact between these two. And the only certainty one had was that this had to be achieved, in one way or another, in terms of political representation. As a consequence, the issue of political representation – an issue that one could discuss quietly and dispassionately in other countries (as was even the case in the USA in the years before 1787) – was here truly a matter of life and death. Moreover, decisions about it could not possibly be postponed, but should have been reached yesterday rather than today.

One of great merits of Rosanvallon's trilogy is that it shows to what extent the shock of these terrible events became inscribed in the French political collective memory, and to what extent this has determined French thought about political representation. He begins by emphasizing that the obligation to begin with point zero after the destruction of all that existed before 1789 could only further reinforce all the rationalist tendencies that French political culture had inherited from the Enlightenment. Reason was the only instrument one could rely on, as the past and the political experience taught by the past had so mercilessly been wiped out. What Rosanvallon refers to as *l'évidence* – what should be evident to anybody regardless of his or her historical and social background – could at that moment be one's only compass (Rosanvallon 1992, 152ff.). There was no accepted empirical basis one could rely upon. This allows us to understand why the issue of who would have or not have the right to vote and to be represented could at that moment be answered only with an appeal to 'natural' and not to 'social' categories. As the social had been destroyed, to be reconstructed anew together (Rosanvallon 1992, 70ff.) with the political order, natural differentiations were the only distinctions one could rely upon – distinctions with regard to age, sex, or mental capacities (Rosanvallon 1992, 106, also 101ff.). Who is and who is not to be a citizen was no longer a simple social datum, but a profound philosophical problem. And more importantly, it can be understood why representation should be for the French revolutionaries (and for later generations!) such an odd problem, combining the features of both inevitability and insolvability. It presented an inevitable problem, since only in terms of political representation could a political link be established between the revolutionary government and the masses of the population that might legitimate the government's actions. The insolvable problem was what purpose representation could possibly serve. Rosanvallon has most perceptively defined it as follows:

> *il y a une seconde raison qui explique pourquoi la représentation comme technique politique est extérieure à tout ce rationalisme politique française du XVIIIme siècle: c'est que le processus représentatif, en tant que technologie politique, a besoin d'hétérogénéité pour exister. S'il n'y a pas d'hétérogénéité acceptée comme telle dans la société, la représentation est un processus impossible et impensable. La représentation ne peut s'opérer que si l'on reconnaît des états, des parties, des classes, des territoires,*

*clairements distingués et identifiés. Il faut que la société puisse se figurer
dans des divisions, dans des différences, s'appréhender dans ses dénivelés.
(Rosanvallon 1992, 156)*

So the paramount difficulty was that anything that could possibly have given
meaning and content to political representation – heterogeneity, social and political
distinctions and so on – had been eliminated from French society by the Revolution
itself. The Revolution had dissolved society into a myriad of isolated individuals
(a fact that would provide Tocqueville with the intrigue of his books on democracy
and on the French Revolution). So the Revolution needed representation in order
to legitimize itself, but it had, at the same time, eradicated all that could possibly
give meaning to representation.

Finally, we can now also understand the deep-rooted fascination of the
revolutionaries (a legacy they would also leave to later generations) for the
resemblance theory of political representation and for the 'projection rules' always
accompanying this theory. For resemblance might really reveal here something
that 'did not immediately meet the eye', to use the most appropriate phrase in this
context. After the destruction of the political landscape of the Ancien Régime, one
really walked in complete darkness as far as the socially and politically crucial facts
about the nation were concerned. This placed the (revolutionary) politicians in a
situation that one could best compare to someone having only a representation
(drawing, painting or photo) to obtain an idea of someone's physical appearance.
And then one's only worry is that the representation should resemble as closely
as possible its forever inscrutable original – all other 'functions' (Gombrich!) that
a representation might have are then gladly sacrificed for resemblance. Next,
under such circumstances, the start of a passionate search can be expected for the
kind of 'projection rules' that will be most successful in guaranteeing 'objective'
resemblance (recall cartographical debate about normal, transversal, azimuthal,
orthogonal and so on projection in the sixteenth and seventeenth centuries). And
since debates about such projection rules should not be prejudiced by purely
empirical coincidences, we need no longer be surprised by the tendency towards
rationalist and a priorist patterns of reasoning in French political thought.

As a result, the idea of political parties, in so far as they attempt to do justice to
social and historical contingencies, would never obtain in France the political self-
evidence that it had in other major Western democracies (Rosanvallon 1998, 310ff.).
Finally, this may also help to explain the, for foreigners, so amazing addiction of
the French to constitutional reform and their habit of changing the constitution as
easily as one moves in other countries from one party(-coalition) to another. For if
the constitution offers the most fundamental definition of the relationship between
the state and its citizens, in France this is an issue that is *never* taken for granted,
and therefore an issue that is placed at the top of the political agenda with a certain
regularity.

In sum, after having destroyed all the social and political institutions of Ancien
Régime France, representation simply *had* to become France's main political
problem. And next, when thinking about representation, an embrace of the

resemblance theory and of the idea of the projection rules (that are necessarily part of the theory) was more or less ineluctable.

Alternatives?

From our present perspective, the weakest point of the resemblance theory is its dependence on what I have referred to as these projection rules. For without these projection rules, resemblance cannot be justified: we cannot speak of resemblance *tout court*, but only of resemblance in relationship to what Goodman had called a 'notational system'. For example, we can say that a map 'resembles' some part of the globe (that is, it offers a true representation of it) if and only if a *certain system of cartographical projection* has been applied correctly. Moreover, we should be clear about what projection -system we have in mind, as what may be a correct representation within a particular system could quite well be faulty within a different one.

Well, there are two facts about these notation (or projection) systems that we should always bear in mind. Firstly, these systems may well be so natural and so obvious, and may well be so widely shared by all of us, that we simply tend to forget about their existence. But nevertheless, they will always be there, as we shall have to admit after a moment's reflection. For example, we see a drawing or a painting of a city, and will then all agree that the city has been represented correctly since the representation 'resembles' its represented. And we will then all be inclined to say, so since we all have grown up with the kind of linear perspective that came *en vogue* in the West since Alberti and Masaccio. But there is also such a thing as 'Chinese perspective', where parallel lines in reality are also depicted as parallel lines on the representation. So there is no 'resemblance' and no 'true representation' without there also being certain 'notation systems', 'projection rules' and so on that define what is to *count* as resemblance.

In the second place, these notation or projection systems do not have their source or justification in the world (or in the represented itself). Cities themselves are wholly indifferent to whether they are represented with the help of either linear or Chinese perspective, and they do not require us to opt for either of them. Nor does either of these perspectives give us easier access to the nature of what is represented than the other. In this way, representation can be called 'anti-foundationalist' (see the first paragraph of the last section for an important qualification of this claim) in the true sense of that word: for there is no real *fundamentum in re* for the kind of notation or projection system we adopt for representing the world. One cannot argue for or against some such notation or projection system on the basis of what the world *is like*. In this way, resemblance has been shown to be founded on, or to presuppose, something that cannot be reduced to resemblance *itself*. And this observation is, of course, fatal for the resemblance theory. For it has been demonstrated that the theory implicitly presupposes what it explicitly rejects.

In consequence, we should distinguish between the notion of 'the represented', on the one hand, and what we commonly associate with 'the world', on the other.

Its supreme indifference to what we say makes it into the repository of truth. And at first sight, we tend to identify 'the represented' with 'the world'. For are the trees depicted on this painting by Ruisdael not simply part of 'the world'? But if we recall our argument about the role played in representation by these notation or projection systems, it will be clear that the represented is never given to us (as 'the world' may be) independent of these systems fixing the relationship between a representation and what it represents.

Two conclusions can be derived from this account of representation. In the first place, one may well say that there is something peculiarly 'idealist' about all representation, since you cannot have a represented without its representation (whereas we can quite well have states of affairs in the world without statements correctly describing them). We can therefore agree with Arthur Danto's claim that, in a sense, the represented has no existence without its representation. *The representation precedes the represented.* In order to make clear what he has in mind and in order to avoid an idealist interpretation of his intentions, I had best refer to an example given by Danto himself. He asks himself the question: 'Can one speak of the USA before, let's say 1776?' In a way, yes, of course, since the mountains, rivers and prairies of this marvelous country are supremely indifferent to the name people decided to give to it. But in another sense, no, in so far as the country only came into being when people started to use the name 'USA'. And so it is with representation in general – the represented only acquires its contours thanks to the representations we have of it.

In the second place, whereas the true statement can be checked against the state of affairs of which it is true, no such thing is possible in the case of representation. For each representation also involves the embrace of a certain notation or projection system. And since these systems have no more of a *fundamentum in re* than the styles we know from the history of art, what is expressed in a representation can never be rephrased without loss of meaning in a set of statements or descriptions whose truth (or falsity) can be checked against what the world is like. Empirically, representations will always 'hang in the air', so to speak.

And it is no different with political representation. The implication is that you may have systems of political representation that you like better than others; and it may also be that you have good reasons for your preferences, in the same way that any sensible person will prefer a portrait by Leonardo da Vinci ('Paint the face in such a way that it will be easy to understand what is going on in the mind!') to one by his contemporary Antonio Pisanello, who had no such lofty pretensions. Not *all* is merely a matter of taste in representation. Similarly, somebody preferring political representation *à la* Guizot to proportional representation is either joking or defending an elitist argument under the cloak of one about political representation. However, the discussions about (political) representation are not so easily solved, since each (style of) representation defines a different (set of) represented(s), where these representeds are incommensurable with each other in the sense that there is not an objectively given 'world' that could function as the neutral arbiter between them. We shall never be in the position to claim that we now have a system of political representation which is fully justified or legitimized by actual social and political reality. In this way, *le peuple* will always remain *introuvable*, and in this way *la démocratie* will always remain *inachevée* – to refer to the metaphors Rosanvallon used in the titles of two of the books of his magisterial trilogy.

If we recall in what way the French Revolution formed the French political subconscious, it seems likely that the French must have found it more difficult to live with this inevitable indeterminacy of all systems of political representation than other people. Unsurprisingly, phases can be discerned in French political history, where attempts were made to overcome the disappointments of political representation. Drawing again on Rosanvallon, I shall discuss below two examples – both having their origin in the great Revolution itself. The first concerns what has come to be known since Carl Schmitt as 'identitary representation' – a kind of political representation in which the represented and the representative are 'identical' in some way or other (see Rosanvallon 2000, 372ff.).

This must seem at first sight a rather bizarre ideal – and thus in need of further clarification. Now, to begin with, according to Leibniz's law of the identity of indiscernibles, two things are 'identical' with each other if and only if each true description of one of them is also true of the other. Obviously, in such a situation no room is left any more for the concerns about representation as expounded above. The empirical gap between the representation and what it represents would then have been closed. So it is easy to understand the charms of the idea of 'identitary representation'. Equally obviously, however, it is difficult to see how identitary representation can be realized in actual political practice. But it could be argued that it should nevertheless be our 'democratic' duty to approximate this unattainable ideal as closely as possible. Consider now Rosanvallon's comment on Robespierre's regime of terror and virtue:

> ... *les montagnards font de la vertu du peuple la clef de voûte de leur représentation du politique. 'Jamais les meaux de la société ne viennent du peuple, mais du gouvernement, explique ainsi Robespierre. Comment n'en serait-il pas ainsi? L'intérêt du peuple, c'est le bien public; l'intérêt de l'homme en place est un intérêt privé. Pour être bon, le peuple n'a besoin que de se préférer lui-même à ce qui n'est pas lui'. Ce que Robespierre appelle d'une assez jolie formule 'le problème de l'économie populaire' se trouve du même coup facilement résolu. Il n'y a rien de plus simple que d'organiser le gouvernement. Point n'est besoin de dispositifs compliqués: il suffit de laisser régner la vertu. (Rosanvallon 1992, 176–77)*

To phrase it in the terms of this chapter: indeed, a complete Leibnizian identity of indiscernibles is unattainable. Nevertheless, there is a 'notation or projection system' that will bring us close to it; namely that of the political virtue (that is allegedly shared by both the people and its Robespierrist rulers). For this notation system gives us 'the political essence' of both the represented and its representatives. The message obviously is: beware of essentialism in political representation! And then the identity of the representation and its representation has been achieved in so far as this is humanly possible. If one replaces the term 'virtue' with 'patriotism' (and this certainly would not be wholly at odds with the Montagnard's ideology), much the same is, for that matter, attempted by the Bush administrations after 11 September 2001.

But the 'promises' of identitary representation would only be fully realized by the Second Empire. According to Rosanvallon, this took three different forms: (1) the embrace of 'incarnate sovereignty', that is, of the idea that the nation's sovereignty had been 'incarnated' in the person of the Emperor, (2) the replacement of the existing *corps intermédiaires* by new and more appropriate ones, and (3) the introduction of the plebiscite (Rosanvallon 2000, 184–5) as Napoleon's programme – and that of Emile Ollivier, the regime's shrewd ideologue – was to eliminate all that might stand in the way between the Emperor and the people. Hence the Emperor's many travels through France, his openness to anybody, and his willingness to listen to what people wanted to tell about their wishes and concerns. Hence the attack on the *corps intermédiaires* that might disrupt the communication channels between the Emperor and the people, and especially on the free press, since this undoubtedly is precisely what you do have a free press for. Hence also the rejection of representative democracy, since the aristocracy of elected representatives would place an insurmountable barrier between the Emperor and the people. Hence, lastly, the embrace of the referendum and of the plebiscite, since political issues could then be submitted to the electorate without the static inevitably created by the machinery of political representation (see, for all this, Rosanvallon 2000, 181–225). In sum, much is surprisingly (and worryingly) modern in Napoleon's programme.

One may well wonder whether 'identitary representation' can still meaningfully be called 'representation'. For here the political action of the representative (the Emperor) is presented as an 'emanation' rather than as a 'representation' of the people's wishes. And, ideally, there should be no difference between the two. This would be at odds with the substitution theory. For something can only truly be said to be a substitute of something else, if it is *not identical* with what it is a substitute of. Things are not substitutes for themselves. In sum, in our media-dominated era and their effort to effect a kind of fusion of the citizen and the domain of politics, we have every reason to be deeply interested in what was initially tested in the Second Empire – even though it will not add a new chapter to the history of political representation.

This brings us to a second attempt to circumvent the discomfitures of political representation, which is to see in *public opinion* the direct, undiluted and undistorted expression of the electorate's will. The notion of public opinion came into use in the second half of the eighteenth century, and in the 1770s it was already described as *la reine du monde*. Even more so, one immediately recognized the *political* potential of public opinion. The *philosophe* Jean-Baptiste Antoine Suard (1733–1817) explicitly related public opinion and political representation: 'que signifie ce nom de représentation? *Qu'est-ce que des représentants peuvent représenter sinon l'opinion publique?*' (Rosanvallon 1992, 159; my italics). During the Revolution, the idea was always that public opinion will be (or ought to be) both guide and surveyor of public decision-making. And, as a certain Nicholas Bergasse most ingeniously argued, public opinion is supremely capable of this august task since it is not institutionalized, and thus not subject to the oligarchic temptation inherent in all the institutions of representative government (see Rosanvallon 2000, 46). Rosanvallon insists, furthermore, that for both the *philosophes* and the revolutionaries, public opinion was taken to be a supremely *critical* power and it is instructive, in this context, that it was often associated with Rousseau's *volonté générale*. Much the same is still true of the doctrinaires. For them, public opinion was absolutely indispensable for the search for the dictates of 'sovereign Reason'; public opinion was the domain where this interaction between state and society, which was so central to their political thought, could only be enacted. Or, as Rosanvallon expresses it in a marvelous formula:

> *la publicité crée ainsi un espace public, elle est à la sphère politique ce que le marché est à la sphère économique: elle produit l'autorégulation dans un système que l'on qualifierait aujourd'hui d'informationnel. Comme le marché, elle fait du système des besoins le moteur autosuffisant de la vie sociale. C'est de cette façon que les doctrinaires donnent sa pleine cohérence à leur conception de la représentation. (Rosanvallon 1985, 68; his italics)*

It is therefore no exaggeration if Rosanvallon attributes to public opinion 'une place tout à fait nodale dans la philosophie politique des doctrinaires' (Rosanvallon 1985, 64).

Now, what should we say about public opinion from the perspective of representative democracy? The question is an urgent one, as Rosanvallon emphasizes, since we could now replace representative democracy with some sophisticated system for processing the data gathered by opinion polls, by an active interaction between government and the electorate in the public media, or perhaps even by the introduction on a national scale of some system of so-called electronic voting. Indeed, we presently possess the technical means for exchanging a by now 'archaic' and 'superfluous' representative democracy for the blessings of a direct 'Internet democracy'. Or so it may seem. Our representatives – if we would still need them at all – could then no longer escape for a moment the inexorable dictates of the will of the people as expressed on the websites of our national governments.

Rosanvallon himself has his doubts about these prospects for the future of our Western democracies. His first argument is that a media democracy or Internet democracy would be 'reactionary' in the sense of being primarily intent upon some rancorous settlement with established powers (the kind of powers owing their political existence to representative democracy). For, as Rosanvallon asks himself, what will this 'people' be that will be allowed to express its will in this way? And his answer is: 'c'est en large partie un peuple évanescent. Il ne trouve consistance que dans la présupposition d'une densité native qui résulterait de son opposition à l'univers jugé suspect des élites et des médias.' And, secondly, Rosanvallon fears the populism that will inevitably result from 'l'avènement de ce peuple-opinion'; we would then have to expect nasty and unsavory lunges at cosmopolitan elites, at mysterious powers allegedly threatening the people's integrity, at multinationals, and above all, at immigrants and what is associated with them – in sum, all that Le Pen's Front National stands for (Rosanvallon 1998, 344–5). Undoubtedly, Rosanvallon's fears are wholly justified, but I don't think that advocates of the replacement of representative democracy by some variant of Internet democracy would admit defeat because of this.

Finally: The Superiority of Representative Democracy Over its Alternatives

This is why I would like to add two more arguments to Rosanvallon's. To start with, I would like to recall the argument that there is no represented without a representation, much in the way that there can only be a USA after people began to use that name (as Danto explained). This is one of the miracles wrought by representation: thanks to it, things come into being, that would not have existed without it. Representation creates identities, and with them, the 'things' to which these identities are attributed. Political representation has the same effect. The nation only comes into existence thanks to its being represented *in one way or another.* A people can never be more than a mere aggregate of individuals, prior to its discovery of itself in the 'foundationalist' mirror of its self-representation. And, indeed, political representation is 'anti-foundationalist' in the sense that is has no foundations itself (as was explained in the section 'Implication for Political Representation' above); but it could nevertheless be said to be 'foundationalist', because it founds a political order. Political representation is the nation's foundation-act. It is thus far more than merely a convenient device for overcoming the practical problems of direct democracy: for even if direct democracy were possible (thanks to electronic voting, for example), it would still be far inferior to representative democracy.

Direct democracy could never *found* a nation. In order to see this, I'd like to focus on an aspect of political representation that has, until now, received too little attention. A citizen in a direct democracy can afford to remain an island to himself; it is not necessary for him to take into account the existence of his fellow citizens, nor their needs or wishes. Above all, he has no real reason to be interested in the question of the legitimacy of these needs or wishes. It is sufficient, for him, to know about his own wishes and desires, and how to express them. In sum, the citizen in a direct democracy can remain a political primitive. A citizen, in a representative democracy, however, will have to elect someone to represent him. And if so, as it should be in a proper representative democracy, this will require him to consider a whole gamut of political options, all of them with their own pros and cons. He will therefore have to imagine himself in the theater of political action. He will have to start thinking of how others might look at him, and at what they might take to be his needs and interests. In sum, he will have to divide himself into two persons, of which the former is the simple incarnation of his needs and interests, whereas the other is an objectification of these needs and interests – an objectification that he may expect to find in the mind of others, or, for that matter, in that of his representative and of the latter's presumable political rivals.

Or, to put it in the appropriate terminology: to the political primitive he could afford to remain as the member of a direct democracy, the citizen will now have to add a *second* and *other* self consisting of his *representations* of himself, of others and of the whole of the political order. Only representative democracy obliges the citizen to look at himself from the perspective of others, and to do all this in terms of *representations* of the social and political world he is living in. It is only this, I would suggest, that makes him into a true citizen. Political representation is therefore not only a matter of the representation of the electorate by its body of representatives; political representation is impossible unless the citizen 'represents' the social and political order. That is how an imaginary representational domain comes into being, we all participate in it, and it becomes the universe in which we define ourselves politically and how we relate to others. This political universe is like Leibniz's universe of monads, in which each monad is a mirror – a representation – of all the other monads contained in the universe. As Leibniz put it:

> *and since everything is connected because of the plenitude of the world, and each body acts on every other more or less, depending on the distance, and is affected by its reaction, it follows that each monad is a living mirror, or a mirror endowed with an internal action, and that it represents the universe according to its point of view and is regulated as completely as is the universe itself. (Leibniz 1969, 637)*

It is impossible to think of a better and more profound description of representative democracy and of where it is superior to direct democracy; each element in this quote can be developed into a profound claim about the nature of representative democracy and about how its participants are related to each other. Again, in a direct democracy, the citizen can remain a foreigner, alien to all that is at the heart of neighbors and fellow citizens. He has no incentive ever to be more than a mere brute. Representative democracy requires of us the capacity and the willingness to see what the world might look like from the perspective of others, and it makes us search for a shared background against which we can negotiate our own needs and interests against those of others. It brings us, in one word, from a state of nature to a civilized world inhabited by human beings capable of and willing to see the world through the eyes of others.

From this, a more practical argument can be derived against those variants of direct democracy that might now seem within the reach of what can practically be realized. Indeed, opinion polls *could* be perfected in such a way that at each instant it will be possible to ascertain what percentage of the electorate is either for or against a certain policy with regard to a certain issue. And it might be inferred from this that then, all the conditions have been satisfied for the realization of a direct (Internet) democracy. This might well be true, if this is what direct democracy aims to do.

But, at the same time, against the background of what was said above about the difference between the citizen of a direct democracy and his counterpart living in a representative democracy, we can establish what would be lost with the transition, and where illusions about direct democracy lead to political stultification. For it would eliminate the *moment of representation* taking place in the citizen's mind – the moment where the citizen is compelled to weigh all important political issues against each other in order to assign them their proper place in his representation of the political world. In a representative democracy, for example when making up his mind about for whom or for what party he shall cast his vote, the citizen will have to put together all political issues he considers important and make a decision about how to fit them into a representation of the political universe. *This moment of representation would be lost with direct democracy (in all its variants).*

Admittedly, it may be of the greatest importance to know whether the majority of the electorate is either for or against a certain policy in a certain issue. Nevertheless, of far greater importance is what happens when citizens transcend this level of individual opinions about individual topics and move on to a level where all these things are synthesized into their own representation of the political and social world they are living in. And precisely this is what we shall inevitably lose with direct democracy, since direct democracy *sui generis* can only deal with individual issues, and not with how to fit them into a representational *whole*. Direct democracy inevitably eliminates this moment of the integration of all that we encounter in the political domain into a representation of the whole, and produces an amputation of part of our political selves if we make the transition from representative to direct democracy.

References

Burke, E. (1757 [1990]), *A Philosophical Enquiry into the Origins of our Ideas of the Sublime and the Beautiful*, ed. A. Phillips (Oxford: Oxford University Press).

Danto, A.C. (1997), *After the End of Art: Contemporary Art and the Pale of History* (Princeton, NJ: Princeton University Press).

de Tocqueville, A. (1840 [1945]), *Democracy in America* (New York: Knopf).

Fukuyama, F. (1992), *The End of History and the Last Man* (New York: Avon Books).

Goodman, N. (1968), *Languages of Art: An Approach to a Theory of Symbols* (Indianapolis, IN: Bobbs-Merrill).

Gombrich, E. (1961), 'Meditations on a Hobby Horse', in M. Philipson (ed.), *Aesthetics Today* (New York: Meridian Books).

Guizot, F. (1851), *Histoire des origines du gouvenement représentatif*, vol. II (Paris: Didier).

Kossmann, E.H. (1987), *Politieke theorie en geschiedenis. Verspreide opstellen en voordrachten* (Amsterdam: Bert Bakker).

Leibniz, G.W. (1969), *Philosophical Papers and Letters*, a selection translated and edited with an introduction by L.E. Loemker (Dordrecht: Reidel).

Manin, B. (1997), *Principles of Representative Government* (Cambridge: Cambridge University Press).

Philipson, M. (ed.) (1961), *Aesthetics Today* (New York: Meridian Books).

Rosanvallon, P. (1985), *Le moment Guizot* (Paris: Gallimard).

—— (1992), *Le sacre du citoyen. Histoire du suffrage universel en France* (Paris: Gallimard).

—— (1998), *Le peuple introuvable. Histoire de la représentation démocratique en France* (Paris: Gallimard).

—— (2000), *La démocracie inachevée. Histoire de la souveraineté du peuple en France* (Paris: Gallimard).

Further Reading

Ankersmit, F.R. (1994), *History and Tropology* (Berkeley, CA: University of California Press).

—— (1997), *Aesthetic Politics* (Stanford, CA: Stanford University Press).

—— (2001), *Historical Representation* (Stanford, CA: Stanford University Press).

—— (2002), *Political Representation* (Stanford, CA: Stanford University Press).

—— (2004), *Sublime Historical Experience* (Stanford, CA: Stanford University Press).

Bagehot, W. (1867/1872 [2001]), *The English Constitution* (Cambridge: Cambridge University Press).

Mill, J.S. (1861 [1991]), *Considerations on Representative Government* (Buffalo, NY: Prometheus Books).

Pitkin, H.F. (1967), *The Concept of Representation* (Berkeley, CA: University of California Press).

Schmitt, C. (1928 [1970]), *Verfassungslehre* (Berlin: Duncker & Humblot).

Direct Democracy, Ancient and Modern

Mogens Herman Hansen

Until Alexis de Tocqueville published his *De la démocratie en Amérique* in 1835–40, democracy was almost invariably taken to be direct democracy practiced in a small community, such as ancient Athens or eighteenth-century Basle,[1] and democracy and representation were seen as opposed forms of government.[2] In the wake of de Tocqueville's book, the concept of democracy became rapidly connected with the concept of representation, and in 1842 – before the abolition of slavery – the United States were praised as the 'most perfect example of democracy'.[3] Democracy without further qualification came to mean representative democracy, and direct

---

1   Encyclopædia Britannica, 1st edn. (1771): 2, 415, s.v. 'Democracy: the same with a popular government, wherein the supreme power is lodged in the hands of the people: such were Rome and Athens; but as to our modern republics, Basil only excepted, their government comes nearer to aristocracy than democracy'.

2   As late as 1848, the new Swiss Federal Constitution treated democracy and representation as direct opposites: the *Constitution de la conféderation Suisse du 12 Septembre 1848* prescribes: 'l'exercise des droits politiques d'après des formes républicaines – représentatives ou démocratiques'. The distinction is between cantons governed by an elected Kantonsrat, and cantons governed by a Landsgemeinde. The first really important political movement launched under the banner of (representative) democracy was Andrew Jackson's Democratic Party, set up in 1828 (see Roper 1989, 54–5).

3   The concept of representative democracy appears in Blackstone's *Commentaries on the Laws of England* (1765–69). Another early occurrence is in a letter from Alexander Hamilton of 1777 (to Gouverneur Morris, 19 May 1777). In the short-lived constitution of the Helvetic Republic of 1798, Article 2 proclaimed that the government shall at all times be a 'démocratie représentative', but in the early nineteenth century, the idea of representative democracy lapsed into oblivion and it took a long time 'for the concept of representation to be ingrafted upon the concept of democracy'; see Thomas Paine, *Rights of Man* (1792 [1986]), 170. That happened in consequence of A. de Tocqueville, *De la démocratie en Amérique*, vols. I–II (Paris 1835–1840), echoed in *Encyclopædia Britannica*, 7th edn (1842), s.v. *Democracy*: 'the most perfect example of democracy is afforded by the United States of North America at the present day.'

democracy was from now on relegated to historical footnotes. During the last generation, however, the concept of direct democracy has reappeared as a possible alternative to the prevailing form of representative democracy.

The case for replacing representative by direct democracy is based on a combination of four propositions: The first is the almost universal belief that democracy is a 'good thing' (Rousseau 1762 [1964], Book III, xv). The second is the proposition – often presented as a corollary of the first proposition – that maximum democracy equals optimum democracy (Barber 1984, esp. 117–20, 131–2, 151). The third is the very plausible axiom that direct democracy is more democratic than representative democracy, and thus constitutes maximum democracy (Budge 1996, 190–92). The fourth is the claim that modern technology has made a return to direct democracy possible (McLean 1989, 108–34, 171–2).

These propositions are, again, based on a number of beliefs which are invoked as justifications for direct democracy, ancient or modern. In my opinion, at least five basic beliefs are involved, which I suggest here to call the five pillars of direct democracy (see Budge 1996; Burnheim 1985; Cronin 1989; Fishkin 1997; Gallagher 1996; Schmidt 1993). They are:

1. the belief that ordinary citizens are *intelligent* people who are capable of making sound decisions about themselves and their fellow citizens;
2. the belief that ordinary citizens are prepared to *disregard their self-interest* in case of conflict with the national interest;
3. the belief that ordinary citizens can be kept sufficiently *informed* about the issues at stake;
4. the belief that ordinary citizens are *interested* in participating in political decision-making instead of delegating politics to professional representatives;
5. the belief that rational decision-making can be conducted on an *amateur basis* if one distinguishes between the *expert knowledge* required to prepare and formulate the measures, and the *common sense* required to make a political choice between formulated alternatives.

In the ongoing discussion of direct versus representative democracy, a major problem is that today, direct democracy is attested only at municipal level, for example in the New England town meetings (Sly 1932; Mansbridge 1980) and in village assemblies in Bhutan (Vinding 1998). It is also attested in federations at member state level, for example in some of the smaller Swiss cantons.[4] But it does not exist any longer anywhere as a form of government of a state. Admittedly, referendums are widely used in Switzerland, in Italy and in 26 of the states of the US (Gallagher and Uleri 1996; Budge 1996, 84–104), but even democratic states

---

4   Kellenberger (1965); Carlen (1976). Until recently, the cantonal popular assembly, the Landsgemeinde, existed in five cantons and half-cantons: Obwalden, Nidwalden, Appenzell Ausserrhoden, Appenzell Innerrhoden, and Glarus. During the last decade, however, the citizens have voted their assembly out of existence in Obwalden, Appenzell Innerrhoden, and Appenzell Ausserrhoden.

which allow some political decisions to be made by referendum are far removed from direct democracy in which every major political decision automatically has to be debated and voted on by the people (Gallagher and Uleri 1996; Budge 1996, 84–104).

Consequently, the five pillars of direct democracy have to be tested against historical evidence, and the only major well-attested historical example of direct democracy is the type of democracy practiced in the ancient Greek city-states from *c.* 500 BC down to the end of the Hellenistic period.

It is commonly, but erroneously, believed that the many hundred *polis* democracies were all direct (Meier 1990, 85, 165, 218), and in this respect different from modern indirect or representative democracy. We know that there was a type of Greek democracy in which the principal function of the popular assembly was to choose the magistrates and call them to account for their conduct in office, while all political decisions were taken by the elected magistrates. This is, if not necessarily representative, then at least indirect democracy (Aristotle, *Politics*, 1318b21–2, 28ff.; 1274a15–18; 1281b32–4; see Hansen 1999, 3).

Most Greek democracies, however, were direct, and so was Athenian democracy, which, furthermore, is the only historical democracy for which we have sources enough to reconstruct its political institutions and democratic ideology (Hansen 1999, 1–2). Among modern champions of direct democracy, there are two opposed assessments of Athenian democracy and its merits.

According to some theorists, ancient assembly democracy is essentially different from modern models of electronic democracy. Admittedly, both are forms of direct democracy. But they are so different that next to nothing can been learned from studying the ancient form. These theorists usually take a negative view of Athenian democracy as, in fact, a disguised oligarchy (Budge 1996, 26–7; Arterton 1987; Gallagher 1996, 234). Modern direct democracy is not a return to something which once was, but rather, the introduction of something completely new.

Other theorists, however, hold that the Athenian example is a highly relevant historical example, and that the methods to be used in modern direct democracy are adaptations to new technology of a political system which, essentially, was practiced by the Athenians. There are, admittedly, major differences between ancient and modern direct democracy, both in the form of debate and the way the vote is taken; nevertheless, some of the basic aspects of direct democracy are common to both forms (McLean 1989; Fishkin 1991, 1997; Carson and Martin 1999). Proponents of this more historical view of direct democracy tend to focus on the institutional and ideological aspects of Athenian democracy.[5] The fact that the Athenians excluded women and had slaves is, largely, irrelevant in this context – an obvious parallel is the American Declaration of Independence of 1776 and the American Constitution

---

5   An important nineteenth-century evaluation of Athenian democracy can be found in J.S. Mill, *Considerations on Representative Government*: 'Notwithstanding the defects of the social system and moral idea of antiquity, the practice of the dicastery and the ecclesia raised the intellectual standard of an average Athenian citizen far beyond anything of which there is yet an example in any other mass of men, ancient or modern' (1861 [1958], 53–4).

of 1787–89. We can appreciate the ideas and ideals advocated in these documents in spite of the fact that US women had no political rights before 1920, and that there was a large population of black slaves who were held neither to have been created equal, nor endowed by their Creator with inalienable rights such as life, liberty and the pursuit of happiness.

Thus, in spite of all the important differences between a small ancient city-state and a large, modern, so-called territorial state, one important way of testing merits or drawbacks connected with direct democracy is to study the political system of ancient Athens from 507 BC, when Kleisthenes introduced *demokratia* in Athens, and 322 BC, when this democracy was abolished in consequence of the Macedonian conquest of Athens. The first thing to note is that what I call the five pillars of direct democracy were explicitly recognized by the Athenians as foundations of their political system.

First, the Athenians did believe in the intelligence and sound judgment of the ordinary citizen, and they put their belief to the test by letting all major political decisions be made by ordinary citizens, either in the assembly (in which every citizen was entitled to speak and to vote) or in law courts and legislative committees made up of ordinary citizens (selected by lot for one day from a panel of 6,000 citizens selected by lot for one year).[6]

Second, ancient critics of Athenian democracy, in particular Plato and Aristotle, claimed that the poor, always being in the majority in any political assembly, would avail themselves of any opportunity to soak the rich, especially by confiscation of property. That may have happened occasionally, but Athenian democrats took pride in stating that although the jurors in the democratic courts were sometimes tempted by irresponsible prosecutors to have a rich man convicted and his fortune confiscated, they almost always resisted the temptation and acquitted the defendant.[7]

---

6   Demosthenes 3.15: 'You have among you, Athenians, men competent to say the right thing, and you are the sharpest of all men to grasp the meaning of what is said, and you will at once be able to translate it into action, if only you do your duty' (trans. J.H. Vince). Cf. Euripides, *Orestes* 917–22; Plato, *Protagoras* 319b–d, 322c–d, 323b–c. See also Ober (1989), 158–60. On the degree of participation in Athens, see Hansen (1999), 313.

7   Hypereides 3.33–4: 'There is not in the world a single democracy or monarch or race more magnanimous than the Athenian people, and that it does not forsake those citizens who are maligned by others, whether singly or in numbers, but supports them. Let me give an instance. When Tisis of Agryle brought in an inventory of the estate of Euthykrates, amounting to more than sixty talents, on the grounds of its being public property, and again later promised to bring in an inventory of the estate of Philip and Nausikles saying that they had made their money from unregistered mines, this jury was so far from approving such a suggestion or coveting the property of others that they immediately disfranchised the man who tried to slander the accused and did not award him a fifth of the votes' (trans. J.O. Burrt). One more example is adduced at 35–6. Plato and Aristotle hold that, in a democracy, the majority of poor will inevitably vote according to class interests and soak the minority of rich (Plato, *Republic* 565A; Aristotle, *Politics* 1304b20–24;1320a4–6).

Third, the Athenians believed that regular participation in the political institutions made the citizens sufficiently knowledgeable to make well-informed political decisions; and the democratic government at Athens was accompanied by publicity to a degree otherwise unheard of in past societies. Everything had to be publicized, either orally or in writing: assemblies were not only decision-making organs, they were the forum where many matters were brought to the notice of as many citizens as possible. It was a hallmark of democracy to have a written code of laws available to the public for inspection; and again and again in the inscriptions the formula is repeated that a proposal or decision is to be published so that it can be read by anyone who wishes.[8]

Fourth, for many Greeks and most Athenians, political activity was a positive value, and participation in the decision-making process an end in itself, and not just a means to self-advancement or to obtain some other advantage. According to Aristotle, man was a 'political animal' – that is, the very stuff of human life at its most basic was involvement in social and political organization. It seems that the Athenians derived actual enjoyment from the formal play with complicated procedures like sortition, voting and debates in political assemblies. Accordingly, the citizens' participation in the running of the political institutions was astonishing and unmatched in world history.[9]

Fifth, although the Athenians supposed that every citizen would take an active part in the running of the democratic institutions, they also insisted that no citizen should be forced to engage in political activity at the top level. Political activity was divided into passive participation – listening and voting – and active participation, which included preparing proposals and taking an active part in political argument by speaking in the assembly and council and being an advocate in the popular courts. What the Athenians expected of the ordinary citizen was passive participation only,

---

8   Aristotle, *Politics* 1281b3ff: 'For each individual among the many has a share of excellence and practical wisdom, and when they meet together, just as they become in a manner one man who has many feet and hands and senses, so too with regard to their character and thought. Hence the many are better judges than a single man of music and poetry; for some understand one part and some another, and among them they understand the whole' (trans. B. Jowett), cf. 1282a14–17; Demosthenes 23.109. Political information brought to the attention of all citizens: Aeschines 3.25, 32; Aristotle, *Constitution of the Athenians* 43.4; Euripides, *Supplices* 433–4.

9   Thucydides 2.40.2: 'Here each individual is interested not only in his own affairs but in the affairs of the state as well: even those who are mostly occupied with their own business are extremely well-informed on general politics – this is a peculiarity of ours: we do not say that a man who takes no interest in politics is a man who minds his own business; we say he has no business here at all' (trans. Rex Warner). According to Aristotle, man is a 'political animal' (*zoon politikon, Politics* 1253a3). His purpose in life is to live an active political life (*bios politikos, Nicomachean Ethics* 1095b18ff; *Politics* 1325b16ff), which is identical with being a citizen (*polites*) in a *polis*, and 'citizens in the common sense of that term, are all who share in the civil life of ruling and being ruled in turn ... and under an ideal constitution they must be those who are able and willing to rule and be ruled with a view to attaining a way of life according to goodness' (*Politics* 1283b42–84a2); cf. *Nicomachean Ethics* 1177b4–20.

41

which demanded enough common sense to choose wisely between the proposals on offer, whereas active participation was left to those who might feel called to it.

Democracy consisted in every citizen having the right to speak, *isegoria*, the genuine possibility to stand up and advise his fellow citizens; but the Athenians did not require or expect everyone to do so. Indeed, if every citizen had insisted on making use of his right to address his fellow citizens, assembly democracy would have broken down there and then. The Athenians presupposed a fundamental divide between leaders and followers, and in this respect there is no distinction between ancient Athenian and modern representative democracy. And this divide is connected with the distinction between those who possess expert knowledge – the leaders – and those who possess enough common sense to listen to a debate and choose between the proposals submitted by the leaders.[10]

The difference between the Athenians and us is that in direct democracy, the choice is between the proposals, and has to be made every other day, whereas, in a representative democracy, the only choice left to ordinary citizens is between the leaders, and the choice is offered to the citizens only once every third or fourth or fifth year. The British House of Commons is an obvious example, both historically and today. At this point, I find it relevant to quote what Jean-Jacques Rousseau had to say about the British Parliament: 'Le peuple anglois pense être libre; il se trompe fort, il ne l'est que durant l'élection des membres du parlement: sitôt qu'ils sont élus, il est esclave, il n'est rien. Dans les courts momens de sa liberté, l'usage qu'il en fait mérite bien qu'il la perde'[11] (Rousseau 1762 [1964], Book III, xv, 430).

Moving from basic ideas to institutions, there is a noticeable difference in how modern proponents of direct democracy use the Athenian example. Those who ignore Athenian democracy, or even take a fairly unfavorable view of it, tend to focus on the idea that all the people all the time must vote on all important political issues, and on how this can be done by electronic voting after the watching of political debates transmitted on TV.[12] In a historical context, the problems discussed

---

10   Thucydides 6.39.1: 'I say, on the contrary, first that the word *demos*, or people, includes the whole state, oligarchy only a part; next, that if the best guardians of property are the rich, and the best counsellors the wise, none can hear and decide so well as the many; and that all these talents, severally and collectively, have their just place in a democracy' (trans. R. Crawley). Active participation not expected of ordinary citizens: Demosthenes 18.308; 19.99; 10.70–74; 22.30; Aeschines 3.233; Euripides, *Supplices* 438–41. A philosophical formulation of the different levels of knowledge is found in Aristotle's *Politics*, where he states that there are two forms of knowledge: one concerns how to make a thing, the other how to make use of a thing. It requires expert knowledge to build a house, but it requires common sense to choose a house that fits one's need. And it is not the cook but the guest who decides the quality of a meal (Aristotle, *Politics* 1282a16–23).

11   'The English people believe they are free. They are grossly mistaken. They are free only on the day they elect the members of parliament. As soon as the members are elected, the people are slaves. They are nothing. During the short moments of liberty they enjoy, the use they make of it shows that they deserve to lose it.'

12   The first one to suggest a high number of electronically conducted referendums was Fuller (1971). A recent champion of this form of direct democracy is Budge (1996, 188),

are whether such a debate can replace a proper face-to-face debate in a public assembly like the Athenian, and whether electronic voting by millions of citizens can replace the direct voting by a show of hands taken among those who have listened to the debate (Budge 1996, 24–33).

These problems are certainly relevant, but we must not forget that direct decision-making in a popular assembly was only one aspect of ancient Athenian democracy. Other important aspects were: (a) the appointment of magistrates, jurors and legislators by the drawing of lots instead of by election; (b) a short term of office (usually a year) combined with a ban on iteration to ensure maximum rotation, (c) payment for political participation to make it possible for even poor citizens to exercise their political rights, and (d) the separation of initiative and decision, so that initiative and preparation of all bills was left to highly active and sometimes even semi-professional citizens in collaboration with a council which prepared all business for the popular assembly, whereas decision by vote was what was expected from the ordinary citizens (Hansen 1999).

Those who really find inspiration by studying the Athenian political institutions are less interested in the face-to-face assembly democracy for which they have contemporary institutions to study, such as the New England town meeting or the Swiss Landsgemeinde. They focus instead on the other aspects, particularly selection by lot, for which the only modern parallel is the completely different modern jury.

The extensive use of the lottery in democratic Athens is completely unknown today (Elster 1989, 78–93; Carson and Martin 1999), and if transformed to fit contemporary states and modern technology, the analogy would be to have a small panel of citizens randomly selected from all citizens, but so few that they can carry on a debate, at least by telecommunication, and that they can be sufficiently informed about the political issues at hand. The idea is, then, to transform parliaments into preparatory and problem-formulating institutions whose proposals are to be voted on by deliberative and decision-making opinion poll panels, selected by lot from among all citizens. This form of popular rule is often called 'demarchy' instead of 'democracy', a term invented by John Burnheim (Burnheim 1985, 9, 156–87; Carson and Martin 1999, 102–14; McLean uses 'demarchy' synonymously with what he calls 'statistical democracy': 1989, 157–61).

So sortition instead of election, rotation to ensure maximum participation, payment to stimulate participation, and the acknowledged distinction between active and passive participation are aspects of direct Athenian democracy which have recently been drawn into the debate about a return to direct democracy. In *Democracy and Its Critics*, Robert A. Dahl suggested one model democracy which incorporated such institutions:

> *Suppose an advanced democratic country were to create a 'minipopulus'*
> *consisting of perhaps a thousand citizens randomly selected out of the entire*

---

who imagines a total of *c*. 50 such referendums per year. See also Gallagher (1996), 240–50.

demos. Its task would be to deliberate, for a year perhaps, on an issue and then to announce its choices. The members of a 'minipopulus' could 'meet' by telecommunications. ... The judgment of a minipopulus would 'represent' the judgment of the demos. Its verdict would be the verdict of the demos itself. (Dahl 1989, 340)

By far the most sophisticated and best-tested version of this form of direct democracy, however, is the deliberative opinion poll as developed by, especially, James Fishkin: a couple of weeks before an election or a referendum, some 300–500 randomly selected citizens are first provided with information about the issue at stake, then they are brought together to participate in a weekend of deliberation on the issue. During this session, they debate with one another and listen to experts and political leaders to whom they can put questions and ask for further information. Both before and after the weekend, a vote is taken.

All experiments so far conducted in accordance with this method show that some panelists have changed their mind in the course of the debates, and especially, that a number of 'don't knows' have made up their mind. If the group of citizens is randomly selected and really represents a cross-section of the citizenry, the experiment indicates both how the people would decide the issue if they had to vote offhand without any information and interactive debate, and how they would vote if *all* citizens had access to the same amount of information and exchange of views in a prolonged debate (Fishkin 1991, 81–96; 1997, 161–228; Carson and Martin 1999, 87; for a critical view, see Merkle 1996). The difference between the first and the second vote reveals the importance of information and debate as key aspects of democracy.[13] By contrast with other models of demarchy, Fishkin does not envisage that it is left to the panel to decide the issue. The deliberative poll is intended to be a guideline for the electorate when, a few weeks later, all citizens have to vote.

Today, the champions of modern direct democracy are in fact split between two models: one is the referendum model – to allow all citizens, not only to elect their political leaders but also to decide a large number of key issues by direct vote, which can be conducted electronically. The other is the demarchy model – to replace, or rather supplement, the elected legislators and their government with small panels of randomly selected citizens who can meet and debate the issues before they vote.

In both cases, the decision is 'the voice of the people'. If a panel is enlarged from the *c.* 500 citizens used in most test polls to *c.* 3000, there is a very high probability that the panel will normally arrive at the same decision as that of a referendum with millions of voters (who had the same information). The panel is, in fact, representative of the people in the true sense that the elected legislators hardly ever

---

13   I am pretty sure that if Rousseau had experienced the deliberative polls, he would say that the difference between the vote before and after represents the difference between 'la volonté de tous' and 'la volonté générale'; see *Du contrat social*, Book II, ch. iii.

are, especially if they take the view that they have been selected for their personal qualities and judgment and are not bound to vote as constituents think.

The advantage of referendums over deliberative opinion polls is that all citizens can participate in a referendum. The drawbacks are the absence of a face-to-face debate among all citizens, as well as the difficulty in keeping all citizens sufficiently informed about all the issues that have to be debated and voted on. Conversely, the advantage of deliberative opinion polls over referendums is that a 'minipopulus' of at most 1000 citizens can get access to all the necessary information, they can meet and debate, and they can devote the time and energy necessary to arrive at a rational decision. The drawback, on the other hand, is that only a minute fraction of the population gets an opportunity to be directly involved in the decision-making process. Even in small nations, the possibility of being selected to serve on a panel is minimal.

A possible compromise is, of course, to combine the two procedures, as has in fact been practiced in British Columbia in 2004–2005 (for a short description, see Milner 2005). Like people in other member states of the Canadian Federation, many citizens have long wanted to get rid of the 'first past the post' system for electing their representatives in the legislature and to introduce some form of proportional representation instead. The ruling party – which was against any reform – was ousted in the 2001 election, and the winning Liberal Party decided to implement the reform, as they had promised to do if they won the election. What was unusual and truly innovative was that the Liberals decided to bypass the legislature and leave the whole matter to a 'Citizens' Assembly' composed of 160 ordinary citizens, one man and one woman selected by lot from each district.

The assembly met in weekends, was briefed by experts, arranged public hearings and – in response to its public call – it worked through over 1000 public submissions. In the course of the year during which the assembly prepared the reform, its members became almost experts in the merits and defects of electoral systems. In the end, the assembly opted for a 'single transferable voting system', in which voters rank candidates in order of preference. The assembly's proposal was submitted to a referendum, which took place in May 2005. The reform obtained a majority of 57 per cent of the voters, but that was not enough, since the law about referendums requires a qualified majority of 60 per cent. Almost all experts and political commentators have expressed their admiration for the way British Columbia handled the reform and the remarkable high quality of the performance by the Citizens' Assembly.

A combination of a small randomized panel of citizens with a full-scale referendum about a matter is an obvious solution when the issue is a major reform of the constitution or the electoral system. To have a three-digit or perhaps even four-digit number of referendums every year is, I think, out of the question.

I know of only one model of direct democracy which avoids the dilemma. Inspired by the Athenian example, and explicitly acknowledging his debt to ancient Athens, Marcus Schmidt, a Danish university teacher, has constructed a very interesting model of modern direct democracy which combines all the features mentioned above.[14]

His model democracy is organized along the following lines. Denmark has a resident population of five million, of whom four million have political rights. Danes are full citizens for, on average, 57 years, namely from when they come of age at 18 and till they die at, on average, 75; 4,000,000 divided by 57 makes 70,000. Now, the idea is, on 1 January every year, to have 70,000 Danes selected by lot from among all the 4,000,000 adult Danes. These 70,000 constitute an Electronic Second Chamber, and using push-button phones with PIN codes, they have to vote some 1000 times a year on all major political decisions debated in the Danish Parliament. The following year, another 70,000 electors are chosen by lot, and so on.

The result is that almost every Danish citizen will be directly involved in the political decision-making process for one year by being a member of the Electronic Second Chamber; 70,000 Danes chosen at random is such a large number that the risk of their voting differently from what 4,000,000 would have done is insignificant. All proposals debated in parliament have to be submitted to the Electronic Second Chamber, both those passed and those rejected by the parliament. Every political decision presupposes agreement between the parliament and the Electronic Second Chamber. In the relatively few cases of disagreement between the parliament and the Electronic Second Chamber, the issue has to be decided by a referendum involving the whole electorate of 4,000,000 persons. The parliament will continue to prepare all bills and will be elected on a party-political basis just as before, so that there will be a division between initiative and preparation, left to professional elected politicians, and decision, shared by the parliament and the Electronic Second Chamber.

Of the 70,000 members of the Electronic Second Chamber, those who have a job will have a paid day off every week to study and debate the proposals on which they have to vote; all 70,000 will be sent the relevant material, and they will receive some compensation for their political participation. Every time they vote, they will obtain a reduction in direct taxation amounting to the equivalent of 2 Danish kroner, which means that the reduction in income tax comes to 2000 DKr. in the course of the year they are members of the Electronic Second Chamber. The total costs of such a political system would come to 5 billion DKr per year, or 2.5 per cent of the state budget (in 1993).

Here, direct popular vote on all major issues is combined with sortition, rotation, political pay and the cooperation between professional policy-makers in the parliament and amateur decision-makers in the Electronic Second Chamber. Thus, all the five most prominent aspects of Athenian democracy are involved, and the result is a model which, in my opinion, is a much improved version of the traditional forms of teledemocracy. Rotation and sortition, combined with a ban on iteration, ensure that all citizens for one year are actively involved in

---

14   Schmidt (1993). Marcus Schmidt is Lecturer in Marketing at the University of Southern Denmark, and he runs the largest Danish opinion poll institution with a carefully randomized panel of 1500 persons (GfK Observa).

political decision-making. For the rest of their lives, they have all the political rights they have today under representative democracy. On the other hand, it is feasible and not too expensive to give 70,000 persons sufficient time to keep themselves politically informed; political pay is an extra incitement, and it is possible to have a political debate, thereby precluding direct democracy from degenerating into a vulgar push-button democracy.

If such a kind of direct democracy is workable, it is supposed to have the following beneficial effects: (a) As a result of the increased importance of the decisions left to citizens, there will be increased participation. (b) Direct democracy will counteract corruption. (c) Lobbyism will have to come out in the open, and can no longer be confined to the corridors. (d) The focus of politics will be issues, instead of persons. (e) Political parties will play a less prominent role in politics. If, on the other hand, one of the pillars collapses, the whole building collapses too. If, for example, only *c.* 20,000 out of the 70,000 members of Marcus Schmidt's minipopulus are prepared to take their obligations seriously, it will thwart the whole idea of the reform.

Today, when information technology has brushed away the technical objections to having a more direct form of democracy, the two principal objections are the ignorance and the apathy of the ordinary citizen (cf. pillars 2 and 4 in the list at the beginning of this chapter).

The ignorance of the common citizen has become proverbial, and even among people who believe in democracy as the only acceptable form of government there is an outspoken criticism of the intellectual capacity of ordinary people. An apocryphal saying of Winston Churchill's is repeated over and over again: 'The best argument against democracy is a five-minute conversation with the average voter.'[15] This line of thought testifies to what I would describe as 'doublethink'. Many democracies have jury courts as an essential element of their administration of justice. Members of juries are drawn by lot from among the citizens. The problems which a jury court has to understand and on which the members of the jury have to form an opinion are often very complicated, and certainly not less thought-demanding than the issues which are discussed and voted on in parliaments. If it is true that an ordinary citizen does not possess the intellectual capacity and does not have sufficient knowledge to take a position on the political issues which are decided by governments and parliaments, jury courts ought to be abolished in the countries where they exist, and the administration of justice should be left to professional judges. Conversely, if jury courts are a valuable aspect of the administration of justice in a democracy, then we cannot uphold the view that citizens at large are not intellectually fit to make political decisions.[16]

Apathy and lack of interest for political issues constitute a different but, in my opinion, more serious problem. To have a direct democracy presupposes a population of citizens who feel that political participation is an indispensable and valuable aspect of human life. The citizens must, at least to some extent, be

---

15   In Google, there are 24,500 matches for the quotation.

16   But that was nevertheless the view taken by Thomas Jefferson in his letter to DuPont de Nemours, 24 April 1816.

'political animals' in the Aristotelian sense. But in many Western democracies there is a small and diminishing willingness to be actively engaged in politics. In the US, less than 70 per cent of citizens are registered as voters. Not only poor citizens but many middle-class citizens do not register, and according to an investigation conducted some years ago, the reason is that jury members are selected by lot from among registered citizens, and service on a jury is often time-consuming and in any case poorly paid (Knack 2000). In Denmark in 1992, when the general public showed some interest for direct democracy, opinion polls revealed that only a third of all Danes would vote for a democracy in which a number of political decisions were made directly by the whole people (Schmidt 1993, 166). And those opinion polls were conducted in a much more democratic atmosphere than we witness today all over the Western world. Since the early 1990s, three of the five Swiss Landsgemeinden have voted themselves out of existence.[17] It is simply unlikely that the majority of 70,000 randomly selected Danes during their year of service in the Electronic Second Chamber would devote the required time and energy to the civic duty to which they had been selected by lot.

On the other hand, the history of democracy reveals alternating periods of progression and regression, from the late eighteenth century to the present day. We do not know what the world will look like in a hundred years' time. In the early nineteenth century, universal suffrage was considered an utopian idea never to be implemented, and if implemented, disastrous for the state in question. Since the mid-twentieth century, universal suffrage has become universally accepted as an indispensable aspect of democracy. Perhaps in a hundred years' time, deliberative opinion polls and decisions made electronically by the whole of the people will be as natural an aspect of a democracy as universal suffrage is today. But as the world is now, there are few signs only of such a development.

So whether this form of democracy is inferior or superior to the prevailing form of representative democracy remains to be seen. It presupposes the veracity of the five propositions here called the five pillars of direct democracy. What matters in this specific context is that this and similar model democracies are indisputably based on institutions and principles borrowed from ancient Athens, and – as long as such a system is just a model – one important way to assess its merits is an investigation of the merits or defects of the Athenian political system from Kleisthenes to Demosthenes. I shall round off this investigation by discussing one positive and one negative observation in connection with Athenian direct democracy.

First, it is a common belief that it must be impossible to conduct a consistent line of policy in a state in which all major decisions are made directly by the people. Such decisions will be made on the spur of the moment, and the state will follow a zig-zag course in domestic as well as in foreign policy.[18] If all states were democracies,

---

17   Those in Obwalden, Unterwalden and Appenzell Ausserrhoden.
18   This critique of Athenian direct democracy goes back a long way: see, for example, Lord Acton (1877 [1986]) and Beloch (1884, 18–19). Among the orators, it is Demosthenes in particular who repeatedly complains that the Athenian democracy is an inefficient form of government compared with the Macedonian monarchy under Philip II; cf.

direct popular rule might be feasible, but a direct democracy will always be unable to assert itself against its much more efficiently governed neighbors in which power rests with a single ruler or a government.

In classical Hellas, about half the city-states were monarchies or oligarchies, and half were democracies, most of them direct democracies of the Athenian type (Hansen and Nielsen 2004, 80–86). If it were true that a direct democracy is an unwise and inefficient form of government compared with oligarchies ruled by an elite, or monarchies ruled by a strong leader, it follows that the many hundred ancient Greek democracies would soon have succumbed to the oligarchies and monarchies, and they would have been eliminated from the political map in the course of the many centuries the city-states existed. But that did not happen. On the contrary, if we judge the Athenian democracy by the consistency and efficacy of its policy, we have to note that democratic Athens was much more efficient and much stronger than its oligarchic neighbors, though these neighbors were as populous as Athens.[19] Like Athens, Thebes was strongest, in fact the strongest city-state in Hellas, in the fourth century when the *polis* was democratically governed (Buckler 1980, 20). So direct democracy can be a highly efficient form of government, and again, both in the fifth and in the fourth century there is little evidence, if any at all, that the Athenians followed a zig-zag course in their foreign policy (Harding 1995).

It is true that the alliance of Greek *poleis* led by Athens lost the war against Philip of Macedon in 340–338 and that Greece in the following period was dominated by Macedon. But that says more about the *polis* as a type of state than about democracy as a form of state. The alliance formed against Philip consisted of oligarchies as well as democracies, and was, first of all, an alliance of *poleis*. It has always been difficult for a city-state culture to hold out against a strong and aggressive neighboring macro-state, and that has been the case irrespective of whether the city-states were monarchies, oligarchies or democracies (Hansen 2000b). The Hellenic city-state culture prevailed in the war against the Persian Empire in the early fifth century, but it lost the draw in the struggle against Philip of Macedon in the mid-fourth century.

My second observation concerns what is called 'the democratic peace theory', according to which democracy will put an end to wars. It is claimed that democracies do not fight democracies, and if all states in the world become democracies, there will be peace in the world (Weart 1998). The theory is especially popular among US neoconservative politicians. Since the Western democracies are young and even today constitute a minority of the close to two hundred states in the world, historical investigations have been adduced in support of the theory, and ancient Greek history in particular has been in focus. It is held that in the Greek world there is only one example of a democracy waging war against a democracy, namely the war between Athens and Syracuse in 415–13, and some advocates of the democratic peace theory hold that, after all, Syracuse was not a true democracy.

Demosthenes 2.23, 3.14, 8.32–4, 18.235. The best analysis of this issue is still Montgomery (1983).

19   According to Herodotos 5.78, democratic freedom of speech (*isegoria*) had made Athens much stronger than she had been under the tyrants.

The theory does not stand up to scrutiny (Russett and Antholis 1993, 43–71; see Hansen and Nielsen 2004, 85 n. 59; Robinson 2001, 593–608). First, like Athens, Syracuse *was* a democracy in the second half of the fifth century BC. Second, a more careful examination of the historical record reveals that there are in fact numerous examples of wars between democratic city-states. In the second half of the fifth century, Taras, then a democratic *polis*, had a dedication sent to Delphi in which the Tarantines commemorated a victory over Thourioi, colonized in 444–43 and issued with a democratic constitution allegedly written by Protagoras. In 424, Athens attacked the democratically governed *polis* of Herakleia Pontica. In 373 democratic Thebes conquered and destroyed democratic Plataiai. In the 360s, Athens made several attempts to re-conquer Amphipolis, probably a democracy at the time. The Social War was fought in 357–55 between Athens and four members of the Second Athenian Naval League: Byzantion, Chios, Kos and Rhodos. Of these Byzantion, Kos and Rhodos were democracies and only Chios had an oligarchic constitution.[20]

Thus, on the basis of the argument from history, it is not to be expected that democratization of the world will entail peace in the world. Perhaps the converse proposition is more in place: that peace in the world may promote democracy all over the world.

The connection between peace and democracy has been claimed not only by neoconservative hawks, but also by direct democratic doves. Champions of this new form of participatory democracy have argued that the majority of people want peace, and that representative democracies tend to become governed by elites who find it easier to send the citizens to war than the citizens themselves if it had been left to them to make the decision.[21]

The above examples, however, show that this version of the theory cannot be upheld either. The *poleis* in question were probably direct democracies, which indicates that, in each case, the war had been voted for by the people in assembly. Other examples can be found, and they show that a whole people can be as militant and bent on war as a ruling elite or a monarch (Samons 2004, 100, 131 and *passim*), and this in spite of the fact that the people will have to fight in the ranks.[22] In Thucydides and Xenophon there are numerous accounts of popular assemblies in which the war has been decided and later upheld by the majority of the people. And in Euripides's *Supplices*, this fact is formulated as a general truth:

---

20   Hansen and Nielsen (2004), no. 47 (Syracuse); no. 71 (Taras) and no. 74 (Thourioi); no. 715 (Herakleia Pontica); no. 674 (Byzantion), no. 840 (Chios), no. 497 (Kos) and no. 1000 (Rhodos). Demosthenes 15.17 mentions numerous wars fought by Athens against democratic *poleis*.

21   This view goes back to Immanuel Kant's 1795 essay *Zum ewigen Frieden*, 2nd section, 2nd article.

22   In November 1914, the pacifist progressivist Walter Weyl wrote that 'if anything is certain about the war of 1914, it is that the impulse came from the peoples', and when Italy joined the war in 1915, another progressivist, Charles Edward Russel, wrote: 'it looks as if the people were forcing a reluctant government'; see Thompson (1987), 92–102, the quotes are on p. 98.

For, when for war a nation casteth votes,
then of his own death no man taketh count
but passeth on to his neighbour this mischance.
But were death full in view when votes were cast
never war-frenzied Greece would rush on ruin.[23]

In this context, it is pertinent to mention that a somewhat similar hope was crushed in the years after the First World War. War is rooted in masculine aggressiveness, it was said. When women obtain the right to vote, there will be no major wars like the one we have just been through.[24] But the only central European state which kept itself out of the Second World War was Switzerland, in which women had no political rights. Historical examples do not support the view that democracies – representative as well as direct – will make our planet a more peaceful place to live in (Layne 1994).

Acknowledgments

This chapter is a revised version of M.H. Hansen, 'Direct Democracy, Ancient and Modern', in P. McKechnie (ed.) (2002), *Thinking Like a Lawyer: Essays on Legal History and General History for John Crook on His Eightieth Birthday* (Leiden: Brill).

References

Acton, J.E.E.D. (1877 [1986]), 'The History of Freedom in Antiquity', in *Selected Writings of Lord Acton*, ed. J.R. Fears, vol. I (Indianapolis, IN: Liberty Classics).
Arterton, F.C. (1987), *Teledemocracy* (Washington, DC: Sage).
Barber, B.R. (1984), *Strong Democracy: Participatory Politics for a New Age* (Berkeley, CA: University of California Press).
Beloch, K.J. (1884), *Die attische Politik seit Perikles* (Leipzig: Teubner).
Blackstone, W. (1765–69 [1979]), *Commentaries on the Laws of England*, 4 vols (Chicago, IL: University of Chicago Press).
Buckler, J. (1980), *The Theban Hegemony, 371–62 B.C.* (Cambridge, MA: Harvard University Press).
Budge, I. (1996), *The New Challenge of Direct Democracy* (Cambridge: Polity Press).
Burnheim, J. (1985), *Is Democracy Possible?* (Cambridge: Polity Press).
Carlen, L. (1976), *Die Landsgemeinde in der Schweiz* (Sigmaringen: Thorbecke).
Carson, L. and Martin, B. (1999), *Random Selection in Politics* (Westport, CT: Praeger).

---

23 Euripides, *Supplices* 481–5, trans. Arthur S. Way.
24 These views were advanced by, among others, Jane Addams, who in 1915 founded The Women's Peace Party in the USA; see Degan (1939) and Marchand (1972), ch. 6.

Cronin, T.E. (1989), *Direct Democracy: The Politics of Initiative, Referendum and Recall* (Cambridge, MA: Harvard University Press).

Dahl, R.A. (1989), *Democracy and Its Critics* (New Haven, CT: Yale University Press).

Degan, M.L. (1939), *History of the Women's Peace Party* (Baltimore, MD: John Hopkins University Press).

Elster, J. (1989), *Solomonic Judgements: Studies in the Limitations of Rationality* (Cambridge: Cambridge University Press).

Fishkin, J.S. (1991), *Democracy and Deliberation* (New Haven, CT: Yale University Press).

—— (1997), *The Voice of the People*, 2nd edn (New Haven, CT: Yale University Press).

Fuller, R.B. (1971), *No More Secondhand God* (Garden City, NY: Anchor/Doubleday).

Gallagher, M. (1996), 'Conclusion,' in M. Gallagher and P.V. Uleri (eds), *The Referendum Experience in Europe* (London: Macmillan).

—— and Uleri, P.V. (eds) (1996), *The Referendum Experience in Europe* (London: Macmillan).

Hansen, M.H. (1999), *The Athenian Democracy in the Age of Demosthenes*, 2nd edn (Bristol: Bristol Classical Press; 1st edn 1991, Oxford: Blackwell); editions in French (1993, Paris: Les Belles Lettres), German (1995, Berlin: Akademie Verlag), Polish (1999, Warsaw: Wydawnictwo) and Italian (2004, Milan: LED).

—— (ed.) (2000a), *A Comparative Study of Thirty City-state Cultures* (Copenhagen: Kongelige Danske Videnskabernes Selskab).

—— (2000b), 'The Concepts of City-state and City-state Culture', in Hansen (ed.), *A Comparative Study of Thirty City-state Cultures* (Copenhagen: Kongelige Danske Videnskabernes Selskab).

—— and Nielsen, T.H. (eds) (2004), *An Inventory of Archaic and Classical Poleis* (Oxford: Oxford University Press).

Harding, P. (1995), 'Athenian Foreign Policy in the Fourth Century', *Klio* 77: 105–25.

Kant, I. (1795), *Zum ewigen Frieden* (Königsberg: Friedrich Nicolovius).

Kellenberger, M. (1965), *Die Landsgemeinden der schweizerischen Kantone* (Winterthur: P.G. Keller).

Knack, S. (2000), 'Deterring Voter Registration Through Juror Selection Practices: Evidence from Survey Data', *Public Choice* 103:1–2, 49–62.

Layne, C. (1994), 'Kant or Cant: The Myth of Democratic Peace', *International Security* 15, 5–49.

Mansbridge, J.J. (1980), *Beyond Adversary Democracy* (New York: Basic Books).

Marchand, C.R. (1972), *The American Peace Movement and Social Reform 1898–1918* (Princeton, NJ: Princeton University Press).

Marcus, G.E. and Hanson, R.L. (eds) (1993), *Reconsidering the Democratic Public* (University Park, PA: Pennsylvania State University Press).

McLean, I. (1989), *Democracy and New Technology* (Cambridge: Polity Press).

Meier, C. (1990), *The Greek Discovery of Politics* (Cambridge, MA: Harvard University Press).

Merkle, D.M. (1996), 'The Polls – Review: The National Issues Convention Deliberative Poll', *Public Opinion Quarterly* 60: 588–619.

Mill, J.S. (1861 [1958]), *Considerations on Representative Government*, ed. C.V. Shield (Indianapolis, IN: Bobbs-Merrill).

Milner, H. (2005), 'Electoral Reform and Deliberative Democracy in British Columbia', *National Civic Review*, Spring, 3–8.

Montgomery, H. (1983), *The Way to Chaeronea* (Oslo: Universitetsforlaget).

Ober, J. (1989), *Mass and Elite in Democratic Athens* (Princeton, NJ: Princeton University Press).

Paine, T. (1792 [1986]), *Rights of Man*, in *Political Writings*, ed. B. Kuklick (Cambridge: Cambridge University Press).

Robinson, E. (2001), 'Reading and Misreading the Evidence for Democratic Peace', *Journal of Peace Research* 38: 593–608.

Roper, J. (1989), *Democracy and its Critics: Anglo-American Democratic Thought in the Nineteenth Century* (London: Unwin Hyman).

Rousseau, J.-J. (1762 [1964]), *Du contrat social*, in *Œuvres complètes*, ed. B. Gagnebin and M. Raymond, vol. III (Paris: Gallimard).

Russett, B. and Antholis, W. (1993), *Grasping the Democratic Peace* (Princeton, NJ: Princeton University Press).

Samons, L.J. (2004), *What's Wrong with Democracy? From Athenian Practice to American Worship* (Berkeley, CA: University of California Press).

Schmidt, M. (1993), *Direkte demokrati i Danmark. Om indførelsen af et elektronisk andetkammer* (Copenhagen: Nyt Nordisk Forlag). For a summary in English of this model, see Schmidt (2001).

Sly, J.F. (1932), *Town Government in Massachusetts 1620–1930* (Cambridge, MA: Harvard University Press).

Thompson, J. (1987), *Reformers and War: American Progressive Publicists and the First World War* (Cambridge: Cambridge University Press).

Vinding, M. (1998), *The Thakali: A Himalayan Ethnography* (London: Serindia Publications).

Weart, S.R. (1998), *Never at War: Why Democracies Will Not Fight One Another* (New Haven, CT: Yale University Press).

Further Reading

Barber, B.R. (1988), *A Passion for Democracy* (Princeton, NJ: Princeton University Press).

Becker, T. and Slaton, C.D. (2000), *The Future of Teledemocracy* (Westport, CT: Praeger).

Manin, B. (1987), *The Principles of Representative Government* (Cambridge: Cambridge University Press).

Resnick, P. (1997), *Twenty-first Century Democracy* (Montreal and Kingston: McGill-Queen's University Press).

Schmidt, M. (2001), 'Institutionalizing fair democracy: The theory of the minipopulus', *Futures* 33: 3–4, 361–70.

Urbinati, N. 2002), *Mill on Democracy: From the Athenian Polis to Representative Government* (Chicago, IL: University of Chicago Press).

Neither Ancient nor Modern: Rousseau's Theory of Democracy

Gabriella Silvestrini

Rousseau's political theory has been the object of very different, even conflicting, evaluations. In spite of these opposed interpretations, it is undeniable that Rousseau's lexicon does not concede an important position to the word 'democracy', designating it as a form of government for gods, not for men. The political ideal embraced by Rousseau is considered to be republican rather than democratic. He distinguished between 'republic', defined as state ruled by law, and 'democracy', defined as one of the three forms of government, where all the citizens, or the majority, exercise executive power directly (Rousseau 1762a [1964], Book III, iv). By consecrating elective aristocracy as the best form of government, the *Contrat social* is supposed to be only a further example of how the term 'democracy' had almost always been discredited.

Indeed, most historians have underlined the secular eclipse of democracy, of the noun as much as of the reality. Its resurgence dates back to the time of the French Revolution: it was present in Jacobin political discourse, and later in the writings of Tocqueville. The latter made democracy compatible with the representative system, which in the vision of founding fathers such as Sieyès and the American constituents, had been opposed to popular government (Rosanvallon 1993; Pasquino 1998). Nevertheless, the idea of democracy is not totally absent in early modern political thought: studies have pointed out its resurgence in specific historical contexts – in England at the time of the 'Great Rebellion', or in the United Provinces in the mid-seventeenth century – and in the works of Hobbes, Spinoza, Pufendorf and of the Marquis d'Argenson (Wootton 1986; Dunn 2005).

I would first like to emphasize the importance of this reflection on democracy, which emerges in early modern thought on sovereignty. The tendency to underestimate it, in my view, is a relatively recent development, and coincides with the 'rediscovery' of Hobbes's *Leviathan* and the pivotal place accorded to it in the genealogy of political modernity. I will then analyze the notion of democracy in Rousseau, by bringing to light its relation to the concept of 'republic'. Furthermore, I will briefly present Rousseau's theory of election in order to show that very evidently, there is not only an aristocratic notion in his thought, but also a democratic notion of election as a source of rulers' legitimacy.

The Notion of Democracy and the Modern Theory of Sovereignty

A first, almost imperceptible, but undeniable turning-point in the history of the modern notion of democracy is to be found in Bodin's theory of sovereignty. In spite of the fundamentally 'monarchic' character of his concept of sovereignty, Bodin shaped some of the most important traits of the modern idea of democracy. To begin with, the logic of sovereignty itself and the use of a purely numerical criterion to identify its holder lead him to range democracy, or the 'popular state', among the legitimate republics, defining it as a form of republic in which 'all the people, or the greater part thereof hath in it the sovereign power and commaund, as in one body' (Bodin 1606, vol. II, i, 184). The novelty of such an analysis of democracy in the light of sovereignty resides, first of all, in an involuntary rehabilitation of this notion, which no longer corresponded to a degenerated form, but coincided, with one of the three legitimate forms of sovereignty.

Moreover, while sovereignty does not seem to exist in the democratic form from the perspective of indivisibility, on the contrary, its 'absolute' character may be found at its highest degree in popular states. And popular states become exemplary when it comes to proving that the sovereign cannot be obliged to obey the existing laws. In fact, in monarchical and aristocratic governments, the monarch and the aristocrats are separated from the common people; there are therefore two parties that in principle can commit themselves to a pact. This dualism determines the difficulties underlined by those who claim that the sovereign should be subjected to the oath of respecting existing laws. These difficulties, according to Bodin, do not occur in democratic states 'seeing that the people make but one body, and cannot bind it selfe vnto it selfe' (Bodin 1606, vol. I, viii, 99). Thus, according to the principle of Roman law which states that one cannot be bound by a promise made to oneself, the body of the people cannot bind itself to preserve the existing laws. The oath of respecting the law was not taken by the whole body of the Roman people, but by each private person, given that, strictly speaking, the oath may only be made 'from the smallest to the biggest'. Therefore, in principle, democratic sovereignty is the most 'absolute' form (Bodin 1583 [1977], vol. I, viii, 143).

Finally, following the logic of the notion of sovereignty, and the consequent critique of mixed constitutions, Bodin does not hesitate to affirm that Rome was not a mixed government, but a real democracy, a popular state governed aristocratically (Bodin 1583 [1977], vol. II, vii, 338). This definition of Rome as a popular state is a novelty introduced by Bodin's doctrine of democracy. Thanks to the reference to the Roman system, the essential traits of democracy also change. The emphasis shifts to the participation in deliberative assemblies, away from participation in political offices, which, according to Aristotle, qualified the citizen. The minimum criterion for defining a popular state is therefore to assign to the body of the people the promulgation of the laws and the appointment of the most important officials – namely, command in the last resort, and possession of power in its own right. The latter is delegated by the people itself to the magistrates (Bodin 1583 [1977], vol. II, i, 255).

According to Bodin, democracy is not just a form of republic relegated to the most distant times: besides Rome and the Greek cities, the German cities, the Grisons and Swiss rural cantons are brought forth as examples of popular states, in which the body of the people assembles annually and delegates the exercise of sovereignty to the magistrates, who report at the end of their term (Bodin 1583 [1977], vol. II, vii, 336). Bodin's description of the Roman constitution is greatly inspired by Polybius. Aristotle himself had acknowledged that democratic participation could be realized in different ways: ancient democracy could take a variety of forms and models, sometimes very different from the better-known Athenian democracy (Aristotle, *Politics* IV, xiv, 1298a).

It is true that Bodin refutes the Aristotelian definition of citizenship, characterized by participation in public offices and by the exercise of judiciary power, as well as participation in deliberative assemblies. This critique recurs when defining the notion of supreme power and when enumerating its elements. But behind Aristotle, it is not difficult to see the Huguenot theorists, who had integrated lower magistrates as a constitutive part of sovereignty. Through this dualistic theory, they aimed to justify the right to resistance. In order to absolutely deny participation of estate assemblies and intermediary bodies in the sovereign power, Bodin dissociates sovereignty from the exercise of judiciary power, as well as citizenship from the function of magistrate: sovereignty does not consist in the exercise of these functions in general, but in their exercise 'in the last resort'. The mistake of Aristotle – as of all theorists of mixed government from ancient times to the Monarchomacs – was to confuse sovereignty and government, the holding of offices with the exercise of supreme power (Bodin 1583 [1977], vol. II, vii, 337–8).

In spite of his notion of sovereignty, Bodin's theory does not differ much from the vision of his ancient and modern interlocutors. According to him, democracy is fundamentally the sovereignty of the common people, of a social force existing next to, and independently from, others. As a result, no form of sovereignty is derived from others: the political bond originates from sheer force, conquest, namely from the 'fact' of the power of command (Bodin, 1583 [1977], vol. I, vi, 69).

Contract theorists, and Hobbes in particular, later retained various elements of Bodin's notion of democracy. To begin with, Hobbes takes up Bodin's definition of democracy as a legitimate form of sovereignty – namely, the government where power is to be found in a council 'in which any citizen hath the right to vote' (Hobbes 1642 [1988], vol. VII, i, 91–2). At certain moments in its history, Rome is also an example of democracy, rather than an example of a mixed government, which both Hobbes and Bodin deny as a theoretical possibility and denounce as a practical danger. However, Hobbes identifies democracy much more explicitly with a legitimate kind of sovereignty thanks to his opposition between democracy and anarchy. In this view, the latter is not a degenerated form of government, but the result of its absence. Democracy is therefore an authentic form of government, or 'Commonwealth'. Bodin, instead, is not always clear in distinguishing democracy from ochlocracy or mob rule (Bodin 1583 [1977], vol. VI, iv, 939).[1]

However, the most striking difference between Bodin and Hobbes lies in the absence of the notion of contract in Bodin. Hobbes's notion of contract logically entails democracy as the original legitimizing moment of states *per institutionem*; political bodies derived from conquests are ultimately legitimized by consent.[2] It is true that this theory had already been sketched by the Monarchomacs and by the theorists of the right to resistance, who had developed the doctrine of popular sovereignty and assigned the function of constituent power to the people. But they do not describe this power as democratic (Gierke 1880; Ingravalle 2005). On the contrary, Hobbes explicitly links the theory of the covenant to the notion of democracy:

> *when men have met to erect a commonwealth, they are ... a Democracy. From the fact that they have gathered voluntarily, they are understood to be bound by the decisions made by agreement of the majority. And that is a Democracy. Thus, participation of everyone in the vote and majority rule constitutes the original democratic foundation of political society 'by institution'. (Hobbes 1642 [1998], vol. VII, v, 94)*

This statement was not to reappear in *Leviathan*. However, even in this work, the origin of the representative person lies in an electoral procedure founded on majority rule (Hobbes 1651 [1996], vol. XVIII, 123). The theory of representation outlined in *Leviathan* looks more like a development than a break with the arguments in *De Cive*. On the one side, already in *De Cive* Hobbes envisages the holder of supreme power as the person whose will is considered to be the will of all – namely, the will of the 'civil Person', of civil society instituted by the contract (Hobbes 1642 [1998], vol. V, vi–x, 72–3). Thus, unlike Bodin, Hobbes formulates in *De Cive* a theory of the sovereignty of the state, or of the 'Commonwealth', by identifying the unity of the will of the commonwealth with the unity of the will of the holder of supreme power. As a result, he asserts the identity of the people and the sovereign, corresponding to the first outline of the future theory of representation: 'In every commonwealth the *People* Reigns' (Hobbes 1642 [1998], vol. XII, viii, 137).

This identification allows Hobbes to dismiss all the problems which, according to Bodin, threatened the absolute character of monarchical power. By excluding all possibility of a contract between the people and the sovereign, Hobbes provided a solution to the problem raised by the theorists of the right of resistance. He extends to all states, including the monarchical states, the absolute nature of democratic

---

1   Ochlocracy, or mob rule, means, according to Polybius, a degenerate form of democracy.
2   Hobbes distinguishes commonwealths originated in natural power – that is, in the submission to paternal power or to the victor in a war – from commonwealths created by 'determination and decision of the uniting parties' – namely 'by institution' – (Hobbes 1642 [1998], vol. V, xii; Hobbes 1651 [1996], xviii–xx).

states underlined by Bodin, and ascribes it to the commonwealth as such. The theory of representation in *Leviathan* reinforces this thesis, and therefore, the identity of king and people. This makes all contractual limitations of sovereignty impossible, without erasing the original democratic moment of the states established by institution.

It is evident that the democratic component in Hobbes's thought is fundamentally anti-democratic. Its function is to reinforce the critique of the theory of mixed government and of the right of resistance against the 'democratic gentlemen' who would like to subject the authority of the king to some kind of control. Moreover, this democratic component is much more explicit in *De Cive* than in *Leviathan*. Here, the original moment of political society 'by institution' is no longer explicitly called democratic, and the occurrence of the very term 'democracy' is considerably reduced. *Leviathan* does not repeat the whole analysis of the different forms of government present in *De Cive*. On the contrary, it underlines the identity of democracy and monarchy from the viewpoint of sovereign power and freedom of the subjects: the citizens are no freer in a democracy than in a monarchy. At the same time, Hobbes devotes a long passage to demonstrate that the monarchical form is the most appropriate in order to produce the very goal of civil society: peace and security (Hobbes 1651 [1996], vol. XIX, 131).

As on other points, Pufendorf as an interpreter of Hobbes does not hesitate to rectify Hobbes with Hobbes (see Palladini 1990). Actually, Pufendorf is well aware of *Leviathan*'s extreme anti-democratic attitude, and it is chiefly by sticking closely to the text of *De Cive* that he reinforces and universalizes the logical and chronological primacy of democracy, namely the idea of an original popular sovereignty, rooted in the compact as the founding act of political society. Pufendorf develops precisely this idea – this 'Hobbesian' moment from *De Cive* – in Book VII of *De iure naturae et gentium*. On the one hand, he refutes Hobbes's extreme anti-democratic doctrines, and on the other, he mitigates the too 'democratic' conclusions that could be drawn from the idea of a democratic origin of all power 'by institution'.

By restoring the possibility, and even the necessity, of a covenant between sovereign and subjects, Pufendorf denies the identity of the people and the sovereign which Hobbes had introduced in *De Cive*, and on which he based *Leviathan*'s theory of representation. This identity becomes unsustainable once the necessity to separate the act of association from that of submission has been proved. In Pufendorf's view, the fundamental point is that Hobbes's covenant between all individuals (*singulorum cum singulis*) is not adequate as a foundation for an authentic obligation, since it is a mere promise between individuals. This promise is of a conditional nature, because its respect on one side depends on its respect on the other side (Pufendorf 1672a [1998], vol. VII, ii, § 9–11, 646–8). I will focus only on the consequences which ensue from this argument and that are especially relevant for the theory of democracy.

The first consequence is that under the first compact, the people acquires if not a full juridical capacity, at least a political existence independent from the sovereign, and from the king. This covenant gives birth to an assembly (*coetus*) of free persons that acquires a certain democratic feature ('aliquod democratiae obtinet', Pufendorf 1672a [1998], vol. VII, v, § 6, 680), in that everyone has the right to express his opinion on common affairs. This is particularly apparent in the case of *interregnum*, which is similar to the original condition brought about by the first covenant: 'Communities at their first uniting, before the Sovereignty hath been conferr'd ... seem to bear the Semblance of Democracies' (Pufendorf 1672b [1729], vol. VII, vii, § 7, 709). But what is especially important is Pufendorf's analysis of democratic sovereignty, to the extent that it intends to demonstrate that the latter is an authentic *Herrschaftsform*. And, contrary to Hobbes, not only would he affirm the need for a contract of submission in the democratic form of government, but he would also prove the logical and real possibility of a covenant between the people and each citizen:

> *We are therefore to understand, that, in a popular Government, the particular Members and the Sovereign Assembly are not only distinguish'd by different respects, but are really different Persons (tho' not of the same kind) who have distinct Wills, distinct Acts, and distinct Rights from each other ... So that hitherto there seems to be no reason why we may not suppose a Covenant to pass between the general Assembly, and the private Members of the State. (Pufendorf 1672b [1729], vol. VII, ii, § 8, 640)*[3]

Thus, Pufendorf takes up and develops Bodin's remarks concerning the oath of private individuals to the body of the people, underlining both the possibility of really distinguishing the two parties of the contract, the body of the people and the individuals, and the existence of an authentic submission to the sovereign of private individuals in democratic states, which makes democracy a fully constituted form of government. In so doing, he uses Bodin's remarks to refute Bodin's own thesis, according to which there could not be authentic sovereignty outside monarchy. In *De iure naturae et gentium*, Pufendorf targets Bodin's argument through his critique of the German conservative Johann Friedrich Horn. More specifically, Pufendorf devotes particular attention to proving the unsoundness and the falsity of the following theses: that in democracies there is no authentic pact of submission; that if sovereignty lies in the body of the people, there are no subjects, given that one and the same person would rule and obey itself; and that the people cannot enjoy an authentic sovereignty, because it is not compelled to respect the deliberations it has made (Pufendorf 1672a [1998], vol. VII, v, § 5, 679).

Against the impossibility of authentic sovereignty in democracies, sovereignty conceived as the power to set the law and to impose it on the subjects, Pufendorf picks up the distinction between the body of the people and the citizens that are part of it, and who are simple subjects without any sovereign power once they are outside

---

3   'Enimvero sciendum est, in rep. populari singulos cives, & concilium, penes quod est summa rerum, non nudo duntaxat respectu differe, sed esse revera diversas personas (etsi diversi generis), quibus distincta voluntas, distinctae actiones, & iura competant ... Ut hactenus nihil videatur obstare, quo minus inter concilium populi & singulos cives pactum intercedat' (Pufendorf 1672a [1998], vol. VII, II § 8, 644–45).

the assembly. In his view, this is a real distinction between different persons, and not simply between different roles that can be played by the same individual. The theory of moral persons allows him to sustain this argument: he claims that moral bodies have properties, which are different from those belonging to individuals, which make up the body. The whole body is a moral person with a will, actions and rights of its own; and the will of the moral body, the general will resulting from the unity of the will of private individuals, is not only perfectly distinct from the individual will, but can also be known through the voting procedure: 'the Consent of the greater part of those, who make up the Council, shall be deem'd the Consent of All' (Pufendorf 1672b [1729], vol. VII, v, § 5, 672).[4]

Therefore, Pufendorf's theory of moral persons allows him to cancel the difference between monarchy and the two other forms of government, democracy and aristocracy, which he designates collectively as 'liberae Respublicae', and in which sovereignty lies in an assembly or collective body. On the one hand, even though the will of the king, as the will of a physical person, is easier to recognize, the question is not as simple as it seems. In the person of the king, we must distinguish his private will from his will as sovereign – namely, the public will that is supposed to represent the state. On the other hand, in democracies and aristocracies, it is not difficult to recognize the subject of sovereignty, because it lies in the assembly, whose law-making will originates in the unity of its members' will. Thus, the 'monarchist' Pufendorf does not hesitate to defend the 'liberae Respublicae' and their full sovereignty from Horn's charges against them. At the same time, he develops some interesting remarks on the decisional procedures of collective bodies.

We may add that, in this respect, he emphasizes that majority rule, even though it is adopted by various decisional bodies, strictly speaking belongs only to democracy. As a matter of fact, majority vote is not the only voting procedure. Certain bodies may decide on the base of unanimity vote, or may require qualified majorities, as in the case of the college that elects the pope. When unanimity is required, it is very difficult to take decisions, given the plurality of views, which divide the assembly. Therefore, majority rule appears to be the simplest procedure to avoid the drawbacks resulting from a stalemate. The submission to majority rule is, in Pufendorf's view, one of the essential elements of democracy.

In this way, he can set apart the original compact and the democratic form of government, by stressing the fact that the first covenant 'singulorum cum singulis' does not entail the introduction of majority rule, which, according to Hobbes, was at work at the very moment of the covenant. Pufendorf emphasizes that the majority principle does not derive from natural law, since its introduction entails a decision, which may be taken by following different procedures, such as a vote based on unanimity. Therefore, the introduction of this rule takes place exclusively through the pact of submission which gives rise to the democratic form of government (Pufendorf 1672a [1998], vol. VII, v, § 6, 680). Thus, Pufendorf was able to oppose

---

4   '… ut consensus majoris partis eorum, qui in concilium coëunt, habeatur pro voluntate universitatis' (Pufendorf 1672a [1998], vol. VII, v, § 5, 679).

the idea – explicitly stated in *De Cive* – that the two other forms of government, monarchy and aristocracy, logically derive from democracy, in so far as they imply a majority decision.

Nevertheless, Pufendorf dedicates a whole paragraph to show that democracy was historically the first form of government:

> *In the first place, we will examine the Nature of a democratical Government; not that we think it to excel the other Forms, either in Dignity or Splendour, or in real Usefulness and Advantage; but because in the greatest part of the World it appears to have been the most ancient. (Pufendorf 1672b [1729], vol. VII, v, § 4, 670)*[5]

Thus, the logical and chronological primacy of democracy as based on popular sovereignty fully affirms itself in Pufendorf's contractual theory. He clearly states that, being secondary and derivative factors, force and conquest can only intervene after the first consensual and 'democratic' institution of political society. Only afterwards can aristocratic and monarchical regimes emerge. On this point, Pufendorf distances himself significantly from Bodin and Hobbes (Pufendorf 1672a [1998], vol. VII, iii, § 5, 665: 'Imperium civile non fuit productum per bella').

Finally, the essential features ascribed by Pufendorf to democratic government allow him to emphasize its fully 'constituted' character. While following the indications provided by Hobbes in *De Cive*, he declares 'that a certain Time and Place be assign'd for holding those Assemblies, in which the common Affairs are to be debated and determin'd' (Pufendorf 1672b [1729], vol. VII, v, § 7, 673).[6] Otherwise, either its members congregate in deregulated assemblies, leading to the emergence of factions, or else the people do not even assemble, ceasing to be a people. Moreover:

> *Since some Affairs of the Commonwealth occur every Day, and are of inferior Moment; others are less frequent, and affect the main Interest; and since it cannot be convenient, for the whole People to meet about settling the former Concerns, either in daily councils, or at Intervals of so little Distance, as to let nothing of this Nature escape their Examination; it is therefore necessary to appoint certain Magistrates, as Substitutes or Delegates, who, by the Authority of the whole People, may dispatch Business of every Day's occurrence; may, with mature Diligence, search into more important Affairs, and in case any thing happens of greater Consequence, may report it to the Popular Assembly;*

---

5   'Primo autem loco videbimus de democratia, non quidem, quod eam dignitate aut splendore extrinseco, aut commoditate caeteris formis antestare arbitremur; sed quod illam plerasque inter gentes antiquissimam constet' (Pufendof 1672a [1998], vol. VII, v, § 4, 677).

6   'In democratia autem haec inprimis videntur necessaria; primo, ut certus locus, certumque tempus constituatur conventibus, ubi super summa rerum sit deliberandum & statuendum' (Pufendorf 1672a [1998], vol. VII, v, § 7, 680).

and may likewise see the Decrees of the People put in execution: for a large Body
of Men is almost utterly useless in respect of this last Service, as of many others.
(Pufendorf 1672b [1729], vol. VII, v, § 7, 673)[7]

As in Bodin and Hobbes, democracy as defined by Pufendorf in terms of his theory
of sovereignty was not opposed to ancient democracy, although a different emphasis
was gradually emerging. First of all, it is defined by the exercise of sovereign power
in the assembly, by the right to vote in the assembly, and not by the equal right
to hold political offices. The issue of participation in political offices is shifted, as
in Bodin, to the level of the 'method of administration'. Like Bodin and Hobbes,
Pufendorf is not only thinking of ancient republics, but also of modern ones, and of
the experience of the city states.

After having underlined, together with Hobbes, the absence of any difference
between the king and the democratic assembly in terms of the absolute nature of
sovereignty, Pufendorf partially takes up Bodin's theses. Actually, if the king and
the people do not coincide, and if a compact between them is possible, this compact
can give rise to a limitless submission, as well as to a limited sovereignty. The
same applies to aristocracies, while it is impossible in democracies. As a result, in
Pufendorf, democracy is the most absolute and at the same time most constituted
form of government. It is the most absolute form since popular will is limitless:
every law approved by an assembly may be abrogated by that same assembly,
because there is nobody else who may enter into a mutual obligation with it. On
the contrary, the king and the aristocratic senate can make a law perpetual through
a compact with their subjects. It is the most constituted because, unlike a king, who
can express his will wherever he is, in a democracy, as in an aristocratic government,
places and times of regular assemblies must be fixed, as well as the procedures for
calling extraordinary assemblies. Outside these assemblies, citizens do not hold
any portion of sovereign power.

Rousseau's Theory of Democracy

The absolutists' reflection on democracy contributed significantly to the
development of democratic theories in the eighteenth century, precisely because, in
virtue of their monarchic and anti-republican views, these authors were authorities
who could be quoted publicly in regard to democratic sovereignty and which could

---

7   'Denique cum alia reip. negotia sint quotidiana, & minoris momenti, alia rariora, &
    quae summam rerum tangunt; & vero integro populo commodum non sit, ut propter
    ista expedienda assidue in concilium coëat, aut ita modicis intervallis, ut nihil ejusmodi
    curam ipsius effugere queat: igitur necessarium fuerit, certos magistratus, tanquam
    delegatos constitui, qui autoritate totius populi quotidiana negotia expediant; circa
    gravia mature explorent, & si quid majoris momenti occurrat, ad populum convocatum
    referant; simulque decreta populi executioni dent, postquam ad & hoc magnus
    hominum coetus fere ineptus est' (Pufendorf 1672a [1998], vol. VII, v, § 7, 681).

not be accused of being seditious. As an example, I will just mention the debates on popular sovereignty which took place in Geneva at the beginning of the eighteenth century between the supporters of the government and those of the bourgeoisie. The former claimed that the government of Geneva was an aristocratically ruled democracy, the latter that it was a pure democracy. Both claims were founded on the authority of Bodin and Pufendorf, and on their distinction between the form of the state, or sovereignty, and the way in which sovereignty is exercised (Silvestrini 1993, 81–124). For these enlightened Calvinists, Hobbes was certainly of no use as an authority in the cross-fire of pamphlets, but his theories were circulating, at least through the writings of Pufendorf. Likewise, the entire opening of Jaucourt's article on 'Démocratie' for the *Encyclopédie* is an almost literal repetition of the chapter that Pufendorf devoted to democracy, followed by a statement of Montesquieu's doctrine (Jaucourt 1754 [1966], 816–8). Finally, Rousseau, who was simultaneously close to the *Encyclopédistes* and well acquainted with the Geneva debates, picked up and reformulated the heritage of the earlier reflection on democracy that sprung from the current of absolutism.

In the *Contrat social*, Rousseau defines as 'republic' all legitimate states, namely all states 'ruled by laws' (Rousseau 1762b [1997], Book II, vi, 67). In his theory, this means that every state in which the people as a body exercise sovereign power – that is, legislative power – is a republic. On the contrary, democracy is but one of the three legitimate forms of administration, a 'sub-species' of the republic: 'every legitimate Government is republican'. And he adds in a footnote: 'By this word I understand not only an Aristocracy or a Democracy, but in general any government guided by the general will, which is the law' (Rousseau 1762b [1997], Book II, vi, 67). Government is the intermediate body between the sovereign and the subjects and it is in charge of executing the law; democracy is defined as the form in which the 'dépôt du Gouvernement' is entrusted 'to the whole people or to the majority of the people' (Rousseau 1762b [1997], Book III, iii, 89). This looks very much like a return to the ancient model of democracy, a revival of the ideal of the citizen magistrate; but at the same time it would mean its extinction, because 'In the strict sense of the term, a genuine Democracy never has existed, and never will exist' (Rousseau 1762b [1997], Book III, iv, 91). However, at various points in his work, the word 'democracy' exceeds the conceptual field of the term 'government' and seems to place itself in the domain reserved to 'republic'. This oscillation can be observed repeatedly.

In the second *Discours*, Rousseau initially writes that he 'would have liked to be born' in a country were the people and the sovereign are one and the same person, that is to say 'under a democratic government wisely tempered' (Rousseau 1756b [1997], 115). Later, while talking about the origin of government, he describes the birth of democratic government as a continuation of that form of administration, which had been instituted since the very beginning of society: those who formed a democracy 'gardèrent en commun l'Administration suprême' [retained the supreme Administration in common] (Rousseau 1756a [1964], 186). In the *Contrat social*, democracy is logically and chronologically antecedent to the other two forms of government, since the institution of government is only possible 'by a sudden conversion of Sovereignty into Democracy' (Rousseau 1762b [1997], Book III, xvii, 118). But this does not imply any historical derivation, because in the chapter on aristocracy we read that the first societies governed themselves aristocratically. And in the *Lettres écrites de la Montagne*, an even more striking definition is found: 'in a Democracy, where the People is the Sovereign' (Rousseau 1764 [1964], 816). Here, the overlapping with the conceptual field of 'republic' is even more explicit. Do these indecisions depend on a lack of available terms, or on a simple inaccuracy?

A comparison with Pufendorf's argument, which Rousseau follows closely, may be helpful in addressing these problems. In Rousseau's work, we can find, as in Pufendorf's, two meanings of democracy, as the originating moment of all political societies and as a specific form of government. But Rousseau operates in a very different conceptual scheme.

To begin with, Pufendorf demonstrated the possibility of a contract of submission in democracy. Rousseau places his own version of this democratic contract of submission at the origin of all societies: it is the covenant between individuals and community:

> *This formula shows that the act of association involves a reciprocal engagement between the public and private individuals, and that each individual, by contracting, so to speak, with himself, finds himself engaged in a two-fold relation: namely, as member of the Sovereign toward private individuals, and as a member of the State toward the Sovereign. But here the maxim of civil right, that no one is bound by engagements toward himself, does not apply; for there is a great difference between assuming an obligation toward oneself, and assuming a responsibility toward a whole of which one is a part.* (Rousseau 1762b [1997], Book I, vii, 51)

Taking up the arguments that Pufendorf had used against Hobbes to justify the covenant between the people and the individuals, Rousseau dismisses the contract between private persons; he then merges association and submission into one act. This allows him to provide simultaneously the foundations of the obligation that binds each individual to the community and the introduction of majority rule.

In Pufendorf, the first covenant gave birth to a 'sort of democracy', allowing free private individuals to exercise a deliberative activity. Rousseau assumes that society is logically and chronologically antecedent to government and this first society can be considered a 'sort of democracy'. As *Discours sur l'inégalité* states: 'Initially Society consisted of but a few general conventions which all individuals pledged to observe, and of which the Community made itself guarantor toward each one of them.'[8] Contrary to Pufendorf, this society without government is not a society without submission, given that the associates are submitted to the will of the people, which derives from the gathering of the individual wills and which

---

8   'La société ne consista d'abord qu'en quelques conventions générales que tous les particuliers s'engageoient à observer, et dont la Communauté se rendoit garante envers chacun d'eux' (Rousseau 1756a [1964], 180).

expresses itself through the fundamental laws (Rousseau 1756b [1997], 175–6). Thus, the peculiar trait of Rousseau's theory of contract is not the lack of submission, but the equality and reciprocity, without exclusion or exception, of this submission. This is clearly pointed out in the formulation of the social contract, which implies the fact that everyone puts his person and his power in common ('met en commun … sous') under the supreme direction of the general will (Rousseau 1762a [1964], vol. I, vi, 361).

Yet this submission to the supreme direction of the general will does not entail the introduction of majority rule. If the social contract requires unanimous consent, and if majority rule is introduced subsequently (Rousseau 1762a [1964], Book I, v, 359), the voting procedures may vary: the people's assembly chooses them. Rousseau emphasizes that majority rule, being the most efficient method, is the most convenient one when decisions demand rapidity, while 'more important and serious the deliberations are, the more nearly unanimous should be the opinion that prevails' (Rousseau 1762b [1997], Book IV, ii, 124). Thus, in the chapter on voting, he establishes a hierarchy of deliberations and norms, accompanied by a hierarchy of voting procedures: the more the laws come close to what today would be called constitutional norms, or fundamental laws, the higher the degree of required consent; a qualified majority is therefore essential. On the other hand, the more the deliberations come close to government functions, to 'affairs', the more it should be convenient to follow the rule of simple plurality (Rousseau 1762a [1964], Book IV, ii, 441).

Government emerges when the political body generates within itself another body entrusted with 'the task of getting the People's deliberations heeded' (Rousseau 1756b [1997], 176). Continuing the comparison with Pufendorf, we observe that the origin of government in Rousseau corresponds to the third 'moment' of democracy in the pages of *De iure naturae et gentium*, namely when it is necessary 'to appoint certain Magistrates, as Substitutes or Delegates, who, by the Authority of the whole People, may dispatch Business of every Day's occurrence' and 'carrying out' its orders (Pufendorf 1672b [1729], vol. VII, v, § 7, 673). Instead of the distinction between ordinary and extraordinary affairs proposed by Pufendorf, Rousseau introduces his specific language, the articulation of general and particular, of legislation and execution. Rousseau takes up again a conceptual scheme used by the theorists of sovereignty, namely the distinction between forms of state and forms of government in Bodin, or between forms of commonwealth and methods of administration in Pufendorf. But once again he uses it with a completely different meaning, because it presupposes only one legitimate form of sovereignty, namely sovereignty directly exercised by the people in assembly.

However, the very notion of sovereignty has changed. The people's sovereignty seems much more limited in Rousseau's case, compared with Bodin and Pufendorf. The power of the people apparently amounts to very little. The exercise of sovereign power is reduced to the exercise of legislative power, and the latter is restricted to voting on laws proposed by the legislator or by the government in the assembly. Thus, the field of action assigned to the sovereign people is much more limited than in the case of Pufendorf's popular assemblies, since its acts, in so far as it is sovereign, must be limited to legislating:

> *the executive power cannot belong to the generality [of the people] in its Legislative or Sovereign capacity; for this power consists solely in particular acts which are not within the province of the law, nor, consequently, within that of the Sovereign, since all of the Sovereign's acts can only be laws. (Rousseau 1762b [1997], Book III, i, 82)*

And yet this does not mean that the generality of the people cannot exercise the functions of government, that the people gathered in the assembly cannot act as sovereign and as 'prince'. The people act as sovereign and then as prince precisely by instituting government, in a way that is very close to Pufendorf's analysis. A passage in Volume VII, Chapter VII of *De iure naturae et gentium* reveals clearly the sequence of acts which are necessary to give birth to monarchical government, and where the term *electio* as designation and choice is explicitly mentioned:

> *after the original Compact between the Members thus uniting, after a Decree pass'd for the introducing of such a Form of Government; the Community or the deputed Representatives proceed to Election. Which being finish'd, and the Grant accepted, and a Covenant thereupon ratified between the Prince elect, and the People, there immediately commenceth a State perfectly monarchical. (Pufendorf 1672b [1729], vol. VII, vii, § 7, 708; see also § 6)*[9]

In an almost parallel way, Rousseau, while refusing to admit a pact of submission between people and rulers, explains the birth of government as a complex procedure. First, a general act, a law, establishes the form of a certain governing body; then through a particular act the people nominates those who will be in charge of the government. In this context, it can be emphasized that an authentic 'election' takes place and this election is at the same time an act of government institution, a process of legitimization and a choice.

We may conclude, first of all, that Rousseau took up and transformed, while universalizing it, the notion of democracy devised by the theorists of sovereignty, and especially by Pufendorf. At the same time, he 'disguises' it, by calling it 'republic' and by opposing it to the ancient ideal of the democracy of the citizen magistrate.

Before distinguishing the sovereign from the government as separate 'bodies', Rousseau advances the distinction between 'acts', or 'functions'. The general will expresses itself through laws, namely through general acts – general statements. On the contrary, the application of laws concerns particular facts or individuals

---

9   'Ibi post primum pactum, & decretum super forma reip. introducenda ad electionem proceditur ab universis, vel per universos deputatis. Qua peracta, & acceptata, insecutoque inter electum & populum pacto perfecta civitas monarchica existit' (Pufendorf 1672a [1998], vol. VII, vii, § 7, 717–18).

who do not belong to the generality of the people: the citizens as subjects, their actions, as well as all that is 'external' to generality, namely other states and their members. The government's sphere of action, as shown in the *Economie politique*, is very extensive: the guarantee of freedom and rights of the citizens, the domain of internal and external 'security', public education, morality, finances and the dimension of 'subsistence', to summarize briefly. In order to provide for all these public needs, the phenomenology of government's functions is very diversified. It involves different acts, including the exercise of a subordinate legislative activity, which consists of the emanation of rules and ordinances, the judiciary function, all the administrative functions, as well as the command of the militia. All these different functions are gathered under the same concept of 'execution', and the institutional organs in charge of this execution, the 'prince', are, first and above all, *tribunaux* (Rousseau 1762a [1964], Book III, iv, 405).

This is especially visible in the chapter dealing with democracy in the *Contrat social*, where the distinction between the two meanings of the term 'democracy', the two possible forms of democratic government, is clearer. The first is the one in which the people's assembly practices all the functions of sovereignty and government itself, and corresponds to the origin of the body politic, the ground zero of functional differentiation of political activities, the total lack of division in political labour. But this situation is highly unstable: 'It is unimaginable that the people remain constantly assembled to attend to public affairs, and it is readily evident that it could not establish commissions to do so without the form of the administration changing' (Rousseau 1762a [1964], Book III, iv, 91). Thus, there is a second form of democracy, which emerges with the advent of differentiation and when 'commissions' are established in order to manage public affairs without convening the people's assembly. The democratic nature of these commissions is not clearly stated, but can be inferred from other passages in the texts: on the one hand, access to these commissions is open to all citizens, 'so that there be more citizens who are magistrates than citizens who are simple particulars'; on the other, designation by lot is the method for appointing magistrates (Rousseau 1762a [1964], Book III, iii, and Book IV, iii). For this reason, the institution of democratic governments is a simple rather than a complex act: only a law is required to establish it, the people's assembly does not need to elect itself government officials, who are designated by lot, nor to perform the functions of government. As in the *Second Discours*, also in the *Contrat social* continuity is the keynote of the shift from the first form of democracy to the second.

However, the 'law of gravity' of small numbers makes the second form of democracy as unstable as the first one: 'Indeed, I believe I can posit as a principle that when the functions of Government are divided among several tribunals, the least numerous sooner or later acquire the greatest authority; if only because of the case in dispatching business, which naturally leads them to acquire it' (Rousseau 1762b [1997], Book III, iv, 91). As a result, the democratic form tends to contract and to become aristocratic. A two-fold political dynamic becomes apparent. The first one takes place when the first form of democracy changes, owing to the creation of commissions, or tribunals, to which the functions of government are delegated. In this case, the result may equally be a democratic, an aristocratic or a monarchical government. The second takes place when the second form of democracy changes, owing to the force of circumstances and to the prevailing weight of small numbers. The inclination of the government to degenerate is what marks the shift from democracy to aristocracy. Thus, two historical possibilities correspond to these two processes: the first, that of earlier societies, involves the transition from the first form of democracy to a 'natural aristocracy'; the second, that of the historical republics such as Venice, Rome or even Geneva (Silvestrini 2005), is characterized by the transition (corresponding with a tendency towards corruption) from the first form of democracy to the second, and then to elective aristocracy, which degenerates into hereditary aristocracy. It is the 'inherent vice' of the body politic: the existence of a separate body, incessantly acting against it and which tends to destroy it.

The difference between democracy and republic refers primarily to two different types of equality that may exist in a legitimate society. With regard to the concept of republic, equality concerns the identity between those who command and those who obey. It is an identity of sovereign and subjects, of the citizen taking part in the assemblies and the subject who obeys the laws. Proper democracy requires a different, more 'extreme' kind of equality: not only between sovereign and subjects, but also between citizens and magistrates. In 'pure' or 'simple' democracy, there are no political inequalities, nor distinctions founded on political hierarchies, while the republican form is compatible with legitimate political inequalities, namely established by law. Moreover, the very definition of republic, 'any state ruled by laws', refers to an ideal – going back to antiquity – of good government, that is submitted to laws and strives to achieve the public good. As a result, the 'res publica' *qua* the 'public thing' is by definition the 'thing of the people', and it entails an intrinsic democratic moment, the constituent power of the people, which alone can define the public good by the exercise of the general will. Thus, the 'republic' is directly defined by its relation to the general will. On the contrary, the word 'democracy' concerns more precisely the fullness of powers proceeding from the sovereign power, not only of the legislative power, but also of the government functions delegated to the councils, commissions or tribunals established by the state's 'constitution'.

Thus, if we think of Rousseau's statement that there are actually no simple governments, but only mixed ones (Rousseau 1762a [1964], Book III, vii, 413), we could represent real and possible republics as ranged on a straight line made of infinite points, of possible combinations, between two limits that cannot be exceeded – between a minimum degree of democracy, beyond which society ceases to be legitimate, and a maximum degree, which is almost impossible: for beyond it politics ceases to exist. The minimum degree coincides with the conferment of the 'constituent' power to the people's assembly, which is the right to ratify fundamental laws, and the power to create or establish the government. If these two conditions are not fulfilled, it is not a legitimate state. The maximum degree corresponds to simple democracy, but this exceeds the limits of politics, because if men could rule themselves, they would not be men, but gods; in Aristotle's words, they would not need to live in a city.

This distinction between two meanings of democracy allows us to understand Rousseau's theory of elections better. Bernard Manin has aptly analyzed the reasons that led Rousseau to include the act of voting, as a particular act, among the functions of government; he has ably explained the arguments used by Rousseau to link democracy, as a form of government, to the designation of the rulers by lot, while affirming the non-egalitarian and, therefore, the aristocratic character of election (Manin 1997, 74–9). Nevertheless, we must not underestimate the importance of the other meaning of democracy in Rousseau, as constituent power of the people. From this perspective, in Rousseau as Hobbes and Pufendorf before him, democracy is closely related to elections.

Indeed, the people directly perform an act of government and elect the prince at the institution of the government. It is true that if the latter is a democratic government, such an act of voting is unnecessary, but it is required when the government is an aristocracy or a monarchy. Thus, election by the people, directly acting as a magistrate, is the source of non-democratic governments. This original democratic moment is to repeat itself regularly in the course of political life. In democratically ruled republics, the problem of the usurpation of sovereignty in fact does not exist, because the sovereign and the 'prince' are identical. This problem only exists when the government becomes a body separate from the body of the people, with its particular will diverging from the general will. As a result, whereas the 'prince chooses the prince' in the aristocracies, it becomes necessary to introduce correctives in order to prevent the government from usurping sovereignty. The remedy indicated by Rousseau, the sovereign people's periodical assemblies, is a renewal of the founding electoral moment taking place at the institution of government. The periodical assemblies, concerning the 'keeping of the social treatise', must begin by the vote on two questions: 'whether it please the Sovereign to retain the present form of Government', and 'whether it please the People to leave its administration to those who are currently charged with it' (Rousseau 1762b [1997], Book III, xviii, 120).

Just as at the origins of government, 'generality' acts first of all as sovereign, because it renews the law which institutes the form of government; and then it acts as the fulfillment of the functions of government, by taking into account a particular object – the rulers actually in charge of it. In the latter case, 'aristocratically' nominated rulers – those elected by the 'prince' – are submitted to a regular procedure of approval by the people, to an election that is not a proper choice, but a form of control and legitimization. While elections are of an inherently aristocratic nature, and as particular acts, they pertain to the 'prince', the institution of aristocratic governments implies, as a side effect, the fact that the people exercises directly a residual electoral function. A minimum part of the executive power is always inalienable and cannot be transferred to representative officials. It is at the same time a particular and a general act: particular because it concerns particular actors, and general because it is bound to the exercise of the general will. It has the function of opposing the non-egalitarian inclination of non-democratic governments and of preventing their particular will from becoming independent of the general will.

To conclude, we can observe that, while using the essential elements of democracy established by Bodin, Hobbes and Pufendorf, Rousseau distances himself from them not only by making people's sovereignty the only form of legitimate sovereignty, but also by being the only author who condemns in principle all forms of representation at the level of legislative power. Earlier authors had acknowledged that the people, while preserving its sovereignty, could entrust its exercise to representatives. From this perspective, by excluding representation, Rousseau seems to radically dismiss modern representative democracy. However, such distance does not seem too great to overcome. It is the constituent power of the people, the enacting of fundamental laws, as well as the power to establish and regularly control the rulers, which are excluded from representation. The rulers are, on the contrary, allowed to exercise a subordinate legislative function, emanating ordinances which implement fundamental laws. This distinction is quite close to the contemporary distinction between ordinary laws and constitutional norms. Therefore, this kind of direct participation of citizens in the exercise of sovereignty does not bring about an unstable constitution, subject to the incessant changes of electoral majorities. The people as a body must regularly give its consent to the form of government. Since this issue is fundamental, one can assume that in order to bring about changes, a qualified majority is required.

Rousseau may rightly be considered one of the participatory democracy theorists. None the less, from this perspective what is important about his thought is that, unlike what has generally been argued, his democratic republic entails a very high degree of constitutionalization, and above all, has nothing to do with the omnipotence of unstable majorities. It was absolutist authors such as Hobbes and Pufendorf who had identified democracy with simple majority rule.

Acknowledgments

I am grateful to Guido Franzinetti and Michael Eve for their revision of the English translation of this chapter.

References

Aristotle (1988), *The Politics*, ed. S. Everson (Cambridge: Cambridge University Press).

Bodin, J. (1583 [1977]), *Les Six livres de la République* (Aalen: Scientia).

—— (1606), *The Six Bookes of a Commonweale, Out of the French and Latine Copies, done into English by Richard Knolles* (London: Impensis G. Bishop).

Dunn, J. (2005), *Setting the People Free: The Story of Democracy* (London: Atlantic Books).

Franklin, J.H. (1993), *Jean Bodin et la naissance de la théorie absolutiste*, ed. J.-F. Spitz (Paris: PUF).

Hobbes, T. (1642 [1998]), *On the Citizen*, ed. R. Tuck and M. Silverthorne (Cambridge: Cambridge University Press).

—— (1651 [1996]), *Leviathan*, ed. R. Tuck (Cambridge: Cambridge University Press).

Ingravalle, F. (2005), 'Populus', in *Il lessico della Politica di Johannes Althusius*, ed. F. Ingravalle and C. Malandrino (Firenze: Olschki).

Jaucourt, L., chevalier de (1754 [1966]), 'Démocratie', in *Encyclopédie, ou Dictionnaire raisonné des sciences, des arts et des métiers*, vol. IV (Stuttgart-Bad Cannstatt: Frommann).

Manin, B. (1997), *The Principles of Representative Government* (Cambridge: Cambridge University Press).

Palladini, F. (1990), *Samuel Pufendorf discepolo di Hobbes. Per una reinterpretazione del giusnaturalismo moderno* (Bologna: il Mulino).

Pasquino, P. (1998), *Sieyès et l'invention de la constitution en France* (Paris: Odile Jacob).

Pufendorf, S. (1672a [1998]), *De jure naturae et gentium*, ed. F. Bohling (Berlin: Akademie Verlag).

—— (1672b [1729]), *Of the Law of Nature and Nations*, ed. B. Kenneth (London: J. Walthoe et al.).

Rosanvallon, P. (1993), 'L'histoire du mot démocratie à l'époque moderne', *La pensée politique* 1, 11–29.

Rousseau, J.-J. (1756a [1964]), *Discours sur l'origine et les fondements de l'inégalité*, in *Œuvres complètes*, vol. III (Paris: Gallimard).

—— (1756b [1997]), *Discours on the Origin and the Foundations of Inequality among Men*, in *The Discourses and Other Early Political Writings*, ed. V. Gourevitch (Cambridge: Cambridge University Press).

—— (1762a [1964]), *Du contrat social*, in *Œuvres complètes*, vol. III (Paris: Gallimard).

—— (1762b [1997]), *The Social Contract and Other Political Writings*, ed. V. Gourevitch (Cambridge: Cambridge University Press).

—— (1764 [1964]), *Lettres écrites de la montagne*, in *Œuvres complètes*, vol. III (Paris: Gallimard).

Silvestrini, G. (1993), *Alle radici del pensiero di Rousseau. Istituzioni e dibattito politico a Ginevra nella prima metà del Settecento* (Milan: Angeli).

—— (2005), *Genève comme modèle dans la pensée politique de Rousseau*, in B. Bernardi et al. (eds), *Religion, liberté, justice. Un commentaire des* Lettres écrites de la montagne *de Jean-Jacques Rousseau* (Paris: Vrin).

von Gierke, O. (1880), *Johannes Althusius und die Entwicklung der natürrechtlichen Staatstheorien* (Breslau: Koeben).

Wootton, D. (1986), *Divine Right and Democracy* (London: Penguin).

Further Reading

Brett, A. et al. (eds) (2006), *Rethinking the Foundations of Modern Political Thought* (Cambridge: Cambridge University Press).

Conze, W. et al. (1972), 'Demokratie', in Brunner, O., Conze, W. and Koselleck, R. (eds) *Geschichtliche Grundbegriffe*, vol. 1 (Stuttgart: Ernst Klett Verlag).

Dent, N. (2005), *Rousseau* (London and New York: Routledge).

Derathé, R. (1950), *Jean-Jacques Rousseau et la science politique de son temps* (Paris: PUF).

Gildin, H. (1983), *Rousseau's Social Contract: The Design of the Argument* (Chicago, IL: University of Chicago Press).

Held, D. (1996), *Models of Democracy*, 2nd edn (Cambridge: Polity Press).

Masters, R.D. (1968), *The Political Philosophy of Rousseau* (Princeton, NJ: Princeton University Press).

Millar, F. (2002), *The Roman Republic in Political Thought* (Hanover, NE: University Press of New England).

Miller, J. (1984), *Rousseau Dreamer of Democracy* (New Haven, CT and London: Yale University Press).

Orwin, C. et al. (eds) (1997), *The Legacy of Rousseau* (Chicago, IL: Chicago University Press).

Shklar, J.N. (1969), *Men and Citizens: A Study of Rousseau's Social Theory* (Cambridge: Cambridge University Press).

Wokler, R. (ed.) (1995), *Rousseau and Liberty* (Manchester: Manchester University Press).

Representative Government or Republic? Sieyès on Good Government

Christine Fauré

Introduction

Abbé Sieyès (1748–1836), deputy of the Third Estate, constituent, was the promoter of representative government in France. But his conception was in opposition to that of the republicans, who readily practiced a melange of republic and representative government. Sieyès thought that his reply to the English publicist Thomas Paine was clear, even though today we find it surprising: he dissociated representative government from the republican concept of power, too close, in his view, to the direct democracy conceived by Rousseau.

In order to preserve unity of action at the head of the executive, Sieyès wanted to maintain a king, but one that owed nothing to hereditary transmission – an elected king. Sixteen days after the Varennes escape, this stand was audacious. It defied the idea of good government as conceived by most of the new republican patriots, such as Condorcet and Brissot.

Before the king's escape, differences with Condorcet had been latent; they were revealed on the occasion of a common initiative, the 17 June 1791 'Voluntary Declaration' in order to assemble extensively the patriots in spite of their differences of opinion. Then events radicalized the positions of each one of them, even if one should not compartmentalize the involvement of any individual too much.

To what extent was Sieyès involved in the petitioner demonstration on which the republicans laid claim, and which lead to the massacre of the Champ de Mars demonstrators by the National Guard on the 17 July 1791? In any case, it is in the tumultuous context of that summer in 1791 that Sieyès conceived the prerogatives of that elected and electing king, 'irresponsible' head of government, whom he would also call the 'great elector', thus anticipating the contemporary figure of a President of the Republic.

In order to understand Sieyès's thought on the best form of government, it is hard to rely exclusively on his often elliptical texts without weighing the circumstances on which they were dependent.

Even though he was often treated as a 'metaphysician', a rare individual in the turmoil of revolution, Sieyès's texts on political theory cannot be compared to the length of Rousseau's and Montesquieu's, whose *Contrat social* and *l'Esprit des lois* he did not like. His works are always short, but they are characterized by fulgurous formulas, in which his contemporaries readily recognized themselves. He was capable of using the pamphlet form in an uncommonly favorable way for that age when the primary aim was to reach the large public. *L'Essai sur les privilèges* and *Qu'est-ce que le Tiers Etat* were certainly the 'best-sellers' in the initial phases of the Revolution.

In his work *La Révolution 1770–1880*, François Furet shows the importance of 'the circumstances' in the writer's activity, belatedly displayed by Sieyès: 'Sieyès, who was so long that could not write anything else than reading notes, driven by circumstances, published at the age of forty his first twenty pages, but what pages' (Furet 1988, 63).

In spite of his reputation as a theorist, Sieyès is firstly a man of action with a good grasp on the battles of his time, intending to play a part in the country's institutional future. Hence some prudent formulations, some judgments which, without an extensive historical work, may seem enigmatic, but which mark closely the difficulties of the times.

Thus, we see him meandering or even escaping when adverse circumstances become too outrageous and he thinks it useless to continue. His great speeches at the Assemblies, which were relatively rare, proved generally unsuccessful. To name, for instance, his speech on the royal veto on 7 September 1789, which did not prevent the Constituent Assembly from adopting the suspensive veto, or again the 2 and 18 Thermidor speech of the III year (20 July and 5 August 1795), where he illustrates his idea of a 'constitutionary [*constitutionnaire*] jury' or appeal against the laws, forerunner of constitutional control in contemporary constitutions, which was not appreciated at the time.

Sieyès, man of action, but also man of government, who perseveringly holds fast to his opinions within the closed space of the committees – a steadfastness which was to be one of the factors of his political longevity, from the General Estates Assembly in 1789 to the 18 Brumaire of the VIII year (9 November 1799) with Bonaparte.

The Paine–Sieyès Skirmish

In July 1791, Abbé Sieyès, deputy of the Third Estate, constituent, refuses to join the republicans' party. The English publicist Thomas Paine (1737–1809), author of *The Common Sense* (1776), which has just been translated in France in 1791, summons him to choose between 'monarchy and aristocracy', on the one hand, and 'republican system', on the other.

Sieyès's answer, published simultaneously with Paine's letter in one of the most accredited papers of the time, *La Gazette nationale ou le Moniteur universel*, astonished the patriots for its cutting and even elliptical aspects. According to Jacques-Pierre Brissot, for instance, Sieyès had to explain himself and retrieve his former clarity and integrity. None the less, Sieyès expressed himself in a way that could not be clearer, preceding Paine's question, which he knew to be imminent. He had already anticipated on 6 July: 'Ce n'est ni pour caresser d'anciennes habitudes, ni par aucun sentiment superstitieux de royalisme que je préfère la monarchie; je la préfère parce qu'il m'est démontré qu'il y a plus de liberté pour le citoyen dans la monarchie que dans la république.'[1]

Monarchy, as indicated by the etymology of the term, is one; republic is the government of many. Sieyès's anthem on the necessity of unity, which he had defended with might and main since September 1789, concerning the territorial division of the kingdom, and which he kept repeating at every possible occasion, is well known:

> *On voit que la question est presque en entier dans la manière de couronner le gouvernement. Ce que les monarchistes veulent faire par l'unité individuelle, les républicains le veulent par un corps collectif. Je n'accuse pas ces derniers de ne point sentir la nécessité de l'unité d'action; je ne nie pas qu'on puisse établir cette unité dans un sénat ou conseil supérieur d'exécution; mais je pense qu'elle y sera mal constituée sous une multitude de rapports. Je pense que l'unité d'action a besoin pour ne perdre aucun des avantages qu'il est bon de lui procurer, de n'être point séparée de l'unité individuelle.*[2]

As we will see, the idea of representative government could designate both a monarchy or a republic, and thus include some ambiguities. Sieyès's reply is not less ambiguous: he wants a king as head of government, a man who preserves the unity of action, but an elected one, the choice of whom owes nothing to hereditary transmission. Nowadays, Sieyès again writes:

> *à la vérité, on est habitué au mode électif; on y a assez réfléchi pour croire qu'il peut exister une grande variété de combinaisons à cet égard. Il en est certainement une très applicable à la première fonction publique. Elle me*

---

1   'It is neither to cherish ancient customs, nor for any superstitious feeling of royalism, that I prefer monarchy. I prefer it because it has been demonstrated to me that there is more freedom for the citizen in a monarchy than in a republic.' All translations are mine.

2   'One can see that it is almost entirely a question of the way of crowning the government. What the monarchists want to do through individual unity, the Republicans want through a collective body. I do not accuse the latter of not feeling the need for unity of action; I do not deny that such unity may be established in a Senate or a superior executing Council. But I think that it will be badly constituted under a multitude of relations. I think that unity of action should not be separated from individual unity so that none of the advantages needed for it are lost.'

paraît réunir tous les avantages attribués à l'hérédité, sans en avoir aucun des inconvénients, tous les avantages de l'élection sans aucun de ses dangers.[3]

The dangers of heirship are well known; they are emulously repeated by all declared republicans, by Louis de Lavicomterie and Pierre-François Robert; but the dangers of election are not really acknowledged. Of course, they are corruption and favoritism, on which Sieyès does not dwell in this text, but which he discusses in his records, and constitute a significant risk, in his view:

En bonne administration, il ne faut pas que le choix des administrateurs soit fait par les administrés. Où serait la soumission sans réplique à la loi si chacun pouvait répondre: c'est moi qui t'ai créé ce que tu es; si tu m'inquiètes, je te révoquerai. Il est tout aussi essentiel que les administrateurs nommés par les supérieurs ne soient point pris hors de la classe d'hommes connus et honorés soit dans le département, soit dans le district.[4] *(Fauré 1999, p. 370)*

Sieyès's set purpose against the republic is incontestably coherent with regard to his ideas as a whole. Thus, it is out of the question that we endorse Lakanal's version, claiming five years later, on the strength of a confidence expressed by Condorcet, deceased in the mean time, that the Paine–Sieyès controversy was agreed upon by its protagonists:

Depuis longtemps me dit-il, nous nous occupons Sieyès, Thomas Payne et moi des moyens de préparer le peuple français à recevoir la république que les affidés de la cour lui présentaient comme le plus grand des fléaux qu'il eut à craindre. Pour attaquer le trône avec succès, il fallait le faire avec mesure. Il fut convenu que Sieyès aborderait le premier la question de la royauté et prendrait sa défense, nous nous chargeâmes de répondre Thomas Payne et moi.[5]

---

3   'In truth, we are used to the elective mode; we have thought enough about it to believe that a great variety of combinations in this respect can exist. There is certainly a very applicable one to the first public function. It seems to me to combine all the advantages attributed to the hereditary principle, without any of its drawbacks, all the advantages of election without any of its dangers.'

4   'In good administration, the choice of administrators should not be made by those who are administered. Where would submission without a rejoinder to the law be if anyone could reply: I created what you are. If you disturb me, I will revoke you. It is also essential that the administrators appointed by their superiors should not be selected outside the class of men known and honored both in the department and in the district.'

5   'For a long time, he tells me, Sieyès, Thomas Payne and myself have been concentrating on the means for preparing the French people to receive the Republic, which the agents of the Court presented as the most dreaded of curses to be feared. In order to successfully attack the throne, we had do it with moderation. It was agreed that Sieyès would be the

In his records concerning the controversy with Paine, Sieyès does not disclose anything of the sort. On the contrary, he does not hesitate to tackle the republican theme of virtue, a canonical theme for the roussovians:

> *Les hommes dans l'état ordinaire des passions naturelles sont assurés dans la monarchie d'être aperçus, appréciés et récompensés. Ils jouent un meilleur jeu et ils dépendent moins ou de moins de monde. Dans la polyarchie au contraire, l'homme utile est assuré de l'ingratitude publique. C'est son lot certain à moins qu'il ne devienne ambitieux et n'acquière une influence contraire à l'intérêt de son pays.[6] (Fauré 1999, 445)*

Through these few lines, Sieyès's partiality for monarchical unity continues: 'more freedom', 'depending on less people', thus confirming the sincerity of his belief.

It is none the less true that sometimes the alliances between Sieyès and Condorcet have blurred contours. The episode of the *Déclaration volontaire proposée aux patriotes des 83 départements* as a sign for rallying on 17 June 1791, precisely four days before the king's escape, is part of those actions carried out together, whose political aims still remain uncertain today, the speeding up of events contributing to concealing their meaning.

'The 17 June 1791 Voluntary Declaration'

The Sieyès records at the Archives Nationales include many printed copies of this declaration with autograph corrections by Sieyès, which undeniably fills a gap, precisely, as far as the works of Paul Bastid are concerned (Bastid 1939 [1978], 118).

The final printed declaration includes three articles – on equality, on the unity of the representatives' bodies, and finally, on submission to the law. But when one compares the text of this declaration with the project conceived by Condorcet, the difference between the two men's political approaches becomes flagrant.

As a man of principles, Condorcet believes it necessary to recall the Declaration of the Rights of Man and the equality of natural rights, while in the final version modified by Sieyès, the article passes swiftly over the statement of these almost ritual formulas, and merely affirms the egalitarian grounds of public freedom. What constitutes Article II of the printed text 'on the unity of the representatives' is almost non-existent in Condorcet.

---

first one to approach the question of kingship, and would defend it, Thomas Paine and myself set about replying.'

6   'Men in the ordinary state of natural passions are certain of being perceived, appreciated and rewarded in a monarchy. They play a better part and they depend less or on fewer people. On the contrary, in a poliarchy, the useful man is certain of public ingratitude. It is his certain lot, unless he becomes ambitious and acquires an influence which is contrary to the interest of his country.'

On the contrary, the theme of religious freedom developed by the latter is left out of the final text in favour of a rapid inventory of the legitimate means for reforming the law –'le raisonnement, les écrits, les pétitions paisibles' – and especially the constituent's deed as suffragist or member of an Assembly.

In fact, in the final text, it is just the preamble which takes up the rudiments of Condorcet's text on the gravity of the situation and the need to assemble the greatest number of important citizens against the intrigues of the Revolution's enemies.

In Sieyès's records, an intermediate version corrected by Sieyès himself can be found. The initial theme, that of Condorcet, already slightly amended, was transcribed by a secretary and follows a page-and-a-half in Sieyès's hand, planning his own political vision with an impetuous writing.

This is the dilemma: how to consent to the bicameralism demanded by certain patriots while preserving that constitutional unity beloved by him?

> J'entends par une chambre <législative> un corps <complet> qui vote à la majorité [et par section où l'on recueille les voix de part et d'autres sur votes en corps et les traduit à la majorité / il ne peut donc y avoir plusieurs chambres, car la majorité serait mal connue et pourrait être fausse si elle était le résultat de deux majorités …]

> Ce corps ne peut pas former plusieurs touts [ou chambres, il est essentiellement un et si la constitution le partage en plusieurs <sections> fractions ou sections, nulle d'elles ne peut voter en corps, c'est-à-dire à la majorité mais les <voix> / suffrages <individuels> pour ou contre doivent y être comptées pour <connaître>/ qu'on connaisse / par le rapprochement de voix individuelles qui ont été données dans toutes les sections, quelle est la véritable majorité du corps total et unique, par conséquent la véritable volonté générale qui seule peut faire la loi /].[7]

This untimely development in Sieyès's thought becomes in Article II of the final text of the Declaration:

> Je reconnais … que le corps des représentants étant essentiellement un, ne peut pas se séparer de manière à former plusieurs touts ou chambres exerçant

---

7   'I mean by a <legislative> chamber a <complete> body voting by majority [and by section, where the voices of each side are gathered on votes as a body and transferred to the majority/thus there cannot be many chambers, because the majority would be badly known and could be false, if it was the result of two majorities …]. This body cannot form several wholes [or chambers, it is essentially one and if the constitution separates it in several <sections> fractions or sections, none of them can vote as a body, that is to say, by majority but the <voices>/<individual> votes for and against must be counted in order to <know> by bringing together the individual voices within all sections, the true majority of the total and unique body, and consequently, the true general will alone can make the law].'

un veto l'un sur l'autre, soit qu'on attribue à ces chambres les mêmes ou différentes fonctions relativement à la loi.

Que dans le cas où le Pouvoir constituant, d'après son gouvernement de la question des deux sections, les jugerait utiles à la meilleure formation de la loi, on ne peut attribuer à ces deux sections ou comités aucun droit, aucun caractère qui tende à les confondre avec le système des deux chambres.[8]

Sieyès's insistence on dwelling on bicameralism was certainly a way of falling in with the general acceptance of all the patriots, and especially of La Fayette, who on his own admission preferred 'the American system of two elective chambers'. As a result, this strategy made the Jacobins indignant. The Constituent Jean-Baptiste Salle accused Sieyès of being a 'two chambers' advocate.

Before the Jacobins, Sieyès defends himself, but he does not convince; the Voluntary Declaration was his own venture above all, not Condorcet's, who rapidly disappears from the debate. Faced with the uselessness of his explanations, Sieyès renounces returning to the Jacobins during the 20 June session, where desertions multiply – La Fayette (1837–38, vol. IV, 17, 26–8) and his friends hasten to deny their adherence; even Madame Roland considers the venture 'dangerous'.

Is the 'Voluntary Declaration' an anodyne mishap, as it was often declared? It provides the lifelike forms of the debates around great institutional choices. From 13 to 17 June 1791, the 'enactment concerning the organization of the legislative body, its functions and relations with the king' was voted at the Assembly. In Sieyès' opinion, the priority choices which had to be elicited concerned bicameralism, the right of veto of one chamber of the decisions of another, and the majority–minority relationships.

Of course, Sieyès and Condorcet's effort reveals a dimension regarding passions, a conspiracy imaginary set, which can make the understanding of events difficult. But on this occasion in particular, two archetypes of the revolutionary 'intellectual' – if I may be allowed this anachronism – come forward: Condorcet, the last of the philosophers of the Enlightenment, the man of principles for whom questions relating to executive power are less important, in spite of his republican *parti pris*; Sieyès, obsessed by the mastering of electoral techniques, planning complex institutional scenarios, whom the multiplicity of his own hypotheses sometime lead to conceive the political categories of the future.

---

8   'I acknowledge ... that since the body of representatives is essentially one ... it cannot separate in order to form several wholes or chambers, exerting a veto on each other, whether we assign to these chambers the same or different functions concerning the law. In the case in which the constituent Power, according to its management of the question of the two sections, would judge them useful for a better formation of the law, we cannot assign to these two sections or commissions any right, any function that tends to confuse them with the two-chamber system.'

The Republican Predicament

In 1791, the Republic was seen as a disturbance at first, a fuss from a group of patriots rapidly stigmatized as ambitious and dangerous individuals. Nothing in the history of ancient and modern republics could lead the French to want this government. Such was the common discourse opposing the Republicans who appeared after the king's flight. Sieyès himself, in his controversy with Paine, dated the outset of the Republican Party from the 21 June event.

Who formed the Republican Party? Its forerunners were: Louis de Lavicomterie, who since 1790 had punctually admitted his republicanism – 'Je suis républicain et j'écris contre les rois.' His work *Du peuple et des rois* had been quite a success, and had also been translated into English and German. Pierre François Robert from Liège also published *Le Républicanisme adapté à la France* in 1790, a work which he hastily recycled after Varennes under a new title: *Avantages de la fuite de Louis XVI et nécessité d'un nouveau gouvernement* (1791).

But the innovation lies in the patriots' rallying to republicanism. On 5 July, Brissot in his *Profession de foi sur la monarchie et sur le républicanisme* gives the following definition of republic: 'J'entends par république, un gouvernement où tous les pouvoirs sont 1/ délégués par le peuple ou représentatifs; 2/ électifs par le peuple, médiatement ou immédiatement; 3/ temporaires ou amovibles.'[9]

Personalities such as Condorcet, Paine or Achille du Chastellet, in July 1791 gathered to found a journal with a unequivocal title, *Le Républicain ou le défenseur du gouvernement représentatif*, a short-lived newspaper of only four editions.

Sieyès's disproof issued from those republican proclamations, which assimilated republic and representative government. His reply to Paine was dictated by that distrust of 'raw democracy', which he would feel throughout his life.

Sieyès's distrust is echoed by Robespierre's. On 13 July 1791, Robespierre delivered a sibylline speech to the Jacobins, resuming the Enlightenment's vagueness and old-fashioned moralism, and emptying the Republic of all political content:

> *Le mot république ne signifie aucune forme particulière de gouvernement. Il appartient à tout gouvernement d'hommes libres qui ont une patrie. Or, on peut être libre avec un monarque comme avec un sénat. Qu'est ce que la constitution française actuelle? C'est une république avec un monarque. Elle n'est donc point monarchie ni république, elle est l'un et l'autre.*[10] (*Aulard 1892, vol. III, 12*)

---

9 'By republic, I mean a government in which all the powers are 1/ delegated by the people or representative; 2/ elective by the people, directly or indirectly; 3/ temporary or revocable.'

10 'The word republic does not mean any specific form of government. It belongs to every government of free men who belong to a country. Now, one can be free with a monarchy as well as with a Senate. What is the present French constitution? It is a republic with a monarch. Thus, it is neither a monarchy nor a republic, it is the one and the other.'

In French historiography, the origin of the republican movement has been the object of controversial discussions between anti- and pro-Jacobins (Monnier 2003). The historians selected by François Furet and Mona Ozouf in the book entitled *Le siècle de l'avènement républicain* do not mention the 17 July 1791 event, usually termed 'the Champ de Mars Massacre'. Could this event have had no effect on the taking of 'theoretical' stands by the revolutionaries discussed in this work?

In the chronology of the events presented in François Furet's work on revolution, he moderately states: '17 juillet 1791, la garde nationale réprime une manifestation au Champs de Mars'[11] (Furet 1988, 55). One demonstration among others? Further on, Furet none the less acknowledges the importance of the date: 'Pour la première fois, les pouvoirs publics issus de la révolution font ce qu'ils n'ont pas osé faire contre les paysans en août 1789, contre Paris en octobre, ils se retournent contre le peuple, du côté du roi'[12] (Furet 1988, 104).

It is no longer a question of identifying with the concerns of the people of Paris, as Albert Mathiez did in his account of the Champ de Mars Massacre (Mathiez 1910, 128–50). The slightest fluctuations in the petitioners' ferment are accurately recorded there, which makes his dossier the most complete source on the subject. It reproduces the first Champ de Mars petition, written, according to Nicolas de Bonneville, for the Jacobins by Brissot on 16 July.

Brissot is moreover considered an 'honest patriot' by the editor of *La Bouche de fer*. On 10 July, he had delivered an audacious speech to the 'Amis de la constitution' on the question of whether the king could be judged, a question to which he replied affirmatively: 'Le roi peut et doit être jugé.'

Two copies of this first petition are left, countersigned by some distinguished members of the Club of the Cordeliers. The same text is found in the Sieyès archives, copied in his own hand under the title *Vivre libre ou mourir*. Sieyès's copy corresponds to Brissot's first version, including part of the sentence: '… et à pourvoir à son remplacement par les moyens constitutionnels'.[13] This reference to constitutional means lead to animated discussions, and was then cut short by the Republicans.

Could Sieyès have counted for something in the writing of this first petition? When on 16 July 1791 a decree had just passed at the Assembly, 'qui ordonne un projet pour tous les cas où le roi pouvait encourir la déchéance du trône',[14] Sieyès did not stick to his parliamentary activity: the existence of this petition in his records indicates at least the Abbé's interest in a politics transferred out of the Assembly into patriotic associations. His reflection, which he readily expresses as remote, beyond all political contingencies, is none the less founded on a perfect day-to-day understanding of events. Among the various revolutionary circles, there was more circulation and less compartmentalism than the historians deceived by clique disputes would admit.

---

11 'On 17 July 1791, the National Guard represses a demonstration at Champs de Mars.'
12 'For the first time, the public powers arising from the Revolution do what they did not dare to do against the countrymen in August 1789, against Paris in October, they turn against the people, on the king's side.'
13 '… and to attend to his replacement by constitutional means'.
14 'Ordering a project for all the situations where the king could incur dethronement'.

An Elected King, or the Anticipated Figure of a Contemporary Republic's Head of State

In his attempts to reconcile with the Court, Mirabeau had already imagined that Sieyès would refuse the monarchist hereditary principle. In his famous speech on royal veto (7 September 1789), Sieyès did not broach this dangerous problem, which could have deprived him of the public's credence.

He quickly states that the depositary of executive power is hereditary. But after Varennes, while saving the king's place in the construction of executive power, he clearly appeals again to this hereditary principle.

The records, undoubtedly written at the same time, reveal all the bitterness of his thought. Many pages take the prince's designation by ballot into account, without one really knowing whether this prediction follows an ancient republican model, or which one.

Sieyès was always extraordinarily careful about the origin of his sources. Significantly, the interest of this example of the king's designation lies in the fact that 'le roi ne pouvait jamais être remplacé par son frère, son beau-frère, son fils, son gendre ou son neveu',[15] and that the small group of 'nine designated' (one can say that Sieyès almost certainly refers to the election ballot for the Doge of Venice), within which the king was chosen, were not part of his family: 'Ainsi le veut la loi qui n'entend pas que le trône puisse jamais être regardé comme une possession de famille.'[16]

In order to merge with representative government and meet the public utility of a great political society, kingship must be reconsidered: 'Qu'est-ce que le roi?' (Fauré 1999, 428). When Sieyès examined and enumerated the royal functions, he recognized the king: the right of assent on legislative acts, the guard of the Great Seals of France, the honorary representativeness of the nation, the command over the armies; he elected all the heads of the administration, and finally, the President of the Council of State.

Persevering with his project of creating a new political language, Sieyès designated the king by this periphrase: 'L'électeur arbitraire des ministres d'exécution et leur surveillant pour les intérêts du peuple et de la loi.'[17] The king appoints the ministers, but is not responsible for their politics, and Sieyès goes as far as claiming that he is not responsible: 'Le prince est le 1er dans l'ordre civil / politique. Il n'est point dans l'établissement public ou dans le corps des agents de la loi. Il est représentant de la nation agissant comme jury irresponsable, inviolable.'[18]

---

15 'The king could never be replaced by his brother, his brother-in-law, his son, his son-in-law or his nephew.'

16 'So wants the law, which has no intention of ever considering the throne a family property.'

17 'The arbitrary elector of the executive ministers and their supervisor in the interest of both the people and of the law.'

18 'The prince is first in the civil/political order. He is not within the public institution or in the body of the agents of the law at all. He is the nation's representative acting as irresponsible, inviolable jury.'

With this definition of the royal functions, he insists on the formal dimension of the king's prerogatives which are important to preserve.

But the royal non-responsibility is not compared to a form of passivity; on the contrary, the king is above all a citizen:

> *Tous les devoirs, toutes les prérogatives du roi découlent de sa qualité de 1 citoyen ... Du moment que nous reconnaissons un 1 citoyen dans l'Etat, il est premier partout, dans tous les districts, dans toutes les familles politiques. Il est citoyen actif dans toutes les assemblées primaires. Ici se présente la question que nous avons envie de résoudre: la qualité de 1er ne doit pas ôter au roi son droit d'éligible. Mais on sent qu'il ne courra cette chance dans aucun département. Il est éligible, il est élu au même titre qu'il est premier. Le sera-t-il <de fait> /en réalité/ par tous les départements à la fois, de manière qu'on puisse lui supposer 80 voix à l'Assemblée Nationale. Cette supposition choque trop évidemment les meilleurs principes.*[19]

If the king has the right to vote, he is also eligible, but this eligibility does not recur in Sieyès's 7 September 1789 speech on the royal veto. In 1791, still trapped by the hazards which surround his ideas, Sieyès justifies the idea of an executive head who elects and is eligible with some difficulty. Deprived of the hereditary transmission principle, must he still be called a king? In the III year, he calls him 'a great elector':

> *Comment se procurer dans un Etat tous les avantages de l'élection d'un chef sans avoir à en redouter les inconvénients et tous les avantages de l'hérédité sans aucun de ses innombrables dangers ... comment le chef de l'Etat armé de grandes prérogatives peut-il exercer lui-même une partie de ses pouvoirs sans en exercer jamais l'action responsable?*[20]

In this text entitled *Bases de l'ordre social*, Sieyès keeps up his hardly altered position. He shows a less notable radicalism towards monarchic succession, because contrary to ancient oligarchic republics, the breeding-ground for recruitment seems

---

19 'All the duties, all the prerogatives of the king originate from his rank as first citizen ....
    From the moment we acknowledge a first citizen in the State, he is first everywhere, in
    all the districts, in all the political families. He is active citizen in all primary assemblies.
    Here the problem we want to resolve arises: the rank of first citizen must not deprive
    the king of his right as eligible. But one feels that he will not risk this possibility in any
    department. He is eligible, he is elected exactly because he is the first. He will be in fact
    for all the departments together, so that one can assume that he represents 80 votes at
    the National Assembly. This assumption clearly shocks the best principles excessively.'
20 'How to obtain all the advantages of a leader's election in a State without having to
    fear the drawbacks and all the advantages of the hereditary principle without any of its
    innumerable dangers ... how can the head of state armed with great prerogatives exert
    part of his powers without ever exerting responsible action?'

probably difficult to constitute to him, and too frequent elections seem to risk the combination of inevitable troubles and chronic instability.

In a series of hypotheses, he specifies that: 'Nous concentrons l'éligibilité pour cette place dans une famille jusqu'au moment où elle viendrait s'éteindre. / Le roi et / cette famille <sera> indiqué<e>: c'est celle des Bourbon.'[21]

In his *Observations constitutionnelles*, dictated to Boulay de la Meurthe (who was his secretary and who on Sieyès's death pubished *Théorie constitutionnelle de Sieyès, Constitution de l'an VIII*–1836), in the chapter 'Great Elector', Sieyès gives up the term 'king' and writes with his usual brevity: 'Il n'est pas roi car il aurait des sujets.'[22] The term has to change because it is tainted with too burdensome a past, but the definition of the royal functions remains the same: 'On gouverne, on exécute sous son nom, on lui rend compte, il surveille mais / il ne gouverne pas <il n'a pas même la signature car il serait> add / sa signature est apposée par une griffe. Il n'est point responsable.'[23] This great irresponsible elector will be cast out by Bonaparte.

Conclusion

In France, Sieyès actions and work correspond to the birth of the concept of representative democracy. He was undeniably one of the creators of the concept. The debate between republic and representative system shows how difficult it was to break away from the models of government known and experienced by history, as well as to conceive new forms of government.

Sieyès unequivocally and constantly condemned 'raw democracy'. In 1799, in his *Observations constitutionnelles*, he repeated yet again: 'La démocratie brute est absurde fut-elle possible.'[24] In 1789, he justified his term 'raw democracy' 'par analogie aux matières premières et aux denrées brutes que la nature partout a offerte à l'homme mais que partout l'homme a mis son industrie à modifier, à préparer pour les rendre propres à ses besoins et à ses jouissances'[25] (Sieyès 1789, 34).

He had distinguished himself from the Jacobins by wanting to extend the representative regime to the executive part: 'Les plus chauds partisans de la démocratie brute n'entendent cependant pas la mettre dans la partie exécutive,

---

21 'We concentrate eligibility for this position in a family until it dies out. The king and that family will be indicated: it is the Bourbon family.'
22 'He is not king, or he would have subjects.'
23 'Under his name one rules, one accomplishes, one accounts to him, he supervises but he does not rule <he does not even have the signature because it would be> / a mark is put for his signature. He is not in the least responsible.'
24 'Even if it might be possible, raw democracy is absurd.'
25 'By the analogy with raw materials and of unmanifactured produces, which nature everywhere has offered to man, but which everywhere man has used his dealings to modify and adjust them to suit his own needs and enjoyment.'

administrative et judiciaire; ils la veulent seule dans l'ordre législatif.'[26] His words are never too hard when lashing out at these phenomena of massification, which are called, in Rousseau's wake, general interest, general will. In his opinion, modernity does not lie in the application of a popular unanimity, which he saw as 're-total', a neologism which he devised on the model of 're-public' and which can be considered as the distant ancestor of the concept of totalitarianism.

In his view, modernity consists in delegating governmental functions to experts or professionals, on the understanding, none the less, that there is deliberation and trust.

He is the advocate of a twofold citizenship: the active citizen, who contributes to the public institution, and the passive citizen who has 'droit à la protection de sa personne, de sa propriété et de sa liberté'.

This concept of citizenship was not incompatible, in his view, with political equality of rights – a thesis which can sound paradoxical to a contemporary reader. Sieyès remains a theorist of political equality in spite of or due to the numerous institutional restraints which he envisaged according to the periods. Pasquale Pasquino (see Pasquino 1998), and Lucien Jaume (see Jaume 2002) are authorities on the constitutional mechanisms conceived by Sieyès.

These institutions, holding back governmental drifts, are of various kinds. The best-known: the 'constitutionary [constitutionnaire] jury' defined on the occasion of his famous 18 Thermidor speech; the college of conservatives proposed in 1799 – recollecting the Venetian oligarchy – is another of Sieyès's attempts to 'secure the powers against one another'.

Between 1789 and 1799, as Sieyès's political interlocutors changed, he expressed institutional motions supposedly acceptable by his audience, and which expressed the same concern: to safeguard the constituent power through the guarantee provided by the Declaration of the Rights of Man (1789) – a guarantee which soon proved inadequate against anti-constitutional laws, hence the motion of a constitutionary jury, but of a college of conservatives too – a kind of assembling of notables, that is to say, of men known for their competence, rigorousness and integrity – capable of regulating society and preserving it against the natural influences of wealth and aristocracy.

References

Aulard, F.A. (ed.) (1892), La société des Jacobins, juillet 1791 à juin 1792 (Paris).

Bastid, P. (1939 [1978]), Sieyès et sa pensée (Geneva: Slatkine reprints).

Fauré, C. (ed.) (1999), Des Manuscrits de Sieyès, 1773–1799, with the collaboration of J. Guilhaumou and J. Valier (Paris and Geneva: Champion-Slatkine).

—— (ed.) (2007), Des Manuscrits de Sieyès, 1770–1815, vol. II (Paris and Geneva: Champion-Slatkine).

---

26 'The most eager partisans of raw democracy have nevertheless no intention of setting it in the executive, administrative and judicial part; they only want it in the legislative order.'

Furet, F. (1988), *La Révolution* (Paris: Hachette).

Gazette nationale ou le Moniteur Universel, reprint of the former *Moniteur* (1862) (Paris: Plon).

Jaume, L. (2002), 'Sieyès et le sens du jury constitutionnaire, une réinterprétation', *Droits, revue française de théorie, de philosophie et de culture juridiques* 36.

La Fayette (1835), *Mémoires, correspondances et manuscrits*, vol. IV (Paris: Fournier).

Lavicomterie, L. de (1790), *Du peuple et des rois* (Paris: Chez les marchands de nouveatés).

Mathiez, A. (1910), *Le Club des Cordeliers* (Paris: Champion).

Monnier, R. (2003), 'Républicanisme et Révolution française', *French Historical Studies* 26:1.

Pasquino, P. (1998), *Sieyès et l'invention de la constitution en France* (Paris: Odile Jacob).

Sieyès (1789), *Observations sur le rapport de Constitution concernant la nouvelle organisation de la France* (Versailles: Baudoin).

——— (2003), *Political Writings, including the debate between Sieyès and Tom Paine in 1791*, edited with an introduction and translation of 'What is the Third Estate?' by M. Sonenscher (Indianapolis, IN: Hackett).

Further Reading

Fauré, C. (ed.) (2003), *Political and Historical Encyclopedia of Women* (New York and London: Routledge).

— (2005), 'Sieyès, lecteur problématique des Lumières', *18ème Siècle* 37, 225–42.

— (2007), 'Sieyès, Rousseau et la théorie du contrat', in Quiviger, Salem and Denis (eds), *Figures de Sieyès* (Paris: Publications de la Sorbonne).

Furet, F. and Ozouf, M. (eds) (1993), *Le siècle de l'avènement républicain* (Paris: Gallimard).

Guilhaumou, J. (2002), *Sieyès et l'ordre de la langue, l'invention de la politique moderne* (Paris: Kimé).

Monnier, R. (2006), *Républicanisme, patriotisme et Révolution française* (Paris: L'Harmattan).

Quiviger, P.-Y., Salem, J. and Denis, V. (eds) (2007), *Figures de Sieyès* (Paris: Publications de la Sorbonne).

Democratic Politics and the Dynamics of Passions

Chantal Mouffe

Advanced liberal democratic societies are characterized by a growing incapacity to envisage the problems facing them in political terms, as requiring not simply technical but properly political decisions, decisions which are made between real alternatives which imply the availability of conflicting but legitimate projects of how to organize their common life. This is not surprising, since he message that, albeit in different ways, the more recent trends in political theory and sociology are conveying – not to mention the dominant practices of mainstream political parties – is that the adversarial model of politics has become obsolete and that we have entered a new stage of reflexive modernity where an inclusive consensus can be built around a 'radical center'. All those who disagree with this consensus are dismissed as being archaic, or condemned as 'evil' or 'enemies of civilization'.

There are many reasons for the disappearance of a properly political vision. Some have to do with the predominance of a neo-liberal regime of globalization, others with the type of individualistic consumer culture which now pervades most advanced industrial societies. From a more strictly political perspective, it is clear that the collapse of communism and the disappearance of the political frontiers that have structured the political imagination during most of the twentieth century have led to the crumbling of the political markers of society. The blurring of the frontiers between right and left that we have steadily witnessed, and which so many are celebrating as a progress, no doubt constitutes a danger for democratic politics. Indeed, the democratic political public sphere has been seriously weakened by the lack of a properly agonistic debate about possible alternatives to the existing hegemonic order. This is at the origin of the increasing disaffection with liberal democratic institutions which manifests itself through declining electoral participation or the attraction exerted by right-wing populist parties which challenge the political establishment.

The Shortcomings of Liberal Democratic Theory

As a political theorist, I am particularly concerned with the responsibility of political theory in the current incapacity to think politically and the role it has played in the demise of a properly political vision, and this is the first point I will examine.

In recent years the traditional understanding of democracy as aggregation of interests – the 'aggregative' model – has been increasingly displaced by a new paradigm which, under the name of 'deliberative democracy', is fast dictating the terms of the discussion; one of its main tenets is that political questions are of a moral nature, and therefore susceptible to rational treatment. The objective of a democratic society is, according to such a view, the creation of a rational consensus reached through appropriate deliberative procedures whose aim is to produce decisions which represent an impartial standpoint, equally in the interests of all. All those who put into question the very possibility of such a rational consensus and who affirm that the political is a domain in which one should always rationally expect to find discord are accused of undermining the very possibility of democracy. As Habermas, for instance, puts it: 'If questions of justice cannot transcend the ethical self-understanding of competing forms of life, and existentially relevant value conflicts and oppositions must penetrate all controversial questions, then in the final analysis we will end up with something resembling Carl Schmitt's understanding of politics'(Habermas 1996, 1493).

The most fashionable theoretical approach nowadays is to envisage the nature of the political as akin to morality, understood in rationalistic and universalistic terms. The discourse of morality has nowadays been promoted to the place of master narrative, the one which is replacing discredited political and social discourses in providing the guidelines for collective action. It is rapidly becoming the only legitimate vocabulary, as instead of thinking in terms of right and left, we are now urged to think in terms of right and wrong.

This has led to erasing the dimension of antagonism which is ineradicable in politics, and to the displacement of the political by the juridical and the moral, which are perceived as particularly adequate terrains for reaching impartial decisions. This displacement of the political by the juridical is very clear in the work of John Rawls, for instance, who gives the supreme court as the best example of what he calls the 'free exercise of public reason', in his view, the very model of democratic deliberation. Another example can be found in the work of Ronald Dworkin, who in many of his essays gives primacy to the independent judiciary seen as the interpreter of the political morality of a community. According to him, all the fundamental questions facing a political community in the field of, for example, employment, education, censorship or freedom of association, are better resolved by the judges, providing they interpret the constitution by reference to the principle of political equality. Very little is left for discussion in the political arena.

Even pragmatists like Richard Rorty, despite carrying out a far-reaching and important critique of the rationalist approach, fail to provide an adequate alternative. The problem with Rorty is that, albeit in a different way, he also ends up by privileging consensus and missing the dimension of the political. The consensus that he advocates is, of course, to be reached through persuasion and 'sentimental education', not through rational argumentation, but he nevertheless believes in the possibility of an all-encompassing consensus, and therefore in the elimination of antagonism.

In fact, the current situation can be seen as the fulfillment of a tendency which, as Carl Schmitt has argued, is inscribed at the very core of liberalism, whose constitutive incapacity to think in truly political terms explains why it always has to resort to another type of discourse: economic, moral or juridical. The force of Schmitt's critique is that it brings to the fore what constitutes the main shortcoming of liberal thought: its incapacity to apprehend the specificity of the political. In *The Concept of the Political*, he writes:

> *In a very systematic fashion liberal thought evades or ignores state and politics and moves instead in a typical recurring polarity of two heterogeneous spheres, namely ethics and economics, intellect and trade, education and property. The critical distrust of state and politics is easily explained by the principles of a system whereby the individual must remain terminus a quo and terminus ad quem. (Schmitt 1932 [1976], 70)*

Liberal thought must necessarily be blind to the political because of its individualism, which makes it unable to understand the formation of collective identities. Yet the political is from the outset concerned with collective forms of identifications, since in this field we are always dealing with the formation of 'us' as opposed to 'them'. The political has to do with conflict and antagonism; its *differentia specifica*, as Schmitt puts it, is the friend–enemy distinction. It is no wonder, then, that liberal rationalism cannot grasp its nature, given that rationalism requires the very negation of the ineradicability of antagonism. Liberalism has to negate antagonism since, by bringing to the fore the inescapable moment of decision – in the strong sense of having to decide in an undecidable terrain – what antagonism reveals is the very limit of any rational consensus.

This denial of antagonism is what impedes liberal theory in envisaging democratic politics adequately. The political in its antagonistic dimension cannot be made to disappear by simply denying it, by wishing it away, which is the typical liberal gesture; such a negation only leads to impotence, impotence which characterizes liberal thought when confronted with the emergence of antagonisms which, according to its theory, should belong to a bygone age when reason had not yet managed to control the supposedly archaic passions. This is at the root of the current incapacity to grasp the nature and the causes of the new antagonisms which have emerged after the end of the Cold War. It is therefore of the utmost importance to listen to Schmitt when he states that the political can be understood 'only in the context of the ever present possibility of the friend-and-enemy groupings, regardless of the aspects which this possibility implies for morality, aesthetics, and economics' (Schmitt 1932 [1976], 35). Schmitt is right to bring to our attention the fact that the political is linked to the existence of a dimension of hostility in human societies, hostility which can take many forms and manifest itself in very diverse types of social relations. This recognition, I contend, should constitute the starting point for an adequate reflection on the aims of democratic politics.

To be sure, Schmitt never developed those insights in a theoretical way, and it is necessary to formulate them more rigorously. I would like to suggest that this can be done with the help of the critique of essentialism developed by several currents of contemporary thought. This critique shows that one of the main problems with liberalism is that it deploys a logic of the social based on a conception of being as presence, and that it conceives of objectivity as being inherent to the things themselves. This is why it cannot apprehend the process of construction of political identities. It is unable to recognize that there can only be an identity when it is constructed as 'difference', and that any social objectivity is constituted through acts of power. What it refuses to admit is that any form of social objectivity is ultimately political, and that it must bear the traces of the acts of exclusions which govern its constitution.

The notion of 'constitutive outside' can be helpful here to make this argument more explicit. This term has been proposed by Henry Staten to refer to a number of themes developed by Jacques Derrida through notions like 'supplement', 'trace' and 'difference'. Its aim is to highlight the fact that the creation of an identity implies the establishment of a difference, difference which is often constructed on the basis of a hierarchy: for example, between form and matter, black and white, man and women, and so on. Once we have understood that every identity is relational and that the affirmation of a difference – the perception of something 'other' that constitutes its 'exterior' – is a precondition for the existence of any identity, then Schmitt's point about the ever-present possibility of the friend–enemy relation can be better formulated; or to put it in another way, we can begin to envisage how a social relation can become the breeding ground for antagonism.

When dealing with political identities which are always collective identities, we are dealing with the creation of an 'us' than can only exist by the demarcation of a 'them'. This does not mean, of course, that such a relation is by necessity an antagonistic one. But it means that there is always the possibility of this us–them relation becoming one of friend–enemy. This happens when the others, who up to now had been considered as simply different, start to be perceived as putting into question our identity and threatening our existence. From that moment on, any form of us–them relation, be it religious, ethnic or economic, becomes the locus of antagonism.

What is important here is to acknowledge that the very condition of possibility of formation of political identities is at the same time the condition of impossibility of a society from which antagonism has been eliminated. Antagonism is therefore an ever-present possibility, as Schmitt repeatedly stressed. This antagonistic dimension is what I have proposed to call the 'the political', and to distinguish it from 'politics' which refers to the set of practices and institutions whose aim is to create an order, to organize human coexistence in conditions which are always conflictual because they are traversed by 'the political'. To use a Heideggerian terminology, we could say that 'the political' is situated at the level of the ontological, while politics belongs to the ontic.

Agonistic Pluralism

It is my contention that in order to understand the nature of democratic politics and the challenge with which it is confronted, we need an alternative to the two main approaches in democratic political theory. One of those approaches, the aggregative model, sees political actors as being moved by the pursuit of their interests; the other model, the deliberative one, stresses the role of reason and moral considerations. What both of these models leave aside is the central role played by 'passions' in the creation of collective political identities. One cannot understand democratic politics without acknowledging passions as the moving force in the field of politics. It is precisely this deficiency that the agonistic model of democracy is trying to remedy by tackling all the issues which cannot be properly addressed by the two other models because of their rationalist individualistic framework.

In a nutshell, the argument goes as follows. Once we acknowledge the dimension of 'the political', we begin to realize that one of the main challenges for democratic politics consists of domesticating hostility and trying to defuse the potential antagonism that exists in human relations. Indeed, the fundamental question for democratic politics is not how to arrive at a rational consensus, a consensus reached without exclusion; this would require the construction of an 'us' that would not have a corresponding 'them'. Yet this is impossible, because, as I have argued, the very condition for the constitution of an 'us' is the demarcation of a 'them'. The crucial issue for democratic politics, then, is how to establish this us–them distinction which is constitutive of politics, in a way which is compatible with the recognition of pluralism. Conflict in democratic societies cannot and should not be eradicated, since the specificity of modern democracy is precisely the recognition and the legitimization of conflict. What democratic politics requires is that the others are not seen as enemies to be destroyed, but as adversaries whose ideas must be fought, even fiercely, but whose right to defend those ideas will never be put into question. To put it another way, what is important is that conflict does not take the form of *antagonism* (struggle between enemies), but the form of *agonism* (struggle between adversaries). We could say that the aim of democratic politics is to transform potential antagonism into agonism.

According to the agonistic perspective, the central category of democratic politics is that of the 'adversary', the opponent with whom we share a common allegiance to the democratic principles of 'liberty and equality for all' while disagreeing about their interpretation. Adversaries fight against each other because they want their interpretation to become hegemonic, but they do not call into question the legitimacy of their opponents to fight for the victory of their position. This confrontation between adversaries is what constitutes the 'agonistic struggle' which is the very condition of a vibrant democracy (for a development of this argument, see Mouffe 2000). For the agonistic model, the prime task of democratic politics is not to eliminate passions or to relegate them to the private sphere in order to establish a rational consensus in the public sphere, it is to 'tame', so to speak, those passions by mobilizing them towards democratic designs, by creating collective forms of identification around democratic objectives.

In order to avoid any misunderstanding, let me stress that this notion of the adversary needs to be distinguished sharply from the understanding of that term we find in liberal discourse. According to the understanding of 'adversary' proposed here, and contrary to the liberal view, the presence of antagonism is not eliminated, but 'sublimated'. In fact, what liberals call an 'adversary' is simply a 'competitor'. They envisage the field of politics as a neutral terrain in which different groups compete to occupy the positions of power, and their objective is simply to dislodge others in order to occupy their place, without putting into question the dominant hegemony and profoundly transforming the relations of power. It is simply a competition among elites. In an agonistic politics, however, the antagonistic dimension is always present, since what is a stake is the struggle between opposing hegemonic projects which can never be reconciled rationally: one of them needs to be defeated. It is a real confrontation, but one that is played out under conditions regulated by a set of democratic procedures accepted by the adversaries.

Liberal theorists are unable to acknowledge not only the primary reality of strife in social life, and the impossibility of finding rational, impartial solutions to political issues, but also the integrative role that conflict plays in modern democracy. A well-functioning democracy calls for a confrontation between democratic political positions. If this is missing, there is always the danger that this democratic confrontation will be replaced by a confrontation between non-negotiable moral values or essentialist forms of identifications. Too much emphasis on consensus, together with aversion towards confrontation, leads to apathy and to disaffection with political participation. This is why a democratic society requires a debate about possible alternatives. It must provide political forms of identifications around clearly differentiated democratic positions, or to put it in Niklas Luhmann's terms, there must be a clear 'splitting' of the summit, a real choice between the policies put forward by the government and those of the opposition. While consensus is no doubt necessary, it must be accompanied by dissent. Consensus is needed on the institutions which are constitutive of democracy and on the ethico-political values that should inform the political association, but there will always be disagreement concerning the meaning of those values and the way they should be implemented. In a pluralist democracy, such disagreements are not only legitimate, but also necessary. They allow for different forms of citizenship identification, and are the stuff of democratic politics. When the agonistic dynamics of pluralism is hindered because of a lack of democratic forms of identification, passions cannot be given a democratic outlet, and the ground is laid for various forms of politics articulated around essentialist identities of nationalist, religious or ethnic type and for the multiplication of confrontations over non-negotiable moral values.

Beyond Left and Right

We should therefore be suspicious of the current tendency to celebrate the blurring of the frontiers between left and right and of those who are advocating a politics 'beyond left and right'. A well-functioning democracy calls for a vibrant clash of democratic political positions. Antagonisms can take many forms, and it is illusory to believe that they could be eradicated. In order to allow for the possibility of transforming them into agonistic relations, it is necessary to provide a political outlet for the expression of conflict within a pluralistic democratic system offering possibilities of identification around democratic political alternatives.

It is in this context that we can grasp the very pernicious consequences of the fashionable thesis which has been put forward by Ulrich Beck and Anthony Giddens, who both argue that the adversarial model of politics has become obsolete. In their view, the friend–enemy model of politics is characteristic of classical industrial modernity, the 'first modernity', but they claim that we now live in a different, 'second' modernity, a 'reflexive' one, in which the emphasis should be placed on 'sub-politics', on the issues of 'life and death'.

As in the case of deliberative democracy, which I have criticized at the beginning of this chapter, albeit in a different way, what is at the basis of this conception of reflexive modernity is the possibility of elimination of the political in its antagonistic dimension, and the belief that friend–enemy relations have been eradicated. The claim is that in post-traditional societies, we do not find any more collective identities constructed in term of us–them, which means that political frontiers have evaporated and that politics must therefore be 'reinvented', to use Beck's expression. Indeed, Beck pretends that the generalized scepticism and the centrality of doubt which are prevalent today preclude the emergence of antagonistic relations. We have entered an era of ambivalence in which nobody can any longer believe they possess the truth – belief which was precisely where antagonisms were stemming from – therefore, there is no more reason for their emergence. Any attempt to organize collective identities in terms of left and right and to define an adversary is thereby discredited as being 'archaic'.

Politics in its conflictual dimension is deemed to be something of the past, and the type of democracy which is commended is a consensual, completely depoliticized democracy. Nowadays, the key terms of political discourse are 'good governance' and 'partisan-free democracy'. In my view, it is the incapacity of traditional parties to provide distinctive forms of identifications around possible alternatives which has created the terrain for the current flourishing of right-wing populism. Indeed, right-wing populist parties are often the only ones which attempt to mobilize passions and to create collective forms of identifications. Against all those who believe that politics can be reduced to individual motivations, they are well aware that politics always consists in the creation of an 'us' versus a 'them', and that it implies the creation of collective identities. Hence the powerful appeal of their discourse, because it provides collective forms of identification around 'the people'.

If we add to that the fact that under the banner of 'modernization' social democratic parties have in many countries identified themselves more or less exclusively with the middle classes and that they have stopped addressing the concerns of the popular sectors – whose demands are considered as 'archaic' or 'retrograde' – we should not be surprised by the growing alienation of all those groups who feel excluded from the effective exercise of citizenship by what they perceive as the 'establishment elites'. In a context where the dominant discourse proclaims that there is no alternative to the current neo-liberal form of globalization and that we have to accept its diktats, small wonder that more and more people are keen to listen to those who claim that alternatives do exist, and that they will give back to the people the power to decide. When democratic politics has lost its capacity to shape the discussion about how we should organize our common life, and when it is limited to securing the necessary conditions for the smooth working of the market, the conditions are ripe for talented demagogues to articulate popular frustration. It is important to realize that to a great extent, the success of right-wing populist parties comes from the fact that they provide people with some form of hope, with the belief that things could be different. Of course, this is an illusory hope, founded on false premises and on unacceptable mechanisms of exclusion where xenophobia usually plays a central role. But when they are the only ones to offer an outlet for political passions, their pretence to offer an alternative is seductive, and their appeal is likely to grow. To be able to envisage an adequate response, it is necessary to grasp the economic, social and political conditions which explain their emergence. And this supposes a theoretical approach that does not deny the antagonistic dimension of the political.

Politics in the Moral Register

I think that it is also crucial to understand that it is not through moral condemnation that the rise of right-wing populism can be stopped, and this is why the dominant answer has so far been completely inadequate. Of course, a moralistic reaction chimes with the dominant post-political perspective, and it had to be expected. It is worth examining it closely because this will bring us some insights about the form under which political antagonisms manifest themselves today.

As we have seen, the dominant discourse asserts the end of the adversarial model of politics, and the advent of a consensual society beyond left and right. However, I have also argued that politics always entails an us–them distinction. This is why the consensus advocated by the defenders of partisan-free democracy cannot exist without drawing a political frontier and defining an exterior, a 'them' which assures the identity of the consensus and the coherence of the 'us'. In domestic politics, this 'them' is nowadays often conveniently designated as 'extreme right', a term which refers to an amalgam of groups and parties which covers a wide spectrum, from fringe groups of extremists and neo-Nazis to the authoritarian right, and on up to the variety of new right-wing populist parties. Of course, such a heterogeneous construct is useless to grasp the nature and the causes of this new right-wing populism. But it is very useful to secure the identity of the 'good democrats'. Since politics has supposedly become non-adversarial, the 'them' necessary to secure the 'us' of the good democrats cannot be envisaged as a political adversary. So the extreme right comes in very handy, because it allows the drawing of the frontier at the moral level, between 'the good democrats' and the 'evil extreme right', which can be condemned morally instead of being fought politically. This is why moral condemnation and the establishment of a *cordon sanitaire* have become the dominant answer to the rise of right-wing populist movements.

In fact, what is happening is very different from what the advocates of the post-political approach would want us to believe. It is not that politics with its supposedly old-fashioned antagonisms has been superseded by moral concerns about 'life issues' and 'human rights'. Politics in its antagonistic dimension is still very much alive, except that it is now played out in the register of morality. Frontiers between us and them, far from having disappeared, are constantly being established, but since the 'them' cannot be defined in political terms any more, those frontiers are drawn in moral categories, between 'us the good' and 'them the evil ones'.

One of the main shortcomings of this type of politics played out in the moral register is that it is not conducive to the creation of the 'agonistic public sphere' which is the requisite of a robust democratic life. When the opponent is not defined in political, but in moral terms, he cannot be envisaged as an adversary, but only as an enemy. With the 'evil them', no agonistic debate is possible, they have to be eradicated.

The approach which claims that the friend–enemy model of politics has been superseded in fact ends up reinforcing the antagonistic model of politics that has been declared obsolete. By constructing the 'them' as a moral (that is, an 'absolute') enemy, they make it impossible to transform it into an 'adversary.' Instead of helping to create a vibrant agonistic public sphere thanks to which democracy can be kept alive and deepened, all those who proclaim the end of antagonism and the arrival of a consensual society are actually jeopardizing democracy, creating the conditions for the emergence of antagonisms that will not be manageable by democratic institutions.

Without a profound transformation in the way democratic politics is envisaged and a serious attempt to address the lack of forms of identifications which would allow for a democratic mobilization of passions, the challenge posed by right-wing populist parties will remain. New political frontiers are being drawn in European politics which carry the danger that the old left–right distinction could soon be replaced by another one much less conducive to a pluralistic democratic debate. It is therefore urgent to relinquish the illusions of the consensual model of politics, and to create the bases of an agonistic public sphere.

By limiting themselves to calls for reason, moderation and consensus, democratic parties are showing their lack of understanding of the working of political logics. They do not understand the need to counter right-wing populism by mobilizing affects and passions in a democratic direction. What they do not grasp is that democratic politics needs to have a real purchase on people's desires and fantasies, and that instead of opposing interests to sentiments and reason to passions, it should offer forms of identification which represent a real challenge to the ones promoted by the right. This is not to say that reason and rational argument should disappear from politics, but that their place needs to be rethought.

Towards a Multipolar World Order

To end, let me present some reflections concerning the international situation, and enquire about possible scenarios for the future of democracy at the world level. We can broadly envisage two main possibilities. There are those who call for the establishment of a 'cosmopolitan democracy' and a 'cosmopolitan citizenship' resulting from the universalization of the Western interpretation of democratic values and the implementation of the Western version of human rights. According to such an approach, this is how a democratic global order should come about. There are different variants of this approach, but all of them share a common premise: that the Western form of life is the best one, and that moral progress requires its worldwide implementation. This is the liberal universalism which aims to impose its institutions on the rest of the world with the argument that they are the only rational and legitimate ones. I believe that even if it is very far from the intentions of those who advocate the cosmopolitan model, such a view is bound to justify the hegemony of the West and the imposition of its particular values.

Those who argue for the advent of a 'World Republic' with a homogeneous body of cosmopolitan citizens with the same rights and obligations, a constituency that would coincide with 'humanity', are denying the dimension of the political which is inherent to human societies. They overlook the fact that power relations are constitutive of the social, and that conflicts and antagonisms cannot be eradicated. This is why, if such a World Republic was ever established, it could only signify the world hegemony of a dominant power which would have been able to erase all differences and impose its own conception of the world on the entire planet. This would have dire consequences, and we are already witnessing how current attempts to homogenize the world are provoking violent adverse reactions from those societies whose specific values and cultures are rendered illegitimate by the enforced universalization of the Western model.

I suggest that we relinquish the flawed models of 'cosmopolitan citizenship', and that we promote a different conception of the world order, a conception that acknowledges value pluralism in its strong Weberian and Nietzschean sense, with all its implications for politics. Discarding the claims of the universalists, it is urgent to become aware of the dangers implied in the illusions of a globalist–universalist discourse which envisages human progress as the establishment of world unity based on the acceptance of the Western model. By imagining the possibility of a unification of the world that could be achieved by transcending the political, conflict and negativity, such a discourse risks bringing about the clash of civilizations that it claims to be avoiding. At the moment where the United States is – under the pretence of a 'true universalism'– trying to force the rest of the world to adopt its system, the need for a multipolar world order is more pressing than ever. What is at stake is the establishment of a pluralist world order where a number of large regional units would coexist and where a plurality of forms of democracy would be considered legitimate.

At this stage in the process of globalization, I do not want to deny the need for a set of institutions to regulate international relations, but those institutions should allow for a significant degree of pluralism, and they should not require the existence of a single unified power structure. Such a structure would necessarily entail the presence of a centre which would be the only locus of sovereignty. It is vain to imagine the possibility of a world system ruled by reason and where power relations have been neutralized. This supposed 'Reign of Reason' could only be the screen concealing the rule of a dominant power which, identifying its interests with those of humanity, would treat any disagreement as an illegitimate challenge to its 'rational' leadership.

By attempting to impose the Western conception of democracy, deemed to be the only legitimate one, on reluctant societies, the universalist approach it is bound to present those who do not accept this conception as 'enemies of civilization', thereby denying their rights to maintain their cultures, and creating the conditions for an antagonistic confrontation between different civilizations. It is only by acknowledging the legitimacy of a plurality of just forms of society, and the fact that liberal democracy is only one form of democracy among others, that conditions could be created for an 'agonistic' coexistence between different regional poles with their specific institutions. Such a multipolar order will, of course, not eliminate conflict, but this conflict is less likely to take antagonistic forms than in a world that does not make room for pluralism.

References

Habermas, J. (1996), 'Reply to Symposium Participants', *Cardozo Law Review* 17: 4–5.

Mouffe, C. (2000*)*, *The Democratic Paradox* (London: Verso).

Schmitt, C. (1932 [1976]), *The Concept of the Political* (New Brunswick, NJ: Rutgers University Press).

Further Reading

Beck, U. (1997), *The Reinvention of Politics: Rethinking Modernity in the Global Social Order* (Cambridge: Polity).

Dworkin, R. (1977), *Taking Rights Seriously* (Cambridge MA: Harvard University Press).

Giddens, A. (1994), *Beyond Left and Right* (Cambridge: Polity).

Luhmann, N. (1990), 'The Future of Democracy', *Thesis Eleven* 26.

Mouffe, C. (1993), *The Return of the Political* (London: Verso).

—— (ed.) (1999), *The Challenge of Carl Schmitt* (London: Verso).

—— (2004), *On the Political* (London: Routledge).

Rasch, W. (2004), *Sovereignty and its Discontents: On the Primacy of Conflict and the Structure of the Political* (London: Birkbeck Law).

Rawls, J. (1993), *Political Liberalism* (New York: Columbia University Press).

Rorty, R. (1991), *Objectivity, Relativism and Truth: Philosophical Papers*, vol. 1 (Cambridge: Cambridge University Press).

Staten, H. (1984), *Wittgenstein and Derrida* (Lincoln, NB: University of Nebraska Press).

Disobedient State and Faithful Citizen? Re-locating Politics in the Age of Globalization

Olivia Guaraldo

The relationship between the modern state and the monopoly of violence has been one of the main features of Western politics, where the identity of state, nation and territory has been guaranteed by the monopoly of the means of coercion – police and armed forces. One could say that the very notion of representation depends upon the stability of the state borders and the order that an effective monopoly of violence is able to maintain. Today, any observer of the contemporary global situation is struck by the progressive evanescence of such monopoly, and a correspondent proliferation of violence both inside and outside the borders of states. What seems to be at stake, in terms of the loss of efficacy of the modern concept and practice of sovereignty, is the end of the 'contract' between state and citizen, one that, at least since the time of the father of such a concept, Thomas Hobbes, has been founded on the mutual relationship of obedience in exchange for protection. What happens when the compact that was founded on the famous agreement *protego ergo obligo* is broken? How can we imagine a politics to come that can be freed from the representative procedural structures that are unable to guarantee what they have been created for? Acknowledging the end of what has been called the 'immunitarian' function of modern politics,[1] political theory

---

1   What Esposito (1998) calls the 'immunitary theory of politics' is modern individualism, which shapes the human according to a supposed unrelatedness, to an absence of bonds or dependence upon the other – be it another individual, a collectivity, or a political authority. To my knowledge, the best account of Esposito's ideas, together with an original political appropriation of them, can be found in Bortolini (2003): 'The immunization of the subject brings about a new classification of what counts as "the public," for the only "thing" these individuals have in common is the preconditions of their private lives – in John Locke's classical formula, "life, liberty, and property." This deprives politics of its independent meaning and reduces it to a collectively owned *machine* meant to protect the premises of human life. We find a classic statement of this condition in *The Jewish Question*: according to the young Karl Marx, in modernity

must embark on the imaginative task of recognizing the end of that model and its anthropological premises, where the very *measure* of representative democracy – the atomized and self-sufficient individual – can no longer work.

Violence, Order and the State

The relationship between the modern state and violence is one of familiarity, to say the least. As Thomas Hobbes, the father of modern politics, suggests, the fear of a sudden and violent death is the background against which the factuality of a radical equality of men in the state of nature emerges:

> *Nature hath made man so equal in the faculties of body and mind as that, though there be found one man sometimes manifestly stronger in body or of quicker mind than another, yet when all is reckoned together the difference between man and man is not so considerable ... For as to the strength of the body, the weakest has strength enough to kill the strongest, either by secret machination, or by confederacy with others that are in the same danger with himself. (Leviathan, Book XIII, 1)*

Consequently, the living conditions of men in the state of nature – that is, in absence of a common and superior power – is defined by Hobbes as *bellum omnium contra omnes*:

> *Hereby it is manifest that during the time men live without a common power to keep them all in awe, they are in that condition which is called war; and such a war as is of every man against every man. For war consisteth not in battle only, or the act of fighting, but in a tract of time, wherein the will to contend by battle is sufficiently known: and therefore the notion of time is to be considered in the nature of war, as it is in the nature of weather. For as the nature of foul weather lieth not in a shower or two of rain, but in an inclination thereto of many days together: so the nature of war consisteth not in actual fighting, but in the known disposition thereto during all the time*

"political life is declared to be a mere means whose end is the life of civil society,' where 'civil society' means a right to freedom which is 'not based on the union of man with man, but on *the separation of man from man*. It is *the right to this separation*, the rights of the limited individual who is limited to himself" (Marx 1844 [1985], 53–4, my italics). With respect to classical political theory, not only the public changes its content, but it also gets completely devalued in itself. Ever since, the State has been the institutional translation of this immunitary subject, the rational and artificial device aimed to mark, nurture and preserve the only thing that a multitude of individual, immunitary subjects can recognize as the "common": the premises of the pursuit of private goals in the form of *individual rights*. In our conceptual lexicon, then, the modern State is *the form of administration of immunity*' (Bortolini 2003, 9–10).

there is no assurance to the contrary. All other time is peace. (Leviathan, Book XIII, 8)

In order to make life livable, peaceful and productive, it is necessary to institute a common power –Hobbes calls it 'the Leviathan' – that keeps men 'all in awe': namely, a power that overcomes the individual wills and appetites, by force of a univocal will, superior and sovereign, able to abolish the war of every man against every man within the borders of its efficacy.

Once order and peace are established, through the proceedings of the covenant by which every man renounces his individual right to all things and transfers it to a third party, the sovereign, the new form of organization, the state, can be sure of having total control of that 'natural' force possessed originally by every man. It is not by chance that two-and-a-half centuries after Hobbes, Max Weber would define the modern state through what he calls its specific means, namely the monopoly of 'the legitimate use of physical force as a means of domination within a territory' (Weber 1919 [2004]).

Modernity, in other words, transforms the natural disorder of violence – the *bellum omnium contra omnes* – in a monopolistic practice of a unitary subject, and by so doing, expels from its borders all forms of violence that are not legitimized by sovereign decision. As we all know, the political order of modernity is defined in its essence through the monopolistic notion of violence, according to which a unitary subject, within the territorial borders that constitute the state, has legitimate power to exercise the implements of coercion. War and police represent, in the modern model of state sovereignty, the two main paths of this monopoly, the violent sides of that 'superior power' created in order to eliminate diffuse and uncontrollable violence.

The principal aim of sovereign power is that of creating and maintaining peace, eliminating the primordial fear of a violent and sudden death that, in the sublime theoretical construction given by Hobbes, legitimizes the construction of the artificial order of sovereignty.

Protego ergo obligo can be the shortened form for the contract established between frightened individuals and the superior power that originates from a mutual agreement among them. The compact that gives birth to the commonwealth or state is entirely legitimized by the need for protection in exchange for total obedience.

The liberal version of representative democracy does not recognize Hobbes as one of its predecessors, and instead enlists him among the thinkers of absolutism, whereas the functioning mechanism of any representative regime is founded upon what Hobbes conceptualized in the seventeenth century:

> *A COMMONWEALTH is said to be instituted when a multitude of men do agree, and covenant, every one with every one, that to whatsoever man, or assembly of men, shall be given by the major part the right to present the person of them all, that is to say, to be their representative; every one, as well he that voted for it as he that voted against it, shall authorize all the actions and judgements of that man, or assembly of men, in the same manner as if*

they were his own, to the end to live peaceably amongst themselves, and be protected against other men. (Leviathan, Book XVIII, 1)

Representation depends constitutively upon the order of peace and protection that the sovereign is able to maintain within its territory. There can be no form of representation of the actions and words of a disconnected multitude, but only of a well-ordered and obedient people. Hobbes is conscious of the implications inherent in his model of order, and radicalizes them in order to make clear that only a regime based on the equality of votes – inaugurating thereby the modern, as opposed to the medieval, notion of representation – can guarantee a legitimate, therefore orderly and peaceful, commonwealth. When we speak today of representative democracy, we must be aware of the origins of such a notion, and be conscious that, liberal democracy notwithstanding, the functioning mechanism of our 'commonwealths' is the same, and still depends upon a notion of representation that orders the space of its territoriality and the subjects included therein.

Disciplining Conflict: The Modern Solution

Let us examine the theoretical implications of this model of order, leaving aside, for a moment, the concrete historical instances of representation, or to put it more simply, the complex history of representative democracy. The innovative political model construed by Hobbes shapes the space of sovereignty as an empty and pacified territory, protected from the outside by borders, and from the inside by a system of regulations that derive directly from the awesome powers of the Leviathan. Violence is dissimulated as power, instantiated as law, proliferated as norms and regulations, as Michel Foucault would later point out (Foucault 1981). This brings us to the point in question: the threat of violence is what makes power function, at least in the model imagined by Hobbes, where we can speak of consent in light of the continuous threat of punishment or disorder. Violence, in other words, is what lies at the basis of the artificial model of sovereignty: the threat of a sudden and violent death is what *forces* men in the state of nature to escape from it. The covenant is the result of a mutual agreement, a dialogical procedure that, to some extent, exemplifies some sort of primordial example of 'public sphere', but that agreement receives its undeniability only by the necessity of escaping the state of nature. One can speak of consensus in a very weak sense, inasmuch as it is a consensus built on fear.

Indeed, the practical solution to the state of nature, namely the covenant among men to institute a common and superior power, does not eliminate violence, but is founded upon the delayed, deferred violence of the Leviathan, which still threatens men, but, as it were, in an optimized way. While violence in the state of nature is the expression of human passions, the result of an immediate instinct to suppress the other before the other suppresses me, violence in the civil state is the threatening sword of the sovereign, which compels subjects to order in light of a rational, mediated pursuit, namely peace. The first type of threat – violence in the state of nature – is sudden, unpredictable, chaotic, unproductive; the second type of threat is mechanical, predictable, rational and productive.[2] Only under the threat of punishment embodied by the sovereign can economy, trade and arts develop and flourish.

Violence *threatens* life in the state of nature, violence *protects* life in the civil state. Interestingly enough, though, it seems that the same governing principle of human relationships has been transferred from a chaotic condition to an orderly one. Violence, as such, does not change. What changes is the way in which it is deployed. One could argue that the political use of violence, as it is conceived in the Hobbesian model, enables men to live in peace, in accordance with the artificial model of order founded upon the presupposition of a necessary agreement. Nevertheless, the peaceful order of the Leviathan is grounded in a bloody terrain: the terrain of civil war, as well as the terrain of the awesome Leviathan.

Violence, in other words, disappears from the perceivable horizon of the ordered territory of the state, from its official paraphernalia as well as its legitimizing procedures, to re-emerge in disguise in the different instances of what Foucault has called regulatory power. Violence founds the state, and to a certain extent remains the emblem of its powerfulness, of its incomparability, as Hobbes remarks. But in such founding and legitimizing act, violence disappears from the public scene, hidden from view because what the state promises is protection, peace, order.[3] Violence is therefore caught in a paradox, which is at the basis of our notion of 'politics': it must be hidden, invisible, in order to become symbolically relevant, and useful. Violence is both the ever-present instinct to kill your enemy, the one who threatens your life and welfare, and also the rational means of coercion that shapes, controls and punishes the free play of instincts. In order to control a free human nature that tends to annihilate itself in constant mutual killings, the artificial order of the state takes onto itself that mutual power to kill and its potential of threat. In so doing, it eradicates violence from daily human intercourse, subsuming it under its own arbitrary, yet indispensable, will.

To sum up, what role does violence play in the shaping of the modern notion of political order? What is the pre-emptive notion of the 'human' that informs the specific notion of order and peace formulated by the contractarian tradition of thought?

The anthropological premises upon which the modern contract is founded are those of modern individualism, which, as many feminist and post-colonial thinkers have pointed out,[4] is essentially of masculine gender, of bourgeois origins, and of white race. Moreover, the premises of what has been called liberal individualism are 'both the presupposition and the result' of the modern territorial

---

2   Of course, Carl Schmitt would say that the violence of the Leviathan is not 'predictable' in so far as sovereignty is built upon an unpredictable decision on the *Ausnahmezustand*, the state of exception (see Schmitt 1922 [1985]).

3   On the disappearance of violence and death from the public scene and the contemporary birth of a disciplinary power, see Foucault (1990, 1997).

4   See, among others, Cavarero (2004). See also Pateman (1988) and Bock and James (1992).

state. Modernity, therefore, is characterized by a sort of 'immunization project'. It consists of assuming 'individuals as free and autonomous subjects in order to save them from the "contagion of relation"'(Cavarero 2005, 185–6). In short, modern ontology, especially in its liberal version, thinks of human beings as autonomous, isolated and competitive individuals.

In the words of Cavarero, 'No one means anything to anyone else – each is already complete in the self-sufficiency that encloses them in themselves, like a world apart,' immunized from one another. Individuals are thus 'prevented from "recognizing" the other', since what is lacking here is precisely a common context in which each can 'exist and be recognized'. Since they 'replicate the same, each one's worth is *one*'. The union that keeps them together – the state – must have its generating principle in the formal and quantitative mechanism of the majority. 'Modern democracy, as a procedural form that organizes the representative body, is founded on this very principle,' namely a principle consistent with 'liberal individualism, according to which, as Hannah Arendt points out, "the state was supposed to rule over mere individuals, over an atomized society whose very atomization it was called upon to protect"' (Arendt 1994, 209, quoted in Cavarero 2005, 186).

The pacified order of the state, therefore, in order to make its threat function, must posit separate individuals, free and autonomous, who willingly, rationally and collectively decide to bind themselves through the means of a founding agreement, the covenant, to that universal power of the state. Whereas violence was a destructive element in the state of nature, here violence is disguised, dissimulated and at the same time dignified by the authority of the sovereign. The Hobbesian model, in order to work theoretically, posits an essential vulnerability in the state of nature, which will eventually be abandoned in the civil state, where individuals are perceived as protected against each other by virtue of the power of the Leviathan. This artificial bond among men, whether it is dictated by necessity (as in Hobbes) or by personal interest (as in Locke) or by good will (as in Rousseau), is legitimized by a need to relate unrelated beings, individuals who pursue personal interests (whether through pure will to power or rational interest) and perceive of themselves as complete, self-sufficient entities.

Violence, which connected men in a deathly embrace in the state of nature, precisely because it has been abandoned, and precisely because such abandonment is the founding gesture of the new political order, does not play any role in the anthropological model which is at the basis of the natural law tradition. In fact, according to that influential tradition, the model of the human which is its basis is construed according to a 'natural' self-sufficiency by virtue of which men are unrelated, isolated entities who come to the world already formed in their conscious self-sufficiency. Hobbes, efficaciously, proposes to 'consider men as if but even now sprung out of the earth, and suddenly, like mushrooms, come to full maturity, without all kind of engagement to each other' (*Philosophical Rudiments Concerning Government and Society*, Book VIII, 1).

The fiction of the 'individual' therefore requires an even more powerful fiction in order to forget, abandon, hide from view the perpetual state of war from which it emerges. And this is why the juridical institution of the contract is the artificial way of connecting, relating artificial beings: the fiction holds only if both poles of the natural law narrative are presupposed as such, namely as the two protagonists of a story of unrelatedness in need of being instituted as relation. Individual and contract are the two indispensable fictive presuppositions of modern political order.

The model of order of the state therefore promises protection in exchange for obedience, and the artificial boundaries of state territory are the limit – both ideal and literal – of the validity of this exchange. Violence enters this compact only as the mediated repression of disorder (what we could call a violence *ex parte populi*) or as the eventual punishment for non-obedience (*ex parte imperii*). In spite of the violence that founds, theoretically, the modern political order, the state, violence is absent from the internal political scene, and it emerges instead in the continuous conflicting wills of different leviathans, namely in the practice of war.

As far as Hobbes's model offers a solution to a bloody civil war, and to the potential infinity of a war that perpetuates 'natural' conflicts among men, we can easily affirm that it has succeeded in providing a context of peace, of protection, of obedience. At what price these three conditions have been achieved is a rather complex question that cannot to be investigated here.

But what happens if one calls into question this narrative? What happens if one attempts to think of the bond that structures human coexistence in a radically different way? What happens if, instead of perpetuating the natural law fiction – which is still at the basis of our notion of political subject and citizen – we pursue a different path? What happens, in other words, if we stop believing in such a narrative?

Challenging Modern Individualism

It is by no means just a matter of faith, or credulity. It is well known how the debate over the possibilities of *amending* the liberal ontology of individualism has reached a point of epistemic, structural divergence between the advocates of liberalism and the advocates of multiculturalism.[5] My claim is that in order to exit the cul de sac of the eternal opposition between procedure and identity, one should, in a way, dare to question the liberal narrative from a different point of view, not by opposing the individual to the community, but by speculating on the possibility of a *different measure* for the human, a measure which is not based on autonomy and independence, but relation and dependence. Dependence and relation, though, should be considered not (only) from the viewpoint of a culture, a set of norms, a tradition, but basically as the ontological premises of human intelligibility: before the individual comes the relation, a relation that is at the basis of the possibility of existence in the singular, a relation upon which the very possibility of saying 'I'

---

5   For an excellent reconstruction of the debate and its latest developments with reference to the question of 'the human', see Ferrara (2003, 2007).

depends. To amend individualism means basically to get rid of the individual as a measure for the human.

The present moment is propitious for a radical, philosophical, even speculative questioning of the political categories that shape human intelligibility. What does this mean? It simply means that politics is not just a matter of elections, parties, consent, cabinet ministers and the like. Politics relates to an existential dimension that is central to the definition of the 'human'. Because, as Arendt pointed out very well, the question of political rights – the admittance of human beings into the sphere of representative politics – is a question of 'life and death': those who are excluded from the scene of representation – the scene of the covenant and of the protection in exchange for obedience – are those who remain exposed relentlessly to violence, death, vulnerability, as was the case of Jews and other displaced minorities in Europe during the first half of the twentieth century (Arendt 1958b). The debate over the access to humanity, to the frames of representability that admit to political existence and allow subjects to the sphere of representation, is not at all new. What must be recognized as new, though, is the historical emergence of political phenomena that are unreadable and incomprehensible according to the frames of intelligibility shaped by the political discourse of liberal, individualistic, immunitarian ontology. From global warming to migrations, from multiculturalism to anti-globalism, from the 'war on terror' to the hysteria of Muslim fundamentalism, from the legitimization crisis of Western democracies to the expanding role of global corporations, the present scenario warns us that the self-sufficient individual, its autonomy and freedom are nothing more than a fetish. Perhaps, I would like to suggest, they have always been, at least in the way they have been inserted into the rational argument of contractarianism.

According to the contractarian narrative, in fact, the relationship between violence and representation becomes effective only in so far as violence is sublimated in the sword of the sovereign. Representation is strictly dependent upon an order of peace, established by the covenant, in which disconnected entities, individuals, become connected, bind to one another in the person – or assembly of persons – of the sovereign. Only when a multitude, belligerent and chaotic, is transformed into a people can it author the actions and decisions of the sovereign. By the same token, only when there is a power, common and superior, that keeps men all in awe, can the multitude of men be called a people. The simultaneity by which representation and sovereignty are constituted, and the impossibility, as it were, to say which should come first, testifies to the artificiality of the model in an even more explicit way.

But if we take Hobbes' proposal seriously, if we consider the effects of his notion of political order and political obedience, namely the relationship between violence and representation, we are able to detect the extent to which this notion has lost pregnancy. The modern notion of representation, to say the least, has become obsolete. Among the many causes for this obsolescence, we can enlist firstly the progressive evanescence of the notion of state sovereignty, which brings with it the disruption of a compact territory, and the subsequent fragmentation of that ordered and obedient 'unit' that Hobbes called 'people', as opposed to the disorderly, pre-statal, multitude. One could add the progressive de-politicization of a vast majority of the citizens of contemporary democracies, where for de-politicization is intended the constant negative trend of participation to the main events of 'representation', namely elections, the correspondent diminishing membership of traditional parties, excessive bureaucratization, the erasure of most of the welfare state policies and institutions, and so on.[6] On the other hand, though, one could register a correspondent re-politicization, an increase in participation in those non-representative events such as public demonstrations, sit-ins, alternative or non-conventional forms of participation, as political science textbooks term them.

To sum up, the challenges to representative democracy are manifold, and it is obvious that the causes that determine the crisis of the modern notion of representation originate from the very flaws of the modern notion of politics and its anthropological premises. On the one hand, we have a notion of political order – and its subsequent legitimacy – that is based upon a covenant that should guarantee protection. This protection can no longer be guaranteed by the state, since its borders have become porous, fragile, and the very distinction between inside and outside is no longer valid. Among the major consequences of the loss of control by the sovereign state there is the very recent proliferation of violence both inside and outside the borders of the so-called First World. What has come mostly to the fore, in recent years – and please forgive me for this unpredicted shift from political doctrine to 'reality' – is the progressive evanescence of the ordering function of sovereignty, and with it, the undoing of the strict relationship between order and violence, as it ruled over the political arrangement of the system of nation-states. Yet, in spite of the major global changes that have caused a progressive weakening of the state, the mechanism of legitimization and representation remains unaltered. It seems that sovereignty has been caught in a 'turn of the screw' where violence on one hand seems to remain the main feature of the Leviathan, the state, but on the other hand, far from being controlled and implemented by it, becomes privatized, outsourced to professional private armies, as well as practiced by non-sovereign entities such as terrorist groups.

Violence, in other words, *fails to disguise itself* in what was considered the ordering function of the Leviathan, it escapes from the complex mechanism of order, obedience and peace to which modern political theory had consigned it. As a consequence, the role of the state, instead of being one of protection and construction of order, sums up to a paradoxical production of further disorder and chaos.

To put it differently, the crisis of sovereignty – the end of the protective function of the violence of the state – makes violence proliferate, and subsequently renders the Leviathan disobedient as to its protective function, and at the same time expects citizens to remain faithful to the procedures of legitimization – through elections, fiscal imposition, citizenship entitlement, and so on.

---

6   See, among others, the following critical assessments of the recent fate of nation-states: Beck (2006), Held (1996) and for a sharp critique of the post-national, cosmopolitan perspective advocated by both Beck and Held, see Mouffe (2005).

What we in fact witness today is a progressive withering away of the state's protective function, since violence enters the once-rigid and safe boundaries of state territories – New York, Madrid, London, Casablanca, Algiers (not to mention Baghdad, Kabul, Gaza) are just some of the instances of a violence that a supposedly sovereign monopoly is unable to control. Protection is withering away also in the face of global economic policies that freely overcome national welfare measures and expose citizens to a precariousness that, as such, was virtually unknown at least to European citizens of the last half a century. The immunization project of modernity, in other words, no longer works, neither in its premises nor in its results. Some call this new situation 'the Age of Empire', and thereby celebrate the possibility that after state sovereignty, what we are left with is not only a weakened Leviathan, but an insurgent multitude finally freed from the impositions of a violent sovereign will and its exclusionary practices. Interestingly enough, these theorists envisage in the present proliferation of violence an affinity with the pre-modern situation of a civil war, and this is why they define it a global civil war (Hardt and Negri 2000, 2003).

I agree that the current proliferation of violence – in the form of preventive war and in the subsequent explosion of terrorism within the boundaries of the West, but also in the form of the recent suburban riots in France – is a phenomenon that resembles, in some aspects, a pre-modern landscape in which there is no regulating political institution – common and superior, as Hobbes would say – able to transform violence into order. Differently from the theorists of the insurgent multitude, though, I think these phenomena confront us with the urgent need to finally free ourselves from the political imagery shaped by modernity, be it an imagery of order or its mirror opposite, disorder. I prefer to practice an exercise in political imagination that goes beyond the schemes shaped in modernity, and I think that this is possible only by putting into abeyance the modern political anthropology of individualism. In doing this, I am following the thought of two feminist thinkers, Adriana Cavarero and Judith Butler. This critical and imaginative task should question the very presuppositions of modern individualism. It should, in other words, ask: '*What if* we dismiss the modern narrative of individualism and expose the paradox on which it was founded, namely the paradox of an absent yet powerful violence?'

Loss, Vulnerability, Relationality

Moving away from the immunitarian notion of individualism, both Adriana Cavarero and Judith Butler have recently embarked on the effort of re-casting the question of what shape a politics to come should take, and, albeit in different ways, both think that what is needed is a radical shift from the premises of liberal individualism.

According to Cavarero, beyond sexual discrimination, the ontological framework that the philosophical fathers of the modern state – Hobbes and Locke – call 'state of nature' and describe in terms of atomized individuals is characterized by an inherent contradiction, in so far as it claims a universal validity while at the same time founding the political within specific territorial borders. The atomized individual typical of modern political theory not only posits the atomized individual as universal – while omitting its specific gendered and social quality – but also encloses it within the borders of the state. There is an inherent contradiction in so far as the claim to universality remains bounded to a specific territorial political entity, the state: 'The so-called pathologies of democracy that were the object of much debate in twentieth-century political thought and were particularly stressed by the communitarians, depend on this very logic – which is called upon to construct the political bond on the constitutive unbinding that guarantees the autonomy of the individual' (Cavarero 2005, 186).

Since the time of that specific political order is now over, Cavarero stresses the importance of going beyond individualism, and instead thinking of the political as the contract or bond between atomized, unrelated individuals, proposes to think of politics by starting from what she calls embodied singularities that, as such, do not come to the world as unrelated – like mushrooms, as Hobbes would say – but exist primarily in relation to somebody else. Relationality – the name Cavarero gives to this condition of relatedness or mutual dependence upon others – instead of autonomy, would be the starting point of a different political order. In this respect, the overcoming of liberal individualism proposed by Cavarero differs radically from that proposed by Hardt and Negri via the concept of the multitude, in so far as the latter replaces the unbound fictitious entities that inhabit modern ontology with an impersonal, inorganic, chaotic mass that ends up making human beings fictitious, or as Hannah Arendt would say, superfluous in their embodied uniqueness.

It is not by chance that, following Cavarero, I am constantly referring to Hannah Arendt, since as she points out, from Aristotle up to modernity, political models have always been constructed upon an ontology centered on fictitious entities: man, the individual, the subject. Man, the Aristotelian *anthropos*, inaugurates a tradition in which the plurality of unique beings appears from the very beginning as an insignificant and superfluous given. The famous *zoon politikon*, as Arendt claims, is 'founded on a clamorous falsification of the plural and anti-hierarchical matrix of politics'. In fact, 'Man', as a universal *fictio*, assumes and neutralizes the plurality of human beings, thereby relinquishing politics as its horizon. 'Man' in the singular 'cannot be political since, in this horizon, there is no plurality and thus no relation' (Cavarero 2005, 191).

Thus, what the Western tradition calls politics, continues Cavarero, is in reality a 'model of de-politicization that excludes the plural and relational foundation of politics'. Significantly, according to Arendt, even contemporary forms of representative democracy belong to this de-politicized tradition, in so far as they rely completely upon an individualistic 'economy of the One', through a notion of the 'individual' which is 'more or less equivalent to the same' (Arendt 1958b, 305, quoted in Cavarero 2005, 191). In short, 'the basic lexicon of equality and its ontological foundation, while allowing for a pluralism of opinions and political parties that represent them, denies the very possibility of plurality and, therefore, politics' (Cavarero, 2005, 191).

In different ways, but in a similar direction and in constant dialog with Cavarero's positions, Judith Butler, in her book *Precarious Life*, has reflected upon the political impact of mourning in the United States after September 11th (Butler 2004). In her book, she affirms that the shock of the terrorist attack should have been an occasion for the USA to reflect not only upon the effects of its foreign policy, but also upon the changed situation of a globalized world, in which what mostly comes to the fore is a strict interdependence between humans. Acknowledging the unavoidable precariousness of life that we all experience (a precariousness that today affects not only Third World citizens) is what has become most necessary, and such precariousness is what forces us to recognize the interdependency that shapes our lives as humans as an unavoidable starting point to rethink politics:

> ... the dislocation from First World privilege, however temporary, offers a chance to start to imagine a world in which that violence might be minimized, in which an inevitable interdependency becomes acknowledged as the basis for global political community. I confess to not knowing how to theorize that interdependency. I would suggest, however, that both our political and ethical responsibilities are rooted in the recognition that radical forms of self-sufficiency and unbridled sovereignty are, by definition, disrupted by the larger global processes of which they are a part, that no final control can be secured, and that final control is not, cannot be, an ultimate value. (Butler 2004, xii)

This constitutive interdependency with others – or the relationality of which Cavarero speaks – can be seen as a positive occasion to reflect on those famous flaws of modernity I mentioned above. Since the immunitarian project of modernity no longer works – it does not protect, it does not safeguard – perhaps it is exactly because the fictive, artificial premises on which it was based do not correspond to the condition of dependency and relationality that conditions our humanity. Butler is adamant in recognizing that such dependency has nothing to do with a so-called 'human nature' that, as such, she would radically refuse. In a recent debate with Cavarero, Butler argues in favour of what she calls a common human condition of vulnerability, shared beyond geopolitical borders and social differences (see Cavarero and Butler 2005).

Violence, in this context, far from engendering an artificial mechanism of order, as in the modern tradition, calls into question the model of individualism, and evokes instead the fundamental exposure of every human being to every other: 'Despite our differences in location and history, my guess is that it is possible to appeal to a "we", for all of us have some notion of what it is to have lost somebody. Loss has made a tenuous "we" of us all' (Butler 2004, 19).

Butler, in this respect, has fiercely criticized the way in which the United States has tried to misapprehend its exposure and vulnerability after September 11th by restoring its masculinity and its expanding sovereignty.[7] What has been lacking, she says, is a way of recognizing vulnerability and thereby taking violence differently, making it become an undeniable part of our human condition of dependence and precariousness.

Challenging the immunitarian project of modernity, Butler and Cavarero embark in the effort of radically re-thinking the human condition, moving from its essential situation of precariousness, vulnerability. The shift, in this respect, has to do with a displacement of politics away from the immune individual – a fictitious entity that, as such, has nowadays been swept away by the virtually non-existent state – in order to relocate it in the vulnerable – and therefore exposed to others and to an 'outside' – self. Politics and ethics must be thought of within the context of an undeniable violence that, at the same time, is the cipher of an undeniable relationality.

Butler, differently from Cavarero, who relies upon the Arendtian notion of uniqueness as the cornerstone of an interpersonal relationality that has a powerful metaphor in the primary bond between mother and child, is convinced that the dependency that shapes humanity is not merely a dependency upon an 'other' human being, but upon a set of social norms that constitute and determine, up to a point, who we are. She revises the liberal notion of autonomy, claiming that no one can be said to be completely autonomous and self-sufficient, by force of a set of social and cultural norms and regulations that shape who we are – and who we are not. The challenge, for her, is to apprehend these social and cultural norms in ways that should put into question and change the fixity of those very norms, the 'nature' or 'normality' they pretend to represent, in the name of a more open, modifiable, amendable notion of the human (Butler 2003).

In this respect, Butler acknowledges the importance of putting at the centre of a politics to come, or what she calls a 'political community of a complex order', the question of human vulnerability. Far from asserting vulnerability as a new phenomenon, Judith Butler claims at the same time that the fundamental and groundbreaking event of September 11th has brought vulnerability to the fore in the apparently invulnerable US society, which on that day lost its 'First World privilege'. I claim that her effort seeks to situate violence differently, as an undeniable aspect of our humanity, in order to both expand the notion of the human to those subjects who had been excluded from the normative and normalizing sphere of the political, and to expose the immunitarian and paradoxical use of violence to a radical critique. Only by so doing will one be able to detect – and change – the ways in which violence is alternatively foreclosed and perpetrated, hidden and powerfully exercised, in the name of a still modern, still 'Leviathanic' model of order. Given that that order no longer works, the time is right to question such paradoxical violence, as we are uncomfortably living within that paradox.

Vulnerability taken seriously, therefore, does not mean a celebration of suffering and an indulgence in mourning, but suffering and mourning are the starting points

---

7   For a very interesting reading of the essentially masculine feature of the concept and
     practice of the 'war on terror', see Mann (2006).

of a new kind of community, where violence and vulnerability are apprehended as present, undeniable, binding elements that enable each human being to appeal to a commonality, to a 'we' that is not entrenched in national, racial, ethnic, gender or class belonging. She seems to avow some kind of 'community of loss', in which, potentially, each one of us can participate, but which, at the same time does not presuppose a fictive 'sameness' based on an unrelated atomized human type.

The community of loss to which Butler seems to point aims to politicize a traditionally apolitical sphere, that of loss and mourning, where the notion of vulnerability plays a crucial role in positing some kind of universality which, at the same time, is founded upon radical differences. Each human being is vulnerable, but the ways in which vulnerability is distributed over the globe differ radically. To have been displaced from the First World privilege means:

> *to experience strands of vulnerability that need to be interrogated, need to be understood in their sources and their outcomes, in the potential for change they bring forth. Loss and vulnerability seem to follow from our being socially constituted bodies, attached to others, at risk of losing those attachments, exposed to others, at risk of violence by virtue of that exposure. (Butler 2004, 20)*

Rethinking Politics within the Boundaries of Mere Vulnerability

It is difficult to imagine the shape that a politics with such premises would have. What is nevertheless certain is that such a politics implies a withering away of the modern forms of spatialization, namely territorial borders, and its 'qualifying' corollaries: sovereignty, nation, representation, to name a few. Is it possible to look at the era of globalization – an era that sees the crisis of the territorial state and its individualistic ontology – as an opportunity for relocating politics in the Arendtian/ relational sense? Following Cavarero and Butler, I argue that it is.

The community of loss to which Butler points has, in my opinion, something in common with the proposal made by Adriana Cavarero when she speaks of the 'politics of the absolute local' (Cavarero 2005).

It is not by chance that Cavarero argues in favour of a politics of *the local*, since 'local' can be seen as the exact antonym of 'global'. Local, moreover, echoes the Arendtian notion of the political space as 'in between', as an immaterial space that both unites and separates those who are here and now, contingently, occupying the public sphere. 'Wherever you go, you will be a *polis*,' says Arendt, quoting a famous sentence that to her bears witness to the way in which, for the Greeks, the political consists of a space created by acting and speaking together 'which can find its proper location almost any time and anywhere' (Arendt 1958a, 198). The *polis*, according to Arendt, is not physically situated in a territory, but it is the space of interaction that is opened by the reciprocal communication of those present through words and deeds. 'In the era of globalization – which seems to require neologisms in order to withstand the collapse of the modern political lexicon – this interactive space could therefore be called the *absolute local'* (Cavarero 2005, 204). 'Absolute local' is the neologism Cavarero proposes for the contemporary political dictionary. The *absolute local* is thus the name of a 'taking place' of politics that has 'no predefined borders, nor any fixed or sacred confines. It is not a nation, nor a fatherland, nor a land, but, rather, it extends as far as the interactive space that is generated by reciprocal communication' (Cavarero 2005, 204).

Thus, the horizon of the *absolute local* is not simply that which the global creates, but rather an 'opening that globalization, as an extra-territorial and de-territorializing force, allows. In other words, once the cartography of states that makes of the world a coherent system has been taken away, and once the topographic parameters which make of the world a geography of borders has imploded, the world finally presents itself as a space available for the contextual and contingent insurgence of the *absolute local'*. It is an insurgency that, apart form the evocative images given by Cavarero's relational ontology, aspires to political participation beyond the structures of modern liberal democracy because such a model no longer respects the premises on which it was founded. It is an insurgency of politics from unexpected, previously unpoliticized spheres, where the claim to participate, to become public and to be recognized as a fully political subject trespasses on the traditional categories of political intelligibility. Local insurgencies, if on one hand the figures of a politics to come, based on vulnerability and precariousness, but also on relationality and mutual dependence, on the other hand are already here and have to do with locally experienced political actions.[8]

Arendt often spoke of the political impact of local townships during the American Revolution. What we should look at today are the multiple insurgencies of local – even municipal – political activism as an essential challenge to representative democracy. Interestingly enough, most of these local activisms have to do with a shared vulnerability people perceive as bounding, as the essential term of their mutual dependence. To that vulnerability, people respond via new forms of political participation, forms that bypass representative institutions and their immunitarian model of coexistence.

As is always the case, political imagination in some respects anticipates and in some others records political changes. It is interesting to note that a politics of the local – or absolute local – can be seen as a guideline to move away from liberal individualism, and on the other hand it is an already existing practice of political action – both municipal and transnational.

---

8   There are many current examples of 'local insurgencies' that put into play a form of political action that cannot be comprehended within the traditional frames of representative democracy, nor in those of collective multitudes. For example, in Italy, the Val di Susa Movement against Fast-Speed railroad works, and in Vicenza, the municipal movement against the expansion of the Military Nato base, are, in my opinion, two interesting expressions of a new type of community, which puts into play vulnerability and relationality, bypassing completely the individualistic–representative model of democracy. The problem, most of the time, is that these local insurgencies are reduced, by experts and political analysts, to simple NIMBY ('Not In My Back Yard') expressions of parochial and therefore limited political goals.

The central point is to rethink politics by focusing on the modality in which a material practice of plural interaction – whose materiality is deeply rooted in the condition of what Butler calls vulnerability – engenders a political space radically displaced from the space of modern immunitarian politics.

Vulnerability can be a category that enables us to think about a common human condition of suffering and fragility, a universal category that, at the same time, is devoid of the paternalistic and homologating features that are normally associated with 'Western cultural imperialism'. Paradoxically, we are sharing a common condition of precariousness engendered by a permanent proliferation of violence. That which separates us is exactly what binds us. Violence, in the existential and embodied form of human vulnerability, instead of being the disconnecting element, as in the thought of Thomas Hobbes, instead of being the justifying motivation for a state of perpetual war, should become the impediment to a senseless proliferation of aggression and retaliation. Vulnerability, as the cipher of our commonality, could become a way of enabling plurality to emerge in a context of fundamental similarity.

Politics, in the age of globalization, instead of embarking on an apparently endless planetary clash of civilizations, should humbly attempt to move from the undeniable material condition that we, as humans, are related beings, we come to the world in relation to someone, and that our survival, by now, constitutively depends upon our willingness to give this relationality a political shape.

References

Arendt, H. (1958a), *The Human Condition* (Chicago, IL: University of Chicago Press).
—— (1958b), *The Origins of Totalitarianism* (New York: Meridian).
—— (1994), 'The Nation,' in *Essays in Understanding: 1930–1954* (New York: Harcourt Brace).
Beck, U. (2006), *Cosmopolitan Vision* (Cambridge: Polity Press).
Bock, G. and James, S. (eds) (1992), *Beyond Equality and Difference* (New York: Routledge).
Bortolini, M. (2003), 'Hannah Arendt, Council Democracy and (Far) Beyond: A Radical View', paper presented at the conference 'The Question of the Common. European Political Philosophy beyond Liberalism', European University Institute, San Domenico di Fiesole, 19 May 2003, available at <www.scform. unipd.it/~m.bortolini/Arendt.pdf>.
Butler, J. (2003), *Undoing Gender* (New York: Routledge).
—— (2004), *Precarious Life: The Powers of Mourning and Violence* (London: Verso).
Cavarero, A. (2004), 'Politicizing Theory', in S.K. White and J.D. Moon (eds), *What is Political Theory?* (London: Sage).
—— (2005), *For More than One Voice* (Stanford, CA: Stanford University Press).
—— and Butler, J. (2005) 'Condizione umana contro "natura"', *Micromega* 9, 33–42.
Esposito, R. (1998) *Communitas. Origine e destino della comunità* (Turin: Einaudi).
—— (2002), *Immunitas* (Turin: Einaudi).

Ferrara, A. (2003), 'Two Notions of Humanity and the Judgment Argument for Human Rights', *Political Theory* 31:3, 392–420.

—— (2007), 'Political Cosmopolitanism and Judgment', *European Journal of Social Theory* 10:1, 53–66.

Foucault, M. (1981), *Power/Knowledge, Selected Interviews and Other Writings 1972–1977*, ed. C. Gordon (New York: Pantheon Books).

—— (1990), *The History of Sexuality: An Introduction* (New York: Vintage).

—— (1997), *Discipline and Punish: Birth of the Prison* (New York: Random House).

Hardt, M. and Negri, A. (2000), *Empire* (Cambridge, MA: Harvard University Press).

—— and Negri, A. (2003), *Multitude* (New York: Penguin Press).

Held, D. (1996), *Democracy and the Global Order* (Stanford, CA: Stanford University Press).

Hobbes, T. (1839 [1994]), *The Collected Works of Thomas Hobbes*, collected and edited by Sir William Molesworth (London: Routledge/Thoemmes Press).

Mann, B. (2006), 'How America Justifies its War: A Modern/Postmodern Aesthetics of Masculinity and Sovereignty', *Hypathia* 21:4, 147–63.

Marx, K. (1844 [1985]), 'On the Jewish Question', in *Selected Writings*, ed. D. McLelland (Oxford: Oxford University Press).

Mouffe, C. (2005), 'Cosmopolitics or Multipolarity?', *Redescriptions: Yearbook of Political Thought and Conceptual History* 9, 15–26.

Pateman, C. (1988), The *Sexual Contract* (Cambridge: Polity Press).

Schmitt, C. (1922 [1985]), *Political Theology: Four Chapters in the Concept of Sovereignty* (Cambridge, MA: MIT Press).

Weber, M. (1919 [2004]), *The Vocation Lectures: Science as a Vocation, Politics as a Vocation* (Indianapolis, IN: Hackett).

White, S.K. and Moon, J.D. (eds) (2004), *What is Political Theory?* (London: Sage).

Further Reading

Arendt, H. (1972), *Crises of the Republic* (New York: Harcourt Brace Jovanovich).

— (1978), *The Jew as a Pariah: Jewish Identity and Politics in the Modern Age* (New York: Grove Press).

Butler, J. (1990), *Gender Trouble* (New York: Routledge).

— (2005), *Giving an Account of Oneself* (New York: Fordham University Press).

Cavarero, A. (2000), *Relating Narratives* (London: Routledge).

— (2002), *Stately Bodies* (Ann Arbor, MI: University of Michigan Press)

Bono, P. and Kemp, S. (eds) (1991), *Italian Feminist Thought* (Oxford: Blackwell).

Honig, B. (ed.) (1995), *Feminist Interpretations of Hannah Arendt* (University Park, PA: Penn State University Press).

MacIntyre, A. (1999), *Dependent Rational Animals: Why Human Beings Need Virtues* (Peru, IL: Carus Publishing).

Tietjens Meyers, D. (ed.) (1996), *Feminists Rethink the Self* (Boulder, CO: Westview Press).

The Gendered 'Subjects' of Political Representation

Tuija Pulkkinen

The Three Feminist Subject Issues

It can be, and has been, justifiably argued in the Nietzschean vein that representation in itself is a mechanism which effectively brings into being the entities that are to be represented. According to this view, the democratization process of Europe during the past two centuries produced the distinct entities, the very units which were represented in national assemblies as the 'peoples' and the 'nations'. The new political thinking of the time preceding the French Revolution conceived of the 'peoples' and the 'nations' in the form of a distinct will, the will which then was intended to manifest itself through the representative organ, the assembly or the parliament. A nation, in other words, was conceived of in the shape of a single will, as a 'subject' in command of itself (Pulkkinen 2000a). Simultaneously, the emerging democratic ideals and systems re-conceived of individual men as citizens, as political 'subjects' in command of their own political will within the democratic system.

Nations and citizens, nevertheless, were not the only new imagined subjects that can be perceived as the performative effects of the democratization process; in multiple meanings, 'women', conceived of as a politically significant category, can also be seen as such an effect of the democratization process (Landes 1988; Riley 1988; Scott 1996). In this chapter, I will argue that there are three distinct gendered subject issues which were created through the democratization process. I also argue that it makes sense to deal with these three issues separately, which has not always been the case in feminist political theory.

I will discuss the separate gendered subject issues of feminist political theory here with reference to the latest book by one of the leading contemporary feminist political theorists, Linda Zerilli, *Feminism and the Abyss of Freedom*. I discuss Zerilli's argumentation critically, as one example of the merging of different subject issues, while also commenting on it as an interesting attempt to fundamentally re-conceptualize the field. A commentary on Zerilli's book will, I hope, provide a perspective on what is at stake, both philosophically and practically, in conceptual choices when the gendered subjects of political representation are discussed.

The three separate subject issues in feminist political theory are as follows. First, there is the idea of the separate will of 'women' as a group or as an imagined subject, analogous to a 'people' or a 'nation'. This idea was an effect of the democratization processes in which women were singled out as a group which was exactly *not* to be part of the new representative systems. 'Women' as a subject gained its political identity through this negative place. The feminist movement then, later on, carried the position of the subject called women.

Second, as the democratization process during the time of the French Revolution was carried out with ideals that strongly relied on ancient Greek models of gender division, in which the democratic body (*polis*) operated as a counter-concept to the domestic sphere (*oikos*), the European democratization processes also acted as gendering processes generating the markedly domestic 'women'. Apart from being the reason to exclude women from the public politics, the domesticity and the skills associated with it, nevertheless, almost simultaneously also turned into the argumentative basis for the demands of political subject positions for individual women. This process created the second gendered subject issue for subsequent feminist politics: the problematic positioning of women in particular positions of expertise in politics, defining females as a particular type of political subject. Female political subject positions have been related to domestic skills, such as care and education. Up to the present, it has been held, female politicians tend to be placed as people responsible for social affairs, education and the arts rather than those responsible for foreign affairs and financial matters.

Two random examples of the second subject issue of feminist politics that caught my eye in the daily press during the time I was writing this were the new Finnish government and the French presidential elections of 2007. In the newly appointed Finnish ministry of 2007, women outnumber men for the first time (12 women, 8 men), but the division of labour almost ironically follows the internal–external; domestic–public divide. The ministerial posts held by men include the prime minister, the minister of finances, the foreign minister, the minister of defense, the minister of trade and industry, and the minister of foreign trade and development, whereas the female ministers hold such posts as the minister of internal affairs, the minister of justice, the minister of communication, the minister of culture and education, the minister of environment, and the minister of social security and health. It also caught my eye that of the French presidential candidates in the 2007 election, the female candidate, Ségolène Royal, was given credit for having served as the Ministre de famille, à l'enfance et aux personnes handicapées, the Ministre de l'enseignement scolaire and the Ministre de l'environnement. In comparison, her male competitor Nicolas Sarkozy's list of merits included notes of having served, among other posts, as the Ministre d'Etat, Ministre de l'économie and Ministre du budget.

The third subject issue of feminist political thought is a result of the fact that the democratization process can be conceived of, if not as largely responsible for, then at least as essentially concurrent with the major transformation process that produced the cultural norms of the bourgeois 'women' and 'men', gendered 'subjects' that are supposed to desire highly different things in life. Females were/ are supposed to desire the position of a wife and a mother and the responsibility of the domestic, and males fame in the public sphere, civil society and the state. The role of a responsible mother was a new creation of the time of the democratization process, during the late eighteenth and early nineteenth centuries, and it was in clear contrast to earlier aristocratic and peasant systems of organizing life, and the values accompanying those systems. The new clear two-gender system, its norms and values, was not traditional, as the phrase usually goes, but the values were created with a lot of cultural work and effort at the time (Riley 1988; Caine and Sluga 2000; Coontz 2005). This was a process that Foucault would call 'subjectivation': it created subjects though subjecting them to particular gender norms. The explorations of the mechanisms of the subjectivation to gendered norms of psychic development, producing subjects called 'women', is the third subject issue of feminist discussions. The limits and consequences of gendered subjectivation processes were the main interest of the second wave of the feminist movement at its beginning,[1] and they have also been among the subject issues in feminist political theory when it has referred to full citizenship[2] of female citizens (Lister 1997; Young 1990, 2000; Fraser 1994, 1997; Phillips 1998a).

All three forms of creating subjects called 'women' are commonly encountered topics of discussion in feminist political theory literature. Very often, they intertwine with each other, and all of them are equally discussed under the one and the same heading, *the* subject issue. As a result, feminist political theory has for decades sorted out subject questions to the degree that recently there have been several calls to abandon 'the subject question' altogether, as it is said to have taken too much attention. For example, as different feminist political theory scholars as Adriana Cavarero (2005, 12–19), Mary Dietz (2002, 3), Judith Squires (2000, 24, 227, 240–56) and Linda Zerilli (2005, 10) say it is time to discuss the issues of women and politics in different terms. For Linda Zerilli, the preferable different term is the concept 'freedom', which she develops on the basis of Hannah Arendt's work.

In contrast to the call to abandon 'the subject' issue, I argue in favour of differentiating the subject issues from each other. If 'the subject issue' is not

---

1   During the first wave of the feminist movement, the concerns were women's legal status, education and suffrage, which were approached as issues of external liberty. They were issues of the right to choose and of removing obstacles for choice. Second-wave feminism was much more concerned about internal constraints on women in their choices, such as their setting of goals in their lives, and the psychological processes of various desires.

2   'Full' citizenship has, in the feminist discussion, often been the term which has been used in distinction to formal citizenship. Although women have had formal citizenship rights in most First World countries for nearly a century, women have not taken the positions that formal political rights would allow them to take in the same proportion as men. Various feminist studies have concluded that for 'full' citizenship, various other conditions than legal equality need to be fulfilled; those conditions range from economic and social status to recognition and respect of speaking styles (see Lister 1997; Young 1990, 2000; Fraser 1994, 1997; Phillips 1998b; Yuval-Davis 1997).

conceived of as a single one, but if the multiple ways in which the democratization process has functioned as performing gendered 'subjects' are given due attention, it becomes apparent that separate subject issues each have a different degree of urgency and topicality in contemporary politics. Although the subject of feminist movement as the will of the women may be justifiably argued to be an obsolete model for conceiving of feminist politics, the two other subject issues – the problematic gendering of political agents, and the culture of gendering in general – remain topics that feminist politics needs to consider.

Zerilli and the Feminist Movement

The title of *The Abyss of Freedom* is a phrase familiar to many as the title of the last chapter in Hannah Arendt's book *The Life of the Mind*, in its second part, 'Willing' (Arendt 1978). Zerilli connects 'the abyss of freedom' with feminism, which, as she notes, was not a concern of Arendt herself. She highlights the Arendtian ideal of politics as a world-building practice of freedom concerned about the lack of this ideal in feminist movement while also taking up some expressive examples of feminist practices of world-building. The term 'freedom', as I will later discuss in more detail, functions in her text as an important sign of her politics of philosophy.

Zerilli is concerned with the present state and the future of the feminist movement. She is highly aware of the emergence of the movement and the subject called 'women' as a performative effect of the democratization process of representing. In representing women, as in any representation, it is apparent that we should not think of representation as a relation analogous to images, as bringing something present again in a way a picture might be thought to re-present its object. As many theorists, such as Hanna Pitkin (1967), Frank Ankersmit (2002), Bonnie Honig (1993), Wendy Brown (2001) and Anne Phillips (1998b), have emphasized with respect to politics, and as the Latin etymology of the 're-' also suggests (Göring 2003), re-presenting rather means presenting something intensively. As an act, representing is closer to creating the thing than mirroring something pre-existent.

Since representative democracy – as a system and as an idea – intensively created the idea of a nation as *one will*, a subject, which supposedly mirrors what it in fact creates, the system of representative democracy is closely bound up with the idea of the nation and the state as a will of its own, one crystallization of which was the Hegelian theorizing of the state (Koselleck et al. 1990; Pulkkinen 2000b). Building on the Hegelian basis, Marxist political thought also envisioned the conscious working class as the *subject* of history in a similar mode. The Hegelian-Marxian tradition of political thought carries the idea of a movement as *a will*, and this sovereign is sovereign primarily with respect to its own will, it is a self-reflecting subject.

The women's movement, being in multiple waves historically parallel to the working-class movement and having been actively in touch with the Hegelian-Marxian tradition of political thought, has for a long time modeled itself on the same pattern as the nation of nationalism and the historical subject of the labour movement (Pulkkinen, 2001). The subject of feminism, 'women', is also conceived of as sovereign with respect to its own will, a subject with one will. The result in practical feminist politics has been an expectation of a single opinion as the opinion of the movement – as well as clinging to the conception of oneness and sameness in time of the imagined group 'women'. This is a similar kind of oneness and sameness of a group to the imagined sameness of an ethnic people or of a socio-economic class, and the internal sameness was long thought to be the self-evident foundation for any politics called feminist.

It was primarily with respect to the presumption of the sameness of 'women' at background of feminist political subject that Judith Butler asked her well-known question at the beginning of *Gender Trouble* (1990), the book which often stands as the icon for finally breaking this presumption. The question posed by her was whether the identity of women is at all needed as the precondition of feminist politics (Butler 1990, 1–6). It is good to notice that the question of sameness – 'is it necessary to presuppose "women" (an imagined community, as a people or a class) in order to have feminist politics?' – is a different question from the one concerning the subject of a movement, which is: 'Does politics necessarily have to be conceived of in a form of a single subject, a "we", in order to be feminist?' It is the latter, the question of the 'subject' of political action, that is our concern here.

When Zerilli in her book encourages feminists to abandon the subject question, is she primarily spotting the Hegelian-Marxian tradition of political thought within feminism and envisioning other modes of thinking of politics than a mode of a collective subject as an agent? This could easily be seen to be so, as the Arendtian conception of politics as world-building in the condition of plurality, highlighted by Zerilli, is clearly a very different way of conceiving of politics.[3] 'What if instead we, together with Arendt, were to shift the problem of freedom outside its current subject-centred frame?', asks Zerilli (2005, 12). She encourages refuting claims to mastery and acknowledging that plurality is the condition of politics: 'By contrast with the feminist sense of crisis that emerged in relation to the critique of the subject, Arendt holds that politics, the realm of action, is possible only on the condition that there is no agent who can begin a process and more or less control its outcome,' she writes (Zerilli 2005, 13). For Arendt, action is less about the subject than about the world (Zerilli 2005, 14).

However, it is not clearly evident that Zerilli's target is the frame of conceiving of politics in terms of a collective political subject. After all, the main concern in the book is the future of feminism as a *movement*. Does holding to the ideal of a movement make Zerilli inadvertently subscribe to the idea of a sovereign subject, in contradiction to the anti-subject intentions of the book? I suggest that an explanation for the threatening incongruity is that in her discussion, Zerilli employs the concept subject in a way that conflates different meanings of the concept, most importantly the notions of an individual human subject and a collective political subject.

---

3   'Political are not the interests as such but the world-building practice of publicly articulating matters of common concern' (Zerilli 2005, 22).

Zerilli, Arendt and the Three Meanings of the Subject

I hope this is not too confusing, but completely distinct from the three different subject issues within feminist political theory which I have just distinguished, I would like to further differentiate various meanings in which the concept 'subject' itself is used in contemporary theory discussions. There are at least three distinct uses of 'the subject' currently circulating in theoretical discussions, or, even more precisely, there are three distinct primary contexts in which this word is used, lending it a distinct sense in each of them.

The first is the philosophical context, in which the transcendental mind or the human in a non-empirical sense is referred to by this word. The second is the psychological context, in which general statements concerning the individual human psyche, either empirically or psychoanalytically conceived of, are referred to by 'the subject'. The third, then, is the political context in which both collective and individual agents are called subjects. All three senses of 'the subject' are, again, often conflated in feminist discussions involving the 'subject question', as is also the case with Zerilli's text.

Zerilli is not the only well-known feminist theorist who conflates the different meanings of 'subject' or who consciously lets them rhetorically slide from one to another. For example, in the first pages of *Gender Trouble,* Judith Butler explicitly conflates the political sense of the subject with the psychological one by first introducing her topic as the dilemma of the feminist subject (as the question of collective political subject 'women'), and then moving on to discuss the (individual, psychological) subject-formation and its paradoxes (Butler 1990, 1–25).

When Zerilli proposes that feminists should take their cue from Hannah Arendt and dismiss *the* 'subject question', she does this without differentiating between the different meanings of the subject or between the three different subject issues of feminist political theory. Instead, she discusses as if the feminist subject questions were one and the same. Arendt's thought, according to her, helps us to shift the focus from the question of the subject to that of the world.

I would argue that if we take into consideration that there are three different subject issues, Arendt's theorizing is not as clearly advisable for feminists as Zerilli suggests: the effects of Arendt's theorizing for feminist theory differ depending on which subject issue we are dealing with, particularly whether the issue is the first, a political subject (a collective subject), or the third, individual gendered subject-formation. Moreover, there is a philosophical subject issue involved in Zerilli's discussion.

Concerning the first subject issue of political theory, the collective subject 'women', Arendt is clearly an option as an adviser. Arendt theorizes about individual human subjects when she builds her theory of 'the who' that is revealed in political acting. Political movements, like feminist movement-subjects, are not an Arendtian issue at all. She does not look at politics in the mode of group-agents; her political ontology is strictly individual-based.

Zerilli argues that Arendt is useful as a teacher for those feminist political theorists who continue to see the problem of (political) freedom as a (political) subject problem. This can be read as if Zerilli saw the problem in conceiving of the feminist movement as a subject with a mastery of its own one will and sovereignty over the results of its action. Clearly, according to her opinion, there is a problem of paying too much attention to 'the subject problem' in feminist discussion. And she also states that the problem does not vanish when the issue of the collective subject is theorized in its negative space, which, according to her, happens in Judith Butler's work, for example. By this, I would understand, she means that Butler maintains the topic of the (collective) subject even if she denies the need for it.

If Zerilli's critique is targeted at the question of there being too much attention to the (collective political) subject problem in feminist discussion, I do very much agree with her on the issue. I think that the tradition of political ontology which posits collective subjects is a problematic heritage of the feminist movement, and that it makes more sense to think of politics on the basis of individual agents than on the basis of collective subjects. Also, Zerilli may well be right, in that Judith Butler does pay excessive tribute to this heritage. This happens to a certain degree in *Gender Trouble*, but I would actually see more of it elsewhere, particularly in the book *Contingency, Hegemony, Universality* which she edited together with Laclau and Zizek (Butler 1990, 12).

Zerilli has her own solution to the issue of political subject. She is concerned with the 'movement', which she conceives of as the 'we' of feminism. Instead of assuming the 'we' to be a natural consequence of the sameness of 'women', Zerilli suggests thinking of the 'we' of feminism anew 'as the fragile achievement of practices of freedom' (Zerilli 2005, 24). In my view, however, Zerilli here modifies Arendt's approach quite significantly. Arendt herself figures politics as an individually significant enterprise, and is more interested in individual heroes than movements. Although Zerilli's approach is an interesting attempt to refigure the Arendtian approach, one must nevertheless ask whether her solution retains the idea of the subject of movement. Does feminist politics really need the formation of a single 'we'? Is this too much as an assumption even if it is thought of as a fragile achievement of the politics of freedom? Could feminist politics rather be thought of as a rich conceptual resource available for mobilizations through different individuals and groups in various forms in various times and places? Does Zerilli's worry about 'the feminist movement', after all, involve an attachment to the idea of the subject of feminism, sovereign with respect to itself even if with respect to the other subjects of politics?

The issue of political collective subject is, however, only (the first) one of the subject issues of feminist political theory. Although I agree with Zerilli that there is too much attention on the (political collective) subject problem in feminist discussion, I see the matter concerning the third of the feminist subject issues, the question of subjectivation, very differently. The third subject issue is the gendered formation of the individual psyche and its non-sovereignty with respect to cultural norms. In Zerilli's discussion, it appears as if the third subject issue involved the same problem of too much attention as the issue of the political subject, and as if, accordingly, Arendt would help to unravel the issues for feminist theorizing here as well by means of diverting the focus away from unnecessary attention to the subject question.

I strongly disagree on this point: I think that it does indeed make sense for feminists to pay attention to the subjectivation to cultural norms, and that gendered subject-formation is one of the key issues for feminist thought. Arendt is a theorist who does not consider subject-formation. For Arendt, the subjects are thrown to the world, and the attention is on the world, as Zerilli points out.

Concerning the third of the subject issues of feminist political theory, therefore, I think, Arendt is *not* a good guide for feminist theorists. Judith Butler is a good example of feminist subject discussions here as well. She, of course, discusses the third subject issue, individual subject-formation, again and again. And as Zerilli points out, she does this by focusing her attention to the sovereignty of the subject in its negative space. This means that she is pointing out that the subject is not sovereign with respect to cultural norms. For Zerilli, this is too much attention to the subject question, even if it is talked about in its negative space. I would defend Butler on this point: I think Butler's way of discussing the individual subject question, that is, the issue of the individual subject's construction and subjection to cultural law, is highly relevant. Feminists can hardly ignore the power of internalized gender and sexuality norms in the construction of gendered subjects.

What is more, paying attention to gendered subjectivation is crucial with respect to understanding the political problems of representation. Feminist political theory is constantly confronted by the problem of finding formal demand for equality in politics a deficient means for facing the unequal numbers in political participation, since there seem to be gendered hierarchies which work inside the formally equal structures of politics. Looking into subject-formation as subjection to cultural norms helps to grasp and challenge those gender hierarchies which function outside the reach of the formal order of political equality. Desires for how one's life should look and how one's personality should appear play decisive roles in choices about whether to become a politician and how to act as a citizen. These desires intertwine with gendering subjection in a contingent way, and may be much more of a key to changing numbers of participants than formal restrictions are. The always challengeable gendered rules of subjectivation, including processes of doing one's gender through acting as a citizen and a politician, remain a crucial topic of research for any feminist political theory.

Arendt does not consider subjectivation, let alone gendered subjectivation, at all. As an existentialist thinker, she considers the individual subject sovereign with respect to itself; it is only the world it is thrown into and the effects of its own actions that it is not sovereign of. Therefore, the focus is in the world, and not in the subject.[4] Arendt can thus be seen as a highly problematic guide for the feminist problems of politics, and it does appear that the role given to her as a teacher must be motivated partly by greater concerns. With respect to the third subject issue, there is, in my view, a politics of philosophy involved in Zerilli's discussion. Her

---

4   'Foregrounded in Arendt's account of action is something less about the *subject* (for example, its stability/instability or its capacity/noncapacity for agency) than about the world (for example, its contingency into which the subject is arbitrarily thrown and into which it acts' (Zerilli 2005, 14).

implicit reliance on existentialist thought becomes evident through a closer look at her writing on the concept of 'freedom', which I will return to.

Women and the Social

The second subject issue of feminist politics, the gendering of political expertise positions, comes up poignantly in Zerilli's discussion, in her acute criticism of the tradition of connecting women and 'the social'. Zerilli's argumentation goes as follows: she takes up two fusions which she sees as commonly occurring flaws in feminist argumentation when dealing with 'freedom'; and here, freedom is closely connected to what is called 'politics' in the Arendtian vein, meaning more or less the individual's political participation, or public action. The two flaws are: confusing freedom and 'the social question', and confusing freedom and 'the subject question' (arising from the ideal of sovereign subjectivity). Zerilli defends the idea of politics as a non-sovereign world-building practice of freedom, and she offers this Arendtian conceptualization as a useful tool for the project of affirming feminism anew.

I very much agree with Zerilli on the need to separate political freedom and the social question. I believe it cannot be overemphasized that, as she argues, 'if we value women's freedom because it is useful in solving certain social problems, we may not value freedom when it interferes with social utility' (Zerilli 2005, 11). In contemporary politics, women continue to take up arguments for the betterment of the education, political rights and political participation of women because it is good for 'the entire society' or 'for future generations' or simply for 'children', not because it is better for women. These arguments are widely accepted in development politics. It is good to remember, in my view, that refraining from being a vehicle for solving social problems was in fact one of the crucial demarcation lines between the first wave and the second wave of feminism. Radical second wavers (such as Firestone 1970; Millett 1971) were resolutely against the heritage of the earlier feminist movement to act for the 'common' good, and to be the social mothers.

Zerilli echoes Denise Riley in noting that historically, the crucial factor was that the emerging sphere of 'the social' in the nineteenth century was deeply feminized (Riley 1988). The entanglement of women and the social was pronouncedly manifested in the work of the first-wave feminists like Wollstonecraft, Mill and Catt, who tended to justify their claim to freedom in terms of social utility and rely on expediency argumentation (Zerilli 2005, 4–9). The female expertise of care was made into a fact, and the motherly tasks as the role of female politicians a needed resource in the life of nations by feminists themselves. As politicians, also, women were figured as a necessary vehicle for reproducing the nation, and ultimately mankind.

As much as I agree with Zerilli that the bond between political freedom (political participation) and the issue of differently gendered abilities, roles and responsibilities associated with the collective needs and reproduction of the human species should be broken for good, I am not as convinced as she is that this is best done with the help of Hannah Arendt's thought. What troubles me is that the human species and its reproduction operate in Arendt's theorizing as the foundational basis, even if they are placed in the negative space.

Freedom

Let me approach this issue from another angle, as a comment on the concept of freedom in Zerilli's text. Freedom goes through an interesting rhetorical shift from one meaning to another in the course of her argumentation in the first chapter of the book.

For most of the chapter, and particularly in the beginning, 'freedom' consistently refers to 'political freedom', not quite as a quality of a political system, not quite as a quality of a political system comparable to the neo-Roman notion of 'a free state' as Quentin Skinner describes it (Skinner 1998, 26), but as the right to participate and the practice of participation in government, the practice of democratic politics.[5] Zerilli pays attention to the unfortunate entanglement of women and 'the social' in arguing for political freedom, and asks the question: 'What must an argument for freedom look like if it is to be heard as such?' She encourages us to become critically aware of the costs of the social question to political freedom itself. I could not agree more on these points.

Nevertheless, when the discussion turns to 'freedom and the subject question', another concept of freedom emerges, although this shift goes unacknowledged: 'freedom' is discussed as if it were the same as in the previous section. The second meaning of freedom emerges with reference to Hannah Arendt, who in the *Life of the Mind* discusses human freedom through moving from the freedom of will to freedom as an attribute of doing and acting. This is the passage which for Arendt marks the departure from the field of philosophy to the field of politics. Within politics, freedom is not a self-relation – epitomized by the phrase 'I will, I can control myself' – but a relation with others – 'I can, I am not constrained by others, by laws, customs.' The man in the singular holds for philosophy, but does not hold for politics, where the fantasy of sovereignty has no place (Zerilli 2005, 16).

The passage from thinking to willing in Arendt's text marks a passage from philosophy to politics, but simultaneously it is a philosophical statement, constituting, in fact, a critique of the *subject* of philosophy that is distinctive of the phenomenological tradition. Although Arendt emphasizes the passage from philosophy to politics, she does not negate philosophy, she merely leaves philosophy to philosophers. For her, philosophizing is an exceptional state. The normal *human* condition is to be among others, in a political situation (Villa 1996; Taminiaux 1997). Arendt privileges the freedom that is present in the plurality of human beings/men. Freedom is ultimately a *human* capacity, a capacity of the subject in the philosophical sense of the word. A human subject has a capacity to start, to begin completely new processes without preceding causes. In this Augustinian sense,

---

5   '... what once brought me to feminism: the radical demand for women's political freedom, the right to be a participant in public affairs' (Zerilli 2005, ix).

the abyss of freedom, the capacity for absolute beginning, is connected to birth, to the fact that human beings, new individuals/men, appear in the world by virtue of birth (Arendt 1978).

Now, in this latter discussion on freedom, I argue, 'freedom' holds another meaning compared to the previous one of Zerilli. The first discussion is about having (participation rights,) or practicing democratic participation, and not being constrained by the (external, decreed) laws, but the latter is more about *being free as a human being*, having the capacity to begin something new. Arendt makes political speech and action the privileged site of practicing freedom, compared to solitary thought (Villa 1996; Taminiaux 1997). Human freedom reveals itself in the condition of plurality. But freedom in this sense is itself an attribute of the human, the subject in general, not of the political system or a particular type of political action.

Simone de Beauvoir employs a similar existential concept of freedom to Arendt, but with a different emphasis. It is exactly the human freedom de Beauvoir is concerned with in *The Second Sex*. She is worried about women shrinking away from and holding back from their freedom. This concern is not primarily a concern of political participation, but it has a much more general meaning, involving women's individual opportunities and ambitions in life, their own projects of beginning new.

Is there a danger in conflating the existential concept of general 'human' freedom of the subject in its philosophical sense and the particular political freedom? Moreover, and more importantly, what are the implications of this fusion with respect to gender?

I see a matter of concern in that both in Arendt's and in de Beauvoir's case, the demand for freedom is built on a foundational humanist approach: it is attached to the species point of view. At the foundation, in the negative space, there is a primary process which is the 'mere' continuation of the 'species', on top of which the 'projects' of 'freedom' are envisioned. An individual subject is pronouncedly an individual between birth and death, as a part of the life of the species. The continuation of the species and the gendered roles in it function as the background assumption in this theorizing (Pulkkinen 2003).

If the species point of view, the human as a particular species, looms large at the background in the approach, as the negative space of the very human freedom, then what is its effect? In my view, the humanist approach sets the stage for both the necessary difference and the ultimate complementarity of the two sexes. On this ground, it is possible to imagine that had Arendt been a gender theorist, she would probably have been a theorist of sexual difference.

The particular discourse of human freedom that is articulated in the existential frame has not been a dominant one in feminist discussions. As Zerilli also notes, de Beauvoir was adopted in a mode that emphasized 'not being but becoming a woman', which has very little to do with her particular kind existential project

(2005, 11).[6] Zerilli clearly works to change this state of affairs. The consequence of the theory-political move, or the conceptual act, that I see Zerilli achieve in her text is that 'freedom' as an existential concept takes over the other meanings of freedom.

The question, then, is whether bringing the existential concept of freedom into the discussion is a good move within present feminisms. This is a move that brings the concept of human, the man, either in singular or in plural, in any case the humankind/(mankind) as a species, into the centre of theorizing. One must ask what kind of feminism it produces. Hannah Arendt, Simone de Beauvoir and Luce Irigaray all share the philosophical tradition of the human, and all of them subscribe ultimately to the complementarity of the two sexes in the life of the human species. The sexual difference in this tradition is not essentialism with respect to gender, it is a far more profound form of attachment to the binary which postulates that: 'humans come in twos'. For the purposes of feminist politics today, I would ask: why two? Refusing the two is what I consider the most interesting politics that is currently conducted in the name of feminism.

Conclusion

As an example of the calls to abandon the subject issue, Zerilli's *Abyss of Freedom* stands out as a very intriguing one in its way of dealing with distinct concepts of subject and distinct feminist subject issues within democratic theory. To conclude my discussion, I will try to summarize my analysis of how her text engages with respect to the differentiation of the three different distinct subject issues of feminist political theory which I have proposed above.

Zerilli does engage herself with the first of the issues, the issue of the subject of the feminist movement, although her approach is somewhat twofold. On the one hand, she is critical of the political theories which theorize within a framework of a collective subject. Along with Arendt, she would rather theorize about the political as a practice of human freedom. She considers the feminist 'we' as a fragile achievement of practices of freedom instead of presupposing a feminist subject. On the other hand, her prime concern is for feminism as a movement, and she constantly refers to the present state of 'it' as if there was indeed a subject of feminism that merely needs to be refreshed out of its state of doziness in order for feminist politics to be.

The second subject issue of feminist political theory is the issue of women as particular kinds of political subjects, connected to the fact that historically, female politicians have been placed in particular positions of expertise in politics and that women's participation has been defended by the need for these special skills. Zerilli

---

6   Zerilli sees de Beauvoir's version of existentialist thought as much closer to Arendt's than Sartre's with respect to freedom. According to her, in de Beauvoir's thought, freedom becomes a question of transforming the world instead of remaining a relationship of the subject to itself, as it is in Sartre's philosophy (Zerilli 2005, 11).

deals with this issue very firmly. She shows in detail how the 'social' has been problematically intertwined with women, and how problematic it is that female political freedom has earlier been defended by expediency argumentation. Her stand is very clear: women are not special kinds of political subjects.

The third feminist subject issue, the subjection to cultural norms of gendering, Zerilli does not engage with, but rather opposes seeing it as an issue at all. I would see this position as strongly connected with her politics of philosophy in the text which joins her with the Arendtian project based on existentialist humanism. This position, however, connects with clinging to the species point of view in the tradition, and in my view, constrains the possibilities of analyzing feminist problems of politics.

With another politics of philosophy, a different set of issues would be at hand: although the idea of the political subject needs to be abandoned and is not a necessary form of theorizing feminist politics, both the issues of gendering political agents and gendering individuals through cultural norms remain acute feminist subject issues.

References

Ankersmit, F.R. (2002), *Political Representation* (Stanford, CA: Stanford University Press).

Arendt, H. (1958), *The Human Condition* (Chicago, IL: The University of Chicago Press).

—— (1978), *The Life of the Mind* (New York: Harcourt Brace Jovanovich).

Brown, W. (2001), *Politics out of History* (Princeton, NJ: Princeton University Press).

Brunner O., Conze, W. and Koselleck, R. (eds) (1990), *Geschichtliche Grundbegriffe. Historisches Lexikon zur politisch-sozialen Sprache in Deutschland*, vol. 6 (Stuttgart: Klett-Cotta).

Butler, J. (1990), *Gender Trouble: Feminism and the Subversion on Identity* (London: Routledge).

—— (2000), 'Restaging the Universal', in Butler, Laclau and Zizek (eds), *Contingency, Hegemony, Universality: Contemporary Dialogues on the Left* (London: Verso).

——, Laclau, E. and Zizek, S. (eds) (2000), *Contingency, Hegemony, Universality: Contemporary Dialogues on the Left* (London: Verso).

Caine, B. and Sluga, G. (2000), *Gendering European History, 1780–1920* (London and New York: Continuum).

Cavarero, A. (2005), *For More than One Voice: Towards a Philosophy of Vocal Expression*, trans. P. Kottman (Stanford, CA: Stanford University Press).

Coontz, S. (2005), *Marriage, a History: From Obedience to Intimacy or How Love Conquered Marriage* (New York: Viking).

Dallmayr, F.R. and Rosales, J.M. (eds) (2001), *Beyond Nationalism? Sovereignty and Citizenship* (Lanham, MD and Oxford: Lexington Books).

de Beauvoir, S. (1989), *The Second Sex*, trans. and ed. H.M. Parshley (New York: Vintage).

Dietz, M. (2002), *Turning Operations: Feminism, Arendt, and Politics* (New York: Routledge).

Firestone, S. (1970), *The Dialectic of Sex: The Case of Feminist Revolution* (New York: Bantam Books).

Fraser, N. (1994), 'Civil Citizenship against Social Citizenship', in van Steenbergen (ed.), *The Conditions of Citizenship* (London: Sage).

—— (1997), *Justice Interruptus: Critical Reflections on the 'Post-socialist' Condition* (New York: Routledge).

Göring, R. (2003), 'The Concept of Representation: From the Origins to Modern Parliamentary Representation', paper presented in the first PHED Network workshop, 'The Formation of Representative Democracy', October 2003, University of Malaga.

Honig, B (1993), *Political Theory and The Displacement of Politics* (Ithaca, NY: Cornell University Press).

Koselleck, R. et al. (1990), 'Staat und Souveränität', in Brunner, Conze and Koselleck (eds), *Geschichtliche Grundbegriffe. Historisches Lexikon zur politisch-sozialen Sprache in Deutschland*, vol. 6 (Stuttgart: Klett-Cotta).

Landes, J. (1988), *Women and the Public Sphere in the Age of the French Revolution* (Ithaca, NY: Cornell University Press).

Lister, R. (1997), *Citizenship: Feminist Perspectives* (Basingstoke: Palgrave).

Millett, K. (1971), *Sexual Politics* (London: Abacus).

Phillips, A. (1998a), 'Democracy and Representation', in Phillips (ed.), *Feminism and Politics: Oxford Readings in Feminism* (Oxford and New York: Oxford University Press).

—— (ed.) (1998b), *Feminism and Politics: Oxford Readings in Feminism* (Oxford and New York: Oxford University Press).

Pitkin, H.F. (1967), The *Concept of Representation* (Berkeley, CA: University of California Press).

Pulkkinen, T. (2000a), *The Postmodern and Political Agency* (Jyvaskyla: SoPhi).

—— (2000b), 'Valtio – on Conceptual History of the Finnish "State"', *Finnish Yearbook of Political Thought* 4: 129–58.

—— (2001), 'Nations within Nations – Nationalism and Identity Politics', in F.R. Dallmayr and J.M. Rosales (eds), *Beyond Nationalism? Sovereignty and Citizenship* (Lanham, MD and Oxford: Lexington Books).

—— (2003), 'Hannah Arendt and the Politics of Philosophy', *Alternatives* 28:2, 215–31.

Riley, D. (1988), *'Am I That Name?': Feminism and the Category Of 'Women' in History* (Houndmills: Macmillan).

Scott, J.W. (1996), *Only Paradoxes to Offer: French Feminists and the Rights of Man* (Cambridge, MA: Harvard University Press).

Skinner, Q. (1998), *Liberty before Liberalism* (Cambridge: Cambridge University Press).

Squires, J. (2000), *Gender in Political Theory* (Cambridge: Polity Press).

Taminiaux, J. (1997), *The Thracian Maid and the Professional Thinker: Arendt and Heidegger*, trans. M. Gendre (Albany, NY: State University of New York Press).

Van Steenbergen, B. (ed.) (1994), *The Conditions of Citizenship* (London: Sage).

Villa, D. (1996), *Arendt and Heidegger: The Fate of the Political* (Princeton, NJ: Princeton University Press).

Voet, R. (1998), *Feminism and Citizenship* (London: Sage).

Wollstonecraft, M. (1792 [1996]), *A Vindication of the Rights of Woman* (Minneola, NY: Dover).

Young, I.M. (1990), *Justice and the Politics of Difference* (Princeton, NJ: Princeton University Press).

—— (2000), *Inclusion and Democracy* (Oxford: Oxford University Press).

Yuval-Davis, N. (1997), *Gender and Nation* (London: Sage Publications).

Zerilli, L. (2005), *Feminism and the Abyss of Freedom* (Chicago, IL: University of Chicago Press).

Further Reading

Arendt, H. (1968 [1993]), 'What Is Freedom?', in *Between Past and Future: Eight Exercises in Political Thought* (New York: Penguin Books).

Atkinson, T.-G. (1974), *Amazon Odyssey* (New York: Links Books).

Butler, J. (1997), *The Psychic Life of Power: Theories in Subjection* (Stanford, CA: Stanford University Press).

—— (2005), *Giving an Account of Oneself* (New York: Fordham University Press).

—— and Scott, J.W. (eds) (1992), *Feminists Theorize the Political* (London and New York: Routledge).

Cott, N. (1987), *The Grounding of Modern Feminism* (New Haven, CT: Yale University Press).

De Gouges, O. (1791 [2003]), *Déclaration des droits de la femme et de la citoyenne* (Mille et une nuits: <www.1001nuits.com>).

Disch, L. (1994), *Hannah Arendt and the Limits of Philosophy* (Ithaca, NY: Cornell University Press).

Okin, S.M. (1979), *Women in Western Political Thought* (Princeton, NJ: Princeton University Press).

Pateman, C. (1988), *The Sexual Contract* (Cambridge: Polity Press).

PART II

PRACTICES

Political Rhetoric and the Role of Ridicule

Quentin Skinner

Within the European tradition of parliamentary politics, the idea that there is a distinctive art of speaking in public assemblies was first widely put forward in the course of the Renaissance. Within Anglophone political culture, on which I shall concentrate, the question of how to speak publicly in the most effective style first began to be examined intensively in the middle decades of the sixteenth century, after which the study of the art of rhetoric came to be central to educational theory and practice for at least the ensuing century.

When the educational theorists of early modern England spoke about the need to study the art of rhetoric, they were referring to the need to master a specifically Greek and Roman literature, a literature that it was one of the distinctive achievements of the Renaissance to revive. The pioneering analysis had been given by Aristotle in his *Art of Rhetoric*, but the texts on which the early modern teachers of rhetoric mainly relied were Roman rather than Greek. Perhaps the most popular textbook was the anonymous *Rhetorica ad Herennium*, a work that, until the sixteenth century, was widely but mistakenly thought to have been written by Cicero. A number of Cicero's authentic works were also widely used, including his youthful *De Inventione*, and above all, his *De Oratore*. But of all the ancient Roman texts, the one that was generally treated with the greatest reverence was Quintilian's *Institutio Oratoria*, the fullest summary of ancient rhetorical thought.

During the second half of the sixteenth century, a large number of vernacular treatises on rhetoric began to appear in England for the first time. Here, the pioneer was Thomas Wilson, whose *Arte of Rhetorique* was first published in 1554 and was reissued at least eight times in the next half-century. More specialized manuals soon began to appear, including those of Dudley Fenner and Charles Butler, both heavily influenced by Ramism, and those of Richard Sherry, Henry Peacham and George Puttenham, all of whom concentrated on analyzing the figures and tropes of speech. By the end of the sixteenth century, these and other writers had made available to English readers a complete understanding of the classical *Ars Rhetorica*.

The Renaissance writers were in agreement with their classical authorities that there are three distinct forms of rhetorical speech. This typology had originally been put forward by Aristotle, who presents it in Book 1, Chapter 3 of his *Rhetoric*. To quote the earliest English translation (which appeared *c.* 1636 and has generally been attributed to Thomas Hobbes), 'there are three kinds of *Orations*', and these can be listed as *'Demonstrative, Judicial, Deliberative'*. The proper business of demonstrative orations is said to be that of *'Praysing* and *Dispraysing'*, while their proper end is that of pointing out what is *'Honourable,* or *Dishonourable'*. The aim of judicial orations is *'Accusation* and *Defence'*, while their goal is to discover what is *'Just, or Unjust'*. Finally, in deliberative speech, the aim is *'Exhortation* and *Dehortation'*, while the goal is 'to proove a thing *Profitable, or Unprofitable'* (Aristotle 1986, 41).

One implication is that an orator who deliberates must in effect be counseling or proffering advice. This assumption was subsequently much emphasized by the leading Roman writers on the rhetorical arts. They further accept that, in the words of the *Ad Herennium*, the purpose of offering such counsel will normally be to persuade or dissuade someone from acting in some particular way (*Ad C. Herennium* 1954, I. II. 2, 4). Aristotle had added that 'the subject of Deliberatives' will always be 'something in our owne power, the knowledge whereof belongs not to *Rhetorique*, but for the most part to the *Politiques'* (Aristotle 1986, 42). The Roman theorists expanded these observations into the further claim that the chief forum for deliberative oratory will normally be the senate or the assembly of the people. The point on which everyone agreed was that, as Cicero had already argued at the start of the *De Inventione*, 'it is in the giving of an opinion in political argument that the deliberative *genus* has its characteristic place' (Cicero 1949, I. V. 7, 16).

When we speak, then, about political rhetoric, what we are talking about (according to the classical and Renaissance writers on the *Ars rhetorica*) is orations in the *genus deliberativum*. The classical writers in turn assume that this genre can be straightforwardly equated with the form of speech most suited to public assemblies. By contrast, for the Renaissance theorists, the category of deliberation is a more capacious one. With the invention of the printed book, they found it necessary to add that one of the ways in which we can hope to deliberate in the public interest is not merely by speaking to the people's representatives, but also by writing tracts and treatises designed to influence our rulers and governments.

Written contributions to the *genus deliberativum* became increasingly important in the early modern period, and came to encompass religious and economic tracts as well as commentaries on constitutional issues and specific public policies. The greatest outpouring of such deliberative works in England came with the outbreak of the Civil War in 1642. The supporters of the Crown as well as Parliament found themselves obliged to offer explicit justifications for their policies as those most suited to securing the *salus populi*, and it is on this unparalleled production of works in the *genus deliberativum* that I chiefly want to concentrate.

Let me begin by asking how one can hope, according to the theorists I have cited, to write or speak in the deliberative mode in such a way as to succeed in persuading a public assembly to act for the common good? The key to winning the war of words was basically held to depend on recognizing that the art of rhetoric contains five distinct elements, all of which must be mastered and simultaneously brought into play if victory in the courts or public assemblies is to be achieved. The first element is described as *Inventio*, that is, the finding out of the most suitable reasons and arguments to put forward. But the other four elements are all concerned not so much with reasoning as with persuasion, and it is here that the art of rhetoric is said to have its most distinctive and powerful contribution to make to successful public speech.

The rhetoricians accept, of course, that the ability to reason well about whatever issue is under debate is essential to winning an argument. But the rhetorical tradition can virtually be defined as that tradition of discourse which insists that, if I am to persuade you of what I say, logical reasoning will never be enough. If we ask why the rhetoricians emphasize this claim so much, we arrive at perhaps the most basic and characteristic assumption of their thought. The reason, they always stress, is that in judicial as well as deliberative arguments, there will always be two sides to the question. As Quintilian puts it in his chapter on the nature of rhetoric, we are dealing in such cases with the sort of situation 'in which two wise men may with just cause take up one or another point of view, since it is generally agreed that it is possible for reason to lead even the wise to fight among themselves' (Quintilian 1920–22, II. XVII. 32, vol. 1, 338). It follows that, as Quintilian adds, in judicial as well as deliberative cases, we shall find that 'the weapons of powerful speech can invariably be used on either side of the case' (Quintilian 1920–22, II. XVI. 10, vol. 1, 322).

The implication is that, in judicial as well as deliberative arguments, we can never look for closure, so that the only appropriate way to conduct such disputes will be in the form of a dialog. It is worth noting how far we still attempt to do justice to this insight in contemporary forums of judicial and deliberative debate. In representative assemblies, the space is still sometimes organized so that two sides face each other; and in courts of law, juries are still required to reach their verdicts by listening to orations from prosecution and defense delivered from opposite sides of the court. If you are speaking in such circumstances, your aim must therefore be to argue in such a way that – as we still say – you persuade your audience to *come round* to your side. You must bring it about that – as we also say – they come to *stand where you stand* on the issue. These spatial metaphors survive in modern times in the form of the judgment that the greatest feat of parliamentary oratory will always be to cause an adversary to 'cross the floor' – that is, to join your side.

Your basic aim – to invoke another deep play on words that still survives – must accordingly be to speak *winningly*. But how can this be done? Not by reasoning alone, it has already been conceded, because there may often be equally good reasons on either side. So how? Not without some misgivings, the classical and Renaissance theorists of rhetoric answer that you must learn how to supplement your reasoning with the purely passionate force of powerful speech. You must learn, in other words, how to arouse in your audience a purely emotional commitment to your side of the case. As the figure of Antonius in *De oratore* puts it with cynical frankness, after capturing the attention of your auditor, you must try 'to shift or impel him so that he becomes ruled not by deliberation and judgment but rather by sheer impetus and perturbation of mind' (Cicero 1942, II. XLII. 178, vol. 1, 324).

With these contentions, the classical and Renaissance theorists find themselves confronting a question of some practical importance. Are there any specific techniques we can hope to learn and deploy in such a way as to succeed in moving the deepest emotions of an audience, so that we succeed in winning them to our side, thereby discrediting our adversaries at the same time? The answer given in antiquity, and extensively taken up in the Renaissance, is that there are indeed specific techniques to be learned, and that a mastery of exactly these techniques is what the *Ars rhetorica* serves to teach.

What, then, are these techniques? To learn the answer, we first need to return to the four elements that, in addition to *Inventio*, were said to make up the essence of eloquent utterance. Of these, two refer exclusively to spoken eloquence. One is memory, for it is always held to be impressive if a speaker can give the sense of having perfect control over his materials. The other is described as 'pronunciation', by which the rhetoricians meant not merely a mastery of the right tone and modulation of voice, but also of gesture and general deportment. The other two elements were held to apply equally to written as well as spoken eloquence. As the author of the *Ad Herennium* puts it, after *Inventio*, the first of these is *Dispositio*, which he defines as the capacity 'to order and distribute the things we have found out in such a way as to indicate how they can best be placed' (*Ad C. Herennium* 1954, I. II. 3, 6). Finally, the other element is *Elocutio*, which the *Ad Herennium* defines as 'the application of appropriate thoughts and words to describe the things we have found out' (*Ad C. Herennium* 1954, I. II. 3, 6).

We are left, then, with the contention that, if you wish to write in a 'moving' style, what you need to understand is the most appropriate words to use and the proper way to 'dispose' or organize them. Let us first consider what is meant by proper *Dispositio*. There was widespread agreement about how we must organize our utterances if they are to have the greatest persuasive force. By far the most influential analysis was propounded by the author of the *Ad Herennium*, who maintained that any rhetorical oration should be divided into six distinct parts. The first is the *Exordium*, in which you establish your *ethos*, that is, your worthiness to speak on the topic under debate. The second is the *Narratio*, in which you lay out the facts of the case. Next comes the *Divisio*, in which you distinguish where you agree and where you disagree with your adversaries. The fourth part is the *Confirmatio*, in which you support your side of the case. The fifth is the *Confutatio*, in which you rebut your opponents' counter-arguments. And finally comes the *Conclusio*, the grandiloquent peroration to your speech.

Very little study of early modern speeches and writings in the deliberative mode has so far been undertaken with the aim of discovering how far they actually conform to these rules. But in general, the rules were followed with almost mechanical exactitude. Consider, for example, one of the most celebrated of the early seventeenth-century speeches in Parliament attacking the policies of the monarchy, Sir Thomas Hedley's oration in the House of Commons in 1610 in which he dismissed as illegal the Crown's attempts to levy taxes and contributions without consent of Parliament (Foster 1966, vol. 2, 170–97). The speech is not only classical and almost republican in content, but follows to the letter the precepts about good

Dispositio laid down in the *Ad Herennium*. Consider, similarly, the most celebrated defense of the English Parliament's decision to try king Charles I for treason, John Milton's tract *The Tenure of Kings and Magistrates* of February 1649. Here too, the entire argument is laid out exactly along the lines laid down in the *Ad Herennium* for the proper disposition of a deliberative speech. Milton begins with an *exordium* in which he establishes his *ethos*, proceeds to a *narratio* of the king's crimes, offers a *confirmatio* of the justifiability of regicide and a *refutatio* of possible objections, and draws to a close with a magnificent *peroratio* on the true nature of English liberties (Milton 1991, 3–37).

So far, I have been considering the importance of *Dispositio*; I next want to turn to *Elocutio*, the most vital element in forensic as well as political eloquence. It was generally agreed that there are two main aspects of *Elocutio*, and hence two characteristic elements in a fully persuasive style. The first, as the *Ad Herennium* puts it, is the ability to put one's case 'purely and clearly', to speak 'with clearness and lucidity' (*Ad C. Herennium* 1954, IV. XII. 17, 268–70). The other is the ability to add to one's writing or speech the appropriate kind of *ornatus* or *ornamenta*. The figure of Crassus is made to yoke these two requirements together when discussing *Elocutio* in the final book of Cicero's *De oratore*:

> *Whom do people stare at in astonishment when he speaks? Whom do they applaud? … Those who speak distinctly, explicitly and copiously, whose words and arguments are presented with complete clarity, and who in delivering a speech are also able to attain a kind of rhythm – speaking, that is, with what I call ornatus. (Cicero 1942, III. XIV. 53, vol. 2, 42)*

It is easy to misunderstand these claims about *ornatus* and *ornamenta*, especially if these terms are translated, as they often are, as 'ornamentation' or 'embellishment'. This misses the metaphorical force of the argument, much of which turns on the fact that, in classical Latin, *ornatus* is the word ordinarily used to describe the weapons and accoutrements of war. To be properly *ornatus* is to be equipped for battle, powerfully armored and protected. What the rhetoricians are claiming is that the 'ornaments' characteristic of the Grand Style are *not* mere decorations or embellishments; they are the weapons an orator must learn to wield if he is to have any prospect of winning the war of words.

The fullest analysis of *ornatus* in ancient rhetorical theory is contained in Books 8 and 9 of Quintilian's *Institutio Oratoria*. What, then, does it mean, according to Quintilian, to speak and write with the right kind of *ornatus* or *ornamenta*? What it means, he says, is to know how to make the best possible use of the figures and tropes of speech. This is the talent, he argues, that an orator most needs to cultivate if he is to speak in a 'winning' style. Quintilian accordingly examines the figures and tropes at considerable length, devoting Book 8 to the *Tropi*, or 'turnings' of speech, and Book 9 to the much wider range of the *Figurae*. It is specifically by the right deployment of these devices, he maintains, that we can hope to increase the emotional force of our arguments while undercutting our adversaries at the same time.

This appears at first sight to be an astonishingly large claim to make about the persuasive resources allegedly inherent in language itself. How can such purely linguistic devices hope to achieve such deep emotional effects? The classical theorists of rhetoric answer this further question in two different ways. First of all, they claim, the deployment of fresh and arresting figures and tropes can have the effect of lending so much vividness and immediacy to our speech that our audience comes to 'see' what we are trying to describe, and is thereby roused to accept and endorse our vision of events. The suggestion is thus that the most persuasive arguments will be those that enable us to picture 'in the mind's eye' what is being described, and that the best way to produce this pictorial effect will be by the right use of what we still describe as 'imagery' – that is, the most eye-opening figures and tropes.

The rhetoricians also discuss, usually at much greater length, a second way in which the figures and tropes can be used to arouse the emotions of an audience. The fullest analysis is again owed to Quintilian in his *Institutio Oratoria*. He begins by acknowledging that this further suggestion may appear trivial, but he insists that it is vital for anyone who hopes to achieve victory in the war of words. His contention is that the figures and tropes are particularly valuable as means of provoking laughter. To learn how to make use of them in this way, he argues, will be to equip yourself with an exceptionally potent means of arousing an audience against your adversaries, and consequently in favour of your cause. So far is he from supposing this suggestion to be inconsequential that he declares in Book 10 that 'the use of humour, together with the ability to inspire pity, are undoubtedly the two means of stirring the emotions that have the greatest impact of all' (Quintilian 1920–22, X. I. 107, vol. 4, 60–62).

But how exactly is an ability to excite laughter supposed to help us turn an audience against our adversaries? To see the answer, we first need to understand the view that the rhetoricians take about the nature of the emotions that laughter may be said to express. Aristotle had given an arresting answer in discussing the emotions in *The Art of Rhetoric*. The essence of his argument is that laughter is almost invariably an expression of scorn or contempt. He first hints at this thesis in Book 1, Chapter 11, where he affirms that among the things that give pleasure are 'ridiculous Actions, Sayings and Persons' (Aristotle 1986, 57). He makes the point still more explicitly at the end of Book 2, Chapter 2, the passage in which he discusses the manners of youth. There, he roundly declares that '*Jesting* is witty Contumely', having already informed us that '*Contumely*, is the disgracing of another for his owne pastime' (Aristotle 1986, 70, 86).

Quintilian's argument is based on very similar premises. He too stresses that laughter 'has its source in things that are either deformed or disgraceful in some way', adding that 'those sayings which excite ridicule are often false (which is always ignoble), are often ingeniously distorted and are never in the least complimentary' (Quintilian 1920–22, VI. III. 8, vol. 2, 440–42). But while these remarks are reminiscent of Aristotle, they owe a more immediate debt to the discussion of laughter in Cicero's *De oratore*. The figure of Caesar discourses at length in Book 2 about the situations that cause amusement, beginning by offering a restatement and elaboration of Aristotle's point. 'The proper field and as it were the province of laughter', he declares, 'is restricted to matters that are in some way either disgraceful or deformed. For the principal if not the sole cause of mirth are those kinds of remarks which note and single out, in a fashion not in itself unseemly, something which is in some way unseemly or disgraceful' (Cicero 1942, II. LVIII. 236, vol. 1, 372).

We can now see why the rhetorical theorists think of laughter as such a potentially lethal weapon of debate. If we can manage to expose our opponents as laughable, we can hope to bring them into scorn and contempt, thereby augmenting our own standing at their expense. This is the promise that Cicero holds out in Book 2 of the *De oratore*, in which he argues that humor possesses a power 'that can break up your opponent's case, obstruct his argument, deter him from speaking and undermine what he has said' (Cicero 1942, II. LVIII. 236, vol. 1, 372). Quintilian strongly agrees, adding that the primary value of humor 'is that we can use it either to reprehend, or undermine, or make light of, or repel, or deride our opponents' (Quintilian 1920–22, VI. III. 23, vol. 2, 448).

We still need to know, however, which particular figures and tropes are capable of producing such dramatic emotional effects. Quintilian first considers how the *Tropi* can be used to excite scorn and contempt. Some, he notes, can easily be adapted for purposes of ridicule, one obvious example being *Hyperbole*. More important, he adds, is the fact that a number of tropes possess an inherently ridiculing character. One is *Aestismus*, the trope we use when we mockingly exploit some ambiguity in a word or turn of phrase. But by far the most powerful is *Ironia*, the trope we employ whenever, as Quintilian expresses it, 'we speak in derision by saying the opposite of what is to be understood' (Quintilian 1920–22, VIII. VI. 56, vol. 3, 332). The English rhetoricians likewise have much to say about *aestismus* and irony, to which some of them add some reflections on the relations between irony and sarcasm. They also discuss a number of mocking tropes not mentioned by their classical authorities. One is *Mycterismus*, the use of scoffing and sneering speech in order, as Henry Peacham puts it, to 'rebuke folly and taunt vice'; a second is *Diasyrmus*, the trope we invoke when, in Peacham's words, we put forward 'some ridiculous example to which the adversaries obiection or argument is compared' and thereby discredit it (Peacham 1593, 37–8, 39–40).

Besides discussing the mocking tropes, the classical rhetoricians had noted that a number of *Figurae* can also be adapted to produce satirical and derisory effects. Among the *Figurae verborum*, Quintilian mentions *Dubitatio*, the ironic expression of doubt or ignorance, as well as singling out various patterned forms of speech – such as *Anaphora* and *Antithesis* – by which we can hope to contrive a tone of disparagement or ridicule. These observations were likewise much extended by the English rhetoricians of the Renaissance. One device they emphasize is *Anaphora*, the repetition of words and phrases, which, as Sherry notes, can easily be used with 'gravitie and sharpnes' (Sherry 1961, 47). A further technique they like to single out is *Percontatio* or *Erotema*, the technique of asking rhetorical questions which, as Puttenham observes, can similarly be used 'by way of skoffe' (Puttenham 1970, 210–11).

As well as considering the *Figurae verborum*, the rhetoricians note that a number of *Figurae sententiarum*, or figures of thought, can be used even more powerfully to produce scornful and satirical effects. Here again, the rhetoricians of the Renaissance build extensively on their classical authorities. One device they like to emphasize is *Meiosis*, the use of ironical understatement, which, as Quintilian had already observed, is especially susceptible of being applied in contemptuous or reproachful ways. Finally, some of them add to the list of satirical *Figurae* a number of examples not mentioned by their classical authorities. One is *Litotes*, a specialized form of *meiosis*, while a second is *Synchoresis*, the trope in play, according to Charles Butler, whenever 'a statement or an argument is seemingly accepted', but when 'that which we concede is harmful to the person to whom the concession is made' (Butler 1629, Sig. M, 4^v to Sig. N, 1^r).

I am now in a position to summarize the advice put forward by the rhetorical theorists about how to win the war of words. They present us, in effect, with three connected arguments. First, the key to victory is said to be to enlist the deepest emotions of your audience. Next, one of the best means of inducing this effect is to cause your adversaries to appear laughable and absurd. Finally, the best way to obtain this result is to make use of the full panoply of the mocking figures and tropes I have now singled out.

Suppose we now return to the political oratory of early seventeenth-century England, and in particular to the period immediately preceding the outbreak of the Civil War in 1642. How far were the views I have been presenting about how to triumph in public assemblies actually taken up and put into practice? By way of answering, I shall concentrate on the replies to the Remonstrances of Parliament published by the Crown in the opening months of 1642. The Crown began to issue these replies in the face of Parliament's demand, in February 1642, to be granted control of the Militia. Charles I vetoed the proposal, and when Parliament responded with the revolutionary contention that it had sufficient authority to legislate in the absence of the royal assent, the battle between the two sides was irrevocably joined. Charles I declared the claim treasonous, Parliament refused to back down, and by the end of June, both sides began actively to prepare for the war that finally broke out in August 1642.

The numerous Remonstrances presented by Parliament in support of its case maintain a tone of grave and even paranoid seriousness. By contrast, the king's replies strike an increasingly strident note of scorn and contempt. Unable to make Parliament accept his arguments, but secure in the belief that the parliamentarian view of the constitution was without foundation, King Charles I and his advisers seek to discredit the Parliamentarian cause by deploying every technique recommended by the theorists of rhetoric for winning an argument by contriving a tone of mockery and ridicule. As I shall next seek to show, it is even possible to summarize the entire chronology of the Crown's reactions to the Parliamentary Remonstrances of spring 1642 in terms of the range of mocking figures and tropes with which the Crown sought to ornament its case.

Charles's speech of 9 March to the Committee of both Houses begins with one of his favorite techniques, that of *percontatio*, the asking of questions in a tone of irony or contempt: 'What would you have? Have I violated your Lawes? Have I denied to passe any one Bill for the ease and security of my Subjects? I doe not aske you what you have done for Me' (Husbands 1643, 103). His *Declaration* to Parliament of the same date opens with a withering use of *meiosis*, the device of ironic understatement. 'We have little encouragement', he begins, 'to Replyes of this nature, when We are told of how little value Our words are like to be with you' (Husbands 1643, 106). To which he adds, repeating the figure, that 'Wee could wish, that our Owne immediate Actions which Wee avow, and Our owne Honour might not be so roughly censured and wounded' (Husbands 1643, 106). Turning to Parliament's objection that he has violated its privileges by withdrawing from London, Charles responds with a dismissive use of *dubitatio*, the ironic expression of ignorance. 'Wee wisht', he replies, that 'it might be so safe and Honourable, that We had no cause to absent Our Selfe from *White-Hall*, and how this can be a breach of Priviledge of Parliament Wee cannot understand' (Husbands 1643, 109). Moving to Parliament's claim that too little in the way of reform has so far been achieved, Charles reverts to his favorite device of *percontatio*, augmenting it by *anaphora*, the figure of repetition: 'Are the Bills for the Trienniall Parliament, For relinquishing Our Title of Imposing upon Merchandize, and Power of Pressing of Souldiers, for the taking away the Star-Chamber, and high Commission Courts, For the Regulating the Councell Table, but words? Are the Bils for the Forests, the Stannery Courts, the Clerke of the Market, And the taking away the Votes of Bishops out of the Lords House, but words?' (Husbands 1643, 109–10).

The Crown produced a further *Answer* to Parliament at the start of May 1642. This opens with a derisive use of *synchoresis*, the pretence of not taking up an argument: 'We very well understand how much it is below the high and Royall dignity … to take notice, much more to trouble Our Self with answering those many scandalous, seditious Pamphlets … But we are contented to let Our Self fall to any Office that may undeceive Our People' (Husbands 1643, 173). Commenting on Parliament's claim that it presented the Militia Ordinance with all due humility, Charles allows himself a tone of broad irony when he responds that the extent of their humility is 'very evident in the Petitions and Messages concerning it' (Husbands 1643, 175). Warming to his task, he uses the trope of *hyperbole* to counter Parliament's insistence that it has the power to make its own ordinances legally binding on the people. The two Houses, he scornfully retorts, appear to be claiming that there is 'a secret of the Law, which hath lain hid from the beginning of the world to this time, and now is discovered to take away the just Legall Power of the King' (Husbands 1643, 175).

The Crown produced a yet fuller *Answer* to Parliament at the end of May. Reiterating his position, Charles opens with an elegantly mocking antithesis, expressing the hope that his defense of himself 'shall no more be called a Scandall upon the Parliament, then the opinion of such a part be reputed an Act of Parliament' (Husbands 1643, 241). Parliament had complained that the king's attitude had given comfort to the rebels in Ireland. Charles responds with another *dubitatio*, or ironic expression of ignorance: 'What that Complaint is against the Parliament put forth in Our Name, which is such an evidence and countenance to the Rebels, … We cannot understand' (Husbands 1643, 247–8). Parliament had once more objected to the king's removal from London, denying that there had been any tumults or disturbances sufficient to justify his departure. Charles responds with a taunting use of *mycterismus*, the trope of sneering speech, coupling it with his favorite device of *perconatio*:

> They knew no Tumults. Strange! Was the disorderly appearance of so many
> thousands people with Staves and Swords ... no Tumults? ... Were not
> severall Members of either House assaulted, threatned, and ill intreated? and
> yet no Tumults? Why made the House of Peers a Declaration and sent it
> down to the House of Commons for the suppressing of Tumults, if there were
> no Tumults? (Husbands 1643, 249)

Finally, Charles responds to Parliament's attempt to brand his own supporters as treasonous with yet another withering use of *mycterismus*, coupling it as before with *percontatio*: 'If they have Power to declare the Lord *Digbies* waiting on Us to *Hampton Court*, and thence visiting some Officers at *Kingston* with a coach and six Horses, to be leavying of War, and high treason: And Sir *John Hothams* defying Us to our face, ... to be an Act of Affection and Loyalty, what needs a Power of making new Laws? Or is there such a thing as Law left?' (Husbands 1643, 250).

Charles I's fullest *Answer* to Parliament was published in early June 1642. The king opens with a condescending use of *meiosis*, the figure of ironic understatement. Whoever looks over the late Remonstrance submitted by Parliament, he observes, 'will not think We have much reason to be pleased with it' (Husbands 1643, 282). He continues in tones of deepest irony. Nevertheless, he adds: 'We cannot but commend the plain dealing and ingenuity of the Framers and Contrivers of that Declaration [who] ... like Round-dealing men tell Us in plain English, *That they have done Us no wrong*, because we are not capable of receiving any' (Husbands 1643, 282).

The king thereupon settles down to comment on Parliament's specific objections and arguments. One of their more paranoid claims, endlessly repeated, was that they were protecting the nation from a party of malignant advisers bent on tyranny. Raising the volume of his contempt, the king has recourse once more to the device of *mycterismus*, the sneering trope: 'Nothing is more evident by their whole Proceedings', he retorts, 'then that by the Malignant Party they intend all the Members of both Houses, who agree not with them in their Opinion' (Husbands 1643, 283). A further argument constantly put forward by Parliament had been that, when it prevented the king from gaining access to munitions in the north of England – its first act of overt hostility – it was acting in defense of the property of the English people. Charles reacts to the implicit definition of private property with a disdainful use of *diasyrmus*, the technique of dismissing an argument by comparing it with one of unquestionable absurdity. 'Do these men think', he replies, 'That as they assume a power of declaring Law ... they have a power of declaring Sense and Reason, and imposing Logick and Syllogismes on the Schooles, as well as Law upon the People?' (Husbands 1643, 286). Reflecting on the absurdity of the claim that the munitions were really the people's property, he finally allows himself a note of pure sarcasm. The munitions, he notes, are said by the Parliamentarians to have been bought *'with the publike Money*; and the proofe is, *They conceive it so*; and upon this conceit have Voted, That it shall be taken from Us: Excellent Justice!' (Husbands 1643, 286).

Charles next comments on the general claim, frequently put forward by Parliament, that the people have entrusted it to act on their behalf. Here, he mocks their presumption with a scornful *aestismus* based on exploiting the dual meaning of the word 'presume'. According to Cotgrave's *Dictionarie* of 1611, for someone to *presume* could either mean to 'imagine, coniecture, suppose' or else 'to over-value his owne person' (Cotgrave 1611, Sig. SSSiiiᵛ). Charles's satirical intentions are therefore very evident when he asks, speaking of the two Houses: 'Can it be presumed (and presumptions go far with them) that We trusted them with a power to destroy Us?' (Husbands 1643, 287). Commenting on Parliament's ensuing claim that it needed to prevent the king from undermining the law, Charles once more allows himself a tone of pure sarcasm. They tell us, he notes, 'that they will never allow Us ... *to be Judge of the Law'*. To which he parenthetically adds: 'An humble and dutifull Expression' (Husbands 1643, 288).

Turning to dissect some of Parliament's additional claims, the king makes derisive use once more of the figure of *synchoresis*, the pretence of not taking up an argument: 'We will not', he assures them, 'accuse the Framers of this Declaration (how bold soever they are with Us) that they incline to Popery ... Neither will We tell them (though they have told us) that they use the very language of the Rebels of *Ireland'* (Husbands 1643, 288). Having considered the details of the Parliamentary case, the king summarizes with a mocking use of *anaphora*, the figure of repetition. They are telling us, he scornfully concludes, that 'Calamitie proceeds from evill Counsellors, whom no body can name; from Plots and Conspiracies, which no man can discover; and from Fears and Jealousies, which no man understands' (Husbands 1643, 292). Pointing to the catastrophe now facing the kingdom, he draws to a close with another elegant, if melancholy, antithesis: 'What their own Method has been, and whither it hath led them, and brought the Kingdom, all men see; What Ours would have bin, if seasonably and timely applied unto, let all men judge' (Husbands 1643, 293).

The tone of these exchanges was unique in the parliamentary debates of early modern England. Normally, the rhetoric of politics was strictly controlled by two factors that militated against any possible recourse to such mockery or ridicule. One was the fact that the members of the Privy Council who sat in Parliament were taken to be speaking in the name of the king, and were consequently taken to be entitled to the same high and dutiful respect. The other was that, to any gentleman sitting in either House of Parliament, to be addressed in scornful or contemptuous terms would have been a dishonor so acute as to be intolerable. As a result, it came to be agreed at an early stage that any such abusive speech should be condemned as 'unparliamentary' and wholly proscribed. So strongly was mocking or insulting speech debarred that, by the early seventeenth century, the phrase 'to speak in an unparliamentary way' had come to *mean* (and still means) to speak in just such an insulting way as would never be accepted in Parliament.

It has often been asked at what moment the war between Crown and Parliament in England became unavoidable. It is arguable that the answer is contained in the political rhetoric I have been examining. When the king began to respond to Parliament with the full range of the mocking figures and tropes, he was signaling that he regarded Parliament as beyond argument, and that he was now prepared to do everything in his power to discredit and overturn the Parliamentary cause. He finally raised his standard of war in August 1642, but by that stage there was a sense in which he had already been fighting rather than arguing with Parliament for several months.

References

Ad C. Herennium de ratione dicendi (1954), ed. and trans. H. Caplan (London: Heinemann).

Aristotle (1986), *A Briefe of the Art of Rhetorique*, trans. Thomas Hobbes, in *The Rhetorics of Thomas Hobbes and Bernard Lamy*, ed. John T. Harwood (Carbondale and Edwardsville, IL: Southern Illinois University Press), pp. 33–128.

Butler, C. (1629), *Rhetoricae Libri Duo* (London: Haviland).

Cicero (1942), *De oratore*, ed. and trans. E.W. Sutton and H. Rackham, 2 vols (London: Heinemann).

—— (1949), *De inventione*, ed. and trans. M.M. Hubbell (London: Heinemann).

Cotgrave, R. (1611), *A Dictionarie of the French and English Tongues* (London: Islip).

Foster, E.R. (ed.) (1966), *Proceedings in Parliament 1610*, 2 vols (New Haven, CT: Yale University Press).

Husbands, E. (ed.) (1643), *An Exact Collection Of all Remonstrances* (London: Husbands).

Milton, J. (1991), *Political Writings*, ed. M. Dzelzainis (Cambridge: Cambridge University Press).

Peacham, H. (1593), *The Garden of Eloquence ... corrected and augmented* (London: Iackson).

Puttenham, G. (1970), *The Arte of English Poesie*, ed. G. Willcock and A. Walker (Cambridge: Cambridge University Press).

Quintilian (1920–22), *Institutio oratoria*, ed. and trans. H.E. Butler, 4 vols (London: Heinemann).

Sherry, R. (1961), *A Treatise of Schemes and Tropes*, ed. H.W. Hildebrandt (Gainesville, FL: Scholars' Facsimiles & Reprints).

Further Reading

Adamson, S., Alexander, G. and Ettenhuber, K. (eds) (2007), *Renaissance Figures of Speech* (Cambridge: Cambridge University Press).

Brett, A. and Tully, J. (eds) (2006), *Rethinking the Foundations of Modern Political Thought* (Cambridge: Cambridge University Press).

Colglough, D. (2005), *Freedom of Speech in Early Stuart England* (Cambridge: Cambridge University Press).

Hexter, J.H. (ed.) (1992), *Parliament and Liberty from the Reign of Elizabeth to the English Civil War* (Princeton, NJ: Princeton University Press).

Kahn, V. (1994), *Machavellian Rhetoric: From the Counter-Revolution to Milton* (Princeton, NJ: Princeton University Press).

Mack, P. (2002), *Elizabethan Rhetoric* (Cambridge. Cambridge University Press).

Palonen, K. (2003), *Quentin Skinner: History, Politics, Rhetoric* (Cambridge: Polity Press).

Skinner, Q. (1996), *Reason and Rhetoric in the Philosophy of Hobbes* (Cambridge: Cambridge University Press).

—— (2002), *Visions of Politics*, 3 vols (Cambridge: Cambridge University Press).

Van Gelderen, M. and Skinner, Q. (eds) (2002), *Republicanism: A Shared European Heritage*, 2 vols (Cambridge: Cambridge University Press).

Political Times and the Rhetoric of Democratization

Kari Palonen

Parliamentary Democracies as Time Regimes

Politicians are extremely sensitive to time. Both journalists reporting on their activities and politicians themselves constantly speak of periods and situations, rhythms and tempi, urgency and delay, temporizing and precipitating, occasions and deadlines, schedules and calendars. 'In politics ... the essence of the game is "timing",' writes Harold Macmillan in his memoirs (1975, 105). Politics is not merely an activity in time, but simultaneously a play with time. In other words, time marks both a restraint and a resource for political activity, as Pierre Rosanvallon puts it (2003, 32).

Speaking on times is nowhere more prevalent than in the parliamentary democratic regimes. It is a part of their historical legacy. The actual political use of time as a medium in political struggle at certain decisive moments of rupture serves as the main source of inspiration in my rhetorical analysis of the times of democratization.

Understanding the politics of democratization requires an inversion of certain powerful rhetorical *topoi*. The priority of the long duration over the short is a *topos* of the classicist as opposed to the romantic style of rhetoric, as Perelman and Olbrechts-Tyteca (1958 [1983], 131) put it. Democratization marks an irrevocable break with this classical *topos*. The temporal practices of parliamentary democracies operate with figures of rupture opening up distinct chances for political agency. This radical *timeliness* is a condition for all democratic politics, and may be conceptualized through distinct figures of rupture which are inherently connected to repetition and recurrence.

Another venerable *topos* that requires reversion in order to help us better understand the conceptual break in democratization lies in the priority of long over the short time, although without a romantic celebration of the instant. On the contrary, my point is to distinguish three relatively short yet non-instantaneous temporal layers as characteristic of the parliamentary-cum-democratic style of politics. Although it is seldom recognized as such by either scholars or politicians, the willingness and competence to play with limited times is one of the most significant advantages parliamentary democracies have over other regimes.

The political implications of democratization challenge me to discuss the distinctly political layers of time and their rhetorical uses in the understanding of the democratization in parliamentary regimes (see also Palonen 2004b). In this chapter, I will use a Weberian ideal typical approach (see Weber 1904) in order to explicate the conceptual links between the break with the old regime and the new possibilities to play with time, by constructing four ideal types representative of the political constellations of democratization. The main point is to clarify the specific forms of temporal rhetoric that correspond to the operations of democratized parliamentary regimes.

Progress Toward the Future, or Rupture with the Old Order?

Reinhart Koselleck presented an ingenious vision of the temporalization of concepts and experiences. His concept of *Verzeitlichung* contains three partly independent and partly intertwined aspects (see, in detail, Palonen 2004a, 264–86). The first is *detraditionalization*, most famously expressed in his thesis of the growing gap between the space of experience (*Erfahrungsraum*) and the horizon of expectations (*Erwartungshorizont*) (Koselleck 1979, esp. 300–349). The second aspect is *denaturalization*, which is the increasing replacement of the criteria of 'natural' time with the human-made requirements of time (see Koselleck 2000, 130–202). The most original aspect in his thesis is the *despatialization* of concepts and experiences. Koselleck insists on the replacement of the original spatial meaning of many concepts with a temporal one (Koselleck 2000, 304).

Koselleck also discusses temporalization through the paradigms of progress and acceleration (see Koselleck 1979, 363–8; 2000, 195–202, and the debate in Koselleck et al. 2003). These paradigms imply a one-dimensional view of time; the main opposition continues to be between promoting and resisting progress, or accelerating and tempering change. Strangely enough, questions related to the perspective and direction of progress and acceleration as well as those whom it affects are not posed at all. This does not, however, necessarily imply that Koselleck himself subscribes to the philosophy of history involved in the progress and acceleration paradigms (see, for example, Koselleck 1980). None the less, his discussion of historical and political times is conducted within this horizon.

The temporalization of experiences and the daily political uses of concepts refers to mundane political struggles. Max Weber's famous formula of politics as a slow drilling movement, 'langsames Bohren von harten Brettern mit Leidenschaft und Augenmaß zugleich' (Weber 1919 [1994], 88), gives us an indication of why politics requires different temporal figures than the one-dimensional and forward-looking movement of progress and acceleration.

Let us take the Weberian metaphor of drilling seriously. It indicates that the activity of politics is not directed 'towards' a future state of affairs, but rather towards a rupture 'with' the existing order, which is a move away from the closed order and toward a 'free stage', as Weber (1917a [1988], 99–100) describes the liberating role of universal suffrage. The finalistic moment of politics is the negating moment of the dissolution of an order, of getting rid of something. Politics opens up opportunities, but does not ensure success. The primary aim of politics in Weber's formula on striving for power sharing, *Streben nach Machtanteilen und Beeinflussung der Machtverteilung* (Weber 1919 [1994], 36), is also related to the possibilities to do something, to share power (for *Macht* as a *Chance*, see Weber 1922 [1980], 28) and its distribution.

The boards or planks (*Bretter*) to be drilled are always plural. Overcoming the resistance to each of them will open up different types of chances, depending also on the constellation of adversity that exists at the moment of the rupture. For Weber, politics is not a single, continuous Sisyphus-like attempt to break down the resistance of the others, but rather a series of singular moves which also leave time to move from one plank to another.

Furthermore, one crucial aspect of Weber's conception of politics is the reciprocity of the drilling, each and every person being both an agent and a patient. The slow movement is a sign of respect for one's human adversaries, and represents the willingness to reserve time for a response. Success is never guaranteed, and managing to drill a hole may have critical unwanted consequences. For Weber, political struggle often has unanticipated, yet not always undesired, consequences; the horizon of that what is realizable often ends up being broader than any participant in the struggle had anticipated, and therefore nobody controls the situation (Weber 1919 [1994], 75–6).

This simple Weberian metaphor renders the linear processes of progress and acceleration inappropriate in the discussion of the times of politics. As a contingent struggle to open up new chances to act and redistribute the old ones, politics operates through the figures of both the rupture with (some aspects of) the existing condition, and the recurrent actualization of the chances that are available in the existing condition. Or, in other words, politics consists of the interplay between politicization and politicking, the opening up of new chances and the application of the currently available chances (see Palonen 2003). Politics as a temporal activity is not 'progressive' as such, but also subversive (politicization) and opportunistic (politicking).

Koselleck's metaphor of temporal layers (see Koselleck 2000) is none the less worth retaining. It allows us to overcome the simple oppositions between cyclic and linear movements, and the ordinary times of the *Kronos* and the extraordinary ones of the *Kairos*. My point lies in insisting that the activity of politics has temporal layers of its own, which have thus far remained unexamined, although Rosanvallon (2000, 2003), for example, does allude to them.

Democratization and the Political Layers of Time

Democratization breaks down the ancient frames of politics – 'L'avènement de la démocratie a brisé des anciens cadres de la société politique' – as Moisei Ostrogorski once put it (1903 [1993], 41). By democratization, I am referring here to three distinct ruptures with the old order, all of which have been tacitly or openly accepted in European parliamentary regimes: universal and equal *suffrage*, the *alternation* in governments and parliamentary majorities, and a parliamentary paradigm of rhetorical procedure that is based on speaking *pro et contra* and the incarnation of dissensus, all of which also transform the political forms of playing with time.

A common implication of these democratizing ruptures is the devaluation of the classical priority of the long time over the short one. The first implication of democratization for political agents is that political times are always scarce. Only bureaucracies and monarchies can even imagine not being affected by the struggle for temporal power sharing, and they too are unable to escape the existential condition of scarcity, to which Sartre refers as the passive motor of history (Sartre 1960 [1985], 234). Politicians in a democratized parliamentary regime accept the limits of their *Spielzeitraum*, and have accepted that they must learn to play with limited times.

It is precisely in their time orientation that the democratizing aspects of politics most manifestly break with the old order. Accordingly, the temporalization of politics can also be seen as an elective affinity, *Wahlverwandtschaft*, between the principles of democratized politics and the changing relationship to time. The constitution, electoral law and parliamentary procedure refer to certain possibilities to operate with time politically (see Rosanvallon 2003, 49, 62).

In this chapter, I will construct precisely such elective affinities between the three dimensions of democratization and the three layers of political time, although one of them will be discussed from two directions. Individual and equal suffrage, alternation in government, and parliamentarianism as a procedural principle have, of course, been defended in various other terms. My point is to accentuate their rhetorical role in marking the rupture from and enabling the play with temporal distinctions and the units of time created by them. The ideal types of political change can thus be seen as corresponding to the rhetorical possibilities that refer to the different layers of political time.

The rupture created by universal suffrage is directed against the supra-individual entities which legitimize the sacrifice of the lives of individuals. Referring to the French Revolution, Pierre Rosanvallon emphasizes the decisive role of individual autonomy for the democratization of suffrage: 'l'individu autonome est donc centrale dans la réflexion sur le suffrage' (Rosanvallon 1992, 108). He distinguishes the mere *suffrage-appartenance* of the 1848 Revolution from *suffrage-souveraineté* (Rosanvallon 1992, 338), which corresponds to the individuality and equality of suffrage in the proper sense of the Musilian figure of a *Mann ohne Eigenschaften* (Rosanvallon 1992, 446). For the Weberian *Staatsbürger*, suffrage forms a medium of persons acting in the ballot box politically, independently of the diversities in their socio-cultural being (Weber 1917b [1988], 170–72). The individual and equal suffrage accentuate the contingency of the doing of political agents, as opposed to their previous personal and socio-cultural identity (see also Sartre 1965 [1991]).

The second aspect of democratization consists of the alternation of parliamentary majorities and of governments based on them. The rupture from life-long tenure distinguishes parliamentary governments from monarchies and bureaucracies. Every chance to govern remains temporary, and is dependent upon the results of recurrent parliamentary elections and the confidence of a parliamentary majority. The political changes in periodic elections and the composition of the government depending on the parliamentary majority interrupt the routine practices in the administration. There will always be next elections and new chances to alter parliamentary majorities and governments. If the possibility for alternation of governments exists but only seldom occurs, it is a sign of the lack of fairness of the electoral procedures and practices.

The core of the parliamentary style of politics is the debate, the exchange of opinions and arguments for and against a proposition. Its origins date back to the Renaissance rhetorical political culture (see especially Skinner 1996, 2002, and his Chapter 8 in this volume). The parliament is a paradigm for a political institution that is based on the systematic procedure of searching for opposing views. In his classical study of English parliamentary procedure, Josef Redlich regarded the role of *Rede und Gegenrede* as decisive for the rhetorical intelligibility of parliamentary politics as such (1905, 586–7). The core of parliamentary politics lies in the dyad of speaking for and against, with the duration of this dyad representing the minimum temporal unit of politics. Parliamentary time has a dual character in which the lapse of quantitative time is joined to the interruption of this time through the act of speaking. The 'mood of the moment', as Gladstone put it (1838 [1953], 269), the priority of the present in the speech and debate between the speakers, is crucial for persuading MPs to alter their previous views on the topic in question or their previous political identities. The parliamentary procedure consists of dealing with a succession of items on the agenda, and their inclusion in and addition to the parliamentary agenda has become an increasingly prevalent topic of political controversy.

According to my thesis on elective affinity, we may draw a parallel between the three aspects of democratization and three temporal layers of politics. Individual and equal suffrage marks a time limit of parliamentary democracies. Correspondingly, if we can speak of a political *longue durée* in the horizons of agents, it is the individual *lifetime*. The condition of one person, one vote expresses the notion that the individual lifetime is an indispensable existential condition of political agents. The aspect of individual and equal suffrage links democratization with the politicization of time as something that depends on the conflicts, acts and decisions of contemporary living individual agents. No principle can legitimize the sacrifice of contemporary living individuals in favour of either past or future ones. This does not, however, necessarily imply a disregard for the effects of things like nuclear waste, for example, but the transformation of questions of this kind to matters to be decided by the contemporary voters and parliamentarians.

The middle range of political time concerns the periodic recurrence of key political events, particularly those occurring in a democratized parliamentary polity of elections. This aspect of political time consists of the interval between elections or, considered from the reverse angle, of the temporal power shares of the incumbent parliaments. This time consists of both a rupture and a duration, of recurrence and

155

singularity, which distinguishes it from both the routine duration of bureaucratic times and the irregular *kairotic* rupture of revolutions and constitutional reforms.

The regular political intervals may be examined from two opposite directions. Viewing them from behind the rupture creates the possibility for a political *momentum* – that is, a singular combination of a definite rupture and the continuation of its political force beyond its original breaking point. For example, every electoral victory provides the victors with a certain momentum of chances that depends on the rules of the polity, the character of the victory and their own competence as regards to the actualization of the momentum beyond the point of victory.

From the reverse angle, the interval appears as a *time-span*, as limited by a terminal point, a 'deadline', and the horizon of time that is still disposable as a chance to act before the deadline. The action programme of a government, for example, has the chance to also be a plan outlining what can be achieved before the deadline, which may intensify the activity level of those involved in the name of chances that might not be available after the deadline of an election has passed.

'A week is a long time in politics' is a slogan that has occasionally been attributed to Harold Wilson. It illustrates the need to divide the disposable political time into shorter units than the interval between elections. The parliamentary procedure offers the paradigm for short yet regular political times. Parliamentary time is broken down into different items to be dealt with by the parliament on a daily, weekly, annual and electoral term-length basis (for the history, see Redlich 1905). In other words, the short political time takes the form of a political *calendar* for which the parliamentary distribution of time into different items serves as a paradigm. In the calendar perspective, every question to be dealt with by the parliament must be transformed into an item which must both be added to the agenda and related to the other items on it. The calendar of politics highlights the primacy of the 'when' questions, which is dependent on their presence and succession on the agenda of items rather than on their weight and relevance as questions *per se*.

In the following sections, I will discuss briefly the rhetoric of each of the temporal layers of parliamentary-cum-democratic politics separately. I will refrain from providing any detailed examples of specific historical cases, but aim instead at carrying out a reinterpretation of the outlines of democratization.

The Politics of Lifetime

A historical link between individual and equal suffrage and the non-legitimacy of the endangering of one's own life without one's own consent has been expressed in various manners and by various writers. With his historical sensitivity, Koselleck has directed attention to the changing character of war memorials since the world wars. The demand to sacrifice oneself in the name of those who have fallen in past wars has increasingly lost ground: it refers to a different concept of death than is acceptable today (Koselleck 1997, 333).

The main implication of individual and equal suffrage lies in the principle that it is impossible to transfer one's own experiences and opinions to any other person. It is impossible for entirely unproblematic 'we'-relationships to ever exist between two individuals. Any reference to the existence of a political 'inheritance' in families, relatives, localities, nations, religions and so on is simultaneously an affirmation of a dependency that is incompatible with the principle of 'one person, one vote'. According to a nineteenth-century formula, 'A statesman thinks about the next generations, a politician thinks about the next elections' (see, for example, Tange 2000, 38). Democratization, as defined in terms of individual and equal suffrage, marks the transition to the era of politicians. 'A statesman is a dead politician,' writes Henry Fairlie (1968, 15), for example. To combine these proverbs, we could claim that a statesman more easily legitimizes the sacrifice of individual lives, whereas politicians, who are dependent both on the electorate and the parliamentary majority, are more reluctant to send 'their' citizens off to war.

Hence, the individual lifetime of presently living persons serves as both the *longue durée* and the upper temporal limit for the politics of democratized regimes with individual and equal suffrage. Contemporary doomsday prophets who express concern over the upcoming majority of the retired people or even suggest that we implement a maximum age limit for voting clearly do not take seriously the individuality and equality of suffrage as a presupposition of democratic polities.

Even more crucial is the possibility to turn the fragile individual lifetime into a chance for the openness of political aims. Any given purpose or task, including the appeal to the 'common good' or 'reason of the state', may thus appear as *a priori* suspicious, because they are outside the range of the deciding power of individuals to choose their own aims. Political goals are not given or inherited, but are inherently contingent and subject to the conflict, debate and choices surrounding the shifting situations.

The individualization of politics can be seen, for example, in the decline of clientele voting. Instead of 'being', for instance, a life-long Social Democrat, voters tend to have more complex voting biographies, in which every election poses a new challenge to their 'political identity'. In each and every election, voters not only choose their candidate and party, but also regenerate themselves as political agents. Indeed, the criterion of the individual lifetime allows us to broaden the genre of political biographies to include the political narratives on the lives of any citizen as an occasional politician. A political biography allows us to analyze the links between the events in voters' personal lives, the intellectual turns they take, their mode of encountering world events and their shifting choices in various elections and assemblies.

The individual and equal basis of suffrage also supports the growing acceptance of the ever more diversified individual decisions citizens make about their lifestyle. There is, however, no guarantee that even democratic majorities won't severely limit the chances to choose highly individualized lifestyles. The Weberian figure of the occasional politician may thus be complemented with the professional politician of one's own life, which appears necessary for those whose choices are easily threatened by conformist majorities – in other words, in situations in which the everyday decisions concerning food, clothes, habitation, sexuality, travel and so on are all experienced as contingent, as politicized (see, for example, Greven 2001, Palonen 2003). In the present situation, particularly those individuals who make conscious and contested choices in their 'private' life develop an attitude towards their choices that resembles that of professional politicians in the parliamentary arena.

The Politics of Momentum

Momentum and the time-span are mirror images with regard to political intervals. Both of them refer to a dual temporality that connects the moment of rupture with that of the duration. Momentum alludes to the past instant of rupture, whereas time-span is always a future rupture. Still, the parallel between them is not complete, and the historical uses of these two types of interval of time appear to be quite different. Because of this, momentum and time-span should be dealt with separately.

John Pocock's *The Machiavellian Moment* (1975) offers us a paradigm for dealing with an event in political thought and agency which combines a rupture and the follow-up period in a specific momentum. For Pocock, Machiavelli's role in the genre of political thought is neither unique nor represents a simple turning point that was followed by later thinkers. Rather, momentum refers to a mode of thinking for which the Machiavellian rupture, which accepts the contingency of a republic, would later serve as a point of reference for a number of authors in various contexts which might not initially appear to have much in common with Machiavelli's. The reference to momentum is the result of a rhetorical effort by these authors to establish degrees of convincing similarity – either in their own eyes or those of the interpreter.

In Weberian terms, a momentum is an event which opens up of new and distinct chances that do not remain – unlike in the unique *kairos* – momentary, but which can be prolonged for a certain period – or even reactivated later – even if the initial instance of rupture has passed. Sooner or later, however, the critical impulse of the momentum fades, and the chances involved in it are exhausted. The political question thus frequently centers on whether a past momentum still retains its vigor, or whether it has been lost.

There are no criteria dictating the kind of event that can become a momentum. As illustrated in Sartre's formal narrative of *Critique de la raison dialectique*, the momentum might be a rare and extraordinary event, such as the capture of the Bastille during the French Revolution, which has retained the proverbial character required of a paradigm. In this sense, historically memorable calendar dates are good candidates for becoming momentums, although they also might signify the end of one, as the 'Prague August' (1968) did for the 'Bolshevik momentum'. It is always possible to evoke an old momentum or even to reactivate a lost one, as is illustrated by Benjamin's (1940 [1980]) metaphor of a tiger jump to old Rome during the French Revolution.

The origins of democratization in revolutionary constitutional reform may serve as a kind of primary momentum which is more significant in some contexts than in others. The US Constitution is a paradigm example of an initial momentum to which US political debates continue to refer to this day. More mundane recurrent events, such as elections and governmental changes, are, however, of equal value, although one can never be sure whether or not they will ultimately come to be judged as examples of a crucial momentum. The risk of losing future elections is an ever-present and enduring aspect of the everyday experience of politicians.

A momentum thus consists of a rhetorical combination of both a rupture and the period which follows it. The element of continuity in a momentum is, however, neither that of an unbroken line nor that of an ongoing process, but rather the continuous possibility to evoke the momentum during the subsequent period. A momentum always has a distinct beginning, but no definite point of termination. The political force of the momentum is subjected to a process of erosion from the beginnings, and it is impossible to pinpoint when it is ultimately lost. We can imagine a number of different forms that the end of a momentum might take, such as marginalization, routinization, normalization and integration with opposite forms of momentum (see Palonen 1992). The last example also indicates that political agents do not usually operate just with one past momentum, but that any number of historical references might serve as potential momentum for the analysis of what can be done in the current situation.

A re-actualization of a lost momentum is also conceivable when the possibility for the establishment of a rhetorically plausible parallel with a past momentum exists. Even then, however, the question remains whether such a connection is plausible in a political situation. A past electoral victory that was inconsequential in its original context may serve as an exemplary model in a later electoral campaign, although it still hardly deserves to be referred to as a momentum in the broader sense of the word.

The Politics of Time-span

The politics of time-span differs from the strictly opportunistic endeavor to prepare oneself to utilize any future occasion for change. The temporary character of politics and the principle of alternation are incarnated in the setting of deadlines that cannot simply be ignored or overcome. Politically crucial deadlines are based on the decision to control the politics of parliaments, governments and individual MPs at regular intervals. Focusing on the 'next elections' implies an obvious possible deadline for parliaments, governments and policies. The success of government or the praise it receives from abroad is inconsequential if the voters decide to overthrow its parliamentary majority. Although even certain West European parties have dominated the governments in their countries for decades, every election marks a deadline for them, or, from the reverse perspective, a chance to overthrow them.

The future time for politics is a deadline in the literal sense of its marking a terminal point for the incumbent political agents, which cannot in practice be suspended or changed. Simultaneously, it – like the individual lifetime – marks a definite horizon of chances. Until the deadline, political agents have distinct and temporary power shares with which to make certain changes, and they cease to exist once the deadline has passed. It is within this context that a governmental programme is accepted for an electoral term, a budget for a year, and so on. Using the deadline as an opportunity requires the concretization of the available choices by setting priorities regarding the changes one intends to implement prior to the passing of the deadline. Without the existence of a definite deadline, many such intended reforms would never be realized.

The governmental paradigm of politics strongly favors a coordinated and internally organized policy, which is something that oppositional parties are seldom able to construct. Under strong parliaments, however, there is good reason to practice, when facing a deadline, a more opportunistic style of politics, shrewdly utilizing the changing situations and shifting constellations as occasions for change. The reorganization of the priorities and significance of the moves one plans to make on the basis of the (assumed) policies of one's adversaries is essential in the politics of both governments and parliamentary oppositions.

Similarly to momentum, the orientation towards acting prior to the passing of a future deadline cannot be implemented as a consistent policy line. When the aim is to actualize the available chances in the available time, a number of questions arise regarding the assessment of their urgency, their degree of realizability in the context of the specific audience, their compatibility with each other, the possibility to make deals with the opposition, or their popularity in the electorate. Not only do the measures have their own temporal implications, but their interrelationships also vary according to the timing, rhythms, tempi and so on. As such, the deadline must be considered part of the internal temporal succession and taken into consideration when determining the agenda of the programme to be realized prior to a given deadline.

The ranking of the policies and situations depends on the deadline. The crucial opposition lies between unique and recurrent deadlines. When it can be assumed that there will always be next elections, a candidate or a party may survive a defeat in the upcoming elections, which means that a temporary electoral setback may not be decisive. None the less, a number of crucial agents and their projects will never get a second chance: some reforms mark a *fait accompli* which has already altered the political constellation. The political styles of acting in anticipation of a deadline may thus appear as highly distinct, depending on whether they take place while waiting for a second chance or in what we might refer to as a 'now or never' situation. The first alternative corresponds to the Weberian slow drill in slow and steady preparation for breaking through at the next occasion, whereas the 'now or never' style may require taking high risks and having to face major hurdles and challenges as a result of regarding the occasion as a unique one.

Learning to play with deadlines and to turn them into opportunities that are realizable within a limited period is a necessary aspect of the politician's competence in parliamentary democracies. When the time before a deadline is scarce, politicians are obliged to learn how to organize and subdivide it, how to prioritize the items on the agenda, how to allocate different temporal shares of power to different parts of the policy, and so on. The crucial point in politics is to be more competent than one's adversaries in terms of playing with deadlines.

The Politics of the Calendar

We can detect numerous markings of political time, such as anniversaries of people's personal and political milestones, such as the voluntary and involuntary ends of their careers, or occasions of personal remembrance, which together form the political calendar. Signs of both the extraordinary and ordinary forms of political momentum are visible either as publicly celebrated events or as more subtle references to the memories of the insiders.

For the politics of the calendar, all of the extraordinary items have to be related to the ordinary ones. The temporal units must be turned into items on the agenda, to be dealt with and distributed according to their succession and weight. Quite exceptionally, Walter Benjamin realized that in democratized parliamentary politics, not only does everything depend on timing, but the temporal succession of items on the agenda has become the organizing principle of political activity as such. Politicians live according to the items on their calendars: 'Nur in Terminen rechnet der wahre Politiker' (Benjamin 1928 [1988], 77). In the organization of one's own political activity, the question of *when* to act has gained priority over the questions of *how*, *who* and *what* as regards the determination of the agenda.

This loss of the priority of substantial questions over procedural ones, or the resignation to the fact that the agenda is dictated by the external and alienating power of the calendar, is frequently lamented. Both accusations are fueled by the misunderstanding of the temporalities of the parliamentary style of politics.

The parliamentary style of politics is based on the rotation of speeches for and against, concerning specific items on the agenda and their succession, both of which allow for the rhetorical actualization of opposing points of view. This also indicates the priority of the procedure over the content of the items to be discussed, illustrating the decisive role of the play with time. No content is so crucial or fatal that it would allow for the suspension of the procedure, for example that of the time limits applied to the various readings of a bill. In exceptional cases, however, certain suspensions may be applied by the parliament in the proper procedural order. The calendar paradigm leaves time for reflection and reconsideration as a crucial aspect of the calendar of parliamentary politics. The procedures themselves may be debated, but a relatively stable procedure that the speakers and the parliamentary officials keenly observe also enables them to use it to the best of their advantage (see Pierre 1887).

The procedural character of parliamentary politics thus provides special chances for intervention and debate. The procedure offers the MPs regular occasions upon which to affirm their own profiles if they are able to locate their points under the category of the items to be discussed or manage to get their favorite items on to the parliamentary agenda. Only those who are competent at playing with the agenda have the opportunity to direct parliamentary attention to the speeches which interrupt the ordinary lapse of time, and thus – to a certain degree and for a certain time – transcend the calendar requirements which exist in the parliament. Instead of protesting against the calendar, it is much more beneficial to parliamentarians to use it in order to highlight the persuasive force of their speeches.

It is here that we encounter an interesting link between democratization and the changing temporal requirements in parliamentary rhetoric. In eighteenth-century Britain, parliamentary eloquence was an art which had been cultivated by quite few master speakers in the face of the majority of silent MPs. One central aspect of the process of democratization was the obligation of every MP to speak, to intervene personally in parliamentary politics (see Curzon 1913). This both reduced the time allowed for speeches and set new criteria for speaking in democratized parliaments. It became necessary to relate the speeches to the debates at hand, to rely increasingly on spontaneity, improvisation, replies to the previous speakers, and even interruptions. This shift from learned orations towards lively debates was also a part of the calendarization of the more democratized parliaments (see Cormenin 1844 [2000], 39). Gladstone's above-quoted reference to the 'mood of the moment' may be seen as an early insight into the strong present-orientation of parliamentary speaking, which has been radicalized over the course of the democratization of parliaments.

Before the First World War, disputes about the agenda itself did not play a decisive role in parliamentary politics. The items on the agenda, their succession and relative weight were determined by the speakers, parliamentary officials or government, occasionally also in accordance with the opposition. Unlike the discussion of single items, no major debate surrounding the procedure of setting the agenda has been conducted, although political controversies have increasingly shifted from answers to questions, from the content of the items to their place on the agenda. One of the chances to activate the parliamentary style of politics lies in extending the application and systematization of the procedure of speaking for and against to the practices of agenda setting.

Democratization as a Rhetorical Re-description of Political Time

Democratized parliamentary politics operates with time-intensive procedures and practices. The temporal aspects of the opportunities, limits, resources and instruments of politics are indispensable components of the political constellation.

The individual lifetime, the temporal interval (with momentum and time-span as its two opposite angles) and the calendar refer to the temporal layers with which the political agents in democratized parliamentary regimes are required to operate. They also simultaneously represent various combinations of the aspects of rupture and duration. The individual lifetime alludes to the duration of the available chances as experienced by the agents. The adoption of the individual lifetime as a criterion also indicates a break with the actions of previous agents that creates new opportunities for those introducing the rupture. Both momentum and time-span refer to the possibility of the combination of the point of rupture and the subsequent or preceding period constituted by this breaking point. The politics of the calendar combines the play with the succession of discrete items with their inherent singularity, each of them serving as a chance to interrupt the routine time-lapse for a moment, particularly in the mode of speaking for and against. In a sense, succession and interruption refer to two different kinds of rupture, both of which may be positioned along a line of relative continuity.

The distinctly political time can be most obviously detected in various occasions and their mutual relationships, as opposed to the experiences of exhaustion and boredom resulting from repetition. The relative continuity of democratized parliamentary regimes is primarily due to the systematized recurrence of certain types of occasions for change, which are manifested in both the calendar and its intervals, and for which the individual lifetime serves as both a limitation and horizon for the agents. Occasions always require both the actualization of chances and the assessment of their relative significance in relation to other occasions. In this sense, in addition to the question of when to act, the question of how long to adhere to a particular calendar datum, to a distinct momentum or a specific future deadline instead of choosing other references for action also arises.

The actualization of various layers of political time and the interrelationships between them serves as a heuristic tool not only for the political agents themselves, but also for those who study democratized politics. The rhetoric of political times offers us a perspective in the analysis of the history of the formation of and changes in parliamentary democratic regimes. Political competence is highly dependent on the assessment, adjustment and balancing of the temporal layers of a given situation and the deliberation over the corresponding modes of acting politically.

To sum up, the democratization of politics signifies a rhetorical break with the old temporal order. Individual and equal suffrage, alternation in government and the parliamentary style of speaking *pro et contra* all allude to two different moves of rhetorical re-description (in the sense of Skinner 1996, Ch. 4), which deserve to be differentiated from one another.

One concerns the weight of time as a political instance, namely the legitimization of the transference of the temporal aspect from the background to the foreground, the metamorphosis of time into an operative medium of politics. The second move refers to a revaluation of timeliness over timelessness, as well as of short over long time, both of which serve as constitutive conditions of the procedures and practices of parliamentary and democratic politics. Democratization thus marks an acceptance of the fragility of political rule, and a willingness to play with it.

References

Aronson, R. and van den Hoven, A. (eds) (1991), *Sartre Alive* (Detroit, MI: Wayne State University Press).

Benjamin, W. (1928 [1988]), *Einbahnstrasse* (Frankfurt am Main: Suhrkamp).

—— (1940 [1980]), 'Über den Begriff der Geschichte', in *Illuminationen* (Frankfurt am Main: Suhrkamp).

Cormenin, L.-M. [Timon] (1844 [2000]), *Le livre des orateurs* (Geneva: Slatkine).

Curzon, G. (1913), *Modern Parliamentary Eloquence* (London: Macmillan).

Fairlie, H. (1968), *The Life of Politics* (London: Methuen).

Gladstone, W.E. (1838 [1953]), 'Public Speaking', *The Quarterly Journal of Speech* 39, 266–72.

Greven, M.T. (2001), 'Dimensions of Politics: A Critique of the Common One-dimensional Concept of Politics', *Finnish Yearbook of Political Thought* 5, 89–112.

Koselleck, R. (1979), *Vergangene Zukunft. Zur Theorie geschichtlicher Zeiten* (Frankfurt am Main: Suhrkamp).

—— (1980), '"Fortschritt" und "Niedergang" – Nachtrag zur Geschichte zweier Begriffe', in Koselleck and Widmer (eds), *Niedergang* (Stuttgart: Klett-Cotta).

—— (1997), 'Vom Sinn und Unsinn der Geschichte', *Merkur* 51, 319–34.

—— (2000), *Zeitschichten. Studien zur Historik* (Frankfurt am Main: Suhrkamp).

—— and Widmer, P. (eds) (1980), *Niedergang* (Stuttgart: Klett-Cotta).

—— et al. (2003), 'Zeit, Zeitlichkeit und Politik. Sperrige Reflexionen. Reinhart Koselleck im Gespräch mit Wolf-Dieter Narr und Kari Palonen', in Kurunmäki and Palonen (eds), *Zeit, Geschichte und Politik/Time, History and Politics* (Jyvaskyla: Jyvaskyla Studies in Education, Psychology and Social Research).

Kurunmäki, J. and Palonen, K. (eds) (2003), *Zeit, Geschichte und Politik/Time, History and Politics* (Jyvaskyla: Jyvaskyla Studies in Education, Psychology and Social Research).

Macmillan, H. (1975), *The Past Masters: Politics and Politicians, 1906–1939* (London: Macmillan).

Ostrogorski, M. (1903 [1993]), *La démocratie et les partis politiques* (Paris: Fayard).

Palonen, K. (1992), *Politik als Vereitelung. Die Politikkonzeption in Jean-Paul Sartres 'Critique de la raison dialectique'* (Münster: Westfälisches Dampfboot).

—— (2003), 'Four Times of Politics', *Alternatives* 28:2, 171–86.

—— (2004a), *Die Entzauberung der Begriffe. Das Umschreiben der politischen Begriffe bei Quentin Skinner und Reinhart Koselleck* (Münster: Lit).

—— (2004b), 'Parliamentarism: A Politics of Temporal and Rhetorical Distances', *Österreichische Zeitschrift für Geschichtswissenschaft* 15, 111–26.

Perelman, Ch. and Olbrechts-Tyteca, L. (1958 [1983]), *Traité de l'argumentation. La nouvelle rhétorique* (Brussels: Editions de l'Université de Bruxelles).

Pierre, E. (1887), *De la procédure parlementaire. Etude sur le mécanisme intérieur du pouvoir législatif* (Paris: Maison Quantin).

Pocock, J.G.A. (1975), *The Machiavellian Moment: Florentine Political Thought and the Atlantic Republican Tradition* (Princeton, NJ: Princeton University Press).

Redlich, J. (1905), *Recht und Technik des englischen Parlamentarismus* (Leipzig: Duncker & Humblot).

Rosanvallon, P. (1992), *Le sacre du citoyen. Histoire du suffrage universel en France* (Paris: Gallimard).

—— (2000), *La démocracie inachevée* (Paris: Gallimard).

—— (2003), *Pour une histoire conceptuelle du politique* (Paris: Seuil).

Sartre, J.-P. (1960 [1985]), *Critique de la raison dialectique* (Paris: Gallimard).

—— (1965 [1991]), 'Kennedy and West Virginia', trans. Elisabeth Bowman, in Aronson and van den Hoven (eds), *Sartre Alive* (Detroit, MI: Wayne State University Press).

Skinner, Q. (1996), *Reason and Rhetoric in the Philosophy of Hobbes* (Cambridge: Cambridge University Press).

—— (2002), *Visions of Politics*, vols 1–3 (Cambridge: Cambridge University Press).

Tange, E.G. (ed.) (2000), *Zitatenschatz zur Politik* (Frankfurt: Eichborn).

Weber, M. (1904), 'Die "Objektivität" sozialwissenschaftlicher und sozialpolitischer Erkenntnis', *Archiv für Sozialwissenchaft und Sozialpolitik* 1, 23–87.

—— (1917a [1988]), 'Das preussische Wahlrecht', in *Max-Weber-Studienausgabe* 1:15 (Tübingen: Mohr).

—— (1917b [1988]), 'Wahlrecht und Demokratie in Deutschland', in *Max-Weber-Studienausgabe* 1:15 (Tübingen: Mohr).

—— (1919 [1994]), 'Politik als Beruf', in *Max-Weber-Studienausgabe* 1:17 (Tübingen: Mohr).

—— (1922 [1980]), *Wirtschaft und Gesellschaft* (Tübingen: Mohr).

Further Reading

Anderson, M.L. (2000), *Practicing Democracy: Elections and Political Culture in Imperial Germany* (Princeton, NJ: Princeton University Press).

Ankersmit, F. (2002), *Political Representation* (Stanford, CA: Stanford University Press).

Angenot, M. (2003), *La démocratie, c'est le mal* (Laval: Les Presses de l'Université Laval).

Hirschman, A.O. (1991), *The Rhetoric of Reaction: Perversity, Futility, Jeopardy* (Cambridge, MA: The Belknap Press of Harvard University Press).

Llanque, M. (2000), *Demokratisches Denken im Krieg. Die deutsche Debatte im Ersten Weltkrieg* (Berlin: Akademie).

Meisel, J.S. (2001), *Public Speech and the Culture of Public Life in the Age of Gladstone* (New York: Columbia University Press).

Mergel, T. (2002) *Parlamentarische Kultur in der Weimarer Republik. Politische Kommunikation, symbolische Politik und Öffentlichkeit im Reichstag* (Düsseldorf: Droste).

Palonen, K. (2006), *The Struggle with Time: A Conceptual History of 'Politics' as an Activity* (Münster: Lit).

Riescher, G. (1994), *Zeit und Politik* (Baden-Baden: Nomos).

Steinmetz, W. (1993), *Das Sagbare und Machbare. Zum Wandel politischer Handlugnsspieräume England 1780–1867* (Stuttgart: Klett-Cotta).

Tomkins, A. (2005), *Our Republican Constitution* (Oxford: Hart).

Turkka, T. (2007), *The Origins of Parliamentarism: A Study of Sandys' Motion* (Baden-Baden: Nomos).

Urbinati, N. (2006), *Representative Democracy: Principles and Genealogy* (Chicago, IL: University of Chicago Press).

Democratization and the Instrumentalization of the Past

Irène Herrmann

Democracy's present revived popularity comes, among other things, from its supposed capacity to reflect each and everyone's opinion. Indeed, it is a governmental system that encourages expression and dialog, whether electoral or parliamentary. If we consider these different aspects, democracy was not truly experimented with until the end of the eighteenth century, and it took more than two hundred years for it to become the undisputed Western, or even global, model it is today. Compared with other types of administration of the *res publica*, democracy is a recent creation. Given its 'youth' and, considering the importance it confers to discourse, one can legitimately attempt to examine the place of history in democracy-promoting rhetoric.

This particular matter is part of the vast topic of the political uses of the past. This field of research, in its time, was affected, if not actually initiated, by *The Invention of Tradition*, a founding book underlining not only the novelty of tradition, but also the need for its creation in periods of rapid changes (Hobsbawm and Ranger 1983, 1–8 and *passim*). In the introduction, Eric Hobsbawm makes it clear that these very traditions 'normally attempt to establish continuity with a suitable historic past' (Hobsbawm and Ranger 1983, 1) opportunely adapted for the occasion (Hobsbawm and Ranger 1983, 4). His statements brought about reflections on the social or political role of the official narrative of the past.[1] Some chose to investigate the interactions between the more or less mythical narration of the origins, and the justification, or even (de)construction, of the national (Nora 1984–94; Andrieu, Lavabre and Tartakowski 2006). Others explored the different modes of instrumentalization to which history was submitted in the handling of periods of crisis or within the functioning of totalitarian regimes (Hartog and Revel 2001). Finally, and more importantly, a number of historians have questioned their own influence in the partisan manipulation of their knowledge (Letourneau 2000; Iggers 2000).

---

1   For historical reasons, this reflection had already been started in Germany, where it was conceptualized in terms of *Geschichtsbewusstsein* (K.E. Jeismann), giving rise to a *Geschichtskultur* (J. Rüsen), including a *Geschichtspolitik* (E. Wolfrum).

But in spite of the generality of the phenomenon, in Scandinavian countries especially, researchers have seldom looked into the exploitation, and more rarely yet the reception, of past facts in the case of interiorizing the norms of self-discipline indispensable to the good functioning of any democratic regime (Macedo 1990). In other words, little has been said of the importance of the collective narrative of the past for the formation of a civic conscience, meaning the elaboration of a sense of responsibility in Hans Jonas' acceptation, 'by virtue of which I feel responsible, not in first place for my conduct and its consequences but for the *matter* that has claim on my actions' (Jonas 1984, 92), and which would apply, precisely, to the *res publica*. How the understanding of past, experienced or reported facts may forge the awareness and then the political attitudes of individual self-regulation thus remains a wide-open question (Weigl 2001).

The fact is that this specific conjunction of political aims and discursive means is difficult to uncover. Nevertheless, this configuration is clearly one which is offered by countries on the path to democratization, this being a time when a government, wanting to innovate by considerably broadening the base of popular rights, is tempted, like Quentin Skinner's 'innovating ideologist' (Skinner 1974), to call upon the assent and therefore (appropriate) participation of the citizens, and in parallel, to summon the past in such a delicate procedure. In this respect, it seemed sensible to analyze as diverse cases possible, in the hope that the discovery of recurrences in totally dissimilar examples would allow a better grasp of the global character of the examined phenomenon. And, in terms of democratization, it seemed difficult to consider cases less similar than those of 1798–1813 Switzerland and 1993–2003 Russia.

Switzerland

Democracy?

On the eve of the invasion of the French Revolutionary troops in 1798, the confederate alliance and its constituent institutions formed a sort of archaic residue of medieval systems of government. At the time, the Swiss entity was a constellation of sovereign cantons, bound to one another by various, but ultimately not very compelling, treaties. The impression of a coherent ensemble is due to the homogeneity of the different state systems (de Capitani 1986). In fact, preserved from the annexationist drives of surrounding autocracies for strategic reasons, the Helvetian body kept the power structures characteristic of 'freed cities' or territories under direct imperial rule. And if, over the centuries, the nature of political decision-making diverged more and more from proto-democracy, certain procedures persisted which provided the Helvetians with the feeling of enjoying rights unparalleled in Europe – an illusion powerfully entertained by an age-old tradition in historiography which was strengthened in the eighteenth century. Better yet, the learned elite of the Enlightenment started using this version of the past to create a sense of identity which up to then had been almost non-existent.

By doing so, they tended to promote the association of medieval privileges and the notion of freedom, so much flaunted by their French counterparts (Walter 2005).

It is therefore not surprising that the enlightened minds in Paris also started circulating an embellished version of the Swiss political systems, discerning in them the possibility of a realization of the egalitarian precepts they advocated.[2] Nor is it surprising that the revolutionaries inspired by their writings thought that with Switzerland, they had found an ideal place to institutionalize their ideological principles.[3] In fact, it was under their patronage that the first Constitution of Switzerland, which had become one and indivisible, was drafted. Enforced from 12 April 1798 onwards, this text not only put an end to the federalist dispersion of the Helvetian entity, but also rooted the core of democratic notions in the new state's political functioning. It thus declared the inalienable freedom of the individual.[4]

Likewise, it abolished all judicial distinctions among citizens (Arlettaz 2005). Moreover, it stipulated that sovereignty lay in the people, whose male, adult and Swiss representatives enjoyed a limited, although incontestable, right to vote. Thereafter, the population deliberated on the approval of the Constitution and on the election of representatives at a national level. In fact, and for the first time in its history, the Helvetian entity was endowed with a real parliament, whose lower chamber was composed of some 150 deputies. Following a series of *coups d'état*, changes were made which reduced the body of representatives and modified its socio-political composition. Initially constituted of young republicans from the bourgeoisie, the country's higher authorities returned imperceptibly under the control of the aristocracy. The revolutionary parenthesis seemed definitely closed when, on 19 February 1803, Bonaparte imposed the acceptance of a Mediation Act on Switzerland, leaving to the cantons the responsibility for their internal organization.

The former political elites, firmly reinstated at the head of the cantons, considered the ills they had suffered to be the consequence of revolutionary aspirations whose resurgence had to be avoided at all costs. The fact was that this process was both made easier and, simultaneously, obstructed by Napoleon. Actually, while he encouraged the return to traditional structures of power, entailing the disappearance of any parliamentary organ at a national level, he preserved certain equality among the cantons and among citizens. Be that as it may, popular participation to political decision-making was limited by both qualitative and quantitative measures. In the

---

2   At the end of the eighteenth century, the cliché of a free and happy Switzerland was already so widespread that it was often the object of caricatures (Reichler and Ruffieux 1998).

3   The 'primitive' cantons, still governed by a system of direct democracy, were considered as 'le berceau de la liberté, comme le pays de Guillaume Tell, aux institutions sacrées jusque-là préservées' ('the cradle of freedom, William Tell's country, whose sacred institutions had been preserved up to that moment') (Berchtold 2004, 30ff.).

4   'La liberté naturelle de l'homme est inaliénable; elle n'est restreinte que par la liberté d'autrui et des vues légalement constatées d'un avantage général nécessaire' (art. 5, al. 1) ('The natural freedom of the individual is inalienable; it is restricted only by the freedom of others and of entities legally found to be of general necessary advantage').

urban cantons, the right to vote was limited according to social criteria, and the elections themselves were only meant to designate the legislative authorities, in a procedure often moderated by balloting or indirect suffrage. In rural states, in spite of the official restoration of a certain equality through direct democracy, the true power remained in the hands of a few families, even in cantons with *Landsgemeinde* (Dufour and Monnier 2003; Andrey and Czouz-Tornare 2003). In order to impose this political orientation, non-compliant with Napoleon's official *desiderata*, the reactionary magistrates curiously resorted to a historical rhetoric quite comparable to that used by their predecessors.

History?

From 1798 to 1813, the Swiss political elite used to frequently refer to the past. Most public speeches at the very least mentioned the 'Fathers of the homeland' when the essential part of the argument did not rest upon an episode or a remarkable figure of the Helvetian saga. Such profusion brings to the fore certain dynamics at the quantitative as well as qualitative levels. Indeed, we clearly observe that the historical rhetoric stopped when the time came for action, as if history lost its relevance when the present became animated. The invasion of foreign troops or the episodes of chaos, or even internal conflict, did not leave time to reflect on past influences. However, periods of calm and, even more, oncoming danger gave rise to a specific rhetoric which eagerly drew on the profusion of past-time deeds and misdeeds. That the 'French era' was more abounding in threats than real dangers also contributes to explaining why the celebration of the past was so important at that time (Strickler 1886–1966).

The secret of such discursive profusion also resided in the accessibility of the erudite account of the Helvetian origins. There is nothing anecdotal in this finding, given the extent to which the history of Switzerland is, in itself, a narrative account whose linearity is difficult to establish. By means of omissions, exaggerations and other literary measures, it presupposes combining the destinies of some 15 different and often hostile cantons into one single path.[5] The problem was solved by focusing, on the one hand, on the report of the origins of the Confederation, and on the other, by unwinding an axiological *Leitmotiv*, represented by the hypothetical aspiration to independence which supposedly incited all the future Helvetians to unite and form Switzerland.

Drawn up at the end of the Middle Ages, this argumentative outline underwent a considerable development during the Enlightenment. At first, researchers provided this account with a scientific gloss, at times acquired in the archives and through a critical reading of the sources. Better yet, they transformed its ideological message, by turning the development of Switzerland into a constant progression towards freedom. Finally, this evolution was carried through by extremely talented men, capable of moving their readers. Caspar Lavaters's *Schweizerlieder*, and then, foremost, the five volumes of Jean Müller's *Geschichte schweizerischer Eidgenossenschaft*

---

5   A total of 13 Cantons until 1803, then 19 from that date on, and 22 since 1814.

(1786–1808) (Walter 2005), inspired a host of political leaders whose most prominent representatives personally produced historical works. If the patriots Peter Ochs, Albert Stapfer and Frédéric-César de Laharpe wrote works which they believed to be erudite (Schenk 1998), it is not surprising that they sprinkled their public allocutions with references to the past – and that the conservatives retorted in the same tone.

In fact, the political use of the past was not the prerogative of a single party, but recurred alternatively, or even simultaneously, among the revolutionary partisans of a French-style democracy as well as among the counter-revolutionaries willing to maintain the traditional system of popular participation. The former, brought to power thanks to the armies of the Directory, carried out the offensive by massively resorting to an argumentation based on the past. The operation was aimed at putting a certain distance between them and the French, who rejected history, by pointing out that the advocated political overthrow was deeply and locally rooted. Here, the evocation of the origins was classically instrumental in proving and claiming ownership of an (ideological) good which had been confiscated for a long time, thus suggesting, in a timid but more modern way, the notion of progress. Therefore, the patriots legitimized their action by presenting the change of regime as the return to the days when the Swiss were free (Strickler 1886–1966, vol. III, 60). Moreover, in order to justify their centralizing project for the country, they stated that the Helvetians were united in this supreme aspiration, and that they belonged, even unconsciously, to a single people whose natural boundaries the present nation had merely reclaimed (Strickler 1886–1966, vol. IV, 115–16). According to this narrative, this golden age had taken place before the roman conquest; it had been momentarily recovered thanks to the revolution (*sic*) brought about by William Tell, and now needed to be wholly retrieved thanks to the contemporary revolution. Switzerland could hence become a universal model due to the precociousness of the indigenous revolutionary phenomenon (de la Harpe 1864).

This conception of the revolution and of its legitimizing antiquity also required the people to strive to live up to the heroes of Helvetian freedom. This enterprise was encouraged by means of at least two complementary discursive procedures. On the one hand, its effect was not so much solicited as affirmed. In other words, the Swiss were not being told that they *needed* to prove worthy of the 'Fathers of the Homeland', but that they already *were*. It was a cunning device, given that people are all the more inclined to adopt a line of conduct if they are supposed to have already been observing it for some time (Joule and Beauvois 2004). On the other hand, the political elite were careful to expound this truth through the mediation of emblematical Helvetian figures. At the beginning of the period which is considered here – because of the French influence – the figure most likely to achieve the call for unity of the Swiss and their acceptance of the new system of government was William Tell. Eventually, the task was transferred to Saint Nicolas of Flüe, a hermit who in the fifteenth century distinguished himself for his conciliatory abilities (Strickler 1886–1966, vol. II, 1081ff.). This evocation promptly established its influence due to its great usefulness. Indeed, it did not recall the invader, and effectively countered the Catholic conservatives whose criticisms were becoming increasingly virulent – and historical.

Undoubtedly, the opponents of the revolutionary regime did not wait long to reinforce their case with the help of historical arguments. One of their advocates, Jean-Jacques Mallet-du Pan from Geneva, had actually written an *Essai historique sur la destruction de la Ligue et de la liberté helvétique* as early as 1798, summarizing their viewpoint on the question. The fact remains that both for institutional and rhetorical reasons, it was not until *c*. 1800 that this historical discourse was heard at the national level. On the one hand, it was at that time that the opponents of the French system grasped the power that, inch by inch, following *coups d'état* and internal crises, they ultimately secured in 1803.[6] On the other hand, this was the interval needed by the conservatives to formulate a coherent vision of the past which distinguished itself in a fundamental way from that of their rivals.

As a matter of fact, the conception of the past, as seen in the reactionaries' writings, was at the same time contrary and similar to that of the patriots. Proceeding less from a progressive than from a Ciceronian concept of history, they presented the revolution as the incarnation of absolute evil, which marked a novel and eminently detrimental break in the Helvetian temporal and axiological substratum. In the cantons of the proto-democratic tradition, it was conceived as a rupture of the fine continuity established since William Tell. In the ancient patrician cantons, it was considered as an ill-fated disruption of a social organization favorable to all. Here again, and whatever the origin of the conservative discourse may have been, the citizens' effort was required to re-establish the order destroyed by the armies and the henchmen of the French outsider. By not imitating their powerful neighbor, the Helvetians could (once again) be an example of a small happy people, chosen by God. The means employed to provoke such commitment resembled those used by the partisans of change a few years before. The process rested upon injunction as well – that is, on the affirmation of a relationship between the nineteenth-century and fourteenth-century Swiss, implying a duty of family loyalty; finally, they also favored personification.[7]

Better yet, it can be noted that the gradual restriction of popular rights during the Helvetian Revolution, their suppression after Bonaparte's Mediation, and the external dangers threatening the country during these two periods conferred the same finality to the political discourse. Whatever the government in power, the effort for which the people were called upon through a fit of historical references

---

6   That is to say, until 1848; the sources examined allowing the statement of the continuity of historical reference in conservative discourse are the accounts of the federal assemblies, and more precisely, the speeches delivered at the opening of these assemblies, where the cantons' common politics was decided (Federal Archives: C/3–5; 29–39; 44; 296; 306; 311; 325; 327. C0/002–004).

7   On 27 December 1801, the authorities of Vevey (Canton of Vaud) complained about a wrongdoing which indicated their opponents' inventiveness and led them to a 'democratic use of personification', that is to say, by using an alleged letter from William Tell calling for the union of the Canton of Vaud with that of Berne (Strickler 1886–1966, vol. XI, 788).

was not to practice democracy with restraint, but to remain peaceful, and should the occasion arise, to sacrifice their own lives for a country protected by God.[8]

Reception?[9]

Like other European populations more or less brought into submission by the 'Ogre', the Swiss paid their tribute of deaths to the Napoleonic conquests. And yet, a proportion of the deaths accounted for during this violent period were also due to revolts against the authority (Simon 1998). We are led to believe by this situation that the Helvetian citizens did not feel particularly concerned by the calls for peace addressed to them. In fact, numerous uprisings are recorded, which for the most part aspired not to enforce, but to abolish revolutionary values. That being said, one may be led to infer that the historical rhetoric drawn on throughout this period had not in the least touched those it was supposed to permeate.

Actually, the opposite is observed. Petitions and other requests made to the different governments reveal a copious use of heroic examples from the past. This is easily explained to the extent that, in order to ensure at least minimum attention from the solicited power, one had better master its line of argument. True, these writings predominantly originated from the so-called primitive cantons, namely those reputed to have been the scene of the events celebrated in the Helvetian saga. They were also states where the proto-democratic practices had more or less persisted, which may allow us to presume that their citizens had fewer qualms about making their wishes known. The fact is that in the vast majority, these petitions relied on history in order to demand the return to the ancient order of things (Strickler1886–1966, vol. I, 291).

Under these conditions, recalling the past, even skillfully presented under the appropriate colours, was not enough to allow representative democracy to be implanted in Switzerland, but on the contrary, hindered its establishment in the country. The political uses of history probably only contributed superficially to such an evolution. Nevertheless, it is symptomatic that in 1848 – that is, fifty years after this first attempt – when the Helvetian radical leaders were to successfully set about the transformation of the country into an authentic democratic republic, they carefully avoided referring to the founding myths which had so inspired their predecessors.

At least two factors explain this generally disregarded phenomenon: undoubtedly, the concern not to recall the unitary period, but also the concern not to lay claim to the original heroes of the cantons opposed to the new regime, given

---

8   This takes place up to the end of the period considered; see, for instance, the Federal Archives: C0/004 Bd 3, Recès de la Diète ordinaire de 1812 à Bâle, *Discours de Son Excellence Monsieur le Landammann de la Suisse Monsieur Pierre Burckhardt, Bourgmestre du canton de Bâle, à l'ouverture de la Diète générale de la Confédération le 7ᵉ juin 1812*, Bâle, 1812, fo. 358.

9   According to the definition carried here, reception is assessed according to the public's abilities to, itself, make a political use of history and/or to observe the slogans conveyed by it.

extent to which this evocation threatened to lead to a perfectly counterproductive opposition to progress, or even to resistance (Herrmann 2006). And initially, this sagacious silence contributed to turning the confederation into a democracy which the Swiss considered as exemplary, until it fell out of this role because of, among other things, the turmoil created by the fall of the Soviet empire.

Russia

Democracy?

The collapse of the Soviet system has sometimes been conceptualized as a revolution (McFaul 2001). Regardless of how problematical such a characterization may appear, it calls parallels to mind which may be drawn between cases as different as those of Switzerland at the turn of the nineteenth century and Russia at the beginning of the twenty-first century. Indeed, in spite of the temporal and contextual distances separating them, they both underwent a radical change of political regime, and more broadly, of their understanding of the world. Moreover, they both saw this crucial turn as the outcome and the patent proof of a great internal weakness. Finally, and more importantly, in each of the cases studied, this overthrow came with a desire for democratization largely 'inspired' – if not imposed – by foreign countries.

The collapse of the USSR was, of course, essentially produced from within. Nevertheless, in the Cold War context, it could easily be interpreted as the tangible sign of the triumph of the capitalist side. In fact, as of the *coup d'état* in August 1991, a majority of the Soviet structures were abolished. The most drastic change certainly occurred in the economic field, where Boris Yeltsin, anxious to win the favour of the West, abruptly got rid of the communist system. This wish for a clean break from the past also became apparent on the political level, as no more than three years were needed to dismember the empire and dismantle the former power structures, and primarily, the once-omnipotent Communist Party of the Soviet Union.[10] A decisive step in this direction was made at the end of 1993, when the population voted massively in favour of a new constitution, creating a parliament supposed to represent the differences of opinion within the population: the Duma.

The new assembly adopted the name of the legislative body that the last Tsar, Nicolas II, was forced to establish after the 1905 revolution (Grankin 2001). Thus (re-)invented, the Lower Chamber of the Russian Parliament consisted of 450 deputies elected by universal suffrage for four years. Essentially, the members of parliament gather in the most diverse parties. Beyond this diversity, there is a certain regularity out of which four great ideological trends may be detected (Barygin 1999; Zotova 2001). The most exotic is, unquestionably, the populist movement, epitomized for many years by the impetuous Vladimir Zhirinovskij,

---

10   <www.cprf.ru/kpss/>, accessed 19 September 2006.

who dominated the parliament during the first legislature.[11] Strangely, these deputies wooing the far right were not that far apart from the communists who ruled the political arena from 1996 to 1999. These ostensible heirs of the Soviet ideology are generally presented as the opponents of a liberal democracy, advocating more or less clear intervention by the state, and which, as of 2004, no longer had representatives in parliament. In between these two groups are, traditionally, the centrists, whose miscellaneous congregation has, since 2000, given Vladimir Putin an overwhelming majority.[12]

Yet another factor contributing to such homogeneity is these politicians' background. Indeed, for social and generational reasons, the MPs are still mostly the product of an education, and even at times of careers, marked by communism (Rigby 1999). This situation favored, in many respects, the pacification of conflicts with a minimum of violence – conflicts which were and are liable to interfere with rapid change of the regime. Nevertheless, it required skillful handling of references to the past, as the goal was mainly to set oneself apart from the former system without disavowing one's own destiny – or that of one's fellow citizens.[13] And in fact, in spite of a persistent reputation according to which the members of the two chambers are essentially concerned with their personal interests, they are duty bound to please the electorate in order to hold their position. Consequently, and especially towards the end of their mandate, they are driven to take decisions or positions which they consider appropriate for their constituents (see Palonen, Chapter 9 in this volume). And while the Duma is not in possession of true decision-making power,[14] the references to the past scattered in parliamentary debates none the less reveal the relation to its history of post-Soviet society as a whole.

History?

Contrary to the practical confrontation with the past characteristic of the beginning of the Yeltsin era, or contrary to its symbolical treatment, which has been the concern of the Russian political class at the turn of the millennium (Smith 2002), the rhetorical use of history is a constant trait during the whole period considered here. Within this framework, one can simply state that the phenomenon becomes more extensive when national pride, rather than the nation itself, is affected (Herrmann 2004, 71–88).

---

11   <www.nupi.no/russland/elections/1993_state_duma_elections_Russia.htm>, accessed 19 September 2006.

12   On 7 December 2003, 68 per cent of the votes and 306 seats were given to Edinaja Rossija, Vladimir Putin's party, against the 11.56 per cent of the votes and 56 seats to the Communists; <www.st-petersbourg.org/gouv_ru/douma_2003.htm>, accessed 15 June 2006.

13   In 1996, more than 70 per cent of the deputies at the Duma and nearly 100 per cent of the federal government had been members of the Soviet Communist Party (Werning Riviera 2000, 419).

14   <www.gov.ru/main/konst/konst15.html>, accessed 15 June 2006.

History is, in fact, often summoned for reasons and within contexts which are hardly related to it. Actually, when the reference is precise, it is not scientifically proven. This was obvious under the Yeltsin administration, when the parliamentarians mentioned the different medieval entities as having experienced the early stages of the parliamentary, if not democratic, system (19 May 1999 session),[15] or when they called attention to the entirely liberal material prosperity that characterized the empire just prior to the First World War (16 October 2002 session, A.M. Fedulov). The purpose of the game was then to emphasize the precociousness of the political and economic phenomenon on Russian territory. By doing so, they sought to claim certain continuity, so that the institutional and economical experiments in contemporary Russia would be considered as a revival of an already attested, if not ancestral, practice. By doing so, the deputies partly avoided the fears to which innovations could give rise, and moreover, they justified their positions as well as their course of action. 'Historical truth' was of little importance (20 March 2002 session).

In any case, the evocation of the past generally remained vague, whether it took in an exceedingly vast period or was limited to the mentioning of History with a capital 'H' as a sort of absolute tinged with Marxism, providing the standard against which all human action could be judged (10 March 1999, I.D. Kobzon, or 20 February 2002, V.A. Lekareva). The vagueness that characterizes historically motivated arguments has two main causes. First of all, it is the result of the status of historical sciences in Russia. Under the communist regime, knowledge of the past was admittedly one of props of the power structure, which did not refrain from dictating the official account that the professionals were duty bound to compose. This situation brought about suspicions (Chechel' 2005, 41–56) which the general mediocrity of academic work under Yeltsin (Chervonnaja 2001, 695–715) was not able to clear up, in spite of the fact, and all the more that at present, Putin's administration shows great enthusiasm in controlling this discipline (Berelowitch 2003, 203–20; Sveshnikov 2004; Ferretti 2004).

And yet the vagueness of historical rhetoric stems less from scientific reasons than from the political efficiency expected to be earned from it. In a country with such a painful and conflicting past, where yesterday's enemies sit next to each other in the same parliamentary seats, it is important to exploit the emotional potentialities of past times, but without recalling their destructive abilities. For this reason, and furthermore, inasmuch as the reference to the past motivates decision-making less than it justifies it, the deputies only rarely start diatribes which aim to confront their colleagues with painful memories. The occasion for such antagonizing rhetoric only arises essentially in order to support real chamber skirmishes and to bring together the parties into presence, as was the case at the time of the dismissal measure

---

15   In the 19 May 1999 session, for instance, V.N. Lysenko (Democrat) said: 'It is here [in the medieval city of Novgorod] that democracy appeared in our state. It is actually here that the rudiments of parliamentarism were established ... and that federative relations were elaborated' (<www.akdi.ru/gd/PLEN_Z/1999/s19-05_v.htm>, accessed 15 February 2008).

advocated by the Communist Party against a declining Yeltsin in May 1999 (*Sbornik dokumentov*). However, according to the same logic, the glorification of the Russian past, and secondarily, the praise of the Russian nation constitute a performance to which politicians lend themselves much more readily. The exercise is flattering and considerably seductive when it is a matter of convincing opponents and voters. Nevertheless, strangely enough, the argument is not fail-safe, since anyone can claim that their stand inscribes itself in the continuity of Russian grandeur.

Unquestionably the argument centered on the notion of suffering provided the most striking rhetorical effectiveness (22 May 1998, S.A. Kovalev, and 24 December 1998, V.V. Zhirinovskij). A number of parliamentary debates turned into the historical overloading of sufferance. Some of these confrontations unfolded in the future perfect tense, the winner being the one who succeeded in proving that his opponent was preparing to inflict on the population an equivalent or even greater evil than that endured during the civil wars with which its history is bestrewn.[16] As a general rule, none the less, the winner of the debate is the one who successfully proves that he represents those citizens who suffered most in the past. In other words, he who made the greatest sacrifices (personally or vicariously) decides. Ever more exploited, this rhetoric has two main repercussions. First, it contributes to 'purifying' the status of the victim. It is as if the sufferings inflicted on the individual or on a group of individuals serve to clear and to absolve possible embezzlements, misdeeds or even crimes in which these persons would have been involved. Thus, a tempting and often attempted equivalence is made, turning every victim into an innocent. As anyone in Russia can legitimately consider themselves the holders of a painful family history, this process of getting rid of one's guilt through grief is a powerful vehicle of national cohesion.[17] Better yet, the parliamentary discourse tends to associate the account of the country's sufferings with the narration of its indisputable power. The result is often a sort of glorification of the victim, who, as such, may believe to have made a crucial contribution to the Russian greatness. Far from being anecdotal, this valuing of grief not only allows social homogenizing, but also, ultimately, the construction of a chronological continuity beyond the turmoil of transition.

This use developed essentially after 1995 – that is to say, from the celebration of the fiftieth anniversary of the victory over fascism onwards. Not only did the event lend itself to this sort of instrumentalization, it also created the opportunity for imperceptibly reintroducing Soviet history into the pool of examples exploitable by political discourse. Throughout Yeltsin's second presidency, this tendency strengthened to such an extent as to become the rule under his successor's mandate. True, Putin's ascent to power corresponded with a spectacular economic

---

16 In the 14 March 1997 session, V.A. Ryzhkov (Centrist) declared to his opponents: 'I ask you to think about the decision you are about to make. It would mean the return of these tragic events, when the country was on the verge of civil war. This decision would divide us between "whites" and "reds", those who are right and those who are not'; <www.akdi.ru/gd/PLEN_Z/1997/s14-03_d.htm>, accessed 15 February 2008.

17 An idea developed by Sergei Zhuravlev, on the occasion of the international conference 'Gulag, le peuple des zeks', Geneva, April 2004.

improvement and with an unquestionable revival of international prestige. The use of a rhetoric centered on the power of the USSR therefore no longer seemed insulting, but legitimate, and all the more accepted as it restored the Russians to their traditional destiny. Within this axiological scheme, they are supposed to have suffered, and to be still suffering, since this eminently passive action finds itself 'transitivized'[18] by the global importance of their country. Taken to the extreme, it is their role as victims, of which their history gives testimony, that gives this very history meaning.

Reception[19]

It is undoubtedly difficult to evaluate the impact of this rhetoric on the population, and even more delicate to draw conclusions on the country's possible democratization from it. Through surveys and private accounts, and thanks to the results of the elections during that period, it is nevertheless possible to get a sense of how the Russian people 'received' their deputies' historical message.

Thus, everything leads us to think that the victimization discourse was well received, seeing as it corresponded to a public tendency born in the wake of *Perestroika*. As of the end of the 1980s, *Glasnost* and its demands for publicity had been the occasion for a reappraisal of the Bolshevik period. There was then an intense activity in the publication of sources and certain effervescence in the circles close to the Memorial Association, whose ambition was to expose all the horrors of Stalinism. Nevertheless, at the beginning of the 1990s, this interest faded and gave way to an enthusiastic (re-)discovery of the realities of the ancient regime. Very soon, this movement intensified, as if Russian society as a whole, sickened by what it had learnt or had been confirmed, and convinced of having finally shed light on all the darkest aspects of the Soviet era, allowed itself a period of deliberate oblivion of the recent past so as better to dive into a wave of nostalgia for a more distant past (Ferretti 1995; Scherrer 2002).

This amnesia essentially characterizes the beginning of the Yeltsin years, when, in a context of loss of international prestige and drastic decline of the standard of living, citizens seemed not only to use history to escape from a too burdensome reality, but also to remember their past glory. In 1995, on the occasion of the fiftieth anniversary of the victory against Nazism and on the eve of Yeltsin's re-election, a crucial turning point was reached. At that time, a slow reappearance of the Soviet period as a positive reference for the public could be observed (Levada Centre 2003; Nikonov and Bunin 2003, 189 and *passim*). The Russian people hence selected in their recent collective memory those episodes which were likely to increase the standing of the population. In this instance, their reflection returned to an immemorial rhetoric boasting the Russian, and then Soviet exploits. As long as this argument is refuted by present events, it will go unheeded as petty propaganda.

---

18   According to Tzevetan Todorov's beautiful expression. In Russian, the term *zhertva*, meaning 'victim', produced a verb, *zhertvovat'*, which means 'to sacrifice', thus giving an object to this essentially passive notion.

19   For a 'monumental' approach to this question, see Forest and Johnson (2002), 537ff.

However, as soon as the discourse massively becomes part of the commemorative acts, and especially as soon as it seems to actually correspond to current events, it will most likely encounter an overwhelming success and change into an innermost conviction.

The very idea of a necessary Russian greatness is then combined with a real personal or family life marked by traumas. The conjunction of these two apparently contradictory elements leads to a fruitful axiological configuration, glorifying suffering – that is to say, bestowing meaning and value on it. Moreover, it allows for transforming a form of passivity into activity, or even political action. At least, this is the hypothesis which the consensus that seems to have formed around the personality of Vladimir Putin over the last few years[20] gives rise to. Indeed, popular will seems to subtend Russian power's imperceptible evolution towards authoritarianism, in that the former encourages citizen passivity while granting a renewed global splendor. If so, is it not the best expression of the political aspirations of a people of glorious victims?

Conclusions

Russia's current evolution may only be transitory, and it is possible that it will only take a few generations to turn this country into a democracy in the full meaning of the term. However, it may be that its present autocratic drift was not created, but rather encouraged by the political handling of the past. In Switzerland, partisan uses of history, even though perfectly suited to the desired ideological bent, were also unable to achieve the installation of an egalitarian system in 1798. And as we know, fifty years later, the radicals managed to do so by carefully keeping silent about the myths so complacently evoked by their predecessors. This silence was deliberate, and is also revelatory of the difficulties created by the use of the past when promoting a new regime.

These problems are first of all linked to the mode of construction of an account of the origins supposed to support what, at the onset, is no more than a dissident movement. In principle, this narration is drawn up starting from the traditional elements of 'stigmatization', such as the revolutionary phenomenon in Switzerland (Römer 2005) or the Russian proto-democracy (*Bol'shaja sovetskaya Enciklopedija* 1974, 165, 169), or even the liberalism orchestrated by the last tsars. The game then consists of reversing the trend, and in turning this 'anti-principle', handed down by the previous historiography into a glorious founding moment. If such mystification can work, and if, feeding on it, the social actors set the course of the national destiny in a new storyline, at least they cement the whole narrative thus recreated by anchoring it to a more consensual factual or axiological framework. In other words, partisan history, conceived in this instance to 'prove' democracy's seniority, takes in the elements, and especially the fundamental message, previously conveyed by the official national account. Partisan narration reaffirms the position,

---

20   <www.levada.ru/prezident.html>, accessed 22 May 2007.

and hence the mission that those whose destiny it relates consider having in space and time. Thus, Helvetian patriots strove to present the confederates as heroes endowed with exemplary wisdom, discreetly favored by Providence. And the USSR's gravediggers soon perceived that they had to underline the power of their country, as well as the glorious although painful role taken on by their compatriots in the affirmation of that very status.

The similarity among the discursive strategies elaborated in Switzerland at the end of the eighteenth century and in Russia at the end of the twentieth century allows one to advance a number of more general hypotheses concerning partisan uses of history and the conditions of their effectiveness on populations required to live in a democracy – that is to say, applying the rules of self-discipline that such a regime entails. First, it seems that the benefits yielded by a political use of history are related to the broadness of the audience it is likely to touch. That is to say, the political uses of the past would become more complex because of the psychological usefulness of their reception. In the event of competition between proposed versions, the variation which is closer to the ancient historical, and especially messianic, interpretation of what happened seems to win the public's assent. More precisely, citizens would regularly lean towards whichever among the historical and axiological arguments they considered most capable of warding off their fear of discontent and legitimizing their search for greater welfare. This attitude would betray a double force of inertia. On the one hand, it would reveal the importance of feelings, such as fear or humiliation in the choice of political options. On the other, it would report the existence of 'axiological invariants' conveyed by culture and history.

Given these conditions, it can be presumed that the invention of traditions revealed by Hobsbawm follows a similar scheme and dissimulates a long-term axiological and formal anchorage which would inform their success. And while the narration of the past to which these symbolical practices are attached is also mostly imagined, at any rate the logic it follows can be called historical. According to Nietzsche, these findings would allow us to understand why the allusion to the past often leads to the preservation of already established structures, if not to the failure to act (Nietzsche 1874 [1990]), 91–169).

Better yet, these results bring into question the effects which historically connoted rhetoric is likely to actually exert on the population. Even worse, one might ask whether history is not detrimental to the establishment of democracy. As an element of discourse, it encourages a passivity that is contrary to change and to the very spirit of a regime based on the expression of the citizens' opinions. On the factual level, it generates oppressive cultural referents which are capable of making democracy less attractive than its current popularity would lead us to believe.

References

Andrey, G. and Czouz-Tornare A.-J. (2003), *Louis d'Affry, 1743–1810, premier landamman de la Suisse: la Confédération suisse à l'heure napoléonienne* (Geneva: Editions Slatkine).

Andrieu, C., Lavabre, M.-C. and Tartakowski, D. (eds) (2006), *Politique du passé. Usages politiques du passé dans la France contemporaine* (Aix-en-Provence: Presses universitaires de Provence).

Arlettaz, S. (2005), *Citoyens et étrangers sous la République Helvétique (1798–1803)* (Geneva: Georg).

Barygin, I.N. (ed.) (1999), *Politicheskie partii, dvizhenija i organizacii sovremennoj Rossii na rubezhe vekov* (St Petersburg: Mikhailov).

Berchtold, A. (2004), *Guillaume Tell. Résistant et citoyen du monde* (Geneva: Editions Zoé).

Berelowitch, W. (2003), 'Les manuels d'histoire dans la Russie d'aujourd'hui: entre les vérités plurielles et le nouveau mensonge national', in *Un 'mensonge déconcertant'? La Russie au XXe siècle* (Paris: L'Harmattan).

Bol'shaja sovetskaja Enciklopedija (1974), 18 (Moscow: Izd-vo sovetskaja Enciklopedija).

Chechel', I. (2005), 'Sovetskoe obshchestvo 1985–1991 godov: novoe izuchenie istorii', in Herrmann et al. (eds), *Istoricheskoe znanie v sovremennoj Rossii: diskussii i poiski novykh podkhodov* (Moscow: RGGU).

Chervonnaja, S. (2001), 'Geschichtswissenschaft Russland in den 1990er Jahren. Problematik, Methodologie, Ideologie', *Osteuropa* 6, 695–715.

Conrad, C. and Conrad, S. (eds), *Die Nation schreiben. Geschichtswissenschaft im internationalen Vergleich* (Göttingen: Vandenhoeck & Ruprecht).

de Capitani, F. (1986), 'Vie et mort de l'Ancien Régime', *Nouvelle histoire de la Suisse et des Suisses* (Lausanne: Payot).

de la Harpe, F.-C. (1864), *Mémoires de Frédéric-César Laharpe concernant sa conduite comme Directeur de la République helvétique adressés par lui-même à Zschokke* (Paris and Geneva: J. Cherbuliez).

Dufour, A. and Monnier, V. (eds) (2003), *Bonaparte, la Suisse et l'Europe: Actes du colloque européen d'histoire constitutionnelle pour le bicentenaire de l'Acte de Médiation (1803–2003)* (Brussels: Bruylant).

Ferretti, M. (1995), 'La mémoire refoulée. La Russie devant le passé stalinien', *Annales. Histoire, Sciences Sociales* 50:6, 1237–57.

—— (2004), 'Obretennaja identichnost. Novaja "oficijal'naja istorija" putinskoj Rossii', originally published online at *Neprekosnovennij zapas* (<www.nz-online. ru>), available at <http://forums.polit.ru/index.php?showtopic=4726>, last accessed 19 June 2008.

Forest, B. and Johnson, J. (2002), 'Unraveling the Threads of History: Soviet-era Monuments and Post-Soviet National Identity in Moscow', *Annals of the Association of American Geographers* 92:3, 524–47.

Grankin, I.V. (2001), *Parlament Rossii* (Moscow: izd-vo gumanitarnoj literatury).

Hartog, F. and Revel, J. (eds) (2001), *Les usages politiques du passé* (Paris: Editions de l'EHESS).

Herrmann, I. (2004), 'L'histoire entre Eltsine et Poutine. La vision du passé dans le discours politique russe', *Traverse* 2, 71–88.

—— (2006), *Les cicatrices du passé. Essai sur la gestion des conflits en Suisse (1798–1918)* (Berne: Peter Lang).

—— et al. (eds) (2005), *Istoricheskoe znanie v sovremennoj Rossii: diskussii i poiski novykh podkhodov* (Moscow: RGGU).

Hobsbawm, E. and Ranger, T. (eds) (1983), *The Invention of Tradition* (Cambridge: Cambridge University Press).

Iggers, G.G. (2000), 'The Uses and Misuses of History and the Responsibility of the Historians, Past and Present', *Actes, rapports, résumés et présentation des tables rondes. XIXe Congrès International des Sciences Historiques* (Oslo: University of Oslo).

Jonas, H. (1984), *The Imperative of Responsibility: In Search of an Ethics for the Technological Age* (Chicago, IL and London: University of Chicago Press).

Joule, R.-V. and Beauvois, J.-L. (2004), 'La psychologie de l'engagement', *Pour la science* 3, 52–5.

Klepikova, E. and Solovyov, V. (1995), *Zhirinovsky: The Paradoxes of Russian Fascism* (London: Da Capo Press).

Létourneau, J. (2000), *Passer à l'avenir. Histoire, mémoire, identité dans le Québec d'aujourd'hui* (Montréal : Editions du Boréal).

Levada Centre (ed.) (2003), *Obshchestvennoe Mnenie*, 2003: <www.levada.ru/om2003html>, accessed 29 September 2003.

Macedo, S. (1990), *Liberal Virtues: Citizenship, Virtue and Community* (Oxford: Oxford University Press).

Mallet du Pan, J.-J. (1798), *Essai historique sur la destruction de la Ligue et de la liberté helvétique* (London: Impr. W. and C. Spilsbury).

McFaul, M. (2001), *Russia's Unfinished Revolution: Political Change from Gorbachev to Putin* (London and Ithaca, NY: Cornell University Press).

Nietzsche, F. (1874 [1990]), *Considérations inactuelles, II: De l'utilité et des inconvénients de l'histoire pour la vie* (Paris: Gallimard).

Nikonov, V. and Bunin, I. (eds) (2003), *Sovremennaja rossijskaja politika* (Moscow: Olma Press).

Nora, P. (1984–94), *Les lieux de mémoire* (Paris: Gallimard).

Reichler, C. and Ruffieux, R. (1998), *Le voyage en Suisse. Anthologie des voyageurs français et européens de la Renaissance au XXe siècle* (Paris: Robert Laffont).

Rigby, T.H. (1999), 'New Top Elites for Old Russian Politics', *British Journal of Political Science* 29:2, 323–43.

Römer, J. (2005), *Revolution und Tradition: die Helvetische Revolution in der Schweizer Geschichte und Geschichtsschreibung* (Geneva: Université de Genève).

Sbornik dokumentov … po ocenke sobljudenija pravil … protiv El'cina (1999) (Moscow: Gos. Duma).

Schenk, C. (1998), *Das Geschichtsbild der Helvetiker: helvetische Politiker als Geschichtsschreiber: Peter Ochs, Philipp Albert Stapfer und Frédéric-César de Laharpe* (Freiburg: Université de Fribourg).

Scherrer, J. (2002), '"Sehnsucht nach Geschichte". Der Umgang mit der Vergangenheit im postsowjetischen Russland', in Conrad and Conrad (eds), *Die Nation schreiben. Geschichtswissenschaft im internationalen Vergleich* (Göttingen: Vandenhoeck & Ruprecht).

Simon, C. (ed.) (1998), *Résistances et contestations à l'époque de l'Helvétique* (Bâle: Schwabe).

Skinner, Q. (1974), 'Some Problems in the Analysis of Political Thought and Action', *Political Theory* 2:3, 277–303.

Smith, K.E. (2002), *Mythmaking in the New Russia: Politics and Memory in the Yeltsin Era* (Ithaca, NY: Cornell University Press).

Strickler, J. (ed.) (1886–1966), *Actensammlung aus der Zeit der Helvetischen Republik (1798–1803)* (Berne and Freiburg: Stämpflische Buchdruckerei and Fragnière).

Sveshnikov, A. (2004), 'Bor'ba vokrug shkolnykh uchebnikov istorii v postsovetskoj Rossii: osnovye tendencii i rezul'taty', *Neprekosnovennij zapas*, <www.nz-online. ru>, accessed 30 September 2006.

Walter, F. (2005), 'Historiographie', <www.dhs.ch>, accessed 20 September 2007.

Weigl, M. (2001), *Political Legitimation and Justification – The Value of History*, conference, Londonderry, <www.cap.uni-muenchen.de/download/2002/2002-Realism_Weigl.doc>, accessed 1 October 2003.

Werning Riviera, S. (2000), 'Elites in Post-Communist Russia: A Changing of the Guard?', *Europe–Asia Studies* 52:3, 413–32.

Zotova, Z.M. (2001), *Politicheskie Partii Rossi* (Moscow: Ros. Centr obuchenija izbirat. tekhnologijam).

Further Reading

Andrey, G. et al. (eds) (1986), *Nouvelle histoire de la Suisse et des Suisses* (Lausanne: Payot).

Erll, A. (2005), *Kollektives Gedächtnis und Erinnerungskulturen. Eine Einführung* (Stuttgart: Metzler).

Gessat-Anstett, E. (2007), *Une Atlantide russe. Anthropologie de la mémoire en Russie post-soviétique* (Paris: La Découverte).

Hettling, M. (1998), *Eine kleine Geschichte der Schweiz* (Frankfurt: Suhrkamp).

Langenohl, A. (2000), *Erinnerung und Modernisierung: die öffentliche Rekonstruktion politischer Kollektivität am Beispiel des neuen Russland* (Göttingen: Vandenhoeck & Ruprecht).

Marchal, G.P. (2006), *Schweizer Gebrauchsgeschichte: Geschichtsbilder, Mythenbildung und nationale Identität* (Basle: Schwabe Verlag).

The Rhetoric of Intellectual Manifestos from the First World War to the War against Terrorism

Marcus Llanque

What We're Fighting For

In February 2002, about sixty scholars and intellectuals wanted to demonstrate their support for the war in Afghanistan as a part of the broader concept of war against terror, and published a manifesto called 'What We're Fighting For'. Signatories were, among many others, distinguished scholars from the field of social sciences, history and philosophy like Jean Bethke Elshtain, Amitai Etzioni, Francis Fukuyama, William Galston, Mary Ann Glendon, Samuel Huntington, Harvey Mansfield, Robert D. Putnam, Theda Skocpol, Michael Walzer and James Q. Wilson. All of them are independent intellectuals, Republicans as well as Democrats. No one was paid by the government, or even commissioned or instructed to write down a manifesto, and no one expected to make a better career by doing so. Some of them had expressed their deepest concerns about the government's politics in other areas before, but now they tried to justify this war.

The moral argumentation of the manifesto is close to the just war tradition. The authors try to demonstrate that the war is not only justified in moral terms, but also claim that this war is 'morally necessary'. Although the war in Afghanistan is justified along terms of the just war tradition, the argument differs from the classical just war tradition in so far as it is said that universal values are at stake. The attacks of September 11th are called 'evil', by which they mean an attack on these universal norms they now try to defend.

Those universal values are humanity in general and the values of the US democracy in particular. It is said that 'the clearest expression of a belief in transcendent human dignity is democracy', which claims an intense relationship between humanity and democracy. Hence, many times the text identifies US democracy and universal principles, an argumentation based on the view that all citizens can be seen as potential immigrants, so that 'anyone, in principle, can become an

American'. The core phrases are 'we fight to defend ourselves' and at the same time 'universal principles'.

The basic values they refer to are those of the Founding Fathers, which, as the authors claim, are still the basis of the American way of life today. These principles are held to be 'self-evident', which is a reference to the famous expression in the Declaration of Independence. By referring to 'Holy Scriptures', the authors obviously meant normative texts like the Holy Bible or documents mentioned earlier like the Declaration of Independence or the Gettysburgh Address of Abraham Lincoln. In addition, universally intended documents like the United Nations Declaration of Human Rights are interpreted as enshrining the fundamental principles the authors refer to.

Later, Elshtain published the manifesto again in her book *Just War against Terror* as an appendix (2003, 182–207), and revealed that she was one of the principal authors of the manifesto (Elshtain 2003, 64). In her view, the 'rhetoric' of the manifesto was modeled after Abraham Lincoln's second Inaugural Address (Elshtain 2003, 65). This makes clear that Elshtain was aware that manifestos of that kind differ from articles and books published on the same topic. While articles and books are mostly written by one or two persons, manifestos give the impression of being a collective work; articles and books are written for a specific group of readers, manifestos are addressed to a broad public. And so their arguments differ from those in articles and books by the attempt to convince a public, referring to moral convictions that are based on as general a level as possible. Readers are imagined and treated analogously to the audience of a speech. Therefore, manifestos are more close to an oratorical attempt to persuade an audience, and less intend to make an argument as strong as possible. Like oratorical speech acts, their purpose is not only to give evidence for a thesis or to show certain relationships; their purpose is to persuade the public that certain general principles are connected with a specific action.

Participation of Intellectuals in Times of War

The question raised here is to what extent this particular way of public participation of intellectuals in times of war is ideological, necessarily so or unintended. According to a thorough study debating whether the war in Afghanistan and the war in Iraq may be justified by just war terms, the conclusion is that the former is much more likely justifiable than the latter (Dolan 2005, 206–10). On the other hand, the war in Afghanistan was a test case for other steps in the beginning war against terror. In the months before the publication of the manifesto, doubts began to rise whether the unilateral concept of fighting the 'axis of evil', including Iran, Iraq and North Korea, could be seen as the start of permanent warfare (Gitlin 2002). In 2005, a leading military historian spoke of 'lessons not learned', referring to the 'dirty wars' of the 1990s in the Balkans and in Chechnya, and criticized Western governments for their unwillingness or inability to turn their military victories into lasting peace (Parker and Murray 2005, 412).

Afterwards, anybody can see the errors of the past. The lesson seems to be to steer clear of such errors in the future, and not to repeat erroneous activities. On the other hand, the intention of anxiously trying to avoid errors leads to inactivity. One should learn about the difficulties of political judgment. Unlike historical judgment, any political judgment is concerned with the future, and not with the past (Aristotle 1959, Book I, ch. 3), and nobody has objective knowledge about the future. If inactivity is no real alternative (because inactivity tends to support what is going to happen anyway), every participant in public discourse of matters of political decision must face the dangers of misjudging the situation or giving justification for actions that were not intended to be justified at first.

Since the intellectuals entered the stage of politics as a specific type of actors, their collective actions were accompanied by manifestos as a modern type of addressing the public. If we talk about the role of intellectuals in politics, we inevitably think of an intellectual in terms of the French intellectual. The paradigm of the French intellectual was set during the Dreyfus affair at the end of the nineteenth century, and has its place in French politics since then (Drake 2002, 2005). It was Emile Zola and his criticism of the government for how the Dreyfus affair was handled that could be seen as the starting point of the modern intellectual (Charle 1990; Drake 2005, 21–3). The particular role of the intellectual, according to the French model, suggests interfering with politics without being involved in politics. This means intellectuals participate in the political process not through the channels of parties or parliament, but rather through public opinion. They attend demonstrations, campaign for single issues or have roles in parliamentary elections as public supporters. The classical way to interfere is to publish one's opinion. Very often, intellectuals don't make clear that they just expressing their own opinions, but pretend to represent the public position, although without a mandate.

The representative character is more likely to be achieved by demonstrating collectively one's conviction in a published manifesto. Unsurprisingly, Zola's letter in L'Aurore was followed the next day by a short statement, which was later dubbed the 'Manifesto of the intellectuals'. Over a hundred leading scientists, men of letters and education who expressed their support for Zola signed it. Since then, manifestos have belonged to the campaigning routine of intellectuals. Manifestos published by groups of intellectuals to back or oppose concrete politics are a remarkable example for the participation of intellectuals. Without being elected by the people, without being representatives, intellectuals are free to speak out, but lack responsibility other than to the principles they consider a priority. Through manifestos, intellectuals can demonstrate convictions that allegedly not only rest on their private thoughts, but on general principles.

In most cases, intellectual manifestos criticize and oppose specific policies carried out by official or other groups. It is not difficult to take sides against politics by referring to general principles, because politics will seldom meet moral principles without compromises with interests. Distance from politics seems to be an appropriate position for an intellectual. Intellectuals supporting politics are a different matter. Then, manifestos back governments by appealing to principles the signatories believe to be the guiding horizon of a government's policy. Instead of discussing politics in terms of interests, intellectuals try to justify it morally. In these cases, intellectuals expose themselves to the danger of treating the moral principles in question ideologically.

Times of war are difficult times for sound reasoning (Strauss 2003). Those who feel attacked and who try to express their views in moral terms must beware of moral arrogance and self-righteousness. All intellectual manoeuvres oscillate between principle-based political engagement and an ideology (Goldfarb 1998, 13–6), separated by only a thin borderline.

The only way to circumvent safely either ideology or engagement would be inactivity. This would mean alienating intellectuals from the political system they are interpreting. Hence, the great danger of treating moral arguments ideologically always persists. To examine this aspect of intellectual behavior, it is helpful to have C.B. Macpherson's definition of ideology in mind:

> I take ideology to be any more or less systematic set of ideas about man's place in nature, in society, and in history (i.e. in relation to particular societies), which can elicit the commitment of significant numbers of people to (or against) political change. ... Ideologies contain, in varying proportions, elements of explanation (of fact and history), justification (of demands), and faith or belief (in the ultimate truth or rightness of their case). They are informed by, but are less precise and systematic than, political theories or political philosophies. They are necessary to any effective political movement, hence to any revolution, for they perform the triple function of simplifying, demanding, and justifying. (Macpherson 1973, 157–8)

Macpherson tried to show that unlike political theory or political philosophy, ideology uses a specific mode of argumentation. It covers the field of faith and belief, a way of thinking that reminds us of religious subjects. Because we believe in certain political ideas, we justify political actions even if they are inconsistent with our interests or violate international obligations.

The Intellectual Manifestos and Democracy in the Twentieth Century

It all began during the First World War, when Oxford scholars justified their government's policy to fight Germany in a manifesto called *Why We are at War: Great Britain's Case*, published in 1914. These scholars wanted to outline the fundamental principles of the British political system, and tried to show that the political ideas that ran Britain and those prevailing in Germany were fundamentally opposed to each other, without any hope of compromise. German scholars answered the open letter of their once-befriended colleagues with the manifesto 'An die Kulturwelt' from October, 1914, claiming that the German political tradition was superior to the British, and that no scholars were more capable of judging a people's values than native scholars themselves (von Ungern-Sternberg and von Ungern-Sternberg 1996). Scholars had exchanged friendly correspondence with each other in the years prior to the outbreak of the war, but then changed into furious ideological supporters of their own governments. A wide-ranging debate between British and German scholars started, soon labeled a war of intellectuals (Kellermann 1915). The ideological battle debating whose side could claim to defend the better principles changed into a fight over who had a better understanding what democracy is. In the end, the so-called 'principles of 1789', meaning the classical French–Anglophone understanding of democracy, were opposed to the 'principles of 1914', which were considered to be a modern, organized and state-directed version of democracy. This debate has been especially well examined in Germany. It is common currency to assume that this debate was a clear sign for the German *Sonderweg*. It seemed that German political culture was unaware of the principles of parliamentary democracy, and based itself more on a non-controlled bureaucratic state and its well-organized army than on situations with representatives delegated by the people itself.

Every nation had its own road to democracy, and until the First World War, even the French and the British would have protested against any effort to show that their political systems could be identified with each other. Notwithstanding the question of whether the thesis of a 'German *Sonderweg*' is true, it is worth mentioning that in many cases, British as well as French intellectuals showed the same symptoms of ideological argumentation and expressed their opinions in manifestos similar to the German ones. In all of these countries, intellectuals believed in the truthfulness of the sample of 'blue books' and 'white books' published by their governments, in all cases explaining why the war was provoked by the other side, and why, at the same time, it was at all means necessary to conduct the war. Liberal as well as conservative intellectuals of all countries believed that the information of the enemy's government was mere propaganda, whereas the information of their own government was taken as the truth and nothing but the truth. On all sides, intellectuals tended to claim to defend rightly understood democracy, and tried to show why and how the other side was obviously wrong. Therefore, it seems that the phenomenon of ideological defense of democratic principles by intellectuals is not related to a certain political system, but belongs to intellectual activities in the field of politics whenever public opinion is free to express itself.

Especially in times of ideological challenge, it so happens that defenders of the democratic idea tend to become ideologists themselves. Since the First World War, many ideological debates were fought: beginning with a newly formed intellectual front establishing the idea of 'Western democracy' which was directed against Germany, then taking the case of democracy against fascism, Nazism and all totalitarian systems. The conflict continued after the First World War, when communism was identified as the ideological opponent of democracy. Today, the battle is fought by intellectuals in the name of democracy against terrorism and a fundamentalist version of political theology. Since the end of the nineteenth century, democracy more and more became a highly valued and also a polemical term in political communication. 'Polemical usage' means that it was used in concrete opposition to terms connected with concurring political systems like tyranny, autocracy, sometimes even socialism, and nowadays Islamic fundamentalism. In all these cases, we observe intellectuals and scholars who are eager to express their belief in democracy. Most intellectuals operate for honorable reasons, earnestly convinced of the rightness of their actions. But in most cases, circumstances affect political judgments. The emotional heat and the clear friend–foe distinction seem to seriously restrain sound reasoning. When during the First World War it was said that the aim of fighting was to make the world a better or even safer place for democracy, or when it is used to define who is 'in' and who is 'out', who belongs to 'us' and who doesn't, then democracy is dealt with as an ideology.

Usually, democracy is not treated as a form of ideology by political science and intellectual history. When democracy is studied in terms of ideology, it is closely linked to liberalism as the broader ideology (Rejai 1995; Sargent 1996; Freeden 1996; Eccleshall et al. 2001). Most of these studies discuss the contents of democracy, not the way it is practiced in public discourse, nor do they discuss circumstances created by times of warfare. On the contrary, often democracy is justified by demonstrating how it is opposed to ideology. This is due to the pejorative connotation of ideology, which signals an oppressive character. Within the totalitarianism theory, ideology is one of the characteristic features of totalitarian political systems. This implies that democracies – ranging on the opposite side of totalitarian systems in the amplest possible spectrum of systems – do not have an ideology. Democracy cannot be an ideology because it is not oppressing people, but emancipating them and setting them free. Democracy can plausibly be held to be the best political system to dismantle ideological treatments. Free speech is one of its fundamental principles, and ensures that the temptation of ideological abuse can be faced with democratic means. But democracy is not immune to ideological abuse. Zealots of democracy praise democracy's openness to everybody and its inclusiveness, staunchly thinking that only the moral position they share can be seen as the appropriate foundation for defending democracy, furiously attacking anyone criticizing this moral position. If the believers in democracy give the impression that there are no alternatives to their view, democracy turns into an oppressing concept excluding other moral foundations of the same political system.

Every political system must define the terms of inclusion and exclusion to secure an efficient defense against its ideological foes. A strong democracy must be able to fight its enemies: institutions and procedures are to be established to protect democracy against those who lack the corresponding spirit and are likely to abuse the openness of democratic institutions. The effort to define the moral basis of that spirit inevitably tends to give democracy an ideological surface that must be considered offensive by people who do not share this spirit. The question here is not whether democracy itself, as an idea, has an ideological character, but whether democracy is being dealt with as an ideology or not. This is not always an intentional process. People are inclined to identify themselves with the moral foundations they are discussing. Exceptional circumstances like times of warfare evidence the tendency to ideological treatment. It is always difficult to discuss value-judgment questions unemotionally and rationally instead of ideologically.

To discuss democracy in times of emotional outrage makes reasoning even more difficult. A political judgment and an ideological effort to defend democracy are not the same. It is always a necessary aspect of civic consciousness to stand up when democracy is threatened. But expressing personal conviction differs from a collectively expressed opinion of intellectuals who implicitly claim to speak as representatives for the idea of democracy and speak out what every citizen should if they were skillful enough to do so publicly.

The first candidate for an actor who tries to use democracy ideologically is the government, of course. Governments are interested in and have the resources to advocate democracy not only by mere deeds, but also by means of communication. This is what we usually call propaganda. Every democratic government creates agencies to spread the idea of democracy throughout the country and among other countries. The second group to use democracy ideologically consists of independent intellectuals and scientists, poets and artists, when they try to demonstrate their belief in the fundamental principles of democracy.

Manifestos as Part of Democratic Warfare

Intellectual manifestos treating democracy as an ideology play a role in democratic warfare. To democracies, waging war is not only a question of bringing troops abroad and giving them the best available equipment. Part of the strategy must be to convince public opinion of the just case their country is fighting for. Therefore, any government that decides to go to war has to mobilize public opinion and to make sure that public support will stabilize the military efforts abroad. Intellectuals who voluntarily try to legitimize the politics of the government are meeting these aims halfway. To legitimize war on normative grounds such as justice, human values and democracy can restrict the political strategy of the government and confine the war aims. War of norms and values cannot easily be satisfied by a peace based on compromises. In the normative perspective of someone who is fully convinced of his reasons to go to war, there seems to be no other way of winning the war than by demanding unconditional surrender of the enemy. Any other kind of peace may seem to be unjust, so that both have to be considered: justifying a war to be just and a peace to be just. If public support is achieved, war produces a great surge of patriotic enthusiasm. The history of intellectual manifestos in democracies shows that sometimes among those who are usually most critical, a deep desire of identification with their regime emerges. But once the war has started, intellectuals should better secure democratic control of warfare and discuss in public how the means and goals of politics can meet moral obligation, rather than giving moral credit to the war.

In the First World War, only a few intellectuals tried to calm down the enthusiasm of fellow citizens in their barely controlled identification with politics. Max Weber, for example, called this phenomenon a politics of *littérateurs'* empty phrases (Weber 1919 [1994], 172–3), by which he meant they were reasoning without sufficient information and without considering alternative lines of thought and strategy.

Intellectuals behaved like prophets of a nation's values. Max Weber's theoretical conclusion was the distinction of *Gesinnungsethik* from *Verantwortungsethik*: ethics of conviction from ethics of responsibility (Weber 1919 [1994], 359–69). In German, *Gesinnung* is a term that strongly expresses the aspect of self-identification (close to *Weltanschauung*, which can be taken as a proper translation of 'ideology' in the times of Weber). Without emotional appeal, no common political action can take place. Without responsibility, no political action in democracies can be controlled effectively. It is a rational process escorted by emotions. To find the balance between rational argumentation and engagement within an emotionally heated situation of deliberation seems to be the main intellectual challenge.

Manifestos and Political Judgment

Now let us return to the latest emergence of an intellectual manifesto dealing ideologically with the idea of democracy, the manifesto 'What We're Fighting For' by US intellectuals and scholars dated February 2002. The political action in question seems to be a war of principles, not of interests. The manifesto's argument that the government's decision to wage war in Afghanistan was correct doesn't refer to international law. Instead, it is based on moral grounds alone, which is typical for intellectual argumentation in the field of politics. In fact, the authors can only guess that the government's action is deduced from universal principles, but they cannot give any proof for this assumption, and they do not seem to be concerned to establish whether this is really the case – they take it for granted.

Moreover, the authors of the manifesto seem to consider themselves representatives of the values that, in their view, are literally shared by all Americans: 'united in our conviction' and speaking with 'one voice', representing the opinions of all Americans. On the other hand, all other principles that could apply to the case are rebuffed. To consider the crisis as a matter of interests is called capitulation to cynicism. Finally, the support for the US government's policy to wage war against Afghanistan is expressed without considering conditions under which they would withdraw their support. They just state that this manifesto does not intend to 'endorse or condemn specific future military tactics or strategies that may be pursued during this war' (at the end of the list of signatories). This is a late proviso, after pronouncing the war to be just according to universal principles. In the case of the manifesto *Why We are at War*, democracy is treated like an ideology. The authors are simplifying, demanding and justifying. They declare themselves representatives, but are without delegation; they make a statement that bears clear signs of a confession, as they are not discussing alternatives. They are judging without having full information.

To define political judgment is always a difficult task. In academic discourse, reference to the classical concept of prudence often serves as a definition. Here, Hannah Arendt is a prominent figure (Steinberger 1990; Beiner 1983; Steinberger 1993). Mostly, the contents of prudent judgment are debated, and not so much the prudent way of expressing such judgment. Rhetoric theory shows that not only the content of a judgment is crucial for the message, but also the form in which a judgment is presented and the impression the speaker gives while uttering that judgment. In terms of rhetoric theory, this is called the authority of the speaker. A televised interview with an expert in politics will not take place at the breakfast table or in a pub, though the contents could be the same. The shelved book rows in the background signal the capacity of an expert to talk expertly in the same way the robe of a judge symbolizes the powers its bearer is entitled to. When published, the text itself has to create authority, mostly by means of language. The manifestos' rhetoric try to give the impression of being objective by combining the authority of the authors with the general principles they refer to.

Emotional involvement, personal conviction to support a just case, and the aim to back a government's politics expose intellectuals to many dangers. However, they can learn from their failures. The authors of the manifesto of 2002 faced rather harsh critiques from other intellectuals; further events showed them more and more what the real weight of moral principles in the government's decisions was.

In her book from 2003, Bethke Elsthain reflected angrily on the reactions of other intellectuals to the manifesto 'What We're Fighting For'. She considered the 'Letter from US Citizens to Friends in Europe' to be a rejoinder. One of the most prominent signatories had been Gore Vidal. Elshtain deplored bitterly the 'polemic' language of their intellectual opponents, who (like, most notably, Edward Said) tried to insinuate that this manifesto was sponsored by the military-industrial complex. Elshtain was infuriated by the criticism that the authors of the manifesto were acting in a partisan fashion.

While Americans stated the authors of 'What We're Fighting For' were too involved in politics, they were also criticized for using morally wrong arguments. This was the case of the response to the 2002 manifesto produced by a group of German intellectuals, called 'A world of peace and justice would be different' (originally published in German under the title 'Eine Welt der Gerechtigkeit und des Friedens sieht anders aus'). The Germans claimed to refer to the same basic values as the Americans – basically, universal principles and democracy; but they drew the opposite conclusions, namely that only a pacifist position could be deduced from these universal principles. Hence, they condemned all forms of military means to pass on these values. In their argumentation, the use of force in the attacks of September 11th was just as little justifiable as the war in Afghanistan. Contradicting themselves, the Germans reminded the Americans of the outstanding contribution of the Americans in the Second World War against Nazism, which for them was obviously a case of using force they would have supported. The rejection's waging war upon the moral grounds of pacifism and on the other hand praising the fight against Nazism seems to be consistent. In the response to their German colleagues ('Is the use of force ever morally justified? A Response from Americans to Colleagues in Germany'), the authors of the manifesto consequently asked whether violence to defend principles was justifiable at any case, and on what principles one could classify just and unjust war. Simply opposing any politics that can cause harm is not helpful. The Americans conceded the matter of civilian casualties in Afghanistan during the war to be a serious one, but they strongly insisted on the difference between unintended casualties in the course of the coalition war and the terrorists' intention to cause casualties among civilians. Being unable to distinguish these cases is what the Americans call 'moral blindness'.

Harsh criticism of their government's politics has always been part of the political culture of left-wing intellectuals in the United States. At least since the protests against the Vietnam War, the opposition to the often labeled as imperialistic American foreign policy belonged to the self-image of liberal intellectuals in the United States. But in the 1990s, the question whether public activity of intellectuals was in a process of 'decline' arose (Posner 2001). The events of September 11th changed the situation dramatically. Initially, the war in Afghanistan provoked the common anti-imperialistic criticism. But many liberals changed their attitude and suddenly discovered patriotism. What used to belong to conservative rhetoric was now a field occupied by liberals, too. This discovery was a surprise to many people (Wolfe 2005, 200–203). Up to that time, the relationship between liberal intellectuals and the political system of the United States seemed to lack a certain intensity of commitment (Fink 1997). But the events of September 11th had such an impact on liberal intellectuals that they identified themselves with the political system that was now under attack.

In the aftermath of September 11th, left-wing intellectuals like Michael Walzer (another signatory of the manifesto studied here) considered the question of why liberal intellectuals had so many problems identifying themselves with democracy when considered as the political system they lived in. He proposed to take four factors into account: the left-wing ideology, the powerlessness that caused alienation, moral purism, and the feeling of not being entitled to criticize anyone else due of the imperial structure of US foreign policy (Walzer 2002). Walzer tried to point out that there always had been a decent tradition of liberal criticism of foreign policy without the necessity of alienating oneself. He mentioned the liberal critics of the British Boer War, and George Orwell's claim to be a patriot and socialist at the same time. But Walzer also stressed that two different ways of patriotism exist (Walzer 1987): there is the patriot out of pride regardless of the fact whether country is doing wrong or right, and then there is the patriot who is concerned about the moral position of his country, as Carl Schurz put it: 'Our country, right or wrong. When right, to be kept right; when wrong, to be put right!' Anyway, pride for a country is an emotional engagement, and certainly not the best guide to establishing sound reasoning. The proud patriot as well as the concerned one are affected by all politics carried out in the name of their country, but not only take the advantages seriously, but also the failures, and try to avoid them. Patriotism of that kind is in any case prone to a unilateral approach. So, long before September 11th, intellectuals tried to stress the limits of patriotism and replace it by cosmopolitanism (Nussbaum and Cohen 1996).

The issue of 'What We're Fighting For' can therefore be reformulated as a question of conflicting commitments. What should any patriotically engaged intellectual do when it turns out that the administration's policy doesn't meet the standards set by universal principles? To whom is an intellectual responsible when it comes to such a conflict (McLean, Montefiore and Winch 1990; Fink 1997; Hollander 2006)?

Without distance from politics, no independent position can be maintained. On the other hand, too much distance and too fundamental a criticism alienates the intellectual from the public, and his criticism will not find an audience big enough to make a difference. If the gulf between intellectuals and the public has become too deep, any criticism is spoken into the wind. Michael Walzer discussed three ways to achieve a position of distance for an intellectual: the path of discovery, the path of invention, and the path of interpretation (Walzer 1987). An intellectual can discover principles, or invent them. Both ways establish a moral position so distant from the moral foundations of politics that this distance turns into a gulf too deep to be bridged. Therefore, Walzer prefers the third way, the way of criticizing by interpreting already existing principles the citizenry is committed to. Here, criticism is understood more like a permanent reminder to fellow citizens of the moral norms they are generally committed to, but fail to meet in the particular situation discussed by the intellectual. But this kind of distance implies other dangers for the support for a certain policy. However, to support politics by way of interpreting the moral assumptions underlying the actions may take for granted that this action is in fact motivated by moral assumptions alone. But it seems naive to consider an administration's policy to be motivated by the wish to apply moral principles in the realm of interests and power. The idealistic perspective tends to neglect or overlook the terms of power politics that may dictate many actions in matters of security and interests. Elshtain had this problem in mind when she later defended the manifesto by claiming a position between crude realism (allowing any suitable military means) and pacifism (allowing no military means at all). By referring to St Augustine and Niebuhr, she intended to demonstrate a morally high-minded path of the realistic approach in international relations. But this kind of morality is generally prone to classifying international actors as good or evil ones (Geis 2006). Unsurprisingly, the manifesto itself spoke of defense against evil.

So moral engagement can lead to 'moral overstretch': instead of guiding public argumentation, it is blinded by its own attempt at identification. One can only speculate beforehand whether a government's policy is bound to, and therefore limited to, moral principles. But it is still possible to define the principles considering the ways and goals a government has to meet to the effect that it can be seen as morally guided.

Fifteen months after the war in Iraq began, some supporters of the war turned to sceptics (Wolfe 2005, 200–201). But at that time it was too late: the machinery of war and its peculiar dynamics had taken over – the 'dogs of war' were let loose (Walzer 2004, 155) and it was, and is, much more difficult to bring them back into their kennels than to let them go. What was now painfully visible was that even if one thought that in terms of the just war tradition the aspect of *ius ad bellum* and *ius in bello* could be accepted as just, it was the *post bellum* phase of warfare that failed the test. Also facing the war in Iraq, Walzer's position changed (Walzer 2004). He continued to stick to his earlier view that violence is not to be seen as the last resort in politics, because that would be an excuse for inactivity. But when the war broke out and evidently the problem of a just *post bellum* settlement was not solved in a satisfactory manner (if even planned beforehand at all), he did not reject personal responsibility for the policy in question. His identification now is based on the relationship between government and citizenry in terms of representation: 'So the justice of the occupation is up to the citizens of the United States' (Walzer 2004, 168). Walzer admits how important it is to lay down the moral criteria for the ongoing war in Iraq: 'Here are the tests that the Bush administration has to meet, and that we should insist on' (Walzer 2004, 168).

The intention to give a government moral credit by justifying its actions in moral terms seems to be a natural impulse. Without positive knowledge that these moral convictions are really motivating the actions of the government, any support that is only based on moral grounds can give the impression of an ideological argumentation. The question raised here is not to condemn false judgments *post hoc*. The problem is how to avoid such judgments *praeter hoc*, and why intellectuals became the proud kind of patriots instead of the concerned and critical ones, in a sense that they thought they could give moral credit based on very thin data. This situation may occur again, and we will face again regrettably misleading judgments. There seems to be an intellectual mechanism to compensate for speculative grounds with convictions that lead to the self-induced attitude that there is no other way of judgment. The 2002 manifesto's case reflects the enduring temptation of intellectuals to restrict their own political judgment by identifying themselves with the principles of the political system they live in, with the effect that alternative ways of thinking are unseen, the capacity to understand the opposite position is lessened. Judgments made under circumstances such as in 2002 were based on limited information, speculative arguments, and formed by emotional as well as rational components. These circumstances characterize the usual way followed by the process of public opinion. However, intellectuals and scholars may be expected to come to their judgment in a more enlightened way. A way to enlighten the public is to pilot their conclusions drawn in an atmosphere of fear and among feelings of outrage back into sound and calm waters. To demand that intellectuals should deny or suppress sympathy for the cause of their country would demand totally alienated intellectuals. The challenge for intellectuals involved in politics is to find the right balance between engagement and reason.

References

Aristotle (1959), *The Art of Rhetoric*, trans. J.H. Freese (London: Heinemann).

Beiner, R. (1983), *Political Judgment* (London: Methuen).

Charle, C. (1990), *Naissance des 'intellectuels', 1880–1900* (Paris: Minuit).

Dolan, C.J. (2005), *In War We Trust: The Bush Doctrine and the Pursuit of Just War* (Aldershot: Ashgate).

Drake, D. (2002), *Intellectuals and Politics in Post-war France* (Basingstoke: Palgrave).

—— (2005), *French Intellectuals and Politics from the Dreyfus Affair to the Occupation* (Basingstoke: Palgrave Macmillan).

Eccleshall, R. et al. (2001), *Political Ideologies: An Introduction*, 3rd edn (London and New York: Routledge).

Elshtain, J.B. (2003), *Just War Against Terror: The Burden of American Power in a Violent World* (New York: Basic Books).

Fink, L. (1997), *Progressive Intellectuals and the Dilemmas of Democratic Commitment* (Cambridge, MA: Harvard University Press).

Freeden, M. (1996), *Ideologies and Political Theory: A Conceptual Approach* (Oxford: Clarendon).

Geis, A. (2006), 'Spotting the Enemy: Democracies and the Challenge of the Other', in Geis, Brock and Müller (eds), *Democratic Wars: Looking at the Dark Side of Democratic Peace* (Basingstoke: Palgrave Macmillan).

—— , Brock, L. and Müller, H. (eds) (2006), *Democratic Wars: Looking at the Dark Side of Democratic Peace* (Basingstoke: Palgrave Macmillan).

Gitlin, T. (2002), 'Empire and Myopia', *Dissent* 49, 24–26.

Goldfarb, J.C. (1998), *Civility and Subversion: The Intellectual in Democratic Society* (Cambridge: Cambridge University Press).

Hollander, P. (2006), *The End of Commitment: Intellectuals, Revolutionaries, and Political Morality* (Chicago, IL: I.R. Dee).

Kellermann, H. (1915), *Der Krieg der Geister. Eine Auslese deutscher und ausländischer Stimmen zum Weltkriege 1914* (Weimar: Duncker).

Macpherson, C.B. (1973), *Democratic Theory: Essays in Retrieval* (Oxford: Clarendon).

McLean, I., Montefiore, A. and Winch, P. (eds) (1990), *The Political Responsibility of Intellectuals* (Cambridge: Cambridge University Press).

Nussbaum, M. and Cohen, J. (eds) (1996), *For Love of Country: Debating the Limits of Patriotism* (Boston, MA: Beacon Press).

Parker, G. (ed.) (2005), *The Cambridge History of Warfare* (Cambridge: Cambridge University Press).

—— and Murray, W.A. (2005), 'The Post-war World, 1945–2004', in Parker (ed.), *The Cambridge History of Warfare* (Cambridge: Cambridge University Press).

Posner, R.A. (2001), *Public Intellectuals: A Study in Decline* (Cambridge, MA: Harvard University Press).

Rejai, M. (1995), *Political Ideologies: A Comparative Approach*, 2nd edn (New York and London: M.I. Sharpe).

Rorty, R. (1991), 'Intellectuals in Politics', *Dissent* 38, 483–90.

Sargent, L.T. (1996), *Contemporary Political Ideologies: A Comparative Analysis*, 10th edn (Belmont, CA: Wadsworth).

Steinberger, P.J. (1990), 'Hannah Arendt on Judgment', *American Journal of Political Science* 43, 803–21.

—— (1993), *The Concept of Political Judgement* (Chicago, IL: University of Chicago Press).

Strauss, B.S. (2003), 'On Public Speech in a Democratic Republic at War', *Critical Review of Social and Political Philosophy* 6, 22–37.

von Ungern-Sternberg, J. and von Ungern-Sternberg, W. (1996), *Der Aufruf 'an die Kulturwelt'. Das Manifest der 93 und die Anfänge der Kriegspropaganda im Ersten Weltkrieg – mit einer Dokumentation* (Stuttgart: Steiner).

Walzer, M. (1987), *Interpretation and Social Criticism* (Cambridge, MA: Harvard University Press).

—— (1989), *The Company of Critics: Social Criticism and Political Commitment in the 20th Century* (London: Halban).

—— (2002), 'Can There Be a Decent Left?', *Dissent* 49:2, 19–23.

—— (2004), *Arguing about War* (New Haven, CT: Yale University Press).

Weber, M. (1919 [1994], 'The Profession and Vocation of Politics', in *Political Writings*, ed. P. Lassman and R. Speirs (Cambridge: Cambridge University Press).

'What We're Fighting For: A Letter from America', February 2002, published under the aegis of the Institute for American Values: <www.americanvalues.org/html/what_we_re_fighting_for.html>, accessed 15 May 2008.

Why We are at War: Great Britain's Case (1914) (Oxford: Clarendon).

Wolfe, A. (2005), *Return to Greatness: How America Lost its Sense of Purpose and What it Needs to Do to Recover it* (Princeton, NJ: Princeton University Press).

Further Reading

Eatwell, R. and Wright, A. (eds) (1999), *Contemporary Political Ideologies* (London: Pinter).

Fontana, B., Nederman, C.J. and Remer, G. (eds) (2004), *Talking Democracy: Historical Perspectives on Rhetoric and Democracy* (University Park, PA: Pennsylvania State University Press).

Freeden, M. (2005), *Liberal Languages: Ideological Imaginations and 20th Century Progressive Thought* (Princeton, NJ: Princeton University Press).

—— (ed.) (2007), *The Meaning of Ideology: Cross-disciplinary Perspectives* (London: Routledge).

Heywood, A. (2003), *Political Ideologies: An Introduction* (Basingstoke: Palgrave Macmillan).

Jost, W. and Olmsted, W. (eds) (2004), *A Companion to Rhetoric and Rhetorical Criticism* (Oxford: Blackwell).

Kennedy, G. (1999), *Classical Rhetoric and its Christian and Secular Tradition from Ancient to Modern Times*, 2nd edn (Chapel Hill, NC: University of North Carolina Press).

Kirchner, A. (2000), *Die sprachliche Dimension der Politik. Studien zu Rhetorik und Glaubwürdigkeit* (Würzburg: Ergon-Verlag).

Lukacs, J. (2005), *Democracy and Populism: Fear and Hatred* (New Haven, CT: Yale University Press).

Rorty, A.O. (ed.) (1996), *Essays on Aristotle's Rhetoric* (Berkeley, CA: University of California Press).

City Squats and Women's Struggle: Feminist Political Action as Public Performance

Anna Schober

On Monday 5 October 1789, a large crowd of women from the workers' suburb of St Antoine and market women from the Paris Halles streamed to the city hall in Paris to demand bread. When their requests were ignored, they stormed the city hall, organized weapons and marched on Versailles in a growing stream, in the end, of about 8,000–10,000 people. In Versailles, after hours of discussions, the women managed to force Louis XVI not only to agree to guarantee the supply of flour and to fix prices, but also to confirm the 'August decrees' (abolishing feudal privileges) and the declaration of human rights. The next day, the crowd brought the royal family back to the capital in a triumphal march (Landes 1988, 109ff.; Petersen 1987, 62ff.). Even if the women of Versailles, who immediately after 5/6 October were cast as the 'avant-garde' and 'heroines', were soon being slandered, mocked or passed over in silence, they still remained a repeated reference point for the political awakening of women.

Only a few years later, on 12 May 1793, the Société des Citoyennes Républicaines Révolutionaires addressed the 'women of 6 October' in their founding appeal, and demanded:

> Women of 6 October, come out again! Force these ice-cold men, who watch the dangers of the revolution so calmly, to abandon their disgraceful apathy … companies of Amazons should move out of our suburbs and the halls and markets of this enormous old city. Because there the real citoyennes live, those who in this time of decadence still keep clean morals and who were the only ones that have felt the price of freedom and equality.[1]

---

1   My translation; the original document in French as well as a transcription in German can be found in Petersen (1987), 179ff.

Such a call, urging women to come out of their working and living spaces onto the city streets in order to become political actors, emerged more frequently some hundred years later, *c.* 1910. All over Germany, but also in other European countries such as the Austro-Hungarian empire, the United Kingdom and Italy, demonstrations were held for equal rights for women and the right to vote, where again women (and men) physically brought themselves onto the stage of the city to demand access to political rights (Warneken 1991a, 105). Sometimes, women assembled in collective bodies with their own banners and slogans, and so demonstrated that they differed from the community of workers while at the same time also claiming to belong to it.

In addition, in those years women started social reform campaigns to transform the city, by organizing women's clubs and associations and by developing tactics to change the use of cinemas or theaters. Demonstrations continued in the 1920s, and in the heated political struggles at the end of the Weimar Republic in Germany, for example, women's organizations of the SPD (Social Democratic Party) and the KPD (Communist Party) jointly organized independent demonstrations by women, especially on 8 March, Women's Day. Under fascism as well as state socialism, a public competition of world views was eliminated, and consequently women's city squats went underground – only occasionally did they show up in streets and squares again to exploit the visible presence in the city as political means. This was the case during the women's uprising in Carrara, Italy, on 7 July 1944, were women successfully protested in the main squares in order to hinder the evacuation of the city by the occupying German forces (Lindi and Rasetto 2004).

With the 1960s student movement, one sees a changed but again very frequent use of the city as a stage for public appearance. Women now organized happenings and sit-ins and created artistic interventions in public spaces. In the 1970s, they protested for women's refuges, squatted warehouses, and closed down factories in order to construct women's museums, women's towers, women's libraries and cultural centers for women. Demonstrations became more carnivalesque, involving the wearing of masks and costumes as well as various kinds of artistic action. In parallel, women were being promoted to higher positions in the world of politics, commerce, education and culture, and started to appear on billboards campaigning for political parties, government positions or cultural events. The institutionalization process of feminist projects continued in the 1980s with the creation of women's housing areas, playgrounds for girls as well as special schools, the opening of women's libraries, women's theaters and information centers. In addition, lesbian collectives now started to struggle for political visibility and spread through the city with film festivals, colourful parades, bars and libraries (Doderer 2003, 93ff.). And today, women are still struggling to appropriate the city – be it in the form of housing projects, demonstrations and parades, or by naming streets after women.

This passage through various historical and geographical milieus shows that there is continuity in the visible presence of women in the city – a continuity that is sometimes also expressed explicitly, for example when new spaces for women are named after famous female 'ancestors' or when actions expose references to previous feminist struggles. In such cases, we are dealing with a tradition-building process, an 'invention of tradition' (Hobsbawm 2005), which acts against a 'symbolic homelessness' and a 'lack of relation among themselves' (Zerilli 2005, 115) that – for women, and in a different but nevertheless similar way for men, too – is so noticeable in modern as well as in post-modern cities.

But at the same time, the examples mentioned also show a variety of differences: The women of Versailles, for instance, became political actors not because of identification within themselves as 'women', but because of shortage of food and the disastrous support situation in general. None the less, only a few years later, their activities were remembered by the Société des Citoyennes Républicaines Révolutionaires in order to politicize women as 'women'. The Suffragettes then formed a political movement based on the identification within those excluded from the democratic process. They made themselves visible as 'women', but sometimes also marched together with men. Through demonstrations, rallies and assemblies, they occupied urban space in order to struggle for inclusion of women in the power structures that simultaneously were regarded as frustrating, exclusive and oppressive. In parallel –and increasingly since the student movements of the 1960s and the disappointment of the Enlightenment and socialist projects that accompanied them – they created certain dwelling situations such as feminist cultural centers, bookshops or women's museums as kinds of nodes for the emergence of a counter-society, in which all these real or fantasized potentialities that the contemporary world lacked could take refuge. Later generations of women again questioned these types of situating oneself *vis-à-vis* the current order, and invented political practices that accommodated their reflections. They show up, for example, as *riot grrrls* or create dwellings on the Internet such as 'plotki feminism' or 'gurl'.[2]

If we accept as a starting point that, as Linda Zerilli and Jacques Rancière have shown, 'politics consists in building a relationship between things that have none' (Zerilli 2005, 23; Rancière 1999, 40), then the next question arises of what exactly it is that triggers such processes in connection with 'women', and if they are triggered, what form they are staged in – which is in itself also changing. In this chapter, I will explore further such processes of women's politicization, and in particular how they refer to the environment of the city. In addition, I will ask what historical developments were connected with the enhanced importance of the visible presence in the city, which became so crucial for political struggle, and highlight the historical changes and territorial re-locations that have shaped this tradition of the feminist, or at least politicized, tradition of women's city squats. Because contemporary city dwellings such as women's bookshops, feminist cultural centers, meeting places for NGO groups that focus on sex workers or immigrant women, cafes and places (clubs, university locations, cinemas), where the now so fashionable 'ladies' parties' or 'queer-film festivals' are organized usually exist side

---

2   See: Plotki (homepage), <http://plotki.net/cms/indexplotki.net/cms/index.php?option=com_content&task=view&id=410&Itemid=31>, accessed 12 July 2007; gurl (homepage), <www.gurl.com>, accessed 12 July 2007.

by side, without much interaction and almost no common project between them. I therefore also pose the question why – at least in what we call the 'Western world' – there is such a lack of more universal projects involving women from different city locations, even if today, the city is still used for constructing links between women and for formulating political claims. But at the same time, I am concerned to observe whether there are not other, new forms of movement emerging that confront this very tendency.

Urban Presence and the Modern Conflictual Being-in-the-world

'The shape of the urban space', writes Henri Lefèbvre, 'evokes and provokes ... [a] process of concentration and dispersion: crowds, colossal accumulation, evacuation, sudden ejection. The urban is defined as the place where people walk around, find themselves standing before or insides piles of objects, experience the intertwining of the threads of their activities until they become unrecognisable, entangled situations in such a way that they engender unexpected situations' (Lefèbvre 2003, 39). Out of this polyphonic mingling, collective bodies such as the above-mentioned women's movements emerge by occupying instants, places and occasions, constituting themselves in this way, and entering, via a staging of their particular world views and an establishing of themselves as a group, into a dispute with other political actors. In doing so, they define and name 'women' as a specific and distinct social collective, composed of members who recognize themselves and one another as being in a relation of sharing a certain project. And as such, a 'self-consciously, mutually acknowledging collective' (Young 1994, 724) affirming itself as engaged in a shared enterprise and identifying itself with common experiences, such women's groups distinguish themselves from the looser forms of social clusters in which we are continuously and passively united through our everyday actions and by the dominant classifications in our environments.[3]

The precondition for such a *mise-en-scène* of a political position via the squatting of space and the use of slogans, gestures, banners and things is a conflictual being-in-the-world as it emerged first with the French Revolution and the emancipation movements following it. Because, as Claude Lefort has pointed out, these historical events completely re-ordered the ways in which people set their being-together 'in form' (Lefort 1999, 37): the emblems of the monarchy were publicly burned, the king decapitated, and in this way, the central position of power became

---

3   Iris Marion Young differentiates 'groups' and 'serial collectivities' in this way by referring to Sartre's (1967, 270ff.) description of several levels of social collectivity, distinguished by their order of internal complexity and reflexivity: 'Seriality designates a level of social life and action, the level of habit and the level of unreflective reproduction of ongoing social structures. Self-conscious groups arise from and on the basis of serialized existence, as a reaction to it and an active reversal of its anonymous and isolating conditions' (Young 1994, 728). The purpose of my approach is to further examining the aesthetic dimension of such public processes of group-forming.

empty. A variety of protagonists and their emblems could now offer themselves to occupy this place temporarily, and the representative had to win the represented in a struggle with other competitors, and in turn, the represented had to find a relationship to the representative – they had to affirm or reject and to make voting decisions. According to Hannah Arendt, this change can be read as being part of a broader transition to a being-in-the-world without so-called 'rescuing coasts' of tradition and handed-down authority. People no longer connect to collective bodies because long-established clan or village conventions or traditional religious orders demand it, but because of contingent processes of identification triggered by certain symbols, significant moments of perception or charismatic political leaders which they then translate into judgments and further actions (Arendt 1971, 49ff.).

This new *mise-en-forme* of society, as Lefort calls it, was accompanied by a symbolic restructuring, where creed and belief were not abolished, but were attached to images, things, bodies, sounds and aesthetic tricks of an earthly world, and no longer mainly to a paradise outside this world. Certain spaces, but also images, things, a face, flags and badges, uniforms, gestures and rituals or any other detail of the world of appearances, however small, are in themselves transformed in such a process: they can act as a kind of 'passage' that sets people in motion and unites them into collective bodies. With this, the staging of one's own political belonging, the exhibition of one's own conviction, the visibly and audibly differentiated presence in the public sphere becomes important in a new way. So, for example, in an always slightly different way, by appearing in almost uniform-like, equalizing clothes, the women socialist or communist demonstrators in the 1920s staged their mutual belonging, egalitarian aspirations as well as a difference *vis-à-vis* the others, the male workers and competing political groups.

This shows that the process of group-formation described above is usually triggered by significant encounters – with other persons, but also with challenging information or involving aesthetic appearances – as well as by experiences of frustration, exclusion and disappointment which then are collectively translated into shared judgments, political goals and a certain style of performance.[4] Usually, groups that are then self-consciously named as political entities only emerge through such events.

On the historical level described by Lefort, this process also included the erection of a distinct stage of 'politics', where such conflicts are presented before everyone's eyes as being necessary, irreducible and legitimate. And, simultaneously, who was allowed to step onto this stage of politics and who was excluded from it in themselves became questions of political struggle. In this struggle, the city was transformed – by women and men – in various ways, into a stage for political action.

---

4   Such contingent significant encounters which somehow build the basis for an identification of people as engaged in a shared enterprise are not highlighted in the concept of a 'self-consciously, mutually acknowledging collective' as described by Iris Marion Young (1994, 724).

However, a perspective attentive to gender differences also unearths the following ambivalence: while this overthrow of the ways people set their being-together *in form* created the condition for women's struggle for emancipation, at the beginning of this process women were also for the first time explicitly excluded from participating in the public, political realm. As Geneviève Fraisse has shown, soon after the central events of the Revolution in 1793, the women's clubs were closed and the declarations and articles in the *Code civil* (1804) denied women citizen's rights (Fraisse 1995a). During the Ancien Régime and the events of the Revolution itself, women had already gained public visibility (Godineau 1988). But the idiosyncrasies that had then allowed some women to vote were eliminated with the codification of electoral law after the Revolution, which led to the complete exclusion of women as a group from the voting process. In addition, in the phase immediately after the Revolution, the domains of private and public again became quite separate, and – for example, as 'Republican mothers' – women were strictly placed in the private sphere, and in this way banned not only from active, but also from passive participation in the political realm (Landes 1988, 122). In this function, they were assigned the role of supporting that from which they had been excluded – as the 'Others' of modernity, that is, as those who bear all the qualities such as sensuality, beauty, sexuality and namelessness which simultaneously became excluded from rational, public negotiations.[5] Nevertheless, at the same time, the events of the Revolution paradoxically also opened up the potential for further emancipation.[6] The new lines of exclusion established after the Revolution also triggered new struggles for inclusion in the sphere of politics and of political rights (Fraisse 1995a, 90).

With the proliferation of public forums organized as utopian socialist circles or democratic and nationalistic movements all over Europe since the 1820s, women again started to join such gatherings arranged by men, and then to meet publicly among themselves, to publish feminist newspapers and to form alliances with liberal

---

5   I use the notions of 'modernity' and 'postmodernity' not to differentiate architectural or philosophical 'styles' of constructing buildings or arguments, but to designate a continuously transforming regime of seeing and being-seen. 'Modernity' is used for a regime that emerged mainly with the revolutions of the eighteenth and nineteenth centuries (even if, as early as the sixteenth century, there had been the first signs of such a transformation), and implies ways of relating and differentiating oneself by showing up, speaking out and being seen and heard. Here, older, more traditional forms of how to relate and to differentiate oneself, which were previously guaranteed by the social unities of families and villages, the power of kings and the inherited religions, had shattered. 'Postmodernity', on the contrary, is used to describe the period since approximately the 1960s, where 'modern' paradigms have increasingly been regarded with scepticism and a different, 'post-modern' description of the present setting (Huyssen 1996).

6   The potential for public action as liberation and as the beginning of something new was reframed with this historical process, and became the central quality of the political sphere. But this potential usually realizes itself in a contingent way in response to the specificity of an environment and the fascinations and frustrations it bears.

reformers as well as with socialist protesters (Käppeli 1997, 542ff.). Throughout the nineteenth and in the early twentieth centuries, then, women's right to vote remained a highly contentious issue, and led to political mobilization. Later, in the second half of the twentieth century, the right to decide on one's own body and its reproductive functions again united women in many parts of the Western world. And today, migration and the working and living conditions for women, connected with the questions concerning residence permits or burning, unresolved political conflicts such as in the Middle East or in the territories of former Yugoslavia, are again leading women to use the city in order to raise new demands. Women – like other political activists, too – this way repeatedly used and are still using the potentialities of what, with the revolutionary events of the eighteenth century, became a newly emerging public sphere of appearance in order to question the rules that regulate the access to the realm of politics and exclude them from it. They have exploited and are still exploiting certain city spaces, the staging of their bodies and the activities of walking, marching, standing up and living together, as well as posters, signs, banners, performances and masks as means to open a subject-space, in which potentially every woman could now count herself as adhering to certain ideas and convictions. They thereby try to reveal the place in time and space that they themselves decide to be adequate.

Space and the Constitution of Collective Bodies

As Hannah Arendt, for example, has also shown, public space does not appear as a pre-given entity, but is constituted in a multi-vocal way through people's visible and audible presence, actions, perceptions and speech in an always actual, specific way (Arendt 1998, 250). Here, in this space, women form collective bodies by occupying spaces and by actions that define and name themselves – as 'women', 'lesbians', 'Catholic women', 'Kurdish women', and so on. During such city squats, the participants are temporarily and visibly present for all in the urban space in order to achieve a transformed – 'more emancipated', 'more just', 'liberated' and/ or 'enhanced satisfying' – common world. Their city interventions thereby cross, challenge and bypass each other – sometimes, they also mutually reinforce each other as well as other political movements, and trigger broader re-formations of society.

With regard to interventions that relate to urban spaces in a political way, one can differentiate between two kinds of process which cannot, however, be strictly separated from each other. At certain points, feminist projects, like other political city squatting activities, usually tip over from one into the other. An example of the first process, in which the actions focus on a specific city space, is the creation of a housing project in Vienna by lesbian and gay groups, today known as the 'Rosa Lila Villa' ('Pink-and-Lilac Villa') on Linke Wienzeile. In 1982, lesbian and gay activists, some of them already organized in other groups, moved into a formerly somewhat derelict house belonging to the municipality, painted it in lilac and pink, the colour of the feminist and gay movements of the 1970s, decorated it with a rainbow flag, and wrote on the outside in bold letters, 'Erstes Wiener Schwulen-und Lesbenhaus. Rosa Lila Villa' ('First Viennese Gay and Lesbian House: Pink-and-Lilac Villa'). The occupation of this space, its particular way of 'dressing up' and a certain way of being together in it advertised by photographs in magazines, newspapers and leaflets contributed to the formation of the first gay and lesbian movement in Austria (Repnik 2001, 229; Rosa Lila Tip 1992). In addition to the permanent inhabitants, some guestrooms, a cafe and an information center, various initiatives such as gay 'come-together circles', lesbian and gay 'coming-out groups', and associations such as 'Homosexuality and the Church', 'Lesbian Mothers', 'Gay Fathers', 'HIV-positives and their Friends' and 'Safer Sex' sought accommodation in this space in order to define their identity as a collective or as part of a group.

The various gay and lesbian groups and the activists from the information centre and the cafe formulated claims that were closely related to this space. For life in their 'own' villa, they demanded everything the usual daily experience in Vienna lacked: a liberated lesbian or gay sexuality, public exchange and possibilities for action, the abolition of injustices between heterosexuals and homosexuals, and a party culture that involved all the senses. In this way, the Pink-and-Lilac Villa became a symbol around which people could organize themselves in order to change society, and became a starting point for reclaiming the city as a whole, and with that also 'the world' in general. Attacks from the outside and support from other homosexual initiatives enhanced the bond between the squatters and the importance of the squatted space. In this way, the community constituted itself by staging a sharp distinction from certain 'others', in this case heterosexuals, and by linking the collective being thus formed to a certain mode of aesthetic existence, which – via the pink-and-lilac colour, the flying of the rainbow flag, collective living procedures and a certain style of furnishing the rooms – was intended to make such a distinction tangible. Through such procedures, the Rosa Lila Villa became a space were one's own self was 'located externally'. Differences between the definition of the various 'own villas' led to conflicts –for example, between gay groups and lesbian groups, but also between lesbians who lived inside the villa (together with men) and those outside.

Here, there is a certain space at the centre of the constitution of a political group – it acts as a focal point, around which a movement forms itself; but at the same time, in the case of the feminist and lesbian movements, there is usually a variety of spaces – libraries, cafes, festival spaces, exhibition halls, parks, club rooms – which are used to call oneself into being and to act as an emancipating collective.

The practice of a political art group, 'The Guerrilla Girls On Tour', is an example of the latter – the constitution of a feminist collective that is not bound to one single space, but moves through various urban places. Since 1985, a number of women artists have been acting anonymously under this name in various art spaces, that is to say, hidden behind gorilla masks and with pseudonyms ('Käthe Kollwitz' or 'Georgia O'Keeffe'), using irony as well as statistics in order to raise the issue of the continuous discrimination against women in the field of the arts (The Guerrilla Girls 1995). For example, they paste posters on walls and advertising hoardings with ironic comments on gender statistics concerning galleries and exhibition halls that particularly discriminate against women, leave messages on the telephone answering machines of influential figures in the cultural field, but also show up with their gorilla masks and costumes in the city streets, distributing leaflets as well as bananas. By giving themselves names and a face – here, pseudonyms and a gorilla mask – and by demonstrating their view in public with posters and provocative performances, they too are adding themselves to the political public sphere. They are thereby exploring the use of aesthetic tactics such as irony and parody as means to provoke and to challenge the current order. In 1989, for example, The Guerrilla Girls distributed a poster with the image of the *Odalisque* by Ingres, shown with a gorilla mask and 'Do women have to be naked to get into the Metropolitan Museum?' written over it in thick letters. And at the turn of the millennium, they sought to draw attention to the fact that women continued to be discriminated in the world of theater, and walked along Broadway wrapped in banners saying: 'There's a Tragedy on Broadway and it isn't Electra.'

In the case of the Rosa Lila Villa as well as that of 'The Guerrilla Girls On Tour', emancipatory groups constitute themselves by accommodating themselves – more permanently or temporarily – in certain city spaces. They use these spaces to meet and act as a 'we', to anchor it in the city, and so attempt to gain temporary or permanent visibility and presence. Sometimes, they form by focusing on a single space and by using it is a dwelling place for their view of a 'better society', strictly separated from a 'dominant' one. But at other times, they also constitute as movements by roaming through various locations – as The Guerrilla Girls do. Feminist city squats are thus characterized by an oscillation between an 'identity politics of space' and a 'spatial politics of identity' (Keith and Pile 1993, 13ff.).

Through squatting, activists usually become involved in a conflict concerning the world, concerning being and the qualities of this being, and of the common world. In doing so, they initiate a displacement of bodies and a questioning of the orders that define and control who can be present on a community's stages, and how. They enter a process of political subjectivization, which, according to Jacques Rancière, breaks sensual forms, for example by removing a body from its assigned place or by changing the definition of a place. Political collective bodies are consequently not created *ex nihilo*, but by transforming identities defined by a 'natural order' of distribution of functions and places in entities of an experience of struggle that gains, in a visible and audible way, presence in the urban, public sphere.[7] And since aesthetic means, too, can call ways of being and the qualities

---

7   For Rancière, not every action connected with 'power' can be called 'political'. For him, 'the political' is the field of an encounter and of confusion between what he has called 'policing' and 'politics', meaning by 'policing' an ordering that follows the logic of counting and refers the population to distinct spaces, whereas 'political action' subverts this differentiating logic through the constitution of an egalitarian discourse that challenges established identities (Rancière 1999, 36ff.). Ernesto Laclau uses the term 'political' in a similar way for every action that calls structural principles of society into question. The term 'politics', on the other hand, denotes for him a separate social complex, which has to deal with this precarious logic of the political (Laclau 1990, 68ff.).

of those present at a common stage into question, artistic actions in public space and aesthetic explorations of languages and representations are included in such a definition of the 'political'.

Aesthetic Tactics and the Avant-garde Tradition

The Guerrilla Girls On Tour use aesthetic provocation programmatically to relate their political practice to another strong strand of political and feminist tradition. For it was not only significant encounters with fascinating political leaders, outstanding speakers or interesting and challenging information that worked as a reference point in the constitution of emancipation movements, but the form of being-together and of representation, as well as the form of public performance itself has, especially throughout the twentieth century, also repeatedly served as a hook to bring a specific community into being. In this tradition, feminist avant-gardists such as Germaine Dulac, who was one of the Surrealists and headed the newsreel movement in the 1920s, are linked with the explicitly politically engaged artists of the 1960s and 1970s such as Valie Export, Carolee Schneemann or Yoko Ono, who used the city in a particularly vivid way for feminist urban interventions. In the 1990s, this tradition was reanimated, for example, by the Riot Grrrl movement, which again claims performances of gender involving parody and other aesthetic tricks as politically 'subversive'.[8]

These examples already show that this 'avant-garde tradition'[9] of feminist political struggle has gained in prominence, particularly in the second half of the twentieth century, when political developments since 1956 started to expose the limitations that the previously so prominent socialist and liberal utopias involved for the 'other sex'. With this, the focus shifted more towards an aesthetic practice in order to demystify and interrogate language and representation as a community-forming, universal tool (Kristeva 1986, 210). The form of appearance has thereby sometimes been emphatically celebrated as a means of rejecting usual viewing conventions and of triggering specific versions of a 'better' and 'more progressive' life. In the course of this particular process of inventing an 'avant-garde' tradition, certain political judgments of aesthetic tactics have been passed on through various historical and geographical locations.

One of the groups supporting such a position, the Collettivo Feminista Cinema-Roma, wrote in a manifesto entitled *Per un Cinema Clitorideo Vaginale* ('For a Clitoral, Vaginal Cinema') in 1975:

---

8   On this, see Baldauf and Weingartner (1998), 25ff. One of the most prominent supporters of this position is Butler (1990), 181ff.

9   During the research project 'Aesthetic Tricks as a Means of Political Emancipation' (2003–2006, financed by the FWF Austrian Science Fund), I investigated in detail the invention and transformation of this 'avant-garde tradition' (see Schober 2008).

Creativity becomes revolutionary if it is not limited to an 'artistic' operation, but becomes itself a creation of life ... for us what is at stake is not surviving, but living, forming our own way of being, our body, our thinking; to realize our own desires and not those of patriarchal society, to produce ourselves in an authentic way. ... We use all means, so that our struggle will not remain isolated within domestic walls, where we have always been segregated, or in a sterile discussion in all those groups of women who ask for instructions. ... We use the cinema in order to live our creativity, our fantasy, our imagination. Because this is what amuses us. (Collettivo Feminista Cinema-Roma 1975)[10]

In this statement, the aesthetic forms disseminated by 'patriarchal society' are linked with isolation, lack of authenticity and hence with repression and domination. Their own form of cinema-dwelling is staged as a 'creative' one, closely linked to the realization of desires as well as to an increased vivid notion of 'life', and presented as a kind of nucleus from which a counter-society or parallel society might start. This group thereby also constitutes itself by excluding a certain element, which is here a formal one – the aesthetics of Hollywood or 'mainstream' cinema, which is simultaneously seen as incarnating 'patriarchal society'. But difference was not staged only *vis-à-vis* the 'mainstream' entertainment centers, but also *vis-à-vis* other, feminist strategies, namely, as the manifesto puts it, against those women 'who ask for instructions'.

Other cinema activists who invented the feminist film festival *Bilder Wandel* ('Image Transformation') in 1991 turned explicitly against 'a male-dominated stream of images' and 'cinematographic idols (that) hinder the development of a self-image that could act as a counter-image to the blandishments of screen-reality'.[11] These feminists again emphasize visibility, provocation and presence in the urban space directed at an audience they are trying to attract and to involve by using irritation and a shattering of forms. They claim that the use of certain aesthetic tactics will lead in a quite direct and causal way to certain political effects. But despite of such a seductive rhetoric, like the other feminist movements described above, such

---

10 My translation; the original text reads: 'La creatività diventa rivoluzionaria quando non rimane limitata all' operazione 'artistica', ma diventa creazione della vita stessa. ... Per noi non si tratta più di sopravivere, ma di vivere, di gestire il nostro modo di essere, il nostro corpo, i nostri pensieri; di realizzare i nostri desideri, e non quelli della società patriarcale; di proporci in modo autentico. ... Useremo tutti i mezzi perché la nostra lotta non rimanga isolata tra le pareti domestiche, in cui da sempre ci anno segregate, o in uno sterile dibattito nei gruppi di donne che si vanno formando. E' IN QUESTO SENSO CHE CI INTERESSANO I MEZZI AUDIOVISIVI: per parlare con altre donne, per esprimere un nuovo modo di essere donna senza per questo volere imporre nuovi modelli. ... Usiamo il cinema per vivere la nostra creatività, la nostra fantasia, la nostra immaginazione. Perchè questo ci diverte.'

11 My translation; the original text reads: 'eine männlich geprägte Bilderflut' and 'das kinematographische VOR-Bild (verhindert) die Entwicklung des EIGEN-Bildes, das als GEGEN-Bild zur vorgegaukelten Leinwandwirklichkeit fungieren könnte' (*Bilder Wandel*, 1991).

groups are also involved in public struggles that are fundamentally open and lead to contingent articulations and further actions. So despite all the clearly expressed motivations and goals and despite all the constructions of causal relations between aesthetic forms and certain political subversive effects – which appear so frequent in this tradition – the deeds, images and words used by these groups also escape any control and establish unexpected and sometimes even surprising encounters with other actions and images.

In this way, feminist projects usually participate in a sometimes quite double-edged way in the re-formation of political hegemony. Some of the working-class and Suffragette city initiatives of the 1910s and 1920s, for instance, raised issues similar to those promoted by the contemporary hygiene and social reform movements – and so contributed to the broader streamlining of a previously quite diverse city culture *c.* 1920. Similarly, the actions of groups such as the Collettivo Femminista Cinema-Roma in the 1970s staged a rejection of sexual taboos and a liberating attitude towards the senses, and in doing so they occupied city spaces in an unusual way and were acting visibly against the current dominant tendency to 'neutralize' the city and to 'purge' social relations of anything 'strange'. But at the same time, their public appearances again affirmed other tendencies – for instance, the close connection of 'women' with nakedness, sensuality and sexuality that we can also see in most of the advertising images of the time, which now began to be published on a massive scale throughout the public sphere. Furthermore, some of the feminist or lesbian interventions since the 1970s have also supported a vehement discursive negotiation of 'normal' and 'marginal' sexuality as it has been portrayed everywhere in this epoch – in *Playboy* or the *Kinsey Report*, but even in the tabloid press, in pop culture and on television. But at the same time, all these feminist city squats also exploited the potential to question people's world views as well as the very current political constellations. Sometimes they violated taboos, something that led either to a rapid re-erection of the violated categories or to an oscillating double vision that could then become translated to further political action and questioning.

Displacements, Entertainment and New Urban Rituals

Contemporary feminist city squats show some pronounced differences in respect to those which characterized first- and second-wave feminism. The earlier feminist movements until approximately the 1960s were characterized by a pronounced universalism: women acted as particular activists for the emancipation of 'all women' and 'the working class as a whole', which becomes evident in the names they choose such as 'Weltbund für Frauenstimmrecht' ('World Council for Women's Suffrage', Berlin, 1904) or 'Women's Freedom League' (UK, 1907). Simultaneously, these movements operated with a seduction tactic that usually presented them as already being in a state of emancipation, of liberation, and of the more sensuous life they were telling us they wanted to achieve through their practices. But with the student movement of the late 1960s, such practices increasingly came to be viewed with scepticism. The reasons for this were, for example, a heightened debate over continuities of fascist structures in post-war Europe as well the frustrating experiences of women in Western political movements themselves.

But as already mentioned, the disappointments socialist practices caused through the violations in Hungary (1956) and Czechoslovakia (1968) were also important, as was the continuous ignoring of problematic gender-related issues such as abortion and contraception faced by women in socialist regimes – despite their egalitarian rhetoric and the various efforts to achieve economic, professional and political equality for women and men (Kristeva 1986, 196). These experiences were accompanied by sharply accelerated capitalist development, a strengthening and expansion of globalization processes, and a rising penetration of and influence of the media on various movements (Gibbins and Reimer 1999, 24ff.). Feminist groups now called themselves 'Weiberrat' ('Women's Councils', Frankfurt am Main, 1968), 'Brot und Rosen' ('Bread and Roses', Berlin, 1972), 'Women's Liberation Workshop' (UK, 1968) or 'Redstockings' (USA, 1969). During the 1980s, 'new social movements' (ethnic, national, sexual) emerged out, of as well as alongside, traditional parties, and started to protest explicitly against 'old universalisms' and a 'totalizing ideology' which, according to them, had dominated emancipation politics until then. The names now chosen are often much more telling about the specific group activities or about their members – as names such as 'Frauen Formen Ihre Stadt' ('Women Shape Their City', Bonn, 1981) or 'Southall Black Sisters' (UK, 1984) make evident.

At the same time, differences between the various movements – between radical feminists, Marxist and Catholic women's groups, lesbians and the queer scene – started to widen, and often became insurmountable. These groups – paradoxically, despite a parallel critique of a politics of identity – were now rather led by the normatively articulated assumption that the members inside were all equal, whereas the difference to the outside was absolute. With this, collectives began to exclude differences among their members, as well as to isolate themselves into kind of 'fortresses' of counter-society or parallel society –to an extent that common activities became impossible (Laclau 1996, 47ff.). But at the same time, membership of one of these groups was often not very long-lasting. People usually participate in a plurality of sometimes overlapping collective public bodies, actualizing quite varying facets of their world views according to the situation of the moment (Gibbins and Reimer 1999, 68ff.).

As part of this process, the form of the appearance of political city squats also changed more thoroughly at the end of the twentieth century, as current film and video festivals, the newly established 'Love Parades' and 'Ladies' Fests', anti-globalization demonstrations or feminist movements in the Middle East or in post-communist eastern Europe demonstrate. Groups now call themselves 'Women Without'[12] or 'Damenkraft'.[13] Here, an explicitly articulated political motivation

---

12   The group formed itself in the framework of the preparatory assemblies to the European Social Forum in recent years. The name is inspired by the French *sans papiers*.

13   This is a political music group, currently active in Vienna and involved – among other things – in organizing the annual 'Ladies' Fest'.

sometimes receded into the background, and entertainment and the acting out of one's own aesthetic existence in the world were emphasized – even if urban movements' performances still simultaneously reveal a political and aesthetic sense. Photographs of public protest spectacles often represent situations of polarized conflict and direct confrontation. At the same time, they highlight spectacular performances of individuals, and quite often, extravagant costumes indicate that lifestyle and the possibility of participating in consumer society are now part of political struggles, too. In addition, political collectives much more explicitly expose references to the established image-worlds of comics, advertising, film and TV, but also to avant-garde and high culture. They prefer images, music, sounds and artistic performance to slogans and banners, and avoid references to universal figures such as 'the people'. In this way, the movements communicate not only with a local public sphere, but sometimes, as in the case of the anti-globalization movement, with the 'whole world', and they use an entire media complex – TV, the press, radio, the Internet as well as mobile phones and live acts – for such communication.

Since the 1970s, feminist groups have thereby reinvented several positions that exist simultaneously. On the one hand, there is an enhanced 'mainstreaming' of women into the power structures that simultaneously continue to marginalize and to frustrate them. Besides this, there are other feminist groups that dismiss such integration and – as described above – still seek to create 'islands' of a counter-society or parallel society. But in recent decades, there have increasingly also been efforts to question such political practices and to develop an again transformed style of squatting the public sphere.

Of all such women's movements, one stands out because of the particular vivid, fascinating story it has triggered: 'Women in Black'. This shares a lot of features with the contemporary political panorama described above, but it nevertheless also displays some important differences – and perhaps these can explain something about the particular success and the enduring appropriations this movement has provoked. First of all, 'Women in Black' did not emerge in the centers of the Western world, but on its periphery: the first group was formed in 1988 in Israel, one month after the outbreak of the Intifada.[14] Three years later, in 1991, Italian women formed 'Women in Black' groups all over their country to protest against Italy's participation in the Gulf War, and in the same year a group in Serbia followed as a response to the Milošević regime and the war in the former Yugoslavia in general (Zajović 2001, 11ff.). Today, there are more than 280 such groups all over the world, demonstrating solidarity among women and an anti-militaristic commitment – a huge number of them emerging in the United States after September 11th.

All 'Women in Black' groups are linked to each other by the same appearance: they choose a day, a time and an urban location – a square or a crossroads – and then appear every week in the same way, wearing mostly black, simple clothes,

---

14   The 'Women in Black' in Israel were first active between 1988 and 1993. In 1994, they re-formed, and since then have been active in the framework of 'Bat Shalom/Women for Peace' (Helman and Rapoport 1998, 7ff.).

reminiscent of traditional mourning, or in some contexts, wedding dresses. They always line up in a similar way, barely talking to each other or to passers-by, but communicating solely through their postures, their gazes and with posters or signs they carry in their hands and on which they have painted short statements, solidarity declarations or the dates of military attacks. Sometimes, however, the activists alienate this scenery by distributing magazines, leaflets and sometimes even flowers, or by carrying out small performances – where, for example, they bring some clothes into play that circulate between the various groups around the world and on which the names of former wearers are written inside.

What distinguish these performances from the appearance of other contemporary political movements are a strong ritualizing and an immutability of their visual, urban presence. All 'Women in Black' groups adhere to a set of minimal rules: definite times and locations, the silence of the protest, black clothes, the bodily presence of women, and recognizable signs and slogans. Whereas other contemporary political groups bank on the flexible, the momentary and on current debates and negotiations, this movement concentrates on unbroken continuity in the visual performance and enhanced repetition. And whereas individualized messages dominate the various local public spheres, here the individual women retreat behind an egalitarian way of dressing, behind collectively chosen repetitive messages and fixed frames (Helman and Rapoport 1998, 12).

This way of forming collective bodies in public space was inspired by previous political demonstrations – for example, by the 'Mothers of the Plaza de Mayo' in Argentina in the mid-1970s, who, in a similar silent but persevering and ritualized way, brought their bodies to always the same urban place in order to protest against the silence of Argentinean authorities in relation to the kidnappings, torture and executions of civilians by paramilitary groups (Torre 1996, 241ff.). At the same time, it is also reminiscent of the historical roots of political demonstrations, developing out of funeral processions and funeral rites (Lüdtke 1991, 124ff.). Here, older, rather traditional meanings of clothes concerning magic, societal cohesion or ritualized time are invoked against certain glamour and consumer appearances of the present day. But besides showing such rather unusual connotative lines to persistent commemoration, collective mourning or ritual celebration, the 'Women in Black' are political in the sense that they form visible collective bodies that challenge deep-rooted classifications – of male, female, public and private – as well as everyday urban routines. Their tactics are hence again characterized not by focusing on negotiation and compromise, but on conflict and provocation.

Pivotal for what is raised in this chapter, the activists do not refer to themselves as 'feminists' (Sasson-Levy and Rapoport 2003, 385), but as 'women' or as 'activists'. They are interrupting the above-described tradition, in which women tried to create a feminist counter-society or parallel society usually based on the expulsion of an excluded element – capital, the other religion, the other sex – charged with all the evil of which the so-constituted community then can purge itself (Kristeva 1986, 209). In contrast to this, the 'Women in Black' rather somehow de-dramatize the war between the sexes, by admitting men among them and simultaneously forming a collective body called 'women'. At the same time, they do not, as the first women's movement did, adopt the practice of identifying with a 'Universal Woman', but – while still sticking to a bridge-building figure of 'women' – they are rather concerned with providing themselves with a representation that can act as a kind of political-aesthetic stumbling block in the public sphere. In doing so, they nevertheless challenge the gendered order of their environment – which becomes most visible in the strong reactions their physical presence on the city stage provokes. The activists are frequently verbally abused, insulted, and sometimes even physically attacked. Passers-by, for example, describe the use of their bodily presence for political means as prostitution, or they are called traitors to their countries or abnormal and sexually unattractive (Helman and Rapoport 1998, 15ff.; Zajović 2001, 30ff.).

Like other contemporary political movements, the 'Women in Black' place heightened emphasis on aesthetic style and bodily presence, the inclusion of artistic performances, a simultaneous use of an entire media complex, including especially the Internet, a communication with 'the whole world', and a focus on conflict and provocation rather than on negotiation and compromise. They form collective bodies for which they adopt the name 'women', and at the same time confuse the dichotomy of men and women as an opposition between two rival entities. But above all, it seems to be the relative stability of the visual form of political appearance and the ritualization of the protest in combination with the absence of a detailed elaboration of ideological questions going beyond broader claims for women's solidarity and peace (see Sasson-Levy and Rapoport 2003, 391ff.) that has provoked the creation of so many follow-up groups and further incorporations of various political linkages.

This movement shows that in our contemporary globalized world, besides the more diverse, local, temporary forms of feminist political struggle – which are so often sharply separated from each other – there is again a political imagination at work that manages to invent new, attractive, varying spaces and territory-bridging figures and to situate them in challenging ways in tangible, urban territories. But – and this is also made quite clear by this example – the possibility of being adopted to very different political contexts as a mere form entails also a certain cost: the political representation so achieved is a quite ritualized one that is somehow empty, devoid of any particular political programme or more elaborated position. Seen this way, the practices adopted by the 'Women in Black' seem to share some characteristics with religious or mystic ones, which also rely on bodily presence, visual spectacle and ritualized repetition. But inside this frame, the women (and men) participating in this movement are again reinventing a form of representation and communication that tries to make up for some of the frustrations imposed on them by the current political regimes as well as by previous forms of feminist political organization. In employing a gesture of open-ended searching, they participate in a collective process of re-writing and re-adopting the traditions of emancipation.

Acknowledgments

I would like to thank the following colleagues for critical comments concerning this chapter: Barbara Grubner, Margareth Lanzinger, Kari Palonen, Tuija Pulkkinen and Elisabeth Timm. This chapter was written in the framework of the research project 'City Squats: The Cinema as a Space for Political Action', currently (2006–2009) financed by the FWF Austrian Science Fund.

References

Agrest, D. et al. (eds) (1996), *The Sex of Architecture* (New York: Harry N. Abrams).

Arendt, H. (1971), *Walter Benjamin, Berthold Brecht. Zwei Essays* (Munich and Zurich: Piper).

—— (1998), *Vita activa oder: Vom tätigen Leben* (Munich and Zurich: Piper).

Baldauf, A. and Weingartner, K. (1998), *Lips. Tits. Hits. Power? Popkultur und Feminismus* (Vienna and Bolzano: Folio).

Bilder Wandel (1991), Women's Film Festival leaflet.

Butler, J. (1990), *Gender Trouble: Feminism and the Subversion of Identity* (New York: Routledge).

Carrara, A.N.P.I. (ed.) (1991), *La meglio gioventú. La memoria che resiste* (Carrara: Società Editrice Apuana).

Collettivo Femminista Cinema-Roma (1975), *Manifesto Per un Cinema Clitorideo Vaginale* (Rome).

Doderer, Y.P. (2003), *Urbane Praktiken. Strategien und Raumproduktionen feministischer Frauenöffentlichkeit* (Münster: Monsenstein & Vannerdat).

Förster, W. (ed.) (2001), *Der andere Blick. Lesbischwules Leben in Österreich* (Vienna: MA 57).

Fraisse, G. (1995a), 'Der Bruch der Französischen Revolution und die Geschichte der Frauen', in Fraisse (ed.), *Geschlecht und Moderne. Archäologien der Gleichberechtigung* (Frankfurt am Main: Fischer).

—— (ed.) (1995), *Geschlecht und Moderne. Archäologien der Gleichberechtigung* (Frankfurt am Main: Fischer).

—— and Perrot, M. (eds) (1997), *Geschichte der Frauen, 4: 19. Jahrhundert* (Frankfurt am Main: Fischer).

Gibbins, J.R. and Reimer, B. (1999), *The Politics of Postmodernity: An Introduction to Contemporary Politics and Culture* (London: Sage).

Godineau, D. (1988), *Citoyennes tricoteuses* (Aix-en-Provence: Alinéa).

Helman, S. and Rapoport, T. (1998), 'Frauen in Schwarz. Eine Herausforderung für die Geschlechterordnung und Gesellschaftspolitik in Israel', *Feministische Studien* 16:1, 7–24.

Hobsbawm, E. (2005), 'Introduction: Inventing Traditions', in Hobsbawm and Ranger (eds), *The Invention of Tradition* (Cambridge: Cambridge University Press).

—— and Ranger, T. (eds) (2005), *The Invention of Tradition* (Cambridge: Cambridge University Press).

Huyssen, A. (1996), *After the Great Divide: Modernism, Mass Culture, Postmodernism* (Bloomington, IN: Indiana University Press).

Käppeli, A.-M. (1997), 'Die Feministische Szene', in Fraisse and Perrot (eds), *Geschichte der Frauen, 4: 19. Jahrhundert* (Frankfurt am Main: Fischer).

Keith, M. and Pile, S. (1993), *Place and the Politics of Identity* (London: Routledge).

Kristeva, J. (1986), 'Women's Time', in T. Moi (ed.), *The Kristeva Reader* (Oxford: Blackwell).

Laclau, E. (1996), *Emancipation(s)* (London: Verso).

—— (1990), *New Reflections on the Revolution of Our Time* (London: Verso).

Landes, J.B. (1988), *Women and the Public Sphere in the Age of the French Revolution* (Ithaca, NY: Cornell University Press).

Lefèbvre, H. (2003), *The Urban Revolution* (Minneapolis, MN: University of Minnesota Press).

Lefort, C. (1986), *The Political Forms of Modern Society: Bureaucracy, Democracy, Totalitarianism* (Cambridge: Polity).

—— (1999), *Fortdauer des Theologisch-Politischen* (Vienna: Passagen Verlag).

Lindi, L. and Rasetto, M.R. (2004), 'Le donne del VII luglio', in Carrara (ed.), *La meglio gioventú. La memoria che resiste* (Carrara: Società Editrice Apuana).

Lüdtke, A. (1991), 'Trauerritual und politische Manifestation. Zu den Begräbnisumzügen der deutschen Sozialdemokratie im frühen Kaiserreich' in Warneken (ed.), *Massenmedium Strasse. Zur Kulturgeschichte der Demonstration* (Frankfurt am Main and New York: Campus).

Moi, T. (ed.) (1986), *The Kristeva Reader* (Oxford: Blackwell).

Petersen, S. (1987), *Marktweiber und Amazonen. Frauen in der Französischen Revolution. Dokumente, Kommentare, Bilder* (Cologne: Pahl-Rugenstein).

Rancière, J. (1999), *Dis-agreement: Politics and Philosophy* (Minneapolis, MN: University of Minnesota Press).

Repnik, U. (2001), 'Lesben in Bewegung(en). Die Lesbenbewegung in Österreich seit den 70er Jahren', in W. Förster (ed.), *Der andere Blick. Lesbischwules Leben in Österreich* (Vienna: MA 57).

Rosa Lila Tip (1992), *Rosa Lila Villa. 10 Jahre Lesben- und Schwulenhaus* (Vienna: Verein Rosa Lila Tip).

Sartre, J.-P. (1967), *Kritik der dialektischen Vernunft*, vol. 1, *Theorie der Gesellschaftlichen Praxis* (Reinbek bei Hamburg: Rowolt).

Sasson-Levy, O. and Rapoport, T. (2003), 'Body, Gender, and Knowledge in Protest Movements: The Israeli Case', *Gender & Society* 17:3, 379–403.

Schober, A. (2008), *Ironie, Montage, Verfremdung. Ästhetische Taktiken und die politische Gestalt der Demokratie* (Munich: Fink).

The Guerrilla Girls (1995), *Confessions of the Guerrilla Girls* (London: HarperPerrennial).

Torre, S. (1996), 'Claiming the Public Space: The Mothers of Plaza de Mayo', in Agrest et al. (eds), *The Sex of Architecture* (New York: Harry N. Abrams).

Warneken, B.J. (1991a), 'Die friedliche Gewalt des Volkswillens. Muster und Deutungsmuster von Demonstrationen im deutschen Kaiserreich', in Warneken (ed.), Massenmedium Strasse. Zur Kulturgeschichte der Demonstration (Frankfurt am Main and New York: Campus).

—— (ed.) (1991b), Massenmedium Strasse. Zur Kulturgeschichte der Demonstration (Frankfurt am Main and New York: Campus).

Young, I.M. (1994), 'Gender as Seriality: Thinking about Women as a Social Collective', Signs: Journal of Women in Culture and Society 19:3, 713–38.

Zajović, S. (2001), Women for Peace (Belgrade: Women in Black).

Zerilli, L.M.G. (2005), Feminism and the Abyss of Freedom (Chicago, IL: University of Chicago Press).

Further Reading

Benhabib, S. (2002), The Claims of Culture: Equality and Diversity in the Global Era (Princeton, NJ: Princeton University Press).

Betterton, R. (1996), Intimate Distance: Women, Artists and the Body (London: Routledge).

Dahlgren, P. (1995) Television and the Public Sphere: Citizenship, Democracy and the Media (London: Sage).

Fuoss, K.W. (1997), Striking Performances/Performing Strikes (Jackson, Ml: University Press of Mississippi).

Ingram, G.B. (ed.) (1997), Queers in Space: Communities, Public Places, Sites of Resistance (Seattle, WA: Bay Press).

—, Bouthillette, A.M. and Retter, Y. (1997) 'Making Room: Queerscape Architectures and the Spaces of Activism' in Ingram (ed.), Queers in Space: Communities, Public Places, Sites of Resistance (Seattle, WA: Bay Press).

Massey, D. (1998), Space, Place and Gender (Cambridge: Polity).

Pollock, G. (1994), Vision and Difference: Femininity, Feminism and Histories of Art (London: Routledge).

Said, E.W. (2000), 'Invention, Memory, and Place', Critical Inquiry 26:2, 175–92.

Weintraub, J. and Kumar, K. (1997), Public and Private in Thought and Practice: Perspectives on a Grand Dichotomy (Chicago, IL: The University of Chicago Press).

Wilson, E. (1991), The Sphinx in the City: Urban Life, the Control of Disorder, and Women (London: Virago Press).

Spectres of Totality

Simona Forti

From Accidents to the Event

For many light-hearted liberals, 1989 sealed the ultimate death of totalitarianism. Instead, for the many orthodox-hearted Marxists, totalitarianism had never been anything else but a corpse, or rather, the scientific simulacrum of an ideological war, fought to quench communism. Cumbersome remnant of the past for the former, mystifying rhetorical instrument for the latter, totalitarianism nevertheless succeeded, toward the end of the twentieth century, in making the two agree that the death had come about, and particularly, on the opportunity of removing the problem's grievous heritage.

With what may look like a suspicious zeal, through refined academic arguments and subtle theoretical distinctions, the use of the term was tapered off, and a gentle but constant process of de-legitimization of the concept was undertaken.

The ostracism which struck, and is still striking, the notion of totalitarianism is indeed bizarre. It is almost as if, among the various terms and concepts of our political lexicon, totalitarianism were the only one to have suffered historiographical inaccuracy and ideological adjustment, as if the same ambivalences and possibility of instrumentalization did not inhere to each and every word of politics. This does not mean denying that at a certain point in history the concept of totalitarianism was *also* used as a Cold War weapon.

The politological typologies which followed Hannah Arendt's 1951 book, or rather, the schematic reception of her work, confined in Friedrich and Brzezinski's so-called 'totalitarian syndrome' (Friedrich and Brzezinski 1956), loyally served the professionals of anti-communism.[1] Moreover, they contributed in simplifying a complex category, reducing it, very often, to an aseptic taxonomical instrument.

I believe, none the less, that the reasons for such an aversion do not lie exclusively in the ideological weight that burdened the concept. The refusal also concerns the stratifications of meaning of a category which has been capable of breaking boundaries that were considered untouchable. From Hannah Arendt to Jean-Luc Nancy, from George Bataille to Michel Foucault, from Simone Weil

---

1   On the uses and history of the concept of totalitarianism, allow me to refer to Forti (2005).

to Jean-François Lyotard, from Emmanuel Levinas to Jacques Derrida, a radical and libertarian philosophy was able to formulate a theoretical category from an historical experience, especially that of Nazism and Stalinism, which goes beyond the concrete configuration of those regimes.

Thus, we might distinguish the phrase 'totalitarian regimes' from the lemma 'totalitarianism'. This is, of course, an over-hasty distinction, but it allows us to emphasize a crucial difference: the one between historical reality – whose unrepeatable uniqueness cannot be neutralized – and the philosophical conceptualization which would also like to dig out, among the tangles of the present, the dynamics, started off by the aforementioned regimes, that are still at work.

Thus, as a philosophical concept, to begin with, totalitarianism provides a useful tool for dismantling the metaphysical game of dualistic oppositions, including the contrapositions which have also delimited, in a certain and patent way, the areas of the political field. When we take *that* reflection of the twentieth century seriously which also thought of totalitarianism as a philosophical event, shelter can no longer be found in comforting antitheses: namely, to take comfort in the identification of Nazism or fascism with an irrational and particularistic anti-humanism, and of Stalinism, for instance, with a pathological deviation of a communist route in itself perfectly sound, rationalistic and universalistic.

Evoking the spirit of democracy and humanism will no longer suffice. A whole cultural and philosophical world would not stand up to the test of the extreme, and for this reason it must be investigated with merciless suspicion. And this is why the historical experience of totalitarianism ends up by transforming itself from accident to event; that event-limit which marks the end of an era, but forces us to rethink its dynamics, both backwards and in prospect.

In short, from the mid-twentieth century onward, a large part of philosophy – at least of 'Continental' philosophy – establishes a real hermeneutical circle with totalitarianism, which culminates in the 'scandal' of thinking the continuity between totalitarianism and the Western tradition, namely trying to trace in the totalitarian logic the involvement of reason itself and its way of relating to the world (Forti 2005, 67–120).

Not exactly everyone, then, dismissed the problem. Some, alarmed by such philosophy and frightened by the future, continue to repeat that 'totalitarianism can be said in many ways'. Even though those regimes collapsed, which in the 'most civilized Europe' of the mid-twentieth century attempted to make everyone's life superfluous, this does not mean that the, so to speak, 'ontological' *a priori* inherent in that incident ceased to operate.

And while the twentieth-century debate questioned the reasons for such 'guilt', today's philosophy must ask itself what still remains active of those totalizing and potentially totalitarian dynamics. The past will not present itself again with those specific features. So, perhaps, rather than analytical comparisons between the past history and recent incidents, a certain capacity to perceive the ghosts of the past under certain forms of the present could prove more useful. And while the social, historical and political sciences take charge in watching over the presence of concrete totalitarian drifts – from the dynamics of preventive war to the migration fluxes of 'non-persons' – philosophy, which has never really recovered from its passion for the invisible, must once again take specters seriously. It will have to continue to watch over strategies which for the time being are only totalizing, but might produce real totalitarian effects.

'Thus, there are no dishonoured concepts, betrayed or treacherous' (Blanchot 1980), there are only concepts which require to be re-thought over and over again. This is what philosophy tries to do, rescuing totalitarianism from the vice of vulgarization and refusal. It must be re-thought on the grounds of a cumbersome presupposition, not always accepted by everyone: it became apparent, no longer 'with any shadow of doubt', in totalitarian regimes, that political power – be it actualized in those specific forms or not – has a totalitarian vocation; that is to say, it tends to have a strict control over everything and everyone (Foucault 2001, 383).

From the excess of such domination, philosophy must find the courage to start being concerned again with the present, in order to ask itself again and afresh the relation between life and power, the relation between reality and fiction and the problem of the metamorphosis of evil. These are the specters of totality which worry philosophy today, which are no longer present in their violent materiality, but nevertheless, have not completely vanished. They worry, at least, that kind of philosophy which does not set itself up as an 'analytics of truth', but offers itself as an 'ontology of actuality'.

I enumerate them separately for heuristic reasons, even though the consistency of the one is, every often, connected with the persistence of the others. I suggest calling them, respectively: the specter of 'hyper-humanity' (or the bio-political specter); the specter of absolute deceitfulness (or the specter of the crisis of reality), and the specter of the normality of evil (or the specter of organized irresponsibility).

Hyper-humanity, or the Bio-political Specter

If the end of every totalitarian system is the total transformation of a given reality, especially human reality, then I think it can be affirmed that its aim is articulated in a twofold strategy: the production of the 'Muslim' – 'the non-humanity' – on the one hand, and the realization of the ideal of a 'hyper-humanity' as the only true humanity on the other. Thus, from a philosophical perspective, totalitarianism today assumes the function of a twofold idea-limit, almost in a Kantian sense. Namely, it can be useful to consider the present by comparing it to a twofold imaginary *focus*, hopefully never completely phenomenizable: the situation-limit of total power over life, which attains physical life, transforming it into sheer organic material; the situation-limit of the identification without residual of each and every singular to the great symbolic political body of totalitarian ideology. I believe that what is called, in a Foucaultian term which is perhaps far too abused, the 'biopolitical' tendency of our time is actually one of the most cumbersome legacies of totalitarianism. When politics – once all formal mediations have failed – assumes as its own object life in its elementary and primary form, now stripped of those masks through which an existence relates to the world; when it is directed toward living itself, in its purely biological meaning; when, therefore, dominion overruns the very body, of the singular and of the population, a radical metamorphosis of power relations can be witnessed.[2]

In the totalitarian glorification of blood (Nazism), but also in the ennobling of the working man at arms (Stalinism), generally speaking, in an unheard-of primacy of the body – from the edification of the new man's body to the annihilation of the superfluous or corrupting body – a new use and appraisal of the biological emerges. It brings forth the total involvement of a naked existence in the now capillary web of power. Therefore, beyond its specific contents, the ideological project cannot be understood simply as a secularized religion that requires an assent of absolute faith; nor can it be read exclusively as the justification which legitimizes the dismantling of the juridical and legal system.

Ideology, far more than an *instrumentum regni* to obtain consent and obedience, is a device which allows for shifting and redefining the boundaries of the human, of what is included and excluded, each time, from the great body of humanity, from the organism of hyper-humanity, hence determining that the *Lagers* not only serve the purpose of exterminating, but also of experimenting the modification of human reality, its mass-production as well as its transformation into organic material.

In totalitarian regimes, power exerted itself over life not merely by suppressing it. It was not a question of an enormous, unprecedented, abuse of power which quelled the rights of the singulars. Political power succeeded in turning itself into both a total and capillary dominion, by setting itself, in the first place, as warrant of the *security*, the *health* and the *prosperity* of an entire people, who required the elimination of a harmful and destructive 'living part' in order to incarnate in the ideal of a hyper-humanity.

In other words, totalitarian bio-politics has shown us what a political apparatus can attain which, in the name of security and public health, by appealing directly to the 'productivity' of life, was able to invade, with unparalleled intensity and capillarity, the existence of all and the entire existence. Certainly, it was a paroxysmal logic that availed itself of different strategies and various techniques, but it is nevertheless the inauguration of an exercise of power in which the logic of the legal covenant no longer works. From the perspective of its concern, bio-power no longer concentrates, through the prohibiting force of law, on the person and his or her property, but it attacks the biological processes of the entire population directly, reaching a point that no state, no political power, had ever reached.

---

2   On bio-politics, see Foucault (1976, 2004). For a reflection on bio-politics which develops Foucault's idea, see also Fehér and Heller (1994), among the first contributions which readdressed the issue of bio-politics taking Foucault as a starting point and connecting it to Hannah Arendt's heritage. See also Heller and Puntscher Riekmann (1996). Among the many works which deal with bio-politics from this perspective, see Brossat (1998, 2003); Butler (1997); Haraway (1991); Hottois (1999); Lecorps and Paturet (1999); Shiva and Moser (1995); Geyer (2001); Stingelin (2003); Gerhardt (2004). See also the references to bio-politics in Hardt and Negri (2000); Bodei (2002); Esposito (2002); Bazzicalupo and Esposito (2003); Forti (2004).

But if bio-power proved to be so functional to the edification of total dominion – and this is particularly the case for Nazism – it is not simply due to the fact that it used an enormously powerful instrument of identification, owing to its primeval and 'natural' character: the idea of race, namely the value or disvalue of the body in its organic and biological condition. Certainly, this has allowed for the organization of manslaughter in terms of a planned and systematic enterprise of healing the body politic. But there is also another vector which concurs in driving Nazi bio-politics to its extreme procedures – something far more familiar to our philosophical tradition than evolutionist race theories. Totalitarianism brings the other situation-limit to our attention here. Racism proceeds from a 'metaphysics of the form'. This theory, using much more Plato than the laws of genetics, holds that the 'supreme spiritual value' of a race lies in the achievement of the perfect form, in the sense of the somatic aspect, because such a form is nothing else but the expression and confirmation of the idea or type, or spirit of the people. According to the former, the type, the spirit, have the transcendental function of turning a body into a phenomenon. In such a context, none the less, race and spirit, the 'spirit of the race', are nothing but the outside and inside of that idea which sustains the 'hyper-humanity', namely that 'Great Human Life', offering the perfect model for an identification process of many into One.

This is certainly not the occasion to dwell upon the crucial importance of a certain 'Nazi philosophical anthropology'.[3] Recalling that such anthropology brought

---

3   None the less, it is worthwhile to cite some of the most influent 'anthropologist-philosophers' beside Rosenberg (see Rosenberg 1933, 1934, 1936) and Krieck (1936) (similar anthropological premises can be found in Hitler's *Mein Kampf*). One must also remember those writers who, between 1932 and 1934, linked Plato's philosophy to the National Socialist movement. The most widely read and circulating include Bannes (1933a, 1933b) and Gabler (1934). The most important author is Hans K.F. Günther, defined by Adriano Romualdi and, even earlier, by Evola as the most important theoretician of race in the twentieth century, responsible for reshaping Gobienau's early theories into a solid doctrinal body. He is, indeed, one of the best-known authors of the Nazi era. Among his extremely successful works in the 1920s are his *Rassenkunde des deutschen Volkes* (1922), which was reprinted 16 times in more than 100,000 copies, and could be found in almost every German household in an abbreviated version, called the *Volksgünther*; but also Günther (1928a, 1928b, 1929, 1937). Günther (1929) and (1937) were reprinted, respectively, 17 and 20 times in more than 120,000 copies. On the eve of the National Socialist rise to power, Günther's work was already an organic component of the movement. He taught social anthropology at Berlin University. On Günther's part in the 'philosophy of National Socialism', see Voegelin (1933). On his part in the history of eugenics, see Weindling (1989). In Italy, this thought is followed by Julius Evola (1938; 1942) and later by F. Freda (see Freda 1996, 2001). Evola also conceives the body as phenomenological expression of the soul –not of the individual soul, but of that of the race (*stirpe*). According to Evola, the supreme value of the race lies in the perfect form of its somatic features and of its 'spiritual' aspect, which must coincide. If one keeps in mind this 'Aryanized' Plato, one may understand Karl Popper's anti-Platonic polemic better: his *Open Society and Its Enemies* (1945) appears to take Plato's

about some of the most widespread works in the pre-Hitlerian and Hitlerian period, reaching the home of almost every 'good German', is sufficient.

These are aberrational but precious texts, for they provide a clear answer to the question, 'What is human in the Third Reich?', by confronting us with a number of strategies of truth which conduct an identification process that aims at being total. A short and widely read work of 1937 is, quite significantly, entitled *Humanitas* (Günther 1937). It was to become a kind of founding text for that theoretical movement within the SS which propounded the unity of Europe on racial grounds. It is up to the German people to bring the idea of *humanitas* back into the German context, whose values, like the original Indo-German ones, are the values of life itself, craving for its self-affirmation and self-increase. True *humanitas* is 'a task to achieve, a model to reach, ... an ideal of racial selection'. Nazi 'philo-hellenic' racism – by no means in the minority – exceeds evolutionistic biologism by far, and culminates in a 'monistic ontology', the 'idealism of a perfect identity of body and soul', of idea and reality, or to use a classical expression, of form and matter.

The 'cultivated' Nazi literature elaborated an intense enterprise of re-defining the human, helped by the appeal to a 'true humanism'. While it establishes the *form* of hyper-humanity, the new concept of *humanitas* sanctions contextually the impossibility for a part 'of the living beings' to elevate themselves to participating in the Idea, in other words, to achieve the reality of the human. Thus, what is at work – as many well-intentioned neo-humanists would like – is not simply a rhetoric of the Arian super-man, who despises the vulgar democratic 'little and last men', thus overthrowing the egalitarian and universal values of the noble humanistic tradition.

Europe has not only been the land of civilization, of Enlightenment and reason, or in other words, of the glorious and civilizing power of *humanitas*. What took place on that very land was the tragic shift into action of a form of nihilism which also spoke without hesitation the language of humanism (Sloterdijk 1999). By this, of course, I do not want to say that Nazism is a humanism. I would only like to stir some suspicion toward the comfortable and unquestioned dualistic visions, toward all humanist rhetoric, which often conceals the potential violence of a constructivist and 'domineering' subjectivism. Hence the necessity to dig deeply in order to bring to light the twofold face of humanism, its dialectic open onto the possible complementariness of hyper-human and non-human.

A will to dominate, which points directly at life, continues working under the semblance of solicitude and the promise of security. For instance, how many agents, among private associations, leagues and public actors, are mobilized nowadays in the name of the absolute and illusory ideal of perfect health.[4] Today's 'hyper-humanity' corresponds to a potentially immortal human ideal, for whom the constitutive limits of existence which we have known up to now seem the heritage of an 'antiquated

---

interpretation offered by these authors seriously. On the Aryan myth, see Poliakov (1971).

4   On 'health ideology', see at least Ruffié (1993); Sfez (1995); Fitzpatrick (2005), but still today the 'classic', Illich (1976).

man'. Actually, this struggle against time, sickness and death answers both to the political desire to get a hold over the bodies and to the demand of an individual identification in the perfectly constituted body. From the war against every risk of 'premature death' to the studies in predictive medicine, from bio-technologies to corrective cybernetics, from breast-feeding campaigns to 'lipophobic' methods, everything seems to multiply the possibilities of the administration of life, of a more secure life in terms of health, but 'stripped', almost 'saved', from the bonds of contingency, but confined, probably more than it ever was, to total control. It is almost as if a new democratic and humanist form of eugenics were leading the human to that 'anthropological leap' of which philosophy had already warned us.

Absolute Lie, or the Specter of the Crisis of Reality

Is it possible to reconstruct a history of the lie, or rather, the history of the idea of lie, within which we might single out turns, changes and discontinuities? Is it reasonable that from lie as the concealment of a determined and circumscribed reality, through the totalitarian laboratory, one could pass on to absolute lie, that is, released totally from factual truth which is concealed proof of its untruthful nature?

In order to decide, we would need to specify the statute of the lie: perhaps one of the most difficult to define. It concerns nothing less than the concepts of reality and also truth. But even if we leave out the obviously various and complex epistemological and gnoseological implications of the problem, the fact remains that it is not easy to determine the political repercussions of the lie when the possibility of identifying the criteria of truth in the correspondence between object and representation fails. What follows, to start with, is that the lie cannot coincide with the error. It is therefore possible to misrepresent a fact, not recognize an event or affirm something completely absurd without none the less lying.

Moreover – and now it is becoming more complicated – the lie is not even self-deception.[5] Because, in this case, actually lying to oneself implies the ego's psychological, cognitive or emotional defectiveness which somehow absolves it from the accusation of being a liar. Without even wishing to discuss additional difficulties – from the classical question regarding the nature of a lie which is told for a 'good purpose' to the Machiavellian cunning of telling a truth openly because nobody would believe it – I think that it is nevertheless appropriate to confirm an attestation which is not always borne in mind: lying is a relation. Or rather, it is a *relational* and *intentional* action. It is directed toward another, toward others, with the precise function of deceiving them or of concealing something from them which would be useful for them to know.

Thus, if lying is always relational and intentional, what change would totalitarianism have brought about? 'Modern man – *totalitarian genus* – is immersed in a lie, he breathes lies, he is a slave to lying in every moment of his life.' In his 1945 article 'The Political Function of the Modern Lie', Alexandre Koyré gives voice

---

5   Derrida (1997), 129–61 (Italian trans. Forti 2004, 189–232).

to what will become a widespread feeling about the break, brought about by the totalitarian lie, in respect to what we might be called a 'traditional' form of lie which would have always been used in politics.

In those decades, Hannah Arendt was not the only one to be troubled about the changes that contemporary lies underwent (Arendt 1965, 380–85; Arendt 1967, 227–64; 1972). Since the end of the 1960s, Eastern dissidents have tirelessly repeated, with great vigor even if with a certain naivety, that totalitarian regimes are responsible for particular 'innovations' in this respect. Their warning was not directed exclusively to the then still communist East, but was also extended to the West, which was, they considered, inscribed in a single and identical 'post-totalitarian' fate. Indeed, there is no 'dissident' text, whose arguments do not pivot around *1984* and does not present Orwell's literary dystopia as a hyper-realistic analysis of the actual situation.[6]

If totalitarianisms establish themselves by means of 'gunshots', they are able to keep themselves in power only by means of 'language shots', thus transforming themselves gradually into real 'mass logocracies' (Milosz 1953).

Only through the use of a 'newspeak' can every possibility of a resistance to the regime be prevented. Once the most destructive ideological terror is over, that 'cold totalitarianism' which operates on the preclusion of all autonomous judgement must be considered. Because that power, which demolishes the very criteria of facticity by manipulating information and destroying historical memory, remains totalitarian.

Certainly, when truth, in the sense of facticity, changes in accordance with power's necessities, it becomes impossible to distinguish between what is true and what is false. The transition from normal lie to 'institutionalized lie', securing political power with the monopoly of historical and factual truths, would thus take place. This is what connects Stalinism and Nazism to the various 'thaws' which are able to reduce the onslaught of violence, precisely because they have perfected the mechanism of 'regime deceit', as variable in its contents as it is inflexible in its function.[7]

Thus, totalitarianism seems to have inaugurated the age of performative lie. Unlike 'traditional' political lies, the totalitarian lie not only set to work its destructive capacity, but also its constructive capacity, which, logically, has always been inherent. It has nothing to do with negations, concealments, of certain factual truths which might somehow be saved. Totalitarianism brings us to the confines of a millennarian ontology which had indeed divided the world in truth and appearance, in reality and fiction, but had certainly not foreseen the 'creative' power of lies that were to become the very foundation for the construction of raving political systems.

By providing linguistic expression to aberrant ideological fictions, an existence was conferred to them which ran the risk of reshaping the world. By concealing the 'harsh facts', we came very close to destroying the texture of the entire reality.

---

6   With regard to this subject, allow me to refer to my 'Dalla costruzione di modelli alla pratica del dissenso' in Forti (2005), 41–67.

7   This opinion is shared by dissident writers; see, for example, Kolakowski (1983) and Havel (1989).

Obviously, what is at stake is much more than the damage provoked by the deceiver's ill will and wickedness. The world's very consistency and its possible share is at stake. This means that the problem is ontological before becoming political. Totalitarian regimes have trodden dangerously on the limits, running the risk of precipitating the world toward extinction, outside a sphere in which it is still possible – in spite of all the precautions of hermeneutics and the suspicions of deconstruction – to distinguish between what happens and what politics narrates, briefly, where it is still possible to separate facts from logical constructions.

These regimes have indeed laid the foundations for the lack of distinction between factual and fantastic, making such a distinction ephemeral to the point of paradox, by conferring absolute primacy on deceit and by endlessly manipulating reality. But they have not succeeded in burying it completely, probably because, in their delirium of omnipotence, the exponents of those regimes did not perceive factuality as a stumbling block in the least.

The distinction between real and fictitious, made uncertain and vague by totalitarian deceit, seems today on the verge of disappearing for ever. Or rather, since it is a question of *in*distinction, it is running the risk of transforming the world into a gigantic ghost[8] – or so the most extreme prognoses concerning our future proclaim.

Divided between the enthusiasm for the opportunities offered by the 'virtual' and the apocalyptic condemnation of a cosmos reduced to an image, the diagnostics have no doubt when designating the present age as one of 'crisis of reality'. From this crisis, politics knows how to take catastrophic advantage, running the risk of shattering a by now extremely thin demarcation line into a new totalitarian game of mirror images.

An enormous possibility for lying is provided now by a kaleidoscopic media world, made up of de-composed and re-composed images, almost to the point of convincing us that reality is not given to us, but is weighed, selected, even produced. And we are carried away by the whirl of this spectacle to such an extent that we feel impotent.

However, totalitarian lies still contained specific ideological contents. Adorno, Baudrillard or Debord do not need to be disturbed in order to recognize that the game is becoming more and more inclusive and elusive, widespread and irresponsible. Without surrendering to the complaint of those who deplore a society of entertainment that transforms everybody in passive spectators and consumers, it cannot be denied that lie and factuality integrate each other to the point that no possible way out for efficacious action or thought can be anticipated in their thick web.

We are not immersed in a lie which violates the body of those who are not devoted to it. We are not impotent, passive and conformist just out of fear and cowardice, but also because the 'unquestionable falsehood'[9] skilfully organizes the ignorance of what takes place, and when needed, it could subsequently prepare the oblivion of what one has been able to understand. Thrown into a sort of constant alternation of images, incapable of understanding which ones relate facts and

---

8   See Anders (1992).
9   Debord (1988).

which ones are inventing them, a really powerful leap – probably impossible and utopian – would be needed in order to try and grasp what we have been deprived of again: the experience of the factual world, which resists mediatization.

Normality of Evil, or the Specter of Organized Irresponsibility

For this reason, talking about 'evil' must continue, even though it is not easy to understand where it comes from and in what ways it is conveyed.

But political evil exists, and above all, reveals itself by making women and men passive and conformist, but expert, as never before, in the conjuring tricks which equate facts and opinions, the possible and the actual, the contingent and the necessary. But the singular, irreducible and painful factuality of the world must finally be able to reach us so that talking about evil, this submissive and widespread evil, still makes sense. In short, a wager must be made on the presupposition that somehow it can still be recognized.

After all, contemporary post-metaphysical and post-theological, political evil set itself up precisely on the negation of such recognition. From this derive both the delirium concerning the infinite possibility of manipulating reality, as well as the feeling of our total impotence. Auschwitz demonstrated this, too: that abnormal crimes were made possible thanks to the action, or rather the inaction, of so many 'normal' people who did not find the strength or motivation to oppose what seemed to be the rule at the time. They were the people who unknowingly lubricated a perfect organization, who bound a very efficient interlacement of the many irresponsibilities. Not that there were no absolute culprits or 'wicked demons', but without the support of an obedient and aligned majority – not for this of a murderous nature – the limit would not have been exceeded.

Totalitarianism exposed the paradox of a devastating evil which surpassed all Decalogue through 'normal' actions – not simply in the sense of actions carried out by normal actors, by 'mediocre demons', but in the literal sense of their *Regelmässigkeit*, of the conformity to the norm, to the rule which that reality set forth.

Thus, the 'banality of evil' – the famous phrase which Hannah Arendt coined for Eichmann's trial[10] – does not only refer to the disproportion between the subjective motivations of an action and its objective, potentially or effectively devastating, effects. Instead, I believe it provides an answer to our need for a new conceptual constellation, indispensable now for thinking of evil in the light of its murderous normality. Besides its iconoclastic power, the phrase expresses the consumption of the normative power of the traditional reflections on evil.

This, in fact, is no longer imaginable according to an ontology which conceives it as an autonomous principle, as the rival of good. Nor can we agree with that theology which thought it the instrument of a future good. But it cannot even simply be identified as personal egoism. Briefly, evil, like the lie, must be restored to a relational dimension, and simultaneously to a 'responsibility of the singular'.

---

10   Arendt (1963).

Evil must be stripped of its objective substance and broken up in its contingent elements, it must be reconstructed – undoing it from its claimed metaphysical or demonic nature – back to its 'micro-physical' and prosaic structure.

From a political viewpoint, therefore, the 'specter of the normality of evil' unmasks one of the most long-lived commonplaces about the evil and power *hendiadys*: the dichotomy between an active and guilty pole of power, and a passive multitude of innocent subordinates compelled to obedience. The compliant acquittal that each one concedes to himself in the name of collective impotence and the impossibility of change is actually a great alibi, very often a deception. In this way, the conformism of one is to be found in the conformism of another, forcing everyone to play the same part in the game of power. We are no longer allowed to think of evil as a mere synonym of transgression. In the same way, we cannot console ourselves any longer by the fact that wickedness and evil coincide as intention and effect coincide.

Because, never so much as now, the capacity to resist evil is linked to the force of bringing into question authority or, rather, of contrasting the pressure of a norm. Conformism, obedience, inaction are the new attributes of evil. Totalitarianism has transformed, once and for all, their passive position and acquiescence in a culpable activity, guilty of being the very condition of the possibility of evil's persistence. Today, as then, omission is no less active than action.

References

Anders, G. (1992), *Die Antiquiertheit des Menschen. 1. Über die Seele im Zeitalter der zweiten industriellen Revolution; 2. Über die Zerstorung des Lebens im Zeitalter der dritten industriellen Revolution* (Munich: Beck).

Arendt, H. (1951), *The Origins of Totalitarianism* (New York: Harcourt, Brace; 2nd enlarged edn 1958, New York: World Publishing, Meridian Books).

—— (1963), *Eichmann in Jerusalem: A Report on the Banality of Evil* (2nd enlarged edn 1965, New York: Viking Press).

—— (1965), 'Politik und Verbrechen. Ein Briefwechsel, Hannah Arendt-Hans Magnus Enzensberger', *Merkur* XIX: 205.

—— (1967), 'Truth and Politics', *The New Yorker* 1, 227–64; also in (1968), *Between Past and Future: Eight Exercises in Political Thought* (New York: Viking Press).

—— (1972), 'Lying in Politics: Reflections on the Pentagon Papers', in *Crises of the Republic* (New York: Harvest).

Bannes, J. (1933a), *Hitler und Platon* (Berlin and Leipzig: de Gruyter).

—— (1933b), *Hitlers Kampf und Platons Staat* (Berlin and Leipzig: de Gruyter).

Bazzicalupo, L. and Esposito, R. (eds) (2003), *Politica della vita* (Rome and Bari: Laterza).

Blanchot, M. (1980), *L'écriture du désastre* (Paris: Gallimard).

Bodei, R. (2002), *Destini personali. L'età della colonizzazione delle coscienze* (Milan: Feltrinelli).

Brossat, A. (1998), *Le corps de l'ennemi. Hyperviolence et démocratie* (Paris: La fabrique).
—— (2003), *La démocratie immunitaire* (Paris: La Dispute).
Butler, J. (1997), *The Psychic Life of Power* (Stanford, CA: Stanford University Press).
Debord, G. (1988), *La société du spectacle* (Paris: Gallimard).
Derrida, J. (1997), 'History of the Lie: Prolegomena', *Graduate Faculty Philosophy Journal* 19:2 and 20:3; Italian trans. Forti (2004).
Esposito, R. (2002), *Immunitas. Protezione e negazione della vita* (Torino: Einaudi).
Evola, J. (1938), *Sintesi di dottrina della razza* (Milano: Hoepli).
—— (1942), *Il mito del sangue* (Milano: Hoepli).
Fehér, F. and Heller, A. (1994) *Biopolitics* (Vienna: European Centre).
Fitzpatrick, M. (2005), *The Tyranny of Health: Doctors and the Regulation of Lifestyle* (London: Routledge).
Forti, S. (ed.) (2004), *La filosofia di fronte all'estremo* (Torino: Einaudi).
—— (2005), *Il totalitarismo*, 2nd edn (Rome and Bari: Laterza).
Foucault, M. (1976), *Histoire de la sexualité, 1: La volonté de savoir* (Paris: Gallimard). English trans. (1978), *The History of Sexuality, Volume I: An Introduction*, by R. Hurley (New York: Viking Press).
—— (2001), *La sécurité et l'Etat*, in *Dits et écrits II, 1967–1988* (Paris: Gallimard).
—— (2004), *Sécurité, territoire, population. Cours au Collège de France, 1977–1978* (Paris: Gallimard).
Freda, F. (1996), *Platone. Lo Stato secondo giustizia* (Padua: Edizioni di Ar).
—— (2001), *I lupi azzurri* (Padua: Edizioni di Ar)
Friedrich, C.J. and Brzezinski, Z. (1956), *Totalitarian Dictatorship and Autocracy* (New York: Harper).
Gabler, A. (1934), *Platon und der Führer* (Berlin and Leipzig: de Gruyter).
Gerhardt, V. (2004), *Die angeborene Würde des Menschen* (Parega Verlag: Berlin)
Geyer, C. (ed.) (2001), *Biopolitik. Die Positionen* (Frankfurt am Main: Suhrkamp).
Günther, H.K.F. (1922), *Rassenkunde des deutschen Volkes* (Munich: Lehemanns Verlag).
—— (1928a), *Rassenkunde Europas* (Munich: Lehemanns Verlag).
—— (1928b), *Platon als Hüter des Lebens* (Munich: Lehemanns Verlag).
—— (1929), *Rassenkunde des Jüdischen Volk* (Munich: Lehemanns Verlag).
—— (1937), *Humanitas* (Munich: Lehemanns Verlag).
Haraway, D.J. (1991), 'The Biopolitics of Postmodern Bodies: Determinations of Self in Immune System Discourse', in *Simians, Cyborgs, and Women: The Reinvention of Nature* (New York: Routledge).
Hardt, M. and Negri, A. (2000), *Empire* (Cambridge, MA: Harvard University Press).
Havel, V. (1989), 'Histoires et totalitarianisme', in *Essais politiques* (Paris: Calmann-Lévy); Italian trans. Forti (2004), 141–66.
Heller, A. and Puntscher Riekmann, S. (eds) (1996), *Biopolitics: The Politics of the Body, Race and Nature* (Vienna: European Centre).
Hottois, G. (1999), *Essais de philosophie bioétique et biopolitique* (Paris: Vrin).

Howe, I. (ed.) (1983), *1984 Revisited: Totalitarianism in Our Century* (New York: Harper & Row); Italian trans. Forti (2004), 124–39.

Illich, I. (1976), *Medical Nemesis: The Expropriation of Health* (London: Marion Boyars).

Kolakowski, L. (1983), 'Totalitarianism and the Virtue of the Lie', in Howe (ed.), *1984 Revisited: Totalitarianism in Our Century* (New York: Harper & Row).

Koyrè, A. (1945), 'The Political Function of Modern Lie', *Contemporary Jewish Record* 8:3, 290–91.

Krieck, E. (1936), *Völkisch-politische Anthropologie* (Leipzig: Armanen-Verlag).

Lecorps, P. and Paturet, J.-B. (1999), *Santé publique. Du biopouvoir à la démocratie* (Rennes: Editions ENSP).

Milosz, C. (1953), *Zniewolony umysl*; Italian trans. (1981), *La mente prigioniera* (Milan: Adelphi).

Poliakov, L. (1971), *Le mythe aryen* (Paris: Calmann-Lévy).

Rosenberg, A. (1933), *Der Mythus des XX. Jahrhunderts*, vol. II (Munich: Hoheneichen Verlag).

—— (1934), *Blut und Ehre* (Munich: Hoheneichen Verlag).

—— (1936), *Gestalten der Idee* (Munich: Hoheneichen Verlag).

Ruffié, J. (1993), *Naissance de la médicine prédictive* (Paris: Odile Jacob).

Sfez, L. (1995), *La santé parfaite. Critique d'une nouvelle utopie* (Paris: Seuil).

Shiva, V. and Moser, I. (eds) (1995), *Biopolitics* (Bloomington, IN: Indiana University Press).

Sloterdijk, P. (1999), *Regeln für den Menschenpark* (Frankfurt am Main: Suhrkamp).

Stingelin, M. (ed.) (2003), *Biopolitik und Rassismus* (Frankfurt am Main: Suhrkamp).

Voegelin, E. (1933), *Rasse und Staat* (Tübingen: JCB Mohr).

Weindling, P. (1989), *Health, Race and German Politics between National Unification (1870-1945)* (Cambridge: Cambridge University Press).

Further Reading

Agamben, G. (1995), *Homo sacer. Il potere sovrano e la nuda vita* (Turin: Einaudi).

Brossat, A. (1996), *L'épreuve du désastre. Le XXe siècle et les camps* (Paris: Albin Michel).

Derrida, J. (1996), *Écographies de la télevision* (Paris: Edition Galilée/Institut National de l'audiovisuel).

Esposito, R. (2004), *Bios: biopolitica e filosofia* (Turin: Einaudi).

Forti, S. (2006), 'The Biopolitics of Souls', *Political Theory* 39:1, 9–33.

Foucault, M. (1997), *Il faut défendre la société* (Paris: Gallimard); English trans. (2003) *Society Must be Defended* (London: Allen Lane).

—— (2004), *Naissance de la biopolitique. Cours au Collège de France, 1978–1979* (Paris: Gallimard).

PART III

CHANGES

Women's Partial Citizenship: Cleavages and Conflicts Concerning Women's Citizenship in Theory and Practice

Claudia Wiesner

Introduction

The heart of this chapter's argument is the tension between the (seemingly) universalist claim of citizenship as a universalist standard and an unequal citizenship practice. The normative ideal of citizenship as a universalist standard implies that neither men nor women can be the standard of citizenship (nor any standards of race, class or belief), but that conditions, rights, duties and the active content of citizenship must be defined in such a comprehensive manner that neither is discriminated against. In a nutshell: the formal elements as well as the active contents of a universalist citizenship must be gender-neutral, and also neutral with regard to race, class and religion. It is the aspect of gender that is the central focus here.

When comparing citizenship practice to this ideal, it quickly becomes clear that until today, we have not been successful in realizing a universalist citizenship, neither concerning race and class, nor concerning gender. Women's citizenship status in practice since the beginning of European democratization has been continually different from men's due to persisting gender differences that affect women's equal rights. But the big gap at first existing over the centuries changed in dimension, and also changed its parameters. This chapter will discuss the differences between men's and women's citizenship status, their political and ideological background, and their normative and analytical implications.

The tension between citizenship as a universalist claim and an unequal citizenship practice has been addressed by many pro-feminist politicians and theoreticians since the beginnings of modern citizenship with the French Revolution. One of the persons who indicated it most clearly was Olympe de Gouges in her famous 1791 declaration 'The Rights of Women and the Female Citizen'. Her starting point is the French Revolution's declaration of the 'The Rights of Men and Citizens', and the fact that she realized that the rights it claims for men as citizens did not concern women. In fact, the rights were only valid for men from a certain class. De Gouges's declaration thus departs from a universalist point of view: she was eager to show that the declaration of the rights of men claimed universal rights, and that women should have equal access to them – whereas in practice, they did not at all.

Re-reading de Gouges's declaration today, one notices that the claims she made have not been fully attained even today: she claimed equality for women with men in all aspects of both public and private life – including equal rights to vote, to hold office, to public employment, to speak in public on political topics, to equal public honors, to own and control property, to participate in the military, to education, and to equal power in the family and the Church (de Gouges 1791). In other words, she mentioned several of the topics that have become most crucial for women's equal rights and political representation during the following centuries.

This chapter is divided into five sections. The first contains the development of the analytical framework. The second deals with the history of the development of women's citizenship from 1789 until the obtainment of women's suffrage. The third discusses the problems, contradictions and differences persisting after the obtainment of women's suffrage. The fourth sheds a light on the current situation, and the fifth contains the methodological and normative conclusions resulting from the preceding analyses. Each section will call on illustrative examples taken from European history to explain the overall theses. In particular, the German case is most illustrative for specific problems and contradictions of women's citizenship.

Conditions, Rights and Active Content: Different Elements of Citizenship

What must be understood by the label 'citizenship'? There are different approaches concerning theory, meaning, content and normative aspects of citizenship (see Kymlicka 2002 for a summary and overview). But most of them have several points in common: First, citizenship – as classically defined by Marshall (1950, 10–27) and Tilly (1975, 32) – names the relationship between a polity and its members, which has formalized as well as practical effects. This definition hints at the fact that the *conditions* of that relationship, their *institutionalization*, and the resulting *practices* are at stake.

Moreover, four important elements of citizenship can be distinguished independently of the character, shape or size of a political entity, the political practices implemented or the normative meaning of citizenship presumed: (a) *conditions* for citizenship (in the political practice of Western states, nationality laws); (b) *rights* derived from citizenship and (c) *duties* resulting from citizenship; and finally, (d) citizenship has (or should have) an *active* content that includes participation and representation.

In most modern Western representative nation states, these four aspects are respectively linked to each other and mostly appear in combination: nationality defines the fact that a person fulfils the conditions for citizenship and has access to the rights of a national citizen, but must also fulfill the duties of a citizen (like the duty of military service or to send their children to school). The citizenship rights cover several areas; among others, they guarantee the citizen's possibility to be politically active, to vote and to be elected.

Moreover, citizenship rights can be differentiated into various categories. T.H. Marshall's classical description in this respect has to be complemented and differentiated today. Written shortly after the Second World War, rights have evolved since: some rights he mentioned still are citizenship rights; others have also become human rights since. Moreover, there have been several criticisms concerning Marshall's description (see, for example, Turner 1997, 12). But his idea of defining different categories of citizenship rights (Marshall 1950, 10–27) proves to be helpful even today.

Marshall distinguishes three sorts of citizenship rights: the bourgeois, the political and the social. With this distinction, Marshall describes as well the historical course of the development of the citizenship status in Western national states, where the bourgeois rights appeared first and the social rights last, as the different types of citizenship rights derived from this development: freedom rights, political rights such as the right to elect and to be elected, and the youngest attainment, social rights. In completion of this list, the right to protection through the state (inner security) can be distinguished as the oldest citizenship right. Marshall's categories represent at the same time headlines to something that can be termed the citizenship rights *acquis* of the twentieth century. But this citizenship rights *acquis* over the years was not, and is not today, equally distributed to every resident in Western democracies: whereas all residents were and are subject to the monopoly of violence, most of the political rights, some of the freedom rights and also some of the social rights first were valid only for men, and today are valid only for nationals.

The four elements of citizenship described above – conditions, rights, duties and active citizenship – can be termed different components of citizenship. They will in most of the Western nation states appear in combination. But they do not necessarily do so, and they neither have to appear in a form that guarantees full realization of them all – or full equality between women and men in all of them.

The total of the four components of citizenship – conditions, rights, duties and active citizenship –can accordingly be named the citizenship *acquis* of the twentieth century. The meaning of *acquis* in this case includes that it is the result of a historical development and is now the formal judicial standard in most Western democracies. Thus, this standard also functions as a universalist norm, because it *de facto* represents a standard for complete citizenship. When speaking about citizenship, one assumes that after having obtained access to a polity by fulfilling the conditions for citizenship, a person gets access to the full package of rights and duties. Vice versa, if this were not the case, as in authoritarian states or dictatorships, one would argue that citizenship was defective or not complete. If the citizenship *acquis* in this way is seen as a formally universalist standard, it has to be stated that of course it was derived from centuries of a male-dominated political practice. One could argue that nevertheless, in *theory*, there is no reason for it to not be put into gender-neutral practice – at least this is claimed in most modern nation states, where equality between women and men is often even laid down in the constitution. But an overview of some two centuries of women's citizenship development will show that the practice is not that easy at all.

Taking into account the distinction of four components of citizenship when analyzing the development and the current situation of women's citizenship in Western democracies, one notices that gender differences can occur in different forms and at different periods concerning either the conditions for citizenship, the content and practice of citizenship rights and duties, or active citizenship, that is, representation and participation. The analysis of examples from the centuries following the French Revolution and de Gouges's universalist claim for equality will show that women for most of the time possessed what one could call partial citizenship, meaning that they had a fully realized citizenship status only in some parts of the range men did.

From the French Revolution to the Attainment of Women's Suffrage

The French Revolution is the symbol for several important steps in European democratization, and in particular for the initial step of the creation of the modern political citizenship status and the direct link between the citizen and the state. It also brought, albeit only for a very short period, universal male suffrage. Mostly in a see-saw of restorations and reforms, universal male suffrage was installed in European countries throughout the nineteenth century. In the neighboring countries France and Germany, this was the case in 1871. Even if this is often labeled the introduction of universal suffrage, this is unjust: suffrage left half of the population out until it became truly universalist with the introduction of female suffrage in the course of the twentieth century.

In Germany, female suffrage was attained comparatively early, in 1918, while in France, the home of the French Revolution, it only was implemented in 1944. What were the reasons for these delays? Historical social-structural factors like industrialization, the development of the bourgeoisie, the strengthening of patriarchal culture and an idealization of motherhood are an important part of the explanation. These factors build the background of this analysis, which concentrates on a closer analysis of the respective developments concerning the elements of citizenship mentioned above, and their political and ideological background. The German example provides telling insights.

At the beginning of the nineteenth century in Germany (that is, in the different German countries, Germany being divided into several small and medium-sized states during the period, which were united in the *Deutscher Bund*), as in other European countries, individual citizens in general were males; women, being considered as dependent on husbands or fathers, possessed nationality, but were only subjects – they did not have citizenship rights. This distinction has been derived from the difference between *citoyens* and *sujets* that developed in the course of the French Revolution (Gravert 1973, 162).

Nevertheless, in the eighteenth and the beginning of the nineteenth century, single or widowed women had the possibility to exceptionally obtain a limited, but independent, individual citizenship status on the local level. The precondition was that they were considered heads of households, if for example they had inherited the commerce of their husband. If women possessed communal lands, they were even *obliged* to become citizens in their own right. This individual and exceptional women's citizenship also meant that those women had to pay taxes and perform other citizens' duties, but had no political rights, while male citizens, who in this period did not profit from a broad range of citizenship rights either, nevertheless had the possibility to vote and to be elected (Frevert 1995, 66–70).

But in the course of the nineteenth century, these exceptional possibilities for women to become citizens were constantly limited until they were finally abolished. Beginning with the Prussian Order of the Cities (*Städteordnung*) in 1808, this development lasted for a period of roughly seventy years, the period of transformation that started with the decrease of the *Deutscher Bund* and ended with the foundation of the new federal state, the *Deutsches Reich*. It was also this period that saw a continual expansion of male citizens' rights at the local as well as at state level: All male citizens of cities and villages became to be considered as voters and potential public officers, and citizens' rights in the northern and the southern part of the *Deutscher Bund* became more and more similar. In 1871, the newly founded Reich established male suffrage.

While men's citizenship thus considerably gained in political meaning and potential active content in the nineteenth century, women were increasingly excluded from it. The role of criteria like social situation and class as determining factors for political participation was reduced, while gender, on the contrary, became decisive (Frevert 1995, 82).

Why did citizenship become this gender-determined? One explanation is that as women in the eighteenth century had already been excluded from political rights, the increase in the political content of citizenship made it easy to exclude them from citizenship in general. Another reason is that in the nineteenth century, women in general were considered less apt than men for political activity (Frevert 1995, 74–6). But the German case also shows another decisive factor: this development was closely linked to the extension of state activity – and of citizens' duties. In particular, the development of military service required finding a base that committed the male population more directly and intensively than before to state activity. The military became one important base of the developing nation state, the patriarchal family the other, and both became linked to one another. Women's legal status became completely subordinated to their husbands'. One of the consequences has been that women lost their nationality when they married a foreigner (the same situation occurred in France; see Weil 2005). This also meant that they could be expelled when he was. An ironic consequence is that women – not being liable for military service – could quit nationality by a civil act, marriage, while men needed a dismissal (Gosewinkel 2001, 171–5, 294–8).

At the end of the nineteenth century, women's associations – which were partly supported by the Social Democratic Party, began to criticize this situation. Some of their arguments even found their way into parliamentary motions, and slight changes occurred. In Germany, women obtained the right to be members of political parties in 1908, but still did not have the active or passive right to vote. In preparation of the 1913 reform of German nationality law, two feminist claims were central: female suffrage and an independent female nationality for married women. But suffrage was not to be obtained until 1918 – and an independent nationality for women not until 1949.

On 25 June 1913, the Reichstag passed a new nationality law, with the oppositional ballots of the social democrats and the deputies coming from the Polish areas. The German nationality law reform of 1913 represents an important step in German nationality policy; its basics, like the application of *ius sanguinis*, have remained unchanged until today. The new law did not change women's situation – on the contrary, it even fixed the two lines of thought of the nineteenth century that had become central mainstream claims in the preceding parliamentary and public debates: the state to be a family – an idea that was particularly pushed forward by conservative parties and the Catholic *Zentrum* ('center') – and the state to be a *Wehrgemeinschaft* ('community of defense'). Following this latter idea, adhesion to the state meant also adhesion to the German community of defense, and thus to be prepared to go to war for Germany.

First, this made a clearer definition of the criteria of adhesion necessary. As the idea of the community of defense was inspired by ethnic criteria, it was a logical consequence that the 1913 law offered new possibilities to exclude men of Polish or Jewish origin from German nationality (Gosewinkel 2001, 310–15, 325–8). This orientation to the community of defense very soon – in 1914 with the beginning of the First World War – proved decisive. All German men fit for military service were subject to conscription. Those who did not obey were expatriated or punished as deserters. German men liable for military service could no longer obtain a dismissal from German citizenship.

Second, the link between the community of defense and the patriarchal family became still closer, and defined the criteria of citizenship politics. As the community of citizens should be equivalent to the community of defense, and as military duties were limited to men, it was a logical consequence that only men were full citizens. And as these men were also considered heads of patriarchal families, it was another consequence to subordinate wives and children in civil law and citizenship practice. Laws concerning nationality and citizenship were not adapted to the idea of individual citizens, but to this hierarchic idea of a patriarchal family and to the idea of the community of defense.

Therefore, the 1913 nationality law kept the principle that women lose their nationality with marriage. It just introduced the fact that now the wife had to formally accept her dismissal from German nationality, and that widowed or divorced German women could be re-nationalized more easily. Gosewinkel (2001, 301) names reasons for that:

The reform the women's associations wanted did not only aim at women's equality. It put into question the fundamental relationship that had been established between state and family. In contrast to these ideas, the majority of the deputies imagined 'the state as a family' – understanding family in the sense of the established, patriarchal family that was dominated by the husband and father. ... Who wanted to change gender roles in the family, in the same time aimed at changing the character of the state, and vice-versa. This double challenge of the social base – even if the majority in the Reichstag did rather feel than realize it – explains why the initiative was countered so vehemently. (my translation)

Helene Lange, a feminist activist, commented laconically on the 1913 law by saying: 'women do not have a Fatherland' (quoted in Gosewinkel 2001, 302).

Third, the 1913 law strengthened another decisive difference between women and men. Men had considerable citizens' duties, in particular the obligation to die for the state while doing military service. Women, in practice, had duties as well – in particular to do the reproductive work and give birth, as a consequence of their dependent status in the patriarchal family. But these were not citizens' duties, and women, on the contrary, were free from the citizen's duty to do military service.

Carole Pateman named the development that was sketched and the link between state activity and patriarchal families *The Sexual Contract* (1988). The name indicates that the new social contract in the development of national representative democracy that subordinated men to the institutions of the nation state was based on a sexual contract subordinating women to men and making men heads of patriarchal families. Not only the social, but also this sexual contract was necessary to make the state function.

To sum up the description of this first phase of women's citizenship development in Germany: after a period in the eighteenth and the beginning of the nineteenth century when women could exceptionally obtain a limited share of citizenship rights, in the course of the nineteenth century women's citizenship became more and more limited. At the end of the nineteenth century, it concerned only a small proportion of the conditions – women were nationals, but not citizens of the new national state. Women's citizenship was not only partial, but also unequal in the one part they had a share in. But at the same time, they had other duties than men: while women's duties were seen in the patriarchal family and explicitly were no citizen's duties, men had the obligation to die for the state. In the early twentieth century, this situation gradually changed again, and women also obtained a small share in the political rights.

It has to be added that then, citizenship did not at all aim to be a universalist standard. It was a clear and open base of the citizenship laws that women and men were not only different, but women were to be subordinated to men because of gender roles pre-designed by nature, which made them also less apt for political activity. As these ideas were taken for granted at least by the political mainstream, the decisive differences in men and women's citizenship status represented a problem only for a small avant-garde of political activists.

241

Contradictions and Differences Persisting after the Attainment of Women's Suffrage

While inequality concerning nationality laws or the conditions of citizenship persisted, changes occurred in the two other elements – citizenship rights and active citizenship. They are again well illustrated by the German example.

The attainment of women's suffrage represents a decisive step. In Germany, after the defeat at the end of the First World War and the following breakdown of the political system, it was the case already in 1918. This was related to a considerable expansion of citizenship rights with the beginning of the Weimar Republic. The distinction between nationality and citizenship was abolished, and suffrage was simply extended to all nationals of age, including women (Gosewinkel 2001, 345). Women finally possessed suffrage, and they also had become independent citizens, but only if they were single.

Even in Weimar Germany, women still lost German nationality by marriage to a foreigner – whether they wanted or not. In spite of a variety of law projects, protests and petitions of women's organizations, and in spite of the fact that the position of women in Weimar society in general was considerably better than in pre-war times, this principle remained unchanged until the beginning of the Nazi dictatorship. Throughout Weimar, the patriarchal principle to rank marriage higher than individual citizenship rights stayed predominant as a guiding principle for the definition of citizenship laws (Gosewinkel 2001, 345–50).

This seems surprising, because it would have fitted particularly into the logic of the nationalist policies growing in importance to let women keep their German nationality after marriage, as the following words of Erich Koch-Weser, a liberal and former minister of justice who claimed in 1931 an independent nationality for married women, show:

> We can no longer understand that for example a German female university lecturer in a German university town, who is married to a Swiss national, will be expatriated, while a mulatto who neither knows the German country nor the language will be German national after her marriage to a German, and if she returns to Germany with him, will even have the right to vote. (quoted in Gosewinkel 2001, 351; my translation)

But Germany was not the only case in Europe: in France, until 1927, when then law was finally changed, women also lost their nationality when marrying a foreigner (Weil 2005). It was only the new French Constitution that was voted for in a referendum in 1946 that fixed the equality of women and men. Likewise, the new constitution of the Federal Republic of Germany, the *Grundgesetz*, which was passed in 1949, fixed the equality of women and men and finally abolished the loss of nationality by marriage for women.

Now, how to judge this development? By obtaining suffrage, women received an important share in two elements of citizenship: formal equality in the area of what Marshall calls political rights, and formal equality in one element of active citizenship. But after the attainment of female suffrage, in all four elements of citizenship crucial gender differences still persisted: first, concerning the conditions – women in Weimar Germany possessed suffrage, but not a nationality independent from their husbands. On the contrary, in France in 1927 they obtained independent nationality, but still lacked suffrage. Second, the contradictions between women's formal and real citizenship status were even more evident – while women had the right to vote, they were rarely represented in parliaments and political parties, and they were subject to several laws that made their status inferior to men's. Thus, women possessed formal equality in that element of citizenship, but the practice proved to be heavily unequal. Finally, the factors well known from the nineteenth century still had their impact: material reasons like income status and professional situation and cultural values like the persisting discriminating stereotypes of a certain female character or behaviour counteracted an equal representation and participation of women – and hence an equal citizenship status.

Therefore, the conclusion regarding the period after the obtainment of women's suffrage until the end of the Second World War is that women, concerning the formal as well as the practical aspects, still had only partial citizenship. Even if they now had a share in three of its four elements – (a) conditions, (b) rights, and (c) active citizenship, they did not posses equality with men. In particular, until the Second World War, women had a very limited share in active citizenship – a considerable change in this element only beginning after the Second World War. But still, women also had fewer citizens' duties, and in particular the duty to do military service was limited to men. One reason for this is that until the Second World War, neither in Germany nor in France did citizenship aim at being a universalist norm. The sexes were not considered formally equal. It was only in 1949 in Germany, or 1946 in France, with the new constitutions that women became at least formally equal citizens (while many discriminations in law persisted). Thus, only then did citizenship attain the function of a universalist norm.

Still Partial, but on a Higher Level: Women's Participation and Representation Today

What has been made of the fact that citizenship since the Second World War in Germany or France is formally equal? A short overview shows that less formal inequalities are persisting – despite ongoing abolishment, some still exist. Nowadays, mainly a tension or even a contradiction between the formal citizenship status, including its formal universalist claim, and the reality is evident.

Conditions of access and citizenship rights today in Western nation states being nearly formally equal, the most blatant differences that persist concern the duties and active citizenship. Whereas in several Western nation states military service has either been abolished as a citizen's duty or has been made a duty for female citizens as well, in Germany it still is a *duty* that is limited only to male citizens. In *active citizenship*, there also exits a striking difference between formal equality and practical inequality: considering female representation in the 15 old EU member states, it can be said that parliaments are still dominated by men. The average proportion of female MPs is only 27.5 per cent – which at least shows a continual increase over the years.

It is important here to cite Pippa Norris's statement that 'women do not participate less than men, but participate differently' (Norris 1991, 56): women are much less active in highly institutionalized forms, such as in parties, and much more in non- or less institutionalized forms such as associations. This is, of course, true. But nevertheless, the difference in men and women's institutionalized political representation has a decisive meaning in a representative democracy, because it means that there still exists a gender difference in their basic institutions. The data in Table 14.1 documents the gender difference.

Table 14.1 Female MPs in old EU member states

Rank	State (election month and year)	Female MPs (%)
1	Sweden (September 2006)	47.3
2	Finland (March 2007)	42.0
3	Denmark (February 2005)	36.9
4	Netherlands (November 2006)	36.7
5	Spain (March 2004)	36.0
6	Belgium (May 2003)	34.7
7	Austria (October 2006)	32.2
8	Germany (September 2005)	31.6
9	Luxemburg (June 2004)	23.3
10	Portugal (February 2005)	21.3
11	United Kingdom (February 2005)	19.7
12	France (June 2007)	18.5
13	Italy (April 2006)	17.3
14	Ireland (May 2007)	13.3
15	Greece (March 2004)	13.0

Source: Interparliamentary Union, <www.ipu.org/wmn-e/classif.htm>, accessed 10 July 2007.

A glance at the table shows that the Nordic countries occupy the first ranks concerning women's representation in parliaments, while France is at the bottom, and Germany occupies a place in the middle.

On 1 May 2004, the EU was enlarged by ten new member states. In these countries, the situation regarding the representation of women is even worse, as shown in Table 14.2. The first places have been held for several years by Latvia, Lithuania and Poland (in changing order over the years) – but with rates of only slightly over 20 per cent. It is interesting to notice that in Lithuania, the proportion doubled with the 2004 election (having been only 10.6 per cent in 2000), and there are also other countries, like Cyprus, were the number of female MPs rose considerably

Table 14.2   Women in the parliaments of new EU states

Rank	State (election month and year)	Female MPs (%)
1	Lithuania (October 2004)	22.0
2	Estonia (March 2007)	21.8
3	Poland (September 2005)	20.4
4	Slowakia (June 2006)	19.3
5	Latvia (October 2006)	19.0
6	Czech Republic (June 2006)	15.5
7	Cyprus (May 2006)	14.3
8	Slowenia (October 2004)	12.2
9	Hungary (April 2006)	10.4
10	Malta (April 2003)	9.2

Source: Interparliamentary Union, <www.ipu.org/wmn–e/classif.htm>, accessed 10 July 2007.

in recent years (10.7 per cent in 2001 to 14.3 per cent today). Therefore, even if the worst results concerning women's representation are to be found in Hungary and Malta with around 10 per cent, presumably in the new member states there will be a tendency to increase these percentages.

What are the reasons behind this still low female representation, both in old and new member states? There are three decisive factors that Beate Hoecker (1995, 28–30) sums up – political culture, social structure and institutions (see also Ruhl 2006a for a discussion of these aspects and an analysis of the British system). They show that speaking of women's partial citizenship in active politics, we have today left the range of what can be tackled or attained by formal or judicial equality. On the contrary, we have now reached the point were we have to talk about gender inequalities in practical life.

Political culture as it has been classically defined by Gabriel Almond and Sidney Verba in 1963 comprises the total of opinions, values and views relevant for the political life – this means that political culture is also determined by the traditional values and norms of societies, and among them the traditional views concerning women and their role in society and politics. It seems to be a logical consequence that countries showing a more conservative set of values also have a lower degree of women's representation, and vice versa. Countries like Malta, Cyprus or Portugal, and also many of the post-socialist states, show such a conservative political culture. In the latter, this is related to circumstances that can be summed up by saying that women were not dependent on their husband, but on the state.

Social-structural factors like education, professional situation and individual situation in life are also important. It is well known, and has been proven several times since the work of Verba and Nie (1972), that the higher an individual's degree of education, his or her income and professional situation, the more opportunities he or she has for political activity. Traditional role models hinder women's employment, and wages all over Europe are still are considerably lower for them, and this also decreases their chances of being politically active. Finally, women are still the persons mainly in charge for housework and childcare – which hinders not only their employment chances, but also their possibilities to be politically active.

Institutional factors include the structure of the party system, the electoral system and the candidate selection practices within the parties. Proportional electoral systems increase women's chances to become MPs, while majority systems are counterproductive. Great Britain, France and Ireland, which all use a majority electoral system, show the lowest rates of women MPs in the old member states. Majority systems favour mainstream candidates, and tend to hinder members of groups discriminated against in society – be they women or ethnic groups. In countries using a proportional election system (the new member states all have a proportional or a single transferable vote system), it is also the parties' system of finding and nominating candidates that is decisive – and the mechanisms that work in a male-dominated social corps like a political party tend to hinder female candidates. The structure and the demands of party work also are important factors: if meetings take place every evening and last until late at night, if the weekends are also occupied by political activity, women will get into trouble more often than men because they do not have a person at home who will arrange reproductive work for them – which is still the case for most male political activists.

Thus, the question raised in the beginning of this section can be concluded by stating that women's citizenship today is still practically limited in the active part of representation and participation. It is therefore justified to argue that citizenship still is not practically equal. Women's citizenship is still partial compared to that of men. The most decisive differences occur in active citizenship, where women are less represented, and regarding citizenship duties, of which women have fewer, even if being free from compulsory military service rather seems to be an advantage.

Looking at the reasons for the persisting inequality in active citizenship, there not many factors left that could possibility be influenced by formal regulations. Institutional factors seem to be the easiest to be influenced by law. Accordingly, many parties, namely Greens and Social Democrats, began to introduce women's quotas in the 1980s and 1990s. In Germany, the Greens have a 50 per cent quota and the Social Democrats a 40 per cent quota, but it only has to be applied if there are enough women willing to be candidates. France even introduced a law to guarantee equal representation of women in parliamentary seats – but this law has proven to be ineffective, because parties are given the option of paying fines instead of guaranteeing an equal distribution of seats (see the contribution of Laure Bereni in Chapter 15 of this volume).

Formal regulations can also exercise a slight influence on social-structural factors. Policies in childcare, as well as marriage and family laws or tax laws, can help to establish a more equal division of reproductive work between women and men. Political culture proves hardest to change, as indicated by the fact that even those parties which introduced female quotas early on still show today a higher representation of male functionaries, especially in the higher ranks of the hierarchy. But what is at the heart of the persisting citizenship inequalities is a persisting gender inequality in all parts of social life that proves difficult to tackle through formal regulations.

Conclusions and Methodological Consequences

If the development of women's citizenship is compared to the – respectively historically changing – standard of the citizenship *acquis*, it has to be stated first that this *acquis* is the result of a development. This is also true for male citizens who did not posses all of the elements of the *acquis* since the beginning of representative democracy, but were subject to changes and the enlargement of citizenship rights and contents. Thus, the content of the citizenship *acquis* itself was also subject to historical change and development. Second, citizenship for many centuries was *de facto* a male-oriented standard that was opened up gradually to women. This also means that the citizenship *acquis* was derived from a male-dominated political practice. For many years, the basic focus of citizenship laws was not a gender-neutral individual, but a male citizen. Citizenship as well was not gender-neutral. But after the Second World War, events took an interesting turn: women and men were declared formally equal, and therefore citizenship also *formally* became a gender-neutral standard – whereas citizenship practice shows gender inequalities until today.

Third, it can be said that women's share in the different elements of citizenship increased step by step. At the beginning of the nineteenth century, women did not have a citizenship at all, because they were not individuals. Then they gradually obtained their share in different elements of citizenship – each share in the male-oriented norm of citizenship having to be obtained with difficulty.

The development of women's citizenship therefore rather took a mingled and slightly uncoordinated route, more equality in one part coming to coexist with continuing inequality in others. As a result, women for most of the time possessed a *partial citizenship*, meaning that they had a fully realized citizenship status only in some *parts* of the range men did: even the conditions for citizenship – that is, nationality rights – were far from equal in the beginning of representative democracy, women often not even possessing an independent nationality. But today, the conditions for citizenship are formally equal in most Western democracies.

This is equally true for most of the rights ensuing from nationality. Nevertheless, two limitations must be mentioned. First, it took a long time to implement gender equality in most of these rights – one of the last steps was female suffrage. Second, citizenship rights may not be classified as truly universalist today. When it comes to conflicting issues such as abortion, or the right to social protection in case of maternity, it shows that Western democracies do not completely guarantee gender equality.

The duties resulting from citizenship are unequal until today, at least in these Western nation states that, like Germany, have kept the duty for male citizens to do compulsory military service. But in the outcome, the fact that women do not have to accept compulsory service and their potential obligation to die for the state rather seems to be an advantage.

Finally, the formal conditions for active citizenship – rules of participation and representation – today being formally equal, female citizens of Western representative democracies are no longer subject to formal limitations on being politically active or elected, but the practice of active citizenship is the field where the biggest gender differences still persist.

Three conclusions follow. First, if practical gender equality has been attained in one element of citizenship, it does not necessarily mean that this must be the case for the others as well. Second, the attainment of formal equality in conditions rights and in active citizenship does not necessarily result in equal outcomes. Third, gains in women's citizenship status went along with developments in the political culture and the social structure of representative democracies. These can also be seen as decisive for the fact that today, citizenship in most representative democracies is theoretically universalist. But due to persisting differences in social structure and political culture, citizenship practice still cannot be classified as gender-neutral.

What are the overall methodological and normative implications these results have for the analysis of citizenship, understood as the relationship between a polity and its members – be it in contemporary western democracies or in developing democracies, as well on the national level as on the supranational level, like in the EU? If one takes the ideal of citizenship as a (formally) universalist standard as a starting point, several conclusions can be drawn.

It should be taken into account that citizenship is not something static, but in development. It can be termed a process rather than a state. Citizenship should be regarded in a differentiated way. The distinction of different elements – (a) conditions, (b) rights, (c) duties and (d) active citizenship – is helpful as a more exact tool for analysis. Citizenship can be more adequately understood when not seen as a static bunch of conditions, rights and active citizenship, but as a process that can entail developments and differentiations in its elements at different periods.

These differentiations will always be crucial for inequalities and distinctions between different groups. If today women's citizenship is much less partial than in the times of the French Revolution, third-country nationals in the EU can be said to be in a state of partial citizenship now. Citizenship can therefore well be claimed to be a formally universalist norm – but in reality, it will probably never be universalist, since it seems improbable that there will be a time when all adults will profit from practical equality. This means that citizenship practice *per se* is and will remain partial. If one regards the respective citizenship *acquis* as a universalist norm, this means that there will always be groups on the edge of citizenship that will only have limited access to its contents – what seems to be continually changing is the location of the edges and the groups that can be found there.

This tension or even discrepancy between a universalist standard and an unequal, partial reality represents a problem from a normative point of view. One reason for that discrepancy can be related to the old liberal dilemma: formal equality in an unequal society entails inequality. But there is also another dilemma that seems equally important: A democratic subject without an outgroup is a paradox, because exit is no longer possible. Thus, if there always has to be an exit possibility, there always has to be an outgroup – which means there will always be edges that entail further normative problems.

References

Almond, G. and Verba, S. (1963), *The Civic Culture: Political Attitudes and Democracy in Five Nations* (Princeton, NJ: Princeton University Press).

de Gouges, Olympe (1791): *The Rights of Women*, <www.pinn.net/~sunshine/book-sum/gouges.html>, accessed 10 July 2007.

Frevert, U. (1995), *Mann und Weib* (Munich: Beck).

Gosewinkel, D. (2001), *Einbürgern und Ausschließen* (Göttingen: Vandenhoeck & Ruprecht).

Gravert, R. (1973), *Staat und Staatsangehörigkeit* (Berlin: Duncker und Humblodt).

Hoecker, B. (1995), *Politische Partizipation von Frauen. Ein einführendes Studienbuch* (Opladen: Leske & Budrich).

'Inter-Parliamentary Union': *Women in Parliaments*, <www.ipu.org/wmn-e/classif-arc.htm>, accessed 10 July 2007.

Kymlicka, W. (2002), *Contemporary Political Philosophy*, 2nd edn (Oxford: Oxford University Press).

Marshall, T.H. (1950), *Citizenship and Social Class, and Other Essays* (Cambridge: Cambridge University Press).

Norris, P. (1991), 'Gender Differences in Political Participation in Britain', *Government and Opposition* 26:1, 56–74.

Pateman, C. (1988), *The Sexual Contract* (Cambridge: Polity Press).

Ruhl, K. (2006a), 'Women in the House (of Commons)', in Ruhl et al. (eds), *Demokratisches Regieren und politische Kultur. Post-staatlich, post-parlamentarisch, post-patriarchal?* (Münster: Lit).

—— et al. (eds) (2006b), *Demokratisches Regieren und politische Kultur. Post-staatlich, post-parlamentarisch, post-patriarchal?* (Münster: Lit).

Tilly, C. (ed.) (1975), *The Formation of National States in Western Europe* (Princeton, NJ: Princeton University Press).

Turner B.S. (1997), 'Citizenship Studies: A General Theory', *Citizenship Studies* 1:1, 5–18.

Verba S. and Nie, N. (1972), *Participation in America: Political Democracy and Social Equality* (New York: Harper and Row).

Weil, P. (2005), 'Die französische Staatsbürgerschaft – eine wechselvolle Geschichte', Interview, Label France 49:2003, <www.diplomatie.gouv.fr/label_france/49/de/12.html>, accessed 10 July 2007.

Further Reading

Bock, G. (ed.) (1992), *Beyond Equality and Difference: Citizenship, Feminist Politics and Female Subjectivity* (London: Routledge).

Brubaker, R. (1994), *Citizenship and Nationhood in France and Germany* (Cambridge, MA: Harvard University Press).

de Beauvoir, S. (1997), *The Second Sex* (New York: Vintage).

Evans, R.J. (1980), 'German Social Democracy and Women's Suffrage 1891–1918', *Journal of Contemporary History* 15:3, 533–57.

Hufton, O.H. (1992), *Women and the Limits of Citizenship in the French Revolution* (Toronto: University of Toronto Press).

Norris, P. and Inglehart, R. (2003), *Rising Tide: Gender Equality and Cultural Change around the World* (New York: Cambridge University Press).

Phillips, A. (1991), *Engendering Democracy* (Cambridge: Polity Press).

—— (1998), *The Politics of Presence: The Political Representation of Gender, Ethnicity, and Race* (Oxford: Oxford University Press).

Sneeringer, J. (2002) *Winning Women's Votes: Propaganda and Politics in Weimar Germany* (Chapel Hill, NC: University of North Carolina Press).

—— (1996), *Citizenship, Identity, and Social History* (Cambridge: Cambridge University Press).

Gendering Political Representation? The Debate on Gender Parity in France

Laure Bereni

Introduction

For the first time in its legal history, France has an affirmative action policy to help women gain political representation, mandated by a constitutional amendment in 1999 and an electoral law in 2000.[1] In this respect, France is not an exception. These laws are the national translation of a process of redefining the categories of gender equality and fair representation that was already under way in international organizations and in many neighboring democracies (Lépinard and Bereni 2004; Lovenduski 2005; Sawer et al. 2006). However, the gender parity laws, and the controversies they triggered before being enacted, also have a specifically French history. The introduction of affirmative action measures toward women in political representation in France took the form of a forceful reform, through a constitutional

---

1   In the *Loi constitutionnelle no 99–569 du 8 juillet 1999 relative à l'égalité entre les femmes et les hommes*, the French Parliament voted an amendment modifying two articles of the Constitution. First, to the article referring to sovereignty, the following provision was added (Article 3): 'The law favors the equal access of women and men to electoral mandates and elective functions'; second, the article about political parties (Article 4) was made to specify that they 'contribute to the execution of the principle set forth in the last section of Article 3 under the conditions determined by the law'. The *Loi no 2000–493 du 6 juin 2000 tendant à favoriser l'égal accès des femmes et des hommes aux mandats électoraux et fonctions électives* provides (1) a legal requirement of *parité* for the party list system (most notably for local, regional and European elections) and (2) financial incentives through the public funding of political parties for the legislative elections. For elections using list systems (municipal, regional, European and some senatorial elections), parties are required to submit lists with equal numbers of men and women in a defined order. A financial incentive is used for the legislative elections (using a single-member district electoral system): state subsidies to each party are reduced in proportion to the gap in the number of male and female candidates nationwide.

amendment and through a law with constraining arrangements, while in other European countries (like in Sweden or in Germany), gender-based quotas were implemented by political parties on a voluntary basis (Sawer et al. 2006). Yet the adoption of the gender parity reform took place in the context of a dominant republican universalist doctrine, which is *a priori* hostile to such a reform, since it does not accept any collective identity within the political realm. How could a set of laws solemnly promoting women as a group in elected assemblies have been passed in a political context marked by a such a powerful universalistic doctrine? To what extent have the rationales mobilized in support of these laws entailed a gendering of this dominant universalistic doctrine?

In the first section of this chapter, I will explore a set of intellectual and institutional discourses that have legitimized affirmative action toward women in political representation in the recent decades. A set of theoretical works produced by feminist scholars in anglophone academia since the early 1980s drew attention to the exclusive character of the so-called neutral citizenship of the traditional liberal paradigm. They have called for the adoption of public policies increasing the 'presence' of women in the political arena (Phillips 1995). In addition to these theoretical critiques of democracy, feminist claims to promote affirmative action policies toward women in decision-making have developed in several international organizations (most notably the United Nations, the Council of Europe and the European Community) since the late 1970s. These discourses offered a favorable context for French parity campaigners (Bereni and Lépinard 2004; Lépinard 2007a).

In the second section, drawing on a corpus of discourses produced by parity campaigners in different public arenas (women's movement, parliament, media) in the 1990s in France, I investigate the discursive strategies they used in order to fit into the French dominant political discourses, notably characterized by the strength of republican universalism. I eventually demonstrate that such discursive strategies led to a certain *depoliticization* of the parity claim.

Gendering Political Representation: Intellectual and Institutional Sources

Feminist Theories of Political Pluralism: A 'Politics of Presence'

Since the 1980s, feminist critiques of representative democracy have gained momentum in academia. Beyond their diversity, all of these critiques question the universalistic, liberal conception of citizenship and representative democracy, arguing that these categories have proven to be inadequate in solving the exclusion of disadvantaged groups, including women. In particular, theorists of 'political pluralism' (Marques-Pereira 2004; Bereni and Lépinard 2003) have pleaded for a more participatory democracy through an increased presence of members of disadvantaged groups among representatives (Young 1990, 2000; Phillips 1995; Gould 1996; Mansbridge 1999).

According to the liberal universalistic paradigm, political equality between abstract citizens is based on the rejection from the public sphere of all social characteristics and group identities. In this view, the only differences to be taken into account in the public sphere to build the common good are opinions (which supposedly translate interests, beliefs and ideas), which are assumed to be detachable from the identities of the individuals. In accordance with this vision of modern political equality, in which the individual is divided into an abstract citizen and a social individual, liberal theories of representative democracy are based on a strict segregation between 'being' and 'doing', that is to say between the *identity* of the representatives and the *act* of representing (Pitkin 1967). In Pitkin's view, representing 'means acting in the interests of the represented, in a manner responsive to them' (Pitkin 1967, 209). According to this model, the quality of political representation depends on a series of factors, such as the ability of the representatives to aggregate the diversity of interests and opinions of the constituency to build the common good through deliberation, their degree of responsiveness to the electorate, and so on, but does not depend on the degree of resemblance between the representatives and the represented. Moreover, in the liberal paradigm, the model of a 'mirror' representation is strongly devalued, and presented as an obsolete legacy of direct democracy. In this view, the absence of women – and other social groups – from representative bodies does not constitute a democratic problem. What is important is to *act for* and not to resemble the represented. As Phillips writes: 'the role of a politician is to carry a message. The messages will vary, but it hardly matters if the messengers are the same (Those who believe that men have a monopoly on the political skills of articulating policies and ideas will not be surprised that most messengers are men)' (Phillips 1995, 6).

However, in the last couple of decades, feminist theorists of political pluralism have challenged the sacrosanct division between being and doing. In their view, a better *descriptive* representation of women will improve their *substantive* representation (a better translation of their interests). In Mansbridge's words: 'representatives are in their own persons and lives in some sense typical of the larger class of persons whom they represent' (Mansbridge 1999, 629). Young was among the first scholars to call for a better descriptive representation of women in a feminist perspective. Her view is based on a deep criticism of the ideal in which impartial citizens stand apart from past experiences to reach a universal point of view. A democratic public, she argues, 'should provide mechanisms for the effective recognition and representation of the distinct voices and perspectives of those of its constituent groups that are oppressed and disadvantaged' (Young 1990, 184).

In her book *The Politics of Presence* (1995), Phillips also made a central contribution to the feminist critiques of representative democracy. In her view, the interests of the represented built through deliberation process in the public arena can be divided into two categories. On the one hand stand 'ideas', which are detachable from the individuals who carry them, and which can be elaborated by deliberation between interchangeable representatives in accordance with the liberal model. On the other hand are 'perspectives', which are strongly embedded in the 'shared experiences' of group members. Phillips argues that representatives who are outside of these groups cannot discern the perspectives of the groups being excluded from representative bodies. Consequently, Phillips calls for a higher proportion of members from disadvantaged groups (including women) in representative bodies in order to improve the articulation of their interests in the public arena. Thus, real equality requires 'participatory equality', defined as the 'equal right to be politically present' (Phillips 1995, 33, 36).

Mansbridge also calls for a more descriptive representation of disadvantaged groups (Mansbridge 2001). She draws a line between the two dimensions of political representation: the 'aggregative' function, which consists in bringing into the public arena the diversity of interests and opinions, and the 'deliberative' function, in which the representatives build the interests of the represented through free discussion, in a very autonomous manner. Mansbridge argues that this second dimension of representation does not work fairly in historical contexts in which the interests of disadvantaged groups are 'uncrystallized', that is, not fully articulated. In line with Phillips, she argues that in such contexts, the presence of representatives who embody – through their experience – the perspectives of disadvantaged groups can facilitate the expression of the interests of these disadvantaged groups in the public sphere.

However, the assumption that the descriptive representation of women improves the substantive representation of their interests, which is at the very basis of a politics of presence, has been recurrently questioned. Critiques of such a perspective have been grounded both on theoretical and empirical arguments. At a theoretical level, a set of works drawing on post-modern theories has argued against the viability of the categories of women and gender (Butler 1990; Mohanty 1997). It has been shown that feminist thinking tends to essentialize women as a monolithic 'interest' group, and therefore tends to obscure the fluctuating, instable subjectivation process of individuals, at the intersection of several potentially conflicting identities. Along with this theoretical critique, empirical studies have stressed the shortcomings of the basic assumptions of 'critical mass' theories, according to which, 'when there is a critical mass of women present (defined somewhere between 15 and 30 percent) politics will reflect to a much greater extent women's concerns' (Childs 2006, 8). A recent set of works (Dodson 2001; Childs 2004, 2006) shows that there is no direct link between descriptive and substantive representation, and that female representatives do no automatically *act for* women.

Feminist theorists of political pluralism have been aware of this critique, and have responded in several ways. Two main arguments can be mentioned here. First, as several of them have argued, the 'interests' of marginalized groups are constructed through past and present *power relations*. Interests are not considered as essential and permanently attached to the groups, but linked to the oppression process from which certain groups suffer. For example, Mouffe distinguishes political 'pluralism', which she calls for, from the liberal, traditional conception of pluralism. In the latter conception, she argues, there is a 'fact' of pluralism, that is, existing differences in society, and 'procedures ... whose objective is actually to make those differences irrelevant and to relegate pluralism to the sphere of the private' (Mouffe 1996, 246). Against this 'liberal' view, Mouffe argues in favour of an 'anti-essentialist' conception of pluralism, which would not be a 'fact', but 'an axiological principle' 'to celebrate and enhance' (Mouffe 1996, 246) The type of pluralism she advocates 'gives a positive status to differences and ... refuses the objective unanimity and homogeneity which is always revealed as fictitious and based on acts of exclusion' (Mouffe 1996, 246). A modern democracy should recognize the ineradicable character of the agonistic dimension of pluralism. In the same perspective, Gould advocates a 'compensatory view of differences', in which differences are defined as the result of social and historical discriminations which preferential treatments measures should redress (Gould 1996, 182). This argument is distinct from the idea of 'essentialist multiculturalism', which advocates the representation of 'diversity' thought as permanent and essential (Gould 1996, 182). Gould writes:

> the injuries of difference – of race, gender and ethnicity, which have been the
> basis for discrimination and unequal treatment in the past – are to be openly
> recognized as grounds for affirmative action to rectify them. Differences are
> recognized in order to eliminate their negative effects ... It is not being black
> or female that constitutes the group difference but being subject to oppression
> as black or as female. (Gould 1996, 182–3)

In order to limit the risks of essentialism, Mansbridge suggests that 'fluid remedies' (such as special training and targets within political parties) are preferable to quotas embedded in laws, and that these remedies should be grounded 'explicitly in historical rationales' to make the power relations visible (Mansbridge 2001, 30).

Second, in line with empirical works stressing the limits of the critical mass theories, theorists of political pluralism have argued that there is no absolute link between descriptive and substantive representation of women. On the question of how strong the presence of women in elected assemblies should be, Phillips gives a *pragmatic* answer: it should be a 'threshold' presence, sufficient to facilitate the expression of the antagonisms of views and experiences within the group to breach a reifying, uniform vision of it, not necessarily a proportionate presence (Phillips 1995, 67). Mansbridge supports this perspective: 'Getting the relevant facts, insights, and perspectives into the deliberation should be what counts, not how many people advance these facts, insights, and perspectives' (Mansbridge 1999, 636). According to Phillips, the politics of presence does not mean that a system grounded on the *delegation* of ideas should be replaced by a system that would be only based on the *presence* of group members. She pleads for a permanent tension between the two principles of a fair democratic representation: the logic of 'ideas', based on the existence of accountability procedures, and the logic of 'presence', through a certain amount of descriptive representation (Phillips 1998a).

> There is no consensus among feminist theorists working on pluralism –
> neither about the degree in which liberal principles of representation should
> be renegotiated through descriptive representation, nor about the concrete
> procedures to be implemented to solve the political exclusion of women.

However, these theories have provided an intellectual framework for women's movements to challenge political representation through affirmative action. As will be shown in the following, one of the first sites of institutionalization of these feminist critiques can be found in several international organizations which have been increasingly concerned with the under-representation of women in elected assemblies.

International Organizations: The Promotion of Gender-based Quotas to Enhance Women's Presence in 'Decision-making'

Since the second half of the 1970s, several international organizations, such as the United Nations and the European institutions, have given a growing importance to the women's rights issue on their political agendas, engaging in a redefinition of their gender equality framework (Hoskyns 1996; Mazey 2002; Bereni and Lépinard 2004; Lépinard 2007a). These organizations have shifted from a conception of equality restricted to 'formal equality' between the sexes to an anti-discrimination frame seeking to promote 'effective' equality. More precisely, they shifted from a 'direct discrimination' conception, which focuses on the perpetrator's intention to negatively discriminate, to an 'indirect discrimination' frame, in which discrimination is evaluated through the objective positions of both sexes without considering the intention of discrimination. In their new anti-discrimination frame, the respect of equality in treatment has to be enriched with the active promotion of women, to compensate their effective disadvantaged position. Among the means to actively promote gender equality, international organizations have encouraged 'affirmative action' policies. These policies consist in allowing preferential treatment toward a category to compensate the current negative consequences of a major, legal disadvantage it suffered in the past (see, for example, Sabbagh 2007). This extensive, renewed conception of gender equality concerns all sites of social activities, including the sites of political power. This section examines how international organizations have been the venues of a redefinition of universalistic democratic representation by promoting affirmative action measures toward women in politics.

It is within the UN that affirmative action was first promoted as a tool to enhance women's representation in politics. A better 'participation' of women in all kinds of decision-making sites (political, but also economic and social) was recommended by the UN as early as the Mexico Conference in 1975, and subsequently defined as a 'necessity' by the Nairobi Conference in 1985. The UN was not only a place of construction of the 'scandal' of the under-representation of women in corridors of power, but also for the elaboration of appropriate legal tools to effectively increase women's representation in politics. The Convention on the Elimination of All Forms of Discrimination against Women (CEDAW), adopted by the UN General Assembly in 1979, encourages member states to take all appropriate arrangements, including preferential treatments, to facilitate women's access to all decision-making sites, including political representation:

adoption by States Parties of temporary special measures aimed at accelerating de facto equality between men and women shall not be considered discrimination as defined in the present Convention, but shall in no way entail as a consequence the maintenance of unequal or separate standards; these measures shall be discontinued when the objectives of equality of opportunity and treatment have been achieved.[2]

In line with this new UN gender equality framework, the Council of Europe engaged, by the late 1970s, in a new, extensive vision of gender equality. The question of women's participation in politics imposed itself as a central theme of action of the Council, which is traditionally concerned with democratic and human rights issues. Throughout the 1980s, the Council conducted several surveys and studies assessing the discrepancy between women's formal right to vote and their marginal presence in representative assemblies all over Europe. In 1986, the first ministerial conference dedicated to 'equality in political life' in Strasbourg was concluded by a resolution inviting the political parties, trade unions and other representative instances to adopt 'positive action' policies in order to promote and increase the participation of women in political decision-making. Three years later, a seminar on 'Equal participation of men and women' in democracy, organized by the Committee on Gender Equality for the commemoration of the forty years of existence of the Council of Europe, sanctioned the term 'parity democracy' and recommended the adoption of special temporary measures (including quotas) to promote a balanced participation of the sexes in political and public decision-making (Conseil de l'Europe 1992).

Finally, the legitimacy of 'positive action' measures, including gender quotas, as a means to promote gender equality in the political arena was encouraged by the European Community by the early 1990s. For the first time in 1976, the European Community (EC) had recognized the necessity of positive action to achieve gender equality in the labour market.[3] Then, throughout the 1980s, the EC broadened its conception of gender equality, going beyond its initial scope of competence, which was limited to the job market. Considering that gender equality in work could not be achieved without a change in dominant cultural views on gender relations, the EC considered that the presence of women in representative bodies was an important element to fight the prevailing traditional gender roles in society (Mazey 2002; Bereni 2004; Lépinard 2007a). The EC began to produce a corpus of soft law, including positive action measures to improve the representation of women in political arenas. The third 'Community Action Programme on Equality of Opportunities between Men and Women' (1991–1995) was concluded by a Recommendation of the Council of Ministers encouraging the member states

---

2   Convention on the Elimination of All Forms of Discrimination against Women, Article 4–1 <www.un.org/womenwatch/daw/cedaw/text/econvention.htm>, accessed 6 June 2007.

3   Council Directive of 9 February 1976 on the implementation of the principle of equal treatment for men and women as regards access to employment, vocational training and promotion, and working conditions (76/207/EEC).

to 'adopt a comprehensive, integrated strategy designed to promote balanced participation of women and men in the decision-making process and develop or introduce the appropriate measures to achieve this, such as, where necessary, legislative and/or regulatory measures and/or incentives'.[4]

The growing concern of international organizations about women's presence in political bodies had a direct impact on the emergence of the parity demand in the French women's movement. The campaign for parity started in France just after the Athens Conference organized by the European Commission in November 1992, during which a group of prominent female politicians from several European countries (including France) signed a declaration in which they supported the purpose of gender parity in political assemblies. The parity demand, which emerged in the French women's movement in the early 1990s, and which was translated into a set of laws at the end of the decade, is thus a national translation of a broader renegotiation, at the theoretical and institutional levels, of the meaning of the category of fair political representation through 'affirmative' or 'positive' action toward women (Lépinard 2007a). A number of modern democracies – especially in Europe – have adopted affirmative action strategies to raise the proportion of women elected in the 1980s and 1990s (Lépinard and Bereni 2004). The central question of the following section is how deeply the parity demand in France reshaped the meaning of modern political categories, in particular the liberal conception of representation, in a national context where the universalistic credo is particularly strong.

Nationalizing Affirmative Action: How the Parity Demand was Shaped in France

Arguments to Support Gender Quotas

Women's movement scholars have shown that activists campaigning for the introduction of gender quotas in political representation recurrently make use of four main types of arguments (Squires 1996; Sawer 2002; Bereni and Lépinard 2003, 2004; Lépinard 2006, 2007a). The first argument presents gender quotas as a means to improve the equality of opportunities between individuals regardless of their sex. In this view, as Phillips puts it:

> if there were no obstacles operating to keep certain groups of people out of political life, we would expect positions of political influence to be randomly distributed between the sexes. There might be some minor and innocent deviations, but any more distorted distribution is evidence of intentional or structural discrimination. In such contexts (that is, most contexts) women

---

4   Council Recommendation of 2 December 1996 on the balanced participation of women and men in the decision-making process (96/694/CE).

are being denied rights and opportunities that are currently available to men.
(Phillips 1995, 63)

The affirmative action frame adopted by most international organizations is based on this first argument: preferential treatments toward women, including gender quotas, are justified by the persistence of effective inequalities of opportunities between the individuals because of their sex, and by the necessity to redress them.

The second rationale relates to the necessity of allowing a better representation of the particular *interests of women*, considered as a disadvantaged group. This argument is based on the idea that the exclusion of women from elected bodies is an obstacle to the representation of their specific interests. In other words, more women in elected assemblies would be a means to bring about women's interests onto the political agenda. This idea of a better representation of women's interests by a stronger presence of women is quite similar to the pluralist feminist theories discussed in the previous section.

A third recurrent line of reasoning consists in arguing that the *completion of representative democracy* requires an increased presence of women. According to this argument, the presence of women is not only desirable because women's interests would be better represented, but because the body of representatives would resemble more closely the body of the represented, that is, society consisting of about 50 per cent women. What must be stressed in this third kind of argument is that the higher proportion of women is expected to guarantee that the elected assemblies would be a better 'mirror' of the represented, but only in a *symbolic* or figurative, and not a substantial manner (Rosanvallon 1998).

According to the last argument, the legitimacy of the political presence of women is related to the *revitalization* of the representation. This view is related to traditional gender roles in society, and is based on the importation of these roles (women as mothers and spouses) from the private to the public sphere. Women are assumed to have specific behaviours and values, different from those of other groups: they are seen as less competitive, more prepared to listen to and care for others, more generous in their political commitment, and so on. Accordingly, an increased proportion of women in politics are expected to diversify, and therefore improve the ways politics is practiced. In other words, in this utilitarian conception of gender quotas, the institutionalization of gender difference is expected to improve the efficiency of politics.

Theorists of collective protest have shown that the success of social movements often depends on their ability to resonate with the dominant cultural context in which they take place (Gamson and Meyer 1996; Benford and Snow 2000; Ferree et al. 2002). At the time they formulated their claim, parity campaigners were faced with (1) a powerful doctrine of 'republican universalism', which was presumed to be the essence of French democracy, and (2) a recurrent media discourse stressing the 'crisis' of the legitimacy of representative democracy. In order to make their claim widely acceptable, French parity campaigners tried to 'bridge' (Benford and Snow, 2000) their demand of gender parity with these two major features of the cultural context (Bereni and Lépinard 2003, 2004; Lépinard 2006, 2007a).

Universalizing the Gender Difference and Bracketing Power Relations

When it emerged in the early 1990s, the demand for parity was chiefly constrained by the particular strength of the republican universalistic rhetoric mentioned above. This rhetoric, which stems from the French Revolution and the Declaration of the Rights of Man and the Citizen, asserts that the individual is the only category on which political representation may legitimately be grounded. During the public debate over parity, opponents recurrently raised this argument of republican universalism (Bereni and Lépinard 2003, 2004; Scott 2005; Lépinard 2006, 2007a, 2007b). Parity, they said, would be an unacceptable inscription of gender in the political order, and would jeopardize the principle of the indivisibility of national sovereignty into categories. This argument referred to a 1982 French Constitutional Council ruling which had censured a parliamentary bill implementing gender-based quotas in local elections.[5] Not only would parity open a breach in the frame of universalism, but it would also, according to its opponents, open the 'Pandora's box of particular claims', that is, the breakdown of national sovereignty into as many categories as there are social groups. According to Elisabeth Badinter, a prominent French intellectual who strongly opposed the parity claim in the media, 'the argument [of parity] introduces a fatal drift in our secular and universalistic Republic. Because the numerical argument will inevitably lead to parity claims from other communities, racial, religious, even cultural and sexual' (Badinter 1996, 15).

In sum, 'republican' opponents to the reform framed the debate as a stark choice between parity and French republican universalism. Faced with these recurrent arguments, which had been responsible for the failure of quotas in the early 1980s, parity advocates recurrently rejected the idea that their claim was a form of 'quota' or 'affirmative action'. They presented their demand as a *deepening* of, rather than a *derogation* from, the universalistic framework. To do so, proponents of parity redefined the status of 'sexual difference', from then on described as an immutable principle prevailing over all other differences (class, age, ethnicity, race, and so on).

In support of this conception, they used three main arguments (Bereni and Lépinard 2004). First, a *statistical* argument: because women had always constituted at least 'half of humanity', they could not, unlike ethnic groups for example, be compared to a disadvantaged 'minority' such as may be targeted by affirmative action programs. Second, the specific status of gender difference was based, for many parity proponents, on a *technical* argument: the fact that, unlike many other distinctions, gender groups have clearly and easily identifiable frontiers, since gender is one of the permanent characteristics of the civil identity of each individual. As parity campaigner Françoise Gaspard wrote: 'categorization as male or female cannot be regarded as comparable to social status, religion, or skin

---

5   A legal provision stating that party candidate lists in local elections should include no more than 75 per cent of persons of the same sex was canceled by the Constitutional Council (*Conseil Constitutionnel*) in a ruling of 18 November 1982 (Decision no. 82–146 DC). The Council stated that two of the founding principles of the French Republic (Article 6 of the *Déclaration des Droits de l'Homme et du Citoyen* and Article 3 of the French Constitution of 1958) were 'opposed to any division of voters or candidates by category'.

colour – contingent features that are not taken into account in the civil status of individuals. The division into sexes has a very special character' (Gaspard 1998, 27). Last but not least, parity campaigners used an *anthropological* argument. According to this argument, the sexual divide structures all known societies, and the sexual bi-categorization is a permanent, 'universal' characteristic of humanity itself. Parity's champions in the media and parliamentary public debates endlessly raised this argument. For example, Gisèle Halimi, a prominent advocate of parity, wrote:

> *Women are not a community, and have among themselves no community ties as they are defined by social scientists. They are not a race, not a class, not an ethnic group, not a category. They belong to all these groups, engender them, and cut across them. Sexual difference is the original parameter. Before being of a class, a race, a corporation, etc., a human being is first of all female or male. (Halimi 1997, 14)*

In sum, opposing sexual difference to diversity, proponents of parity managed to define the gender divide as the only acceptable criterion of distinction in a universalistic, republican framework, and to make their claim a genuine French product, defined in self-conscious opposition to the American model (Scott 1997, 2005; Fassin 1999; Bereni and Lépinard 2003, 2004; Lépinard 2006, 2007a, 2007b). But in the same move, such discursive strategies contributed to depoliticizing the category of gender.

As some feminist critiques of parity have pointed out, during and after the debate, on the ground of materialist feminist and/or queer theories (Varikas 1994, 2006; Delphy 1997; Bourcier 2007, Lépinard 2007a, 2007b), parity advocates have tended to obscure the idea that duality is as much a social product of power relationships as is hierarchy. The agonistic dimension of gender was replaced by the idea – based on the metaphor of the heterosexual couple – of an eternal and necessary complementarity between the two sexes, considered as 'partners'. Significantly, prominent parity advocate Sylviane Agacinski (philosopher and wife of Prime Minister Lionel Jospin) raised the same argument of the 'Symbolic Order', based on what she calls the 'natural' heterosexuality of humanity, to support parity and to make her case against homosexual families during the debate over the 'PACS' (same-sex contract of union), which took place at the same time as the debate over parity in 1998–99 (Scott 2005).

In this sense, while there has been a reconfiguration of universalism in pro-parity discourses, it was accompanied by a reaffirmation of the norm of gender binarism that precludes the proliferation of sexes, sexualities and genders. Last but not least, such a vision has led to denying other oppressed minorities the benefits of the 'breach' made by women 'in the bulwark of the Republic' (Lépinard 2007a, 392). By drawing a border between sexual difference and other social differences, this discourse has tended to reinforce the homogenization of the category of gender, and has tended to neglect the intersection of gender and other categories, such as race and ethnicity.

Improving Political Representation, Silencing Women's Interests

Along with the rejection of affirmative action discourses, the way parity was framed had another essential feature: during the public debate, parity campaigners tended to present their claim as a means to perfect political representation rather than to promote gender equality. Jane Jenson and Isabelle Giraud have shown how in France in the 1990s, the recurrence of a public discourse on the supposed crisis of the legitimacy of political elites provided a 'window of opportunity' for parity campaigners (Jenson and Giraud 2001).

Indeed, from the very beginning of the parity campaign, the demand for an increasing proportion of elected women was framed as a means to perfect democracy. Accordingly, some parity proponents argued that an increased presence of women in politics would make the body of representatives more similar to the body of citizens. This argument is the logical consequence of the discourse about the universality of gender difference: since gender difference prevails over all other social differences, as it is part of the 'universal' identity of the individual, therefore its natural extension in political representation is the 'figuration' of this gender difference in the representative body (Bereni and Lépinard 2003, 2004; Lépinard 2006, 2007a, 2007b).

For example, according to parity advocate Sylviane Agacinski, inscribing the gender difference in political representation reflects the universal duality of human beings, who are either male or female: 'We must at last recognize the mixed character of humanity, its originally sexual character …. If we take for granted that the two sexes universally constitute humanity, it is legitimate to rethink the people's sovereignty with allowance for its dual composition' (Agacinski 1999, 1). As parity proponent Claude Servan-Schreiber said, women and men are the 'two legs' of a 'single body', the human species, and are 'not interchangeable' (quoted in Scott 2005, 61). Not only has gender difference been invoked – through parity – to achieve the faithful figuration of the gendered nature of citizenship, but women have also been celebrated as a means to make political representation more efficient. This was done by emphasizing the very qualities and competences that they are assumed to provide because they are women. According to ten prominent female politicians who called for parity through a manifesto in the press: 'our propositions are supported by a large part of public opinion … which finds astonishing that our society cannot benefit from a feminine political representation, liable to enhance the efficiency and the quality of public action' (Barzach et al. 1997, 10).

Thus, the claim of parity was often framed as a means to improve representative democracy. Such a discursive strategy had a great advantage: by linking gender parity to the improvement of representative democracy, both in a more figurative and a more efficient manner, it allowed an 'increase in generality' (*montée en généralité*) (Boltanski and Thévenot 1991) of the claim, and facilitated the construction of a broad consensus around it among the political elites and public opinion. In other words, these arguments made it possible to define parity as a means not only to solve a gender question, but also to solve more general political issues (Lépinard 2006, 2007a).

But if parity was based on a series of arguments celebrating gender difference as a means to enhance political democracy, to what extent did it actually reshape political representation in a feminist perspective? Among the many discourses calling for the introduction of gender 'difference' in representative democracy, the question of women's *interests* has very scarcely been raised by parity proponents in the public space. Even if this critical mass argument was in many parity campaigners' minds, only a small number of feminists and a few female members of parliament openly pointed out the link between the claim for a more descriptive representation and the question of the political interests of women articulated by the feminist social movement.

If the gender difference was celebrated in the public space, it was often as a means of reflecting a so-called 'eternal' gender difference and increasing the performance of political representation through the importation of competences that are supposed to be specifically feminine. Parity campaigners recurrently claimed that the role of a representative, whether male or female, is to represent *all* the people. They rarely argued that female representatives could voice women's specific interests – as a disadvantaged group. Therefore, it seems as if the dominant framing of the parity demand did not significantly challenge the traditional, universalistic meaning of political representation from a feminist perspective.

Conclusion

The parity demand emerged in the context of intellectual and institutional challenges to representative democracy claiming for a stronger presence of women through affirmative action measures. However, analysis of the rationales used in the public space to support the parity demand shows that the dominant framing of parity contravenes the principles of its intellectual and institutional sources. First, most parity advocates refused to define parity as a 'quota' or as an 'affirmative action' measure, evicting the political, antagonist dimension of gender. The two sexes have been presented as eternal, complementary partners, and not as categories constructed through power relations. Second, the parity demand was recurrently justified as a means to improve representative democracy, rather than to fight gender discriminations. Parity was expected to enhance political representation, making it resemble the body of citizens, and making it more efficient, but parity was not presented as a means to include the substantial interests of 'women' into the public arena.

It remains to be seen in the future to what extent the dominant justifications of parity are liable to affect the practical implementation of the reform. Did the emphasis on a supposedly eternal gender difference and the euphemization of power relationships between the sexes entail new social constraints for female politicians? What are the effective changes induced by the parity reform on how citizens and political elites define and practice representative democracy? This question has to be explored through a further study of the implementation of the reform (Lépinard 2006, 2007a), and can only be assessed in the middle or long term.

References

Agacinski, S. (1999), 'Contre l'effacement des sexes', *Le Monde*, 6 February, 1.

Badinter, E. (1996), 'Non aux quotas de femmes', *Le Monde*, 12 June, 15.

Balme, R. et al. (eds) (2002), *L'action collective en Europe* (Paris: Presse de Science-po).

Bard, C. et al. (eds) (2004), *Quand les femmes s'en mêlent. Genre et pouvoir* (Paris: La Martinière).

Barzach, M. et al. (1997), 'Assez de paroles, des actes', *Libération*, 26 March, 10.

Benford, R. and Snow, D. (2000), 'Framing Processes and Social Movements: An Overview and Assessment', *Annual Review of Sociology* 26, 611–39.

Benhabib, S. (ed.) (1996), *Democracy and Difference* (Princeton, NJ: Princeton University Press).

Bereni, L. (2004), 'Le mouvement français pour la parité et l'Europe', in Jacquot et al. (eds), *Les usages de l'Europe. Acteurs et transformations européennes* (Paris: L'Harmattan).

—— and Lépinard, E. (2003), 'La parité, "contresens de l'égalité"? Contraintes discursives et pratiques d'une réforme', *Nouvelles Questions Féministes* 22:3, 12–31.

—— and Lépinard, E. (2004), '"Les femmes ne sont pas une catégorie". Les stratégies de légitimation de la parité en France', *Revue française de science politique* 54:1, 71–98.

Boltanski, L. and Thévenot, L. (1991), *De la justification: les économies de la grandeur* (Paris: Gallimard).

Bourcier, M.-H. (2007), *Sexpolitiques: Queer Zones 2* (Paris: La Fabrique).

Butler, J. (1990), *Gender Trouble* (New York: Routledge).

Carroll, S.J. (ed.) (2001), *The Impact of Women in Public Office* (Bloomington, IN: Indiana University Press).

Childs, S. (2004), *New Labour's Women MPs: Women Representing Women* (London: Routledge).

—— (2006), 'The Complicated Relationship between Sex, Gender and the Substantive Representation of Women', *European Journal of Women's Studies* 13:1, 7–21.

Conseil de l'Europe (1992), *La démocratie paritaire. Quarante années d'activité du Conseil de l'Europe (actes du Séminaire de Strasbourg, 6 et 7 novembre 1989)* (Strasbourg: Editions du Conseil de l'Europe).

Delphy, C. (1997) 'Pour en finir avec l'exclusion des femmes', *Le Monde diplomatique*, March, 6–7.

Dodson, D. (2001), 'Acting for Women: Is What Legislators Say, What They Do?', in Carroll (ed.), *The Impact of Women in Public Office* (Bloomington, IN: Indiana University Press).

Fassin, E. (1999), 'The Purloined Gender: American Feminism in a French Mirror', *French Historical Studies* 22:1, 113–38.

Ferree, M.M., Gamson, W.A., Gerhards, J. and Rucht, D. (2002), *Shaping Abortion Discourse: Democracy and the Public Sphere in Germany and the United States* (Cambridge: Cambridge University Press).

Gamson, W.A. and Meyer, D.S. (1996), 'Framing Political Opportunity', in McAdam et al. (eds), *Comparative Perspectives on Social Movements* (Cambridge, MA: Harvard University Press).

Gaspard, F. (1998), 'La parité: principe ou stratégie?', *Le Monde diplomatique*, November, 26–7.

Gould, C. (1996), 'Diversity and Democracy: Representing Differences', in Benhabib (ed.), *Democracy and Difference* (Princeton, NJ: Princeton University Press).

Halimi, G. (1997), 'Parité hommes-femmes: un débat historique?', *Le Monde*, 7 March, 14.

Hoskyns, C. (1996), *Integrating Gender: Women, Law, and Politics in the European Union* (London: Verso).

Jacquot, S. et al. (eds) (2004), *Les usages de l'Europe. Acteurs et transformations européennes* (Paris: L'Harmattan).

Jenson, J. and Giraud, I. (2001), 'Constitutionalizing Equal Access: High Hopes, Dashed Hopes?' in Klausen et al. (eds), *Has Liberalism Failed Women?* (New York: Palgrave).

Klausen, J. et al. (eds) (2001), *Has Liberalism Failed Women?* (New York: Palgrave).

Lépinard, E. (2006), 'Identity Without Politics: Framing the Parity Laws and their Implementation in French Local Politics', *Social Politics* 13:2, 30–58.

—— (2007a), *L'égalité introuvable. Les féministes, la parité et la République* (Paris: Presses de Science po).

—— (2007b), 'The Contentious Subject of Feminism: Defining Women in France from the Second Wave to Parity', *Signs* 32:2, 375–403.

—— and Bereni, L. (2004), 'La parité ou le mythe d'une exception française', *Pouvoirs* 111, 73–85.

Lovenduski, J. (ed.) (2005), *State Feminism and Political Representation* (Cambridge: Cambridge University Press).

—— and Norris, P. (eds) (1996), *Women in Politics* (Oxford: New York: Oxford University Press).

Mansbridge, J. (1999), 'Should Blacks Represent Blacks and Women Represent Women? A Contingent "Yes"', *The Journal of Politics* 61:3, 628–57.

—— (2001), 'The Descriptive Political Representation of Gender: An Anti-essentialist Argument', in Klausen et al. (eds), *Has Liberalism Failed Women?* (New York: Palgrave).

Marques-Pereira, B. (2004), 'L'inclusion des femmes en politique et la théorie politique anglo-saxonne', in Bard et al. (eds), *Quand les femmes s'en mêlent. Genre et pouvoir* (Paris: La Martinière).

Mazey, S. (2002), 'L'Union européenne et les droits des femmes: de l'européanisation des agendas nationaux à la nationalisation d'un agenda européen?', in Balme et al. (eds), *L'action collective en Europe* (Paris: Presse de Science-po).

McAdam, D. et al. (eds) (2006), *Comparative Perspectives on Social Movements* (Cambridge, MA: Harvard University Press).

Mohanty, C. (1997), *Feminist Genealogies, Colonial Legacies, Democratic Futures* (New York: Routledge).

Mouffe, C. (1996), 'Democracy Power and the "Political"', in Benhabib (ed.), *Democracy and Difference* (Princeton, NJ: Princeton University Press).

Phillips, A. (1995), *The Politics of Presence* (Oxford: Oxford University Press).

—— (1998a), 'Democracy and Representation: Or, Why Should it Matter Who our Representatives Are?', in Phillips (ed.), *Feminism and Politics* (Oxford: Oxford University Press).

—— (ed.) (1998b), *Feminism and Politics* (Oxford: Oxford University Press).

Pitkin, H.F. (1967), *The Concept of Representation* (Berkeley, CA: University of California Press).

Rosanvallon, P. (1998), *Le peuple introuvable. Histoire de la représentation démocratique en France* (Paris: Gallimard).

Sabbagh, D. (2007), *Equality and Transparency: A Strategic Perspective on Affirmative Action in American Law* (New York: Palgrave).

Sawer, M. (2002), 'Representation of Women in Australia: Meaning and Make Believe', *Parliamentary Affairs* 55:1, 5–18.

——, Tremblay, M. and Trimble, L. (eds) (2006), *Representing Women in Parliament: A Comparative Study* (London, New York: Routledge).

Scott, J.W. (1997), '"La Querelle des Femmes" in the Late Twentieth Century', *New Left Review* 226, 3–19.

—— (2005), *Parité: Sexual Difference and the Crisis of French Universalism* (Chicago, IL: University of Chicago Press).

Squires, J. (1996), 'Quotas for Women: Fair Representation?', in Lovenduski and Norris (eds), *Women in Politics* (Oxford: New York: Oxford University Press).

Varikas, E. (1994), 'Refonder ou raccommoder la démocratie? Réflexions critiques sur la demande de la parité des sexes', *French Politics and Society* 12:4, 1–34.

—— (2006), *Penser le genre* (Paris: PUF).

Young, I.M. (1990), *Justice and the Politics of Difference* (Princeton, NJ: Princeton University Press).

—— (2000), *Inclusion and Democracy* (Oxford: Oxford University Press).

Further Reading

Bereni, L. (2007), 'French Feminists Renegotiate Republican Universalism: The Gender Parity Campaign', *French Politics* 5:3, 191–209.

Childs, S. and Krook, M.L. (2006), 'Gender and Politics: The State of the Art', *Politics* 26:1, 18–28.

Lovenduski, J. (2005), *Feminizing Politics* (Cambridge: Polity Press).

Randall, V. (1991), 'Feminism and Political Analysis', *Political Studies* 39:3, 513–32.

Squires, J. (1999), *Gender in Political Theory* (Cambridge: Polity Press).

Political Professionalism and Representative Democracy: Common History, Irresolvable Linkage and Inherent Tensions

Jens Borchert

Introduction

The three-step argument I wish to make in this chapter is as simple as it is cumbersome for the proponents of democracy. First, historical democratization, as it occurred in Europe and North America, by necessity caused political professionalism. Second, political professionalization – also by necessity – has created a certain logic of action among the practitioners of politics that tends to violate democratic principles. Third, attempts at reform are either futile, counter-productive or short-lived – but still vital to maintain the democratic project. Thus, in other words, the revolutionary movement that brought us democracy also infected it with a virus that since then has spread, and now threatens to erode the strength of democracy. The trick is to keep the democratic patient alive, not to heal her.

What is Political Professionalization, and What Do We Mean by Democracy?

Let us first make clear what we mean by democracy: In Robert Dahl's (1971) minimalist definition, democracy is based on two essential elements: political participation and public contestation. Political participation here refers to the chance of all citizens to have a meaningful impact on the selection of both personnel and policies. Public contestation, by contrast, concerns the supply side of politics: there has to be an equally meaningful competition of candidates for public office and of policy solutions. These two elements, then – participation and competition – define the essence of modern democracy.

Participation entails a norm of social inclusiveness. In democracy, there is no justification for the exclusion of citizens from decision-making based on social criteria such as origin, wealth, status, race or gender. Historically, the process of democratization characteristically started with limited concessions being granted to *some* hitherto excluded groups. Mass democracy, however, was not to be stopped at any given point. Its continuous extension of social scope remained one of its defining features. Today, there is no legitimate argument left to delimit the inclusiveness of the democratic principle. Suffrage has ever been extended to include non-landowners, the property-less classes, women, people of colour, immigrants (not yet fully) and other formerly underprivileged groups.

However, the extension of the *right to participate* has not necessarily meant a tendency toward greater *actual participation*. Voter turnout, as one major indicator of political participation, was larger in the United States, for example, in the second half of the nineteenth century than in the twentieth. That led some US social scientists in the 1950s and 1960s to point out that the motivation to participate in most cases is discontent with politics as it is (mostly based on Downs 1957). By way of logical reversion, they concluded that low rates of turnout reflect widespread political satisfaction, and thus are a sign of democratic maturity and stability (see, for example, Lipset 1960, 185, 226–9). It seems more reasonable, however, to conclude, as contemporary critics did at the time (see, for example, Schattschneider 1960), that the urge to participate is strongly influenced by the attractiveness of the choices offered. If none of the options seems appealing, voting becomes less meaningful and abstention quite a rational choice to make. This turns us to Dahl's second norm, that of contestation or competition.

Competition (which seems a more adequate term than contestation) entails a norm of meaningful choice, of real alternatives to be offered. While the structure of political competition has undergone deep changes since the beginnings of mass democracy, it has not seen anything like the pattern of extension we found for participation. Typically, the number of recognizable alternatives is limited. Hence, the alternatives change while their number remains roughly constant. The most basic change in the structure of political competition has been from a stylized struggle between large social interests organized as political actors who register the support of their 'natural' clientele to a contest between professionalized political actors who try to win over a more or less free-floating electorate on an *ad hoc* basis. Where workers used to battle employers and both were opposed to agrarian interests, now parties try to reconstruct their electoral base from election to election using the modern marketing techniques of political communication experts. While in the former model political change was a reflection of social change (or of new social coalitions), in the latter politics has gained a more autonomous quality, making competition at the same time less principled and more personal, less important and more intense.

In Western democracies, there is a universal perception that the choices offered represent a smaller spectrum of political options and a less attractive tableau of persons standing for election than used to be the case. This feeling of decay might in some respects reflect a certain romanticism and a longing for a better past whose superior quality lies above all in the fact that we do not have to live through it (any more). But there is also some truth to the perception of a narrower political spectrum and of less competition. This presents a puzzle. Why would the opening up of the political sphere lead to less meaningful competition? Weren't the two categories positively related in Dahl's thinking? Participation was to spur contestation, and more (or more profound) competition was to bring about more participation as well. So what has happened, and what is the role of political professionalism in all of this?

Before we come to that question, we have to lay out what we mean by the 'professionalization of politics'. Unfortunately, the notion of political professionalization carries two different meanings: one refers to politics becoming an occupation, while the other takes that for granted and uses the term 'professionalization' to refer to the 'professions' as a distinct group of occupations with special qualities setting them apart from others. While I have argued elsewhere (Borchert 2003a, 133–201) that it is analytically fruitful to look at politics as a profession like law and medicine, here I am simply referring to the former process that turned politics into an occupation.

This process has hardly gone unnoticed in social science. Weber's classical lecture *Politik als Beruf* is still the principal text to look at.[1] Weber, who experienced the ongoing process of political professionalization in Germany at first hand, directs our attention to the simple but consequential fact that politicians turn into professionals under the conditions of modern democracy. This professionalization of politics proceeds on three levels: of the individual, of political offices, and of political institutions (Borchert 2003a). *Individually*, political professionalization entails the giving up of a prior occupation and moving into politics. This move changes both the time budget and the monetary budget of those who make it. Based on earlier observations by James Bryce (1888 [1995], 731–2; see also Portinaro 2001, 298), Max Weber made the three decisive distinctions in this regard: 'habitual' versus 'occasional' politicians, 'full-time' versus 'part-time', and 'living off politics' versus 'living for politics' (Weber 1919 [1994], 171–2, 1994a, 316–18; see Borchert 2003a, 72–8).

The first two indicators for political professionalism concern time spent in and for politics. A 'habitual' involvement in politics refers to both: a certain intensity of the political activity, and a certain permanence. In his notes for the lecture, Weber referred to 'habitual and continuous politicians' (Weber 1919 [1994], 139). While 'we all are occasional politicians' (Weber 1919 [1994], 167), habitual politicians are distinguished by their intense and long-term involvement in politics. It is with the further step from part-time to full-time habitual politician that the line to professionalism is crossed.

---

1   Translations of the title vary, and convey different meanings: 'Politics as a Vocation' (Weber 1946, 2004b), 'Politics as a Profession' (the title Gerth and Mills originally envisaged; see Oakes and Vidich 1999), or the compromise solution, 'The Profession and Vocation of Politics' (Weber 1994b). For reconstructions of the lecture, see Palonen (2002) and Borchert (2003a, 64–94). For a critique of the various translations and their impact, see Borchert (2007).

The increasing time demands on modern politicians, however, raised the question of 'dispensability' that Weber (1919 [1994], 170–71) stressed so much: Who was so dispensable in his civil occupation that he could engage in politics habitually? Weber's answer to that question emphasizes the 'elective affinities' of certain occupations to politics. Two occupations in particular were so close to politics in various regards that their practitioners became the natural politicians of the late nineteenth century: lawyers and journalists. Lawyers were privileged because they could relatively freely dispose of their time. Also, their political activities, while time-consuming, won them additional clients as their name recognition was enhanced. Often, then these clients could be handled by their partners, which served to reconcile the time demands of politics and the interests of even small law firms. In terms of the personal qualities emphasized in both arenas, Weber pointed out that the politician is representing interests in just about the same way as the lawyer. Thus, lawyers also seemed to be particularly well qualified for the political business. In addition, their high social status turned them into attractive candidates and their oratory skills made them effective campaigners.

Journalists, on the other hand, had a much lower social status, yet were also dispensable. They were rather free in their organization of work as well. Also, the qualities of a journalist in terms of being able to aptly summarize an issue, in making an argument and in applying rhetorical skills were well suited for politics. As Weber clearly saw, the kind of professionalization associated with journalists differed profoundly from that based on lawyers. While the latter represented notables in their own right, the former depended on a (party) organization to employ them as journalists and to provide them with the necessary resources to run for political office. Lawyers much easier fit the role of political entrepreneur, while journalists tend to stick to that of the loyal party official. Thus, the two occupations that served as the primary recruitment grounds for politicians also stood for two different types of political professionalism – entrepreneurship versus officialdom (see Borchert 2003b).

With full-time involvement in politics, however, the issue of dispensability recedes in importance. If somebody is to enter politics on a full-time basis, the issue is no longer one of reconciling politics with a regular occupation. Rather, the issue becomes one of making a living out of politics. This is the core of Weber's sharp observation: Once politics becomes a full-time endeavor, there are but two choices. Either you provide the opportunity for a 'periodic and reliable income derived from politics', or you 'by necessity have a plutocratic recruitment of the leading political strata' (Weber 1919 [1994], 171–2; my translation): 'Politics can either be "honorary" and then is made by "independent", that is wealthy, people, above all rentiers. Or it is made accessible to those without personal wealth and then it has to be paid for' (Weber 1919 [1994], 172).[2] Full-time politics, then, is either socially exclusive or it has to provide its practitioners with a decent income. This is the link between democratization and professionalization, to which we shall return briefly.

---

2   Weber further distinguishes income derived from bribery and other fees, and that from regular salaries.

Once the professionalization of politics has begun in a polity, professionalization of individuals is a recurring process. Political positions open up at each election. The people filling certain positions then tend to enter politics full-time and with the expectation of deriving their income from their political activity. Typically, they have held various honorary political positions in local and party politics before. The way into professional politics is usually anything but arbitrary. Rather, it follows an established pattern of recruitment and careers characteristic of a certain political system. This pattern is primarily based on the professionalization of certain *offices and institutions*. The offices which are available in a polity and the hierarchy in which they are organized by common perception together present the 'structure of opportunity' (Schlesinger 1966) for political professionals. In a similar way, political institutions may be more or less professionalized according to the resources they provide.

Politicians running for professional offices – most often these are public rather than party offices – are fully aware beforehand that election to that office is linked to professionalization in politics. If a certain office is already established as requiring full-time involvement and offering its holder a decent income, the newly elected holder becomes a professional politician right away, and without having to struggle for that status. By endowing political offices with a competitive salary, their professionalization becomes institutionalized. The array of professionalized political offices then basically provides the aspiring politician with the menu to choose from. Honorary offices serve as apprenticeship, home base, and fall-back position, but they are clearly distinct from professionalized offices in the view of politicians.

The analytic distinction between professionalization of individual and office allows for the incongruence between the two. That is, there may be political amateurs taking over a professionalized office, or there may be political professionals coming into an office that has not yet been professionalized. While these instances are rather rare, they do occur, and most often signal a transitory state that usually is resolved by way of professionalization of the as yet amateur side. Amateurs elected into professional offices tend to acquire the norms and habits of professionals rather quickly. This can be seen in formerly anti-professional parties like the German Greens as well as in the proverbial 'Mr Smith' coming to Washington or to any other capital (see Canon 1990; Docherty 1997). Professionalism most often proves to be a rather infectious disease.

The reverse situation of politicians who pursue politics full-time while the position they hold is not yet adequately reimbursed is usually part of a historical (rather than an individual) process of transition. If possible, these office-holders will struggle for the introduction of salaries. Otherwise, they will devise individual strategies of professionalization, with their income coming from other sources without requiring work outside of politics. Parties and interest groups are the most likely candidates to bear the financial burden in these cases. Historically, most of these misfit situations have been resolved in favour of the professionalization of the office. However, as professionalization proceeds further, new conflicts of this sort emerge. One case that was recently analyzed is the hidden professionalization of city councilors in the larger German cities. Many of them spent more than 80 per cent of their working hours in politics. Yet their public mandate pays only for part of their costs. The rest is covered by various sources such as employers (for no-show jobs), parties and interest groups, and public pensions (Reiser 2006).

How Democratization Made Political Professionalism Necessary

Let us return to the causal nexus between democracy and political professionalism. 'Democratization necessary result: living *off* politics' is the relevant entry here in Weber's original manuscript (Weber 1919 [1994], 141). Democratization contributed to the professionalization of politics in a number of ways.

With political issues being moved from a sphere of discretionary decision-making – be it by hereditary rulers and their entourage, be it by bureaucracies – to one of public scrutiny and majority decision-making, the arena of politics was greatly enlarged. This created a demand for additional personnel, but also changed the time demands on each individual practitioner. The tendency towards full-time involvement in politics was not a conscious choice made by politicians, but rather was a result of enlarging the public sphere containing now many more issues to be resolved.

Democratization also created all kinds of demands directed to the state. Public office-holders were increasingly held accountable for the degree of public welfare. Thus, policy areas emerged that did not even exist before. The rise of first the interventionist state and later the welfare state was a reaction to economic needs, but also to social rights being deduced from political rights as T.H. Marshall framed it. Democracy meant participation, but participation without sharing in a nation's wealth seemed a hollow right indeed. On the other hand, politicians ran for public office and increasingly came to rely on it for their income. Thus, the re-election interest provided the gate through which material demands could effectively enter the political arena. That led to a rapid expansion of the modern state under democratic government. This greatly enlarged state needed even more personnel and needed them for longer than was called for by democracy alone.

Finally, democratization meant opening up politics to new social groups. It was no longer acceptable to restrict politics to a narrow sector of the population. This was true for the extension of the franchise, but even more so for the right to be elected. As Michel Offerlé (1999b, 11) has pointed out, the 1848 introduction of universal male suffrage in France multiplied the electorate by 80, but the group of potential office-holders by 400. Consequently, it was seen as profoundly illegitimate to exclude all men without independent wealth from public office. Here, then, enters the logic analyzed so well by Weber.

Democratization thus created increasing time demands on politicians, and thereby the need for an income derived from politics. This is reflected in the struggle for the introduction of legislative salaries as well as in various ways to make up for the lack of these salaries. In the struggles for the compensation of legislators, it was almost uniformly the democratic and liberal left that supported legislative salaries, while the conservative right often opposed them. While this constellation may seem surprising in the light of current debates, it seems quite logical if we look at the interests of historical actors. Germany is a good case here: the German struggle over the introduction of legislative salaries that goes back to reforms in the German states during the 1820s and 1830s and to the debates of the National Assembly of 1848–49 was successful (in that allowances, later to be transformed into salaries, were introduced) only in 1906 (see Butzer 1999; Jansen 1999). The National Assembly convened in Frankfurt in 1849 had agreed without much controversy on the general need for financial compensation of representatives, as it was already practiced by that time in most German state parliaments. Some representatives even explicitly demanded to 'give the representatives a salary from which they can live' (Jakob Venedey, quoted in Jansen 1999, 47).

Yet this effort at constitution-building failed. When it was taken up again for the constitution of the Norddeutscher Bund and then the German Reich in 1867–71, Bismarck achieved almost single-handedly an article in both constitutions that explicitly ruled out state payments to legislators ('The members of the Reichstag in that capacity may not receive a salary or a compensation', Article 32). Although liberal voices like the leading newspaper *Vossische Zeitung* called for an end to 'dilettantism in parliament' and vigorously demanded the establishment of 'politics as a profession' (7 February 1867, 23 February 1867; quoted in Jansen 1999, 51), Bismarck effectively vetoed any step into that direction. He flatly declared that the compensation of legislators amounted to 'salaries for the educated proletariat for the purpose of professional demagoguery' (quoted in Jansen 1999, 49). For him, the ban on legislative salaries was a corrective mechanism to keep the effects of the universal suffrage under control (Jansen 1999, 52).

There was no shortage of later attempts to introduce legislative salaries during the Kaiserreich. The standard argument by conservatives, however, was brought forward by the President of the Reichstag, von Levetzow, who stated that the ban was to be upheld, since the lack of salaries was the last barrier against 'bringing the Reichstag down to the lowest level of a purely democratic representative of the people' (quoted in Molt 1963, 39). This quote demonstrates that the participants in this eighty-year debate were fully aware that professionalization was both a result of democratization and a prerequisite for its further extension into the parliamentary sphere. The battle over legislative compensation was basically one about democracy and the social opening of the political sphere.

This interpretation is reinforced when we take a look at the 'old democracies' and their position regarding payments to politicians. Members of Congress in the United States were paid a per diem from the very beginning. Payments themselves were never controversial – although the amount has always been a matter of debate. Similarly, the post-revolutionary French Constitution provided for compensations, and additionally made it illegal for representatives not to accept these payments (Jansen 1999, 36). This was a provision aimed at wealthy populists who might otherwise embarrass other politicians by forgoing their compensation.

Among the old democracies, the United Kingdom was a late-comer in introducing legislative allowances: British MPs were not paid until 1911–12. During the nineteenth century, almost half of the British representatives were wealthy rentiers. In the UK, then, early democratization coincided with a highly stratified class system reaching well into politics. As in Germany, Conservatives (but Liberals, too) were reluctant to open the gates of politics to new entrants. However, when a Liberal government needed Labour votes in Parliament, it knew what it had to do (Rush and Cromwell 2000, 471, 488).

The British and German cases also show clearly that a ban on legislative allowances was not sufficient to prevent political professionalization altogether. Labour politicians, against whom the denial of salaries was primarily directed, were 'sponsored' – mostly by the unions (Rush and Cromwell 2000, 471). Likewise, German Social Democratic leader August Bebel proudly declared that his party did not depend on legislative compensation and had always been able to fund its representatives in the way it saw fit (Jansen 1999, 50). Basically, in Germany there were four ways to circumvent the ban on allowances:

1. private salaries from parties, interest groups, and from funds collected among the citizens;
2. employment as an official or a journalist by parties and interest groups;
3. dual mandates in state legislatures that continued to pay compensations; particularly sought after was the combination of a seat in the Reichstag with one in the Prussian legislature that was also conveniently based in Berlin;
4. jobs within the bureaucracy, as public officials continued to receive their salary while they were on leave to fulfill their legislative duties.

All of these detours receded in importance once legislative allowances or salaries were introduced. The historical trend ever since has been toward legislatures as the most important institutions for professional politicians and toward legislative salaries as the most important source of income. Wherever possible, parties have externalized the cost of their personnel to the state by way of parliamentary allowances and salaries. Legislatures were of central importance not only because they provided the bulk of political jobs, but also because their members were in charge of the (self-)regulation of the political profession. While parliaments may have lost power in general political terms, they have retained their importance as bodies of professional autonomy.

Further professionalization occurred in three ways. First, allowances were transformed into salaries that underscored the character of political work as a quasi-regular occupation. The introduction of parliamentary pension schemes (usually after the Second World War) constituted another major step toward a legislative-based political professionalism. Also, the number of staff was dramatically increased, and by now represents a new layer of political professionals often hoping to run for public office in their own right some day.

The second tendency of professionalization was its diffusion within political systems. Gradually, it was extended to other territorial levels of government (regions/states, municipalities). The third pattern was one of a progressive 'colonialization of state and society' (von Beyme 1993, 39) – or at least of relevant parts thereof.

Parties in many countries took control of state institutions and organizations, and subsumed the available positions to their personnel portfolio.

The Logic of Political Professionalism, and the Tension with Democracy

Overall, then, the number of professionalized positions has multiplied in all advanced democracies, and is still growing. If we define political professionalization as a result of democratization, then this success story should signify the victory of democracy. Yet criticism of political personnel is more prevalent than ever. One line of criticism is directed against supposed deficiencies of representation. In this view, the under-representation of women and ethnic minorities in legislatures throughout the world is a serious flaw of that peculiar democracy of political professionals. And indeed, political professionalism does not allow for a miniature version of the population at large, but rather tends to create a more or less coherent professional group with certain common attributes regarding educational background and social class. If under pressure, however, professionalized institutions have been remarkably flexible in accommodating female or ethnic minority candidates. The latent conflict is more profound than the debate over descriptive representation would have it. The common history of professionalism and democracy conceals an inherent tension: while democracy demands participation and competition, professionalism is based on social exclusion and political collusion.

Adam Przeworski (1991, 12–14) has characterized democratic politics as the 'institutionalization of uncertainty'. This uncertainty is created by the electoral mechanism. Elections feed the hope for re-election and prolonged political careers. But this hope is necessarily of an uncertain kind, as elections may turn out differently from what one expects. With the professionalization of politics, uncertainty gains a new quality. Once politicians have become *professional* politicians, they stand to lose at election time not only power, status, prominence or influence, but also their job. This threat would be less cumbersome for those affected if they would not mind returning to their prior occupation or if there were similarly attractive positions outside the electoral mechanism. However, most politicians do not return to their old job even if they lose an election. Non-electoral political positions, on the other hand, are limited in number and usually are either entry positions or dead-end jobs amounting to the end of one's career.

One need not assume that politicians are primarily interested in re-election for its own sake. Yet whatever their primary interest – power, status, certain policies, representing certain social groups or interests, or even representing the 'common good' – they simply *have* to be re-elected to pursue it. With their professional careers always at the mercy of voters, politicians are confronted with a degree of uncertainty that is unheard of in other occupations – even in times of mass unemployment. But they are not helpless, either: professional politicians within parliaments are in a unique position in terms of their autonomy and their capacity to influence their terms of competition. They not only distribute campaign resources, they can also shape the electoral system. Thus, they are in a privileged position to positively influence their chances of re-election, and thereby reduce their uncertainty.

Avoiding open competition on a level playing field, there are basically three options: setting favorable institutional rules, awarding themselves superior resources, and keeping a check on intra-party challengers.

First, the most important type of institutional rule that is open to manipulation is electoral systems. Historically, there is a tendency in democratic countries from plurality to proportional electoral systems (Nohlen 2000, 200–202, 209). While this has the democratic advantage of reflecting more accurately the partisan vote, it also means less control by voters over the actual composition of parliament. As most proportional representation systems have closed lists and incumbents tend to be placed at top of the lists, this amounts to an effective safeguard against electoral threat.

Even in first-past-the-post electoral systems that tend to carry the highest degree of uncertainty, some informal safety mechanisms have been installed. For example, British politicians tend to be placed to contest uncertain or impossible constituencies at the beginning of their career. Waging a losing campaign is considered a sort of apprenticeship. Later, these candidates are transferred to relatively safe constituencies.

With safer seats, inter-party competition becomes less central to politicians' fortunes. This is bad news for democracy, since it renders electoral competition – one of the two defining aspects of democracy according to Dahl – less important. Safeguarding the careers of incumbents via institutional rules is a non-partisan game, and leads to cartel-like structures. Only the reliable cooperation of all players, their 'silent agreement' (Kirchheimer 1944 [1964], 83) across party boundaries, secures everybody's advantage *vis-à-vis* the challengers (also see Kirchheimer 1957 [1964]; Katz and Mair 1995, 22–3).

Second, incumbents may also be awarded superior material resources. This is particularly important in highly personalized electoral systems like that of the United States, where advantages in campaign finance are crucial to making incumbents' seats safer. But also in European party democracies, party and campaign finance laws are means to exclude new forces from the electoral arena. Party and campaign finance regulations typically favour those parties that are already represented in parliament, and thus serve as a safeguard against new competitors on the scene.

Third, while competition between parties is affecting political careers less than used to be the case, the electorate within parties has become more important. The most threatening competitors for professional politicians thus tend to come from *within* their own parties, rather than from competing political forces. This puts a premium on measures to control the nomination process within one's party. Therefore, strategies that are based on the accumulation of political mandates and positions across territorial levels become highly rational. In this way, office-holders keep their ears to the local ground and are more aware of potential threats.

The vertical accumulation of offices is a very common phenomenon in advanced democracies, precisely because additional offices on the 'lower' levels of the political system are closer to the nomination process. The office that is considered the best safeguard varies from system to system. In France, the *député-maire* – the national representative who is concurrently mayor of his or her town – is the classical figure. In Germany, many professional politicians from the Bundestag as well as from the state legislatures hold both party and local public office beside their main 'bread-winning' position. The crucial career safeguard, however, is the county chairmanship of one's party (see Borchert and Stolz 2003).

How vulnerable do all these measures of active career politics leave the political practitioners? Subjectively, many are still 'running scared', as Anthony King titled his book on professional politicians trying to maintain their careers. Yet looking at the data in European democracies, we find a turnover rate of only about 30 per cent (Cotta and Best 2000). This may sound high, but of course it includes voluntary retirements and deaths in office. Much of the rest of the fluctuation concerns small parties hovering around the electoral threshold. For most other incumbents, their seat is safe at least after the party lists have been nominated. While in every election there are involuntary losses of office or mandate, the conscious deselecting of politicians deemed unfit is practically impossible. The struggle against uncertainty has been extremely successful in the history of European democracies. The result is precisely that 'social closure' of democracy that Athenian democracy sought to avoid by relying on the lot to determine office-holders.[3]

While Athenian democracy was based on the idea that everybody should have equal access to public office, modern democracy placed the emphasis on the equal right of citizens to select representatives ('one person, one vote'). This includes the right to 'recall' as a central check on the abuse of power or the loss of responsiveness (Manin 1997, 12). 'Accountability' is to keep public office-holders 'virtuous' (Madison) and responsive to the interests of those they represent (see Manin 1997, 234). With the success of the insulation strategies professional politicians have devised, accountability loses its meaning. As Andreas Schedler has shown, accountability consists of two parts: the duty of the office-holder to justify his actions before the voters, and the voters' capacity to sanction the office-holder – in Schedler's words, 'answerability' and 'enforcement' (Schedler 1999, 14–17). Both aspects are hollowed out if elections only ratify co-option mechanisms within the political class of professionals (on co-option, see Löwenstein 1973).

Representative democracy gives citizens the task of selecting the political personnel as their most important chance of influencing politics and policy-making (Schumpeter 1950). Once the political personnel succeed in taking away that task from citizens, the democratic promise is turned into a meaningless 'offer of inconsequential participation' (Greven 1977). The mechanism which leads to this decay of democracy is the 'collusion and cooperation between ostensible competitors' – de Jouvenel's prescient vision of a 'république des camarades' (Katz and Mair 1995, 16–17; de Jouvenel 1914). Stefano Bartolini (1999, 2000) has developed an elaborate analysis of how democratic competition is necessarily based on the

---

3   On the notion of 'social closure', see Weber (1922 [1972], 23–5). Bourdieu (2001, 44–5) has explicitly applied the concept to the social closure of politics by way of professionalism.

'collusion' of political actors. As I would add, the motivation for collusive behaviour arises out of common interests of professional survival and career advancement that unite professional politicians across party boundaries. This is the motivational base for Bartolini's (2000, 63) apt diagnosis: 'In politics, cooperation and negotiation – that is, collusive interactions – between political leaders are the rule; competitive interactions are a small island in the big sea of collusion.'

The simultaneous decline of both competition and participation has not gone unnoticed. As various studies have found, citizens still overwhelmingly support democracy as a political system, yet are discontent with its practice and personnel (see Kaase and Newton 1995; Pharr and Putnam 2000; Dalton 2007). As Hibbing and Theiss-Morse (2001) have shown for the US, this discontent is directed primarily against the democratic *process*, not its results. The quality of the democratic process that is bemoaned is its inaccessibility for the ordinary citizen. The act of voting is more and more seen as pure symbolism. This, however, is perceived as a deficiency. The professional politician is identified as the character that is mainly responsible for the shortcomings of modern democracy. In turn, politics as a profession becomes even less popular than ever before – and it was never popular to begin with (see Damamme 1999). The democratic suspicion of political professionalism is seen as justified by history – even though, as has been shown, professionalism is a product of democracy.

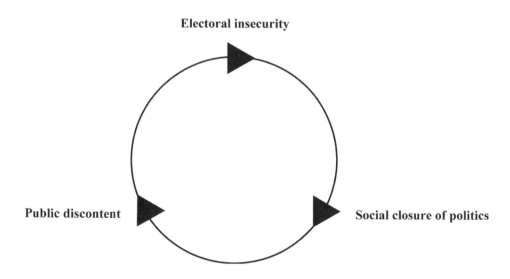

Figure 16.1 The vicious circle of political professionalism

This, then, is the vicious circle of professionalism and democracy (see Figure 16.1). Professional politicians understandably want to maintain their positions in a situation where electoral loss could mean de-professionalization. With increasing partisan volatility, they grow even more nervous about those 'unreliable voters'. They thus devise various strategies to protect themselves against potential challengers and to close the selection process to the outside. Once citizens realize this, they react with frustration about politicians' lack of accountability. This in turn increases the feeling of insecurity among elected politicians, who start to think about yet other mechanisms of insulation. And so on ....

How to Cope with a Destructive Necessity: The Need for Permanent Reform – and for Critical Theory

Professional politicians are not only necessary in order to keep democratic institutions open to people from different social backgrounds. They also tend to stabilize democracy, in which they have a common stake. Yet if modern democracy needs professional politicians but professional politicians tend to subvert modern democracy, we have a little systemic problem.[4] What can be done about it? The answer is fairly simple, but not very inspiring – not much! At one level, we simply have to live with the tension I described. Yet at a second level, we have to limit its destructive consequences. That entails the need for what I call 'permanent reform' – we must have the courage to continuously adapt our institutional order so as to create incentives to enhance participation and competition, rather than to restrict it. This requires sound analysis and institutional imagination.

The solution, however, cannot be to abolish political professionalism, as the good reasons that led to its creation still prevail. Rather, we have to see to it that a loss of office does not amount to a personal catastrophe. But we also have to insist on competition and personal accountability in order to keep political participation meaningful. Thus, any reform – which I will not discuss in any detail here (but see Borchert 2003a, 202–24, for some ideas) – would have to counter the tendency toward self-insulation and self-referentiality within professional politics. But any success in this effort can only be temporary, as the logic of political professionalism would not change in principle. Therefore, the need for reform is perennial. The reconciliation of professionalism and democracy is a continuous, never-ending task, and does not allow for a 'quick fix'. And yet fixed it always needs to be.

The role for theory in all of this is a rather old-fashioned one: enlightenment. As of now, the precarious relationship between professionalism and democracy is poorly understood in public discourse, which is dominated by populist attacks and apologetic defenses. A critical theory of modern democracy might start right here: looking at the mutual drift between citizens and politicians. More than forty years ago, Otto Kirchheimer (1964a, 17) in an unpublished paper talked about the 'mutual loss of control' in 'the contemporary Western political system': 'the political subjects' over the political organization and the political organization's over the political subjects'. This means that citizens are losing control over their

---

4   For a similar diagnosis with a much more sceptical prognosis, see Zolo (1997).

representatives, who deny them accountability, while politicians are losing control as well – over citizens who, with good reason, do not trust them any more.

A critical theory of democracy would have to acknowledge, on the one hand, the democratic virtue of political professionalization: it is only with professional politicians that the idea of democratic self-government can be upheld under present conditions. De-professionalizing politicians would mean restoring either Weber's plutocratic rule or handing over power to bureaucracies and interest groups – actors without any democratic legitimacy. On the other hand, the vices of political professionalism endanger the very essence of democracy. Using Weber's terminology once more, one might say that in modern democracy, the people as sovereign are under the permanent threat of 'expropriation' at the hands of the political personnel (see Weber 1919 [1994], 165–67). Democracy both needs political professionals and constantly has to be defended against them. But then who said democracy was simple?

References

Bartolini, S. (1999), 'Collusion, Competition and Democracy, Part I', *Journal of Theoretical Politics* 11, 435–70.

—— (2000), 'Collusion, Competition and Democracy, Part II', *Journal of Theoretical Politics* 12, 33–66.

Best, H. and Cotta, M. (eds) (2000), *Parliamentary Representatives in Europe 1848–1998* (Oxford: Oxford University Press).

Borchert, J. (2003a), *Die Professionalisierung der Politik. Zur Notwendigkeit eines Ärgernisses* (Frankfurt: Campus).

—— (2003b), 'Professional Politicians: Towards a Comparative Perspective', in Borchert and Zeiss (eds), *The Political Class in Advanced Democracies* (Oxford: Oxford University Press).

—— (2007), 'From Politik als Beruf to Politics as a Vocation: The Translation, Transformation, and Reception of Max Weber's Lecture', *Contributions to the History of Concepts* 3, 42–70.

—— and Stolz, K. (2003), 'Die Bekämpfung der Unsicherheit: Politikerkarrieren und Karrierepolitik in der Bundesrepublik Deutschland', *Politische Vierteljahresschrift* 44, 148–73.

Borchert, J. and Zeiss, J. (eds) (2003), *The Political Class in Advanced Democracies* (Oxford: Oxford University Press).

Bourdieu, P. (2001), *Das politische Feld* (Konstanz: UVK).

Bryce, J. (1888 [1995]), *The American Commonwealth*, new edn, 2 vols (Indianapolis, IN: Liberty Press).

Butzer, H. (1999), *Diäten und Freifahrt im Deutschen Reichstag* (Düsseldorf: Droste).

Canon, D. (1990), *Actors, Athletes, and Astronauts: Political Amateurs in the United States Congress* (Chicago, IL: University of Chicago Press).

Cotta, M. and Best, H. (2000),. 'Between Professionalization and Democratization: A Synoptic View on the Making of the European Representative', in Best and

Cotta (eds), *Parliamentary Representatives in Europe 1848–1998* (Oxford: Oxford University Press).

Dahl, R.A. (1971), *Polyarchy: Participation and Opposition* (New Haven, CT: Yale University Press).

Dalton, R.J. (2007), *Democratic Challenges, Democratic Choices: The Erosion of Political Support in Advanced Industrial Democracies* (Oxford: Oxford University Press).

Damamme, D. (1999), 'Professionel de la politique, un métier peu avouable', in Offerlé (ed.), *La profession politique, XIXe–XXe siècles* (Paris: Belin).

de Jouvenel, R. (1914), *La république des camarades* (Paris: Grasset).

Diamond, L. and Plattner, M. (eds) (1999), *The Self-restraining State* (Boulder, CO: Lynne Rienner).

Docherty, D. (1997), *Mr. Smith Goes to Ottawa: Life in the House of Commons* (Vancouver: University of British Columbia Press).

Downs, A. (1957), *An Economic Theory of Democracy* (New York: Harper and Row).

Gerth, H.H. and Mills, C.W. (eds) (1946), *From Max Weber* (New York: Oxford University Press).

Greven, M.T. (1977), *Parteien und politische Herrschaft* (Meisenheim: Anton Hain).

Hanke, E. and Mommsen, W.J. (eds) (2001), *Max Webers Herrschaftssoziologie* (Tübingen: Mohr, Siebeck).

Hibbing, J. and Theiss-Morse, E. (2001), 'Process Preferences and American Politics: What the People Want Government to Be', *American Political Science Review* 95, 145–53.

Jansen, C. (1999), 'Selbstbewußtes oder gefügiges Parlament? Abgeordnetendiäten und Berufspolitiker in den deutschen Staaten des 19. Jahrhunderts', *Geschichte und Gesellschaft* 25, 33–65.

Kaase, M. and Newton, K. (1995), *Beliefs in Government* (Oxford: Oxford University Press).

Katz, R.S. and Mair, P. (1995), 'Changing Models of Party Organization and Party Democracy. The Emergence of the Cartel Party', *Party Politics* 1, 5–28.

King, A. (1997), *Running Scared* (New York: Free Press).

Kirchheimer, O. (1944 [1964]), 'Zur Frage der Souveränität', in Kirchheimer, *Politik und Verfassung* (Frankfurt am Main: Suhrkamp).

—— (1957 [1964]), 'Wandlungen der politischen Opposition', in Kirchheimer, *Politik und Verfassung* (Frankfurt am Main: Suhrkamp).

—— (1964a), 'Elite – Consent – Control in the Western Political System', unpublished manuscript, Otto Kirchheimer Papers, University at Albany Libraries, State University of New York.

—— (1964b), *Politik und Verfassung* (Frankfurt am Main: Suhrkamp).

Lipset, S.M. (1960), *Political Man* (Garden City, NY: Doubleday).

Löwenstein, K. (1973), *Kooptation und Zuwahl. Über die autonome Bildung privilegierter Gruppen* (Frankfurt: Alfred Metzner).

Manin, B. (1997), *The Principles of Representative Government* (Cambridge: Cambridge University Press).

Molt, P. (1963), *Der Reichstag vor der improvisierten Revolution* (Cologne: Westdeutscher Verlag).

Nohlen, D. (2000), *Wahlrecht und Parteiensystem* (Opladen: Leske & Budrich).

Oakes, G. and Vidich, A. (1999), *Collaboration, Reputation, and Ethics in American Academic Life: Hans H. Gerth and C. Wright Mills* (Urbana, IL: University of Illinois Press).

Offerlé, M. (ed.) (1999a), *La profession politique, XIXe–XXe siècles* (Paris: Belin).

—— (1999b), 'Professions et profession politique', in Offerlé (ed.), *La profession politique, XIXe–XXe siècles* (Paris: Belin).

Palonen, K. (2002), *Eine Lobrede für Politiker. Ein Kommentar zu Max Webers 'Politik als Beruf'* (Opladen: Leske & Budrich).

Pharr, S.J. and Putnam, R.D. (eds) (2000), *Disaffected Democracies* (Princeton, NJ: Princeton University Press).

Portinaro, P.P. (2001), 'Amerika als Schule der politischen Entzauberung. Eliten und Parteien bei Max Weber', in Hanke and Mommsen (eds), *Max Webers Herrschaftssoziologie* (Tübingen: Mohr, Siebeck).

Przeworski, A. (1991), *Democracy and the Market* (Cambridge: Cambridge University Press).

Reiser, M. (2006), *Zwischen Ehrenamt und Berufspolitik: Professionalisierung der Kommunalpolitik in deutschen Großstädten* (Wiesbaden: VS Verlag).

Rush, M. and Cromwell, V. (2000), 'Continuity and Change: Legislative Recruitment in the United Kingdom 1868–1999', in Best and Cotta (eds), *Parliamentary Representatives in Europe 1848–1998* (Oxford: Oxford University Press).

Schattschneider, E.E. (1960), *The Semi-sovereign People: A Realist's View of Democracy in America* (New York: Holt, Rinehart and Winston).

Schedler, A. (1999), 'Conceptualizing Accountability', in Diamond and Plattner (eds), *The Self-restraining State* (Boulder, CO: Lynne Rienner).

Schlesinger, J. (1966), *Ambition and Politics: Political Careers in the United States* (Chicago, IL: Rand McNally).

Schumpeter, J. (1950), *Kapitalismus, Sozialismus, Demokratie*, 2nd edn (Munich: Lehnen).

von Beyme, K. (1993), *Die politische Klasse im Parteienstaat* (Frankfurt am Main: Suhrkamp).

Weber, M., (1919 [1994]), 'Politik als Beruf', in *Max-Weber-Studienausgabe* I:17 (Tübingen: Mohr).

—— (1922 [1972], *Wirtschaft und Gesellschaft*, 5th edn (Tübingen: Mohr).

—— (1946), 'Politics as a Vocation', in Gerth and Mills (eds), *From Max Weber* (New York: Oxford University Press).

—— (1994a), *Political Writings*, ed. P. Lassman and R. Speirs (Cambridge: Cambridge University Press).

—— (1994b), 'The Profession and Vocation of Politics', in Weber, *Political Writings*, ed. Lassman and Speirs (Cambridge: Cambridge University Press).

—— (2004a), *The Vocation Lectures*, ed. D. Owen and T.B. Strong (Indianapolis, IN: Hackett).

—— (2004b), 'Politics as a Vocation', in Weber *The Vocation Lectures*, ed. D. Owen and T.B. Strong (Indianapolis, IN: Hackett).

Zolo, D. (1997), *Die demokratische Fürstenherrschaft. Für eine realistische Theorie der Politik* (Göttingen: Steidl).

Further Reading

Best, H. and Cotta, M. (eds) (2000), *Parliamentary Representatives in Europe 1848–1998* (Oxford: Oxford University Press).

Borchert, J. and Zeiss, J. (eds) (2003), *The Political Class in Advanced Democracies* (Oxford: Oxford University Press).

Mastropaolo, A. (1984), *Saggio sul professionismo politico* (Milano: Franco Angeli).

Norris, P. (ed.) (1997), *Passages to Power: Legislative Recruitment in Advanced Democracies* (Cambridge: Cambridge University Press).

Offerlé, M. (ed.) (1999), *La profession politique, XIXe–XXe siècles* (Paris: Belin).

Riddell, P. (1993), *Honest Opportunism: The Rise of the Career Politician* (London: Macmillan).

Democratization and Professionalization: The Disappearance of the Polling Officer in Germany and the Introduction of Computer Democracy

Hubertus Buchstein

Introduction: The Price of Democracy

It is well known today, that democracy does not come for free, but that it is a costly political order. How to calculate the price tag for democracy is less well known, however. Some normative political theorists who defend the intrinsic value of political participation will probably answer that the infinite normative superiority of democracy always makes democracy cheaper than all other forms of political order which leave less or no room for political engagement. Utilitarian political theorists would probably prefer a sober cost–benefit analysis of all components and implications of democratic regimes before they come to a final judgment. But even if we avoid the tricky question of the 'value' of political participation, some other questions are left unanswered. Is the price we want to accept for a democracy relatively fixed over time, or can changes in its cost factors be observed? Will a cheaper democracy always be a worse democracy, or can it even provide, under certain circumstances, a better democracy? What exactly should be included into the long list of the costs and benefits of democracy in addition to its general normative value? What are the main cost factors which can make a modern democracy a less or more expensive political system?

Questions like those are normally not asked within the academic field of normative political theory. Modern normative theories of democracy start with the agreement that democracy has an intrinsic value, and that any cost–benefit analysis of democracy is, from a normative point of view at least, dubious. Even rational choice approaches and empirical measurements of the performance of democracy flinch before such questions. The reason why modern political theory avoids such questions probably has to do with the fact that some politicians in the past (like Pinochet in Chile in 1973) have exploited such considerations in order to substitute a democratic order with a dictatorship.

But this is only one aspect of the 'price question'. Citizens and politicians do raise and answer the question of the price of democracy in their day-to-day political interaction all the time and everywhere (and not only in Afghanistan after NATO fought the Taliban regime), and it would be at least unwise for normative political theory to counter these kind of considerations with only one general answer – 'The value of democracy is infinitely high-period!' – instead of contributing to the debate over the adequate price of a democracy on a more concrete level.

One essential component which defines the price factor of a democracy is the cost of holding elections. And like oil, elections worldwide are recently growing increasingly more expensive – the cost for the last presidential elections in the US increased by nearly 30 per cent, and in most European democracies the amount of money spent on elections has risen by 15–25 per cent for each national election.[1] And even if we focus purely on those expenses which are necessary to guarantee every citizen the chance to cast his or her ballot, expenditures in all European democracies have increased tremendously over the last two decades.[2] These costs can rarely be found clearly set out in any state budget, but they have become – depending on the way elections are organized – a matter of public concern not only in new democracies like Estonia and Bulgaria, but in old democracies like Italy and Germany as well.

Until today, European democracies have had various methods of arranging their elections. Despite their agreement on some basic rules which are included in common European law (like equality of the vote, secret voting), European democracies differ in a remarkable degree with respect to concrete details which govern the way voters are supposed to cast their ballot.[3] These differences not only include matters of proportional representation versus the winner-takes-all model or competing systems to take the count (d'Hondt or Hare/Niemeyer or Saint Laguës); these differences even include practices of casting the ballot on election day. In some European countries, for example, people can cast their vote personally before election day in a ballot box which is located at a post office; in other countries, they are allowed to fill out the ballot paper at home and mail it to the ballot office; in yet other countries, they have to show up at the voting booth in person on election

---

1   My own estimates, based on numbers from newspapers and television news between 2002 and 2007. To my knowledge, no national or cross-national collections of data which include the cost for elections exist at present.

2   Information based on several interviews with state officials in different European countries over recent years.

3   For an overview of the historical variants in Europe, see Reeve and Wade (1992) and Katz (1997).

day.[4] Other differences concern the use of new technologies with respect to casting or counting votes. Some countries have chosen to introduce modern computer technology in order to hold elections, whereas other countries are hesitant in this regard.

I will focus my attention on another aspect of election day: the persons overseeing the premises in which we vote, those checking during election day whether people are entitled to vote, and those counting the votes after the ballot has been cast. European countries also differ in the ways they deal with this organizational issue. Most European countries have chosen the public sector model: civil servants are on duty on election day, and it is their job to make sure that the procedures and the count will proceed according to the rules. Other countries, however, differ in this respect. Among this group of European democracies, Germany may represent, in a historical perspective, a somewhat special case. On the one hand it has historically switched the models for organizing elections, and on the other hand it is currently undergoing another switch of model. But with respect to the ongoing reform debate about the best ways to organize elections, the troubles faced by the traditional German model have lead to a reform agenda, which has striking similarities to other discussions around the globe.

Unfortunately, no comparative studies about the ways elections are organized on a day-to-day level in different countries have been published so far. These day-to-day questions not only include issues of different political cultures, but also different way of organizing matters, and extend to all phases of the voting procedure, from the publication of the electoral day until the last legal challenge.[5] The recruitment of staff to take care of the voting offices during election day and conduct the count after the electoral offices are closed is a crucial aspect among these sets of voting procedures. Nevertheless, political scientists have ignored this issue to date. One of the reasons for this deficiency can be explained by the fact that the legal norms in a country do not explicitly describe the ways in which the recruitment takes place in reality. In addition, the ballot laws or legal regimes in most European countries do not even make any statement about this issue.[6]

Therefore, I want to focus my attention in the first section of this chapter on only one case – Germany – and start with a historical overview of the rise and fall of the polling officer in modern German democracy. Secondly, I will present the key components which are presented in order to find a new technological solution to the problem of the missing polling officer. In the third second of the chapter, I will take a more general as well as critical look at this technological reform agenda, which can be found in all European democracies today, under the headline of 'outsourcing democracy'. In the final section of the chapter, I will argue that the

---

4   For some of these differences in the ways of casting votes, see Ohms and Rieser (1989).

5   For a tentative list, see the collection of criteria for fair elections by Elklit and Svensson (1997).

6   It would be an interesting international research project not only to compare the different methods of recruiting polling officers, but to discuss the advantages and disadvantages of some of these models more extensively.

level of professionalization which is implicit in the new technological solutions to cast and count the vote is violating the normative basis of democratic equality as we know it.

The Rise and Fall of the Polling Officer in German Electoral History

As was stated above, democracy has its price. For example, the last election to the German Bundestag (federal parliament) in 2005 cost the federal government 65 million euros merely to cover organizational expenses. In addition, the costs for the elections to the Landtage (state parliaments) amount to 13 million euros on average, which adds up to more than 200 million euros per legislative period. Furthermore, the costs of municipal elections and decisions using methods of direct democracy on the municipal level must be added to this figure.

Considering the general public financial problems, it is not surprising to see the efforts that are being made to reduce the costs of elections. Such attempts have recently led to some changes in the electoral law in the Federal Republic of Germany, like getting rid of the so-called 'second envelope' for the ballot. However, the amount of money so far is minimal compared to the amount some self-declared foresighted reformers hope for. Their goal is to lower the costs of elections and to look for the largest cost factors.

Recently, polling officers have been identified as one of the main expense factors. Polling officers – their official title in Germany is *Wahlhelfer*, members of the electoral committees – are indispensable personnel when holding elections. Their work starts with the receipt of the electoral roll before the opening up of the polling stations, and ends late at night with the preliminary declaration of the joint count of votes. The number of polling officers that are needed for an election to the German Bundestag amounts to 630,000. They work in 90,000 polling stations (80,000 polling stations for people voting in person , and 10,000 postal vote polling stations).

A brief historical overview shows that today's regulation concerning polling officers can by no means be taken for granted. The question of who may and who may not act as a polling officer was strongly disputed even during the last third of the nineteenth century. The situation in Prussia illustrates the German case at its best.[7] In 1849, the Prussian government installed an electoral law. This law was oriented on an *authoritarian state* model, and stood in the tradition of anti-democratic political thought. According to the electoral law, which was in force from 1849 until 1918, only civil servants of the Prussian state were allowed to supervise elections. They were responsible for establishing the veracity of voters as well as their ballot papers. In addition, these civil servants decided upon possible challenges to the count and other potential irregularities of the election in the first instance. In addition to this system, it is noteworthy that all public officials in the

---

7   The politics of Prussian electoral rules is discussed in Anderson (2002).

civil service received instructions from the government with regard to the party they were supposed to vote for. And to make the authoritarian model a full picture, it should be mentioned that polling officers were also informed by government officials about the kind of election results which were to be achieved in their polling stations.

The opposition in Prussia, consisting of the left liberals and social democrats, strongly opposed this practice for decades without any success. They demanded that the government should stop manipulating elections, and suggested that all citizens should be entitled to act as polling officers on a voluntary basis. According to the opposition, only such a transparent system would prevent the manipulation of elections by the government. And in addition, they argued that a voluntary job in a polling station would provide a good schooling in democracy for every citizen. I call this way of organizing elections the *republican model* of the polling officer. The ideas that were behind these demands were based on democratic cooperation and the social value of self-government. If democracy means that its citizens are sovereign in the field of politics, then citizens are not only responsible for participating in elections and votes, but also for holding them themselves, as far as possible.

For decades, the Prussian government did not give in to any of these demands for polling station reform. Until the end of the First World War in 1918, public officials in Prussia held the chairmanship of every group of polling officers during elections not only to the Prussian Landtag, but to the German Reichstag as well. The chairman was responsible for the co-option of 'trustworthy' citizens, who were in charge of acting as polling officers. It was also up to the chairman to choose the premises for the polling station – his own office, his own apartment, his brothers' bar or the favorite pub of the most nationalistic Germans near the Polish border. Up until the end of the empire, elections in Prussia were staged as a state-led exercise in manipulation during which polling officers wielded power in an authoritarian manner (see Buchstein 2001).

After the revolution of 1918, the volunteer model finally made it to the political agenda. According to the compromise which was worked out by the parties of the Weimar Republic, a mixture between the republican model and a *state-guaranteed* model was introduced. According to the basic idea of the state-guaranteed model, it is one of the main responsibilities of a democratic state to ensure the holding of fair elections. This is the reason why the state is in charge of providing all necessary means and resources for the holding of elections, such as electoral premises and polling station equipment. The state is also responsible for providing polling officers if necessary, should there be a lack of volunteers.

The Weimar Republic relied more on its citizens' commitment in the run-up to the organization of elections than even the Federal Republic of Germany after 1949. Weimar's political parties and their members were not only responsible for the electoral campaigns, but also for the printing of the ballot papers and the distribution of these papers to all potential electors. The parties merely received reimbursements from the state for the cost for printing the electoral lists (see Lipphardt 1975). After the introduction of a new regulation in 1924, only the state printed official ballot papers and distributed them to the polling stations. Henceforth, volunteer polling officers were needed to carry out the entire process of the electoral day from the beginning on the morning until the last count.[8] Some of these activities were accompanied by surges of adrenalin, since the polling officers cooperated with the police to ensure free access to the ballot box for all citizens. During the militant boycotts of the vote on the referendum on the expropriation of the princes in 1926 by the right-wing Weimar parties, this responsibility meant that they had to escort voters through groups of militant boycotters.[9]

After political power in Germany was handed over to the new coalition government led by the National Socialists in January 1933, the Weimar mixed model remained formally unchanged. In reality, the authoritarian state model returned. The members of the election boards were now chosen according to their political loyalty to the new regime. Most election boards consisted exclusively, or at least of a strong majority, of National Socialists, and worked as a mere governmental instrument of manipulation during referendums and elections to the Reichstag (see Hubert 1992, 249).

After the Second World War, the policy regarding polling officers developed in different ways in the two German states. In the German Democratic Republic, the work of the election board became strikingly similar to the authoritarian state model, despite the official republican rhetoric.[10] In the Federal Republic, on the other hand, elections were organized according the baselines of the Weimar mixed model (see Buchstein 2000). This time, however, it included a strong party-oriented component. According to the electoral laws which have been in force since 1949, the preparation and holding of elections and voting procedures are assigned to special election organizations which function as independent institutions and act legally with autonomous status. Due to this particular status, they are not subject to any official supervision except by the courts, which means that the members of the polling bodies can be held responsible by neither the federal government nor the individual states or municipalities in whose territory they work. All offices are required to ensure cooperation between authorities and must place the necessary equipment at the disposal of the polling officers. In the constituencies, the local election boards consist of three groups of people: members of the public sector, who are normally responsible for different administrative jobs on the local level, form the core group; representatives who are nominated by the political parties are a second group, and volunteer citizens make up the balance of members of the local electoral boards. The post of polling officer is honorary, similar to that of a juror. According to the federal and state election rules, every citizen who is entitled to vote may be required to act as a juror or a member of the election board. They can only refuse to do so for good reasons, like being sick or being out of town due to other responsibilities.

---

8   For this reform, see Holste (2005).

9   See the contemporary report by later Nobel Peace Prize winner Carl von Ossietzky (1926).

10   For a description of this practice, see Kloth (2000).

This is how the system is supposed to work in theory. In practice, however, the republican part has been declining continuously for the last two decades. Since the turn of the century, the situation has reached a dramatic extent in the eyes of some local authorities. Cities and municipalities have drastically increased their efforts to recruit enough citizens to act as polling officers. Using their own financial resources, many cities have increased the 'pocket money' of 16 euros which polling officers are entitled to receive from the federal government to 40–50 euros in order to recruit less well-to-do students from high schools. Even the Petition Committee of the Federal Parliament dealt with the problem after an initiative of the Christian Democratic Party to raise the 'pocket money' significantly.

It is worth taking a brief look at the means and rhetoric of those who want to recruit more polling officers over recent years. Some newspaper campaigns have used republican rhetoric when calling upon citizens to work as polling officers: 'We are looking for polling officers – democracy needs your participation.'[11] Other municipalities have elected a 'polling officer of the month' or invited outstanding polling officers to a ceremony at the city hall after the elections.[12] The Bavarian city of Regensburg added modern means to the republican repertoire in their advertisements for the Bavarian state parliament elections by using the following slogan to attract polling officers: 'You win twice: you deliver an outstanding service to democracy and you may win a dream holiday.'[13] In Nuremberg, citizens who acted as polling officers could win free holiday trips to Turkey or free admission to public swimming pools.

Despite these innovative measures, the decrease in the number of polling officers has become a serious problem for the municipalities. For a number of years, counting of votes during election night cannot be guaranteed in several towns. During the election to the Federal Parliament in 2002 in the city of Kassel, for example, 140 out of 300 nominated polling officers decided against fulfilling their civic duty on such short notice that the rest of them were so displeased that they stopped counting and went home after midnight. Kassel was not able to determine its election results until the next day. Similar events have been reported from other cities, and at the state elections of Berlin in autumn 2006 led to a situation where the top candidate of the Christian Democratic opposition did not even know on the day after the election whether he won his seat in parliament. Most members of his local election board had either not shown up at all or had left the office during the count in order to go home.

The problem concerning polling officers has grown to such an extent in Germany over recent years that officials are seriously thinking about ways of reforming the system. The main measure to deal with the problem is not holding more lotteries with big prizes in order to attract more citizens, but recruiting most of the personnel from the civil service. This solution has been chosen by most cities and communities

---

11   Recalling the appeal by the mayor of the city of Regensburg on 10 January 2000.

12   As has been done regularly in Hamburg since 1998.

13   Appeal by the Mayor, Hans Schaidinger, on theoccasion of the elections to the Bavarian Landtag on 21 September 2003.

in the last decade, and it has led to a certain professionalization of an activity which in the beginning of the democratization process in Germany was interpreted as a genuine duty of any democratic citizen.

Computer Democracy as a Reform Agenda

The switch from the republican model to the professional model is less widely discussed because of its implications for the interpretation of a democratic citizen. Instead, it has become the subject of discussions and public concerns for a different reason. It has turned out that the costs of holding elections increase tremendously when members of the public service have to be paid for an activity which sometimes takes up more than 16 hours of an official's normal work time.

Some enthusiastic democrats in the public debate still worry when they look at the decrease in polling officers. However, they are unable to provide a remedy. Faced with this situation, only followers of the rational choice theory feel reassured. They designed the profit-maximizing voter to be the essence of their basic module of democratic theory, and they are neither surprised when it comes to low voter turnouts nor when the number of voluntary polling officers is decreasing. According to their approach, the act of participating in elections, and especially helping to hold elections, are costs that citizens have to bear, and for which they demand compensation on the benefit side of things. According to the logic of rational choice, the solution to the problem of the loss of polling officers lies in adequate payment for the services citizens deliver.

The products to be delivered are 'fair elections', produced by competent personnel. I want to call this approach the *service model* of polling officers. It is not totally new, but its basic logic has already taken root in the existing system by hiring members of the public sector or the lotteries which seek to attract citizens. Once we take the step from the republican and state-guaranteed models to the service model, it is even reasonable to calculate the cost–benefit ratio of the entire service of 'holding of elections' in a rational and efficient way.

This state of the debate has become the new portal for computer companies who sell software and hardware for political elections. Their main promise is that elections of the future can be held more economically through the use of modern computer technology. The activities of computer companies are accompanied by a new business strategy. It is no longer their goal to immediately propagate the great leap forward from the current way of casting votes at polling stations to elections via the Internet or cell phone. Instead, for the time being, they are lobbying for a gradual introduction of computer networks with touch-screens or with voting pencils which carry a small camera at all existing polling stations.

The computer technology is fairly well developed, and has been used not only in the United States, but also in several European, Asian and Latin American countries over the last decade. In Germany, these devices were used in the city of Cologne for the first time during the elections to the Bundestag in 2002, and have been in use in three states since. Nowadays, the technological development of such devices is carried out nearly exclusively by private companies. These professional companies compete with each other on a global market and offer joint stock companies, any kind of civil organization – from parties to associations, as well as state authorities – the service of holding elections.

The advertising campaign for these new devices is hardly addressed to the public in general. In addition, it no longer includes the promise of greater political participation as articulated at the beginning of the euphoria regarding online voting ten years ago. On the contrary, the advertisements are directly addressed to those authorities and persons who deal with the practical problems of holding elections (in Germany, the state election chairmen, for example). The product advertisements by Election.com, VoteHere.net, E-Ballot.net and SaveVote – some of the current leading suppliers of voting software for computer-based voting devices – mainly praise the cost saving opportunities and the effectiveness of the election process they have designed.

The computer industry promises the officials responsible for organizing elections that elections in the future will be a lot cheaper and that the count will be must faster than today – after a certain amount of money has been invested in the new technology in the first place. In addition, they promise that the costly search for polling officers will come to an end: 'Election.com, with its proprietary software and services, lowers costs, enhances accuracy and accountability, improves security and reduces the use of financial, human and natural resources.'[14] The use of computer technology is supposed to make it easier for authorities and municipalities to prepare and hold elections. Elections via the Internet will not only save paper, but will also relieve municipalities of such tasks as training polling officers. As soon as the appropriate identification technology has been developed, it will be possible in the future to have elections without polling officers, once touch-screen devices have been set up at petrol stations, public libraries or shopping malls.

Outsourcing Democracy

The computer industry addresses the interests and needs of those for whom elections are a cost factor in the first place and who suffer most from problems regarding polling officers. And their strategy has had a certain amount of success over the last years. Since 1998, Dieter Otten has been commissioned by the Federal Minister for the Economy and Labor (BMWA) to carry out feasibility studies on legally valid Internet-based elections together with his research group, Internet Based Elections. They play a leading role in the project 'Voting In Electronic Networks' (WIEN) sponsored by the BMWA from 2002 to 2005. Dieter Otten summarized his experiences with actors on the local level as follows: 'when it comes to municipal interest in modernizing, city financial officers and the heads of the election office are most interested' (Otten 2001, 74). Naturally, the involvement

---

14   This is part of the current advertisement by the Website Election.com in their vision statement <www.election.com/us/info/index.html>, accessed 26 September 2007.

of private industry in elections holds great market potential. US economic experts estimate that the company awarded the contract for holding online elections in the US could potentially gain 10 billion US dollars worth of business on a global scale.

With the introduction of a network of touch-screen devices provided by private companies, the 'outsourcing' of one of the core procedures of modern democratic systems has moved a step further. Naturally, the printing of ballots, and devices for voting booths or carrying out postal votes[15] have already been entrusted to companies in the private sector. And in principle, outsourcing is not at all new to the modern state – a number of main responsibilities of the state defined as public goods are already produced cheaply by private concerns. So why should 'outsourcing' not be extended to include the technology for holding political elections? One may argue that, as with other services, the only thing that needs to be done is to clearly define the product 'holding of elections'. A definition could be: elections should be held correctly according to electoral law principles as laid down by the constitution and further determined by the relevant electoral laws. Furthermore, an additional feature could be added to the product to satisfy the proponents of a more participation-oriented democracy: in order to increase the legitimacy of the election results, a high turnout is to be aimed for during the elections. According to this argument, the state need only check the technological qualities of the voting devices for reliability and certify them. The old voting machines in Sweden and the US have been supervised in exactly this way over the past fifty years. According to this line of argument, touch-screen devices merely follow this trend and lead a little further in the direction of online elections.

One may even argue in the following way, to make this optimistic line of argument stronger, that dynamic technological development will automatically further increase the process of outsourcing. Even the technological assessment of voting techniques, now a responsibility of the state, will move into the private sector. So, until recently, all voting devices in Germany (for example, ballot boxes) were subject to a quality check by a state certifying agency named TÜV (Technischer Überwachungsdienst). But TÜV already relies on reports by private agencies when it comes to assessing computer cryptography programs. Thus, the growth of a market for special rating agencies which focus on the certification of computer programs in the private sector must be expected. In a few years, their task will include checking, rating and certifying technological devices and electoral procedures. One could even envision a 'European Voting Security Agency' in the near future which awards the highest rating, 'AAA', to certain voting technologies.

From such a professional management point of view, the outsourcing model follows the normative ideal of the neo-liberal, minimal state. The citizen of the old model was a *Gelegenheitspolitiker* (Max Weber), and acted in various roles as voter, as candidate for office, as polling officer and as tax payer. In the new model, the burden of some roles has been taken away from the citizen. He or she turns from *Gelegenheitspolitiker* into *Verlegenheitspolitiker* (if I may play with Weber's terms),

---

15   During the presidential elections of 2004 in the US, the Election.com Website handled 700,000 online requests regarding the mailing of postal vote ballot papers.

which means that political participation is understood less as a civic duty or a rational option, but more as a form of activity which one chooses from among other activities which are supposed to entertain or express oneself.

If we follow the outsourcing model even further, citizens are relieved of all avoidable costs and burdens. With a touch of fantasy, one could develop this idea in a more radical fashion much further:

- the infrastructure of voting processes could be prepared, supervised and maintained by certified private companies;
- private rating agencies could check the quality of the various voting devices offered on the market;
- citizens could cast their vote from the privacy of their homes, voters themselves ensuring that their vote is secret;
- lottery prizes for voters could be announced in order to raise voter turnout;
- frequent plebiscites could make sure that citizen can articulate their preferences regarding certain political topics on a regular basis, and a higher voter turnout would be encouraged by raffles;
- citizens could put their vote up for auction on eBay or to sell it to a voting broker.

Some of these ideas are less far-fetched than they might appear. Bulgaria, for example, did indeed introduce a lottery system in 2005 in which every voter had the opportunity to win one of three expensive cars. Or we may turn our attention to the debate in the Estonian parliament on the topic of online elections in 2004. When countering the objection that casting one's vote from one's computer at home wasn't safe and that this would cause vote buying, in defense of online elections several Estonian representatives went as far as to say that it was up to each individual to decide why they elected whom. Part of the freedom to elect whomever one wants was the freedom to give away one's vote in exchange for other goods. After all, democracy in general wasn't anything but an exchange of votes for certain services rendered by politics.

However, some of the ideas suggested above are obviously not in line with constitutional democracy in the EU member states. Nevertheless, the case is different in Australia, the US, in Latin America and in most Asian countries. Moreover, these countries claim to play a leading role when it comes to the technological modernization of elections. It will be interesting to see at which point they will overstep the traditional lines which so far keep the state responsible for holding elections.

Democracy and Transparency

Let us go back to the more modest invention of computer democracy. One of the key questions regarding computer technology for elections is still the security problem. On the one hand, computer companies do not tire of claiming that the current technology is absolutely safe.[16] On the other hand, critics who work in the field of computers have for years strongly articulated doubts about the security of touch-screen device networks, concerning their internal screen as well as their safety measures against hackers from the outside (see Rubin 2001). Several hundred computer experts in the US wrote resolutions in spring 2003 and again in the wake of the presidential elections of 2004 in which they raised serious concerns regarding the security in the technology that was used. There are still debates among experts about whether the presidential election of 2004 was really won by George W. Bush again, or whether computers had been manipulated in at least one state. Again in the elections for the US Congress in October 2006, hundreds of technical failures and computer breakdowns were logged, which again raised concern among computer specialists. In addition, hackers have claimed again and again that they have been able to crack computer systems which were supposed to be 'hundred per cent safe'.

For outsiders, it is hard to judge such controversies among computer experts, and I do not want to go deeper into these debates either. What can nevertheless be judged is the manner in which lapses in security and mistakes by governments that strive to lower costs, and by companies in the computer industry that are interested in larger turnouts, have been dealt with in recent times. Three cases that occurred some years ago raise particular scepticism, as they prove how thoughtlessly computer companies and those who hold elections by order of the state can ignore serious security defects for financial reasons.

The first example is a municipal election in England in April 2003 during which election computers that were hooked up to a network were placed in the polling stations where 1.5 million British citizens could cast their vote. Beforehand, a number of computer experts protested, they were able to show that the technology could be manipulated. The British government dismissed these accusations, carried out no checks itself, and referred to statements by the system's producer. They considered the matter to be closed.[17]

The second example took place in the United States. There, Diebold together with the software company VoteHere offers touch-screen voting devices that are connected via a network. They were used during the governors' elections in several states, and were bought for the sum of $50 million each. Computer experts who work with Avi Rubin at the Johns Hopkins University managed to acquire the Diebold code and checked it in July 2003 for its security technology. It turned out that security defects in the software allowed computer hackers who were

---

16   'We have the technology to deal with the worst horror scenarios that anyone can think of in terms of virus attacks or denial-of-service attacks'; CEO Jim Adler from VoteHere on 22 April 2002, quoted on Wired News, <www.wired.com/news/politics/0,1283,51838,00. htm>, accessed 26 September 2007; 'Technologically not a problem'; Dieter Otten in an interview with Politik-Digital, <www.politik-digital.de/archiv/edemocracy/otten. shtm>, accessed 26 September 2007. See also the categorical reply by Erwin Staudt of Initiative 21 in an interview with Politik-Digital, <www.politik-digital.de/archiv/ edemocracy/staudt.shtm>, accessed 26 September 2007.

17   Concerning the technological details, see Dembart (2003).

fairly well experienced to cast several votes per voter and to change the election results afterwards.[18] In contrast, Diebold and VoteHere insisted publicly that their technology was secure. The election remained valid, and the programs are being sold and used worldwide even today.

And in 2004, a panel of computer experts has rejected SERVE, the $22 million system which enabled soldiers and other US citizens overseas to vote via the Internet as inherently insecure (see *New York Times*, 25 January 2004).

The irritating aspect of these three incidents is not that there were controversies regarding the security of the voting procedures. Such controversies have always occurred in the long history of electoral law; even printed ballot papers were for some time thought to ease the forgery of election results. No, more irritating is the *nonchalance* with which government authorities and the computer industry disregard security risks for pure financial reasons.

One has to realize the large extent to which some of the new voting devices debase the role of the citizen in a democracy. The most important source of democratic legitimacy is trust in the procedures of democracy. With respect to the technological aspect of the voting act, one can reduce almost all democratic reforms of electoral laws in the world during the last 150 years to one common denominator: they were all inaugurated in order to base this trust on a larger, more objective – which means, in a democracy, intersubjective – foundation. Those reforms included the public counting of the vote or all legal details regarding the right to challenge an election. Certainly, even printed ballot papers have been stolen, added or forged repeatedly in the history of political elections since they were invented in the nineteenth century – be it in the US and UK for decades,[19] in the GDR, or more recently in Dachau in the state of Bavaria, where the Christian Democratic Party managed to improve its election results with the help of forged postal votes from 1984 to 2002 (see *Süddeutsche Zeitung*, 30 June 2002). But the fact that the judiciary could later deal with this election scandal illustrates more: in principle, ballot papers can be kept safe for a certain amount of time and can be checked and re-counted later on. Forgeries on a larger scale require a number of procedure violations as well as several accomplices.

Safety via democratic transparency is also maintained with technologies which, for example, include a small digital camera inside the voting pen – at least as long as the paper ballots are kept for a possible re-count. It looks different when touch-screen devices connected via a network are introduced in order to get rid of the traditional paper form completely. Then the summer 2006 scandals when computer hackers claimed that they had broken into election computer programs brought two aspects to light. The most successful and ingenious manipulations have two features: first, that no one else knows about them besides the culprit, and second, that they cannot be proven later on. In order to be able to judge the procedures that are supposed to guarantee security, one needs to be competent in computer technology at a high level to which normally only a community of a few specialists

---

18   Concerning the technological details, see Rubin et al. (2003).
19   For an instructive history of voter fraud in the US, see Fund (2004).

can rise. No regular citizen can evaluate how secure the procedures which make use of touch-screen devices really are.

This may have consequences for the political culture of modern democracies. Politics involves contingency, spontaneity and sometimes surprises. Assume that surprising results occur on election day or assume a very close election – doubts will arise, and a certain amount of mistrust that cannot be dispelled will remain regarding the election results. This is difficult, as even the legitimacy of the results cannot be documented in a way which is equally transparent to everyone. The number of claims about computer fraud has grown over the last few years in Latin America and Africa, and in all cases the winners were principally unable to document that they had really had won the elections. In the long run, the new technology will contribute to undermining the legitimacy of democratic elections due to its poor transparency. Even if the new technologies may lower the costs of procedures of democracy in the medium term, the price democracy has to pay in the long run may be much higher and a much more serious matter: it could come to the point where trust in the procedures of democracy is at stake. Once this trust is lost, it cannot be reproduced by any ingenious computer system.

It is obvious that the new computer technology for elections influences the way modern democracies see themselves, not only on the practical level, but in a normative sense as well. So far, democracy not only stands for equal suffrage, it also includes the egalitarian offer of transparency with respect to its procedures. Every citizen has the same right, and in principle the same chance, to comprehend the technology involved in elections, and an equal chance to check the results. For this reason, all elements of the voting procedure in a democracy – not only in principle or after a long period of special training – have to be comprehensible to all citizens. In political practice, the consequence of this comprehensive approach is the right of citizens and candidates to be present in person when votes are counted in public. The role of the voluntary polling officer is the republican incarnation of this democratic demand.

In the digital age, citizens are instead supposed to trust the judgment of professional state authorities, of private companies or of rating agencies when it comes to the security of election technology. Citizens who are willing to delegate this trust to technology professionals, who in their stead evaluate the security of the technology of voting devices, have given their consent to the dominance of a technological elite and a new level of professionalization in democratic politics. The new technology may not lower the cost of democracy in the short term (the investment costs for the new technologies have increased in double digits over the last years), but may perhaps do so in the medium term. But the price democracy has to pay in the long run may be infinitely higher. The new level of professionalization in democratic politics puts the normative interpretation of democracy as a type of rule – that includes equal transparency of all procedural stages – at stake, and opens the door for a new aristocracy.

References

Anderson, M.L. (2002), *Practicing Democracy: Elections and Political Culture in Imperial Germany* (Princeton, NJ: Princeton University Press).

Buchstein, H. (2000), 'Präsenzwahl, Briefwahl, Onlinewahl und der Grundsatz der geheimen Stimmabgabe', *Zeitschrift für Parlamentsfragen* 31:4, 886–902.

—— (2001), 'Démocratie et secret du vote. La controversé entre scrutin public et vote secret dans les luttes électorales en Prusse', *Politix – Revue des Sciences Sociales du Politique* 14, 61–84.

Dembart, L. (2003), 'Are Internet Ballots a Vote-fixer's Dream?', *International Herald Tribune*, 28 April.

Elklit, J. and Svensson, P. (1997), 'What Makes Elections Free and Fair?', *Journal of Democracy* 8, 32–46.

Fund, J. (2004), *Stealing Elections: How Voter Fraud Threatens our Democracy* (San Francisco, CA: Encounter Books).

Holste, H. (2005), 'Die Einführung des amtlichen Einheitsstimmzettels und seine Bedeutung für ein freies und faires Wahlrecht', *Der Staat* 44:1, 101–11.

Holznagel, B., Grünwald, A. and Hanßmann, A. (eds) (2001), *Elektronische Demokratie* (Munich: Beck).

Hubert, P. (1992), *Uniformierter Reichstag. Die Geschichte der Pseudo-Volksvertretung 1933–1945* (Düsseldorf: Droste).

Katz, R.S. (1997), *Democracy and Elections* (New York: Oxford University Press).

Kloth, H.M. (2000), *Vom 'Zettelfalten' zum freien Wählen. Die Demokratrisierung der DDR 1989/90 und die 'Wahlfrage'* (Berlin: Links).

Lipphardt, H.-R. (1975), 'Die Erstattung der Stimmzettelkosten zu Beginn der Weimarer Republik und die Einführung des amtlichen Stimmzettels', *Archiv des öffentlichen Rechts* 100:4, 611–23.

Ohms, B.L. and Rieser, H. (1989), 'Die Briefwahl', *Österreichisches Jahrbuch für Politik*, 209–23.

Otten, D. (2001), 'Wählen wie im Schlaraffenland? Erfahrungen der Forschungsgruppe Internetwahlen mit dem Internet als Wahlmedium', in Holznagel et al. (eds), *Elektronische Demokratie* (Munich: Beck).

Reeve, A.W. and Wade, A.J. (1992), *Electoral Systems: A Comparative and Theoretical Introduction* (London: Routledge).

Rubin, A. (2001), 'Security Considerations for Removal of Electronic Voting over the Internet', <www.avirubin.com/e-voting.security.html>, accessed 22 October 2006.

—— et al. (2003), 'Analysis of an Electronic Voting System', <www.avirubin.com/vote/analysis/index.html>, accessed 26 September 2007.

von Ossietzky, C. (1926), 'Volksentscheid', *Weltbühne*, 22 June, 951–2.

Further Reading

Katz, R.S. (1997), *Democracy and Elections* (New York: Oxford University Press).

Kerstin, N. and Baldersheim, H. (eds) (2004), *Electronic Voting and Democracy: A Comparative Analysis* (New York: Palgrave).

Keyssar, A. (2000), *The Right to Vote: The Contested History of Democracy in the United States* (New York: Basic Books).

Kloth, H.M. (2000), *Vom 'Zettelfalten' zum freien Wählen. Die Demokratrisierung der DDR 1989/90 und die 'Wahlfrage'* (Berlin: Links).

Kühne, T. (1994), *Dreiklassenwahlrecht und Wahlkultur in Preußen 1867–1918* (Düsseldorf: Droste).

Mergel, T. (2002), *Parlamentarische Kultur in der Weimarer Republik. Politische Kommunikation, symbolische Politik und Öffentlichkeit im Reichstag* (Düsseldorf: Droste).

Rosanvallon, P. (2002), *Le sacre du citoyen* (Paris: Gallimard).

Vogel, B., Nohlen, D. and Schulte, R.O. (1971), *Wahlen in Deutschland* (Berlin: de Gruyter).

The History of Parliamentary Democracy in Denmark in Comparative Perspective

Uffe Jakobsen

Introduction

Parliamentary democracy combines parliamentary government, a government accountable to the majority in parliament, with representative democracy, a form of rule with universal suffrage and other characteristics of political competition, political participation and political rights. As institutions, parliaments have a long history, but also cover very diverse types of functions in relation to governments and to the people they represent. The root of parliaments is both the assemblies of the estates, often functioning as consultative bodies for absolutist rulers, and the assemblies of popular movements, serving as negotiating bodies in the revolutionary period that brought about the modern form of representative democracy. Today, representative democracy is challenged and perhaps faltering, especially in Western Europe, where network governance and other new-old forms of political decision-making are increasing together with tendencies of both regionalization and Europeanization of politics. In Eastern Europe, however, the parliamentary model of political order has been widely adopted after the breakdown of Soviet rule following the 1989 upheavals. This chapter takes its point of departure in the recent processes of democratization in Eastern Europe and the former Soviet Union to use this as an *analytical perspective* for a fresh look at the history of democratization in Western Europe, using Denmark as an example. In this way, by comparing recent experiences with historical ones but at the same time avoiding any anachronistic tendencies, the history of democratization can be rewritten to show a more complicated and contradictory political struggle among contemporary actors compared to traditional analyses of the abolition of absolutist rule and the transition toward democracy in Denmark.

In the 'transition to democracy' literature after 1989, the term 'triple transition' (Offe 1991) came to signify the uniqueness of the simultaneously ongoing processes of democratization, transition to capitalist market economy and nation-state formation in the post-Soviet states of Eastern Europe and the former Soviet Union in contrast to the ideal-type picture of historical processes of linear and sequential transition to modernity in the West. It has, however, been questioned whether this applies to the West as such, or whether a 'triple transition' type of development is an appropriate perspective for Western countries and past cases of these grand transformations as well. In partial disagreement with Offe's thesis, Robert E. Wright (1997) maintains that the United States is a historical example of a 'triple transition'. However, he also maintains that the simultaneity of the US case contrasts with the paths to modernization in Western Europe. Thereby, he is actually strengthening the conception of West European development as linear and sequential or non-simultaneous, implicitly present in Offe's account, and explicitly stating that West European countries *first* developed nation states, *then* market economies, and *finally* democracies (Wright 1997). In this chapter, however, a closer look at the case of Denmark as an example of a classical West European transition to modernity will show whether the transformations of state, nation, economy and democracy after the abolition of absolutism in 1848 and the adoption of a constitutional monarchy with a (two-chamber) parliament in 1849 is also a case of 'triple transition'. The demise of the Soviet-type political systems in Eastern Europe and the former Soviet Union and the transition to democracy, the introduction of market economy and the launching of nation-building and state-formation processes in former Soviet-type societies took the social sciences by surprise, and initiated a debate on the proper understanding of these processes. Needless to say, perhaps, this is still an ongoing debate that may further develop into a two-way learning process: from West to East, and from East to West (Kopecky and Mudde 2000). Some, although so far very few, have hinted at the possibility of improving understanding of recent developments in Eastern Europe by comparing them to historical developments in Western Europe. Here, however, the focus is on what can be learned about West European historical developments by comparing them to East European contemporary developments.

While most researchers within comparative politics tended to see these developments as a continuation of the 'third wave of democratization' (Huntington 1991), others took a broader view. By coining the term 'triple transition' of politics, economy and state (Offe 1991) – or even a 'quadruple transition' of politics, economy, state plus national identity-formation (Kuzio 2000) – the need for such a broader view of the transformations of Eastern Europe is indicated. This chapter further develops the characterization of the transformations in post-Soviet societies in recent decades as a 'triple transition' to the characterization of these transformations as 'telescoped modernization', that is, attempts to achieve in decades that which took centuries in Western Europe (Jakobsen 1999). The characterization of the recent transitions as 'telescoped modernization' will here constitute a prism in the study of the historical processes of modernization in Western Europe, to see them from a different perspective than usual, and thereby establish a position from which to rewrite the history of democratization. The chapter will take a closer look at the case of Denmark and the transformations of state, nation, economy and politics, showing that, in a way, this is also a case of 'triple transition'. This closer look, however, will demonstrate that matters are more complicated: in the case of Denmark, it will be maintained that even if the process of modernization transpired more or less sequentially over a longer period, it also, at certain times, *in casu* around the year of 1848, clearly developed simultaneously, that is, also as a 'triple transition'. According to this perspective, and taking Wright's analysis of the United States for granted, Denmark – *contrary* to Wright's claim – joins the US as a historical example of a 'triple transition'.

This analytical perspective is used as an argument for a broader look at the transition to modernity in Denmark instead of only focusing on democratization. In this way, a seemingly anachronistic principle is *consciously* applied in spite of the well-founded criticism from conceptual historians and other contextualists. Inspired by Collingwood's *An Autobiography* (1939), Quentin Skinner developed a new approach to the history of ideas as an alternative to the mainstream essentialism and the study of ideas as 'perennial problems' (see Koikkalainen and Syrjämäki 2002). In order to redesign historical inquiry, Skinner used Collinwood's 'logic of question and answer', according to which ideas and actions should be seen not simply as events, but as attempts to solve problems (Skinner 1969). Also in this chapter, actions of contemporary actors are seen as answers to specific questions. The task, then, is to recover the questions. The idea of a 'triple transition', borrowed from recent research into democratization in Eastern Europe, is used as a prism in the analysis of the Danish history of democratization in order to gain new insights compared to the results of earlier analyses of the historical events. Of course, as in any conceptual history, the task here is also to maintain a principle of contextualism and avoid a projection of 'present-day concepts into the past' (Koselleck 1996, 67). Thus, the struggle of contemporary actors should be seen as answers to contemporary questions. The hypothesis, however, is that a resemblance of these questions and the questions with which actors in the recent transitions in Eastern Europe are struggling makes Eastern Europe an appropriate analytical point of departure.

Post-Soviet Modernization in Eastern Europe

A brief chronology of developments from 1989 to 1991 is useful to point out the pivotal concepts in the process of the transformations: In 1989, developments in Central Europe were caused by popular contestations toward the old regimes, and democracy was the main concern in these upheavals. The demand for a transition from the Soviet-type economy to a Western type of market economy was also introduced almost instantaneously. During 1990, popular national movements in the Baltic republics of the Soviet Union demonstrated for change by means of song festivals and other permitted forms of public manifestations. The main concern of these 'singing revolutions' (Lieven 1993) was demands for national independence from the USSR and nation-building and (further) development of national identity in the three Baltic republics. In addition, in 1991 the world experienced the disintegration of the Soviet Union itself following the August coup that was led by members of the Communist Politburo in opposition to Gorbachev and his reform programme of 'Glasnost, Perestroika and Demokratizatsiya' (Tismaneanu 1999b). The main concern here became state-formation in the earlier Soviet republics, as well as economic reform in the direction of a market economy and capitalism.

The categorization of 1989 is contested. In the literature on regime change and political development in general, it has become commonplace to speak of 'waves of democratization', even if the meaning of the concept of 'wave' is ambivalent and unclear, and the number of actual waves is disputed (cf. Kurzman 1998; Simensen 1999). Huntington (1991) depicts three waves, the first prior to 1919, another subsequent to 1945, and a third after 1974. In so doing, he collects the democratization in Southern Europe in the 1970s, in Latin America in the 1980s and in Eastern Europe and elsewhere after 1989 all in the same wave. However, unlike the transitions from authoritarian rule in Portugal, Greece and Spain since 1974, the transitions in Central and Eastern Europe and the former Soviet Union involve more than the insulated democratization of a political system: the scope is broader, and numerous transitions are transpiring simultaneously. Accordingly, the issues are more complex, and the agenda for change much more contested by different actors. While questions concerning the basic organization of the economy were generally not part of transitions from authoritarian rule in Southern Europe in the 1970s, economic questions are central in the transitions from Soviet rule, complicating the transition process by making it a 'dual transition' (Pridham 2000). Multinational states such as the Soviet Union also had to face a third issue – the defining of state borders and state-formation. The transitions in post-Soviet societies became 'triple transitions', encompassing political, economic and socio-cultural aspects of societal life (Offe 1991). In addition, even a fourth issue, as far as it can be separated from the third one, is on the agenda in countries with a multi-ethnic composition of the population – the issue of nation-building, the formation of national identity, and actual or potential ethnic conflicts (Linz and Stepan 1996). Using a recent expression coined by Taras Kuzio, granted this analytical distinction between state-formation and nation-building is made, the transitions in post-Soviet societies are actually 'quadruple transitions' (Kuzio 2000).

Summing up, post-Soviet political actors encounter a more complex challenge than actors in earlier sets of transitions in the 'third wave' did. Consisting of state-building, nation-building, economic liberalization and democratization, the transitions from communist rule became 'protracted democratization' (McFaul 1999) compared to the democratization processes in Southern Europe and Latin America. At the same time, they were also 'telescoped modernizations' compared to the 'classic' processes of modernization in eighteenth- and nineteenth-century Europe, assuming that states and societies in Eastern Europe would accomplish in decades what, according to standard assessments, took centuries in Western Europe.

Modernization in Western Europe

In the standard construction of political development in Western Europe, the processes of state-formation, nation-building, transition to market economy and capitalism and democratization lasted centuries, and took place more or less separately, or sequentially (Flora 1999; Rokkan 1981; Tilly 1975). In contemporary Eastern Europe, these processes are 'telescoped' to last presumably only decades, and therefore taking place simultaneously instead of sequentially. Independently of the correctness of the hypothesis of a sequential transition in the cases of 'classical' modernizations, reserving the cases of simultaneity to the post-Soviet transitions, the main point in this context is the character of the post-Soviet transitions as processes of modernization, and not only democratization. Therefore, from an analytical point of view, the contemporary post-Soviet cases become 'working laboratories' for the historical process of modernization, thus facilitating deeper insight into the apparently sequential, mutually supportive processes of modernization that took place earlier in history, revealing contradictions and conflicts that have remained concealed in the literature thus far (Grzymala-Busse and Loung 2002).

The purpose in this section of the chapter is to discuss whether the 'telescoped modernization' is a unique post-Soviet characteristic, or whether it is also discernible in some form in other cases, in other geographical spaces, and in other times of democratization. Thus, using Denmark as an example, the process of modernization in Western countries will be discussed, subdividing that process into (1) state-formation, (2) nation-building, (3) transition to capitalist market economy (economic liberalization), and (4) democratization. Again, the purpose is not to use contemporary concepts anachronistically in the analysis of earlier processes of change, but to compare recent European experiences with historical ones in order to reveal hidden or repressed aspects in the traditional analyses of the history of democratization in Denmark (cf. Jakobsen 2005).

Overall, the modernization process in Denmark was long and complicated. Concerning the history of state-formation, Denmark for centuries was a multinational state with several non-Danish areas before it was eventually reduced to a fraction of a nation-state as a consequence of several lost wars that left multitudes of Danish nationals outside the state borders. However, when the northern part of Schleswig was returned to Denmark as a result of referendums held following the completion of the First World War as part of the dictates of the Treaty of Versailles, the Danish state as a result equaled the Danish nation, or more or less so, meaning that the nation-building process has also been long and complicated (Knudsen 2006; Kaspersen 2004; Brincker 2003; Paludan et al. 2002; Østergård 2000; Feldbæk 1991–92). The process of economic liberalization and development of a capitalist market economy started relatively late. It took a different form than in other European cases with small-sized enterprises, cooperative traditions and bottom-up influence (cf. Byrkeflot et al. 2001; Damsgaard Hansen 2001). The process of democratization in Denmark also has a long history, slowly beginning prior to the formal breakdown of absolutist rule in 1848. In 1849, a relatively large-scale (male) suffrage was introduced. However, parliamentarism first became a reality in 1901.

Since then, a growing number of people and issue areas have been drawn into the realm of democratic decision-making (Knudsen 2006; Svensson 1996; Friisberg 1975).

State-formation

The historical processes of state-formation in Europe must predominantly be understood from the perspective of establishing security within a given territory as the very idea of state sovereignty (Tilly 1975). Important aspects of this are the granting of citizenship to the inhabitants of the state territory, and the conditions on which membership of the political community is based. Territorially, some kind of state in parts of the geographical area now belonging to Denmark dates back more than a thousand years. Archeological research has dated Danewirk, a great rampart in the vicinity of the contemporary German city of Schleswig, to 737, and the building of another defensive wall by King Godfrey and his campaigns against other Danish kings are described in Frankish annals from 810. After the Peace of Westphalia in 1648, the territory of the Danish state changed several times due to military defeats, resulting in the loss of primarily non-Danish areas in national terms – in the period up to 1658 territories in southern Sweden and Norway were lost, in 1814 the whole of Norway was lost, which until then, together with Denmark, constituted the 'double monarchy', and in 1864 the German duchies of Schleswig and Holstein were conquered by Prussia. Denmark was thus reduced from a North European empire – a 'conglomerate' or 'composite' multinational state – to a 'small state' comprising only Danish nationals. As a result of referendums held as a part of the Treaty of Versailles after the First World War, the northern part of Schleswig again became part of Denmark. Only from 1920, then, has Denmark been a proper nation-state with the borders of the Danish state practically equaling those of the Danish nation.

The form of the Danish state was also transformed during the period of shifting territories. Following a system with an elected monarch, Denmark became a hereditary absolutist kingdom in 1660. The degree of actual absolutism varied during its almost two hundred years of existence, in some periods earning the reputation of being a 'responsive absolutism', and in 1834 representative consultative chambers were introduced in the form of the four assemblies of the Estates of the Realm covering the four provinces in the Kingdom of Denmark and the duchies of Schleswig and Holstein. Formally, the absolutist rule ended in January 1848, and a constitutional monarchy was established in June 1849. According to the 1849 constitution, political power in the state of Denmark was divided between the king, the government and the parliament; however, parliamentarianism was not realized until 1901, when the king first gave in to parliament's demand to appoint a government in accordance with the parliamentary majority.

In spite of the actual institutional history, the legacy of state-formation and state history in the Danish public debate is typically pictured as a centuries-old nation-state[1] Thus, the former status of Denmark as a multinational state is hardly mentioned, nor is the fact that the history of Denmark as a nation-state only dates back less than a century.

Nation-building

Theoretically, nation-building can be regarded as based on either ethnic kinship or political community construction (Anderson 1991). Nation-building conceived as community-formation can in principle be made on different foundations: cosmopolitan, patriotic, national, cultural, ethnic or other identities. Nations are seen as constructed, both as legitimizing foundations of the state (Hobsbawm 1990), and as a precondition for economic and political liberalization (Rustow 1970). A common analytical distinction in this regard is the civic versus ethnic distinction (Brubaker 1992). Lately, however, this distinction has been widely criticized. Not least the idea that the former is essentially Eastern, while the latter is essentially Western, has been criticized by pointing to opposite examples from East and West (Kuzio 2000). The case of Denmark demonstrates that a shift in the civic versus ethnic dimension within the same state is also a possibility.

The question of the age of Danish nationality is harder to answer than in the case of the age of the Danish state, since the evidence is to a lesser degree artifact than it is mentality and discourse. The Vikings, perhaps the most widely known examples of ancient inhabitants of Denmark, were more 'trans-nationals' than nationals. The famous work of the historian Saxo Grammaticus from *c.* 1200, which bore the title 'The Deeds of the Danes' (*Gesta Danorum*), is more myth than history, and more about the state than the nation of Denmark. Later national histories were likewise more an accounting of state and royal histories than national histories. From *c.* 1740 or earlier, a measure of interest in Danish nationality and national identity began to appear among writers, artists, academics or students, and others (Feldbæk 1991–92). This can be taken as the beginning of the discourse on the Danish nation that underpins contemporary Danish politics.

The first institutional step in this direction was the introduction of the Law of Indigenous Rights in 1776, according to which civil servants were to be citizens of the Danish state. However, due to the multinational nature of the Danish state at that time, this merely meant exclusion of citizens from other *states*, not the exclusion of other *nationalities* within the Danish composite state, such as Germans and Norwegians with citizenship of the composite state. The idea of national identity in Denmark at that time resembled more that later expressed by Ernest Renan in his *Qu'est ce qu'une nation?* from 1882, that is, one of choice – Renan pictured national belonging as an everyday referendum, an anti-essentialist and voluntaristic conception, not culturally or ethnically inspired by, for example, Herder's ideas of nation or *Volk*, as was the case in other European societies at that time, such as Germany (Koselleck 1992). The Danish *pendant* of Renan could

---

1   Cf., for example, the official Website of the Danish Parliament, <www.folketinget.dk/doc.aspx?/samling/20051/menu/00000005.htm>

be N.F.S. Grundtvig, who in a poem on 'Danishness' (*Folkelighed*) from 1848 hints to national identity as a choice – those who belong to a people or nation are those who (choose to) feel they do (Østergård 2000). Later, this was the principle applied by the referendums on where to (re)place the Danish–German border in 1920, and also in the Danish–German government Act from 1955 on Danish and German minorities in the border region of Germany and Denmark.

In 1848, however, during the war between the Danish state and rebellions from Holstein fighting for the independence of the duchy – actually a civil war, since it was fought among citizens of the same (composite) state – and again following the defeat in the war with Prussia in 1864, the civic conception of national identity is contested by a cultural one, close to the Herderian idea of the *Volk* as the key element in the nation, and dependent on the Danish nation-state and the practical congruence between nation and state, nevertheless not established until 1920.

Economic Liberalization

Normally, economic liberalization and the introduction of a capitalist market economy are connected to the growth of individualism, and also in the ongoing debate on internationalization and globalization. However, the case might appear different upon closer examination of specific examples of the transition to market economy and capitalism. In the case of Denmark, the idea of 'the people' was also promoted in economic and social matters. As in Sweden, where the Social Democratic party coined its vision of an ideal welfare society in the 1930s as *folkhemmet* (the 'people's home') (Stråth 2000b), an idea of a care-taking state of the citizens, combined with a strong sense of egalitarianism in economic relations, already began to take form in the period *c.* 1848. Again, N.F.S. Grundtvig very aptly expressed this in an earlier poem from 1820, entitled *Langt højere bjerge* ('Far Higher Mountains'), on the Danish vision of the 'good life'. The motto here was that not only should the state prevent poverty among its citizens, it should also prevent the accumulation of excessive wealth or possessions by individual citizens: in terms of wealth, we have made the largest progress 'when few have too much, and fewer too little' (Østergård 2000). The criteria for the real wealth of the nation, hence, was not merely absence of too many poor people, but also absence of too many rich – this seems to be egalitarianism and anti-elitism far beyond the norm. Danish conceptions of the good society stipulate that the state is to ensure economic and social security in a manner promoting inclusion and popular participation, that is, in a decentralized, bottom-up manner. The project of a Danish welfare state was clearly anticipated as a one-nation project.

The first steps toward economic liberalization involved economic reforms in the 1780s. The abolition of the principle of adscription in 1788, whereby male members of the population were prohibited from moving from the estate upon which they were born without the permission of the estate owner, freed the peasants from the landlords. This created the possibility for a conscripted army and a free labour force. A truly modern liberal economic movement began to appear in the beginning of the nineteenth century, and emerged clearly in the 1830s. Liberal ideas became more prominent, and proposals for economic deregulation and free trade were put forward and discussed. Later, they were also formally adopted, first in the 1849 Constitution, and free trade was finally secured by parliamentary adoption of the 1857 Trade Act.

But the development of a competitive economy and capitalism had a strong egalitarian and participatory trend. In the late nineteenth century, much of agricultural secondary production became organized in cooperatives governed by the principle of one-man-one-vote as opposed to principles of decision-making power in share-holding companies. Also here, the anti-elitism and do-it-yourself ideology salient in Danish political culture has gained much. Later, the welfare state became conceived to be something typically Danish and different from (Continental) European welfare state projects. It has almost become part of the national identity. In this way, economic globalization has also been judged a threat against the welfare state, thereby also representing a threat against the national identity and the tradition of participation in the decision-making processes that concern oneself.

Democratization

Theories of democratization are abundant, and the 1989 changes in Eastern Europe have accelerated the debate on structure versus agency, democracy as institutions versus democracy as practice, the relations of democratization and globalization, to cite the main disputed issues (Grugel 2003). The democratization process in Denmark has been quite protracted. Absolutism was somewhat responsive to the preferences of the citizens voiced in public debate, at least periodically. In 1834, representative institutions – in the form of the assemblies of the general estates – were granted consultative power *vis-à-vis* the absolutist king. The actual end of absolutist rule in January 1848 was quiet and peaceful – a single demonstration in the streets of Copenhagen and a meeting with the king were all that were necessary to solve matters. It was only later when the struggle for democracy resulted in violent confrontations for a nation-state that actually became a civil war. The king, however, retained some measure of power upon the adoption of the Constitution on 5 June 1849 that was elaborated by a constitutional assembly elected in the autumn of 1848.

In certain cases, the king did in fact use this power to appoint governments against the will of the majority in parliament, especially in the period from 1885, when the majority in parliament shifted from conservative to liberal, until the parliamentary principle *de facto* was introduced in 1901. This event is termed the 'system change' in the national history corpus, and represents the introduction of parliamentary government. A constitutional amendment in 1915 granted female suffrage, and in 1920 a proportional electoral system was introduced. Finally, the upper house was abolished in 1953; age, gender, income and social status no longer reduced the principle of universal suffrage and political equality in general, and the parliamentary principle was introduced *de iure*.

A 'Triple Transition' Also in the Case of Denmark?

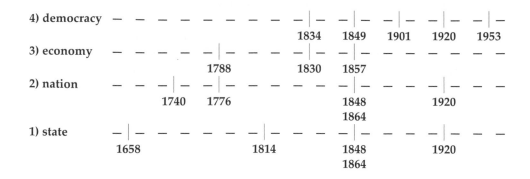

Figure 18.1 Sequence and simultaneity of modernization sub-processes in Denmark

Compared to the contemporary processes of modernization in post-Soviet societies, the development in Denmark is clearly slower and less complex because of the timing and sequencing, although different developments also tend to group temporally, as illustrated in Figure 18.1, where events that significantly made changes in each of the four sub-processes of modernizations are indicated.

Two conclusions can be drawn from this matrix. The first is that Denmark has a longer and more sequential development than the 'triple transition' that contemporary Eastern Europe is undergoing. After the state-formation of 1660 was consolidated, the nation-building processes began in the 1740s, before the economic liberalization began in the late 1880s and the first sign of political liberalization materialized in 1834 in form of consultative assemblies of the estates during the absolutist rule. Denmark (or another similar example) can therefore be expected to be better off concerning consolidation of democracy, levels of economic equality, nationalistic or ethnic tensions, and conflicts and state capacity with a high level of legitimacy *vis-à-vis* the citizenry.

The second conclusion is that, contrary to the view espoused by Wright on West European development as sequential or non-simultaneous (Wright 1997), a certain degree of simultaneity is also present in the Danish case: During the initial phase of the transition from absolutist rule toward democracy in 1848–49, Denmark also experienced the formal economic transitions toward a market economy beginning in 1849, and at the same time the formation of a nation-state and a strong development of national identity as a consequence of what was actually a civil war between Danish and German citizens in Denmark and the duchies of Schleswig and Holstein within the borders of the Danish multinational state. A first war was waged between 1848 and 1851, a second in 1864 that led to a drastic change in state borders and state territory that was partially restored in 1920, almost securing the congruence between the Danish state and the Danish nation and definitely ending Denmark's existence as a multinational empire. Hence, *c.* 1848, Denmark did also have its 'triple transition'!

What can be learned about the West upon examination of the history of democratization in Eastern Europe, then, is that in a way, the same problems appeared during the transition to democracy, and the need to simultaneously produce an answer to the question of who is entitled to be part of 'the people', or a member of the political community, is not a specific 'Eastern' question, but a general question to understand democratization as such. If this is combined with the case that only a very limited democratization took place in 1849 apart from a relatively wide male suffrage – for example, it took another 52 years before governments as a *de facto* principle was appointed by parliamentary majority – or, conversely, that the 'soft' Danish absolutism managed to maintain important positions of power by transforming itself into a constitutional monarchy, then the conclusion from an analysis of the recent East European transitions also holds for the limited democratization in Denmark in 1848–49: 'the faster the transformation, the greater the potential role for norms, practices, and understandings inherited from the past to shape elite decisions' in the new political system (Grzymala-Busse and Loung 2002).

References

Allardt, E. et al. (eds) (1981), *Nordic Democracy: Ideas, Issues, and Institutions in Politics, Economy, Education, Social and Cultural Affairs of Denmark, Finland, Iceland, Norway, and Sweden* (Copenhagen: Det Danske Selskab).

Anderson, B. (1991), *Imagined Communities: Reflections on the Origin and Spread of Nationalism* (London: Verso).

Branner, H. and Kelstrup, M. (eds) (2000), *Denmark's Policy towards Europe after 1945: History, Theory and Options* (Odense: Odense University Press).

Brincker, B. (2003), 'A "Small Great National State": An Analysis of the Cultural and Political Factors that Shaped Danish Nationalism 1760–1870', *Journal of Historical Sociology* 16:4, 407–31.

Brubaker, R. (1992), *Citizenship and Nationhood in France and Germany* (Cambridge, MA: Harvard University Press).

Brunner, O., Conze, W. and Koselleck, R. (eds) (1992), *Geschichtliche Grundbegriffe: Historisches Lexikon zur politisch-sozialen Sprache in Deutschland*, vol. 7 (Stuttgart: Klett-Cotta).

Byrkeflot, H. et al. (eds) (2001), *The Democratic Challenge to Capitalism: Management and Democracy in the Nordic Countries* (Bergen: Fagbokforlaget).

Collingwood, R.G. (1939), *An Autobiography* (Oxford: Oxford University Press).

Damsgaard Hansen, E. (2001), *European Economic History: From Mercantilism to Maastricht and Beyond* (Copenhagen: Copenhagen Business School Press).

Feldbæk, O. (ed.) (1991–92), *Dansk identitetshistorie*, vols 1–4 (Copenhagen: C.A. Reitzel).

Flora, P. (ed.) (with S. Kuhnle and D. Urwin) (1999), *State Formation, Nation-building, and Mass Politics in Europe: The Theory of Stein Rokkan, Based on His Collected Works* (Oxford: Oxford University Press).

Friisberg, C. (1975), *På vej mod et demokrati: Fra junigrundloven 1849 til junigrundloven 1915* (Copenhagen: Fremad).

—— (2007), *Ingen over og ingen ved siden af Folketinget. Partiernes kamp om forfatningen 1848–1920*, vols 1–2 (Varde: Vestjysk Kulturforlag).

Grugel, J. (2003), 'Democratization Studies: Citizenship, Globalization and Governance', *Government and Opposition* 38, 238–64.

Grzymala-Busse, A. and Loung, P.J. (2002), 'Reconceptualizing the State: Lessons from Post-Communism', *Politics and Society* 30, 529–54.

Hobsbawm, E.J. (1990), *Nations and Nationalism since 1780: Programme, Myth, Reality* (Cambridge: Cambridge University Press).

Huntington, S.P. (1991), *The Third Wave: Democratization in the Late Twentieth Century* (Norman, OK: University of Oklahoma Press).

Jakobsen, U. (1999), 'Demokratisering: Begreber, teorier og processer', in Jakobsen and Kelstrup (eds), *Demokrati og demokratisering: Begreber og teorier* (Copenhagen: Copenhagen Political Studies Press).

—— (2005), 'Integration of the Baltic Sea Region in the European Union: Notions of State, Nation, Market and Democracy', in M. Schartau (ed.), *Political Integration and Northern Dimension of EU Order* (Berlin: Nordeuropa-Institut der Humboldt Universität zu Berlin).

—— and Kelstrup, M. (eds) (1999), *Demokrati og demokratisering: Begreber og teorier* (Copenhagen: Copenhagen Political Studies Press).

Kaspersen, L.B. (2004), 'How Denmark Became Democratic: The Impact of Warfare and Military Reforms', *Acta Sociologica* 47:1, 71–89.

Knudsen, T. (2006), *Fra enevælde til folkestyre. Dansk demokratihistorie indtil 1973* (Copenhagen: Akademisk Forlag).

—— (2007), *Fra folkestyre til markedsdemokrati. Dansk demokratihistorie efter 1973* (Copenhagen: Akademisk Forlag).

Koikkalainen, P. and Syrjämäki, S. (2002), 'On Encountering the Past – Interview with Quentin Skinner', *Finnish Yearbook of Political Thought* 6, 32–66.

Kopecky, P. and Mudde, C. (2000), 'What Has Eastern Europe Taught Us about the Democratization Literature (and Vice Versa)?', *European Journal of Political Research* 37:4, 517–39.

Koselleck, R. (1992), 'Volk, Nation, Masse', in Brunner, O., Conze, W. and Koselleck, R. (eds), *Geschichtliche Grundbegriffe: Historisches Lexikon zur politisch-sozialen Sprache in Deutschland*, vol. 7 (Stuttgart: Klett-Cotta).

—— (1996), 'Response', in H. Lehmann and M. Richter (eds), *The Meaning of Historical Terms and Concepts: New Studies in Begriffsgeschichte* (Washington, DC: German Historical Institute).

Kurzman, C. (1998), 'Waves of Democratization', *Studies in Comparative International Development* 33:1, 42–64.

Kuzio, T. (2000), 'Transition in Post-Communist States: Triple or Quadruple?', *Politics* 21:3, 168–77.

Lehmann, H. and Richter, M. (eds), *The Meaning of Historical Terms and Concepts: New Studies in Begriffsgeschichte* (Washington, DC: German Historical Institute).

Lieven, A. (1993), *The Baltic Revolution: Estonia, Latvia, Lithuania and the Path to Independence* (New Haven, CT: Yale University Press).

Linz, J.J. and Stepan, A. (1996), *Problems of Democratic Transition and Consolidation: Southern Europe, South America, and Post-Communist Europe* (Baltimore, MD and London: Johns Hopkins University Press).

McFaul, M. (1999), 'The Perils of a Protracted Transition', *Journal of Democracy* 10:2, 4–18.

Offe, C. (1991), 'Capitalism by Democratic Design? Democratic Theory Facing the Triple Transition in East Central Europe', *Social Research* 58, 865–92.

Paludan, H. et al. (2002), *Danmarks historie – i grundtræk* (Århus: Aarhus Universitetsforlag).

Pridham, G. (2000), *The Dynamics of Democratization: A Comparative Approach* (London: Continuum).

Rokkan, S. (1981), 'The Growth and Structuring of Mass Politics', in Allardt et al. (eds), *Nordic Democracy: Ideas, Issues, and Institutions in Politics, Economy, Education, Social and Cultural Affairs of Denmark, Finland, Iceland, Norway, and Sweden* (Copenhagen: Det Danske Selskab).

Rustow, D.A. (1970), 'Transitions to Democracy: Toward a Dynamic Model', *Comparative Politics* 2, 337–67.

Schartau, M. (ed.) (2005), *Political Integration and Northern Dimension of EU Order* (Berlin: Nordeuropa-Institut der Humboldt Universität zu Berlin).

Simensen, J. (1999), 'Democracy and Globalization: Nineteen Eighty-nine and the "Third Wave"', *Journal of World History* 10:2, 391–411.

Skinner, Q. (1969), 'Meaning and Understanding in the History of Ideas', *History and Theory* 8, 3–53.

Stråth, B. (ed.) (2000a), *Myth and Memory in the Construction of Community: Historical Patterns in Europe and Beyond*, (Bern: PIE Lang).

—— (2000b), 'Poverty, Neutrality and Welfare: Three Key Concepts in the Modern Foundation Myth of Sweden', in Stråth (ed.), *Myth and Memory in the Construction of Community: Historical Patterns in Europe and Beyond*, (Bern: PIE Lang).

Svensson, P. (1996), *Demokratiets krise? En debat- og systemanalyse af dansk politik i 1970'erne* (Århus: Politica).

Tilly, C. (ed.) (1975), *Formation of National States in Western Europe* (Princeton, NJ: Princeton University Press).

Tismaneanu, V. (1999a), 'Introduction', in Tismaneanu (ed.), *The Revolutions of 1989* (London: Routledge).

—— (ed.) (1999b), *The Revolutions of 1989* (London: Routledge).

Wright, R.E. (1997), 'The First Phase of the Empire State's "Triple Transition": Banks' Influence on the Market, Democracy, and Federalism in New York, 1776–1838', *Social Science History* 21:4, 521–58.

Østergård, U. (2000), 'Danish National Identity: Between Multinational Heritage and Small State Nationalism', in Branner and Kelstrup (eds), *Denmark's Policy towards Europe after 1945: History, Theory and Options* (Odense: Odense University Press).

Further Reading

Bunce, V. (2000), 'Comparative Democratization: Big and Bounded Generalizations', *Comparative Political Studies*, 33:6–7, 703–34.

Campbell, J.L. et al. (eds), *National Identity and the Varieties of Capitalism: The Danish Experience* (Montreal: McGill-Queen's University Press).

Collier, R.B. (1999), *Paths towards Democracy: The Working Class and Elites in Western Europe and South America* (Cambridge: Cambridge Univesity Press).

Goldblatt, D. (1997), 'Democracy in the "Long Nineteenth Century": 1760–1919', in D. Potter et al. (eds), *Democratization* (Cambridge: Polity Press).

Lauwerys, J.A. (ed.) (1958), *Scandinavian Democracy: Development of Democratic Thought and Institutions in Denmark, Norway and Sweden* (Copenhagen: The Danish Institute, The Norwegian Office of Cultural Relations and The Swedish Institute in cooperation with The American–Scandinavian Foundation).

Svensson, P. (1993), 'The Development of Danish Polyarchy or How Liberalization also Preceded Inclusiveness in Denmark' in T. Bryder (ed.), *Party Systems, Party Behaviour and Democracy* (Copenhagen: Copenhagen Political Studies Press).

Sørensen, G. (2007), *Democracy and Democratization: Process and Prospects in a Changing World* (Boulder, CO: Westview Press).

von Beyme, K. (2000), *Parliamentary Democracy: Democratization, Destabilization, Reconsolidation, 1789–1999* (Houndmills: Macmillan).

Whitehead, L. (2002), *Democratization: Theory and Experience* (Oxford: Oxford University Press).

PART IV

CONTEXTS

A Long and Hard Process of Democratization: Political Representation, Elections and Democracy in Contemporary Spain

Gonzalo Capellán de Miguel

... un appel fait à ses droits en faveur de ses intérêts [du peuple].
Je dis quand les élections sont libres: car quand elles ne sont pas libres,
il n'y a point de système représentatif.
(Benjamin Constant, *Principes de politique*, 1872, 34)[1]

Introduction: Joining Theory and Praxis for a Conceptual History of Politics

The aim of this chapter is to analyze the long, complex and far from linear historical evolution of contemporary Spanish politics from the point of view of two key elements: on the one hand, the concept of representation and its political expression, representative government, which was something totally new on the Spanish nineteenth-century scene dominated by the existing absolute monarchy; on the other, elections as the basic political mechanism whereby the governed exercised their sovereignty and governments were legitimized. In fact, the true or false nature of electoral practice proves vital in Spanish contemporary politics when judging the various governments, whether for the quality of their parliamentary regimes or for the extent to which they could be regarded as being more or less democratic – or not at all.

In the first place, one has to remember that the very idea of political representation was something entirely new for Spain in the nineteenth century. Moreover, it

---

1   '... a call made to their rights in favour of their interests [of the people]. I say when the elections are free: because when they are not free, there is no representative system at all.'

presented an alternative political regime to the existing absolute monarchy, along with other options for a political system, such as direct democracy. It must not be forgotten that the absolute monarchy prevailed, with two brief liberal parentheses (1808–1812 and 1820–1823), until 1833, and it had numerous supporters during the following decades, even giving rise to various civil wars – the so-called 'Carlist wars'. Such a difficult and slow establishment of the liberal state in Spain during the nineteenth century had as its colophon, once into the twentieth century, the two periods of dictatorship (1923–31 and 1939–75) which made political representation, the parliamentary system and elections a pure fiction. At the same time, the two pioneering attempts at establishing a political system on foundations of a democratic nature proved tumultuous and short-lived (1868–73 and 1931–36).

In each of these superficially described periods, various definitions and concepts were put forward, not only of political theory – ideas on democracy, sovereignty, rights – but also of political praxis – the nature of the legislative bodies, of the constitutions, of the electoral body. Hence, fully aware of this reality, this chapter seeks to carry out an analysis of conceptual history which does not scorn the political practices underlying the concepts; a conceptual history which moves from political rhetoric and language, through the players and their actions, to the reality which accompanies and shapes their discourse at any given moment and in each particular historical context. To put it in a nutshell, the aim is to trace the nature of the concepts beyond the merely semantic level to the very conduct of those who construct the political discourse, as well as those who received this discourse, and thereby see their interaction.

Starting with 1808, the date when the first liberal period in Spain began, it is not possible to understand the formation, debate and definition of the concept of representation by the various political players without the parallel process of holding elections, the convening of Parliament and the establishment of a Constitution (1812), since each of these practices was impregnated in the ideas and meanings which formed part of the concept of representation itself. All these elements together are what made it possible to give shape and sense to a first system of representative government in the Spanish state of the early nineteenth century.

By the final decades of the nineteenth century, once this concept of political representation and the resulting parliamentary regime had fully settled down, the debate focused increasingly on the mechanisms and practices whereby the elected government expressed itself and ruled. When the main authors and parties accepted the theories of representative government as the official framework for the political game, which lasted nearly half a century, embodied in the 1876 Constitution, some thinkers realized that such government meant nothing in itself. If, for example, the Parliament did not represent the opinion of the country or the elections were not free and fair, the elected government was not representative – it was false.

This is why, in this second phase, having overcome the ups and downs of the absolutist monarchy and its supporters, the text focuses its attention on the effective functioning of political representation through another key notion, elections, because elections are more than a simple political practice, more than a legal or technical mechanism for making representation effective. In twentieth-century

Spain, it becomes a whole concept in its own right, associated with other basic concepts such as freedom – everyone can vote without being coerced or pressured; conviction, the word must replace violence – such as equality – the rich and poor, women and men must vote on the same terms – such as democracy itself, as the Spanish saw the act of being able to go to the polls in order to vote in 1977. In other words, the term 'elections', like 'representation', formed an essential part of the rhetoric of democratization.

As a consequence, the existence of elections, the nature of these elections, their scope and the way in which the electoral process takes place prove to be the keys to defining the political system. And at the same time, they are a symptom which illustrates the nature of the political system, which is reflected in theoretical debates, in Parliament or in the press. Thus, the evolution and changes in the way of understanding, of defining political representation, as well as electoral practice itself, are a good guide, if not the only one, to analyzing the evolution of the political history of contemporary Spain until it achieved democracy.

The Concept of 'Representation' in Nineteenth-century Spain

It was common among nineteenth-century writers examining the origins of political representation to focus on the meetings held in the Cortes, Houses or General States – depending on the country – during the final stages of the medieval period in Europe. Admittedly, this form of primitive representation was flawed: four knights per county in England, or the deputies of the voting cities in the Cortes in Spanish Castile. Furthermore, these representatives had limited functions: 'free voting for subsidies and a few humble requests for reform' (see *El Censor* 1, 5 August 1820, 39–40). It was, therefore, a representative model linked to the so-called 'imperative mandate', a notion later abandoned by the political philosophy of liberalism and replaced with the 'representative mandate' (González Encinar 1984, 809–11).

The opinion of early liberals, however, regarding this type of representation was not at all positive. For them, the principle of representation meant an expression of general free will. It was, to them, a new phenomenon associated with liberalism, despite the differing opinions of some of the more historicist authors, such as Martínez Marina. Sovereignty lies in representation of the nation. On the basis of this idea, political representation can be defined as an 'artifice', a means by which the nation can be present in government. At the same time, however, representation is a need that can be justified in territorial terms. Along the same lines of thinking as those established by Montesquieu in *De l'esprit des lois*, the size of the republic was to be, for Spanish liberals, a determining factor in the extent to which national sovereignty could be exercised directly and democratically.

In accordance with this principle, immediate and direct participation of the people in government affairs can only occur in small republics. This has been the case throughout history, from the ancient Greek city states to present-day Geneva. For this same reason, in the extensive English, French and Spanish monarchies direct popular government is, in practice, impossible. At the time of the Cortes of

Cádiz, in October 1809, the *Junta Central*, or Central Council, proclaimed that 'in the large states, power is undoubtedly wielded by the hands of few, rather than by the hands of many' (*Biblioteca de Autores Españoles*, 151, 379). This argument was backed up clearly some years later in *El Censor*: 'the people will inevitably delegate their authority' (*El Censor*, 7 October 1820, 261). Here we have the origins of representative government.

Nevertheless, beneath the determining territorial factor for political representation to be able to enter onto the scene, and the parallel argument that democracy is, in practice, impossible, one can find at least two ideas that are very characteristic of the moderate liberalist thinking during the *Trienio* – the liberal period of 1820–23. On one hand, there is the idea which opposes democracy as a form of government. This forms part of a historical period in the evolution of the republics, one which is now confined to the past. On the other hand, if democracy is to be seen as direct popular sovereignty, then this will involve large-scale meetings of the masses. The result of this would be nothing but passion, violence and anarchy. Consequently, the people had to be persuaded that 'their immediate and continued intervention is not only unjust and illegitimate, but also does not offer any security. It creates disorder and damages the representative system, destroys the actions of the government and replaces them with the unhealthy energy of opposing passions' (*El Censor*, 7 October 1820, 278–9). This is what had occurred during the French Revolution. Thus, in defending representation as an imposition of the territorial reality, there is an underlying rejection of the principles and consequences of democracy.

At the same time, there was a firm belief in the virtues of a representative regime. This existed to the extent that national representation formed, along with liberty and the Constitution, one of the three pillars of the political system supported by Spanish liberals *c.* 1820. As well as the virtues that made representation preferable to both democracy and the despotism of an absolute monarchy, there were the many arguments put forward by European liberals. Among these was that presented by Sieyès, in which the quality of representative government came from its being based on the division of work. As Burke and Guizot argued, the representatives of a nation would be 'the most able' or the most skilled members of the new bourgeois society (Guizot 1851, 106–8). This would result in the best government possible, as it would be a government of the best people for the job, not chosen by birth, but by their abilities. At the same time, this reasoning implied that the rest of the population were not capable of exercising authority over themselves. One must not forget the point raised by Constant, in which political representation corresponded to modern liberty. This liberty was to be found in the personal sphere of each individual. Representation thus became a positive liberation for the citizens, who, having delegated their sovereignty, were now able to spend more time for themselves and their private lives. This is where they could find true liberty.

Thus, in liberal spheres, representation is seen as something necessary in practice, legally just and legitimate, politically efficient, and finally, positive for the individual. On the other hand, the exact nature of political representation was yet to be seen. For the majority of liberals, representation was not synonymous with sovereignty: the representatives were not the same as the nation, but were merely the nation's delegates. In their opening session, the Cortes Generales of 1810 had declared themselves to be sovereign, but some liberals quickly corrected this statement, making it clear that national sovereignty, which is one, indivisible and everlasting, is not sacrificed when delegated. Thus, as can be seen in Article 27 of the 1812 Constitution, the Cortes are representative, not sovereign (see González Casanova 1998, 299).

During the *Trienio*, *El Censor* distinguished between 'radical – or primitive – sovereignty', which remains inherent in the nation and 'current sovereignty', which is that possessed by governments, reflected in the laws and held only temporarily by the representatives. Therefore, if sovereignty were to be transferred on a lesser scale, the representatives were only there because of the wishes of the nation. The representatives were answerable to the ministry, and as they could potentially be removed from office by the wishes of the nation, the people held a vital mechanism in their grip: electoral power, or as Bentham called it, the right not to re-elect them (see Manin 1997, 164).

Following these years of effusive theorizing, there were plenty of visions, even some official ones, of representative government as something 'terrible' (*Gaceta de Madrid*, 1834). From this time on, representation was referred to as 'representative government'. The idea of political representation as the basis of a constitutional system was strengthened, which put Spain in line with other European countries, where around the 1850s liberals still sang the praises of this type of government. Of course, there was no lack of critical voices either. Criticism came not only from sworn enemies of representative government, but also from those who shared the principles but who believed that they were being misinterpreted by certain liberal sectors.

The position of the former is revealed in works such as that of Taparelli, *A Critical Examination of Representative Government in Modern Society*, translated into Spanish by the neo-Catholics, who shared his deep rejection of liberalism. For them, the representative system, which they identified with mixed government, was 'essentially damaging and anti-Catholic'. The criticisms of the latter, the liberals themselves, were not as vicious. One good example of these is to be found in the work of the French politician Henri Fonfrède, translated into Spanish in 1841 as *Preocupaciones por el gobierno representativo*. The book reveals the views of a sector of conservative liberals who were opposed to the supremacy that the popular chamber had gained over the other two powers, those of the king and the *pares*, or peers – in France, as a result of the Revolution of July 1830. Fonfrède believed that representation of the French nation would not be complete without the monarchy and the chamber of peers, who were also legitimate representatives, even though they had not been elected.

A similar way to look at representation is that which was used by the Spanish liberals who drew up the 1834 Charter. They appealed to the historical legitimacy through which the nobility and the clergy had been represented in the royal court up until the time of Charles I. They also held that these two groups would create the necessary balance needed for good government. The council of ministers would introduce a second chamber in the Cortes, as opposed to the single-chamber model of Cádiz. This chamber would house the class known as *próceres del Reino*, or 'notable citizens of the Kingdom', and would include archbishops, bishops, grandees, Castilian nobility, landowners, as well as other well-known individuals from the world of education, science or the arts (Sevilla Andrés 1969, 261–71). From 1837 onward, this chamber would be known by its modern name, the Senado, or Senate, the senators either being appointed by the king or queen or chosen by suffrage, depending on the historical period. Either way, it was significant that representatives from various socio-economic, cultural and religious fields were accepted as a necessary element in the legislative branch of power.

The dominant model of representation in early Spanish liberalism was the individualist or inorganic model. Around 1850, however, the so-called 'Krausist school of thought' would incorporate into Spanish political thought the idea that society is made up of a series of social creatures that are orientated towards fulfilling different objectives in life, be they economic, scientific, religious or any other. As a result, true representation would mean that all of these fields would need a presence in the political system. This 'proto-corporatism', which had an influence on the partially organic make-up of the Senado in the 1876 Constitution as well as on many writers of the time, was intended to replace individualist liberalism.

In practice, however, it did little but give rise to a very different movement: the traditionalists. This movement did agree with the notion that there are a series of social bodies that ought to be represented in the state. The difference lay in the fact that, unlike the complementary nature of organic representation with regard to the individual, as supported by the Krausists, traditionalists stayed with the old idea that class representation should do away with any trace of individual sovereignty, something which they had never accepted. For them, individuals did not exist apart from the community of which they were part. For this reason, corporative representation would be adopted in the early part of the twentieth century.[2]

In any case, the Krausists believed that representation within the state would always be subject to certain well-defined rights and obligations. Hence their insistence on representation of general interests rather than individual, selfish ones. This is an idea that was made very clear in numerous electoral manifestos and was used as a theoretical weapon against the rampant administrative and political corruption of the time (Azcárate 1877, 145–83). Burke's theory of virtual representation, by which an elected *diputado* could represent, at the same time, both the general interests of the nation as well as his specific constituency (see Pitkin 1967, 168–89), was not considered by those Krausists who sat in Parliament as representatives of the general public.

According to theorists such as Azcárate, the means by which the interests of all could be guaranteed was through public opinion. This apparently novel idea had been circulating since the beginnings of Spanish liberalism. Domeq, in the Cortes of Cádiz, said: 'public opinion ought to aid us with its indications and warn us of our mistakes, and put us back on the right path should we stray from it'.

---

2   This was of utmost importance to authors (especially during the dictatorship of Primo de Rivera) who followed in the wake of others who, like Gil Robles, had started this regression around the end of the nineteenth century (see García Canales 1977, 25–65).

Likewise, French doctrinaires would stress the importance of *publicité* as the most characteristic element of representative government (Rosanvallon 1989, vol. III, 421). Also, from the ranks of the Spanish republicans, José María Orense, following the English saying that one must have a majority both in and out of parliament, wrote in 1863: '*Congreso* is nothing if it is not a mirror which reflects public opinion' (Orense 1863, 15). This became a means of reconnecting the representatives with the represented, since the independence of the *diputados* had caused the distance between the two parties to grow and the old imperative connection to weaken (Gress 1980, 543–46).

Voting and Representative Government in Nineteenth-century Spain

Undoubtedly the most direct and greatest mechanism by which the citizens could control the representatives, as well as being the instrument that gave voice to the nation's will, was the electoral process, as opposed to the ancient democracies' characteristic allotment, or sortition, a mechanism characteristic of the ancient democracies. This, in turn, brings us to the mechanism that makes representation possible, that is, elections. From the time of the *Cortes* of Cádiz on, the fact that representatives were elected meant that any type of class representation was automatically excluded. That is to say, a fundamental element of the old regime was denied, with liberals insisting that representation have a strictly modern nature: it was to be, in their eyes, a political victory over the past. Although representation was on occasions linked historically with the old *Concilios*, or religious councils, it was expressly recognized that this form of representation had disappeared in Spain under the absolutist system which national representation now rightly opposed, as argued by the famous deputy Argüelles in 1812.

The new criteria for representation now had to be laid out. This led to a heated debate. At the time of the Royal Statute of 1834 and the new electoral law of 1836, the position amongst liberals had evolved towards two criteria which came to be known in liberal Spain as material (economic) and intellectual (cultural) or alternatively, property and enlightenment. The *Encyclopédie* had defined the representatives as 'citizens who are more enlightened than others, more interested in politics, whose possessions link them to the patria' (Ruiz Otín 1983, 89–90). Spanish liberals could not find a more efficient criterion – or, of course, more convenient for the liberal bourgeoisie – to establish representation, than by linking votes with wealth (contributions) and culture (capacity) of the voters (*Diario de Sesiones de las Cortes*, 25 January 1862).

In practice in nineteenth-century Spain this meant having an electoral system based on direct census suffrage – as opposed to the indirect universal suffrage of the 1812 Constitution or the direct universal suffrage of the law of 1890 – in which the fate of the nation fell into the hands of a select minority, These so-called 'modern aristocracies', became, for many liberals, according to Royer-Collard, a kind of 'natural representatives' of the nation (see Garrorena Morales 1974). From the republican ranks, Pi y Margall (1854) described the situation as a 'political monopoly' of capital, which could only be broken by means of popular sovereignty and its counterpart, universal suffrage. Conservative liberals, on the other hand, felt that class equality and the conditions that this entailed, namely democracy, were incompatible with representative government.

The will of the people was therefore reduced to the will of a small oligarchy in whose hands political power would rest from the very beginnings of the liberal state. The struggle between moderates (*moderados*) and progressives (*progresistas*) during the reign of Isabel II (1833–1868) over this question led to an extension of the electoral body, the nation, several thousand voters. The qualitative nature of representation was not altered, however, only the quantity of voters, which grew from over 15,000 voters in the 1830s to nearly 40,000 before the 1868 revolution.

The *de facto* oligarchy was one of the initial endemic defects to be found in nineteenth-century Spanish liberalism, but we should also look at another, no less damaging, that created a wide gap between political theory and practice: the 'boss system', one of whose manifestations was electoral fraud. As far back as the 1820's, liberals had warned that the principle of political representation would collapse unless it were put into effect by popular authentic suffrage, and would be equally threatened if the government rigged the elections by buying votes, offering employment or threatening voters (*El Censor*, 1 September 1821, 172). There are two issues at stake here: universality and the veracity of the vote. Some authors, such as Bentham and J. S. Mill, went as far as to calculate the value of representative government itself by its capacity to allow unrestricted political participation for all citizens. Between 1860 and 1861 Mill wrote his *Considerations on Representative Government*, based on the British case. At that time, Mill believed that 'the two great improvements that representative government is yet to make' were to introduce 'proportional representation' – proportional to the number of voters in each constituency – and 'suffrage for women' (Mill 1873, 257–58).

In this sense Spain was to go down the same path as Britain and would also undergo a continuingf extension of suffrage, driven by the more progressive liberals. During the *Restauración* (Restoration, 1875–1923), the Conservative Party of Cánovas would systematically refuse to introduce universal suffrage. Unlike the republicanism of Pi y Margall, conservatives did not consider that every man had the inherent right to vote, simply because he is a man. Conservatives still believed that the strictly contributive criterion, which excluded the working classes from the process, was the best possible option. Cánovas himself expressed this very clearly during the debates over local electoral law in 1878:

> *Viewed from these pitiful limits, who can be denied the right to contribute in Spain? Who? The simple journeyman? The prole? In any case, can Señor Castelar tell us in truth that modern political science, even amongst its more liberal representatives, if they are truly deep and as long as they truly study the social organism, maintains the need for representation of the proletarian class? Not long ago I read one of the more illustrious ones who had written:*

'The proletariat does not need representatives. It needs patrons.' (Diario de Sesiones de las Cortes, 17 November 1876)[3]

Perhaps the most worrying question toward the end of the century was that of the necessary purity of the elections. This was the basis of the very idea of representation. In England, the problem of electoral fraud was of concern to politicians, and in 1847 in France Duvergier wrote that 'representative government cannot truly exist without three conditions', one of which was that 'elections must be pure and free' in order to create 'an assembly that represents in just proportions ... the opinion of the people of the country' (cited in Lacché 2000, 535). The political class in Spain was also concerned about the denaturalization of representative government in practice and about the necessary means to improve it. In the heyday of the liberal period, the conservative Marqués de Orovio told the congress that 'electoral truth is what this country really needs' and that it should be the banner of 'all genuine supporters of the representative system' (*Diario de Sesiones de las Cortes*, 12 November 1878). The in-depth study of elections by historiographers throughout the country in recent years has revealed widespread systematic and institutionalized falsification in electoral mechanisms by various governments. The introduction of universal suffrage in 1890 exacerbated this situation.

One last question remains: was there truly representative government in nineteenth-century Spain, even if we take the parameters defined by the liberals themselves as a reference point? It is here where theory and practice differ, where the speeches and the actions create an obstacle that is often difficult to overcome. There is no doubt that the principle of representation (however it was put into practice) was efficient enough for the liberals to take political control of the new state. Neither the despotic government nor the modern democratic mechanisms, such as the referendum, were able to rival the principle of representation in 'popularity'. It was a principle that the liberals successfully transferred from the realm of individual rights to the very heart of politics, the public realm. It was a principle to which they gave a specific structure, that of representative government, and in which representative legitimacy was gradually absorbed by the legislative powers, the 'parliamentary regime'.[4]

Elections as a Pathway to Democracy: Spain, 1898–1978

The circumstances which appeared *c.* 1898 to some extent represent a milestone in Spanish history in the cultural, political and social sphere, but they did not entail significant changes in the concept of elections. The notably pejorative vision

---

3   Castelar was an old democrat leader, President of the Republic in 1873, who was regarded as the best orator in the Spanish Parliament at that time.

4   And which, following the crisis suffered by liberalism, ended up preserving some of its more fundamental features after the advent of the modern democracy – 'representative democracy' (see Conde 1945).

which, ever since nineteenth-century liberalism had introduced the election of representatives to town councils, provincial councils and parliaments into the political system, had accompanied the whole electoral process, was still in evidence at the beginning of the new century. Not even the arrival of one of the great demands for democracy of the previous century, universal suffrage (1890), had been capable of changing this situation, but rather, as has been shown by subsequent studies, the fraudulent practices had spread to every corner of the country as soon as the time for elections came round (see Yanini 1991, 99–114).

The only perceptible changes in this situation, as crude as it was well known, were perhaps linguistic ones, since the network of concepts and lexical terms of the electoral family was enriched by the contribution of Joaquín Costa to Spanish political vocabulary. While it is common to speak of *caciquismo* (dominance by a local despot) when analyzing political, and especially electoral, practices in Spain in the nineteenth century, only after 1898 and the famous survey instigated by Costa from the Ateneo of Madrid were the two concepts coined which perfectly defined the structure and functioning of elections under the Restoration: 'oligarchy' and '*caciquismo*'. That was then the form of government, and one of the evils 'regenerationists' wanted to eradicate from the country since 1898 until the 1930s, since for Costa, a sad truth lay behind these two concepts: 'Spain is not a free and sovereign nation' (Costa 1901 [1993], 17–24). That is, that within the deep semantic structure of the concept of 'elections' there were such far-reaching realities as sovereignty, freedom or democracy, which remained amputated in the face of the fraudulent electoral reality of Spanish and European liberalism.

One of the elements which would contribute to the persistence of this negative opinion of elections as being synonymous with fraud, violence and farce was an essential part of the local despot's network: the executive arm of the 'oligarchy', the civil governors. According to the provincial press, these were 'the worst from every house' and they were assigned huge powers in municipal and provincial life, authority which rather than being used to the benefit of the populace, 'they used for electoral and political ends, protecting their friends and pursuing their enemies' (*La Rioja*, 18 July 1899). This is why, after 1936, the deep-rooted electoral tradition would pass into collective consciousness as a synonym of turbulent times, of coercion and confrontation in the towns and villages of Spain.

The first systematic attempt to tackle this problem was right at the start of the new century, the result of Prime Minister Antonio Maura's policy, as he set himself the goal of 'uprooting *caciquismo*'. His programme of 'revolution from above', of the regeneration of political life, was built up on two key pillars: making the administration morally responsible, and ensuring clean elections. Maura tried to make the 1903 elections a genuine and sincere exercise capable of attracting the so-called 'neutral mass' into public life, those people who, disillusioned with the system, had decided to take no part in the electoral process. The report sent to his government by the British Ambassador sheds some light: 'As far as I can judge, Mr Maura is trying to prevent the abuses honestly; but his own party supports him with little enthusiasm and the abuses continue' (González 1997, 50).

Nevertheless, Maura adopted new measures, set out in the controversial electoral law of 1907 and the aborted plan to reform local administration. The former sprang from the desire to change the way people perceived elections, making them appear more dignified by associating them with the ideas of 'transparency and veracity'. To do so, among other things, it was necessary to draw up an accurate census, which until then had been manipulated so as to supplant the popular vote: votes cast by dead people or a total poll with more votes cast than the number of registered electors had become commonplace in all the elections. These efforts were not limited to the person of Maura, since other leading political figures, such as the reformer Melquíades Álvarez, made 'electoral sincerity' and the 'purity of the vote' their party's slogan and a condition *sine qua non* for the rule of democracy (Suárez Cortina 1986, 136).

Such efforts once again seemed in vain, to the point where a local despot of the day was able to scoff at the 1907 law in the following terms: 'Bless my soul! But I don't cheat any more than with the previous one [1890] .... All these mechanisms just make me laugh' (González 1997, 145–47). In fact, alongside the general crisis in the political system of the Restoration during the second decade of the century, electoral corruption continued *in crescendo*. This is corroborated by the unanimous testimony of the level of scandal that was reached in the 1918 elections, 'the most corrupt in living memory' in the opinion of Spanish writer Pérez de Ayala. Prior to these, he points out, as well as coercion there had always been economic corruption, but discreetly: 'In these elections, buying votes took place with the blinkers off, without ceremony or squeamishness. The voters offered their votes the highest bidder; candidates bid up the price of the vote', the price ranging between 0.40 and 500 pesetas (Pérez de Ayala 1918, 157).

This kind of practice simply exacerbated the loss of prestige that elections in particular and the system in general gained for themselves at the time across the length and breadth of the ideological spectrum of the country. Thus, from the left, the socialist Luis Araquistain, after the 1918 election, coined a new expression, 'plutocratic electoral machinery'. In fact, Araquistain assures, in a country of free, that is, incorruptible citizens, any kind of electoral apparatus would be unnecessary. In the absence of such conditions, 'While by law it has existed for some time, we can say that in fact there is no suffrage in Spain.' His pessimism was based on a deep-rooted belief, 'In Spain the electoral regime means total vexation of any will of representation', and from this the 'atrophy of the Parliament' had sprung (Barrio Alonso 2001, 157–60, 230).

From the opposite end of the political spectrum, the Catholic newspapers agreed in denouncing that 'Our elections are a school for political corruption and depraving of the people', and asked the following question: 'Is there anything more demoralizing than seeing how the authorities throw themselves on the stages of delinquency, in its various forms, in order to falsify the will of the electors?' (*El Debate*, 5 May 1923).

If we add to these fiercely critical sectors that, as late as 1923, according to a provincial newspaper, 'There is still, then, a large mass of opinion which is not moved or interested by the elections', we can understand part of the general apathy and reigning discontent when in this same year, Primo de Rivera led the military coup which started the dictatorship (Garrido Martín 1998, 134). As we will be able to understand, too, the dictator himself made use of the regenerationist rhetoric which proclaimed fighting against *caciquismo*. In practice, however, there was no chance to find out, since the electoral question vanished over the horizon, leaving the cafe gathering and the Ateneo, or local literary circles, as the only parliament, 'open' to all and fully democratic, of course.

This parenthesis for the electoral custom was going to conclude precisely as a result of elections which, for once, seem to have served what was their purpose in pure terms: to express the will of the people. That was the interpretation that the newspaper *El Socialista* made of the municipal elections held by the Berenguer government in 1931 and which represented the beginning of the end for the dictatorship: 'The elections have been truly constituent because, while they were only for the municipal authorities, people with a lot of foresight and more political sense than the government, realized that they constituted a plebiscite and have expressed their opposition to the monarchy in a perfectly unequivocal way.' And the king himself, Alfonso XIII, corroborated such an interpretation in his farewell speech: 'Sunday's elections have shown me clearly that I no longer maintain the affection of my people' (Gil Pecharromán 1999, 197). It also meant a radical and positive shift in the concept of elections, since for the first time they had proven an effective instrument for peaceful change.

This was a shift which came together with deeper changes in the social and political structure itself, with the advent of the Second Republic, reform of the electoral law and the new Constitution. The recently inaugurated Republic called elections for the Constituent Assembly in June, to be held under the criteria which the 1907 law had partially modified, for example, by lowering the voting age from 25 to 23 or making it possible for women to be elected, although not to vote (*Royal Decree*, 8 May 1931). The result was a triumph for the Republican forces which drafted the new Constitution. The new system also saw a new political vocabulary, so prolific and active was the political life which flourished during these years. As for the 'electoral lexis', with respect to the 'central term' *elections* there were no significant changes, but one should highlight the appearance of linguistic 'alternatives' such as the syntagms 'consulting the electorate', 'going to the country', 'asking the voters' or the term *comicios*, another word for 'elections'. The use of war vocabulary also spread, metaphorically transplanting these to the electoral field, where 'battles', 'struggles' and 'fights' are waged between the candidates (see García Santos 1980, 366–67).

The sense of the elections would be modified in the very concept, quite apart from the strictly technical aspects of such a complex mechanism as an electoral system. The great landmark in this change was Electoral Law Reform Bill which was passed in July 1933. The most heated debate was over the majority or proportional character of the law. Azaña defended the majority option as the lesser of the two evils, since 'the ideal of perfection and representative justice' was impossible to achieve. Hence, everything related to the elections belongs more to political 'physics' than to 'metaphysics'. With the question firmly planted in the field of practice, then, he defended that 'the majority regime ... is a truly democratic regime', against the criticisms of (radical) deputies who considered in as a 'crushing of the minorities' which allowed the famous *copo electoral* by the majorities. The preference, according to Azaña, is due to the fact that it favors the 'electoral group which is strong enough for it'. That is, even though the elections were a political mechanism for obtaining parliaments in accordance with the 'general will', which for Azaña was the same as 'the majority of the country', far from being a neutral instrument in its design and conception, it could overturn a whole philosophy, in this case the 'popular front' tendency, and a particular electoral geography (Azaña 2001, 707).

The above is all explained in a historical context that, more or less explicitly, shaped a first electoral sociology of Spain, although still without the sophistication of the analysis of later social sciences, but not for this less present: conservative and/or reactionary votes came from the rural milieu, while town votes and those of the intellectual sectors belonged to the Republic. For this reason, the design of the electoral system took into account this sociology and mobilized the different currents of opinion based on a calculation of opportunity and benefit in terms of franchise for their political interests. In the 1931 elections, the big working-class centers of Madrid, Barcelona and Bilbao had been converted into constituency cities, for example. Azaña was thinking in the interests of the Republic in terms of 'left-wing currents', while the journalists of *El Debate* dismissed this generalized electoral sociology, yet at the same time shared his complaints: 'They say that the socialist votes in Madrid are of aware, educated, free men while the right wing votes of the people from the country are from backward, uneducated, enslaved peasants. The statement of the proposition itself is irritating because of its injustice' (*El Debate*, 5 December 1933).

The effect of such sociology was no less in one of the points which caused most commotion both inside and outside Congress, which related to the vote for women. Electoral participation had been at the very roots of the modern women's movements – the suffragettes – in the United States and Europe. When the time came for their constitutional recognition, however, the forces of the Republic split. The Catholic and socialist 'extremes' supported the cause, while the parliamentary minorities, like the radicals, including the female deputy Margarita Nelken, were against due to the danger that it could entail for the Republic, convinced as they were that the female vote would favour reaction, almost always arguing the lack of freedom and the educational shortcomings in order to dismiss women's participation in elections. When finally Article 34 of the constitutional bill was approved, giving the franchise to women (by 161 votes to 121), it was due to the fact that overwhelming ideological reasons were used to defeat more pragmatic considerations.

Enfranchisement in that context meant a key right in woman's equality with man, a right which could not be denied in a system which aspired to call itself democratic. Moreover, together with these values, the vote was identified with the idea of citizenship, as well as with liberty, justice and equality. All this wide, positive semantic field remained an integral part of the electoral concept, not so much of suffrage, of the vote itself, as of the action of emitting it, of what elections really meant in the end: a right, yes, but an exercise of responsibility too, and consequently a capacity. During these tumultuous times, the newspaper *El Crisol* was able to transmit very well the beneficial implications of an ideal which, through exercising it, was able to change the very reality of women and the country. 'It is convenient for the future of Spain', one can read in its pages, 'for women to be spurred to exercise a function which, consisting in the most vital operation of voting, awakens the awareness of her personality and responsibility' (Capel 1992, 125). Elections are therefore not only the exercise of a right, but a means of participating in public life, an act of citizenship, a purifying, educational experience for the person.

The political implications for the members of parliament of 'overturning these six million votes at the ballot boxes' would become evident in the elections held immediately afterwards, in October, which brought victory to the Confederación Española de Derechas Autónomas (CEDA), and in the elections of February 1936, won by the National Front, in which women became the main target of propaganda for parties of all colours, making it necessary to modify the messages and strategies which had been dominant in the electoral process until then, elections which by then had already become the central focus for all the tensions which had built up in the political system itself and which were again transferring to the very heart of the electoral process such negative realities as coercion and violence.

In March 1936, the socialist and former minister Fernando de los Ríos denounced in Congress the intimidation to which Andalusian casual farm labourers had been subjected, and pronounced words to define the elections which recalled former times that seemed to have been surpassed: 'he who has the land has the man' (de los Ríos 1999, 737). De los Ríos himself had revealed in Parliament years earlier that it was precisely due to a belief in elections that part of the Spanish socialist movement had opted for the path of law rather than resort to revolutionary options. That is, when elections work properly, they are a factor for peaceful change and of legitimate constitution of political power. And it was precisely the fact of not settling ideological differences peacefully through the elections, of not accepting the results of the ballot box, which would lead the socialists to resort to violent methods of gaining access to power which had appeared to belong to past.

Epilogue: From the Representative Mask of the Dictatorship to the Electoral Truth of Democracy

With the bloody civil war which began that same year, a dark era opened up, which, among other things, brought the suppression of elections and everything they implied: participation, freedom, democracy. This is no surprise if we take into account the words of General Franco in 1938: 'We do not believe in a government which is produced by the ballot box' (*Time* 27 June 1977, 1). Nevertheless, Franco's dictatorship was soon to put in place a dense legal framework which would regulate the peculiar Spanish electoral process of the time. Thanks to these ground rules, a succession of elections to town councils, regional councils, assemblies and trade unions would be verified in the central decades of the century. The regime saw elections as the way of making 'the participation of the people in the tasks of the state through the family of the Movement and the Syndicate' a reality (*Royal Decree*, 29 September 1945). In this way, the inorganic nature of the franchise gave way to the corporate vote which supposedly represented the different interests of society (and clearly undermined the electoral body by restricting the census to 'heads of family').

Under the so-called organic democracy, an elite belonging to a single 'party' (the Movement) elected, often indirectly, by co-opting its representatives (*tercios*) into the various institutions of the regime. Thanks to the predominance of direct appointment ('anti-election') to the main and most numerous posts, the concept of elections was removed from areas which until then had made them more or less free and competitive, adapting to the model which political scientists call 'elections without choice'. This non-competitive election model could serve, all the same, for purposes of external accreditation, to present a fictitious appearance of participation or to legitimize power (Vallés and Bosch 1997).

In spite of everything, when this new electoral practice started, in *ABC* they wrote enthusiastically that 'With the elections which begin today, the Spanish town hall confirms its strictly representative character.' 'The voter ... is the one who must meditate and judge the integrity and capability of the future councilors. There lies the responsibility of the inexcusable duty which today will take you to the polls' (25 November 1951). The same philosophy spread to the area of the trade unions where Francoism also put into law a similar electoral system to that which until then had only been practiced in the political sphere. Again, there was a contrast between the reality of the vertical syndicalism of the Francoist regime and the rhetoric present in the regulation of elections in which all the workers and company owners could participate through 'free, equal and secret ballot' (*Royal Decree*, 14 May 1966). At this point in the dictatorship, there was no lack of discordant voices which, like those emanating from the Confederación Nacional del Trabajo (CNT-AIT)[5] in Asturias, denounced that 'Elections with an appearance of democracy, since we are free to elect whoever we want for trade union links, were aimed at impressing people abroad' (CNT-AIT 1963, 4).

In the same text, they expressed a desire for a future in which this freedom of choice would be an inalienable right of all workers. This moment was to arrive a few years later, following the death of the *caudillo* in 1975, when a period in Spanish history began in which the word 'elections', with all that implies, became fundamental to political debate and social change. Right from the start of the transition, from the presentation of the Political Reform Bill as a mechanism for political transformation in the democratic sense and without ruptures, the electoral question was the subject of as much attention as commotion in the heart of the political class (in both the government and the opposition). It was then when it became completely clear that the electoral system was in no way a mere aseptic mechanism whereby the sovereignty of the people was translated into votes, into seats, into representation within the political power and nothing else. It is when

---

5   CNT-AIT was set up in Barcelona in 1910. Rooted in the anarcho-syndicalist ideology, it was the most important trade union in Spain before the dictatorship.

the theories of Duverger or Sartori on the influence of electoral systems on political parties, in shaping the political map of a country, were shown as a tangible reality in which the various groups pushed for an electoral law which would benefit their interests or expectations of representation in the new regime. In the Spanish case, the proportional representation system did not prevent the polarization of votes and the consolidation of a two-party system (see Gunther 1989, 73–106).

The first big debate in the Assembly, as under the Second Republic, focused on whether the electoral system should be by majority or proportional representation. Given the constituent assembly character which was being attributed to the coming elections (which in the end were held in June 1977) from the most advanced sectors of opinion, except for the most reactionary deputies, the tendency was to prefer the proportional system of representation. This, in theory, would allow for the wide range of views existing in Spain at that time to be reflected, as one can see from the 'alphabet soup' created by the initials of all the parties which stood at the 1977 elections (*El País*, 6 November 1998).[6] But even in the precision of the system within the different possible formulas for determining the proportional distribution between votes and representatives, the one produced by the Belgian mathematician V. d'Hondt which was adopted in the Royal Decree law of 18 March 1977 aroused bitter criticism from the outset. It encouraged the final distribution of seats among the 'remains' of the votes to the parties receiving the most votes, an option which favored the bigger parties so that criticisms have continued over a length of time. Hence, at the 1999 local elections, the candidate for mayor of Madrid, Fernando Morán, demanded the 'urgent correction' of the electoral system because it 'has led to an estrangement between political representatives and the citizens'.

Among the requirements that the democratic opposition demanded to support these first and transcendental elections was freedom and fairness in the process, but above all else, neutrality: 'legal and political guarantees' from the state. In fact, although on the election day of 15 June some irregularities were still detected in some villages, polling stations and particular individuals, even the sectors critical of the opposition considered them 'formally acceptable' (*Triunfo*, 16 June 1977). In fact, the turnout at these elections was very high, with a participation of around 80 per cent – which reflected the popular enthusiasm for the elections – and in which, according to the French daily *Le Monde*, 'an extraordinary lesson in public spirit' was given. The *New York Times* highlighted the 'surprisingly peaceful character' of the elections, so that the old concept forged during the Restoration and fed right up until February 1936 seemed finally to shake off in this new phase that connotation of violence which had made elections something conflictive, which divided people and set them against each other (see Ministerio Asuntos Exteriores 1977).

In this whole debate opened up in 1976, the technical and political pressures on the definition of the electoral system were resolved not to hinder a greater goal: seeing off the existing authoritarian regime and establishing full democracy. In this process, the elections, and especially those of 1977, had a lot of symbolic importance which made the concept of elections something much more than a mere legal and

---

6   For the pre-election atmosphere, see *El País*, 9 November 1976.

political mechanism. In the first place, the peculiar historical context had the effect of identifying elections, the electoral practice, with democracy itself.

The judgment on the inaugural nature of this democratizing process that the elections had was unanimous. The foreign press saw the elections as the 'farewell to Francoism', as the 'birth of the democratic era in Spain', as an expression of a political normalization which brought Spain closer to Europe. For Spain, it was 'its return to political civilization' (*Frankfurter Allgemeine Zeitung*, 18 June 1977) – that is, that both inside and outside the country, the elections were a synonym of the exercise of freedoms and democracy. They were, as the king would say at the opening of the new Parliament, 'the recognition of the sovereignty of the Spanish people', and thence the legitimizing function of power which is intrinsic to the concept of elections (see Cotarelo 1992, 494).

Over and above specific results, what was more important was the advance it represented and the return of their sovereignty to the people. No subsequent election, not even those of such relevance as in 1979 (the first strictly democratic ones in Spanish local authorities) or those for the autonomous governments of 1983, again roused such enthusiasm, massive turnout and significance as those of 1977, when people felt that something was being recovered from Spanish history, at the same time as, from an electoral point of view, a conscious break was being made with historical precedents (see Montero 1997, 396–427). It was during the 1970s that the word 'elections' acquired its increased importance and a positive tone as a central element of Spain's democratic system.

References

Azaña, M. (2001), *Discursos parlamentarios* (Madrid: Congreso de los Diputados).

Azcárate, G. (1877), *El self-government y la monarquía doctrinaria* (Madrid).

Barrio Alonso, A. (ed.) (2001), *Luis Araquistain. La revista España y la crisis del Estado liberal.* (Santander: Universidad de Cantabria).

Capel, R.M. (1992), *El sufragio femenino en la II República* (Madrid: Horas y Horas)

CNT-AIT (1963), *Nuevamente en la brecha* (Gijón: CNT-AIT).

Conde, F.J. (1945), *Representación política y regimen español* (Madrid: Subsecretaría de Educación Popular).

Costa, J, (1901 [1993]), *Oligarquía y caciquismo*, in *Oligarquía y caciquismo; Colectivismo agrario y otros escritos* (anthology) (Madrid: Alianza).

Cotarelo, R. (ed.) (1992), *Transición política y consolidación democrática. España (1975– 1986)* (Madrid: Centro de Investigaciones Sociológicas).

de los Ríos, F. (1999), *Discursos parlamentarios* (Madrid: Congreso de los Diputados).

del Aguila, R. (ed.) (1997), *Manual de Ciencia Política* (Madrid: Trotta).

García Canales, M. (1977), *La teoría de la representación en el siglo XIX* (Murcia: Universidad de Murcia).

García Santos, J.F. (1980), *Léxico y política de la II República* (Salamanca: Universidad de Salamanca).

Garrido Martín, A. (1998), *Favor e indiferencia. Caciquismo y vida política en Cantabria (1902–1923)* (Santander: Universidad de Cantabria).

Garrorena Morales, A. (1974) *El Ateneo de Madrid y la teoría de la monarquía liberal* (Madrid: IEP).

Gil Pecharromán, J. (1999), *La Segunda República* (Madrid: Historia 16).

González Casanova, J.A. (1998) 'La cuestión de la soberanía en la Historia del constitucionalismo español', *Fundamentos* 1, 295–328.

González Encinar, J.J. (ed.) (1984), *Diccionario del sistema político español* (Madrid: Akal).

González, M.J. (1997), *El universo conservador de Antonio Maura. Biografía y proyecto de Estado* (Madrid: Biblioteca Nueva).

Gress, F. (1980), 'Representación', in *Diccionario de Ciencia Política* (Madrid: Alianza).

Guizot, F. (1851), *Histoire des origines du gouvernement représentatif en Europe* (Paris: Didier).

Gunther, R. (1989) 'Leyes electorales, sistemas de partidos y élites: El caso español, *Revista de Investigaciones Sociológicas* 47, 73–106.

Lacché, L. (2000), 'Constitución, Monarquía, Parlamento: Francia y Bélgica ante los problemas y "modelos" del constitucionalismo europeo', *Fundamentos* 2, 467–543.

Manin, B. (1998), *The Principles of Representative Government* (Cambridge: Cambridge University Press).

Mill, J.S. (1873) *Autobiography* (London: Longmans).

Ministerio Asuntos Exteriores (1977), *Las elecciones en España vistas por la prensa extranjera* (Madrid: Ministerio de Asuntos Exteriores).

Montero, J.R. (1997) 'Elecciones en España', in R. del Aguila (ed.).

Orense, J.M. (1863), *Treinta años de gobierno representativo en España* (Madrid).

Pérez de Ayala, R. (1918), *Política y toros* (Madrid: Renacimiento).

Pitkin, H.F. (1967), *The Concept of Representation* (Berkeley, CA: University of California Press).

Rosanvallon, P. (1989), 'Les doctrinaires et la question du gouvernement représentatif', in *The French Revolution and the Creation of a Modern Political Culture* (Oxford: Pergamon Press).

Ruiz Otín, D. (1983), *Política y sociedad en el vocabulario de Larra* (Madrid: Centro de Estudios Políticos).

Sevilla Andrés, D. (1969), *Constituciones y otras Leyes y proyectos políticos de España* (Madrid: Editora Nacional).

Suárez Cortina, M. (1986), *El reformismo en España* (Madrid: Siglo XXI).

Vallés, J.M. and Bosch, A. (1997), *Sistemas electorales y gobierno representativo* (Barcelona: Ariel).

Yanini, A. (1991), 'La manipulación electoral en España: sufragio universal y participación ciudadana (1891–1923)', *Ayer* 3, 99–114.

Further Reading

Criado de Diego, M. (2007), *Representación, Estado y democracia* (Valencia: Tirant lo Blanch).

Forner, S. (1998), *Democracia, elecciones y modernización en Europa. Siglos XIX y XX* (Madrid: Cátedra/Instituto Juan Gil-Albert).

Fraile Maldonado, M. (2005), *Cuando la economía entra en las urnas: el voto económico de España (1979–1996)* (Madrid: Centro de Investigaciones Sociológicas).

Gunther, R. Montero, J.R. and Puhle, H.-J. (eds) (2007), *Democracy, Intermediation, and Voting on Four Continents* (Oxford: Oxford University Press).

Moreno Luzón, J. (2007) 'Political Clientelism, Elites, and Caciquismo in Restoration Spain (1875–1923)', *European History Quarterly* 37: 3, 417–41.

Sierra, M. (ed.) (2006), *La representación política en la España liberal*, monographic issue of *Ayer* 61 (Madrid: Marcial Pons).

Suárez Cortina, M. (ed.) (2003), *Las máscaras de la libertad. El liberalismo español 1808–1950* (Madrid: Marcial Pons/Fundación Sagasta).

Do Political Parties Matter? Direct Democracy and Electoral Struggles in Switzerland in the Nineteenth Century

Pierre-Antoine Schorderet

Introduction

In a recent study of literature dedicated to the question of the emergence of political parties in nineteenth-century Europe, Susan Scarrow has reminded us of the importance of two simultaneous processes: parliamentarization on the one hand, and the universalization of the right to vote on the other (Scarrow 2006). While refusing to enter a debate over the choice of which of these processes has been a determining factor in the development of modern political parties, she lays an invitation to describe their influence in different configurations, in time and space.

Scarrow's propositions highlight, albeit with some nuances, the accepted facts, the knowledge gained by the numerous researches dedicated to this issue, and which have resulted in a fairly common consensus shared by the scientific community. With regard to the understanding of the Swiss political parties, however, there remains a particularly interesting discussion, for three main reasons.

First of all, one must emphasize the fact that the volume of literature produced in Switzerland on this subject is quite insignificant: in the fields of both history and political science, the political parties have long been a neglected matter, and have usually been treated according to analytical formats that show but a slight interest in their origins (David et al. 2007). Therefore, there have been, and here lies the second reason, researches led since the 1960s by a team of historians and political scientists, united under the guidance of Erich Gruner, which have extensively studied this problem, but which have bred followers in neither political science nor history.

Focused on reviewing the evolution of the political competition at the federal level as well as at the level of the cantons, these studies have shown the extent to which elections and the evolution of parliamentary work contributed to the emergence of the political parties in Switzerland. There is a theory associated with these results which deserves reconsideration because it remained somewhat unnoticed: in the only analytical study of the Swiss political parties in existence to this day, written in 1969, Gruner put forth the idea that 'the parties are the offspring of people's rights' (Gruner 1969, 11).

He thus points out an idiosyncrasy of the political dispute in Switzerland, paced, of course, by elections, but also by popular ballots; he also, however, highlights a particularity of the process of parliamentarization in Switzerland at which we shall take another look: it is at the same time precocious, having begun in the 1830s, and uninterrupted. The legislative power's competence shall never be reconsidered by the executive, but restrained by the introduction of instruments of direct democracy limiting its development.

And finally, the third reason: the importance of the process of the universalization of the right to suffrage in Switzerland, and its influence on the forms of political modernization, can only be recorded adequately by filling in important gaps, and by correcting some of the persistent untruths related to the history of the right to vote. In this respect, Switzerland is actually a peculiarity in nineteenth-century Europe: having been in existence since 1830, the universality of the right to suffrage unfolded under extremely strict conditions that drastically limited its influence on the evolution of the morphology of the electoral body.

By considering the emergence of political parties as the result of one or more processes, we avoid a trap – that of the establishment of a single origin – because rarely do the different elements of what are considered constituent of a political party today (a statute, a doctrine, a programme, members, an etiquette, and so forth) appear simultaneously, thus enabling accurate pinpointing of a moment of formation. We shall consider 'political party' here as the form taken by what we shall call the 'political enterprise' at a given moment (Offerlé 1987). This Weberian-inspired term has been notably redefined by French political science, and enables us to pick out different moments in the process of refining the means of gaining political support: primarily individual, local and irregular at first, the political enterprises gradually became collective, national and long-lasting. Only then do they take the form of what can be called a 'political party'. This process is sustained on one hand by the universality of the right to vote, and on the other by parliamentarization.

Indeed, from the moment when the right to suffrage was extended to an ever-growing proportion of the male population, the individuals engaged in the political dispute and the pursuit for support had to deploy new efforts and refashion their resourcefulness in order to convince a greater number of voters. In other words, the extension of the right to suffrage tended to dismantle an elite system dominated by the notables, that is, those individuals who need not necessarily campaign in order to get elected and who 'owe their election to that which they are'; it permitted, on the other hand, the emergence of a system where individuals inject primarily collective resources into the ambit of explicitly political campaigns. It can be said of these new individuals that, contrary to the archetypal notable, they owe what they are to their election, and tend to live for, and make a living from, politics.

This specialization process is equally visible from within the walls of Parliament. What we call 'parliamentarization' refers primarily to a historical moment, common among a number of nineteenth-century European political regimes, when the legislative powers abandon their status of being just a chamber for registering the executive decisions, and become the main arena for political confrontations. However, it also refers to a process which will bear more immediate consequences on the constitution of partisan political enterprise: it is actually by and for parliamentary activities that somewhat loose groups gathered purposely around one opinion, gradually organize into more structured fractions, often identified by a label and/or a program.

It is therefore advisable, in the case of Switzerland, to take note of the process specifications to which we refer here in a very general manner. These eventually fashioned the shape that Swiss political partisan enterprises would take in the second half of the nineteenth century.

A Formative Moment: The Regeneration (1830–48)

In order to more accurately describe the particularities of the considered procedures and to evaluate their impact on the formation and the development of the political parties in Switzerland, it is necessary to revisit a particular moment: the Regeneration. It is a period that constitutes, seen from the point of view of the right to vote as well as from that of parliamentarization, a formative moment which left a permanent mark on Swiss political history.

The Right to Vote: A Conditional Universality

The history of the right to vote in nineteenth-century Switzerland is not a simple tale. The first difficulty, also common to most histories of suffrage in federal states, is that it was deployed at two different and partially autonomous levels. The respective prerogatives of the Confederation's cantons in the matter have been the object of several debates, and the adopted measures have revealed occasionally contradictory, not quite comprehensible and very heterogeneous legal and political situations between one canton and another.

In regard to this matter, it is incorrect to say that male universal suffrage was introduced in Switzerland in 1848 – the date of the creation of the federal state – or in 1920 – after the adoption of proportional representation at the federal level. First of all, its history started earlier, since the 1830s, and furthermore, it was far from being universal. The rupture did not come about so much at the moment of creation of the federal state and the adoption of the first constitution of modern Switzerland, but rather at the time of the so-called liberal revolutions which affected the cantons in the 1830s. Favoring these political and judicial changes of regime, the liberal elites that come to power suppressed the electoral census. This tendency would spread progressively, and in 1848, all of the Swiss cantons, with few exceptions, had abolished this measure. The suppression of the electoral census, however, was not quite yet the same as an introduction of universal male suffrage: this liberal bourgeoisie in command of the so-called regenerated cantons has no intention to concede the right to vote to just any male citizen having come of age. Two sets of clauses would in fact delimit the outlines for Swiss citizenship, establishing powerful restrictions: place of residence, and exclusion clauses.

Alongside age and gender, the place of residence constitutes one of the conditions for the right to vote, now called objectives.[1] It constitutes an answer to the main question of how voters can be identified in order to assure, for instance, that they indeed exist, and that they do not vote twice in two different constituencies. This question would fuel a number of debates, first at the cantonal level and then at the federal level, because it is an essential aspect in the definition and the positioning of the electoral body. Before 1848, the cantons naturally had the authority to settle the modalities of residence and their connection to the exercise of the right to vote. Without going into the details of the different cantonal legislations, let us just say that by general rules, all citizens of a canton can vote if they are born in the canton, or if they have acquired 'nationality'.[2]

Concerning the matter of residence, the federal Constitution of 12 September 1848 innovated on two important points: first of all, it restored a right to Swiss citizenship, briefly in effect under the République Helvétique (Arlettaz 2005). However, it was formulated in a different manner by restoring the priority of cantonal membership which had disappeared between 1798 and 1803, by stating that 'every citizen of a canton is a Swiss citizen'.[3] It furthermore stipulated that every Swiss citizen could establish residence at will anywhere within Swiss territory. These innovations took shape around a complex question: the right to vote of Confederates, in other words, of cantonal citizens who, by taking advantage of the recently acquired freedom of establishment, took up residence in a different canton from the one where they had citizen's rights. This new federal right was not only minimal, it was also ambiguous. It mobilized categories that would lead the Swiss political scene on a constant basis: the place of residence, the abode and the home – three different ways of defining the territorial ties of every citizen, and which appear equal in the nascent electoral law, although their definition and their weight in the framework of the right to vote remain, at this point, unclear and subject to many interpretations. These categories would collide with the habits in the cantons, which, of course, generally had legislation on the matter, but with different phrasings.

If the notion of the universal right to vote was challenged by the clauses dealing with the place of residence, the abode and the home of Swiss citizens in 1848, it

---

1 That is to say, those conditions which are independent of the actual behaviour of an individual: age, place of residence and nationality. Today, only age remains a necessary condition. One can vote without residing within the national territory (Swiss abroad); however, in certain cantons foreigners can vote and stand for office at the communal level.

2 The term refers to the right to citizenship in a canton.

3 Federal Constitution of the Swiss Confederation, 12 September 1848, Official Compilation of Federal Legislation (1848–50: 3–34).

Table 20.1   Comparative evolution of the electoral corps in several nations between 1850 and 1910

	CH 1[1]	CH 2[2]	France	UK	German Reich	Italy	Belgium	USA
1850	23.4	22.8	27.9	3.8			1.8	13.1
1860	23.9		26.5	4.5		1.9	2.1	14.9
1870	24.9	23.8	29.1	8.1	19.5	2.0	2.2	15.0
1880	24.1		26.9	8.6	20.1	2.2	2.3	18.2
1890	24.5		27.2	11.7	21.7	6.8	2.3	18.4
1900	25.6		28.2	11.9	21.9	6.9	21.4	18.3
1910	25.8	22.1	28.9	13.0	22.2	8.3	23.0	15.8

Notes:
[1] Calculation based on the Swiss population.
[2] Calculation based on the total population.

Sources: Gruner et al. (1978), vol. 1, 92; for Switzerland, these calculations were made by Gruner based on the official figures released by the federal authorities (statistics, communiqués of the official ballots results and so forth). For the other countries, Gruner used information taken from third-party literature (notably Sternberger et al. 1969; Zapf and Flora 1971).

actually became pointless with regard to the clauses of exception which were in effect at the time. In fact, Article 63 of the new federal Constitution stated that all Swiss citizens could vote, under the condition that they were not excluded by the legislation of the canton where they resided. The truth is, most cantons maintained the clauses issued by the Regeneration: taking benefits (or having benefited) from public assistance, being under guardianship or having been bankrupt or a having a penal record all constituted reasons for exception (or of exclusion) common in almost all Swiss cantons, and which partially remained until the twentieth century. After several fruitless attempts led by the Federal Council between 1875 and 1890 aimed at unifying in all the federal territory both the objective and subjective conditions of access to citizenship, as well as the different operational modalities of the electoral corps, no measures were taken before the 1970s and the adoption in 1976 of a federal law dealing with political rights. As a matter of fact, there are still several electoral corps in Switzerland, and there is a very strict separation of authority between the cantons and the Confederation. If nowadays the exclusion clauses are identical throughout, it is not as a result of a federal legislative intervention, but rather due to modifications of the constitutions and the cantonal laws relating to political rights.[4]

---

4   And also after the adoption of laws which carry an exclusion clause of some sort. For example, in the new federal law from 1920 dealing with bankruptcy, it is stipulated that bankruptcy can no longer be considered a justification for exclusion from the right to vote.

The process of universalizing the right to suffrage in Switzerland was evidently very slow, and not marked by a rupture in its foundation such as that of France in 1848, for instance. It is simply impossible to speak of one electoral body in nineteenth-century Switzerland. There have been quite a few, and if, by hypothesis, a relationship between this process and the surge of parties does exist, one must first of all define its relevance at the cantonal level. The development of a federal electoral body, strictly dependent on the constitutional and legislative clauses of the different cantons, is not impressive. In the cantons, situations undoubtedly vary much more. An overall idea of the federal electoral corps can be gained from Table 20.1, which illustrates constancy between 1850 and 1910.

A Parliament Under Control

It was also in the 1830s that the parliamentarization process affirmed itself in Switzerland. This enables us to recall, contrary to the incorrect belief, that seen from a chronological point of view, Switzerland is also a representative democracy. As in other countries, it was in the 1830s that direct election of representatives seated in a parliament with new and general powers became the rule at the cantonal level. In most cantons, the electoral bodies were called upon to elect their deputies for varied but regular periods whose rhythms would accelerate. The St Gallen electors, for instance, would do so every two years, the others being spaced out at three, four, five or six-yearly intervals.

In the ambit of a questionnaire on the structure of the groups engaged in political dispute, the multiplication of the electoral ballots, and above all their predictability, played an important role in the degree of specialization and the types of mobilization. Similarly, the internal organization of legislative work in the parliaments with their now extended powers was modified. What is known about the functioning modalities of the first legislative assemblies in Switzerland resembles the descriptions suggested by other parliaments.

The difference between many Swiss parliaments and other European parliaments at the time is the existence of new institutions which restrained the reach of the legislative power and give a particular colour to the parliamentarization process. As of the 1830s, in fact, a number of cantons introduced what was then called 'the sanction of the Constitution', which obliged the authorities to submit all modifications of the Constitution to a popular vote of approval. In fact, certain cantons introduced in the 1830s what was then called 'the veto', a complicated instrument which authorized a portion of the electoral body to demand a general citizens' vote on all Acts decreed by the cantonal authorities. Progressively, all Swiss cantons would adopt some sort of wide-ranging instrument: the obligatory or the optional referendum, the constitutional or the legislative initiative, the financial referendum, the veto referendum, the empowerment or the destitution of elected authorities, and so on.

If these institutions, which we group together under the generic name 'direct legislation', as opposed to 'direct democracy', a term which did not come into use in Switzerland before the beginning of the twentieth century, are drawn into the history of the establishment of the separation of powers, they are equally interesting with regard to the issue of the origin of political parties in Switzerland. From the moment they were put into use, together with elections, they set the pace for an agenda of political deadlines whereby political groups probably had to take a position, or in view of which they had to get organized. The richness of political life is evident if one considers, for example, the ballots organized in the canton of St Gallen between 1831 and 1841. If one discards the communal ballots (primary assemblies and elections of executive officers), and if one focuses on the cantonal votes (after the veto procedure) and the cantonal legislative elections (every two years), one arrives at a total of 30 ballots whose frequencies vary: six ballots in 1831 and in 1835, four between 1832 and 1833.[5] On the other hand, one can mention other cantons which ignored direct legislation institutions, apart from the sanction of the Constitution, and which experienced a more regular electoral rhythm. In that same period, Argovia had five ballots, and there were four in the canton of Vaud and in Fribourg.

In spite of this cantonal diversity, the Regeneration is evidently a formative moment with regard to the two processes herein: the democracy which gradually consolidated itself in Switzerland in the 1830s was formally full of institutions facilitating the direct participation of the electoral corps in a competitive game with the executive and legislative authorities, but with limited access. There were no considerable modifications in the electoral corps' morphology which would direct political groups toward modification of their ways of amassing political support. It is appropriate to take this matrix as a basis for the analysis of the progressive specialization of the political groups that tackled diverse fronts at different levels: cantonal elections, voting tied to a veto, an initiative or a referendum, and also, from 1848 onwards, to federal elections and voting. Stretching the argument, one can reasonably propose that despite all this diversity in the players, of the rules and of the issues which varied from one canton to the another, the different forms of division of the political work which emerged in the 1830s would endure roughly until the aftermath of the adoption of the Federal Constitution of 1874. Only then did the political groups gradually become structured collective enterprises, permanently and progressively visible on the whole of Swiss territory.

The Notables' Turn (1830–75)

In support of his theory on the origins of the political parties, Gruner mentions the movements which unfolded in the canton of St Gallen at the beginning of the 1830s. Against a background of controversy between rather Protestant Liberals and rather Catholic Conservatives, a new Constitution was adopted which notably foresaw the possibility, for a fraction of the electoral corps, of launching a procedure which could

---

5   Our own breakdown, deduced from third-party literature, from the press and from official documents of St Gallen.

lead to a vote by the whole citizenry on an Act adopted by Parliament. Known in political language as 'the veto', this procedure is very complex and requires intense mobilization on behalf of those who wish to see it abolished (Dietschi 1926).

This veto was the first instrument, besides the sanction of the Constitution, to garnish the panoply of popular rights in Switzerland. In the first years of the Regeneration, the Catholic Conservatives, a minority in the cantonal parliament, would make substantial use of this new right. Considering the constraints on its use, the numerous ballots that they managed to provoke decidedly constituted a feat as well as the manifestation of an efficient political organization. Between 1831 and 1835, the procedure was put in motion for 19 resumptions, and resulted in the rejection of the law in four cases.

Little is known about the course of these mobilizations. They seem to have relied upon the action of some few local notables who managed to meet and to unite the local population, mainly communal, in their support. In 1834, 25 of them, all catholic Conservatives and syndics, deputies, communal counselors, judges or ecclesiasts, called for a popular assembly which would soon be called the Oberegger Verein and which would result in the decision to launch a petition dealing with the question of religion. Following the refusal to entertain matters posted by the Council of State, this same Verein called for a new assembly on the last day of the year at Gossau, with the intention to set in motion a veto. It was on this occasion that statutes were adopted which stated in their first article that, in substance, the association's aim was to guarantee respect for, and the exercise of, the Roman Catholic religion, to preserve liberties, and to do everything possible to demand everything which was good and satisfactory for the canton.

Yet, if this episode can be used by historians to establish a founding date of the Conservative Party of St Gallen, it can hardly be identified as an important moment in the history of the political parties in Switzerland, and even less so as proof in support of Gruner's theory. He himself admits as much when he makes a note that these mobilizations did not lead to the establishment of a long-lasting organization. The Oberegger Verein itself would disappear and leave room for other similar attempts which would emerge from time to time (1847, 1857, 1875) before a long-lasting organization of the Catholic Conservatives of St Gallen saw the light of day in 1896, at a time when the impulse came essentially from the federal level. This slightly chaotic history of the Catholic political organization of St Gallen is no exception. The Liberals, their opponents in the canton, have a similar story of names, tags and founding assemblies, between 1857 and the end of the nineteenth century (Ehinger 1970).

Likewise, when Gruner mentions this example in St Gallen, he refines the importance of direct democracy in the emergence of the party, while recalling the parliamentary origin of the movements. Against a somewhat romantic image, which would present these movements as the result of political work led by a politically responsible people, conscious of their rights, one must recall that although formally led from outside of the walls of the Great Council, they were actually closely linked to the parliamentary dispute. Furthermore, they only barely survived the deadlines of the issues for which they were set up. These two characteristics are constituent of most of these mobilizations, electoral or by referendum, occurring in Switzerland during this period.

Fundamentally, nothing changed after 1848. Considering the weight of the cantonal regulations for the political game, by election or by referendum, the creation of the federal state did not contribute to the modification of the *modus operandi*. It is always this model of a more or less structured group uniting some notables, often supported by an organ of the press, which prevails. The term *Verein* is used frequently, and refers to groups capable of greater mobilizations. Significantly, the Radicals concerned with the revision of the Federal Pact in 1847 reunited under the Volksverein, a generic name found among many radicals at the cantonal level and which we will once again see in 1873, when, following the rejection of the first attempt to review the Federal Constitution, the Radicals launched the review process once again. This model of *Verein* was also taken up by the Catholics, in the pattern of the Piusverein created in 1857 and which, for a long time, would be the minimal organizational basis of the Swiss Catholic Conservatives before the great turmoil of the years 1874–1912 (we will come back to this later). If they could occasionally be used as a support base for potentially massive mobilizations for referendums or protests, they only rarely displayed themselves as such when presenting candidates on electoral lists, an approach which constitutes, for Gruner again, a key moment in the emergence of 'political parties'. To these elements which attest to the absence of political parties, one can add several conclusions unveiled by the conceptual history. The sparse literature dealing with the term 'party' in nineteenth-century Switzerland generally confirms the depicted evolution of other European and Western political scenarios. Long a synonym of 'faction', and therefore a catalyst for division in a society conceived in terms of agreement and unity, it gradually set forth different trains of thought which were tolerated as long as they manifested themselves predictably basis and within the ambit of ballots aimed at a return to harmony.

As proven by this excerpt from a report of the Federal Council of 1854, the associations (*Vereine*), although of uncertain juridical status (His 1939, vol. 1, 559),[6] were considered perfectly legitimate players in political life: 'these three things (the parties, the associations and the press) are closely tied, the associations and the press being the means used by the parties to influence and to sway public opinion in their favour in the elections and in other votes by popular ballot'.[7] Notice here that although the term 'party' is used, it is not yet in the sense of a lasting structured organization, but rather according to the classical liberal understanding of the term, which is the general opinion by a group of individuals during times of a dispute or a ballot.

---

6   Legally, in nineteenth-century Switzerland, the right to unite and the right to assemble were more or less one and the same thing (His 1938).

7   Report and notice from the Swiss Federal Council to the United Federal Assembly concerning the decree from Berne in relation to the Grütli Association', *Feuille Fédérale*, 1854, 1 491.

Only after the second half of the nineteenth century did the party refer to a more organized form and gradually acquire the status of legitimate player in parliamentary life, at first political and then obtaining a constitutional sanction in most of the Western countries at the end of the Second World War.[8]

The political dispute between 1830 and 1875, electoral or by referendum, at the cantonal and the federal level, did not pit political parties against one another, but rather more or less structured political groups of very limited general scope that rarely survived the term for which they were elected, but which were, however, sometimes capable of rallying considerable mass support. To speak of 'political parties' after the example of the *Vetobewegungen* in the canton of St Gallen, or even more broadly, to consider direct democracy as a factor for the emergence of political parties in Switzerland, is certainly too premature. Not only did these groups lack structure and durability, but furthermore, their actions often resulted from the initiative of individuals who were members of Parliament themselves. These mobilizations often appeared as just a continuation of parliamentary disputes led on different grounds and by other means. Only as of 1875 did the Swiss political parties gradually emerge, from the point of view of real history as well as from that of conceptual history.

The Transformation of Political Enterprises (1875–1912)

'Considering the current overall political situation, one cannot but notice that it is peculiar: the customary political groups change everywhere and new propositions seek to supplant the old discourse' (quoted in Widmer 1992, 248). This citation, taken from the conservative *Urner Zeitung* in 1878, intervened in a new political context. For nearly three years, an aftermath of disputes took place dealing with the implementation of the new federal Constitution adopted in 1874, in an ambiance marked by the *Kulturkampf*. Mainly, they opposed the Federal Council and Parliament, leaning toward a centralizing radicalism, victor of both the *Sonderbund* of 1848 and of the 1872–74 revision, over a rather conservative federalist Catholic minority. This minority discovered, with a certain glee, the profits it could reap from the optional referendum, a new popular prerogative introduced some years before. On several occasions, the laws adopted by the councils were indeed rejected by a majority of the electorate mobilized for different ballots. This rise to power of a catholic Conservative minority would be buttressed by the electoral defeat suffered by the Radicals at the federal elections in the autumn of 1878. For the first time since 1848, in fact, they lost seats to the Catholic Conservatives and they ran the risk of becoming a minority.

---

8   In Switzerland, it was only in the 1999 Constitution that the 'political parties' made their appearance at the constitutional level. For the first time since 1848 and the creation of the modern federal state, they were called upon and their role 'in the formation of the popular opinion and will' was underlined.

If the editorialist rightfully evokes the changes in discourse and stance, he neglects to mention that these were also the methods for doing things and the structural means of the political groups that began a process of transformation, through both Parliament and referendums. With regard to the preceding period, important changes intervened: the referendum was introduced at the federal level, opening a new battlegrounds no longer limited to cantonal borders; the political struggle tended to structure itself through organizations that survived electoral and referendum processes, and whose creation seemed to accompany an ever-increasing competitive logic between the different groups engaged in the struggle; the political tickets diversified and settled themselves, whereby interactions seemed increasingly inter-dependent, one's blows being reactions to the blows from others. We will try below to illustrate this by using two examples. The first grants certain strength to Gruner's theory on the emergence of political parties, even if it only concerns a marginal group. The second has to do with the transformations that affected the Catholic Conservative movement, which were much more a result of the existence and the use of the new popular rights introduced at the federal level between 1874 and 1891 than of direct parliamentary or electoral disputes.

From Referendum to Electoral Struggle: The Eidgenössischer Verein Case

During the whole period considered (1875–1912), the creation of this *Verein* constituted, without a doubt, an example confirming Gruner's hypothesis on the importance of direct democracy in the origin of political parties. The history of this small group is primarily that of a society, the Gesellschaft vom alten Zürich, which evoked the ancient regime and Protestant conservatism. It brought together notables from Zurich, Basle, Bern and Neuchatel, with no former experience or federal political mandates, who decide to enter the political arena in the name of federalism and to defend of the interests of the commune.

The occasion for this first involvement was the adoption by the councils in December 1874 of the law on the right to vote, and the law on civil status and marriage.

Flagships of the Radicals' centralizing and secular policy, they struck at the heart of the representations and interests defended by Conservatives and federalists, Protestants and Catholics alike. An irony in the history of Swiss political parties, this law on the right to vote intended to suppress the different established cantonal regimes by simultaneously unifying the exclusion modalities and the residency issues by granting the right to vote, under certain conditions, to those in the so-called 'sojourn', a category until then largely excluded from the exercise of political rights. This law of 24 December 1874 had the power to universalize the right to suffrage, and would probably have considerably modified the rules of the political game, bestowing it with a status equivalent to the Cormenin Decree that established universal right to suffrage in France in March 1848.

Soon supported by the Catholic Conservatives, who also started a movement from their side, this group, arising from the Gesellschaft vom alten Zürich, began a campaign to collect signatures. Its organization did not seem to differ from the practices in effect at the cantonal level. A few individuals rallied acquaintances, mostly by means of letters, published appeals in the media and could largely count on the logistical support offered by a newspaper, the *Allgemeine Schweizer Zeitung*, one of whose editors, Andreas Heusler, was a prominent member of this small circle of Conservative notables. The important difference, however, was the national dimension that was now at the heart of the referendum campaigns. Considering the number of signatures required (30,000) and the new prerogatives allocated to the Confederation, the shift to the federal level was a necessary one. This is what Heusler expressed in a letter to his friend Georg von Wyss on 15 February 1875, two weeks after the official publication of the law on marriages announcing the beginning of the signature-collection period:

> the situation is such that we must fight on the only federal terrain in hopes to recover a tolerable situation for our canton. What we can obtain at the federal level exerts an effect on the cantons which is exactly opposite to that before the new Constitution. I must say that, if there is not much we can do for the moment in our canton, we must then unite and try to obtain results in a wider battlefield. We will also write to Appenzell, Schaffhausen and the Graubünden in order to collect signatures everywhere possible, and launch an appeal. (Rinderknecht 1949, 17)

We shall not enter the details of the campaign, whose outcome was the popular ballot and the rejection of the law on the right to vote on 23 May 1875, due primarily to the signatures collected by the Catholic Conservatives. Let us also note that it was in the midst of this mobilization, as success was drawing near, that this group united around Heusler decided to create the Eidgenössischer Verein, aimed at 'reuniting in a solid way the comrades of opinion spread around Switzerland'. Who were these comrades of opinion? After several hesitations, they decided to call for action and reunite the Conservatives of reformed Switzerland, which meant the exclusion of the Catholics, who were already 'organized'. This first sign of stabilization of a political identity in relation to the existing ones was joined by the aspiration of the *Verein* to present candidates at future federal elections and to undertake all the necessary means to prepare. A programme would even be adopted in 1879, but for several reasons, would never be followed by any autonomous participation in federal elections. The *Verein* would content itself with its participation in a few signature-collection campaigns launched by others during later mobilizations.

Statutes, a program, the will to stand for elections (federal), a label established in relation to the existing ones and a permanent organization conscious of the need to be present in several cantons – the history of this group, rallied together at the referendum level prior to venturing out on the electoral grounds proper, is exemplary support for Gruner's hypothesis. Its story is short-lived, the *Verein* formally disappearing in 1913, but it left its brand in a process that also had to do with other political families, among them the Catholic movement.

The Repeated Resurrections of the Catholic Movement

Since 1848, the Catholic Conservatives have always been sceptical about the development of a federal state. Basing themselves on their cantonal fiefdoms (Central Switzerland, Fribourg and Valais in particular), they only took part in federal political life reluctantly, especially through the parliamentary faction headed between 1848 and 1878 by the Catholic Conservatives' strongman, Philipp Anton von Segesser. The Catholic associative world was less active than the Radicals' and rested on two pillars: the Studentenverein, founded in 1841, and the Piusverein, founded in 1856.

For the Catholics, as for the Radicals and the Liberals for that matter, the essence of the resources mobilized toward the political struggle were at that time allocated at the cantonal level. It was only at the time of the litigation for constitutional revision, on the basis of *Kulturkampf*, and later at the time of the post-1874 referendum mobilizations that the issue of a more structured and centralized organization arose at the core of the Catholic movement. Even if the Catholics' unity was sustained in the face of the common enemy, secular and confining radicalism, internal divergences emerged as soon as the new Constitution was adopted. Taking advantage of the new instrument, the referendum, the Catholic Conservatives fought every inch against the application laws issued by the new Constitution, negotiating at a federal level which they had so far resisted to enter, and whereupon they in fact accepted the new rules of operation.

During the 1872–74 struggles concerning the constitutional revision, the Conservative Catholics attempted to block the Radicals on their own field and with their own methods: the foundation of a short-lived Conservative Association in 1874 was the answer to the reactivation of the Radicals' Volksverein of 1873, an alteration of the one created in 1847, and which contributed to the success of the Federal Pact's revision. This Conservative Association would not survive the adoption of the new Constitution.

Defeated, in a minority at both federal councils, it was on the new grounds of referendums that the Catholics initially organized themselves. They thus greatly contributed to the rejection of the law on the right to vote, which was contested by the referendum mentioned above. A period of relative euphoria followed, during which the Catholics, through the joint mobilization of their parliamentary faction and public authorities of the Catholic cantons and municipalities, notably the sections of the Piusverein, managed to petition for referendums, thus blocking several laws adopted by the federal councils. The unity of this movement, which seemed to prolong the *Kulturkampf* by fighting inch by inch against the power of the Radicals, would progressively crack. Not all Catholics agreed to pursue the struggle against centralization. Internal struggles and dissent will be more apparent as the issue of a new revision of the Constitution was raised through an initiative originated by the Radicals.[9]

---

9   It was on the initial impulse of a Radical maverick, Wilhelm Joos, that an initiative was submitted. The purpose of this atypical member of Parliament close to the labour

Three trends emerged among the Catholics who disagreed with this project (Altermatt 1972): a Conservative and federalist trend represented mostly by the cantons of central Switzerland and at the core of the parliamentary faction in Bern, which tended to reject all centralization on principle and continued to be very reticent about the new Constitution, but remained receptive to the reformed Conservatives; a more ultramontane trend which also defended federalist positions while rejecting any collaboration with the Protestants (Fribourg and Valais), and finally a younger trend, originating mostly from the Studentenverein and which united mainly the Catholics from the mixed cantons and from the diaspora and which was more tolerant toward the federal state and to some form of centralization.

Until 1912, these tendencies would in turn try to establish themselves as the legitimate voice of a Catholic Conservative movement whose identity and reference group became more and more problematic. The moments of foundation would succeed each other according to the actions and mobilizations of the different tendencies. In 1881, it was the younger and more modern trend, relatively open to centralization, that created a Conservative Union which would not resist for more than a year the reluctance from the parliamentary faction and from the representatives of Fribourg who were very influential in the movement. In 1894, this time the ultramontane and ultra-federalist trend raised a Swiss Catholic People's Party. At last, it was in 1912 that the struggle over the movement's identity (Primarily Catholic? Conservative? Both?) was settled by the victory of those who called themselves Conservative above all, and who aspired to an opening toward the other faiths by founding the Swiss Conservative People's Party.

Albeit not a birthday, 1912 indisputably marks a stage in the specialization process. Since then, indeed, the political organization of the Catholics (because, in spite of its official name, the party would for a long time remain a party run for and by Catholics) would be continuous, collective and present in an extensive part of the national territory. At first sight, it was indeed the referendum and its usage that forced the Catholics to organize. But it was a double-edged instrument: in a way, it admittedly allowed following the *Kulturkampf* initially through other means, but it also signified the Catholics' tacit acceptance of the rules of a political game now widespread at the federal level. As it happens, if there was a struggle within the Catholic movement between the several trends mentioned, it was because of the discord over the recognition of what appeared to be a new political arena. Before 1875, the Catholics conducted politics backwards, basing themselves in their cantonal strongholds and refusing to fully play the democratic game which they considered to be a submission to the centralizing and secular radical state. The creation of the Swiss Conservative People's Party in 1912 marks without a doubt

---

movement was to ask for a federal monopoly on the issuing of banknotes. Since there was no initiative process allowing a call for partial revision of the Constitution (it would be introduced in 1891), he was forced to collect signatures to demand a total revision. Without going into the details, this initiative would also divide the Radical movement, from which a labour- and socialist-oriented wing would gradually emerge.

the 'coming out from the ghetto' (Altermatt) and the recognition of a federal state in whose operation the Catholics now actively took part.

The successful creation of this party definitely testifies to the restructuring of labour division within the Catholic community. While they resisted participating in federal political life after 1848, at the same time the Catholics signaled to their opponents that they did not intend to renounce their perception of the world, where religion prevailed over politics. During the creation of the Piusverein in 1856, the first article of the new association's status indeed specified: 'Piusverein's policy consists: 1. not to engage in politics, but to claim the liberty for each and every one, as well as for the Church, to do good and to banish evil ...' (Jenny 1974, 21). The internal struggles of the late nineteenth century also certainly had something to do with the relevancy of this distinction. In any case, in 1905 the Catholics managed to reorganize and federate the associative and religious milieu under a Swiss Catholic People's Union whose main purpose still remained, like the Piusverein's, to 'maintain and encourage faith and Catholic life, vigorously protect the Church's rights and freedom and take a stance in public life according to its religious conviction', leaving aside 'day-to-day' and 'party' politics (Gernet 1988, 6). In other words, perhaps one of the conditions for the success of the party in 1912 was to have previously established this distinction between the 'political' and the 'associative', or even between the 'political' and the 'religious'. The creation of the Swiss Conservative People's Party marks without a doubt the acknowledgement by the Catholic movement of a place for activities endowed with rules of its own, distinct from the other spheres of social activities.

Conclusion

The specialization process that we have identified here from the internal history of the Catholic movement also affected the other political groups and allows us to return to the hypotheses proposed for the origins of the Swiss political parties.

The Radical family went through difficult times after 1875. The Radical Party set itself up formally in 1894 on the ashes of a dismantled Volksverein, divided between trends, some of which would crystallize in partisan-like organizations (the Grütli, which for the first time appointed candidates for the National Council elections in 1881; the Socialist Party in 1888; the Social Political Group in 1896, for example). If there also lies an internal history here to retrace, with its own actors and stakes partially different from those of the Catholic movement, a common dynamic presides over the creation of these partisan enterprises, and it becomes difficult to identify whether the determining factors were actions taken at the parliamentary level, the electoral level (classic hypothesis defended by Scarrow) or rather in the field of referendums (Gruner's hypothesis).

All of these actions ultimately depended on the existence of rules in the political game, which were used in different ways and worked as a resource as much as a constraint in for political parties' development. However, this process was not merely the result of playing by the rules, it was also the outcome of the competition process itself, which took place not only within the political groups, but between them as well.

Everything happened, in fact, as if the actions of one party were reactions to the actions of another. In 1882, for example, the Radicals reorganized themselves and adopted a programme for the first time since the 1878 debacle, equipped with a set of rules for procedures for the parliamentary faction. The same year, the Catholics also adopted regulations and a programme which transformed the group, until then somewhat informal, into an organized parliamentary faction. Likewise, it was in 1894 that the Radical Democratic Party was created, the same year as the Catholic Conservative Party and two years before the formal creation of the Social Political Group. In other words, many examples could certainly be mentioned, and unless these chronological coincidences are haphazard, they demonstrate that intra- and inter-partisan struggle gradually provoked the foundation of an arena of competing relations, within which on one hand positions became clearer (conservatism, radicalism, socialism, political Catholicism, and so on), and on the other hand it became necessary to organize on a long-term basis.

It is therefore hopeless to try to identify a parliamentary origin for the Swiss political parties, or one based on the referendum process. What seems to be determinant is the emergence of new rules of a political game now extended to the federal level. In their own rhythm, depending on their expectations and interests, the political groups intervened within this new arena, and the actions taken contributed progressively to their structure, shaping them into political ventures that tended to become permanent, organized to be long-lasting and to intervene at the electoral and referendum levels and at both the federal and the cantonal level. This redefinition of the rules contributed to multiply the terms and to gradually structure a proper 'political' arena, distinct from the other spheres of social activities.

References

Altermatt, U. (1972), *Der Weg der Schweizer Katholiken ins Ghetto* (Zurich: Benziger).

Arlettaz, S. (2005), *Citoyens et étrangers sous la République Helvétique, 1798–1803* (Geneva: Georg).

David, T. et al. (eds) (2007), 'Plaidoyer pour un renouveau de l'histoire des partis politiques en Suisse', *Traverse* 1 (Zurich: Chronos).

Dietschi, U. (1926), *Das Volksveto in der Schweiz. Ein Beitrag zur Geschichte der Volksgesetzgebung* (Olten: Dietschi & Cie).

Ehinger, P.H. (1970), 'Die Anfänge des liberalen Parteiwesens im Kanton St Gallen. Ein Beitrag zur Geschichte und Soziologie des organisierten Liberalismus in seinem Frühstadium (bis 1870)', doctoral dissertation, University of Zurich.

Gernet, H. (1988), *Der Schweizerische Katholische Volksverein im Spannungsfeld von katholischer und politischer Aktion 1930–1960* (Freiburg: Universitätsverlag).

Gruner, E (1969), *Die Parteien in der Schweiz* (Bern: Francke).

—— et al. (eds) (1978), *Les élections au Conseil National Suisse: 1848–1918* (Bern: Francke).

His, E. (1938), *Geschichte des neuern schweizerischen Staatsrechts*, vol. 3, 1848–1918 (Basle: Helbling and Lichtenhahn).

Jenny, J. (1974), *Le Piusverein à Fribourg: une association politico-religieuse 1857–1899* (Fribourg: Editions Universitaires).

Katz, R. and Crotty, W. (eds) (2006), *Handbook of Party Politics* (London: Sage).

Offerlé, M. (1987), *Les partis politiques* (Paris: Presses Universitaires de France).

Rinderknecht, P. (1949), *Der 'Eidgenössiche Verein' 1875–1913. Die Geschichte der protestantisch-konservativen Parteibildung im Bundesstaat* (Affoltern am Albis: J. Weiss).

Scarrow, S. (2006), 'The Nineteenth Century Origins of Modern Political Parties: The Unwanted Emergence of Party-based Politics', in Katz and Crotty (eds), *Handbook of Party Politics* (London: Sage).

Sternberger, D., Vogel, B. and Nohlen, D. (eds) (1969), *Die Wahl der Parlamente* (Berlin: de Gruyter).

von Beyme, K. (1978), 'Partei', in Brunner, O., Conze, W. and Koselleck, R. (eds), *Geschichtliche Grundbegriffe*, vol. 4 (Stuttgart: Klett-Cotta).

Widmer, T. (1992), *Die Schweiz in der Wachstumskrise der 1880er Jahre* (Zurich: Chronos).

Zapf, W. and Flora, P. (eds) (1971), 'Zeitreihen als Indikatoren der Modernisierung: einige Probleme der Datensammlung und Datenanalyse', *Politisches Vierteljahresschrift* 6, 29–70.

Further Reading

Balmelli T. (2001), *Le financement des partis politiques et des campagnes électorales. Entre exigences démocratiques et corruption* (Fribourg: Editions universitaires).

Borchert, J. and Zeiss, J. (eds) (2003), *The Political Class in Advanced Democracies* (Oxford: Oxford University Press).

Geser H. et al. (eds) (1994), *Die Schweizer Lokalparteien* (Zurich: Seismo).

Gruner, E. (1957), Zur Sozial- und Parteigeschichte des 19. und 20. Jahrhunderts', *Revue Suisse d'Histoire* 7, 362–78.

—— (1966), *Die Schweizerische Bundesversammlung 1848–1920* (Bern: Francke).

—— et al. (eds) (1978), *Les élections au Conseil National Suisse: 1848–1918* (Bern: Francke).

Hasler, T. (1998), *'Dienen, nicht verdienen, soll das oberste Gebot des Politikers sein'. Wie der Staat seine Bundesräte, Nationalräte und Chefbeamten besoldet* (Zurich: Ruegger).

Jost, H.-U. (1986), 'Critique historique du parti politique', *Annuaire suisse de science politique* 36: 317–32.

Klöti, U. (ed.) (2007), *Handbook of Swiss Politics*, 2nd edn (Zurich: NZZ Verlag).

Ladner, A. (ed.) (2001), *Die Schweizer Parteien. Von Mitgliederparteien zu professionalisierten Wählerorganisationen?* (Zurich: Seismo).

—— (2004), *Stabilität und Wandel von Parteien und Parteiensystemen. Ein vergleichende Analyse von Konfliktlinien, Parteien und Parteiensystemen in den Schweizer Kantonen* (Wiesbaden: VS Verlag).

—— (2007), 'Political Parties', in Klöti (ed.), *Handbook of Swiss Politics*, 2nd edn (Zurich: NZZ Verlag).

Vatter, A. (2002), *Kantonale Demokratien im Vergleich. Entstehungsgründe, Interaktionen und Wirkungen politischer Institutionen in den Schweizer Kantonen* (Opladen: Leske & Budrich).

Wiesli, R. (2003), 'Switzerland. The Militia Myth and Incomplete Professionalization' in Borchert and Zeiss (eds), *The Political Class in Advanced Democracies* (Oxford: Oxford University Press).

Glossary of Terms and Peculiarities of Swiss Political Vocabulary

Conseil Fédéral	Federal Council (Swiss executive authorities).
Conseil National	National Council (Swiss legislative authorities).
Initiative	Request submitted by a minimum of 100,000 voters to the Federal Assembly to undertake a complete revision of the Federal Constitution or to adopt, repeal or amend any provision of the Constitution or of any other federal Act (<www.admin.ch>).
Referendum	Popular vote by means of which voters can accept or reject new or amended constitutional provisions, federal Acts and certain other decrees of the Federal Assembly (federal decrees) (<www.admin.ch>).
Sonderbund	League formed on 11 December 1845 by the seven Catholic Swiss cantons (Luzern, Uri, Schwyz, Unterwalden, Zug, Fribourg and Valais) to oppose anti-Catholic measures by Protestant Liberal cantons. The term *Sonderbund* also refers to the civil war that resulted from this conflict (<www.concise.britannica.com/ebc/article-9360862/civil-defense>).

The Breakthrough of Universal
Suffrage in Finland, 1905–1906

Jussi Kurunmäki

Introduction

This chapter addresses the question of the relationship between universal suffrage and democracy by analyzing a case that does not fit into a general trajectory of parliamentary democratization. Why and how did Finland, a country that was the last in Europe to have an estate-based representation and was socio-economically and politically underdeveloped, introduce universal and equal suffrage in parliamentary elections as early as 1906, making it the first country in Europe to do so? Finland's four-estate representation was replaced by a unicameral parliament, which was also an exceptionally radical solution at the time. Was there something special about Finland, a Grand Duchy within the Russian Empire, or about Finnish universal suffrage? Did parliamentary reform deal with democracy or not?

Contemporary theories of representation as well as democracy and democratization are of little help in understanding the emergence of universal suffrage in general (see Pateman 1994, 333, 343), and particularly in regard to Finland. The implementation of universal suffrage has often been taken as a sign of the breakthrough of democracy. Accordingly, a closer analysis of the relationship between universal suffrage and democracy has seemed more or less futile. This view is often accompanied by a linear understanding of democratization, according to which the progress of democratization follows more or less automatically the ideological and/or socio-economic development of society. In addition, theories of democracy and representation have a tendency to discuss their problems in today's context, rather than that of the past, thereby rendering them largely ahistorical.

However, when asking questions about democracy, we should not claim any agreement regarding the meaning of the concept, although it is often treated as one without a history (see, for example, Ankersmit 2002, 92; Markoff 1999, 661). For most of its career, the concept of democracy was seen in negative terms. It was only toward the end of the eighteenth century, when it became associated with the concept of representation, that it began to be seen in a more positive light (see, for example, Dunn 2005, 20; Urbinati 2006, 4–5). This change was far from self-evident or peaceful. As Albert O. Hirschman has put it: 'inasmuch as the extension of the franchise in Western Europe in the course of the nineteenth century was achieved in a fairly gradual and peaceful manner, the temptation is to think that opposition to that process was not particularly strenuous. Nothing can be farther from the truth' (Hirschman 1991, 20; see also Keyssar 2000, xvii–xx).

Explanations of the Finnish reform emphasize the exceptional and sudden nature of the political situation. According to common explanations, the revolutionary unrest in Russia forced the imperial government to loosen its grip on Finland. This opened up an opportunity for a thorough reform in the country. As the argument goes, the Finns exploited the situation when the Russian Great Strike was followed by a Great Strike in Finland at the end of October 1905. Within a couple of days, an agenda for reform was set and immediately accepted by the Russian Emperor. Nicholas II signed the November Manifesto on 4 November 1905. According to the manifesto, a reform of Parliament based on universal and equal suffrage should be prepared. An extraordinary session of the Diet was called to implement the parliamentary reform. The process developed quickly. Eight-and-a-half months later, on 20 July 1906, Nicholas II signed the new Parliamentary Act of Finland (see Mylly 2006; Seitkari 1958; Teljo 1949).

Universal suffrage emerged in Finland after a short campaign. This reform is an example of a sudden parliamentary democratization, in contrast to countries like the United Kingdom and Sweden, where there had been a long history of gradual reforms (see Rokkan 1999, 233–34, 251). The principle of universal suffrage was already decided upon before the reform bill was discussed in the Diet and in the Senate (the Finnish Government). As a consequence, the reform process was characterized more by different rhetorical strategies of legitimization than arguments in favour of universal and equal suffrage. The reform had to be explained, rather than demanded. Despite this, it is necessary to pay attention to the contexts in which demands for universal and equal suffrage were made. We must begin, therefore, with the topic of revolution.

On Revolution and National Assembly

The Finnish parliamentary reform took place in the shadow of the revolutionary events in Russia, and arguments concerning revolution were voiced also in Finland. There was a short period during the one-week-long Great Strike when both the political and the coercive apparatus were more or less paralyzed (Alapuro 1988, 114–15). Popular pressure for change was considerable during the days of the strike. Compared to the Baltic provinces and other parts of the Russian empire, however, Finland remained relatively calm in 1905 (Raun 1984), though the rhetoric of revolution played a considerable role during and shortly after the days of the strike. Revolution as a domestic topic was discussed in Finland for the first time when the principle of universal suffrage was accepted.

There was an animosity between political parties concerning the political goals of the strike, although many reports immediately after the strike testified to a patriotic enthusiasm in the country. The most controversial issue was the Social Democrats' demand for a national assembly that would have been authorized by a provisional government. The constitutionalists (the Young Finns and the Swedish Party) tried to reach an agreement with the Russians on the recovery of the autonomous status of the country, but they soon realized that a radical solution to the question of the franchise was needed. The Old Finns tried to get hold of the political situation by introducing the idea of 'a lawful national assembly' authorized by the Senate. The party that had had a leading position in the political life of the country referred to the need of 'the poor in the country', 'the workers' and 'the public opinion among the people' in its rhetoric (see, for example, *Uusi Suometar*, 7 November 1905; see also Roos 1906, 305, 396). In the Constitutionalists' view, the Old Finns flirted with the social democrats and the demonstrating masses (*Helsingin Sanomat*, 29 November 1905; see also Teljo 1949, 52–4). After the strike, the demand for a national assembly was associated with the concept of revolution in many disappointed non-socialists' comments (Alapuro 2003, 534–36).

The idea of a national assembly had been presented six months earlier, after the Diet had turned down the previous reform bill (Kujala 1989, 119–20). Ultimately, the inspiration came from the French Revolution. One socialist intellectual, N.R. af Ursin, drew a strong parallel between the Finnish situation and the Third Estate in France in the wake of the French Revolution. His point was that the Third Estate had not acted in accordance with the prevailing laws when it had declared itself the national assembly. However, this unconstitutional act had received the total support of 'the real people'. The same, therefore, should have been possible in Finland. According to af Ursin, a law became 'a paper law' when it did not meet the people's idea of justice (*Kansan lehti*, 14 November 1905). The socialists viewed the concept of a national assembly as a counter-concept (see Koselleck 1972) to privileged representation, and in this sense it was used in the Sieyèsian manner (Sieyès 1789 [1963]). The Old Finns denied any associations with the French Revolution. For them, 'a legal national assembly' would not 'be anything else than the unicameral Eduskunta that was wanted somewhat unanimously by our people' (*Uusi Suometar*, 14 December 1905).

In many respects, the Social Democrats described the November Manifesto as a kind of fraud, where bourgeois leaders had succeeded in getting the emperor to believe that the content of the manifesto accorded with the will of the people, whereas it was really meant to benefit the bourgeoisie (*Kansan lehti*, 9 and 18 November 1905). Despite such forceful statements, the Social Democrats did not really want a revolution in 1905. The majority within the party were national-minded rather than revolutionary-minded. They viewed the general strike and the political demands in favour of universal suffrage as a national defense against Russian rule. In addition, those who considered themselves revolutionaries held a doctrinaire view of revolution, which ruled out the possibility for a revolution in an underdeveloped periphery like Finland (see Kautsky 1902 [1906], 5–6). In accordance with the Kautskyan doctrine, *Sosialistinen Aikakauslehti* ('Socialist Journal') stated that a Great Strike and revolution would take place when the time was right. However, universal suffrage was considered a political goal that deserved all possible effort. The periodical explained that it had been right to call for a national assembly, but the timing had been wrong. Despite this, it was possible to think of suffrage reform as 'our internal revolution' (*Sosialistinen Aikakauslehti*, 1906, 2, 145, 283).

A national assembly and universal suffrage were clearly closely linked political goals, yet they were considered separate issues. It was possible to reject plans for a national assembly while simultaneously arguing in favour of universal suffrage, but not vice versa. To be sure, universal suffrage was the main topic and a point of departure in mass demonstrations and party meetings, as well as in negotiations between different delegations during the strike. It soon became clear to everyone during the strike that the strike was not only about the recovery of the constitutional rights of the country. In fact, all political parties wanted to take the credit for having succeeded in including universal suffrage in the November Manifesto (see, for example, *Helsingin Sanomat*, 14 November 1905; *Uusi Suometar*, 8 November 1905). During the days of the strike, universal suffrage was a topic that was, in a peculiar way, both discussed and 'silent'. It was silent in the sense that, to many on the non-socialist side, it was an unexpected and also an uncomfortable topic. It was also silent in the sense that it was negotiated behind closed doors. The result, the November Manifesto, was suddenly there before it could be discussed. However, the principle of universal suffrage was also widely accepted before the strike had started. Consequently, the national assembly was a more controversial issue than voting rights during and immediately after the Great Strike.

Continuity and Contingency: Women's Suffrage

A recent study has emphasized continuity in the reform process (Mylly 2006, 10–13). A reform of the four-estate system had been discussed since the 1880s. The main goals had been an abolition of the gradual vote in the Burgher Estate and a reform of the Peasant Estate. The idea of an individual voter and equal vote were commonly held at the turn of the century. Some arguments in favour of a bicameral legislature had been presented as well. However, any substantial reform had turned out to be impossible due to the language conditions in the estates, where the Nobility and the Burghers had a Swedish-language majority, while the Clergy and the Peasants had a Finnish majority within their respective estates. Reform was further hampered by Russia's autocratic and bureaucratic rule of Finland.

Women's right to vote arrived on the political agenda in the 1890s, although the topic was already being discussed in 1869, when J.S. Mill's *The Subjection of Women* was reviewed in a newspaper (Pohjantammi 2003, 386). Early calls for female suffrage argued that women should have the same voting rights as men. This was also the case in the first petition for women's right to vote in 1897, presented in the Burger Estate. However, the petition did not survive in the Committee of Law, in which the majority regarded women as unsuitable for political life (Sulkunen 2007, 36-8; Mylly 2006, 73–5; Koskinen 1997, 29–30). As a matter of fact, introducing women's right to vote to the level of qualified male voters did not succeed anywhere in Europe. Such a demand was always open to criticism from both the socialists' and the conservatives' point of view (Bock 2002, 148).

The women's suffrage movement was radicalized in the early 1900s. Some Social Democrat women saw the franchise question in terms of class conflict rather than a gender issue. In general, however, women's struggle for the vote was considered a shared issue with that of unenfranchised men. Women's struggle for the vote should be seen as a part of the popular mobilization in which the difference between men and women was not as significant as it was, for example, in the United Kingdom and the United States or in Germany (see Sulkunen 2007, 38–41, 79–81; Alapuro 2006, 53; Sulkunen 1989, 185–89; Evans 1980, 533–57). Only in Finland, the Netherlands and Ireland were women enfranchised at the same time as men. If there is a pattern in the democratization of women's suffrage, it would seem that those countries in which men have a longer history of voting rights, such as France and Switzerland, took the longest time to introduce female suffrage (see Bock 2002, 146, 156).

Universal suffrage, and in particular women's right to vote, were briefly but importantly discussed during the last days of the 1904–1905 Diet. A range of arguments in favour of the extension of the franchise were raised during this debate. 'Justice for everyone!' was the slogan of the day, finding its way into several parliamentary speeches in the estates (see, for example, Peasants II 1905, 1122–7, 1138–40; Burghers II 1905, 994–6). The principles of natural rights, justice, humanity and equality were advanced alongside practical reasons for a reform in the pro-reform arguments put forward in the estates. It was also stated that women had the same responsibilities as men, and that they should therefore also have the same citizenry rights as men. Women were regarded as both equal with men and complementary to them (Peasants I 1905, 180–81, 202–5; Peasants II 1905, 1126–7; Burghers I 1905, 432–34). Moreover, advocates of female suffrage argued that Finnish women had proven to be 'more independent and freer than women in European civilized countries' (Peasants II 1905, 1132–3). Importantly, the issue of the enfranchisement of women was linked to the question of national unity. As the petition in the Burghers put it, 'our small nation cannot afford not to use any of the mental capacities that prevail in the people, but it must take use of them in all spheres of life in the uneven struggle for national survival' (Burghers I 1905, 433). Consequently, the right to vote was considered as a means of engaging everybody in the duties of the nation. In this context, universal suffrage was not thought in terms of an overthrow of the entire system of representation.

There were, of course, critical opinions in the Diet, as well. Universal suffrage was considered a risky step that would lead to uncertainty in political life. For example, it was held that the abolition of the gradual vote and census would be 'a sudden and thoughtless leap' in the system of representation (Clergy 1905, 842). Moreover, a stated willingness to introduce universal suffrage was often accompanied by strategic preconditions. The more important reform was thought to be universal male suffrage in the estates of the Peasants and the Burghers (Burghers II 1905, 982). In addition, it was always possible to point out that a woman's right to vote had not been accepted by other European countries yet, so why should it be in Finland (Clergy 1905, 826–29)?

In understanding the reform process, it is also important to acknowledge an element of contingency alongside the obvious continuities. Most radical arguments in favour of reform were put forward in another context and for other purposes than those for which they were later used. Apart from the Social Democrats and some non-socialist radicals, universal suffrage as a political goal was only accepted by most parties briefly before the November Manifesto set the reform agenda. The Labor Party had claimed universal and equal suffrage in 1899. The Old Finns decided on the same thing in their party meeting in June 1905 (Polvinen 1989, 99), while the Young Finns came to a similar conclusion during the summer and autumn of 1905. The Swedish Party accepted universal suffrage after the November Manifesto. Despite this seeming consensus, the meaning of 'universal suffrage' remained a topic of controversy during the Great Strike (Hultin 1935, 217–18, 223–25, 269).

The Rhetoric of Foreign Examples and the Question of Bicameral Representation

The reform agenda went beyond the general European pattern of parliamentary systems. Most European parliamentary systems were based on extended or universal male suffrage and a bicameral body of representation. There was, then, a certain difficulty in drawing on the experiences of other countries. This was different from the situation a year earlier, when it had been possible to mean quite different things when speaking of universal suffrage and easier to find foreign examples. Earlier arguments in favour of parliamentary reform had been made with a bicameral system in mind. In 1906, bicameralism had become an object of somewhat nostalgic reflections.

The newspapers as well as discussions in the Parliamentary Reform Committee, consisting of four members from the Young Finns, four from the Swedish Party, three from the Old Finns and three from the Social Democrats, clearly show that there was a considerable willingness among the political elite to establish a bicameral system (see, for example, *Hufvudstadsbladet*, 15 November 1905; *Finsk Tidskrift*, 1905, 3–16). Supporters of bicameralism thought that a unicameral parliament could not secure the position of political minorities, and would instead lead to political extremism thanks to the radical voting rights. In spite of such opinions, the memorandum of the Parliamentary Reform Committee explained that the advantage of a bicameral system was less obvious when the upper chamber would be based on universal and equal suffrage, as the Imperial Manifesto presupposed (Reform Committee 1906, 57–8).

There was a certain dilemma in making references to bicameralism. On the one hand, it was argued that the bicameral system was in use in 'freer countries' (see Mylly 2006, 125–28). For example, the Young Finns' paper *Helsingin Sanomat* presented the bicameral system of the US as a model of democratic representation (*Helsingin Sanomat*, 16 November 1905). On the other hand, it was important to show that there was something wrong with bicameralism. The example of the UK was held up for this purpose. This was because it was believed to have a weak upper chamber. Sweden and Denmark were examples of countries in which the political system had suffered from a long-lasting conflict between the upper and lower chambers (*Uusi Suometar*, 11 November and 12 December 1905; Clergy 1906, 546–47). It was also claimed that 'millions of people' in the UK, France, Belgium and Sweden demanded the abolition of the upper chamber (*Kansan lehti*, 14 November 1905). The Norwegian Stortinget was regarded in principle as unicameral, but in practice it was divided into two parts. To the members or the Reform Committee, it served as a good example for the Finnish Parliament. As it was proposed, the Finnish Eduskunta would elect from within a Grand Committee that would scrutinize motions and function as an extra control mechanism before laws were passed. It was explained that the role of the Grand Committee was to fulfill many of the functions that would have fallen to the upper chamber in a bicameral system (Reform Committee 1906, 58–63).

If universal and equal suffrage means that all citizens are treated equally, then the proportional system of voting can be viewed as a means of ensuring that their views are fairly respected (see Urbinati 2002, 79–80). In the Finnish case, proportional representation was motivated not only by egalitarian arguments, but also more conservative considerations. Once the unicameral system was accepted in the Reform Committee, proportional representation became a priority topic in securing the political role of minorities. The discussion concerning the size of electoral districts and the number of candidates on the ballot as well as the pros and cons of the proposed Belgian d'Hondt's system in comparison to other arithmetical solutions revolved around the question of how to de-dramatize the effects of the reform. The Reform Committee, for example, maintained that the proposed system would be a safeguard against strong parties and professional politicians (Reform Committee 1906, 59). The Constitutional Committee of the Diet stated that the Electoral Act must not force citizens to join political parties (Documents 1906, V.M. – Esitys No. 11, 29).

It was held that experiences in other countries were so positive that those countries would not want to return to elections with a majority principle (Documents 1906, 7, 40–41). However, the proportional system was in use only in Belgium and Serbia, as well as in Danish elections for the upper chamber (Törnudd 1968, 30). Belgium also fitted well in the rhetoric of the Social Democrats because of its history of a strong franchise movement and a General Strike in the early 1890s. The Marxist journal *Sosialistinen Aikakauslehti* gives us an illustrative example of how international examples and advice were put to use. The periodical asked several prominent comrades for help in deciding whether there should be a majoritarian electoral system of elections, or a proportional system. They learned that Kautsky was in favour of the majority system, Bebel for proportionality, the leader of the Swedish Social Democrats Hjalmar Branting preferred the proportional system in the Finnish case, and so on, but the Finnish Social Democrats remained divided in the question (*Sosialistinen Aikakauslehti*, 1906, 28–9, 78).

'Universal suffrage' was often used to mean the right of men to vote even in the early twentieth century. This fact was pointed out by women's suffrage movements in different countries (Bock 2002, 130–33). In the Finnish debate, other countries' examples were sometimes used in favour of universal and equal suffrage as if these countries really had universal suffrage for both women and men (see, for example, *Uusi Suometar* 26 November 1905). Concerning the Finnish case, this was nevertheless more or less out of the question after the November Manifesto, although there were many detailed issues concerning the age limit and the qualification criteria still left to be decided (see Harjula 2006, 368–81; Kurunmäki 2005, 122–3). The eligibility of women did provoke some discussion in the Reform Committee. The chairman of the committee, Professor Hermansson, even opposed the right to vote for women, arguing that women tended to favour political extremes. The majority of the committee, however, maintained that married women were politically moderate (Reform Committee 1906, 64–5, 121–4).

The People and the Nation

The most striking feature of the legitimization of universal suffrage and the electoral system was the dominant role of the rhetoric of the unity of the people and its inter-connectedness with the perceived national cause of the country. According to the Reform Committee, it was crucial that 'all were included' in a non-independent country like Finland (Reform Committee 1906, 58). The Constitutional Committee of the Diet maintained that the purpose of the proportional system was to ensure that 'all ideological groups' would have a fair say in the assembly (Documents 1906, V. M. – Esitys No. 11, 4). The final debate in the Diet was characterized by a widespread willingness among the representatives to emphasize the wholeness and unity of the people (see, for example, Peasants 1906, 789–90; Clergy 1906, 544, 590), although there were also some dissenting voices, especially in the Noble Estate (see, for example, Nobles 1906, 347–50, 358–63, 378–86).

It is possible to view this rhetorical emphasis on the unity of the people as 'a sacrament' of social inclusion, to draw on Pierre Rosanvallon's famous interpretation on the breakthrough of universal male suffrage in France in 1848 (Rosanvallon 2006, 98–114; Rosanvallon 1994; Rosanvallon 1992, 372–87). The period of universal male suffrage between March and May 1848 has often been seen as a consequence of exceptional circumstances and the 'spirit of 1848' in France. However, Rosanvallon argues that it was not a parenthesis in the French history of democracy, but instead an example of the illiberalism of French democracy. His main point is that the introduction of universal male suffrage was thought to be a means of strengthening the unity of the people, rather than radically expanding the possibilities for the political participation of individual voters. The reform was not so much about the rights of citizens, but the social unity of France.

To a large extent, Rosanvallon's analysis could be applied to Finland in 1905–1906, especially when seen from the political elite's point of view. However, there is an important difference in the rhetoric of the unity of the people between France in 1848 and Finland in 1905–1906. As Risto Alapuro has noted, the rhetoric of unity in Finland was compatible with the idea of social and ideological plurality in a way that was impossible in the French political culture (Alapuro 2006, 46–8,

51–5; see also Pohjantammi 2003, 386–89, 394). In Finland, 'ideological groups' and social diversity were accepted, but at the same time subsumed under the idea of a shared national interest, whereas in France there was a tradition, since Rousseau's revolutionary reception, to reject any associational plurality as artificial and illegitimate. The unenfranchised people were invited to the national campaign under a paternalistic tutelage that had been cultivated by the leaders of the Finnish-language movement during the second half of the nineteenth century. The idea of a diligent and patriotic people allowed for the existence of different groups and strata in society, though not necessarily those based on (the Swedish) language.

There are also some similarities between the Finnish rhetoric of reform and the Anti-Federalist rhetoric during the drawing up of the US Constitution in the 1780s. According to Bernard Manin, the Anti-Federalists claimed that the most important feature of representation was that the representatives ought to be like their constituents. In other words, they should resemble the electorate. However, this does not mean, Manin argues, that it was a question of the 'mandate theory' of representation. Rather, it was thought that the representatives would spontaneously do as the people wished (Manin 1997, 108–11, 129–30). Neither in Finland was the aimed resemblance between representatives and the people 'in its entirety' supposed to result from any kind of binding relationship between the voters and the representatives. 'The people's representatives' were never thought of as delegates of the constituency (save some doctrinaire Social Democrats who stuck to the Kautskyan idea of party delegates). The principle of imperative mandate had already been denied in the 1869 Diet Act. Moreover, the candidates were not to be bound to any home district in elections, which also marked the idea of their independence from the local interests of the electorate (Documents 1906, Valtiosäät. Vast – Esitys No. 11, 11).

There is a striking resemblance between the reform in Finland and the suffrage reforms in New Zealand and Australia, the two countries which were ahead of Finland in granting women the right to vote. Like Finland, New Zealand and Australia also had a peripheral position within a large empire, and the campaigns for universal suffrage in these countries were fuelled by national goals *vis-à-vis* the British Empire (Sulkunen 2007, 16–31). It has been argued that the reason why Finland became the first European country to grant the vote to women was the enthusiasm for national liberation from the Russian yoke, to which women had contributed as significantly as men (Bock 2002, 143). Although this is an over-simplification of the reasons for reform, the Russians gave the Finns both a rationale and the possibility for the reform.

As a matter of fact, the rhetoric of nation is a regular bedfellow of parliamentary reform. Representative bodies have often been identified with 'the nation', at least since the eighteenth century, although representative political institutions often originated as instruments of the ruler. As early as the 1640s, the Parliamentarian opponents of the Stuart monarchy in England presented their case in the name of 'the nation' and 'the people' (Skinner 2005, 155–84). In eighteenth-century France, 'nation' was used to signify the opposition against despotism and monarchy in the confrontations between the king and privileged estates (Fehrenbach 1986, 83–91).

The French Revolution, and in particular Sieyès's use of 'nation' as a counter-concept to the estates' privileges, is the paradigmatic case with regard to the rhetoric of nation and its relationship to political representation. The creation of the National Assembly was viewed as a re-creation of the nation (Sieyès 1789 [1963]). Since then, the rhetoric of nation has been linked to the idea that a parliamentary reform should not only mirror the existing nation, but also re-create the nation. These constitutive and descriptive aspects of national rhetoric are often intertwined in political language (see Kurunmäki 2000, 12, 80–81).

In Finland, the Marxist socialists made fun of the pompous slogan of 'the rebirth of the nation' (*Sosialistinen Aikakauslehti*, 1906, 97). Not even af Ursin, who drew a parallel between the French Revolution and the Finnish calls for a national assembly, took up the question of the nation. The Social Democrats were, by and large, considered to be as national-minded as the rest of the (Finnish-speaking) population. If there were any speculations regarding the re-creation of the nation in 1905–1906, it was in connection to the language division in the country. In the view of some Old Finns, reform was seen as a way of reducing the considerable influence of the Swedish-speaking minority (see, for example, *Uusi Suometar*, 26 November 1905; see also Seitkari 1958, 26–8). It is also possible to understand the introduction of a unicameral parliament in the same light. An upper chamber that quite probably would have been dominated by a Swedish-speaking economic and cultural elite would certainly not have been welcomed even by a conservative Finnish-language nationalist.

The word 'nation' was used mainly in circumstances that related to the country's position *vis-à-vis* the Russian Empire. In general, however, this term was replaced by 'the people' in the rhetoric of reform. 'The nation' and 'the people' have always been closely connected in national rhetoric, particularly in Finland. This is because of the peculiarity of the Finnish language, in which 'the people' (*kansa*) is the root word for 'nation' (*kansakunta*) and 'citizen' (*kansalainen*). The semantic closeness of these concepts made it possible to use 'the people' when one actually meant 'the nation'. Despite several usages echoing revolutionary and other radical slogans, 'citizens' were primarily thought of as members of the people, not as individuals who would take an unforeseen active role in politics. Equal voting rights, however, are the rationale of *Staatsbürger*, as noted by Weber (1917 [1994], 103). In this sense, the parliamentary reform created political citizens who were politically emancipated from the constraints of societal privileges. This was, though, intended to create the political unity of the nation, to follow Weber, rather than to emancipate people from social inequalities (Nobles 1906, 412; cf. Weber 1917 [1994], 121–22).

Democracy, the People's Power and Democratization

In addition to the concepts of nation and citizen, the concept of democracy was also built on the concept of the people. 'The people's power' (*kansanvalta*) was more often used than 'democracy' (*demokratia*) by Finnish-speaking debaters in 1905–1906. The choice of words was not only a matter of finding a genuine Finnish translation for the classic key word of politics, in which *demos* and *kratein* have found their equivalents *kansa* ('the people') and *valta* ('power') in Finnish, but also a matter of promoting and handling the situation that opened up in the autumn of 1905. It has been noted that the Finnish word *kansanvalta* did not necessarily refer to the idea of the sovereignty of the people in the early twentieth century, but rather, to the Finnish-speaking majority of the population, to the nation, and to the institution of political representation, the Diet (Hyvärinen 2003b, 36–44). In the debate over the reform, 'the people's power' referred to the people as the nation or as the Finnish polity. For example, the Young Finns' periodical *Kansanvalta* stated that the greatest menace to 'the people's power' came from Russia (*Kansanvalta* 1906, 52). It was also argued that reform would strengthen the people both internally and externally (Clergy 1906, 597; Nobles 1906, 366). To be sure, 'the people's power' also referred to 'the common people', 'all' and sometimes 'the proletariat' in the rhetoric regarding reform. Natural rights, humanity, solidarity and the idea of the sovereignty of the people belonged to the rhetorical arsenal of many protagonists of the bill (see, for example, Peasants 1906, 810, 819–20, 853; Burghers 1906, 616, 618–19), as well as to that of some opponents, like Professor Hermanson, the chairman of the Reform Committee, who was critical of them (Clergy 1906, 528–29; see also, for example, Nobles 1906, 348).

This oscillation between the two sides of the people – that is, between the sovereign people and the national people – is actually built into the concept of democracy. As Bernard Yack has argued, there is an important connection between popular sovereignty and nationalism. According to him, 'the doctrine of popular sovereignty contributes to the rise and spread of nationalism by introducing a new image of political community, an image that tends to nationalize political loyalties and politicize national loyalties' (Yack 2001, 523). It is arguable that this connection was expressed in the word *kansanvalta* more explicitly than in the word *demokratia*. Thus, the idea of the sovereignty of the people was fused with the idea of the people, which was the nation defending its rights against an external threat. Moreover, *kansanvalta* could have its roots in the people and the nation, whereas such a link was less obvious if one used the word *demokratia*.

The concept of 'the people's power' was contested, however. The Young Finns criticized the Social Democrats for their exclusive and class-based use of the concept (*Kansanvalta* 1906, 52). This was actually in response to the ironic comment that 'it seems that we do not have any reactionaries nowadays; ... everyone is extremely democratic [the people's power-minded] and almost a friend of the workers' (*Sosialistinen Aikakauslehti*, 1906, 25). The most vehement attack on 'the people's power' and 'democracy' came from a small number of reactionaries in the Noble Estate, who associated all that was happening with future chaos, anarchy and socialism, and who thought that the reform would destroy the society and culture of the country (Nobles 1906, 347–48, 358–63, 378–84).

Most of the critical voices were more cautious. The speeches of opponents of reform suggest a sense of resignation to the seemingly inevitable (see, for example, Peasants 1906, 831, 839; Burghers 1906, 580–81, 597–8; Clergy 1906, 542, 550). In some speeches in the Diet, it was pointed out that the whole situation was a product of the revolutionary upheaval (see, for example, Nobles 1906, 347). More common was to speculate about what would have happened if the reform work had started earlier. Several reflections that were heard in the Diet concluded that there would not have been any need for a radical reform if gradual reform had occurred earlier (see, for example, Clergy 1906, 531, 551–52). This, however, was sometimes viewed as a virtue. If gradual reform had begun already, 'the most democratic reform' being proposed would have been impossible (Peasants 1906, 843; see also Burghers 1906, 583).

As these comments show, the debaters were well aware of the peculiarity of the pace of democratization in Finland. It can be argued, however, that neither the peripheral position of Finland nor the suddenness of the reform were particularly unique in the history of parliamentary democratization. Theories and analyses of democratization often emphasize the role of national mobilization and war in democratization processes (see, for example, Keyssar 2000, xxi; Goldblatt 1997, 58–70; Cohen 1996, 721). The Finnish case can be viewed in this light. Reform in Finland took place in a revolutionary context that followed the war between Russia and Japan. In addition, Finland was not the only peripheral nation advancing the case for wider voting rights. New Zealand (1893), Australia (1902) and some US territories or states, which were the first to enfranchise women (Wyoming 1869, Utah 1870, Colorado 1893, Idaho 1896) were all in a peripheral position in an empire or a federal state (see Markoff 1999, 680). Consequently, the democratization of voting rights has not followed any 'from centre to periphery' pattern. Rather, 'the history of democracy is profoundly polycentric' (Markoff 1999, 689).

Parliamentary government is viewed as a crucial part of representative democracy (see Manin 1997, 195), although it has not always been linked with any kind of idea of democracy (Weber 1917 [1994], 210). The topic of parliamentary government did not gain a central place in the debates on reform. True, there had been some veiled efforts in the Reform Committee and in the Senate to interpret the Manifesto as if it had promised that the Senate would be legally and even politically responsible to the Parliament (see Mylly 2006, 156–59). It was, however, felt far more important that the franchise reform should be accepted in St Petersburg. The most eager supporters of parliamentarism were, as a matter of fact, the Finnish Marxists. They pointed to the fact that any kind of reform of voting rights would not make the political system truly democratic because the government always had the final say (*Sosialistinen Aikakauslehti*, 1906, 121–23, 145, 171–73, 247). Even such conservatives who otherwise disliked parliamentary rule may have been willing to create a political dependence between the representation and the government, provided that the government in question was Finnish. At the same time, there was a risk that such a relationship between Parliament and the government would have allowed the Russian government too much influence over the Finnish Parliament.

In May 1906, when the Diet discussed the bill, the lack of parliamentary rule was less important for the representatives of the Finnish estates. Self-congratulatory voices proclaiming that Finland would take first place among civilized countries in Europe and the world in terms of voting rights were the most common ones in the Diet. The reform would show the way to the rest of the world. A new era was about to begin (Peasants 1906, 797, 827; Burghers 1906, 576–77). Although the reform would mean 'a leap into the unknown' (Clergy 1906, 552), it was transformed into national pride. It was stated that 'universal suffrage suits Finland well' (Clergy 1906, 563–64) and that the people knew the right thing 'by instinct' (Burghers 1906, 578). One representative of the Burghers likened the reform to an invention of a scientist, who first makes his discovery, and can only explain it afterwards (Burghers 1906, 613).

References

Ahtisaari, E. et al. (eds) (1997), *Yksi kamari – kaksi sukupuolta: Suomen eduskunnan ensimmäiset naiset* (Helsinki: Eduskunnan kirjasto).

Alapuro, R. (1988), *State and Revolution in Finland* (Berkeley, CA: University of California Press).

—— (2003), 'Vallankumous', in Hyvärinen et al. (eds), *Käsitteet liikkeessä. Suomen poliittisen kulttuurin käsitehistoria* (Tampere: Vastapaino).

—— (2006), 'The Construction of the Voter in Finland, c. 1860–1907', *Redescriptions* 10, 41–64.

Ankersmit, F. (2002), *Political Representation* (Stanford, CA: Stanford University Press).

Bock, G. (2002), *Women in European History* (Oxford: Blackwell).

Brunner, O., Conze, W. and Koselleck, R. (eds) (1972), *Geschichtliche Grundbegriffe. Historisches Lexikon zur politisch-sozialen Sprache in Deutschland*, vol. 1 (Stuttgart: Klett).

Cohen, P.N. (1996), 'Nationalism and Suffrage: Gender Struggle in Nation-building America', *Signs: Journal of Women in Culture and Society* 21, 707–27.

Daley, C. and Nolan, M. (eds) (1994), *Suffrage and Beyond: International Feminist Perspectives* (New York: New York University Press).

Dunn, J. (2005), *Setting the People Free: The Story of Democracy* (London: Atlantic Books).

Engman, M. and Kirby, D. (eds) (1989), *Finland: People, Nation, State* (London: Hurst).

Evans, R.J. (1980), 'German Social Democracy and Women's Suffrage 1891–1918', *Journal of Contemporary History* 15, 533–57.

Fehrenbach, E. (1986), 'Nation', in Reichardt et al. (eds), *Handbuch politisch-sozialer Grundbegriffe in Frankreich 1680–1820*, Heft 7 (Munich: Oldenbourg).

Finsk Tidskrift 1905.

Fontana, B. (ed.) (1994), *The Invention of Modern Republic* (Cambridge: Cambridge University Press).

Goldblatt, D. (1997), 'Democracy in the "Long Nineteenth Century", 1760–1919', in Potter et al. (eds), *Democratization* (Cambridge: Polity Press).

Harjula, M. (2006), 'Kelvoton valtiokansalaiseksi? Yleisen äänioikeuden rajoitukset ja äänioikeusanomukset Suomessa 1906–17', *Historiallinen Aikakauskirja* 104, 368–81.

Helsingin Sanomat 1905–1906.

Hirschman, A.O. (1991), *The Rhetoric of Reaction: Perversity, Futility, Jeopardy* (Cambridge, MA: Belknap Press).

Hufvudstadsbladet 1905–1906.

Hultin, T. (1935), *Päiväkirjani kertoo 1899–1914 I* (Helsinki: Sanatar).

Hyvärinen, M. et al. (eds) (2003a), *Käsitteet liikkeessä. Suomen poliittisen kulttuurin käsitehistoria* (Tampere: Vastapaino).

—— (2003b), '"The people's power" (democracy) as an argument in Finnish party manifestos', *Finnish Yearbook of Political Thought 7*, 36–67.

Kansan lehti 1905.

Kansanvalta 1906 – *viikkolehti valtiollista ja yhteiskunnallista valistusta varten* 1906.

Kautsky, K (1902 [1906]), *Yhteiskunnallinen vallankumous* (Pori: Kehitys).

Keyssar, A. (2000), *The Right to Vote: The Contested History of Democracy in the United States* (New York: Basic Books).

Koselleck, R. (1972), 'Einleitung', in Brunner et al. (eds), *Geschichtliche Grundbegriffe. Historisches Lexikon zur politisch-sozialen Sprache in Deutschland*, vol. 1 (Stuttgart: Klett).

Koskinen, P.K. (1997), 'Äänioikeuden lainsäädäntöhistoriaa', in Ahtisaari et al. (eds), *Yksi kamari – kaksi sukupuolta: Suomen eduskunnan ensimmäiset naiset* (Helsinki: Eduskunnan kirjasto).

Kujala, A. (1989), *Vallankumous ja kansallinen itsemääräämisoikeus. Venäjän sosialistiset puolueet ja suomalainen radikalismi vuosisadan alussa* (Helsinki: SHS).

Kurunmäki, J. (2000), *Representation, Nation and Time: The Political Rhetoric of the 1866 Parliamentary Reform in Sweden* (Jyvaskyla: Jyvaskyla Studies in Education, Psychology and Social Research).

—— (2005), 'A parliament for the unity of the people: On the rhetoric of legitimisation in the debate over Finnish parliamentary reform in 1906', in Landgrén and Hautamäki (eds), *People, Citizen, Nation* (Helsinki: Renvall Institute).

Landgrén, L.-F. and Hautamäki, P. (eds) (2005), *People, Citizen, Nation* (Helsinki: Renvall Institute).

Manin, B. (1997), *The Principles of Representative Government* (Cambridge: Cambridge University Press).

Markoff, J. (1999), 'When and where democracy was invented?', *Comparative Studies in Society and History 41*, 660–90.

Mylly, J. (2006), *Edustuksellisen kansanvallan läpimurto. Suomen Eduskunta 100 vuotta 1* (Helsinki: Edita).

Pateman, C. (1994), 'Three Questions about Womanhood Suffrage', in Daley and Nolan (eds), *Suffrage and Beyond: International Feminist Perspectives* (New York: New York University Press).

Pohjantammi, I. (2003), 'Edustus', in Hyvärinen et al. (eds), *Käsitteet liikkeessä. Suomen poliittisen kulttuurin käsitehistoria* (Tampere: Vastapaino).

Polvinen, T. (1989), *J. K. Paasikivi. Valtiomiehen elämäntyö I 1870–1918* (Porvoo: WSOY).

Potter, D. et al. (eds) (1997), *Democratization* (Cambridge: Polity Press).

Raun, T.U. (1984), 'The Revolution of 1905 in the Baltic Provinces and Finland', *Slavic Review* 43, 453–67.

Reichardt, R. et al. (eds) (1986), *Handbuch politisch-sozialer Grundbegriffe in Frankreich 1680–1820*, Heft 7 (Munich: Oldenbourg).

Rokkan, S. (1999), *State Formation, Nation-building, and Mass Politics in Europe: The Theory of Stein Rokkan*, ed. P. Flora, S. Kuhnle and D. Urwin (Oxford: Oxford University Press).

Roos, S. (1906), *Nationalstrejken i Finland* (Helsingfors: Lindberg).

Rosanvallon, P. (1992), *Le sacre du citoyen* (Paris: Gallimard).

—— (1994), 'The Republic of Universal Suffrage', in Fontana (ed.), *The Invention of Modern Republic* (Cambridge: Cambridge University Press).

—— (2006), *Democracy: Past and Future* (New York: Columbia University Press).

Seitkari, O. (1958), 'Edustuslaitoksen uudistus 1906', in *Suomen Kansanedustuslaitoksen historia* (Helsinki: Eduskunnan historiakomitea).

Sieyès, J.E. (1789 [1963]), *What is the Third Estate?* (London: Pall Mall Press).

Skinner, Q. (2005), 'Hobbes on Representation', *European Journal of Philosophy* 13, 155–84.

Sosialistinen Aikakauslehti, 1, 1906.

Sulkunen, I. (1989), 'The Women's Movement', in Engman and Kirby (eds), *Finland: People, Nation, State* (London: Hurst).

—— (2007), 'Suomi naisten äänioikeuden edelläkävijänä', in *Naiset Eduskunnassa. Suomen Eduskunta 100 vuotta 4* (Helsinki: Edita).

Teljo, J. (1949), *Suomen valtioelämän murros 1905–1908* (Porvoo: WSOY).

Törnudd, K. (1968), *The Electoral System of Finland* (London: Hugh Evelyn).

Urbinati, N. (2002), *Mill on Democracy: From the Athenian Polis to Representative Government* (Chicago, IL: University of Chicago Press).

—— (2006), *Representative Democracy: Principles and Genealogy* (Chicago, IL: University of Chicago Press).

Uusi Suometar 1905–1906.

Weber, M. (1917 [1994]), *Political Writings*, ed. P. Lassman and R. Speirs (Cambridge: Cambridge University Press).

Yack, B. (2001), 'Popular Sovereignty and Nationalism', *Political Theory* 29, 517–36.

Further Reading

Allardt, E. et al. (eds) (1981), *Nordic Democracy: Ideas, Issues, and Institutions in Politics, Economy, Education, Social and Cultural Affairs of Denmark, Finland, Iceland, Norway, and Sweden* (Copenhagen: Det danske Selskab).

Bryce, J. (1921), *Modern Democracies* (London: Macmillan).

Canovan, M. (2005), *The People* (Cambridge: Polity Press).

Haavio-Mannila, E. et al. (eds) (1985), *Unfinished Democracy: Women in Nordic Politics* (Oxford, Pergamon Press).

Hentilä, M. and Schug, A. (eds) (2006), *Von heute an für alle! Hundert Jahre Frauenwahlrecht* (Berlin: Berliner Wissenschafts-Verlag).

Koselleck, R. (2002), *The Practice of Conceptual History: Timing History, Spacing Concepts* (Stanford, CA: Stanford University Press).
Markoff, J. (1996), *Waves of Democracy: Social Movements and Political Change* (Thousand Oaks, CA: Pine Forge Press).
Pitkin, H.F. (1967), *The Concept of Representation* (Berkeley, CA: University of California Press).
Rosanvallon, P. (1998), *Le people introuvable. Historie de la représentation démocratique en France* (Paris: Gallimard).
—— (2000), *La démocratie inachevée. Historie de la souveraineté du people en France* (Paris: Gallimard).
Sulkunen, I. (2006), 'Finnland – Pionier des Wahlrechts für Frauen', in Hentilä and Schug (eds), *Von heute an für alle! Hundert Jahre Frauenwahlrecht* (Berlin: Berliner Wissenschafts-Verlag).

Parliamentary and Official Documents

[Burghers I 1905] *Borgareståndets protokoll vid Landtdagen i Helsingfors åren 1904–1905. Första delen. Från Landtdagens början till och med den 31 december 1904.*
[Burghers II 1905] *Borgareståndets protokoll vid Landtdagen i Helsingfors åren 1904–1905. Andra delen. Från och med den 24 januari till Landtdagens slut.*
[Burghers 1906] *Bårgareståndets protokoll vid landtdagen I Helsingfors åren 1905–1906. Andra delen, från och med den 22 maj 1906 till landtdagens slut.*
[Clergy 1905] *Suomen Pappissäädyn pöytäkirjat valtiopäiviltä v. 1904–1905 ynnä jäsen – ja aineluettelot.*
[Clergy 1906] *Suomen Pappissäädyn pöytäkirjat valtiopäiviltä v. 1905–1906. Edellinen osa.*
[Documents 1906] *Asiakirjat väliaikaisilta valtiopäiviltä Helsingissä vuosina 1905–1906. Toinen osa.*
[Nobles 1906] Protokoll förda hos Finlands Ridderskap och Adel vid landtdagen år 1905–06. Första häftet. Från landtdagens början till och med den 31 Maj 1906.
[Peasants I 1905] *Suomen talonpoikaissäädyn keskustelupöytäkirjat 1904–1905 vuosien valtiopäiviltä. Ensimmäinen osa. Joulukuun 6 päivästä 1904 tammikuun 30 päivään 1905.*
[Peasants II 1905] *Suomen talonpoikaissäädyn keskustelupöytäkirjat 1904–1905 vuosien valtiopäiviltä. Toinen osa. Tammikuun 31 päivästä huhtikuun 15 päivään ynnä Jäsen – ja sisällysluettelo.*
[Peasants 1906] Suomen talonpoikaissäädyn keskustelupöytäkirjat 1905–1906 vuosien valtiopäivillä.
[Reform Committee 1906] *Eduskunnan uudistamiskomitea 1906*, Helsinki.

Nationalism, Constitutionalism and Democratization: The Basque Question in Perspective

José María Rosales

This chapter deals with the difficult accommodation between nationalism and democracy. Based on a case study on political negotiations to end terrorist violence in Spain, I shall argue that any secure advancement in that direction should be grounded on the compliance with the constitutional order, which to nationalist parties appears as a disputable source of authority. By imposing limits to politics, namely to political negotiation, this condition makes agreements harder to work out, but legitimate and effective. Otherwise, as the Basque experience on the changing trade-offs between the constitutional order and the claims for self-determination shows, the best of political intentions produce at most an ever-delayed promise of democratization.

The set-up of democracy depends on a series of conditions: constitutional, institutional and civic. Constitutional conditions lay the fundamental principles and procedures for democratic ruling, which basically means self-government by citizens, while institutional conditions put into practice the elements of the model. Democracies, unlike dictatorships, are civic regimes: their institutional performance rests heavily on their civic resources and practices. These conditions correlate with each other, though not in a linear order, since institutional and civic factors operate as prerequisites for democratic constitutions. Moreover, they tend to affect the normative provisions of constitutional models in ways that uphold or revise them, not to mention the normative disputes themselves that nurture and influence democratic constitutionalism.

Nationalism challenges democracy this way, not only as an ideology, but also as a normative disposition of politics. Even though constitutions aim at exerting a transformative effect on politics, sometimes the reverse is the case. Formally, most if not all types of nationalism in current democracies endorse the principles of democratic theory and of liberal constitutionalism. To that extent, it should not be contradictory to speak of democratic nationalism. Admittedly, there are hundreds of nationalist parties competing regularly in elections in liberal democracies, and Europe is home to nationalist parties from all sides of the political spectrum.

Yet, constitutionally considered, the normative consistency of democratic nationalism is but partial, and probably unattainable in full, for a recurrent problem arises when nationalism is confronted with some basic tenets of liberal constitutionalism. In the main, constitutionalism embodies the principle of legally limited government (Waluchow 2007). From that legal constraint, a number of sub-principles derive, most notably that the state has the obligation to enforce and protect the system of rights, being the individuals, not the groups, the legitimate bearers of rights. Consequently, as a constitution gives rise to a conventional, contractual order, the idea that natural, pre-contractual collective entities should be constitutionally recognized involves a controversial accommodation.

As it happens, the belief in collective political subjects, be they peoples or nations, is one of the main features of nationalism. As a rhetorical motif, it exerts an undeniable allure in politics, but it turns out to be a self-defeating constitutional aspiration. This lack of adjustment is but inconsequential, since the aspiration to acknowledge a constitutional status for nations directly affects the very meaning of democratic government, and more precisely, of democratic representation. For example, recognition is granted at the expense of this democratic principle when electoral engineering makes possible that minority nationalist parties do not gain representation in national parliaments in a proportional way, which would give them a very limited say. Correction devices thus allow for nationalist interests to be over-represented in national parliaments (Lago Penas 2004).

This is not the only intriguing aspect of the relation between nationalism and democracy. In the pages that follow, I shall examine other aspects through the exceptional view of terrorist violence in the name of a nationalist cause. Undoubtedly, nationalism is not by itself the cause of terrorism. At times, terrorist actions are claimed in the name of some nationalist goal. When that happens, this very association benefits terrorism's ideological background while undermining nationalism's political reputation, thus making it even more difficult to reconcile it with democracy. The Basque case is an illustrative example of such irony.

The Basque Question: Terrorism and the Uses of Nationalism

At stake is the issue of self-rule in the Basque Country, as interpreted in both constitutionalist and independentist terms. Next, the Basque question refers to the consequences of a secessionist project imposed by force, where self-determination is associated with the demand for territoriality. What distinguishes it from other devolution cases is the intimidating role played by the terrorist organization ETA (Euskadi Ta Askatasuna, 'Basque Homeland and Freedom') and its lengthy history of ties with the nationalist cause.

Irreducible as political autonomy and independence are to each other, since no democratic constitution acknowledges independence as a right, their tension divides Basque society along nationalist lines. Furthermore, the Basque question has proved a major influence on Spanish politics, to the point that after thirty years of democracy, tackling ETA's terrorism remains one of Spain's foremost political challenges. So enmeshed are the ideas of political autonomy and independence in Basque politics that it is necessary to distinguish institutional from violent forms of nationalism. To be precise, ETA's terrorism constitutes strictly the most radical expression of independentism, hence it should be spontaneously linked neither to separatism as such nor to nationalism in general. There are other, non-violent ways of vindicating nationalist and secessionist projects. The problem is that ETA's ascendancy over those political alternatives has resisted the passage of time ever since its foundation in 1959.

So violence alone does not explain this disturbing endurance. One reason is to be found in ETA's interventions in politics through violence and through periodic appeals to the Basque citizenry. One episode I consider particularly representative of this singular mixture of terrorism and rhetorical communication: the unilateral cease-fire declared by ETA in March 2006, which was interrupted only *apparently* by a bomb attack in December 2006, and resumed again in January 2007 as if the blasting had only been an accident that killed two people, just meant as a warning that the organization's objects and strategy had not ceded to the government's demands.[1]

My argument is that the nine-month cease-fire, which came with the promise of democracy made for an episode of fictitious democratization, where expectations for change had been heightened while the proofs of democratic advancements had been low, and even contradictory. If compared with previous truces, the circumstances surrounding the suspension of terrorist attacks were too reminiscent of similar tactical moves in the past, intended to gain advantage in the aftermath dialog with the Spanish government. Of particular interest was the fact that the peace talks proceeded, whereas ETA's activity was not properly interrupted and was even excused by the organization's accustomed nationalist arguments. And yet, paradoxically, the truce unveiled more clearly than ever the possibility of ETA's dissolution (Unzueta 2006).

Short-lived as the episode was, it gave rise to a notably different scene in Spanish politics, where the basic consensus on the fight against terrorism was undermined, and where the ending of violence seemed still a long way off. But most of all, it was patently representative of the thirty-year history of terrorism under democracy, marked by an astounding record of failed attempts at negotiating with ETA (Alonso and Reinares 2005). Over those years, Spain has experienced a remarkable transformation into a modern society whose democratic system has accommodated nationalist demands to extremes hard to match by other federal or federal-like states in the world (Pérez-Díaz 1993; Moreno 2001). In the meantime, ETA has intensified its pressure both on Basque society and on the state, while

---

1   Apart from official electronic sources, the information referred to in this chapter is easily accessible via the online editions of Spain's two main, ideologically opposed, newspapers: *El País* (<www.elpais.com>) and *El Mundo* (<www.elmundo.es>). These can be contrasted with the account given by the separatist *Gara* newspaper (<www.gara.net>). Likewise, the BBC provides a useful chronology of ETA's history at <http://news.bbc.co.uk/2/hi/europe/545452.stm>, last accessed 24 February 2007.

persisting in the old rhetoric of hatred against a supposedly invader state, and the promise of liberation.

Even if the assumption cannot be demonstrated empirically, the claim of 'non-Spain' is a powerful nationalist motif, in spite of its dubious economic viability (Buesa 2003). In political terms, secession might be addressed in due course, on condition that terrorism ends. The Constitution could be amended to allow for a referendum on independence. Then an example like the Canadian constitutional procedure on eventual secession of Quebec would be much needed, thereby contemplating a separation from the state through multilateral negotiations. Secession, coherently, would imply both the end to mutual obligations and the loss of mutual benefits. And yet there would be always a barrier to overcome, since independence bears two divergent meanings when interpreted in constitutional and in irredentist terms, and also a far-reaching political problem, for Basque society is strongly divided about the issues of self-determination and territoriality.

In this line of reasoning, this chapter's next two sections will examine the expectations that the truce raised in the spring of 2006. It produced the illusion of democratic change, which was tragically denied after the resuming of terrorist violence some nine months later. Moreover, it had been almost daily refuted by the continuation of other forms of violence. While discussing ETA's moves, my purpose is not to assess the Spanish government's performance, but to describe its responses to such an odd interlocutor as a terrorist organization, thereby pointing out some serious obstacles to a genuine dialog.

ETA's rhetoric, symptomatically appealing for peace and democracy, is hard to resist by a political actor, all the more if it is a legitimate government and if the nationalist idea is upheld by the threat of violence. The promise of democracy has exactly two opposing meanings in Basque politics: the ending of terrorist violence and the democratization of political life on the one hand, and the achievement of an irredentist scheme to establish a new state on the other. All this makes the Basque question a political puzzle – fascinating, but distressing. A way to understand it, and to try to solve its inextricable difficulties, is by widening the view of analysis both in comparative and in theoretical terms.

The world is full of entrenched ethnic conflicts, and the Basque case is not the biggest, although it is one of the most enduring and perplexing (Horowitz 1985, 250–53; Connor 1994, 165–91; Lake and Rothchild 1998). The fact that it happens in a democratic state bespeaks alike of its paradoxical condition and of the hopes for its resolution. In the fourth section, a comparison with the Northern Ireland conflict is made, with the aim of shedding some light on the Basque predicament. The fifth section discusses the Quebec case as an instructive example of constitutional limits to secessionist politics. In the last two sections, I shall comment on the rarefied political context of the Basque question and argue for an interpretation of the prospects for democratization.

Democratic Expectations for a 'Permanent Truce' that was Not Indefinite

Ever since the retrieval of democracy in 1977, Basque nationalism has demanded of the central government a growing transfer of power to the regional administration. Similar negotiation strategies are used by the other 16 Spanish autonomous regions, but the claims are stronger, and the dividends bigger, in the Basque Country and in Catalonia, the two communities where peripheral nationalisms are in power.[2] Although diverse forms of nationalist violence are present in Catalan political life, the main difference lies in the presence of terrorist violence. Not surprisingly, the beginning of negotiations between the central government and ETA had been claimed by each party as a new chance for peace and democratization.

That was only partially true. After some speculation over ETA's internal divisions since the arrest in France and Spain of its main leaders in 2004, the terrorist group announced a 'permanent cease-fire' in March 2006 'with the aim of promoting a democratic process in Euskal Herria'.[3] Previously, from 1981 to 1998, a number of short unilateral truces had also been adopted, at times to attempt negotiations, always presumably to rearm. The initiatives were invariably followed by renewed terrorist attacks. One of the most significant moves came in September 1998, when ETA declared 'an indefinite, unconditional truce' immediately after the so-called Lizarra Agreement was signed by all nationalist parties, unions and organizations, excluding all non-nationalist parties from negotiations with ETA. The truce lasted until November 1999.

Violence has run on since, but the latest attack that killed people took place in May 2003. The perspective of time was a strong reason for the Prime Minister, José Luis Rodríguez Zapatero, to ask for support in Parliament as early as in May 2005.[4] All groups agreed except the Popular Party, adducing that the Congress resolution in fact revoked the 2000 Antiterrorist Pact subscribed by the two main national constitutionalist forces, the Socialist Party (PSOE) and the Popular Party (PP). The same reason led the Prime Minister in June 2006 to announce in Congress the start of 'a dialog with ETA, while keeping the non-negotiable principle that

---

2   The exception has been Galician nationalism, until recently, as the Galician Nationalist Bloc (Bloque Nacionalista Galego) formed a coalition government with the Socialist Party of Galicia after the regional elections of June 2005. See the official electoral data at the Website of the regional government, Xunta de Galicia, at <www.ige.eu/ga/index.htm>, accessed 27 April 2006.

3   The name Euskal Herria ('Basque People') refers to the three provinces of the current Basque Autonomous Community or Basque Country, the Community of Navarre and the French Basque Country, as if together they form, or are entitled to form, a political entity.

4   'Lucha contra el terrorismo' ('fight against terrorism'), resolution passed by the Congress of Deputies, *Boletín Oficial de las Cortes Generales*, 206 (20 May 2005), pp. 28–34: <www.congreso.es/frames_publicaciones.htm>. See the parliamentary debates in the *Diary of Sessions of the Congress of Deputies*, 90 (17 May 2005) at <www.congreso.es/pdf/plenos/05/mayo_05.htm>, accessed 12 December 2006.

political issues should only be dealt with the legitimate representatives of popular sovereignty'.[5]

For the second time, none the less, the government did not receive the backing of the Popular Party, on the grounds that political negotiations were already under way according to police sources. A different, though related, matter was the way the government had pushed through its initiative, thereby isolating the main opposition party. Finally, later evidence confirmed the existence of previous contacts between the Socialist Party of the Basque Country and ETA at least from 2002, pointing out the strength shown by ETA in the negotiations (Aizpeolea 2007). The question is: how politically reasonable was the decision to proceed, considering these antecedents and the fact that talks had begun without a full cessation of violence and other illegal activities?[6]

A permanent cease-fire, the promise behind all this, seemed to envisage a future without violence and a future built upon democracy, as the declaration profusely stated. However, no mention was made of disarmament, nor a definitive abandonment of violence. The declaration referred to a 'democratic process that needs to take place in the Basque Country'. The initiative maintained continuity with previous statements by adhering to the same conditions: decriminalization of the organization's activities, including amnesty for ETA prisoners (not a modest bidding in view of a record of more than 800 people killed), halting of the constitutional order, self-determination and the constitution of a new state, Euskal Herria, out of a series of territories from Spain and France. What, if anything, had changed?

A look at the political scene during the first nine months of the cease-fire shows that no remarkable progress had been made, except for the rise of a new horizon of expectations of a future without violence in the Basque Country. Before the truce was broken, it was difficult to conclude whether the hopes were reasonable or not, precisely because acts of urban violence, together with extortion, persisted. This was odd enough for a so-called peace process. After the resuming of terrorist attacks, the response seemed clear, but the political consequences were hard to imagine (Wieland 2007).

Change, arguably, was the fruit of the imagination of political leaders, namely nationalists and socialists, and persisted despite the evidence otherwise – or, ironically, because of the stubborn evidence, notably in the case of nationalists. So the expectations for change were due to the proper anticipation of political hope

---

5   <www.la-moncloa.es/Presidente/Intervenciones/Discursos/Rdez.Zapatero-DialogoETA290606.htm>, accessed 12 December 2006.

6   A ruling by Spain's High Court (Tribunal Supremo) in 2003 had established that ETA was an organization with a network structure including terrorist commandos, fundraising extortion activities, cultural associations, media, political parties and numerous emerging groups dedicated to sowing panic among civilians through different forms of urban violence (*kale borroka*): Sentencia del Tribunal Supremo (Sala Especial) of 27 March 2003, available at <www.poderjudicial.es/jurisprudencia>, accessed 19 September 2006.

and the alluring effect of persistently reiterated well-intentioned statements more than any significant change in ETA's strategy.

One of the most revealing factors of how the nationalist question has been addressed in Basque politics over the years is precisely what happened once again: the permanent promise of overcoming violence, plus the enduring hope fulfilling this wish, with the usual result, creating a never-ending cycle of good intentions and disappointing acts. This time, the argument returned with renewed strength, against the rebuttal of political reality, and against some fundamental political and legal principles, as the cease-fire depended on a number of demands that do not fit international law, nor match the normative assumptions of the rule of law.

Conditions Unchanged, Foreseeable Outcomes

ETA's bulletin, *Zutabe*, of October 2006 threatened to resume its activities unless the Spanish and French governments acceded to its demands. In fact, the application of the law in both countries, which had involved the arrest of ETA suspects, was interpreted by ETA as an act of aggression: 'We have said it clearly, should these attacks to Euskal Herria continue, ETA will respond.' On 30 December 2006, a car bomb exploded at Madrid's Barajas Airport killing two Ecuadorian citizens. More than twenty people were wounded. The Spanish Prime Minister gave the order to suspend negotiations, admitting that this move would not entail the complete abandonment of the talks.

Had the truce been only apparent? According to ETA, absolutely not. In a communiqué published by the *Gara* newspaper on 10 January 2007, the organization claimed that 'the permanent cease-fire still stands'. As in previous reports, and particularly in the March 2006 declaration, at least four kinds of arguments appeared in the communiqué. Later in this chapter, another example of nationalist argumentation will be presented – the draft for a new political statute for the Basque Country. The means are logically different, but the aims, the ideological justifications and the rhetorical arguments look quite similar.

First, there is the rhetoric of self-sacrifice and victimization. ETA, 'the Basque socialist revolutionary organization for national liberation', gave the strongest proof of its genuine will to seek peace when calling a *unilateral* cease-fire. The blast had been announced, claimed the band, with enough notice to avoid casualties. This time, it offered its condolences for the dead. ETA, so it argued, was ready to make new efforts to relaunch the peace process, given its self-assumed condition of representative of the Basque people, meaning the people of Euskal Herria, not merely the current Basque citizens.

Secondly, there was the denunciation by the government. Was the cease-fire properly honored by the government? Not at all, continued the statement. Instead, it had blocked the peace process by imposing 'the limits fixed by the Spanish Constitution and the legal system', which are deemed 'mechanisms of war and repression'. Besides, 'the Spanish government has not fulfilled its cease-fire compromises'. But the government, significantly, has always denied any compromise with ETA, and has only acknowledged the existence of peace talks.

Third, there was the appeal to democracy and peace. For ETA, 'the way that will lead steadily to a genuine democracy' passes through the recognition 'of a new legal and political framework grounded both on the right to self-determination and on territoriality'. That would be the only option left for the 'recognition of the national rights of Euskal Herria'. According to ETA, it 'could change the current situation and give rise step by step to the chance for opening a new path toward a conflict resolution'.

Fourth, there was the threat of violence, still preceded by a call for peace, or precisely because of it, to judge from the rhetorical content of the message. After warning the governing Socialist Party that ETA expected political measures 'before it is too late', the statement became straightforward: 'ETA's decisions and reactions will depend on the behaviour of the Spanish government.' Despite proclaiming ETA's will to resume the process, it was made clear that if the existing impasse continued, 'ETA will show its full determination to react.'[7] Finally, some months later, in June 2007, ETA used quite similar arguments to announce that the cease-fire had officially expired.

The Basque Question in Perspective, Part I: Negotiating a Conflict

The international media often present ETA in euphemistic terms as a mere separatist group, or just another terrorist band. Rather, it is an organization, a conglomerate of groups – a big business, somehow similar to the mafia business in Sicily, but not competing with the Spanish security forces to keep law and order in the region. In fact, ETA's extortion network is closer to the IRA's organized crime, although the similarities between the two cases are scant. The different command structures of the IRA and ETA, Sinn Fein having a clear ascendancy over the IRA and ETA tightly dominating Batasuna, explain why the Irish and the Basque questions are only loosely comparable (Alonso 2004). Furthermore, the order of the measures taken in each process has been quite the opposite.

Concerning the Northern Irish case, the peace process began after a number of conditions were in force. It has been a long-lasting, exigent procedure. The decommissioning of weapons by the IRA has taken more than ten years, since the November 1995 agreement by the British and Irish governments to launch a parallel attempt at disarmament and at starting all-party negotiations. The process was supervised in 1996 by the then International Body on Arms Decommissioning, and from 1997 onward by the Independent International Commission on Decommissioning. Its January 2007 report ratified previous accounts confirming

---

7   ETA's communiqué of 10 January 2007, translated from Euskara into Spanish by Vasco Press Agency, available at <www.elmundo.es>, accessed 29 January 2007.

that the arms under the IRA's control had been put beyond use, and hence that the 'deterioration of terrorist capability' continued.[8]

Only when the withdrawal of weapons was under way was a pact reached by the governments of the UK and Ireland. The British–Irish Agreement of April 1998, which replaced the Anglo-Irish Agreement of November 1985 that had failed to eradicate violence, initiated a new peace process with enduring consequences which have transformed the political scene in Northern Ireland. New power-sharing institutions were established. And although contested initially, over the years their legitimacy has been recognized by political actors on both sides.

Presumably, the decommissioning of ETA weapons could also take a long time, not to mention the dismantling of its illegal activities. But unlike the Northern Ireland conflict, the Basque question does not involve two parties in a power-sharing dispute, namely Spain and the Basque Country (as assumed, for example, by Danis and Sanjurjo 2006). Nor has the Basque Country been invaded by Spain. Besides, there is no historical record of the Basque Country being an independent state. Euskal Herria, the longed-for state of nationalists, is simply an imagined community. The experience of self-government in the Basque Country is a creation of the Spanish Constitution of 1978. Taking these facts into consideration, the comparison with the Northern Ireland conflict is instructive, but should not lead to easy interpretations, since they are not symmetrical cases.

To begin with, taking the Basque case as a *conflict* between the Basque Country and Spain (and France) would be a political mistake. Furthermore, the basic problem is the presence of terrorism and other forms of violence, compromising the civil and political freedoms of Basque citizens. Solutions to this threat can spring from combined action by the democratic political leadership, a nationwide political consensus in support of the constitutional order, and international cooperation in policing and security matters. Lastly, it should not be forgotten that ETA is not the rightful political representative of Basque citizens, nor is it at all a legitimate political actor.

If in Northern Ireland the withdrawal of IRA weapons preceded the launching of the peace process, in Spain all peace talks have begun without that fundamental condition being met. This mediating concession has been a practice of conservative and socialist governments alike, with questionable results, for a negotiation not conducted under contractual terms becomes unreliable for the parties involved. As a further matter, ETA has always shown itself to be a rational actor that calculates its moves and the government's (Sánchez-Cuenca 2001). Conversely, all governments are supposed to be fully aware of its tactics when approaching ETA.

After long exploratory contacts with ETA's representatives, the Spanish government asserted before Congress in May 2005 its conviction that 'politics can and should contribute to the ending of violence'. A dialog was deemed viable if based on 'a clear will to end violence and on unequivocal attitudes that can lead to

---

8   See the complete proceedings at <http://cain.ulst.ac.uk/events/peace/decommission/iicdreports.htm>, last accessed 9 September 2006. CAIN is the Conflict and Politics in Northern Ireland Archive on the Internet, based at the University of Ulster.

that conviction'. The resolution was not sufficiently detailed, at least if compared, for example, with the 'Document on Decommissioning' signed in Belfast in June 1997 by the participants in the multi-party negotiations.[9] But by then, ETA's leadership was divided, its finances in bad shape, and its structure debilitated.

In fairness, no decommissioning was explicitly required, so when the talks officially began in the summer of 2006, the circumstances were not similar to those of 1998 in Northern Ireland. The irony of the attempt was that during the truce, ETA had rearmed, according to French and Spanish police sources (Chambraud 2006), and its network's finances had improved. Interrupting the talks, the government was right in leaving some room for further manoeuvre. Understandably, it asked Parliament for a second chance in January 2007.[10] The issue was whether a real possibility existed, and how to make it work. For any government, it would be extremely difficult to get rid of this trap created by ETA's claims, because an immediate consequence of their acceptance would be a partial suspension of the rule of law. Under question was not, and is not, the negotiation in itself, but its timing and the method chosen. ETA's expertise in the timing of violence needs to be matched by the government's skillfulness in conducting negotiations – a variant of the 'temporalization of scarcity' (Palonen 2006, 294–8).

The Basque Question in Perspective, Part II: Constitutional Limits to Politics

After all, both sides claimed the dialog was an opportunity for peace and democracy, although ETA's ideas of peace and democracy (peace after ethnic cleansing, and ethnic democracy, *Euskal demokrazia*, through revolutionary means) have nothing to do with their constitutionalist meanings. As shown by the comparative experience of the Northern Ireland case, the success of a democratizing experience relies mostly on the capacity to meet the conditions, not of constitutional, but of normal politics (Dahrendorf 1990, 30–31). Indeed, the role of constitutional politics has to do more with the mapping of reasonable itineraries than with the designing of models (Grimm 1991, 338–73), but not that alone.

In practice, the rationality and the viability of the changes envisaged (constitutional politics) are tested by the political response to both the foreseeable and the unexpected consequences of their implementation. That explains much of the failure and the success of democratizing experiments all over the world. Another reason lies in the effective application of constitutional limits to politics as a way of setting the legitimacy conditions for democratic politics. Secessionist debates are a unique illustration of this challenge.

Leaving aside hardly comparable examples, like Montenegro's independence from Serbia in May 2006, the Quebec case provides a learning experience for the

---

9   <http://cain.ulst.ac.uk/events/peace/docs/ai25697.htm>, accessed 9 September 2006.
10   *Diary of Sessions of the Congress of Deputies*, 207 (15 January 2007): <www.congreso.es/pdf/plenos/07/enero_07.htm>, accessed 30 January 2007.

Basque question. For decades, Quebec has been claimed as a model of secessionist struggle. The presentation by Basque nationalism, though, had been traditionally ambiguous, borrowing selected aspects of the secessionist debate while omitting others, until they wholeheartedly endorsed the passing by the Canadian House of Commons in November 2006 of a motion recognizing Quebec as a nation 'within a united Canada'.[11]

A formal rejection of secession had been expressed in two referendums held in the province in 1980 and 1995 at the request of the then governing Parti Québécois. In the second referendum, held in June 1995, 49.42 per cent voted yes, while 50.58 per cent said no to secession.[12] Such a narrow margin encouraged independentists to interpret the result loosely by criticizing the formulation of the referendum question. And the Quebec government claimed that, reading the outcomes, international law would sanction a process of independence where the Canadian government would not be competent to interfere.

In response, in September 1996, the federal government referred three questions to the Supreme Court on the constitutionality of a unilateral secession of Quebec from Canada. On 20 August 1998, the Supreme Court made public its decision, stating on the one hand that 'Quebec could not, despite a clear referendum result, purport to invoke a right of self-determination to dictate the terms of a proposed secession to the other parties to the federation.' On the other hand, it argued that 'Nor, however, can the reverse proposition be accepted: the continued existence and operation of the Canadian constitutional order could not be indifferent to a clear expression of a clear majority of Quebecers that they no longer wish to remain in Canada.'

This was a remarkable advance, but what clarity meant was still unsettled, since the Supreme Court had argued that it was up to political representatives to determine what constituted 'a clear majority on a clear question' to be submitted to referendum.[13] In an attempt to eliminate ambiguities, the Canadian government presented to Parliament in December 1999 the project for a Clarity Act, drafted by the then minister Stéphane Dion. The bill was finally passed by the House of Commons and by the Senate in March and June 2000, respectively.

In a detailed procedure, the Act established, among other provisions, that secession requires, first, a clear formulation of its consequences in a referendum question. Secession accordingly involves a multilateral negotiation between the federation and the provinces to agree upon the terms the separation would bring about, and the public circulation of information about the conditions and the effects. Second, what constitutes a "clear majority" could not be predetermined, but rather, should be definitely established by assessing the referendum outcomes. And third,

---

11   *House of Commons Debates*, vol. 141, No. 087, 1st Session, 39th Parliament: <www2.parl. gc.ca/housechamberbusiness/ChamberSittings.aspx?View=H&Language=E&Mode=1 &Parl=39&Ses=1>, accessed 24 February 2007.

12   Centre for Research and Information on Canada: <www.cric.ca/en_html/guide/ referendum/referendum1995.html>, accessed 8 September 2006.

13   Reference re Secession of Quebec, [1998] 2 S.C.R. 217: <http://scc.lexum.umontreal.ca/ en/1998/1998rcs2-217/1998rcs2-217.html>, accessed 8 September 2006.

should that happen, then a process would begin to amend the Constitution of Canada involving 'at least' the governments of all the provinces and the federal government (Dion 1999, 183–254).[14]

During the parliamentary debates on the granting to Quebec of national status, the Clarity Act was present, even though it was mentioned on just a few occasions. The coda of the motion, 'within a united Canada', was reminiscent of its constitutionalist spirit. The Clarity Act has been contested strongly by Canadian nationalists since, and some possibilities exist that it may be modified or revoked in the future. At any rate, it has contributed to strengthening the legal protection of the Canadian Constitution. The discussion will likely be resumed at election times, but the outcomes of the debates in Parliament sent a clear message to secessionist adventures – the constitutional rules of democracy cannot be altered to accommodate electoral interests. It is for that reason that the comparison with Quebec, and particularly with Canadian constitutionalism, is so inappropriate for Basque nationalism.

Solutions Postponed

For all the attempts to enter political life, ETA has defended the same programme through the same means ever since its founding in 1959. All peace talks so far have been conditioned by its unrenounceable demands. But some negotiations have produced hopeful results. From 1977 onwards, a series of contacts between the then centrist Spanish government and ETA's representatives culminated in the dissolution in September 1982 of a faction of ETA, the politico-military ETA VIIth Assembly. Most of its members entered the political left-wing party Euskadiko Ezkerra, which in March 1993 merged with the Socialist Party of the Basque Country (Domínguez Iribarren 2006). The other faction, military ETA, has since continued the terrorist program.

Maximalist as its conditions were, they have proven powerfully authoritative over time. The problem is not merely ideological. The imagined legitimacy of ETA's demands has been transmitted from generation to generation, thus nurturing the belief that the claims even justify fighting and dying for the cause. The resentment induced and re-created by various forms of hatred lies at the heart of terrorist violence, which is arguably one of the main reasons explaining a migration movement to other Spanish regions of some 200,000 Basque citizens over the past thirty years, more than 10 per cent of the total population (Barbería and Unzueta 2003). Worst of all, violence has threatened and threatens the lives and freedoms of thousands of citizens, and the prospects for an effective solution to this problem look somber.

Next to violence, the other major effect of this legacy has fallen upon the civil fabric of society, wounded by the pressure of a persistent threat. As a result, Basque

---

14   Clarity Act (Bill C-20): <http://laws.justice.gc.ca/en/c-31.8/228755.html>, accessed 8 September 2006.

society is divided along nationalist lines in a dramatic way (Llera 1993; Pérez-Agote 2006, 121–91). Citizens are strongly moved by a tragedy that has separated them, although not in irreparable ways. Political language, a symbolic example of this breach, has become trapped in a web of confusing intentions and meanings. Over time, the Basque political vocabulary has become pervaded by the double meanings, nationalist and non-nationalist, of words (González 2004). This would not be a major problem in normal circumstances, where political actors use different language games to interpret reality, and accordingly, to justify their stances and actions.

What singles out the Basque experience is that violence has transformed public life by prompting the alteration of meanings in precious concepts and ideas like democracy, human rights, peace, tolerance or dialog. This has made possible a disquieting cultivation of ambiguity, especially painful for the victims of violence, first and foremost by members of ETA's network, which, taken to the extreme, leads to the non-condemnation of terrorist violence or its imaging through euphemistic terms such as 'acts', 'actions', 'facts' or 'accidents', and to a much lesser degree by nationalist politicians, who clearly condemn violence although they cannot help but appeal to a potential electorate among ETA's supporters.

It is within this rarefied context that an institutional attempt to reform the regional autonomy statute came about. The so-called 'Ibarretxe Plan' came with the promise of eradicating violence, and received the endorsement of Batasuna. But the promise was linked to the traditional pro-sovereignty aspiration of ETA.

The plan, named after the Basque premier, had been drafted in 2002 as a nationalist alternative to the 1979 regional statute, introducing a formula of associated statehood with the rest of Spain (Ibarra and Ahedo 2004, 380–82). The change, arguably a constitutional reform, was to be negotiated bilaterally with the Spanish government, thereby circumventing the other 16 autonomous communities in a move of dubious constitutionality. The draft, passed by the Regional Parliament in December 2004, was rejected by the Spanish Congress in February 2005. By then, the foreseeable negotiations of the central government with ETA had seized the attention of public opinion. The initiative has since remained dormant, but was revived by the regional premier after December 2006 as an alternative to self-determination by force.

As a political proposal, the Ibarretxe Plan was not definitely illegal, according to Spain's Constitutional Court.[15] The relevant point for our discussion is that a nationalist government induced a nationalist debate among the citizenry through Parliament and other public institutions, with the odd result of furthering the nationalist divide within Basque society. Under the title 'Proposal for the Political Statute of the Community of the Basque Country', the initiative envisaged an eventual merger of the seven 'historical' Basque territories. It was claimed that Euskal Herria was not a mere dream, but a rightful goal founded on the self-

---

15   Decision 135/2004, of 20 April 2004: <www.tribunalconstitucional.es/AUTOS2004/ ATC2004-135.html>, accessed 19 September 2006.

determination right of the Basque people that the current statute and the Spanish Constitution were deemed unfit to acknowledge.

In order to proceed towards independence, the initiative advanced the idea of a transitory free association status with the rest of Spain, reminiscent of the status defended by the Parti Québécois in its 1968 programme (later abandoned in favour of full independence). The acceptance of this provisional regime, reads 'Article' 12.2, 'does not represent any waiver of the historical rights of the Basque People, which may be updated at any time in accordance with their own democratic wishes'. Hence, non-recognition of this demand would entail a flagrant violation of the 'right' to self-determination of the Basque people.

Three reasons are argued to support the move. First, a legal entitlement: the project itself is based upon the idea that the Basque people 'have the right to decide their own future', a claim already endorsed by the Basque Parliament in 1990, taking it as a legitimate expression of the will of the people, even though no legal procedure applied to assess that will. Second, political legitimacy: the Basque government is supposedly entitled to proceed with the initiative in the name of the Basque people. Third, economic interest: the new political settlement would be 'compatible with the possibilities of developing a pluri-national and asymmetric state'.

Still, if the secessionist demand is not consistent with international law's provisions on self-determination, the hopeful tone of the preamble turns into a severe warning at the end of the proposal. Thus, when the sequence of arguments leads to the transitory provision regulating the implementation of the statute through a referendum procedure, the *suaviter in forma* style disappears. Instead, *a fortiter in re* approach concludes the document by warning that should no agreement be reached, the 'Community of the Basque Country' would be entitled to proceed unilaterally with secession.[16] In sum, the project aimed to set up a democratic ethnic state. A gentle rhetoric of inclusion surrounds the idea of constituting Euskal Herria. But an implicit rhetoric of exclusion derives from the nationalist notion of a Basque people. Such a claim brings the initiative closer to ETA's project.

Prospects for the Future

After the breakdown of the 2006 cease-fire, the political scenario resembled that of preceding broken truces – again, frustrated expectations after a failed attempt to bring violence to an end. Public opinion thought the government handled information badly. Moreover, the sequence of optimistic statements by the government in previous months, underlining that ETA's end was closer than ever, proved overblown.[17]

---

16   Official English version: <www.nuevoestatutodeeuskadi.net/propuesta.asp?hizk=ing>, accessed 15 March 2007.

17   See, for example, the interview of *Die Zeit* with Prime Minister Zapatero on 7 September 2006, 'Haben wir etwa gewonnen?': <www.zeit.de/online/2006/36/zapatero-interview>, accessed 1 February 2007. The assumptions were almost uncritically shared

So what went wrong? At least three hypotheses can be argued. The first is that the assessment of the conditions that would undermine and finally defeat ETA's leadership was inaccurate. ETA's leaders were divided on the need to negotiate with the government, but the government's more recent offers (a regroupment of ETA's inmates was expected in the coming months) were not enough, even if they represented a major concession. Under what circumstances was there any chance to corner ETA's hard-line faction? Compared to other negotiations, the pragmatic faction was not in full command of the organization. And worse – the very existence of a pragmatic faction was questioned, which dramatically reduced the chances of a change of leadership, as confirmed by ETA's communiqué on 10 January 2007 and by a *Gara* newspaper interview on 8 April 2007.

The second is that civic trust in public institutions was damaged, the main reasons being that ETA's political wing, Batasuna, even if outlawed in 2003, had since received innumerable tokens of recognition from other political parties. The price to be paid for political deals should not overstep the limits of the law. The Basque government had held meetings with Batasuna during and after the cease-fire, in this way sending mixed signals to Basque citizens about the legitimacy of illegal political contacts.

A final hypothesis is that while the conditions for the unthreatened exercise of basic freedoms were lacking, it was politically imprudent to embark on any form of negotiation. The first condition – indeed *the* precondition – following the instructive example of Northern Ireland, should be the abandonment of all forms of violence.

It is an understandable aspiration of any government to eradicate violence and to lead to ETA's dissolution. But not at any price. The 30 December bomb attack reduced prospects for a resolution in the near future, but the situation was not completely hopeless. It was also a reminder that the fight against terrorism is a matter of state, and thus requires to build the amplest possible inter-party consensus within the constitutional order. In other words, it should not become an electoral issue (De Blas 2007).

All in all, it is interesting to note that the peace talks were not really a dialog, as each party adopted different procedural assumptions (negotiated steps and non-negotiable gains following the government's secession), pursued different ends (peace and self-determination) and, most important, resorted to different means to negotiate (concessions to ETA's demands and threats of violence).

Terrorism, argues Michael Ignatieff, 'has damaged liberal democracies, but it has never succeeded in breaking their political systems'. That is indeed one of the main hopes for democratization. 'One further assumption of the terrorists has proven wrong: that democratic peoples lack the will to fight for democracy.' The reverse is true: 'Terrorist emergencies have shown ... that democratic elites and publics alike can show a surprising tenacity when attacked' (Ignatieff 2004, 73).

No doubt, this kind of civic reaction is an encouraging factor in the fight against terrorism. The episode commented upon was arguably a case of

---

by newspapers like the *New York Times* and *The Economist*, while treated with some scepticism by *La Libre Belgique* and the *Frankfurter Allgemeine Zeitung*.

rhetorical democratization that reproduced the incommunicable condition of two contradictory discourses on democracy and peace, and showed the political actors in a state of disarray. The crucial hope was provided by the endurance of democratic institutions and by the response of citizens who once again took to the streets peacefully in hundreds of cities across Spain to show their rejection of terrorism. The government had the citizens' backing, though not their unconditional support. Something went wrong, and new chances should not mean revisiting former strategies. In the end, the experience proved dramatically how extremely difficult it is for a democracy to tackle the threat of terrorism within the limits of the rule of law. Furthermore, it shows the puzzling adjustment of nationalism to the civic and institutional conditions of constitutional democracy.

Acknowledgments

I am grateful to Javier Fernández Sebastián, Eloy García, Kari Palonen, Manuel Toscano and to the anonymous reviewer of this book for comments on earlier versions of this chapter.

References

Aizpeolea, L.R. (2007), 'Así fue el diálogo con ETA', *El País*, 10 June, Sunday Supplement, pp. 1–5.

Alonso, R. (2004), 'Pathways Out of Terrorism in Northern Ireland and the Basque Country: The Misrepresentation of the Irish Model', *Terrorism and Political Violence* 16:4, 695–713.

—— and Reinares, F. (2005), 'Terrorism, Human Rights and Law Enforcement in Spain', *Terrorism and Political Violence* 17:2, 265–78.

Barbería, J.L. and Unzueta, P. (2003), *Cómo hemos llegado a esto* (Madrid: Taurus).

Buesa, M. (2003), 'Secesión y los costes de la no-España en el País Vasco', *Cuadernos de Alzate* 28, 171–89.

Chambraud, C. (2006), 'Malgré le cessez-le-feu, l'ETA ne renonce pas aux armes', *Le Monde*, 26 September.

Connor, W. (1994), *Ethnonationalism: The Quest for Understanding* (Princeton, NJ: Princeton University Press).

Dahrendorf, R. (1990), *Reflections on the Revolution in Europe* (London: Chatto & Windus).

Danis, V. and Sanjurjo, D. (2006), 'Difficile adieu aux armes pour le Pays basque', *Le Monde diplomatique*, November, 4–5.

De Blas Guerrero, A. (2007), 'Las lecciones del proceso de paz', *El País*, 6 January.

Dion, S. (1999), *Straight Talk: On Canadian Unity* (Montreal and Ithaca, NY: McGill-Queen's University Press).

Domínguez Iribarren, F. (2003), *Las raíces del miedo. Euskadi, una sociedad atemorizada* (Madrid: Aguilar).

—— (2006), 'El enfrentamiento de ETA con la democracia', in Elorza (ed.), *La historia de ETA* (Madrid: Temas de hoy).

Elorza, A. (ed.) (2006), *La historia de ETA* (Madrid: Temas de hoy).

González, S. (2004), *Palabra de vasco. La parla imprecisa del soberanismo* (Madrid: Espasa).

Grimm, D. (1991), *Die Zukunft der Verfassung* (Frankfurt am Main: Suhrkamp).

Gunther, R. (ed.) (1993), *Politics, Society and Democracy: The Case of Spain (Essays in Honor of Juan J. Linz)* (Boulder, CO: Westview Press).

Horowitz, D.L. (1985), *Ethnic Groups in Conflict* (Berkeley, CA: University of California Press).

Ibarra, P. and Ahedo, I. (2004), 'The Political Systems of the Basque Country: Is a Non-polarized Scenario Possible in the Future?', *Nationalism and Ethnic Politics* 10:3, 355–86.

Ignatieff, M. (2004), *The Lesser Evil: Political Ethics in an Age of Terror* (Princeton, NJ: Princeton University Press).

Lago Penas, I. (2004), 'Cleavages and thresholds: the political consequences of electoral laws in the Spanish Autonomous Communities, 1980–2000', *Electoral Studies* 23:1, pp. 23–43.

Lake, D.A. and Rothchild, D. (eds) (1998), *The International Spread of Ethnic Conflict* (Princeton, NJ: Princeton University Press).

Llera, F.J. (1993), '*Conflicto en Euskadi* Revisited', in Gunther (ed.), *Politics, Society and Democracy: The Case of Spain (Essays in Honor of Juan J. Linz)* (Boulder, CO: Westview Press).

Moreno, L. (2001), *The Federalization of Spain* (London: Frank Cass).

Palonen, K. (2006), *The Struggle with Time: A Conceptual History of 'Politics' as an Activity* (Münster: Lit).

Pérez-Agote, A. (2006), *The Social Roots of Basque Nationalism*, trans. C. Watson and W.A. Douglass. (Reno, NV: University of Nevada Press).

Pérez-Díaz, V.M. (1993), *The Return of Civil Society: The Emergence of Democratic Spain* (Cambridge, MA: Harvard University Press).

Sánchez-Cuenca, I. (2001), *ETA contra el Estado. Las estrategias del terrorismo* (Barcelona: Tusquets).

Unzueta, P. (2006), 'Epílogo: Regreso a casa', in Elorza (ed.), *La historia de ETA* (Madrid: Temas de hoy).

Waluchow, W. (2007), 'Constitutionalism", *The Stanford Encyclopedia of Philosophy* (Spring 2007), ed. Edward N. Zalta, <http://plato.stanford.edu/archives/spr2007/entries/constitutionalism>.

Wieland, L. (2007), 'Terror und Dialog', *Frankfurter Allgemeine Zeitung*, 25 January.

Further Reading

Antxustegi-Igartua, E. (2007), *El debate nacionalista. Sabino Arana y sus herederos* (Murcia: Universidad de Murcia).

Conversi, D. (ed.) (2002), *Ethnonationalism in the Contemporary World: Walker Connor and the Study of Nationalism* (London: Routledge).

Douglass, W.A. (2002), 'Sabin's sin: Racism and the founding of Basque nationalism', in Conversi (ed.), *Ethnonationalism in the Contemporary World: Walker Connor and the Study of Nationalism* (London: Routledge).

Etxeberria, X. et al. (2002), *Derecho de autodeterminación y realidad vasca* (Vitoria: Servicio Central de Publicaciones del Gobierno Vasco).

Manswelt-Beck, J. (2005), *Territory and Terror: Conflicting Nationalism in the Basque Country* (London: Routledge).

Martínez-Herrera, A. (2002), 'Nationalist Extremism and Outcomes of State Policies in the Basque Country, 1979–2001', *International Journal on Multicultural Societies* 4:1, pp. 16–40.

Reinares, F. (ed.) (2000), *European Democracies Against Terrorism: Governmental Policies and Intergovernmental Cooperation* (Aldershot: Ashgate).

—— and Jaime, O. (2000), 'Countering Terrorism in a New Democracy: The Case of Spain', in Reinares (ed.), *European Democracies Against Terrorism: Governmental Policies and Intergovernmental Cooperation* (Aldershot: Ashgate).

Salbidegoitia, J.M. and Montaña, J. (2002), *Vocabulario democrático del lenguaje político vasco* (Vitoria: Asociación Ciudadanía y Libertad).

The Dis-/Appearance
of the *Demos*

Meike Schmidt-Gleim

The routine of the current representative democracies in Europe makes us unaware of their fundamental condition. Moments of seeming dysfunction give a hint as to what is left out in these presumably well-working systems. In this sense, the uprisings in the *banlieues* of France's metropolitan areas in fall 2005 shed a light on basic questions of democracy. Giving a negative example of the public understanding of representative democracy, we can – by analyzing the riots – unravel what is often forgotten in the operations of modern democracies or reduced to a meaningless point of reference: the sovereignty of the people.

Sovereignty of the people tends to be merely associated with elections. But elections widely decline to a tautological system, in that they stand for the representation of the people by creating representation according to specific voting measures and by restricting representation to these procedures.

In the following pages, I shall argue, on the basis of the reactions toward the riots in France in 2005, how the people are taken as unable to lead their own discourse, and in consequence, remain politically unrepresented. The analysis concentrates on the accounts of the unrest transmitted by international media. It does not seek to illuminate more authentic details on behalf of the rioters, but focuses on what is missing in the media debates. It is in these discourses that a specific concept of politics is constructed, which is leaving out the question of popular sovereignty.

The chapter starts by giving an overview on the events happened, then looks for what was considered to be the reason for the riots. This will be followed by an analysis of the political practice that is suggested to be applied, and by asking which political practice is missing in this panorama. The second half of the chapter treats more theoretical aspects by defining governmental representation and its counterpart, democratic representation.

The riots started off on 27 October 2005 in the Paris suburb of Clichy-sous-Bois after two youngsters died. Zyed Benna (17) and Bouna Traoré (15) were accidentally electrocuted while trying to escape a police identity check by hiding in a power substation. On 1 November, the riots spread out from Clichy-sous-Bois to Seine-Saint-Denis, and subsequently to other parts of Île-de-France. Then they jumped south to Nice, east to Strasbourg, west to Nantes, and to other cities in and outside France.[1] On 8 November, the French government adopted a law decree dated 3 April 1955, instituting a state of emergency,[2] authorizing curfews and house searches without an official mandate by a judge.[3]

Four weeks after the riots started, the score sheet summed almost 9,000 cars torched, 96 public buildings, schools, community centers, post offices and police headquarters burnt out, more than a hundred people injured, including police officers (Cobbe, 7 November 2005), and 3101 people arrested, with 562 held in detention (Lagrange 2006, 47).

A brief view into history tells us that torched cars as a political means to draw the attention of the public to the *banlieues* have a tradition that goes back to 1980. There have been uprisings in these suburbs ever since. Even before the riots, an average of 3,500 cars were burnt across France every month.[4] The current unrest was merely unusual in terms of its duration and the way it had spread (Holmes 2006).

Reasons for the Riots

What goes wrong that parts of the people[5] fight against their elected representatives in a democratic state? What goes wrong that this group of people doesn't feel represented by their state? Is this a crisis of *representation*?

The general answer to these questions is that it is a problem of *integration* – not of representation. The rioters are not well integrated into French society. The word 'representation' was only mentioned once by the contemporary President Jacques Chirac, but not in connection to political representation. Instead, he asked the media for a better reflection of French diversity.[6]

---

1   'Banlieue à savoir', *Libération*, 15 November 2005, 2.

2   The law instituting the emergency state is Law no. 55–385, from 3 April 1955, text of the law: <www.fil-info-france.com/actualites-monde/etat,uregence,france.htm>, accessed 15 November 2005.

3   'Banlieue à savoir', *Libération*, 15 November 2005; 'France, in disorder, declares emergency; Curfews are aimed at quelling riots', *The International Herald Tribune*, 9 November 2005. The state of emergency was abolished on 4 January 2006 ('Chirac met fin à l'état d'urgence', *Libération*, 2 January 2005).

4   'Saturday: What we've learned', *Guardian*, 19 November 2005.

5   The actual number of active participants is, interestingly enough, never mentioned in the media. But as the riots spread all over France, causing severe damage and leading to about 3,000 arrests, the number involved should not be underestimated.

6   'Le chef de l'Etat a annoncé lundi, dans le cadre de la lutte contre les discriminations, qu'il rencontrerait 'l'ensemble des responsible de l'audiovisuel', afin que les médias reflètent mieux la diversité française d'aujourdhui' ('Les télés favourable à davantage de diversité mais contre les quotas', *AFP/L'Agence France Press*, 15 November 2005). Yet *Le nouvel Economiste* warned that 'même si Jacques Chirac converse avec un casting de jeunes gens sur TF1 pour déviser laborieusement du traité européen, ou intervient

So who are the rioters, why is their problem mainly seen as a problem of integration, and not of representation? The majority of the involved rioters are the offspring of immigrant families. But they were born in France, raised and educated in France, and carry a French passport – legally, they are French citizens, and at the age of 18 they can vote and hence participate in the representative system.

The fact that many of the rioters were under 18, approximately a third of those arrested (Lagrange and Oberti 2006, 49), does not contradict this perception. Participation in the representative system only requires some patience. So representation is taken for granted, and integration seems to be the right answer to the problem. (Apart from these basic data, little information was given about the rioters in the media. No common organization existed, nor any collective declarations toward the public.)

Everybody seems to agree on the point that integration is lacking. The reflections on the questions of who and what is responsible for it, however, vary from different political angles:

The *social* explanation refers to the high unemployment rate in the *banlieues*: France has the highest unemployment rate in Western Europe. And for young people in project housing (the so-called *cités*, degraded and stigmatized, with a high level of segregation; Lagrange and Oberti 2006, 14), it is at least twice as hard to find a decent job than for middle-class youth – the average unemployment rate in the poorer suburbs is more than twice the national average, at 20.7 per cent. And in some of the hardest-hit areas, 50 per cent of young people are jobless.[7]

The *criminalistic* explanation claims that there are 'others' behind some of the violence. Some of the project housing schemes are 'no-go' zones, where drug dealers and criminal gangs rule. According to Nicolas Sarkozy, in those days the French Interior Minister, two-thirds of those arrested were known to the police services (Lagrange 2006, 46). The French daily newspaper *Libération* wrote that the Prime Minister Dominique de Villepin connected the riots to organized criminality (Tourancheau, 16 November 2005, 4).[8]

The *cultural* explanation blames differences in customs for the lack of integration of immigrants. Nicolas Sarkozy said: 'Let us put it as it is: polygamy

---

à 20 heures pour admettre qu'il a compris l'exaspération des banlieues, les jeunes ne semblent avoir aucun autre relais dans la société que la Star Academy et Top of the pop. Consomme, télécharge et tais-toi' ('Evènement – Le péril jeune – Expression spoliée, faible représentativité, émiettement des solidarités et valeurs en demi-tente: le jeunisme véhiculé par les pouvoirs médiatiques et économiques masque difficilement les frustations réelles des nouvelles générations. Attention, société bloquée', *Le nouvel Economiste*, 17 November 2005).

7   'L'emploi. Mission impossible', *L'Express*, 17 November 2005; 'France's Failure – of riots and failure', *The Economist*, 12 November 2005: 'The biggest lesson of the French riots is that more jobs are needed.'

8   '"Je refuse que les réseaux du crime et des traffics de drogue profitent des déordres pour prospérer", a martelé Dominique de Villepin le 3 Novembre face à l'explosion des violences urbaines, qu'il liait au crime organisé.' (P. Tourancheau, 'Les émeutes, aubaine policière; Evènment 1. Banlieue', *Libération*, 16 November 2005, 4).

and a-culturalization of a certain number of families are the reasons why it is more difficult for a young French woman of African origin than a young French of any other origin to integrate.'[9] Two other political representatives of the center-right Union pour an Mouvement Populaire (UMP) held similar views: the Delegate Labor Market Minister, Gérard Larcher,[10] and Bernard Accoyer,[11] President of the UMP faction at the Assemblée Nationale.

It is obvious how these different arguments are distributed across different political parties. The left contested vehemently Sarkozy calling the young people 'scum' or 'hooligans' – he used the French term *racaille* – and criticized strongly the repeated reference to polygamy.[12] The question of what and who triggered the riots is a contentious political subject. Thus, the correct interpretation, explanation and ideas of how to deal with the incidents differ very much from each other and are a source of conflict.

The anti-racist NGO SOS Racisme – founded in 1984 – declared in a press release its indignation about the reference to polygamy, arguing that this assimilation of polygamy and uprisings reveals a crude intention to distract the public from the real problems.[13]

So what are the suppressed real problems? According to SOS Racisme, responsible politicians are incompetent to intervene and respond to the difficulties the populations of the banlieues face – meaning the social exclusion of these areas.[14]

At first sight, the gap between a position such as the government's 'hardliners', who blame disorder in families and criminality, and a position such as SOS Racisme's, which blames the government, seem unbridgeable. But do the positions of the right and the left really differ so much?

It has already been said that both sides hold the lack of *integration* responsible for events. And who should take care of improving integration of excluded youth?

---

9   Nicolas Sarkozy: 'Mais disons les choses comme elles sont: la polygamie et l'a-culturation d'un certain nombre de familles font qu'il est plus difficile d'intégrer un jeune Français originaire d'Afrique noire qu'un jeune Français d'une autre origine' (J. Denis, 'Nicolas Sarkozy contre-attaque: Une interview exclusive', *L'Express*, Spécial banlieue, 17 November 2005, 28).

10   'M. Larcher fait le lien entre polygamie et violences urbaines', *Le Monde*, 16 November 2005; 'Polygamy played part in French riots', *Financial Times*, 16 November 2005, 8.

11   'L'essentiel de la semaine', *L'Humanité*, 19 November 2005.

12   'France unable to stop rioting for an eighth night', *The Independent*, 14 November 2005; 'Opinion: What Sarko did wrong; France's top cop has erred in statement and more important in policy', *Newsweek*, 14 November 2005.

13   'Quand l'indécence sert à masquer l'incompétence', SOS Racisme, at <www.sos-racisme.org/index.php?option_com_content&task=view&id=509&Itemid=77>, published online 15 November 2005.

14   'Ce que les émeutes urbaines ont montré, c'est avant tout la crasse incompétence des responsables politiques à apporter une réponse aux difficultés rencontrées par les populations vivant dans les quartiers difficiles': *SOS Racisme*, at <www.sos-racisme.org/index.php?option_com_content&task=view&id=509&Itemid=77>, published online 15 November 2005.

In substance, all positions, whether they are from the left or from the right, agree in that institutions have failed – the state, the family,[15] and Claire Brisset, Director of the Défenseur des enfants institution, adds the role of the school as an important factor in the crisis.[16]

Whether it is the state held responsible for unemployment, the family held responsible for not keeping young people at home or the school held responsible for their bad education, it seems that there is a common agreement that the riots broke out because young people have not been taken sufficient care of, and hence have not become normal and docile citizens. All of these approaches are basically looking for integration of this 'second or third'-generation immigrant population by paying greater attention to them, be it at school, at home or in the work sphere.[17]

Racism as an independent motor of exclusion is mentioned very rarely in the French media as a cause for the riots. The universalist French state does not consider race a political category. Keith Richburg writes: '… it is considered unlawful even to keep statistics by race religion or ethnicity'.[18]

Contrary to that, the anglophone media consider it to be a crucial factor. The CBS reported, for instance, that Nasser Ramdane, a member of SOS Racisme who is of Arab descent, said that after the 1998 World Cup victory with its multi-racial team, they were French; after September 11th, they were Islamists, victim of the generalized idea that all Muslims are Islamists – another source of discontent among these people. Educated alongside Jean-Charles and Sandrine, who have gone on to good jobs, it is no wonder Mohamed and Mustapha feel the French slogan of 'liberté, égalité, fraternité' is colour-coded.[19]

Interestingly enough, the government admits failures in respect to the youth of the poor suburbs. But racism is a good example to have a closer look at what is considered to be the failure of the state. It becomes clear that the state does not give itself an active role in the racist exclusion of young people from French society. No discussion led by the government recognizes racism as being embedded in the structures of the state in order to conserve power relations and exclude newcomers in the traditional institutions.

Supposedly, the failures of the state do not lie in the state's practices. Instead, the public receives the image of an innocent state, which is perceived as a paternal

---

15   'Chirac blames riots on parents', *The Mirror*, 15 November 2005; 'Immigrant parents pressured in France; Unrest brings calls to control children', *International Herald Tribune*, 14 November 2005.

16   'Tout ce qu'on a dit sur le chômage, la pauvreté, la précarité, etc., est tout à faite juste', même si 'on a peut-être un peu sous-estimé le problème lié à l'école' ('Communiqué de presses lors de l'entretien de la défenseure des enfants, Mme Claire Brisset avec Jacques Chirac', *AFP/L'Agence France Press*, 17 November 2005).

17   'Chirac says riots rooted in "deep malaise"; French leader urges hiring of Minorities, More Integration', *Washington Post*, 15 November 2005.

18   K. Richburg, 'The other France, separate and unhappy', *Washington Post*, 13 November 2005.

19   E. Cobbe, 'Reporter's notebook from Paris', *CBS News*, <www.cbsnews.com>, published online 7 November 2005.

institution. What the state is to blame for – according to state officials – is that it was not there when the people (the minors) were in need of it. It failed to take enough care of everyone (because it was busy). It failed to take care of the job market, it failed to prevent criminality, it failed to discipline the families, and it failed to install a good educational system. And other political groups agree.

Regardless the background of the political groups, parties and institutions, the demands are commonly shared. They ask for improvements in administration of the difficult areas, which means a stronger presence of the state – not in the sense of a repressive state (repression is only considered to be a short-term measure against the uprisings). Whether left or right, everybody demands a paternal state, a caring family or a protective school system, which takes young people under their wing. Political proposals to deal with the situation are putting new formation and job programs for them on the agenda, programs to form and educate them.[20]

Governmentality

What does this mean for the question of where the problem is located? Detecting the problem in institutions like the state, the school and the family means locating it in the disciplinary apparatus, and asking for state administration of the problems means that it is widely considered to be a crisis of *governmentality*.

According to Michel Foucault, governmentality is a tradition of government which is deducted homologically from the *oikos*; the state is formalized as an extended family (Foucault 1978 [2001], 635–57). This means on the one hand that the government follows the principles of a household, the economy of a household. It regulates the distribution and exchange of the individuals who form the state's population. It is politics as economy, political economy. Jean-Jacques Rousseau was among the authors who developed the concept of *political economy*. (Ahead of his times, Rousseau had already given an account of governmentality, although without the critical impetus which fuels the writings of Foucault.)

Governing is not merely about ruling and decision-making. Governing instead means optimizing society's goods. Foucault wrote: 'quel peut être son but? … d'améliorer le sort des populations, d'augmenter leurs richesses, leur durée de vie, leur santé'[21] (Foucault 1978 [2001], 652).

On the other hand, in order to achieve this goal, the government takes care of every single member of the society with the same amount of care and diligence, as in paternal custody, it cares for the economic growth as well as the health of each individual of the population. Rousseau asked: 'l'engagement du corps de la nation

---

20   P. Gouillaud and B. Jeudy, 'Service civil, nouvelle urgence du gouvernement', *Le Figaro*, 18 November 2005.

21   'What can be its goal? … It is to improve the destiny of the population, increase their goods, their lifetime and their health.' All translations are mine.

n'est-il pas de pourvoir à la conservation du dernier de ses membres avec autant de soin qu'a celle de tous les autres?[22] (Rousseau 1762a [1964], 78).

The subject of the state is conceived of as a sum of distinguished and distinguishable parts, individuals who are administrated separately, each individual specifically, or as Foucault says, each is disposed in space and time. It establishes an organization of the people.

Why is it useful to institute such a governmental principle? The aim of governmentality is to make the laws loved by the people: 'Mais quoique le gouvernement ne soit pas le maître de la loi, c'est beaucoup d'en être le garant et d'avoir mille moyens de la faire aimer. Ce n'est qu'en cela que consiste le talents de régner?'[23] (Rousseau 1762a [1964], 72). Only a government which takes care of every single member of society can guarantee loyalty to the state. But loyalty is not a very precise expression, as the governmental state produces the subjects it needs. The subjects subjectify the dominant norms, and consider themselves the authors of their deeds, which correspond to these norms. In other words: people become what the state wants them to be, and consider this to be their very specific nature. Rousseau wrote: 'S'il est bon de savoir employer les hommes tels qu'ils sont, il vaut mieux encore les rendre tels qu'on a besoin qu'ils soient; l'autorité la plus absolue est celle qui pénètre jusqu'à 'intérieur de l'homme'[24] (Rousseau 1762a [1964], 73).

Going back to the current crisis in Paris, this analysis underlines what the different representatives argue: the institutions are in a crisis. Apparently, the French state did not take care of every single member of society with the same amount of care and diligence to guarantee love of the laws by all of its members.

But what does it take to strengthen this sort of government, of governmental principles? It means focusing the reforms on the means of the classical *disciplinary society* implementing disciplinary and regulatory practices – a system including the state, the workplace, the school and the family which organizes the lives of the individuals in order to optimize society.[25] New job programs, more family control and better public education are the common answers to the difficulties.

Where is the Political Community?

In the governmental account of politics, the political community is replaced by a different kind of community that is deeply unpolitical, in that it oppresses

---

22 'Isn't the engagement of the body of the nation to take care of the last of its members with the same diligence as all the others?'
23 'Even though the government is not the master of the law, it is very much its guarantor and has a thousand ways to make it loved. Is this not what the talent to rule is about?'
24 'If it is good to know how to employ people as they are, it is even better to make them into what we need them to be; the most absolute power is the one that penetrates people to their interior.'
25 According to Michel Foucault, both were developed in the eighteenth century (Foucault 1997).

collectivity by restricting everyone to a predesignated place: society. The French case made this very explicit when Jacques Chirac, during the riots, demanded a more accurate representation of the different groups of the population on television screens, reflecting the mixture of skin types in French society.[26] This could appear a step forward toward opening up representation to the excluded. A closer look, though, will show that it is part of the disciplinary governmental practice.

What is society? And in which sense is it unpolitical? Hannah Arendt claims that society emerges after the extension of the public sphere to the economic (Arendt 1958, 38ff.). It is a form of community which considers the household, with its practices, forms of organization and concerns, matters of public interest. Until then, politics was understood to only emerge 'after' economic problems were solved. 'A system of political economy would have been a contradictory term.'

This emergence of the social in the public is, to Arendt's eyes, a negative turn: society describes a horizon, within which people are conducted toward conformism (see Arendt 1958, 39). Their private matters become the object of public concern, and thus societies set up norms according to which people have to behave (Arendt 1958, 45ff.).[27]

The model of politics in antiquity demanded the opposite: private matters should be left behind, in order to be liberated from these concerns and to be free for political action and to concentrate on collective matters.

The conformist effects of society should not be mistaken as constituting equality among citizens (Arendt 1958, 41). In a society, individuals have unequal positions, thus forming a community of inequality. Whereas the political sphere was constituted through the appearance in the public space, individuals in society are allocated to different places, and are bound to stay in them. The social provides secure identities, but no freedom, because it restricts individuals to these assigned identities. Freedom, yet, demands leaving the secure place and being ready to risk one's life (Arendt 1958, 36).[28]

In society, the individual is discovered, every single member is registered and captured with their specific needs via opinion polls, statistics or even lobby groups. The people thus becomes individualized, and the individuals identifiable. The people become a population – as Foucault has put it in his account of bio-power[29] – disposing and disseminating individuals on separate places in the social space (Foucault 1978 [2001]).

26　'Les télés favourable à davantage de diversité mais contre les quotas', *AFP/L'Agence France Press*, 15 November 2005.

27　'It is decisive that society ... excludes the possibility of action, which formerly was excluded from the household. Instead, society expects from each of its members a certain kind of behaviour, imposing innumerable and various rules, all of which tend to "normalize" its members ...' (Arendt 1958, 40).

28　'Whoever entered the political realm had first to be ready to risk his life, and too great love of life obstructed freedom, was a sure sign of slavishness' (Arendt 1958, 36).

29　The population is constituted in the second half of the eighteenth century by new regulatory practices such as demographical statistics that coexist with disciplinary ones (Foucault 1997, 218ff.).

When Chirac demands to represent the diversity of the people, he is referring to the people as population with different identities and needs. And even though he demands to shift and extend the assigned places for these identities, they remain prefigured places in society.

His proposal fits all too well into the realm of disciplinary governmental programs, which indeed try to satisfy the necessities of each particular individual. Slavoj Zizek comments: ' … a vast legal-psychological-sociological network of measures, from identifying the specific problems of each group and subgroup (not only homosexuals but African-American lesbians, African-American lesbian mothers, African-American single unemployed lesbian mothers) to proposing a set of measures ("affirmative action", etc.) to rectify the wrong' (Zizek 1999, 34). In the case of the French uprisings in the *banlieues,* one could cite the young second-generation North-African Islamic unemployed school drop-out immigrant from a polygamous household.

A governmentally acting government pretends to do what the people really want. It attempts to accommodate the concrete heterogeneity of the people, of subjecting its representation to the specific particularities of each member of society. Each social group receives specifically adapted treatment.

The heterogeneity that this system seems to introduce finds its boundaries in any attempt to transcend what one is supposed to be, according to such instruments as opinion polls and statistics. The system eliminates anything that transcends the sum of particular wills – any collectivity is abandoned before it can appear. Political struggle for recognition is avoided by the routine of personal treatment.

The distribution of individuals knows of no exteriority, of no one and nothing that is not represented. It constructs a society that is identical with itself – full integration of each of its members.

Everyone is represented, and everyone is transparent. Everyone is what he or she empirically is. The individual cannot recognize any difference between himself and his representation, because the individual is only what is represented. It is integrated. So what seems to be a demand for political representation of the people is in fact an offer to integrate them into society.

People as *Demos*

Something else: a different form of community is, strangely enough, completely left aside in the current debates for reform and political answers to the crisis – the people as *demos.* The *demos* that has given democracy its name and that is supposed to rule in a democracy, is never a subject in the public debate.[30]

---

30   Rancière writes that on the one hand the *demos* is the term for those who are not integrated in the parliament or *polis.* But it is at the same time the ground on which the poor or excluded identify with the whole of the community. Rancière distinguishes two subjects of the *demos*: the poor crowd, and the political community of equals. The political moment happens when the excluded *demos* calls for its rights to represent the

Nowhere in the political analyses of the crisis is it mentioned that the *demos* is apparently not well represented, that there is apparently no public arena where the *demos*, the young people, can appear other than destructive – although in a way that was very media-savvy.

So where is the *demos*? It is on the streets rioting, or at least a part of it. What does it want? Why are people rioting? Here we stumble over another strange fact. We don't know. Who is giving us the different explanations for the political unrest? Who is telling us why youths are torching cars? All we know, all explanations and interpretations of the events whether from the right or the left, everything that is said is an interpretation by institutional representatives. But the question, 'Who is talking?' is never asked.

So the young people rioting do not seem to say anything. 'They have nothing to say,' is what people responded to me whenever I asked. 'They only know how to destroy, torch cars and burn public buildings.' And they are minors. But did the French state authorities ever challenge the qualities of public speech and negotiation of the young rioters, announcing: 'We, the state authorities, would negotiate with you when you send us a delegate? Who speaks for you?'?[31] This might sound naïve, but isn't it just as naïve to presume to know what is at stake in the unrests?

The brother of one of the victims, Siyakah Traore, called on RTL radio[32] for youths to 'calm down and stop ransacking everything', adding: 'This is not how we are going to have our voices heard.'[33] So maybe there are more people who want to make their voices heard than the media and political representatives suppose. A politics that is only directed toward better governmentality means again a yet more efficient way to shut young people up. The fact that many of the rioters were very young facilitates the state's intention to keep them as minors. I do not doubt that it can be a very efficient way to cope with the recent problems of violence on the streets. But what is the role of democracy in this scenario? Maybe, apart from the crisis of the disciplinary institutions, a democratic deficit can be found: the disappearance of the *demos* as sovereign.

---

people and thus brings the non-coincidence of the two subjects to the fore (see Rancière 1997, 99 ff.).

31   Olivier Masclet gives a very interesting analysis in his article on the gap between left-wing parties in France and second-generation immigrants, which leads to the problem that there is no political participation of these youths, and their voices remain unrepresented (Masclet 2006).

32   'French Youths still on Rampage', *Birmingham Post*, 5 November 2005, 7; 'French unrest spreads outside Paris', *Guardian Unlimited*, <www.guardian.co.uk/france/ story/0,,1634739,00.html#article_continue>, published online 4 November 2005.

33   Gary Younge argued that 'Riots are a class act – and often they're the only alternative: France now accepts the need for social justice. No petition, peaceful march or letter could have achieved this': *Guardian*, 14 November 2005, 31.

Sovereignty

Rousseau describes the *gouvernement* as a governing concept that exists in addition and next to another principle, the *sovereignty* of the people.

What is sovereignty? In contrast to the principle of governmentality, it is not a principle of organizing, disposing and disseminating individuals, but of making decisions by imposing laws on the community. The sovereign founds new laws, instead of administering the existing laws as the *gouvernement* does. The sovereign is the legislative, whereas the government is the executive, the magistrate – the police, the social and educational system.

The sovereign was traditionally the king. In a democratic state, the sovereign is the people, the people as *demos*, but who is the demos? The demos shall stand for the political subject of the people. It is a collective being, which appears in the public as a political community. In contrast to society, the *demos* is a community of equals – to be precise, it is equals by law, not sociologically defined equals.[34]

Who belongs to this community of equals? Who is part of the *demos*? Everybody who appears as such belongs to the *demos*. The margins of the *demos* cannot be preconceived. It cannot, for example, be restricted to the community of voters or legal citizens. Joseph Vogl reminds us that the convention founds the people, and not the other way round: the people are not the condition of the convention. The people do not anticipate the convention.[35] The people consists of everyone who is assembled in the convention. Therefore, it remains a precarious and ephemeral object. The people does not have one voice, but many. It does not build a unity, but heterogeneity. So the *demos* can potentially interrupt any confined society (Vogl 1994a, 9). The appearance of the *demos* challenges the existing society and its specific inequality.

In this sense, the current uprising has to be recognized as an appearance of the *demos*. The young people joining the uprising moved away from the places they were assigned to in society, and thus they called the given society into question.

It can be considered as an appearance of the *demos*, but it signifies at the same time the disappearance of the *demos* as sovereign. The *demos* does not have any competencies. On the contrary, one can detect that sovereignty does not even fully lie in the hands of elected representatives, but is to a great extent taken over by the executive – while pretending to fulfill merely executive tasks. Figures like the state of emergency – which was declared by the French state officials facing the *banlieues'* unrests – serve as an official form to justify what is daily practice: measures are implemented without going through the law-making process which would publicly present the sovereign's moves and could be called into question by the popular sovereign. Advisers, experts and magistrates make decisions by

---

34　'Pour que la communauté politique soit plus qu'un contrat entre des échangeur de biens ou de services; il faut que l'egalité qui y règne soit radicalement différente de celle selon laquelle les marchandises et les dommages se réparent' (Rancière 1995, 24).

35　'… die Versammlung der Gemeinschaft gründet … [die Gesellschaft]' ('the convention of the community founds [the society]') (Vogl 1994a, 9).

translating statistics – formally infallible results of scientific research – into action programs. The mere execution of the 'people's will' in fact eliminates the people's will.

Furthermore, the existing exclusion of areas such as the poor *banlieues* is only deepened, in that the government operates via means of inclusion and exclusion. The public widely discussed instruments like the curfew, but other measures implemented, such as interrupted bus services, have an equally excluding effect on people and are much more invisible to the public. This latter operation is sustained by decisions made by the administrative apparatus – thus, it is the government that acts sovereign. Did popular sovereignty disappear?

Representative Democracy and Popular Sovereignty

How can these young people become politically represented? Does the actual appearance of the *demos* in riots reveal a moment of dysfunction of the representative system? Where can popular sovereignty be retrieved? And more fundamental: what is the role of popular sovereignty in the current system of representation?

In Rousseau's classical concept of popular sovereignty, representation has to be self-representation in order to render the people sovereign. Any representation that stands in for the people suspends popular sovereignty. He writes: 'Que la souveraineté est inaliénable … Je dis donc que la souveraineté n'étant que l'exercice de la volonté générale ne peut jamais s'aliéner, et que le souverain, qui n'est qu'un être collectif, ne peut être représenté que par lui-même; le pouvoir peut bien se transmettre, mais non pas la volonté' (Rousseau 1762b [1964], 190).

It is the actual performance, the moment, where the people enter the stage that characterizes sovereignty. The meaning of representation converges with the presence of the people. Joseph Vogl puts it, in his reading of Rousseau, in the following words: 'Where the represented are found there are no more representatives' (Vogl 1994a, 9). This perception is at first sight contradictory to our current system of representative democracy, as the focus lies on the appointment of representatives acting in the place of the people, representatives who act sovereign.

So how is the role of these representatives to be considered? Are they simply undemocratic? At first sight, the gap between Rousseau's account of popular sovereignty and our representative system is unbridgeable. The people are mostly not much more than a point of reference, representatives act in the name of the people while the people are absent. But is there no possibility of conceptualizing these two forms of representation in their interaction, the actual appearance of the people or *demos*, and the operations of elected representatives? And could it not be that the popular sovereign is reappearing in the relation of presence and representation?

I would argue that democratic representation lies exactly in the duality that is opened up between the presence of the people and their representation. In the latter, the continuum of the system is inscribed, the first can provide a chain of democratic moments where the people appear in public, which guarantees democracy. Elections, demonstrations and other forms of reunions of the people are moments of an appearance of the people – as well as the riots in the *banlieues*. But where can the popular sovereign reappear?

So far, I have claimed that unrests are an event where the *demos* appears, but at the same time disappears as sovereign because the people remain without discourse and the legislative lies in the hands of the elected representatives. The mere presence of the people is apparently not enough to constitute popular sovereignty. Now I would like to take a closer look at the interaction between the *demos* and elected representatives in order find out whether there is not a popular sovereign hidden in this relationship.

Rousseau defines popular sovereignty as the general will of the people. All particular wills are given up in favour of the formation of a general will: 'Chacun de nous met en commun sa personne et toute sa puissance sous la suprême direction de la volonte générale; et nous recevons en corps chaque membre comme une partie indivisible du tout' (Rousseau 1762b [1964], 183).

The community of the rioters, now, is clearly not the realization of Rousseau's ideal conception of the general will. On the contrary, the riots in the *banlieues* of Paris started off because this group of people is excluded from the common will. The parts of the people emerging in self-representative moments such as demonstrations or unrests do not build a part of the whole. Still the general will plays a role. It is the reference point of the protesters, the ideal against which the exclusion becomes a disadvantage. Moreover, it is the form of the political claim. The claim becomes political because the rioters claim: 'We are the people – and not a sociologically defined interest group. We, a part – in the case of the part, which has no share of the whole – claim to be universal' (see Rancière 1995).

If this performative enunciation, 'We are the people,' of the protesters is strong enough to confront the representative claim, 'in the name of the people', of the officially nominated representatives, then a gap between these two forms of 'representation', which contests the legitimization of the latter, appears.

This gap at first sight seems to point at a failure of democratic representation. But in fact it is viable for democratic representation, because this is where one can find remnants of popular sovereignty. Popular sovereignty is precisely the capacity to bring the gap between self-representation and appointed representatives to the fore.[36] This gap serves as a starting point, foundation and background for any claim of the excluded, the non-represented, to be included in representation. Hence, democratic sovereignty is inscribed in a steady reformulation. It is the challenge of the current representation by the elected parliament.

I started off by asking, 'How can these young people become politically represented?' The analysis undertaken now shows that the question is rather which form these moments of self-representation should take. And this depends on the facilities and forums provided to appear in public. Elections, in general, cannot guarantee the appearance of a formerly unrepresented part of the people, because

---

36   'C'est au nom du tort qui lui est fait par les autres parties que le peuple s'identifie au tout de la comunauté' (Rancière 1995, 28).

their appearance only takes place if the non-represented can actually transcend their status and redefine the situation in which they act, and not only choose between given alternatives of representations (that include only the already considered). Hence, elections can only offer representation to a formerly unrepresented group when the scope of representation is transformed, for example by the formation of a new faction or party.[37]

Conclusion

The unrests show that people do not only want to be *integrated*, but *represented* politically. They do not only want to participate economically in society (by finding a decent job), but also in the creation of the community. The riots portray a claim to take part in the political community as somebody worthy of listening to. That this claim takes a violent form is not always avoidable, but it is fueled by the lack of understanding of the role of popular sovereignty in democratic representation – the people, who represent themselves and put into question governmental representation – the *demos* as sovereign, which challenges the continuous inequality of society and drives toward the inclusion of the excluded.

Violent outbreaks can only be avoided if the people can participate actively in politics. Instead of providing such forums, the government tends to apply governmental measures and shuts down again all possibilities for appropriate self-representation of young people. The little attention that is paid to the problem of racism in relation to recent events is equally linked to the trend of *governmental* reforms in the current political debates. A reflection of the representation of the *demos* by sovereignty would go right to the heart of the questions of 'Who talks and who decides for whom?', and thus includes the claim of equality and access which can be avoided by a discourse that intends to give everyone their specific place in society.

The 'integration' that is referred to is not understood as a demand to include new voices, but as the assimilation of these voices in order to prevent their saying something new and different.

In the classical concept of Rousseau, the *gouvernement* had a bridging role between the various particular wills of individuals and the democratic sovereignty that represents the common will. The democratic sovereign makes the laws according to the common will, the *gouvernement* takes care of the particular wills.

In recent developments, the role of the *gouvernement* has been to annihilate the existence of the *demos* by producing subjects that become identical with the norms of the existing society, and thus sovereignty becomes a *governmental* principle. No need to make new laws if the subjects comply perfectly with the existing ones.

---

37   As Slavoj Zizek argues: 'die wirklich freie Wahl ist eine Wahl, bei der ich nicht einfach zwischen zwei oder mehreren Alternativen innerhalb eines festgelegten Sets von Koordinaten wähle, sondern ich entscheide mich dafür, dieses Set von Koordinaten selbst zu ändern' (Zizek 2001, 154).

Representative democracy, then, refers to sovereignty of the people, which is a crowd of preconfigured identities, a crowd of voters allocated to their specific places and predictable voting behavior. No need to expect any surprises from unheard voices which claim something that is unheard up to this day, and thus call the current representation into question. Representative democracy is, in a way, always threatened by the appearance of the popular sovereign. To be oblivious of the role of the sovereign is not merely a failure of memory, but due to the potential of the sovereign to turn current relations in society upside down.

References

Arendt, H. (1958), *The Human Condition* (Chicago, IL: University of Chicago Press).

Foucault, M. (1978 [2001]), 'Gouvernementalité', in *Dits et Ecrits*, vol. 2, ed. D. Defert and F. Ewald (Paris: Gallimard).

—— (1997), *Il faut défendre la société* (Paris: Gallimard).

Holmes, B. (2006), 'Images of fire. The banlieue riots and the unanswered question of the welfare state', in *Multitudes*, <http://multitudes.samizdat.net/article2468. html>, published online 28 March 2006.

Lagrange, H. (2006), 'Autopsie d'une vague d'émeutes', in H. Lagrange, H. and M. Oberti (eds).

—— and Oberti, M. (eds) (2006), *Emeutes Urbaines et Protestations* (Paris: Presses de Sciences Po).

Masclet, O. (2006), 'Des quartiers sans voix. Sur le divorce entre la Gauche et les enfants d'immigrés', *French Politics, Culture & Society* 24:3, 3–22.

Mouffe, C. (ed.) (1999), *The Challenge of Carl Schmitt* (London: Verso).

Rancière, J. (1995), *La Mésentente* (Paris: Galilée).

—— (1997), 'Demokratie und Postdemokratie', in *Politik der Wahrheit* (Vienna: Turia und Kant).

Rousseau, J.-J. (1762a [1964]), 'Discours sur l'économie politique', in R. Derathé (ed.), *Du Contrat social* (Paris: Gallimard).

—— (1762b [1964]) 'Du Contrat social', in R. Derathé (ed.), *Du Contrat social* (Paris: Gallimard).

Vogl, J. (1994a), 'Einleitung', in Vogl (ed.), *Gemeinschaften. Positionen zu einer Philosophie des Politischen* (Frankfurt am Main: Suhrkamp)

—— (ed.) (1994b), *Gemeinschaften. Positionen zu einer Philosophie des Politischen* (Frankfurt am Main: Suhrkamp).

Zizek, S. (1999), 'Carl Schmitt in the Age of Post-politics', in Mouffe (ed.), *The Challenge of Carl Schmitt* (London: Verso).

—— (2001), *Die gnadenlose Liebe*, trans. N.G. Schneider (Frankfurt am Main: Suhrkamp).

Further Reading

Balibar, E. (2004), *We, the People of Europe?: Reflections on Transnational Citizenship (Translation/Transnation)* (Princeton, NJ: Princeton University Press).

Burchell, G., Gordon, C. and Miller, P. (eds) (1991), *The Foucault Effect: Studies in Governmentality* (Chicago, IL: University of Chicago Press).

Dean, M. (1999), *Governmentality: Power and Rule in Modern Society* (London: Sage).

Foucault, M. (2004), *Naissance de la biopolitique*, ed. F. Ewald (Paris: Gallimard).

Kastoryano, R. (2002), *Negotiating Identities: States and Immigrants in France and Germany* (Princeton, NJ: Princeton University Press).

Lemke, T. (1997), *Kritik der politischen Vernunft. Foucaults Analyse der modernen Gouvernementalität* (Hamburg: Argument Verlag).

—— (2001), 'The Birth of Bio-politics: Michael Foucault's Lectures at the College de France on Neo-liberal Governmentality' *Economy and Society* 30:2, 190–207.

Maus, I. (1992), *Zur Aufklärung der Demokratietheorie* (Frankfurt am Main: Suhrkamp).

The Past, Present and Future of Democratization

Kari Palonen

The high value of democracy cannot be interpreted as an expression of a consensus. On the contrary, as, for example, Reinhart Koselleck claims, it is precisely those concepts which are universally accepted that become extremely controversial upon closer inspection (see, for example, Koselleck 2006, 534). Conceptual 'movements', such as democratization, are always contested as regards the specific concept around which they revolve, and it is always possible to uncover further aspects or dimensions of democratization.

Several of the authors in this volume (for example, Frank Ankersmit, Olivia Guaraldo, Hubertus Buchstein and Chantal Mouffe) have expressed their discontent with the current situation of European democracy. In his recent book *La contre-démocratie* (2006), Pierre Rosanvallon suggests an alternative interpretation of the current *malaise dans la démocratie*. He has directed our attention toward new types of measures which can be used to complement the representative regime. 'Counter-democratic' moments accentuate the political role of measures such as vigilance, prevention, judicial control or the calls for transparency. The counter-democratic programme can be traced back to a number of historically relevant yet overlooked aspects of the histories of democratization. In his analysis, Rosanvallon ultimately remains critical of the depoliticizing and paralyzing effects of counter-democratic measures.

Majority Rule and its Limits

In this discussion of the past, present and future of democracy, I shall take a fresh look at an old discussion surrounding representative democracy: the relationship between government and parliament and majority rule. My perspective is above all connected to the opposition between two historical forms of political rhetoric: deliberation and negotiation. Deliberation *pro et contra* has its paradigmatic site in the parliament, negotiation in the diplomacy aiming at compromises between given partners. Theorists of the so-called *Parteienstaat*, such as Gerhard Leibholz

(1957 [1974]), have attempted to understand parliamentary government in terms of negotiation. My point is to affirm the deliberative character of the parliament, and correspondingly, to reconceptualize parliamentary democracy in terms of placing a stronger emphasis on the deliberative style of parliamentary politics.

Of course, in a democracy, votes are counted and not weighted, as, for example, Max Weber explained in his *Wahlrecht* pamphlet (1917 [1988], 167–69). We can, however, question the degree to which majority rule should be extended and how it should be exercised. Despite the fact that any governmental majority is constantly under the control of the electorate, the rule of the majority often seems to be quite inimical toward deliberation and debate. Contractarian and quasi-contractarian theorists from Thomas Hobbes (1651 [1991]) to Carl Schmitt (1923 [1979]) tend to accept democracy only on condition that the issues are voted on without deliberation and debate. Conversely, Alexis de Tocqueville (1835–40 [1986]) and John Stuart Mill (1861 [1991]), for example, realized that the democratization of the polity might be compatible with intolerant or even oppressive majority rule. In order to prevent this danger, the possibility of overthrowing an oppressive majority in free and fair elections is not enough. This is particularly the case for those who never have any real chance to gain the support of the majority.

If we take a more disillusioned view, we might claim that the support for democratization through free and fair elections has been historically linked to the possibility for parties to obtain governmental power. Most parties accepted democratization during the nineteenth- and early twentieth-century reforms for precisely such tactical reasons; there was little difference between liberal, democratic, socialistic, nationalistic or agrarian parties in this respect. The democratization of suffrage and other political rights and powers did not exclusively aim to get rid of the privileges of an old aristocracy. Nor did it intend to ensure that all individuals had the right to live, act and form associations of their own.

For most parties, the parliamentary majority and the governmental powers that came along with it were tools with which to 'realize' their political program. There was no way of entirely avoiding the potential danger that the democratized regime might ultimately be just as uniformistic and controlling of the lives of the individuals as the old order had been. There was absolutely no tolerance for bohemians, eccentrics, subversive elements and so on in the manifestos of the main parties at the time. The potentially intolerable and even oppressive consequences that the full realization of any such programme might have had has only recently been truly recognized.

There are, of course, numerous ways of preventing a majority realizing its programme too completely. Measures such as proportional representation, qualified majorities and the use of quotas for women and minorities are among the most obvious. All of them have been attempted in various contexts and with varying degrees of success, although none have proven entirely effective.

In this context, the classical relationship between government and parliament deserves rethinking. The traditional power struggle has shifted over the course of the parliamentarization of government from that between the parliament and the Crown to that between government and opposition within the parliament. Walter

Bagehot's classical expression for this new reality was the 'cabinet government' (Bagehot 1867 [2001]). The main power of the parliament was to elect and dismantle governments, and the role of the parliamentary majority was to support the government in the parliament. The chance for opposition is limited to overthrowing the governmental majority in the next elections, and parliamentary criticism and other attempts at controlling the government are means of achieving this end.

Of course, the practice of cabinet government is valuable in many respects. The fact that voters have clear alternatives to the parliamentary majority and the possibility to alternate governments gives it an advantage over regimes with similar governments, almost independent of electoral results. In Finland, for example, voters have only really had realistic alternatives to governing coalitions since the 1990s. Nobody wants to return to the short-lived governments of the French Third and Fourth Republics, even if historians such as Nicolas Roussellier have identified their *raison d'être*.

With the conscious exaggeration of a true system theorist, Niklas Luhmann (2000, 97–102) refers to the government versus opposition divide as the 'political code' of democratic regimes. The power of parties and politicians is decisively dependent on their belonging either to the government or the opposition. The metaphor of the code alludes to the government's quasi-monopoly on political action; the opposition's next chance to overthrow the government is in the next elections.

The Luhmannian code makes me wonder whether the old opposition between parliament and government as such should be re-actualized after all. Political resources are always asymmetrically distributed, even in parliamentary regimes. The government has a huge bureaucratic apparatus at its disposal, which plans, prepares, interprets and executes its policies and sets the agenda for the entire electoral term. It is frequently evident that government ministers have only limited power to intervene. As such, it might well be in the best interest of the government itself to increase parliamentary control of the bureaucracy by various means (Max Weber's *Parlament* pamphlet from 1918 contains an entire range of such measures).

The Empowerment of Parliament

While the bureaucratic apparatus has a duty to serve the government, the opposition parties and politicians depend on the benevolence of bureaucrats. Despite all their claims of transparency and citizens' control over administration, state officials cannot serve the opposition parliamentarians as effectively as the government. The main means of increasing the power of parliament is to empower its own staff as a counter-power to the bureaucracy. Although there is the danger that parliamentarians will become overly dependent on their personal secretaries and staff members, the self-identity of parliamentary officials tends to be opposed to the government bureaucracy and loyal to the powers of the parliament.

The main justification for strengthening the powers of the parliament and parliamentarians over the government and its bureaucracy is to increase the chances for deliberation and debate. While officials tend to monopolize their knowledge of the issues (*Fachwissen, Dienstwissen, Geheimwissen*, as Weber put it; Weber 1918 [1988], 236–38), the parliamentary powers are, on the contrary, based on the rhetorical principles of discussing every item *pro et contra*.

The very notion of parliamentary government disputes the claims of expert knowledge. The dissensus between opposed perspectives has been an inherent part of the parliamentary procedure since the English Renaissance, as Quentin Skinner illustrates in Chapter 8 of this volume. Rhetorically speaking, the items on the agenda and proposals put forth by the government can only be properly understood when and if they are discussed from opposite perspectives. Political questions are not just questions of knowledge, but also of judgment and choice, and the knowledge required to discuss them properly can be judged from a number of opposing points of view. Actualizing the political role of parliamentary deliberation and debate is perhaps the most powerful means of controlling the government and the rule of officialdom.

From a rhetorical perspective, the idea that a government should follow a single unified and consistent policy should be contested. Overly consistent government policies have frequently had oppressive consequences, even in parliamentary regimes. The undesired consequences of a given governmental policy are the result of an obvious lack of interest in discussing alternatives to it – a *deformation professionnelle* of majority parties and government officials.

In addition, a government seldom has the patience to consider why there would be any resistance to what it considers to be a superior policy. The individualization and pluralization of the lifestyles, human situations and daily practices of everyday life is something that has yet to be fully realized by any government. In some cases – recently, for example, in the case of so-called 'population policy' – governments have even intentionally set out to punish those who are not prepared to make personal sacrifices for the 'common good'.

The effects of the new empowerment of parliament will be limited to the parliament itself, and will thus not concern the opposition parties as such. In post-war thought, the parliament was frequently regarded solely as an arena of party conflicts and compromises, thus rendering it a negotiating rather than a deliberating assembly, 'a congress of ambassadors', as Edmund Burke put it in 1774. In a negotiating assembly, the mutual persuasion of parliamentarians would be no more effective than that of the ambassadors of different states or opposing sides in a labour dispute. At the end of the day, we would fall back into a corporative or neo-feudal assembly in which speeches are irrelevant and votes are not counted.

In other words, the actualization of the parliament as a deliberating assembly requires a revitalization of the role of the free mandate of individual MPs. For example, the party quotas of speakers in a parliamentary debate should not be taken as a given. The constitutional lawyer Adam Tomkins (2005) has also suggested that parliamentary party whips should be abolished altogether.

Compared with the situation in the 1970s, party discipline has none the less lost its strength. Parliamentarians' ties to a specific doctrine, to the party apparatus outside parliament and to their constituents are weaker now than they have been in recent decades. One unintentional consequence of all this is that individual parliamentarians have regained certain lost chances to construct and manifest their own personal profile, both inside and outside parliament.

Above all, the character of politics has changed in recent decades. Its emphasis has decisively shifted from a politics of different answers to the same questions, toward struggles over the agenda. This shift opens up *Spielräume* for individual initiatives toward and interventions in the introduction of new items to the agenda and the alteration of the rank of existing ones. A parliamentarian has virtually endless opportunities to politick, to add his or her own thread to the web, to quote Hannah Arendt's classical formula (Arendt 1960 [1981], 174).

The distinct deliberative character of parliament also may be manifested in the political significance of deliberation and debate beyond the government versus opposition divide. The parliamentary procedure is built on the rhetorical assumption that proper judgment of any proposal can be made only through a discussion *pro et contra* inside the parliamentary process, both in the plenum and in the committee stage. If one has no objections to the government's proposals readily at hand, one can always imagine new ones and think of possible grounds to contest further aspects in the proposals. The parliamentary conflict between government and opposition as well as a number of other dividing lines among MPs will conspire to construct objections and alternatives, as well as to enable the discussion of their merits and demerits.

This re-visioning of our understanding of the parliamentary style of politics in terms of a paradigmatic arena of deliberative rhetoric also indicates possibilities for democratization. Against intolerance, uniformity and repression, parliamentary procedure and the practices of parliamentary speaking incarnate the politics of dissensus, of the value of presenting and weighing opposite alternatives and contesting every claim to unity or consensus. Parliamentary democracy is a political regime of dissensus.

Voting as Deliberation

Today, it is common to protest simultaneously against overly powerful and powerless parliaments. This protestation tends to downplay the act of voting as irrelevant or uninteresting, thus both neglecting and misjudging the political opportunities inherent in voting (see Hubertus Buchstein's Chapter 17 in this volume). Highlighting the political resources inherent in the elementary act of voting in parliamentary elections is thus worth closer discussion.

According to Max Weber's formula in *Politik als Beruf* (1919 [1994], 41), voting is a paradigmatic way for the individual citizen to act as an 'occasional politician'. Voting is an exemplarily contingent situation in which both the choice of individual voters and the net result of the elections can always be different. It is this double contingency that is the source of the power sharing involved in the act of voting.

Some of the more classical theories of voting have lost their hold on the electorate. The act of voting as the mere fulfillment of one's civic duty has now become inherently unpolitical; voting without regard for the candidates would be its purest expression. The idea of voting purely on the basis of 'objective interests' is also becoming less and less plausible, as there is no such thing as inherently quasi-natural 'interests', and hardly anyone is prepared in this day and age to admit that any single party can monopolize the representation of certain 'objective' interests. Sharing the same 'preferences' with candidates is also considered rather implausible grounds for voting for a definite candidate when the point of the election is to choose a member of parliament for a certain time span. It is the competence, trustworthiness, innovativeness and political judgment of the prospective members of parliament that matters at the ballot box.

The voters of today thus always have choices to make, and correspondingly, chances to politick in elections. Electoral choice can be understood as a serious personal matter of deliberation *pro et contra*, manifesting itself in the choice made at the ballot box. Today, most voters tend to be 'floating voters', and we can refer to them as having their own personal electoral biographies. Even if someone has voted for the same party, say, in the last ten elections, a new election offers always the chance to reconsider this choice in each new election. When voting in an election, one chooses, as Jean-Paul Sartre wrote in 1965, not only a candidate, but also 'oneself', a political identity. Or, alternatively, one may strategically choose to vote for a party that one does not particularly like, but which has a good chance of beating an even less attractive party.

Perhaps the most common complaint of voters in elections is that there is no one worth voting for. This kind of sentiment indicates a lack of political literacy regarding the actual contest itself, the candidates and their chances of winning, as well as one's own electoral biography. Hardly any election marks a real historical turning point, but none the less, the margins of deliberation and choices to be made by a politically literate voter in any election are real. The voters of today need to have patience for detail in order to make their electoral choices.

As Mogens Herman Hansen notes in Chapter 2 of this volume, Jean-Jacques Rousseau claims in *Du contrat social* (1762, Book II, ch. xv) that the English are only free on election day. The obvious response to Rousseau would have been that the French were not even free then, because there were no elections under the *ancien régime*. For the voters of today, Rousseau's main point can be reinterpreted: there is much to be deliberated and many choices to be made on any election day. In this sense, free and fair elections also distinguish election day as an extraordinary occasion for every citizen to act politically. If there are no attractive alternatives, one must deliberate even more over how to act in the elections.

The freedom of the voter at the ballot box is inherently linked to the understanding of parliament as the paradigmatic arena of the deliberative style of politics. Indeed, from the perspective of deliberation, the voting of individual citizens can be understood as an extension of the activity of the parliamentarians. In deliberative terms, the ideal voter would be one who is able to imagine him- or herself to be a member of the next parliament. In other words, a deliberating voter might consider him- or herself as a member of parliament on election day.

References

Arendt, H. (1960 [1981]), *Vita activa oder Vom tätigen Leben* (Munich: Piper).

Aronson, R. and van den Hoven, A. (eds) (1991), *Sartre Alive* (Detroit, MI: Wayne State University Press).

Bagehot, W. (1867 [2001]), *The English Constitution* (Cambridge: Cambridge University Press).

Burke, E. (1774 [1996]), 'Mr. Edmund Burke's Speeches at his Arrival in Bristol, and at the Conclusion of the Poll', in *The Writings and Speeches of Edmund Burke*, ed. Paul Langford, vol. III (Oxford: Oxford University Press).

de Tocqueville, A. (1835–40 [1986]), *De la démocratie en Amérique*, vols I–II (Paris: Gallimard).

Hobbes, T. (1651 [1991]), *Leviathan*, ed. R. Tuck (Cambridge: Cambridge University Press).

Koselleck, R. (2006), *Begriffsgeschichten*, ed. C. Dutt (Frankfurt am Main: Suhrkamp).

Leibholz, G. (1957 [1974]), *Strukturprobleme der modernen Demokratie* (Frankfurt am Main: Fischer 1974).

Luhmann, N. (2000), *Politik der Gesellschaft* (Frankfurt am Main: Suhrkamp).

Mill, J.S. (1861 [1991]) *Considerations on Representative Government* (Buffalo, NY: Prometheus Books).

Rosanvallon, P. (2006), *La contre-démocratie. La politique à l'âge de la défiance* (Paris: Seuil).

Rousseau, J.-J. (1762 [1966]) *Du contrat social* (Paris: Garnier-Flammarion).

Sartre, J.-P. (1965 [1991]), 'Kennedy and West Virginia', trans. Elisabeth Bowman, in Aronson and van den Hoven (eds).

Schmitt, C. (1923 [1979]), *Die geistesgeschichtliche Lage des heutigen Parlamentarismus* (Berlin: Duncker & Humblot).

Tomkins, A. (2005), *Our Republican Constitution* (Oxford: Hart).

Weber, M. (1917 [1988]), 'Wahlrecht und Demokratie in Deutschland', in *Max-Weber-Studienausgabe* I/15 (Tübingen: Mohr).

—— (1918 [1988]), 'Parlament und Regierung im neugeordneten Deutschland', in *Max-Weber-Studienausgabe* 1/15 (Tübingen: Mohr).

—— (1919 [1994]), 'Politik als Beruf', in *Max-Weber-Studienausgabe* 1/17 (Tübingen: Mohr).

Index